D0575995

Bottom Line's
HEALTH BREAKTHROUGHS 2011

Bottom Line Books

www.BottomLineSecrets.com

HealthDay

Articles in this book were written by reporters for HealthDay, an award-winning international daily
consumer health news service, headquartered in Norwalk, Connecticut.

Bottom Line Books® publishes the advice of expert authorities in many fields. The use of this
material is no substitute for health, legal, accounting or other professional services.
Consult competent professionals for answers to your specific questions.

Telephone numbers, addresses, prices, offers and Web sites listed in this book are accurate
at the time of publication, but they are subject to frequent change.

Bottom Line Books® is a registered trademark of Boardroom® Inc.
281 Tresser Boulevard, Stamford, Connecticut 06901

www.bottomlinesecrets.com

Bottom Line Books® is an imprint of Boardroom® Inc., publisher of print periodicals,
e-letters and books. We are dedicated to bringing you the best information from the most
knowledgeable sources in the world. Our goal is to help you gain greater wealth,
better health, more wisdom, extra time and increased happiness.

Printed in the United States of America

Contents

Contents

Contents

13 • PAIN TREATMENT

14 • SAVVY CONSUMER

15 • STROKE PREVENTION & RECOVERY

16 • WOMEN'S HEALTH

Contents

Preface

We are proud to bring you *Bottom Line's Health Breakthroughs 2011*, a new book filled with the year's latest health discoveries.

When you choose a Bottom Line Book, you are turning to a stellar group of experts in a wide range of specialties—medical doctors, alternative practitioners, nutrition experts, research scientists and consumer-health advocates, to name a few.

We go to great lengths to interview the foremost health experts. Whether it's cancer prevention, breakthrough arthritis treatments or cutting-edge nutritional advice, our editors talk to the true innovators in health care.

How do we find all these top-notch professionals? Over the past 20 years, we have built a network of thousands of leading physicians in both alternative and conventional medicine. They are affiliated with the world's premier medical institutions. We follow the latest research and we regularly talk to our advisors in major teaching hospitals, private practices and government health agencies. We also tap the resources of HealthDay, an award-winning news service devoted to consumer health issues.

Bottom Line's Health Breakthroughs 2011 is a result of our ongoing research and contact with these experts, and is a distillation of their latest findings and advice. We hope that you will enjoy the presentation and glean helpful information about the health topics that concern you and your family.

As a reader of a Bottom Line Book, please be assured that you are receiving reliable and well-researched information from a trusted source. But, please use prudence in health matters. Always speak to your physician before taking vitamins, supplements or over-the-counter medication…changing your diet…or beginning an exercise program. If you experience side effects from any regimen, contact your doctor immediately.

The Editors, Bottom Line Books, Stamford, Connecticut.

Aging & Senior Health

Hip Fractures: Why They're a Bad Break for Your Health

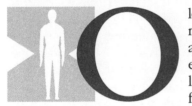 lder men and wo-
men who break
a hip are five to
eight times more
likely to die in the
first three months
after the fracture, a new study by Belgian researchers has found.

And, while the death rate after a hip fracture
diminishes substantially during the first two
years after the break, it never returns to the
death rate seen in similar people who did not
fracture a hip, the study authors said.

THE STUDY

For the study, a team led by Patrick Haentjens,
MD, PhD, of the Centre for Outcomes Research
and the Laboratory for Experimental Surgery at
the University Hospital in Brussels, examined 22
studies that included more than 578,000 women

and 17 studies that included more than 154,000
men with hip fractures. All study participants
were 50 or older.

The researchers found that older women who
had a hip fracture had a slightly more than 50%
greater risk of dying in the first three months
after the break, and men had a nearly 80% increased risk of dying during that time.

The risk increased with the person's age. For
80-year-old women with hip fractures, the increased risk of dying was 8% at one year, rising to 22% at 10 years, compared with women
without hip fractures.

For 80-year-old men, the increased risk of
death at one year was 18%, and 26% at five
years, compared with men who did not break a
hip, the study found.

The findings were published in the *Annals of
Internal Medicine.*

Elton Strauss, MD, associate professor, chief of orthope-
dic trauma and adult reconstruction, Mount Sinai School of
Medicine, New York City.
Annals of Internal Medicine.

IMPLICATIONS

"These findings may be helpful when performing cost-effectiveness analyses of hip fracture prevention strategies or designing treatment strategies in patients with hip fracture," the researchers concluded.

EXPERT COMMENTARY

"A hip fracture is a major blow to the body," said Elton Strauss, MD, an associate professor and chief of orthopedic trauma and adult reconstruction at Mount Sinai School of Medicine in New York City, who was not involved in the study. The main problem is not repairing the fracture itself but the toll it takes on older people, he added.

SUPPORT SYSTEM REQUIRED

Dr. Strauss said that one key to surviving and recovering from a hip fracture is to have a good family or other support system when the person leaves the hospital.

"Most of these patients are discharged from hospitals before they can be optimized to the very best condition," he said. "Most Medicare patients stay in hospitals three days after [a] hip fracture, and three days is just not enough to get these patients back on their feet."

COMPLETE HEADING TAKES TIME

It takes time to fully heal, especially for people who are old and suffering from other medical conditions, Dr. Strauss said.

"If the patient does not have a family unit, if the patient doesn't have finances to pay for a nurse or a homemaker or somebody to drive them to the doctor's office, somebody to help them shop—the resources out there are minimal," he added. "Most patients get three to four hours of home health aid a day, and that's not enough."

info For more information on hip fractures, visit the Web site of the American Academy of Orthopaedic Surgeons, *http://orthoinfo.aaos. org*, and click on "hip" under "parts of body."

Chronic Pain "Trips" Up Seniors

Suzanne G. Leveille, PhD, RN, professor of nursing, University of Massachusetts-Boston and Beth Israel Deaconess Medical Center, Boston.
Colin Milner, founder and CEO, International Council on Active Aging, Vancouver, BC, Canada.
The Journal of the American Medical Association.

Falls are a leading cause of death among older Americans, and new research confirms that chronic pain contributes to those accidents.

"Chronic pain, no matter how we measured it, was associated with an increased likelihood of falls," said lead researcher Suzanne Leveille, PhD, RN, from Beth Israel Deaconess Medical Center and the University of Massachusetts, both in Boston. "Pain has not traditionally been thought of as a risk factor for falls."

Health-care costs associated with falls account for more than $19 billion each year, but the role pain plays in those falls was not explored before, the authors said.

THE STUDY

For the study, published in *The Journal of the American Medical Association*, Dr. Leveille's team asked 749 people, ages 70 and older, about any pain they suffered. The participants also kept a record of each time they fell.

At the start of the study, 40% of the participants said they suffered from chronic pain in more than one joint, and 24% had pain in only one joint.

During 18 months of follow-up, there were 1,029 falls. More than half (55%) reported falling at least once.

Those people who had pain in more than one joint were more likely to fall, compared with people who reported no pain or pain in only one joint. Severe pain and pain that affected participants' ability to do daily activities also made falls more likely, the researchers found.

In addition, people who reported severe pain in one month had a 77% increased risk of falling the next month. Even people reporting very mild pain were more likely to fall the following month, the group found.

POSSIBLE EXPLANATIONS

The authors noted that the neuromuscular effects of pain could cause leg muscle weakness or slow neuromuscular responses to a loss of balance. Attempts to ease pain by changing gait may also cause balance problems, and chronic pain may be a huge distraction, making people less aware of hazards, according to the report.

IMPLICATIONS

Pain tends to be thought of as part of growing old, Dr. Leveille said. "People tend to be dismissive of it, but this study shows that it may not be such a minor thing. There could be some very serious hazards related to chronic pain," she noted.

Colin Milner, chief executive officer of the International Council on Active Aging, welcomed the findings. "This study shows us the importance of recognizing that pain typically has a cost associated with it, as it may be a symptom of a greater issue that, in this case, if left unattended can have serious consequences."

Health, fitness and wellness professionals now have another tool in creating fall-reduction programs, Milner said. "Now, if they have not before, they may have a better understanding of how pain impacts many systems in the body and how these can impact falls," he said.

"If we look at the population as a whole, the number of people with pain is significant," Milner added. "This study shows that addressing this pain early is not only preventative in nature, but cost-effective, as the long-term costs associated with falls is significant."

ADVICE

Based on these findings, Dr. Leveille thinks that pain should be a factor in assessing the risk for falls. She also said effective pain management might reduce the risk of falls.

Patients should discuss pain and falling with their doctor and work out a plan to prevent falling, she added.

■ ■ ■ ■

When Dizzy Turns Deadly

Accidental falls kill an estimated 13,000 seniors each year in the US and result in more than 1.5 million visits to hospital emergency rooms, according to a recent survey. An inner-ear disorder, known as *vestibular dysfunction*, can make you suddenly dizzy, throw you off balance and lead to a serious fall.

Important: Be sure your doctor gives you a balance test, including screening for vestibular dysfunction, as a routine part of your checkup.

Lloyd B. Minor, MD, Andelot Professor and director, department of otolaryngology, head and neck surgery, Johns Hopkins Medical School, Baltimore, *www.hopkinsmedicine.org.*

Simple Test Gives Doctors a Hand in Helping Elderly

Canadian Medical Association Journal news release.

Decreased handgrip strength in the elderly is associated with increased risk of death, researchers say.

STUDY FINDINGS

In a new study of 555 men and women in the Netherlands, handgrip strength was measured at age 85 and again at age 89. The researchers found that low handgrip strength at ages 85 and 89, and a greater decline in strength over time, were associated with increased risk of death from all causes. They also concluded that the association between handgrip strength and risk of death increases as people age.

The reasons for the link between muscle strength and risk of death aren't clear, said Dr. Carolina Ling, of the department of gerontology and geriatrics at Leiden University Medical Center in the Netherlands. The researchers weren't able to determine if muscle strength has a direct effect on death risk or if it's associated with other factors that ultimately lead to death.

IMPLICATIONS

Assessing handgrip strength can help doctors identify elderly people at risk and improve their chances of survival by taking measures to maintain their muscle strength, the researchers concluded.

"Handgrip strength is an easy measurement for clinicians to obtain," said Allen Huang, MD, a geriatrician at McGill University Health Centre in Montreal, Canada. "Handgrip *dynamometers*, though not commonly found in physicians' offices, are simple, low-maintenance devices."

The findings were published in the *Canadian Medical Association Journal*.

info For more information about strength training for older adults, visit the Web site of the US Centers for Disease Control and Prevention, *www.cdc.gov/physicalactivity/growingstronger.*

Forgetful? It Might Not Be Alzheimer's

Lara Jehi, MD, an epileptologist (a neurologist who specializes in treating epilepsy) and clinical neurophysiologist at the Epilepsy Center at the Cleveland Clinic and director of the clinic's Epilepsy Outcome Program. She is a recipient of the Young Investigator Award from the American Epilepsy Society and has published several medical journal articles and book chapters on epilepsy.

I f you experience occasional confusion—so-called "senior moments"—or times when you "zone out" by staring into space, your doctor may suspect a heart problem or early-stage Alzheimer's disease. But one possible cause that is often overlooked is epilepsy. A disorder caused by abnormal electrical activity in the brain, epilepsy has symptoms that vary widely, depending on a number of factors, including the area of the brain that is affected and the person's age.

Epilepsy is widely known to strike younger adults, but researchers estimate that one out of every 20 people over age 65 has the condition. Many experts believe the true number is even higher because data count only people who have had obvious seizures, which don't necessarily occur in older adults with epilepsy.

What you need to know...

EPILEPSY IN OLDER ADULTS

Epilepsy is caused by abnormal electrical activity in the brain. In younger people, this tends to express itself in very noticeable movements, such as full-body fidgeting, jerking movements or uncontrollable shaking. In older adults, the abnormal brain activity typically produces a much milder physical response. The reason

isn't known, but researchers theorize that as the brain ages, connections between its regions weaken, so the spread of electrical activity—which is what produces seizures—becomes less pronounced.

When epilepsy begins later in life, it typically results from a health problem that alters the brain's function. *Cerebrovascular disease* (reduced blood flow to the brain)—which can result in a stroke—causes one-third of new epilepsy cases in older adults. Other conditions that can lead to epilepsy include head injury...a brain tumor...infectious diseases, such as meningitis and encephalitis (both of which cause inflammation in the brain)...and excessive drinking (which damages parts of the brain where seizures are likely to arise).

WHAT ARE THE RED FLAGS?

Besides occasional confusion and staring spells, signs of epilepsy in an older adult can include...

•**Uncontrollable twitching of a specific body part.**

•**Numbness or tingling on one side of the body (typically in the arm).**

•**Dropping things for no reason.**

•**Falling or passing out due to a brief loss of consciousness.**

In some cases, symptoms are so mild that family members describe an older person with epilepsy simply as being "a little out of it" or "not acting himself."

Important tip-off: Each episode typically involves the same sensation in the same part of the body. Symptoms often occur for a few minutes then go away, only to return later. They may recur many times in a day or appear as rarely as once a week or even once a month.

GETTING A CORRECT DIAGNOSIS

Untreated epilepsy is dangerous because it puts the person at serious risk for brain damage from continued attacks, as well as driving mishaps, falls and other epilepsy-related injuries.

If epilepsy is suspected, the patient should see an epileptologist (a neurologist who specializes in the treatment of epilepsy) or a general

*To find an epileptologist near you, contact the Epilepsy Foundation of America, 800-332-1000, *www.aesnet. org.* Under the tab "Patients," click on "Find a Doctor."

neurologist.* The brain's electrical activity will be recorded with an electroencephalograph (EEG), a device that uses small, adhesive sensors (electrodes) that are placed on a person's scalp. The procedure is noninvasive and painless. If the EEG shows abnormal brain activity that is characteristic of epilepsy, the diagnosis is made.

BEST MEDICATIONS

Antiseizure medication is the first step in treating epilepsy. Older adults are typically prescribed one of three antiseizure medications—*levetiracetam* (Keppra), *lamotrigine* (Lamictal) or *gabapentin* (Neurontin).

Levetiracetam's primary side effects are depression or anxiety...lamotrigine can cause a skin rash...and gabapentin is generally safe but has to be taken at high doses in order to be effective. In people who respond to one of these drugs, symptoms are usually eliminated within two months.

Latest development: The antiseizure drug *pregabalin* (Lyrica) was recently approved by the FDA for the treatment of partial onset seizures, the most common form of epilepsy in adults. Pregabalin now must be used in combination with other epilepsy medication, but it shows promise as a primary drug treatment. Its side effects include depression and anxiety.

Caution: The FDA has reported that the drugs mentioned above and other antiseizure drugs have been linked to increased risk for suicidal thoughts and behavior and advises that patients who take these medications should pay close attention to changes in mood.

THE SURGICAL OPTION

If medication does not relieve epilepsy symptoms, surgery is considered. The procedure, which involves removal of the part of the brain from which the seizure originates, effectively relieves epilepsy symptoms about 70% of the time. The surgery typically requires a hospital stay of three to five days, often followed by a week or two of rehabilitation to help the patient regain strength and balance. Normal activities usually can be resumed within six weeks.

If surgery isn't possible—for example, the brain location where the seizure originates may be too close to an area vital for a basic function,

such as speech or mobility—then vagus nerve stimulation may be recommended.

With this procedure, an electrical wire is wrapped around the vagus nerve (a large nerve that stretches from the side of the neck into the brain) and connected to a small lithium battery that is implanted under the skin, where it sends regular electrical impulses through the nerve.

For reasons that aren't completely clear, this form of stimulation disrupts epileptic episodes. The downside: In about 50% of cases, this procedure reduces—but does not eliminate—the frequency of epileptic attacks.

Secret to Slowing Down The Aging Process

Bruce Ames, PhD, professor of biochemistry and molecular biology at the University of California, Berkeley, and a senior scientist at the Children's Hospital Oakland Research Institute. Dr. Ames has published more than 540 scientific articles, including many on the role of mitochondria in health and aging. He is the winner of several major awards, including the US National Medal of Science, the Linus Pauling Institute Prize for Health Research and the Japan Prize.

Most people associate aging with an inevitable decline in overall vitality and well-being. Over time, our bodies' major organs just don't seem to work as well, and our bones and muscles weaken.

But what if it were possible to slow down this process before such age-related damage can occur?

Breakthrough thinking: The best way to fight aging may be to attack it on a cellular level. By focusing on the health of our *mitochondria* (tiny energy-producing structures in each cell of our body), we can minimize age-related decay to our organs and other major bodily systems.

WHAT ARE MITOCHONDRIA?

There are hundreds of mitochondria within each cell (except for red blood cells) of your body. Each mitochondrion is a miniature energy factory that turns fuel (dietary fat and sugar) into *adenosine triphosphate* (ATP), the primary energy source in every cell.

Though your doctor is unlikely to talk to you about the health of your mitochrondria, you should be aware of various factors that can weaken these important cellular structures…

•**Certain medications.** Statins, for example, block the body's natural production of coenzyme Q10, which plays a crucial role in normal mitochondrial functioning.

•**Inadequate intake of key nutrients.** Low levels of nutrients, such as iron, magnesium or biotin (vitamin B-7), cause damage to mitochondrial DNA.

•**Age-related wear and tear.** To produce the cells' energy source, ATP, mitochondria burn up (oxidize) fuel—a process that generates free radicals, unstable molecules that can damage mitochondrial structures.

If mitochondria are weakened, a domino effect is created, thereby weakening cells, tissues and, eventually, organs.

This harmful process may affect your brain (with poor memory and concentration)…heart (with irregular heartbeats that increase your risk for a heart attack)…muscles (with pain and fatigue) and overall vitality (with energy levels that are only one-fourth to one-half of what you enjoyed in your youth).

Mitochondrial decay also may play a role in the development of cancer, Alzheimer's disease and Parkinson's disease.

How to supercharge your mitochondria…

MUST-HAVE NUTRIENTS

Your mitochondria require most of the roughly 40 essential nutrients to function at optimal levels. *These include…*

•**The "Heme Seven."** Seven nutrients are required for the synthesis of heme (a molecule that contains iron and is made in—and used by—mitochondria).

The heme-synthesizing nutrients are riboflavin (vitamin B-2)…*pantothenate* (vitamin B-5) …*pyridoxine* (vitamin B-6)…biotin…and the minerals zinc, copper and iron.

Inadequate levels of heme can damage mitochondrial DNA…promote mitochondrial decay…and accelerate cellular aging overall.

My advice: Take a daily multivitamin/mineral supplement that supplies most essential nutrients (megadoses aren't necessary).

Caution: Most multis don't contain enough calcium, magnesium, potassium, vitamin K, vitamin D and omega-3 fatty acids—or lack some of those nutrients entirely.

Therefore, it's important to also eat a balanced diet that contains more fish and poultry than red meat, as well as fruits and vegetables, whole grains, legumes and some low-fat dairy products.

•**Magnesium.** About 55% of American adults get inadequate amounts of magnesium in their diets (leafy green vegetables are a good source of this mineral). Low levels of this nutrient can damage mitochondrial DNA.

Magnesium also is a key element in calcium absorption, so the ratio between the two nutrients is important. The body needs more than twice as much calcium as magnesium.

My advice: A good rule of thumb is to take supplements that supply a total daily intake of 500 milligrams (mg) of calcium and 250 mg of magnesium. (These doses can be adjusted depending upon your dietary intake of these minerals.)

Important: Some experts recommend higher daily doses of calcium supplements, but research shows that it's preferable to get these minerals from dietary sources, whenever possible, since foods also contain other important nutrients.

Good calcium sources: Low-fat yogurt (300 mg per eight-ounce serving)…spinach (115 mg per one-half cup, cooked)…and pinto beans (45 mg per one-half cup, cooked).

Bottom line: Get 1,200 mg of calcium daily—from all sources—if you are age 51 and older. Do not exceed 350 mg of magnesium daily (some people may experience diarrhea).

•**Acetyl-L-carnitine (ALCAR).** This nutrient helps move fatty acids into the mitochondria, produce the cells' energy sources, and transport waste products out of the mitochondria.

Important human evidence: In an analysis of 21 studies focusing on the use of ALCAR to help prevent Alzheimer's and mild cognitive impairment (the stage of memory loss before Alzheimer's), researchers found that people who took the supplement had less mental decline compared with those taking a placebo.

•**Lipoic acid (LA).** This compound performs several functions, including acting as an antioxidant, which protects the mitochondria from free radicals.

Compelling animal research: In studies conducted at the University of California at Berkeley in which older rats were given a combination of LA and ALCAR, the two nutrients reduced the amount of mitochondria-damaging free radicals produced by oxidation…increased mitochondrial oxygen consumption (a sign of increased energy production)…and reversed age-associated decay of mitochondrial structures.

In a study on aged beagles, the dogs improved their ability to learn and remember when taking the nutrients in supplement form.

My advice: Ask your doctor about taking a dietary supplement that combines ALCAR and LA. One such product is Juvenon Cellular Health Supplement,* which contains 1,000 mg of ALCAR and 400 mg of LA. The supplement is available from Juvenon (800-567-2502, *www. juvenon.com*).

As an alternative to Juvenon: Consider taking one of two other supplements that contain ALCAR and LA and are specifically formulated for mitochondrial health—Anti-Age/Energy Formula from Body Language Vitamins, available at 877-548-3348, *www.bodylanguagevita min.com*…or MitoForte: Energy, Memory and Anti-Aging Support from Nutritional Biochemistry, Inc., available at 406-582-0034, *www.mon tanaim.com* and click on "Shop."

FOR OPTIMAL RESULTS

Exercise is an important adjunct to the use of the supplements listed above. That's because frequent physical activity improves the number and functioning of mitochondria in muscles.

Standout scientific evidence: When researchers studied the effect of regular exercise on mitochondrial health in adults (average age 67), there was a 53% increase in mitochondrial DNA…and a 62% increase in energy-making mitochondrial enzyme activity.

My advice: Follow the standard recommendation for regular exercise—a minimum of 30 minutes of moderate exercise, such as brisk walking, most days of the week.

■ ■ ■ ■

Early Alzheimer's Harms Driving Skills

Warning signs include loss of memory and cognitive abilities, such as needing more help than before with directions or a new route…getting lost on once-familiar roads…having trouble making turns, especially left turns…becoming confused when exiting a highway…being honked at frequently by other drivers…drifting in and out of the proper lane.

What to do: If you notice these signs in yourself or a family member, talk to a doctor.

Also: Consider consulting a specialist in driver rehabilitation who can provide a comprehensive evaluation to determine one's ability to drive and/or provide rehabilitation to strengthen driving skills—find one through the American Occupational Therapy Association, 301-652-2682, *www.aota.org/olderdriver*.

Jeffrey Dawson, ScD, departments of biostatistics and neurology, University of Iowa, Iowa City, and leader of a study of 155 older people, including 40 with early-stage Alzheimer's, funded by the National Institute on Aging and published in *Neurology*.

■ ■ ■ ■

Postretirement Work Helps Guard Against Illness

Researchers who interviewed 12,189 adults found that those who took "bridge jobs"—full-time, part-time or self-employment—after official retirement had fewer major diseases (such as diabetes, cancer and arthritis) and performed better at daily tasks than those who stopped working.

Theory: The increased physical and mental activity—as well as social interaction—required for working protects against chronic illness and functional decline.

Yujie Zhan, researcher, department of psychology, University of Maryland, College Park.

*Dr. Ames is the volunteer chairman of the scientific advisory board for Juvenon. He accepts no pay from the company.

Meaningful Life May Help Fight Alzheimer's

Aron S. Buchman, MD, associate professor, department of neurological sciences, Rush University Medical Center, Chicago.

Greg M. Cole, PhD, neuroscientist, Greater Los Angeles VA Healthcare System, and associate director, Alzheimer's Disease Research Center, UCLA David Geffen School of Medicine, Los Angeles.

William H. Thies, PhD, chief medical and scientific officer, Alzheimer's Association, Chicago.

Archives of General Psychiatry.

People who say their lives have a purpose are less likely to develop Alzheimer's disease or its precursor, mild cognitive impairment, a new study suggests.

As the population ages and dementia becomes a more frequent diagnosis, there's increasing impetus to determine the causes of the disease, associated risk factors and how to prevent it, explained study coauthor Aron S. Buchman, MD, an associate professor in the department of neurological sciences at Rush University Medical Center in Chicago.

"There has been a lot of interest in psychosocial factors and their association with cognitive decline and dementia in later life," he said.

THE STUDY

The study looked at the positive aspects of life and their possible effect on keeping dementia at bay, "looking at happiness, purposefulness in life, well-being and whether those kind of concepts are associated with a decreased risk of dementia," Dr. Buchman explained.

For the study, published in the *Archives of General Psychiatry*, Dr. Buchman and his colleagues collected data on 951 older people without dementia who participated in the Rush Memory and Aging Project. The participants were asked to respond to statements such as: "I feel good when I think of what I have done in the past and what I hope to do in the future," and "I have a sense of direction and purpose in life."

After an average four years of follow-up, 16.3% of the people in the study developed Alzheimer's disease. Taking into account other factors that could account for Alzheimer's, the researchers found that people who responded most positively to statements about their lives were the least likely to develop the condition. Also, people who said they had more purposeful lives were less likely to develop mild cognitive impairment and had a slower rate of cognitive decline.

People who scored 4.2 out of 5 on the purpose-in-life measure were about 2.4 times less likely to develop Alzheimer's disease compared with people who scored 3.0, the study found.

POSSIBLE EXPLANATION

It's not known whether there is a biological reason for this finding, the researchers noted.

"One possibility is that, truly, somebody with high purpose in life might have a lower risk of developing dementia because of what's involved in purpose in life," Dr. Buchman said.

IMPLICATIONS

"The importance of the study," he added, "is this doesn't prove anything, but it points researchers in the direction of a link between purpose in life and cognition in late life. And now we have to find out what the biological basis is."

Still, the researchers think these findings could have implications for public health.

"More social activity, more physical activity, higher cognitive activities, high purpose in life—all these psychosocial factors seem to be linked with longer life, decreased mortality, decreased disability and provide important clues to a public health approach to try to increase independence in older people in later life," Dr. Buchman said.

EXPERT REACTION

Greg M. Cole, PhD, a neuroscientist at the Greater Los Angeles VA Healthcare System, wondered if the study is really measuring depression, not a purposeful life.

"I am unclear about how low scores on the purpose-in-life measures can be separated from mild depression," Dr. Cole said. "Depression has been repeatedly associated with increased Alzheimer's disease risk. So psychiatrists can make a distinction, but they seem likely closely related.

"One wonders whether this is a treatable psychiatric condition contributing to risk or an early symptom of decline," he added.

William H. Thies, PhD, chief medical and scientific officer at the Alzheimer's Association, said the new study "contributes to the literature that says there is a linkage between behavior and disease."

The question is do more people lack a sense of purpose and develop Alzheimer's disease or is lacking a sense of purpose an early, subtle, sign of dementia, he said.

"As we get better and better at having biological measures of the disease, we will shed a lot of light on these kinds of studies and whether these behaviors are simply a symptom or they are a place where you can intervene," Dr. Thies said.

info For more on Alzheimer's disease, visit the Alzheimer's Association, *www.alz.org*.

Hospital Stays Increase Dementia Risk by 40%

The Journal of the American Medical Association news release.

Elderly people who have been hospitalized have an increased risk of cognitive decline, according to a new study.

THE STUDY

Researchers analyzed data from a period of 13 years on 2,929 people, ages 65 and older, who did not have dementia at the start of the study. Average follow-up was 6.1 years. Of the 1,287 who were hospitalized for a non-critical illness, 18% developed dementia. While 12% of the 41 hospitalized for a critical illness developed dementia, only 9% of the 1,601 participants who were not hospitalized during the study period were diagnosed with dementia.

THE RESULTS

After adjusting for various factors, the researchers concluded that patients hospitalized for a non-critical illness were 40% more likely to develop dementia than those who weren't hospitalized. Seniors hospitalized with a critical illness also had a higher risk of dementia, but the result wasn't significant, possibly because of the small number of people in that group, the study authors explained.

The study findings are published in *The Journal of the American Medical Association*.

POSSIBLE EXPLANATION

"The mechanism of this association is uncertain," said study leader William J. Ehlenbach, MD, of the University of Washington, Seattle. "These results also could suggest that factors associated with acute illness, and to a greater degree with critical illness, may be causally related to cognitive decline."

There are a number of possible mechanisms through which critical illness could contribute to cognitive decline, including hypoxemia (decreased partial pressure of oxygen in blood), delirium, low blood pressure, glucose dysregulation, inflammation, and sedative and analgesic medications, the report indicated.

"Further studies are needed to better understand the factors associated with acute and critical illness that may contribute to cognitive impairment," according to the researchers.

info The AGS Foundation for Health in Aging Web site offers cognitive vitality tips at *www.healthinaging.org*. Click on "Public Education" and choose "FHA Tip Sheets" and then "Cognitive Vitality."

■ ■ ■ ■

Cell Phones Could "Call Off" Alzheimer's

Mice predisposed to Alzheimer's disease were exposed to cell phones' electromagnetic waves for two hours daily for seven to nine months. Younger mice did not get Alzheimer's...older mice who had the disease showed cognitive improvement.

Theory: Cell-phone waves may reduce beta-amyloid protein plaques that are believed to cause Alzheimer's.

Gary Arendash, PhD, research professor, Florida Alzheimer's Disease Research Center, University of South Florida, Tampa, and author of an animal study.

New Criteria for Alzheimer's Diagnosis Proposed

Martin Goldstein, MD, assistant professor, and director, department of neurology, Mount Sinai School of Medicine, New York City.

William Thies, PhD, chief medical and scientific officer, Alzheimer's Association, Chicago.

Mony de Leon, EdD, professor, department of psychiatry, and director, Center for Brain Health, NYU Langone MedicalCenter, New York City.

David Loewenstein, Ph.D., professor of psychiatry and behavioral sciences, University of Miami Miller School of Medicine.

Alzheimer's Association meeting, Honolulu.

A draft proposal that would update the diagnostic criteria for Alzheimer's disease for the first time in 25 years has just been presented to Alzheimer's experts.

The key change would put more focus on the various stages of the condition, according to the drafts from three workgroups convened by the US National Institute on Aging and the Alzheimer's Association.

While these criteria are still in use, experts say the field has changed a great deal since they were created in 1984.

"These changes are inevitable, given the forward movement of the scientific knowledge regarding Alzheimer's-how it develops, how it progresses and how it impacts the patient," said Martin Goldstein, MD, director of the department of neurology at Mount Sinai School of Medicine in New York City.

Developing methods to identify Alzheimer's in its early stages is essential to the early diagnosis of the disease, he added. This can also lead to new treatments.

DETAILS OF PROPOSED CHANGES

The proposed changes were presented at the Alzheimer's Association International Conference on Alzheimer's Disease 2010.

Among the reasons the criteria need to be updated is the new understanding that Alzheimer's starts years before symptoms are apparent, experts said. The earlier the disease can be identified, the better are the chances to slow its development, they added.

Among the ways researchers are identifying Alzheimer's are through genetic analysis of the blood, biomarkers in the cerebrospinal fluid and changes that can be seen on PET and MRI scans.

In addition, since 1984 there has been a better understanding of the differences between Alzheimer's disease and other types of dementia.

Much more is known about dementia caused by *Lewy body disease* (a build up of microscopic protein deposits known as Lewy bodies in the brain) as well as *Pick's disease* and other *frontotemporal dementias* (degeneration of the front and side parts of the brain).

The proposed changes in diagnosing Alzheimer's will take into account preclinical disease, which can help identify Alzheimer's before symptoms appear, and mild cognitive impairment, which can be the first signs of Alzheimer's. The evaluation of recommending specific biomarkers, which can aid in diagnosis, has also been proposed.

EXPERT REACTION

"The proposals would change the 1984 criteria by better reflecting the various stages of the disease and the inclusion of Alzheimer's disease biomarkers," said William Thies, PhD, chief medical and scientific officer at the Alzheimer's Association.

"While the role of biomarkers differs in each of the three stages, much remains to be understood concerning their reliability and validity in diagnosis. This makes it critical that we thoroughly test any new recommendations," Dr. Thies added.

Dr. Goldstein noted that these proposed changes would lead to new questions, including who should be screened and at what cost. "These changes have significant economic service delivery implications. It has significant public health implications, but it's ultimately a worthy goal," he said.

There are no effective treatments for Alzheimer's. "Current treatments are primarily symptomatic," Dr. Goldstein said. "The ultimate goal is stopping the pathological process long before it develops a momentum that can't be stopped."

Another expert, Mony de Leon, EdD, director of the Center for Brain Health at NYU Langone

Medical Center in New York City, called the proposed changes "long overdue."

The ultimate goal is to find a treatment for Alzheimer's, de Leon said. "But unless you know who needs the drug, how do you develop a drug?" he stated. "You need the early diagnosis before you can even consider the prevention work."

David Loewenstein, PhD, a professor of psychiatry and behavioral sciences at the University of Miami Miller School of Medicine, added, "a diagnosis of Alzheimer's used to be a diagnosis of exclusion."

If a patient had cognitive impairment that interfered with their social functioning, then Alzheimer's disease was only diagnosed after all likely causes were excluded, he explained.

"These new criteria are based on the fact that new science is showing that we actually have biomarkers that are sensitive to early Alzheimer's disease," Dr. Loewenstein said.

info For more information on Alzheimer's disease, visit the National Institute on Aging's Web site, *www.nia.nih.gov*, and click on "Alzheimer's Disease Information."

Breakthrough Jellyfish Treatment Makes You Smarter in Days

Mark A. Stengler, NMD, naturopathic medical doctor in private practice, La Jolla, California...adjunct associate clinical professor at the National College of Natural Medicine, Portland, Oregon...author of many books, including *The Natural Physician's Healing Therapies* and coauthor of *Prescription for Natural Cures* (both from Bottom Line Books)...and author of the *Bottom Line/Natural Healing* newsletter.

Scientists have found that a naturally occurring protein in one of the planet's oldest sea creatures—the jellyfish—might hold the key to improved memory and comprehension. The substance, *apoaequorin* (a-poh-ee-kwawr-in), found in the *Aequorea victoria* jellyfish species, has a unique way of working in the brain that is different from other natural memory enhancers. Many of my patients already are benefiting from it. Apoaequorin not only seems to reverse some of the effects of aging on the brain but also might help alleviate the effects of serious neurodegenerative diseases such as Alzheimer's disease, Parkinson's disease and ALS (Lou Gehrig's disease).

THE JELLYFISH CONNECTION

Scientists first discovered apoaequorin and its companion molecule, green fluorescent protein (GFP), in the *Aequorea* jellyfish, found off the west coast of North America, in the 1960s. The natural glow of GFP enables researchers to observe microscopic processes within cells that were previously invisible, such as how proteins are transported or how viruses enter cell membranes. Apoaequorin, which binds to calcium and becomes luminescent once it does, has been used since the 1990s in a similar way to track the activity of calcium in the body's cells. Later, three researchers who played key roles in developing these chemical markers were awarded the Nobel Prize in Chemistry.

MEMORY-BOOSTING PROPERTIES

Apoaequorin's value as a memory-boosting supplement also depends on its calcium-binding properties but in a different way. In the brain, calcium plays an important role in the chemical process that allows nerve cells to recharge before firing. It has to be present in just the right amounts. If too much calcium builds up inside a nerve cell, it interferes with the nerve-firing process and causes the cell to die. One of the key roles of calcium-binding proteins is to prevent the toxic buildup of calcium by removing excess calcium from the nerve cells.

In the normal course of aging, beginning at around age 40, the number of calcium-binding proteins in our brain cells starts to decline, resulting in the gradual buildup of toxic calcium inside these cells. This leads to impaired cellular function and eventually brain damage as the toxic calcium kills off brain cells. The symptoms of this age-related deterioration start slowly but then accelerate as we get older.

Because apoaequorin is similar to the naturally occurring calcium-binding proteins in the brain, the theory is that by taking daily supplements, you can replace the calcium-binding proteins that are lost through the aging process—allowing your brain cells to function optimally again while also preserving them from the long-term toxic effects of excess calcium.

A "EUREKA" MOMENT

The jellyfish protein went from "scientific" discovery to "supplement for the brain" because of the efforts of Mark Underwood, cofounder of the biotech firm Quincy Bioscience, the company that makes Prevagen (888-814-0814, *www.prevagen.com*), the only commercially available form of apoaequorin. Underwood's "eureka" moment came when he was reading about an Australian swimmer who developed multiple sclerosis–like symptoms after being stung by a jellyfish. Underwood wondered what protected the jellyfish from its own venom…and whether apoaequorin's calcium-binding abilities could have neuroprotective properties.

His company conducted a number of studies in conjunction with the University of Wisconsin–Milwaukee that found that apoaequorin did seem to have a powerful protective effect on brain cells. In one study, 56 people ranging in age from 20 to 78 showed significant improvements in memory after taking 10 mg of Prevagen daily for 30 days. More than half the group reported gains in general memory and information retention…two-thirds did better at word recall…and 84% showed improvement in their ability to remember driving directions.

Most of my patients and others report that taking Prevagen helps them feel mentally sharper, improves their memory and gives them more mental energy. Some even say that their mood is enhanced and that they sleep more soundly.

HOW TO USE IT

Prevagen is best taken in the morning (because cognitive function is more important during the day than at night), with or without food. I recommend it for anyone over age 40 who wants to improve memory and focus. While 10 milligrams (mg) daily is the recommended starting dose, apoaequorin also is safe at higher doses. I recommend that my own patients who have suffered a noticeable decline in cognitive function start out with 10 mg daily for four weeks. If they don't notice an improvement in memory and focus, they can increase to 20 mg daily. Most of my patients benefit from taking 10 mg or 20 mg daily. Research has shown that Prevagen is safe to take with other memory-enhancing supplements, such as omega-3 fish oils, or medications, such as *donepezil* (Aricept). People with allergies to fish or shellfish can use it because jellyfish is neither. The manufacturer of Prevagen is exploring apoaequorin's potential as a medical treatment for conditions such as Alzheimer's disease and Parkinson's disease.

With Age Comes Wisdom—Really!

Richard E. Nisbett, PhD, professor of psychology, University of Michigan, Ann Arbor.

Colin Milner, founder and chief executive officer, International Council on Active Aging, Vancouver, British Columbia, Canada.

S. Duke Han, PhD, assistant professor of clinical neuropsychology, Rush University Medical Center, Chicago.

Proceedings of the National Academy of Sciences online.

There just might be plenty of truth to the old adage, "With age comes wisdom," according to new research.

The study finds that seniors are better equipped than younger people to solve social conflicts. Seniors could more easily see multiple points of view, were more interested in searching for compromise and were more willing to acknowledge that there might be things about a difficult situation that they didn't know.

Taken together, those attributes make people age 60 and older generally wiser than younger people, the researchers said.

"People have held the opinion forever that older people are wiser," said senior study author Richard E. Nisbett, PhD, a professor of psychology and codirector of the Culture and Cognition program at the University of Michigan at Ann Arbor. "Now we have some evidence it's true. Independent of social class, older people are wiser, by our definition, for group conflicts and individual conflicts. And this was true independent of their level of intelligence."

The study findings were published in an on-line edition of the *Proceedings of the National Academy of Sciences.*

STUDY DETAILS

For the study, the researchers divided 247 participants into three age groups: 25 to 40; 41 to 59; and 60 and older. The participants were presented with three stories about social conflicts. One story, for example, described immigration tensions between the Kyrgyzes and the Tajiks in Tajikistan in central Asia. The newer immigrants, the Kyrgyzes, wanted to preserve their customs, while the native Tajiks wanted Kyrgyzes to assimilate.

The participants were asked to reflect on the scenarios. Their answers were then rated for their wisdom, or "the ability to use intelligence for the social good," Dr. Nisbett said. Specifically, participants were rated on well-accepted characteristics of wisdom: being able to see the point of view of each side of the dispute; realizing that situations rarely stay static; being able to see multiple ways in which the conflict could unfold; recognizing the limits of their own knowledge; and showing a willingness to search for conflict resolution and compromise.

Though the answers varied, wise responses were those that encouraged immigrants to try to fit into their new country, while also encouraging natives to be more tolerant of new arrivals wanting to hold on to the familiar.

Unwise comments included those such as: "If you can't speak the language, stay at home or get the hell out of there."

Participants ages 60 and older had higher wisdom scores than either of the other two age groups, the researchers found.

In a second experiment, the researchers asked participants to read "Dear Abby" letters involving personal conflicts between spouses, friends and siblings. Participants were asked how they thought the conflict might unfold over time, and what they thought should be done in the situation.

On average, older people also came up with wiser answers by nearly all measures than younger people, according to the study results.

POSSIBLE EXPLANATION

Changes in the brain that occur with aging might help to explain the study findings, said S. Duke Han, PhD, an assistant professor of clinical neuropsychology at Rush University Medical Center in Chicago.

Recent neuroimaging research has suggested that older adults use more of their frontal lobes on memory tasks than younger adults. The frontal lobes of the brain are generally thought to be key to abstract reasoning, problem solving, concept formation and multitasking, Dr. Han said.

"It could be that as older adults learn to use more of their frontal lobes to compensate for declines in other cognitive abilities, the greater use of the frontal lobes allows them to reason more fully about social conflicts," Dr. Han said.

IMPLICATIONS

Dr. Nisbett said the findings should come as good news, given the constant barrage of information about the physical and mental declines that can come with aging.

"We keep finding ways in which older people are cognitively defective. With every passing year, I am made more and more aware of the limits of my ability to learn new things," Dr. Nisbett said. "But if you have a social conflict, look for an older person to give you advice or discuss it. They are going to have perspectives on it that may be useful in helping you understand what the conflict is about and how it might be resolved."

Colin Milner, chief executive officer of the International Council on Active Aging, said the findings confirm what many have believed to be true.

"In eastern cultures, older adults are revered for their knowledge. It's only in western culture that we say the marketers no longer have an interest in you, jobs are harder to get and that you should want to retire and do nothing," Milner said. "The reality is we have all of this life experience that can be very valuable."

info To learn more about the brain and aging, visit the University of Southern California Web site, *www.usc.edu,* and search "aging brain."

How to Have Great Sex at Any Age

The late Robert N. Butler, MD, professor of geriatrics at Mount Sinai School of Medicine in New York City and the president and CEO of the International Longevity Center (*www.ilcusa.org*). He was founding director of the National Institute on Aging and the coauthor of *The New Love and Sex After 60* (Ballantine).

Despite what Hollywood would have us believe, sex isn't limited to people under age 40. In fact, recent research shows that a sizable percentage of Americans are remaining sexually active into their 70s, 80s and beyond. But let's be honest—there are obstacles, both physical and psychological, to maintaining a healthy sex life as we age.

Very good news: After years of research and clinical practice as a specialist in longevity, I have found six key principles that, taken together, can help the vast majority of couples—no matter what age—have a good sex life. And when a couple has a satisfying sex life, their feelings of fondness and intimacy can grow stronger—and that improves every aspect of their lives. *For a great sex life at any age...*

1. Realize that sex and intimacy can literally add years to your life. Numerous studies have shown that close relationships are a key to maintaining good mental and physical health as we get older. Of course, emotional closeness can exist without sexual intimacy—but to the degree that sexuality helps enrich our closest relationships, it can be an important contributor to a long, healthy life.

Bottom line: If you give up on a good sex life, you may die sooner.

2. Ignore what society tells us about aging and sex. The idea of older people having sex is thought of as a rarity. This stereotype couldn't be further from the truth. A study of sexual activity among older Americans, published in *The New England Journal of Medicine*, showed that more than one-half of men and women between the ages of 65 and 74 and more than one-quarter of those between 75 and 85 had been sexually active within the previous 12 months. And among those who reported that they were in good or excellent health, these figures were considerably higher.

Bottom line: Don't let society's false stereotype keep you from one of the great joys of life.

3. Take care of your health. A healthy blood flow to the sexual organs is essential for sexual response. That's why maintaining good cardiovascular health—including managing cholesterol levels and blood pressure as well as exercising—is key to a good sex life. *Also vital...*

•**If you have diabetes, control it.** Diabetes is a killer of sexuality because it damages the cardiovascular system and the body's peripheral nerves.

•**Discuss with your doctor whether any medications you take might be affecting your sexual desire or response.** Examples: Antidepressants can significantly reduce libido, while diuretics and beta-blockers used for high blood pressure can cause erectile dysfunction. Ask about alternative drugs and/or drugs that might counter the sexual side effects.

4. Steer clear of alcohol. A character in *Macbeth* famously said of alcohol, "It provokes the desire, but it takes away the performance." He was right. Alcohol can make us want sex more—and some women, in particular, say that their sexual pleasure is increased after drinking, most likely because alcohol reduces psychological inhibition. But even one drink can reduce a woman's vaginal blood flow and lubrication and intensity of orgasm. For men, intoxication can severely reduce the ability to achieve an erection and the intensity of orgasm—and regular alcohol consumption (even without intoxication) lowers testosterone levels, affecting quality of erection and orgasm.

Bottom line: A little alcohol might help—or at least not hurt your sex life. But it's best to save any imbibing for after sex.

5. Take advantage of medications and sex-related personal-care products. For older people, the introduction of the oral medications *sildenafil citrate* (Viagra), *vardenafil* (Levitra) and *tadalafil* (Cialis), which help men to maintain erections, has been an important development.

Reason: Erectile dysfunction is one of the most frequently cited reasons that older couples are no longer sexually active. While they are safe and effective for most men, talk with your doctor about potential side effects before trying any of these drugs.

What many couples don't realize: It is normal for an older man to need to have his penis physically stimulated to achieve an erection—just thinking about sex, or even kissing and other foreplay, often isn't enough. Ladies, this is not an indication of diminished desire.

As we all know, hormones play a great role in sex…

•**For men.** If you are unhappy with your sexual response after following the advice throughout this article, see an endocrinologist for a check on your levels of testosterone and thyroid hormones. A low level of either can dampen sexual desire and ability. Hormone supplements can be prescribed.

•**For women.** Older women often experience vaginal dryness, which can make intercourse far less enjoyable or sometimes impossible. This problem can be solved by applying an over-the-counter, non-oil-based lubricant, such as K-Y Jelly, Astroglide, or Slip, just before sex…or, to allow for more spontaneity, by using a moisturizing insert such as Lubrin (which lasts several hours) or Replens gel, which lasts several days. (Avoid oil-based lubricants, such as petroleum jelly and baby oil, which tend to remain in the vagina and create a breeding ground for infections.)

Alternative: If a lubricant isn't enough to make sex comfortable, ask your doctor about a topical form of the hormone estrogen, which can be applied to the vagina to increase your body's ability to lubricate itself.

6. Keep all the flames burning. If you're in a long-term relationship and you want a satisfying sex life, it's important to purposely set aside time for nonsexual intimacy on a regular basis. Perfect example: Years ago, I lived next door to a couple who had a weekly candlelight dinner in their backyard. This kind of intimate encounter may not always lead to sex—but it creates a psychological closeness that encourages physical intimacy.

IF YOU ARE SINGLE, DIVORCED, WIDOWED…

For older unmarried people, finding an appropriate sexual (and life) partner is a challenge.

This is especially true for older women, whose longer life span means they outnumber older men by about two to one.

But remember: The loss of a sexual partner wouldn't stop a 30-year-old from seeking a new relationship, so why should it stop you at age 60, 70, 80 or older?

To find a wonderful partner: The key is to frequently participate in activities that will expose you to potential partners, especially activities in which you have a strong interest, such as dancing, politics or art. This will give you the best chance of meeting someone you're attracted to and who shares your interests, an ideal starting place for developing a more intimate bond.

■ ■ ■ ■

Cheers! Wine Helps Men Live Longer

In a study of 1,373 men, those who drank wine—on average, less than one-half glass daily—lived an average of five years longer than alcohol abstainers and two-and-a-half years longer than beer and spirits drinkers.

Theory: Wine's cardiovascular benefits may account for the added longevity. More research is needed to assess whether these findings would also apply to women.

Marinette Streppel, PhD, researcher, division of human nutrition, Wageningen University, Wageningen, the Netherlands.

Aging Reversed For Real!

Paul McGlothin and Meredith Averill, practitioners of calorie restriction for 17 years. They are directors of the CR Way Longevity Center in Ossining, New York, and leaders of the CR Society International. They are authors of *The CR Way: Using the Secrets of Calorie Restriction for a Longer, Healthier Life* (HarperCollins) and the online e-book *The CR Way to Happy Dieting*, a guide to changing your biochemistry so that you feel optimistic most of the time. *www.LivingtheCRWay.com.*

Seventy years of scientific research shows that restricting calories to 30% below normal intake can extend life span by up to 50% in laboratory animals. New research shows that calorie restriction may extend the life span of human beings as well.

Paul McGlothin and Meredith Averill, experts on calorie restriction and authors of *The CR Way: Using the Secrets of Calorie Restriction for a Longer, Healthier Life*, spoke about some of their important findings…

NEWEST RESEARCH

Reporting in *Science,* researchers from the University of Wisconsin revealed the results of a study on calorie restriction in rhesus monkeys, our closest "relatives." The researchers studied 76 adult rhesus monkeys (which live an average of 27 years and a maximum of 40), dividing them into two groups. One group ate a calorie-restricted diet, and one didn't. After 20 years, 37% of the monkeys in the nonrestricted group had died, compared with only 13% in the calorie-restricted group. The calorie-restricted monkeys also had fewer incidences of heart disease, diabetes, cancer and brain disease.

In other research, scientists at Washington University School of Medicine in St. Louis studied the biomarkers of aging of 33 people, average age 51, who ate a calorie-restricted diet for an average of six years. Compared with another group of people who ate a typical American diet, the calorie-restricted practitioners had lab results that are typical of people much younger than themselves. They had lower cholesterol, lower blood pressure, less body fat and lower glucose (blood sugar) levels.

The study participants also had lower levels of insulin (the hormone that regulates blood sugar)…C-reactive protein (a biomarker for disease-causing inflammation)…tumor necrosis factor (a biomarker for an overactive immune system)…and thyroid hormone T3 (lower levels indicate a slower, cell-preserving metabolic rate).

WHY IT WORKS

There are several theories as to why calorie restriction improves health and may increase life span. *It may…*

•**Reduce DNA damage.**

•**Reduce daily energy expenditure,** the most basic of metabolic processes, thereby reducing oxidative stress, the internal "rust" that damages cells.

•**Decrease core body temperature.** The higher your normal body temperature, the faster you age.

•**Improve how the cells handle insulin, which controls glucose.** Poor glucose regulation damages cells.

•**Improve the neuroendocrine system,** the link between the brain and the hormones that regulate many of the body's functions.

•**Activate a type of gene called sirtuins,** which protect *mitochondria*, tiny energy factories in the cells. Mitochondrial failure speeds aging.

EASY WAY TO CUT BACK

The level of calorie restriction probably required to extend life in humans—about 20% to 30% of typical intake—is more than most people are willing to do on a regular basis, but reducing calories by even 5% can produce significant health benefits.

Estimated calorie requirements for a moderately active person age 51 or older are 2,200 to 2,400 calories a day for a man and 1,800 for a woman. Reducing calories by 5% would mean cutting between 110 and 120 daily calories for a man and 90 for a woman.

With just a few changes in your dietary routine, you easily can reduce calories by 5% or more and improve your health…

•**Favor nutrient-dense foods.** A nutrient-dense food has a high amount of nutrients per calorie. They're the healthiest foods to eat. *They include…*

Animal protein: Salmon (Alaskan wild, canned, fresh or frozen), sardines, tuna.

Good fats: Nuts…avocados…grapeseed oil, extra-virgin olive oil.

Beans: Adzuki, limas, black-eyed peas, black turtle beans, garbanzos (chickpeas), lentils (red or green), mung, pinto, soy.

Veggies: Arugula, beets, bok choy, broccoli, cabbage, carrots, chard, collard greens, garlic, kale, kohlrabi, leeks, mushrooms (maitake, portobello, shiitake), mustard greens, onions, romaine lettuce, spinach, squash (butternut, summer), sweet potatoes, tomatoes.

Grains: Barley, quinoa, wild rice, sprouted-grain breads.

Fruit: Apricots, blackberries, blueberries, cantaloupe, cranberries, kiwi, lemons, limes, oranges, peaches, raspberries, strawberries, tangerines.

Spices and herbs: Season foods with herbs and spices rather than salt, butter or sugar. Examples include basil, chives, ginger, parsley and turmeric.

•**Focus on foods with low-to-moderate Glycemic Index rankings.** High levels of glucose and insulin are linked to faster aging and disease. It's just as important to limit glucose as it is to limit calories.

The best way to regulate glucose and insulin is to choose carbohydrates that have a low-to-moderate score on the Glycemic Index (GI)—carbohydrates that digest slowly so that glucose and insulin levels don't suddenly skyrocket.

The beans, veggies, grains and fruits that are nutrient-dense (listed above) have a low-to-moderate GI score.

Other ways to keep glucose low…

•Start your meal with one cup of water with one tablespoon of lemon juice.

•Finish your last meal of the day as early as possible, eating complex carbohydrates and a fat source.

•After your evening meal, take a 45-minute or longer walk.

•**Keep protein intake moderate.** Excess protein can increase blood levels of the hormone *Insulin-Like Growth Factor-I* (IGF-I), which deactivates a sirtuin gene and accelerates aging.

Each day, eat 0.36 grams (g) of protein per pound of body weight—at your healthiest, ideal body weight. That's 43 g of protein a day for a woman whose ideal weight is 120 pounds and 55 g of protein a day for a man whose ideal weight is 154 pounds. For comparison, typical intake for US adults is 65 g to 90 g. One ounce of meat or fish contains about 7 g of protein.

•**Stop eating before you're full.** Always leave the table slightly hungry. This helps you cut calories and prompts the hypothalamus—the emotion-generating part of the brain—to produce the hormone orexin, which boosts feelings of happiness. The Japanese have a concept for this healthful practice—*hara hachi bu*—which means eat until you're 80% full.

Slimming Secrets for Seniors from a Trusted Doctor

Nancy Snyderman, MD, chief medical editor for NBC News and host of MSNBC's *Dr. Nancy.* She is a head and neck cancer surgeon and associate clinical professor in the department of otolaryngology/head and neck surgery at the University of Pennsylvania, Philadelphia. Dr. Snyderman is cofounder of LLuminari, a communications network of health experts, *www.bewell.com*, and author of *Diet Myths That Keep Us Fat* (Crown).

Shedding even just a few pounds can have profound health benefits for people who are overweight. But those of us who have tried to lose weight as we age know how difficult and frustrating it can be.

I'm a veteran of the diet wars. I have binged, dieted and skipped meals. I've tried dozens of diets and exercised in sauna suits, and I even went through one period where I subsisted on nothing but vanilla wafers and black coffee.

What I discovered: The quest for a silver bullet is one of the main reasons people never lose weight and keep it off. We're fascinated by the latest theory about calories or fad diets. But unless the diet fits our lifestyle, it's bound to fail—and then we gain weight again. Finally, I started "making friends" with food—and with exercise. *Strategies that worked for me…*

FOOD AS FUEL

Many Americans have become so accustomed to eating out of anxiety or boredom and using food as a reward or as entertainment that they actually have trouble identifying when they are hungry and when they are not.

Solution: Start thinking of food as nothing more than fuel. This isn't a romantic notion—but it will help you lose weight.

Counting calories isn't fun, but it does work. Calories are important because they are actually a measure of the potential energy in food. Think of calories in terms of a bank account. You make deposits by eating calories and withdrawals by burning calories through exercise—only you want this bank account to have just enough in it.

To lose weight: Most people should aim for 1,200 to 1,500 calories daily, depending on their height and activity level. That's enough fuel to keep you going during the day and help you lose up to eight pounds in a month but not so little that you feel hungry all the time. The best choices when trying to achieve this calorie level are nutritious, low-calorie fruits, vegetables, healthful whole grains (such as brown rice) and lean proteins (such as skinless chicken).

At first, it might help if you keep a food journal in which you write down what you eat and each food's calorie amount. There are many online sites that list calories. A good, free one is *CalorieCount.com.*

My approach: Learn what is contained in 100-calorie portions—such as 15 almonds, one large egg, one-third of an avocado. Once you know these general portion sizes, you can easily count up by 100s your day's worth of food.

EATING STRATEGIES

Some of the best ways to make a friend of food and master weight control…

•**Make sure that your medications aren't working against you.** Many prescription drugs increase appetite or slow metabolism. Drugs that might affect weight include antidepressants, such as *paroxetine* (Paxil), *escitalopram* (Lexapro) and *sertraline* (Zoloft), as well as insulin medication, such as *glyburide* (Diabeta). Your physician may be able to adjust your dosage or switch you to a drug that doesn't have these side effects.

•**Don't deprive yourself.** I believe that depriving yourself of your favorite foods sets you up for failure. If you really want a piece of cake, eat it as an entrée. Allowing yourself the occasional splurge means that you may be less likely to overindulge.

•**Mix low-fat carbohydrates with proteins at every meal.** This combination slows down digestion and allows you to eat less but still feel full.

Example: Rice cakes will satisfy your hunger as a snack more effectively if you eat them with a piece of sliced turkey or a smear of peanut butter.

•**Widen the color spectrum of the fruits and vegetables you eat.** Eat a variety of fruits and vegetables with deep colors, such as blueberries, tomatoes, broccoli, spinach and sweet potatoes. They are densely packed with healthful nutrients, such as cancer-fighting antioxidants, vitamins and fiber.

Helpful: If you are unable to clean or cut vegetables, select precut vegetables at the grocery store. Many people with arthritis, for example, shy away from healthful foods because they are too difficult to prepare.

•**Control your portions.** Using a nine-inch salad plate instead of a dinner-sized 11- or 13-inch plate can help you serve yourself smaller portions.

Another way: Divide your plate into three sections—one each for protein, carbohydrate and vegetable. Having distinct sections cuts back on overflowing—and oversized—servings.

•**Have dessert but take just three bites.** This requires only a little willpower. Researchers have found that taste buds provide the maximum amount of pleasure in the first three bites of a food, and then the eater starts to get bored by the fourth bite. The rest of the dessert offers diminishing returns—you ingest more calories but derive less pleasure.

•**When you feel like bingeing, drink water.** People often blow their diets by bingeing when they feel hungry between meals.

Solution: Drink an eight-ounce glass of water. You will be amazed how full it will make you feel.

Bonus: You stay hydrated. As you age, your body has a harder time recognizing the need for fluids, which is why many seniors get dehydrated.

•**Curb your appetite by eating "wet" carbohydrates when very hungry.** Wet carbs are such foods as cooked oatmeal, yams and brown rice, which are full of fiber and moisture that create a bulk effect in your stomach. You can eat them at mealtimes or as a snack.

Other wet carbs: Fruits and vegetables.

•**Add herbs and spices with strong flavors to your food.** Older people often suffer diminished taste and smell and reach for the salt shaker or butter to enhance food.

Better: Tarragon, ground cinnamon and turmeric, all of which add a strong accent to food, won't raise your blood pressure like salt.

•**Skip herbal supplements for weight loss.** Avoid herbal supplements that contain bitter orange extract, *L-carnitine* (an amino acid derivative that helps fat metabolize within cells) and *hoodia*, the extract from an African cactuslike succulent plant. Flimsy evidence of their safety and effectiveness makes them too speculative for me to recommend.

A word about exercise: Find a physical activity that you like to do—and do it for 30 minutes on as many days as you can. My favorites are walking, hiking and biking outdoors.

Constipation? How to Get Things Moving

Brian Lacy, MD, PhD, director of the gastrointestinal motility lab, Dartmouth-Hitchcock Medical Center, Lebanon, New Hampshire, and associate professor of medicine, Dartmouth Medical School, Hanover, New Hampshire.

The word "constipation" comes from the Latin meaning "to press or crowd together." And that's just what happens in this common digestive disorder—stool becomes hard and compressed…and/or difficult to expel from the body. There are traditional remedies—some of which can work in the right circumstances—and there's also a new drug that has been created to help with chronic constipation.

We all get constipation sometimes. *Here's what you need to know to remedy constipation and keep it from becoming chronic…*

WHAT'S NORMAL?

While most people think of constipation as the inability to have a daily bowel movement, the definition is broader than that. Studies show that the "normal" frequency of bowel movements varies. Some people may have more than one bowel movement per day, while others may routinely have a bowel movement every couple of days. I generally consider someone constipated if he/she typically goes three or four days

between bowel movements. On the other hand, you may have a daily bowel movement that involves lengthy straining—which also qualifies as constipation.

While constipation can cause discomfort and may affect your quality of life, it doesn't pose a health threat in and of itself. Until recently, it had been thought that infrequent bowel movements could increase the risk for colorectal cancer. But a recent large-scale study in Japan found that only very infrequent bowel movements (every 10 to 14 days) could increase the risk. Some of the main health risks associated with constipation arise from the physical stress of passing hard stools—which may cause hemorrhoids and, in some cases, a fissure or tearing of the rectum.

CAUSES OF CONSTIPATION

Most people experience constipation as a temporary condition brought on by a change in diet…medication (constipation can be caused by narcotic pain relievers, high-dose iron supplements and some blood-pressure drugs)…or travel (when you are thrown off your routine, not following your normal diet or not able to make regular bathroom visits). For this group, self-treatment with an over-the-counter laxative will usually restore regular bowel function.

For others, constipation is chronic—it does not go away. *The two main causes of chronic constipation are…*

•**Irritable bowel syndrome (IBS).** This disorder of unknown cause is associated with the abnormal function of the muscles of the colon. It accounts for 30% to 40% of all chronic constipation and is usually associated with bloating and pain in the lower abdomen.

•**Pelvic floor dysfunction.** This condition accounts for another 30% to 40% of chronic constipation. More common in women than men, it occurs when the muscles and nerves in the pelvic floor (the muscles under the pelvis) aren't coordinating properly. Constipation due to pelvic floor dysfunction won't respond to laxatives but can usually be cured through physical therapy.

Chronic constipation also can result from other disorders including neurological disorders (such as Parkinson's, multiple sclerosis and stroke)…

metabolic and endocrine conditions (such as diabetes and an underactive thyroid)…and systemic disorders (such as lupus or *scleroderma*). A problem in the colon, such as *diverticulosis* or cancer, can also cause constipation, although this is not common.

Whatever the cause, constipation becomes much more prevalent over age 65, and women are more likely than men to become constipated.

TREATMENTS THAT WORK

For occasional constipation or constipation due to IBS, the first line of treatment involves establishing a regular bathroom schedule, dietary changes and over-the-counter medications. *What to do…*

•**Establish a regular bathroom schedule.** A wave of motility goes through everyone's GI tract around 5 a.m., which is why many people feel the urge to have a bowel movement in the morning. A similar wave occurs after eating. I encourage my patients to listen to their bodies and to arrange for scheduled bathroom times that coincide with their urges to have bowel movements. Give yourself three to four weeks to adjust to this schedule.

•**Add fiber to your diet.** Dietary fiber speeds movement of food through the GI tract and binds with water, causing stools to become bulkier and pass out of the colon more easily. Optimal fiber intake is 25 to 30 grams a day, but the average American consumes less than half this amount.

Solution: Eat more high-fiber foods, such as legumes (split peas, lentils, black beans, lima beans, baked beans, etc.), fresh fruits and vegetables (artichokes, raspberries, pears, broccoli), whole-wheat pasta and cereals and other foods containing whole bran or oats. You can also boost fiber intake with supplements, such as *psyllium* husk powder (Metamucil, Serutan) or *methylcellulose* (Citrucel). It may take three or four days to notice positive effects.

•**Try an over-the-counter laxative.** If regular bathroom visits and additional fiber don't solve the problem, add an over-the-counter laxative. There are different types—for example, osmotic, which draw water into the area, or lubricant, which help stools move more easily. Milk of magnesia is a safe, effective and inex-

pensive choice. To avoid elevated magnesium levels, however, it shouldn't be taken for longer than two weeks—and should be avoided by anyone with kidney disease. Miralax, another laxative, also is safe and effective for seven days, but some people don't like mixing the powder. Stimulant laxatives, such as *bisacodyl* (Dulcolax), have been shown to improve constipation with short-term use, though they may cause cramping. After two weeks, however, the body develops a tolerance to them. If your constipation is not improved within two weeks, consult your doctor.

Not recommended: Stool softeners. These popular laxatives are a waste of money. They are supposed to work by drawing water into the stool, making it softer and easier to pass. But they bulk up stool by only 3%—and that's not enough to make any difference in your bowel movements.

Also not helpful: Exercise. While regular physical activity is beneficial in many ways, studies have shown conclusively that it has no effect on chronic constipation.

WHEN TO SEEK MEDICAL HELP

Most people are helped by the steps above. But if you see no improvement after several weeks, ask your primary care doctor for a prescription-strength laxative. An osmotic agent called *lactulose* (Chronulac, Constilac)—which is made of sugar molecules that make the gut more acidic and causes more water to be drawn in—makes bowel movements easier. Although side effects can include gas and bloating, people can take lactulose indefinitely. There is also a new medication for chronic constipation called *lubiprostone* (Amitiza) that has been found to be safe and effective. It is the first medication for constipation that works by stimulating intestinal fluid secretions that help the bowels move. Most patients prefer lubiprostone because it comes in a pill, not a sugary drink (like lactulose) and because there is no bloating.

If these prescriptions drugs still don't help, there may be an underlying condition that is causing the problem and you may need to see your primary care provider or a gastroenterologist for testing. This may include a complete blood count (CBC) test to make sure that you are not anemic and a thyroid-stimulating hormone (TSH) test to make sure that you do not have an underactive thyroid gland. This visit should also include a physical exam to check for pelvic floor dysfunction or any neuromuscular disorder. Since constipation can sometimes be a sign of colon cancer, a colonoscopy may be recommended.

Lastly, some patients with severe constipation swallow a capsule with markers to determine how quickly the markers pass through the gastrointestinal tract.

If pelvic floor dysfunction is detected, the patient will be referred to a physical therapist for a series of specific exercises for the pelvic floor and surrounding muscles.

If the constipation still doesn't improve and is seriously affecting quality of life, the last resort is a surgical procedure, called a *colectomy*, in which the colon is removed and the small intestine connected directly to the rectum. While this relieves constipation, it also results in frequent bowel movements—up to four per day.

Smile! New Ways to Keep Your Teeth for Life

Dennis P. Tarnow, DDS, a periodontist and a prosthodontist (a dentist who specializes in the fitting and placing of implants, bridges and dentures) and professor and chairman of the department of periodontology and implant dentistry at New York University College of Dentistry, both in New York City. Dr. Tarnow is a recipient of the Master Clinician Award from the American Academy of Periodontology. He has published more than 100 peer-reviewed articles and coauthored three textbooks.

B y the time we reach middle age, most of us have had a few root canals—or worse. Years of use make our teeth weaker and more vulnerable to decay and breakage.

Surprising statistic: At least two out of every 10 older Americans (about 20 million people) are toothless.

But strong, healthy teeth are important: If you have dental pain or denture problems, it can be difficult to eat fruits and vegetables, which are crucial for adequate nutrition. In addition, numerous studies have linked gum (periodontal) disease—a primary cause of tooth problems—to a variety of serious ailments, including heart disease, diabetes, dementia and some forms of cancer. *How to optimize the health of your teeth…*

• **Use sugarless candy or gum to stimulate saliva.** Salivary flow decreases as we age, creating an ideal environment for mouth bacteria to flourish. Many heart drugs, antidepressants and other medications may further decrease saliva production.

To help lubricate your dry mouth, your doctor may have suggested that you suck on mints or other small candies. But the sugar in such candies—including so-called breath mints—feeds bacteria in the mouth, accelerating tooth decay you may not even see.

My advice: Switch to sugarless candies—or chew sugarless gum. Also avoid "sticky" foods, such as dried fruit (including raisins and prunes), that tend to promote tooth decay.

• **Bite carefully.** Our teeth become more fragile as we age, and any tooth that has had a root canal, crown or filling is more brittle than an intact tooth. A crown (a custom-made structure like a thimble that fits over a trimmed-down tooth that has decayed) typically lasts for seven to 10 years, but the longevity of natural teeth, crowns and fillings may be shortened if you don't take the right precautions.

My advice: If you have crowns, fillings and/or veneers (facings applied to the front of teeth to improve their shape and/or color) in the front of your mouth, biting into an apple, carrot or even a crusty piece of bread could shatter them.

Instead, bite with your side teeth to shift the force on to them. Better yet, cut up apples, carrots or hard bread into bite-sized pieces so you can chew with the teeth in the back of your mouth (molars), which are usually the strongest.

Caution: Never chew ice—even molars can be shattered with one good crunch. Also, don't use your teeth as "tools" to do such things as open plastic packages, cut thread or crack nut shells.

• **Pamper your gums.** Most people have some degree of gum recession (in which the gums have pulled back, exposing the roots of the teeth). It results from brushing too aggressively or from gum disease. Receding gums make teeth more susceptible to cavities at the roots and increase their sensitivity.

Smart idea: If you have receding gums and use "sensitive" toothpaste (such as Sensodyne or Colgate Sensitive), apply it with your finger to the sensitive area, count to 60 (to ensure good absorption), then brush.

My advice: To minimize gum recession, most people know to use a "soft" or "ultrasoft" toothbrush, but it's also important for these brushes to be replaced at least every three to four months. After that point, the bristles usually flare out and become less effective. When brushing, use light pressure. I recommend electric toothbrushes only if you have arthritis in your hands or some other condition that affects manual dexterity.

●**Be vigilant about self-care.** Up to 30% of the population is genetically predisposed to gum disease, which is a major cause of tooth loss. Even people who are not genetically primed for gum disease may wind up with bacterial infections in the tissues surrounding the teeth as a result of changing hormone levels, poor self-care or other health problems.

My advice: For adults with healthy teeth, twice-daily thorough brushing is fine. If you have gum disease or its precursor (gingivitis), which causes such symptoms as swollen gums, bad breath and gums that bleed easily when brushing or flossing, brush your teeth after every meal—or, if that's inconvenient, at least swish your mouth with water after you eat.

Important: Brush for a full two minutes with any fluoride toothpaste. When you floss (any type is fine), be sure to remove the plaque from the sides of every tooth.

Important: Since many people now drink bottled water instead of tap water, which is fluoridated in most municipalities, some experts fear that the incidence of tooth decay may increase. If you live in a community that does not have fluoridated water, look for bottled water brands that are fluoridated. Many companies, including Deer Park and Poland Spring, produce fluoridated bottled water.

For a list of companies: Consult the International Bottled Water Association, 800-928-3711, *www.bottledwater.org/public/fluoride.htm.*

●**Opt for an implant.** In the old days, when you lost a tooth, your dentist would crown the teeth adjacent to an empty space and create a "bridge" to hold a replacement tooth. An implant (a metal post and abutment that are surgically anchored into the jawbone to provide support for a crown) generally is a better option because its placement does not require cutting down adjacent teeth. However, the price of a bridge may be lower than implants initially, and some insurance companies balk at covering the cost of an implant.

My advice: If your dentist recommends a bridge, ask whether an implant can be used instead. If cost is an issue, work out a payment plan with your dentist.

Helpful: If your dental insurance does not cover implants, insist that your case be reviewed by a dentist. About half the time, such appeals result in at least partial reimbursement. Or ask the insurance company to pay you its standard reimbursement for a bridge and apply it to your implant.

If the cost is still too high: Go to a nearby dental school, where students are supervised by professors and the cost is about half of that charged at a private practice.

Secrets to Keeping Your Teeth Forever

Edmond Bedrossian, DDS, director of implant training at the University of the Pacific Oral and Maxillofacial Surgery Residency Program in San Francisco. He also maintains a private practice in San Francisco and is a fellow of the American College of Dentists (FACD) and fellow of the American College of Maxillofacial Surgeons (FACOMS). Dr. Bedrossian is coauthor of *A Patient's Guide to Dental Implants* (Addicus), as well as three dental textbooks.

For generations, removable dentures were the only option for replacing teeth lost to decay, infection or injury. During more recent decades, dental implants have offered a more comfortable and natural-looking alternative. And recent advances in dental technology—including "immediate loading" and computer-guided insertion—have made implants more convenient and efficient.

What you need to know…

WHY IMPLANTS?

Implants have several advantages over traditional bridges and dentures…

•**Bone health.** Like other types of bone, jawbone requires pressure to remain strong. Biting with natural teeth transfers pressure via the root into the bone, but this force is lost when teeth are removed and one is chewing with dentures. Over time, the bone shrinks and deteriorates in a process called *resorption*.

•**Implants allow pressure to be transferred through the post into the bone during chewing,** mimicking pressure from natural teeth and helping to maintain the jawbone.

•**Comfort.** Implants do not irritate the gums or interfere with chewing, taste or speech, unlike dentures. They allow you to chew any and all types of food.

COST

The main drawback of implants is the cost—approximately $2,000 to $3,000 per tooth for implant surgery, plus $1,800 to $3,000 per tooth for the crown. When a full arch is being replaced—the entire upper set of teeth or the entire lower set—$30,000 per arch is an average estimate. Insurance typically does not cover implant surgery, although some plans may reimburse part of the cost of crowns.

THREE STAGES

Traditional implant surgery is a three-stage process over several months. Your own dentist may be trained in performing implant surgery. More likely, an oral surgeon or a periodontist performs the surgery (in consultation with your dentist), and a restorative dentist makes and fits the crowns.

Stage 1: **Insert the implants.** After the dental professional has performed an examination and taken X-rays, implants are custom-ordered to the precise size. During the first surgery, lasting one to four hours under local or general anesthesia, the surgeon places the titanium implant (or implants) by making small incisions to lift away the gum, drilling a small hole in the bone, inserting the post and suturing the gum closed.

The jawbone then is given three to six months to fuse to the implant before the tooth-like crown is placed. This fusing process, called *osseointegration*, is essential to the success of the implant.

Many patients are surprised to find that they have less discomfort after surgery than they expected. One to two days of rest at home is enough for most patients, and pain can be managed with over-the-counter pain relievers and prescription medications, such as Vicodin. Applying ice to the jaw keeps down swelling.

Helpful: A rinse of warm water and salt (one teaspoon of salt in a cup of warm water) should be used four to five times a day, especially after meals, starting on the morning after surgery.

Slight bleeding is not unusual. One way to stop bleeding is to double-wrap a tea bag with slightly dampened gauze and gently bite on it for 45 minutes. Black tea helps the blood to clot.

Only soft food should be eaten for the first few weeks after surgery. If implants are disturbed during the early stages of healing, osseointegration will not occur.

Be gentle brushing the surgical areas. Do not use an electric toothbrush during the three-to-six-month period of implant healing.

During the months after the titanium screw is put in place, the space above it—where the crown will be—usually is left empty if the tooth is in the back of the mouth. If the missing tooth is in the front, the patient is given a temporary, removable denture.

Stage 2: **Connect the abutments.** Three months (for implants in the lower jaw) to six months (upper jaw) after initial surgery, the implant is uncovered and checked manually by the doctor to make sure osseointegration has been successful.

If the implant is firmly rooted in the jawbone, then the surgeon connects the abutment—the foundation for the new tooth—to the implant and places a temporary crown on it. An impression of the mouth is then made for use in making the permanent crown.

Depending on the number of teeth to be replaced, it may take one to eight weeks for the new crowns to be ready.

When many adjacent teeth are being replaced, a special bridge often is used instead of individual implants and crowns. Similar to a traditional bridge, the implant bridge attaches to the titanium implants rather than to other teeth.

Note: If the implant moves at all—which happens in as few as 3% of cases—the implant has not fused to the bone, the procedure has failed and the post must be removed.

After allowing about three months for the bone to heal, the procedure can be tried again. Further implants are likely to be successful.

***Stage 3:* Complete the restoration.** The crown is fitted to the abutment. This phase also is called *loading the implants*.

Care afterward—brushing and flossing—is the same as for regular teeth.

NEWER OPTIONS

•**Immediate loading.** Some specialists use an accelerated process in which they insert implants, attach abutments and place temporary crowns during a single session. The patient still must eat soft foods and return in several months—after the bone has fused to the implant—for a permanent crown.

In addition to being convenient for the patient, immediate loading helps preserve surrounding gum and bone by more quickly filling in the gap left by the missing teeth. It can be a good option for people with receding gums and for patients missing a few or all of their teeth.

The procedure requires a great deal of technical skill—not all dentists are familiar with the procedure—and it costs more than traditional implants.

•**Computer-guided insertion.** Using a CT scan of the patient's jaw, the dentist plans the position of the implant on a computer. A laboratory makes a surgical template (similar to a drill press) to fit the patient's mouth. The technology makes it possible to place implants by drilling through the gum without making incisions. The goal of this treatment approach is to place the implants, connect the abutments and secure the temporary teeth all in a single session. After

three to six months of osseointegration, the final bridges can be made.

WHO SHOULD AVOID IMPLANT SURGERY?

Though many people can benefit from implants, they are not appropriate for everyone.

Usually, children under age 18 should not have implants. The jaw and teeth need to have stopped growing before such a procedure is performed.

Smokers have a higher implant failure rate than nonsmokers. Smoking impairs blood circulation and healing, increasing the likelihood that the implant will not fuse to the bone.

People with uncontrolled diabetes are not good candidates for implants, because diabetes is associated with bone loss, gum loss and difficulty healing in general. Implants can be considered after diabetes is under control.

Patients who have lost substantial bone from the jaw are candidates for replacement of all their teeth with the immediate-loading approach. However, in rare cases, if bone is not available to accommodate implants, bone grafts—using bone from elsewhere in the patient's jaw or body—can sometimes heighten or widen the jawbone enough to make implants possible.

How to Stop Macular Degeneration (Works for Almost Everyone)

Rishi Singh, MD, associate staff member in the department of ophthalmology at the Cleveland Clinic. He has published numerous articles in peer-reviewed journals and currently is leading clinical trials on treatment for eye conditions, including age-related macular degeneration.

The eye condition known as *age-related macular degeneration* (AMD) has long been associated with blindness, since no drug or surgical procedure has been able to halt the disease's progression.

Now: New treatments, including a simple nutritional therapy, have given hope to the up to 10 million Americans who suffer from the early stages of AMD.

If caught before permanent damage has occurred, the most serious form of AMD can be stabilized in 90% of people with the condition—and one-third even may experience improved vision.

ARE YOU AT RISK?

The incidence of AMD is on the rise—primarily due to the "graying" of America. As Americans live longer, AMD, which grows more common with age, affects increasing numbers of adults. Almost one in three Americans over age 75 has it. Obesity, which is strongly linked to increased risk, also remains high. *Other risk factors…*

•**Family history,** which increases risk due to a likely genetic component to AMD. If a close relative (parent or sibling) has had AMD, your own risk is greater.

•**Stroke and "mini" strokes,** which often are referred to as transient ischemic attacks (TIAs). Both result in a substantially higher risk for AMD. This increased risk is thought to be due to injury to the blood vessels, which occurs with strokes, TIAs—and AMD.

•**Cigarette smoking,** which increases oxidative stress throughout the body. It can quadruple the chance of developing AMD. Quitting will reduce the danger, but you're still at higher risk than people who never smoked.

DAMAGE IS PROGRESSIVE

AMD occurs when there is a deterioration of the tissue in the *macula*, the central area of the light-sensitive retina.

There are two forms of AMD…

•**Dry macular degeneration.** In up to 85% of AMD cases, deposits of protein and cholesterol called *drusen* develop among the pigmented cells behind the macula. These deposits cut retinal cells off from their blood supply, depriving them of nutrients and oxygen, leading to the accumulation of waste products.

As the drusen grow, central vision gets blurry. If the degenerative process continues, a blind spot may develop in your central vision.

•**Wet macular degeneration.** This form of AMD, which typically develops from the dry form, is responsible for the bulk of serious vision loss. Damage to the retina spurs the formation of fragile new blood vessels that often leak fluid or blood into the area around the macula. If untreated, wet macular degeneration often progresses rapidly—and within weeks or months, sight may deteriorate to the point of legal blindness.

Don't ignore the red flags: Because the progressive vision loss of AMD often can be halted, it is essential to spot the disease and start treatment as early as possible. If you notice changes in central vision (such as difficulty recognizing faces)…a decline in your ability to distinguish colors and details…and/or night blindness (inability to see in very dim light), see an eye specialist (ophthalmologist or optometrist) promptly.

Important: AMD can start in one eye while the other remains normal. This can make changes in vision difficult to notice until they become pronounced and affect both eyes.

Best approach: Schedule a yearly eye exam, particularly after age 65, to spot early signs of AMD. The doctor should use drops to dilate the pupils so he/she can see the retinas clearly with a magnifying instrument. To monitor your eyesight between visits to your doctor, check your vision daily with an Amsler grid.

NUTRITIONAL THERAPY

A large clinical trial sponsored by the National Eye Institute found that a high-dose mixture of antioxidants and zinc could slow the disease in a substantial number of people with dry AMD.

For patients with varying stages of AMD, a supplement containing vitamin C—500 milligrams (mg)…vitamin E—400 international units (IU)…beta-carotene—15 mg…and zinc—80 mg, with 2 mg of copper to prevent deficiency of that mineral, reduced the risk for progression to an advanced stage of the disease by about 25%, compared with a placebo. This formulation, known as AREDS (Age-Related Eye Disease Study), can be found in a single supplement at drugstores.

If you have early AMD: Increase your dietary intake of dark green, leafy vegetables, which contain the nutrients described above… and cold-water fish, for their omega-3 fatty acids. Red wine, which contains antioxidants, also may protect against AMD. If you smoke, it's crucial that you stop.

If you have intermediate AMD or advanced AMD in one eye: Take the supplement combination described above (along with a daily multivitamin, if you like). In addition, follow the dietary guidelines described above.

NEW DRUG TREATMENTS

Until fairly recently, wet AMD made severe vision loss a near certainty, but new medications have enabled many people to preserve their sight. Anti-VEGF (*vascular endothelial growth factor*) drugs stop production of fragile new blood vessels by blocking the action of a protein that blood vessels need to develop. These drugs are injected into the eye monthly.

•**Ranibizumab** (Lucentis) is the first anti-VEGF drug to receive FDA approval for AMD. In clinical trials, it stabilized vision in nearly all the patients who used it for a year…and up to 34% registered significant improvements in sight. The effects appear to increase over time.

•**Bevacizumab** (Avastin) has been approved for the treatment of colorectal cancer, but appears to be equally effective when administered intravenously for wet AMD.

•**Aflibercept** (VEGF Trap), another anti-VEGF drug, is being studied for treatment of AMD. It is given every other month.

•**Photodynamic therapy** is an older approach that involves the injection of the drug *verteporfin* (Visudyne) into the bloodstream. When a laser beam activates the chemical within the eye, it seals off abnormal blood vessels. Photodynamic therapy is less effective than anti-VEGF drugs and will slow—but may not stop—vision decline. Nowadays, photodynamic therapy has mostly been supplanted by anti-VEGF drugs. A study is under way to determine whether combining the two will be more effective than either alone.

ON THE HORIZON

New scientific research is focusing on AMD prevention. *For example, one recent study suggests that a protective effect may be offered by…*

•**Lutein and zeaxanthin.** Research has found that the plant-based antioxidants lutein and zeaxanthin may reduce the risk for intermediate and advanced AMD in women under age 75. It is believed that these antioxidants provide protective effects for men as well.

Now, a major trial is under way to determine if a supplement with these nutrients and omega-3s might halt progression of the disease.

If you are age 65 or older, call the Foundation of the American Academy of Ophthalmology's EyeCare America at 800-222-3937 to see if you qualify for a free eye exam in your area.

■ ■ ■ ■

Improve Your Vision

In a study of 22 adults, participants who played an action video game for 50 hours over nine weeks had a 43% improvement in contrast sensitivity—one of the first visual abilities to decline with age—while those who played a slow-moving video game did not improve. The benefits lasted for several months after the study.

Theory: Action video games may fine-tune the visual-processing pathways in the brain for challenging visual tasks, such as night driving.

Daphne Bavelier, PhD, professor of brain and cognitive sciences, University of Rochester, New York.

Best Ways to Keep Your Sense of Smell

Alan Hirsch, MD, founder and neurological director of the Smell & Taste Treatment and Research Foundation in Chicago. He is a neurologist and psychiatrist, and author of Life's a Smelling Success *(Authors of Unity) and* What Your Doctor May Not Tell You About Sinusitis *(Grand Central).* www.SmellandTaste.org.

Up to 15 million Americans suffer from a severe-to-total loss of sense of smell. By age 65, up to half of adults have a reduced sense of smell. *What to do…*

CAUSES

It's estimated that the average adult can detect between 10,000 and 30,000 distinct odors. The nasal membranes are lined with cellular receptors that match the shape of different scent molecules. These molecules bind to cell walls at the top of the nose, where they trigger the release of neurochemicals. These, in turn, generate nerve signals that stimulate the parts of the brain that identify different scents.

Cigarette smokers are far more likely to experience a loss of smell than nonsmokers. Damage to the sense of smell also can be caused by brain injury, nasal polyps, a brain tumor or nervous system diseases, such as Parkinson's.

Other causes: Diabetes, a deficiency of some B vitamins and the use of cholesterol-lowering statins or antihypertensive drugs.

Many patients with a diminished sense of smell also suffer from chronic depression or anxiety disorders. It's possible that the air contains yet-to-be-identified molecules with druglike, antianxiety effects—benefits that don't occur in those with smelling disorders.

SMELL TEST

To test for a diminished sense of smell, most doctors take an alcohol pad and hold it beneath the patient's chin. (You can do this at home with an alcohol pad from a first-aid kit.) If you can smell alcohol at that distance, your sense of smell is fine. If you can smell the alcohol only when the pad is raised closer to your nose, you have a problem.

Self-test: Put vanilla ice cream in one bowl and chocolate ice cream in another. Close your eyes, and move the bowls around so that you don't know which is which. Take a taste from each bowl. Because taste is largely determined by smell, an inability to tell them apart indicates that there's a problem somewhere in your olfactory system.

WHAT TO DO

Often, when the underlying problem is corrected, the sense of smell returns. People who quit smoking usually regain all or most of their sense of smell, but this can take years. *Also...*

•**The nutrients thiamine (100 milligrams daily) and phosphatidylcholine (9 grams daily)** can elevate levels of neurotransmitters that improve the sense of smell. In one study, about 40% of patients improved significantly after taking phosphatidylcholine for three months. The success rate with thiamine is somewhat lower.

•**Sniff therapy.** People who expose themselves to the same scent 20 to 50 times a day for several weeks will have an increase in scent receptors and will sometimes regain their ability to smell that particular scent.

Hidden Signs of Thyroid Trouble

Mark A. Stengler, NMD, naturopathic medical doctor in private practice, La Jolla, California...adjunct associate clinical professor at the National College of Natural Medicine, Portland, Oregon...author of many books, including *The Natural Physician's Healing Therapies* and coauthor of *Prescription for Natural Cures* (both from Bottom Line Books)...and author of the *Bottom Line/Natural Healing* newsletter.

I see a great many patients each year with thyroid problems—so many that I and many other physicians believe that thyroid disorders are epidemic in our country. Reasons for the upsurge: environmental toxins, side effects from pharmaceutical medications and stress. The thyroid gland, a butterfly-shaped organ in the front of the neck, produces several hormones that regulate the metabolism of every cell in the body.

Low thyroid activity, known as hypothyroidism, is the most prevalent disorder of the thyroid. About 10 million Americans are diagnosed with it—but I estimate that 30 million have the condition, including those who don't know it. Could you—or your doctor—not know you have an underactive thyroid?

SYMPTOMS

Symptoms such as fatigue...cold hands and feet...gaining weight for no reason...dry skin and/or hair loss...or depression all can be the result of a hectic, stressful lifestyle—or they can be signs of low thyroid activity. Some patients have many symptoms, while others have none at all. My typical hypothyroid patient is a woman in her late 40s or early 50s, but low thyroid activity can affect anyone at any age.

COMMON CAUSES

The most common cause of hypothyroidism is *Hashimoto's thyroiditis*, an autoimmune condition in which the immune system attacks the thyroid gland, causing thyroid inflammation and underproduction of thyroid hormones. Low thyroid activity is five to 10 times more common in women than in men. People with this disorder seem to have a genetic predisposition to it, although there are other possible triggers, such as imbalances of other hormones (especially insulin resistance seen with diabetes), food sensitivities (such as to gluten) and stress. Less common causes are failure of the pituitary gland or a pituitary tumor.

DIAGNOSIS CONFUSION

Many physicians, including both conventional and holistic, fail to properly diagnose low thyroid activity. Often, they run just one standard blood test—the *thyroid stimulating hormone* (TSH) test—which provides a general indication of thyroid activity but misses all of the subtleties of thyroid function. What to do: Have a holistic physician run a full thyroid test panel, which includes an evaluation of free T3 and free T4, the principal thyroid hormones, and tests for thyroid antibodies.

If your free T3 and/or free T4 levels are low, your doctor will see that you have a low thyroid condition. But what confuses the matter is that many patients' free T3 and free T4 levels are on the low side of the normal range. Many conventional physicians consider this low side of normal to be acceptable, but I believe that the standard for normal is too low. When I get my patients' levels closer to the mid-range they feel better.

Keep in mind: Your tests will determine whether you have a normal free T4 level combined with either a low or low-normal free T3 level. Here's why you want to know: Your body should convert T4 to T3. But if your TSH and T4 levels are normal, while your T3 level is low or low-normal, you're probably having difficulty converting T4 to T3. That means you are in need of supplemental T3 or need help converting T4 to T3. Because there is so much underdiagnosed low thyroid in the general population, I believe that patients are greatly helped when they understand the intricacies of these test results.

THYROID HORMONE REPLACEMENT

Most conventional physicians prescribe only synthetic T4 to patients with hypothyroidism.

That's because this hormone (sold as Synthroid, Levoxyl and Levothroid) has been the most heavily marketed. In my practice, I've found that synthetic T4 by itself doesn't work very well. If a person isn't efficiently converting T4 to T3, prescribing more T4 doesn't make a lot of sense.

I prescribe natural, *bioidentical* (chemically identical to hormones made naturally by the body) thyroid hormone replacement therapy, such as Armour Thyroid, Nature-Throid or Westhroid, which are made from dessicated pig thyroid. (These are safe for everyone except people who are allergic to pork.) These provide T3 and T4. Side effects are rare. Those who have Hashimoto's thyroiditis usually take these medications for life.

NUTRITIONAL SUPPORT

For all my patients with low thyroid activity, I recommend several nutrients to help the body make more of its own thyroid hormones. They are safe for everyone.

•**L-tyrosine.** This amino acid is the foundation of thyroid hormones. Take 500 milligrams (mg) about 30 minutes before breakfast.

•**Multivitamin.** These contain many nutrients, such as selenium, zinc and B vitamins, that are needed to convert T4 to T3.

•**Iodine.** This element is an important component of T4 and T3. Take at least 150 micrograms (mcg) daily. Higher doses may be helpful—and these are best prescribed by a nutrition-oriented physician.

Is It Just Old Age...or Should You See a Doctor?

Donnica Moore, MD, president of Sapphire Women's Health Group, a multimedia education and communications firm in Far Hills, New Jersey, and editor-in-chief of *Women's Health for Life* (DK). She is a medical expert on ABC's *Good Morning America Health* and has served on the board of directors of the American Medical Women's Association and Research!America. *www.DrDonnica.com.*

You sigh with resignation when some annoying symptom appears or worsens, dismissing it as an inevitable sign of aging—but that can be a mistake.

Reasons: Often, simple self-help strategies correct the problem. In other cases, a visit to the doctor can prevent unnecessary suffering—or even save your life. *Symptoms to watch for...*

•**Seeing Spots.** Gazing at a blank wall, you notice floaters—tiny dark specks or strings—in your field of vision.

Normal aging: The *vitreous*, a gel-like substance inside the eye, becomes more liquid, allowing microscopic fibers within to clump and cast shadows on the retina.

For self-help: Try nonprescription Dry Eye Relief Tear Stabilization Formula (*www.Cure Floaters.com*). Its omega-3 fatty acids and other nutrients may reduce visual distortion from floaters by improving the cornea's film of tears.

See your doctor if: Floaters are accompanied by gradual blurring or an overall yellowish or reddish hue to your visual field. You may have cataracts (clouding of the eyes' lenses), correctable with surgery.

Seek emergency care if: Floaters suddenly increase significantly in number or are accompanied by flashing lights or hazy vision. You could have a retinal tear or detachment that requires immediate surgery to prevent vision loss.

•**Dizziness.** You stand up and your head spins.

Normal aging: The ear has fluid-filled structures that sense movement and balance. When tiny calcium crystals in the inner ear dislodge and float in this fluid, you may develop *benign paroxysmal positional vertigo* (BPPV). Other possibilities include *orthostatic hypotension* (postural low blood pressure), which occurs when blood pools in the legs, decreasing oxygen-rich blood flow to the brain...or *hypoglycemia* (low blood sugar).

Self-help: Get up more slowly. In mild cases of BPPV or orthostatic hypotension, this prevents dizziness. BPPV also may be corrected with head movements called Epley or Semont maneuvers, which cause the crystals to lodge in a harmless area. For instructions online, see *www.dizziness-and-balance.com* (click on "Dizzy Patients"). To avoid blood sugar dips, each day eat three moderate meals and two healthful snacks that include some protein. Do not drive when dizzy!

See your doctor if: Dizziness persists or is severe enough to create a risk of falling. A physician or physical therapist can guide your head through the Epley or Semont maneuvers. Low blood pressure can be corrected with diet, drugs and/or compression stockings. You also should be checked for medication side effects and underlying disorders (diabetes, anemia, ear or sinus infections) linked to dizziness.

Seek emergency care if: Dizziness is accompanied by impaired vision, speech problems, and/or weakness or tingling on one side of the body. These may indicate a stroke.

•**Indigestion.** You feel a burning sensation beneath your breastbone.

Normal aging: When the sphincter between the esophagus and stomach weakens, digestive acids can move upward into the esophagus and cause irritation.

Self-help: Limit foods and beverages likely to trigger discomfort—citrus, onions, tomatoes, mint, spicy or high-fat foods, coffee, alcohol. Do not eat within three hours of bedtime. Lose excess weight. Wear clothing that is loose at the waist. Do not smoke. Use blocks to raise the head of your bed by about six inches.

See your doctor if: Symptoms occur more than twice per week—chronic heartburn may warrant medication or surgery. If you also experience swallowing difficulties, vomiting, tarry stools or unintended weight loss, get screened for gastrointestinal ulcers and cancer.

Seek emergency care if: Upper abdominal pain occurs along with unusual fatigue, shortness of breath, nausea and/or back pain. These can be signs of a heart attack.

•**Leaking urine.** You sneeze or are hurrying to the bathroom and—whoops! Some urine escapes.

Normal aging: Pelvic muscles that control urination weaken over time...and declining estrogen thins the walls of the urethra, creating a wider and weaker channel for urine to leave the bladder.

Self-help: Six times each day, do "fast-and-slow" Kegel exercises.

How: Contract the muscles around your vagina and anus, lifting them upward and inward...

hold for 10 seconds, then relax for 10 seconds… repeat 10 times. Next, contract for one second, then relax for one second…repeat 10 times. Avoid caffeine and carbonated beverages—they can irritate the bladder.

See your doctor if: You often leak urine or use the toilet more than eight times per day or more than twice at night.

Treatments: A probe inserted into the vagina emits a current that may stimulate and strengthen pelvic muscles over time. Collagen injected into the bladder outlet may improve closure…Botox injected into the bladder lining can reduce spasms. Surgical options include inserting a sling to support the urethra…or implanting a nerve-stimulating device that calms spasms in an overactive bladder.

Seek emergency care if: There is blood in your urine. You must be checked for kidney stones, *pyelonephritis* (a kidney infection), severe urinary tract infection and/or urinary tract cancer.

•**Poor memory.** You made plans to see a friend but cannot remember where to meet.

Normal aging: As the body produces lower levels of chemicals that brain cells need to function optimally, memory worsens.

Self-help: Try daily crossword or Sudoku puzzles or games that challenge brain speed (see *www.GamesForTheBrain.com*). Get regular aerobic exercise to increase cerebral blood flow and promote neuron regeneration. Aim for seven to nine hours of sleep per night. Do not smoke or consume more than one alcoholic drink daily—people with these bad habits develop Alzheimer's disease an average of 2.3 to 4.8 years earlier, respectively, than nonsmokers and nondrinkers.

See your doctor if: Forgetfulness interferes with day-to-day tasks or if loved ones say that they notice behavioral changes. High blood pressure and diabetes increase dementia risk, so work with your doctor to control these conditions. Ask your doctor if memory problems may be linked to medication or an underlying problem, such as a vitamin B-12 deficiency, sleep disorder, anemia, low thyroid or depression.

Seek emergency care if: A memory lapse occurs suddenly and is accompanied by changes in vision, speech and/or balance—this could signal a stroke. Also get immediate help if memory problems occur after a head injury, even a seemingly minor one. This can signal bleeding within or around the brain. Emergency surgery can be lifesaving.

■ ■ ■ ■

Topical Gel Beats Bladder Problems

Gelnique, the first topical gel to treat overactive bladder (loss of bladder control), has been approved by the FDA. The gel is applied once daily to the thigh, abdomen, upper arm or shoulder. In a 12-week study of 789 women and men with overactive bladder, Gelnique decreased incontinence episodes by 10% and urination frequency by 6%, compared with a placebo. Gelnique is not metabolized by the liver, thus reducing side effects. Patients with urinary retention (inability to pass urine) or gastric retention (delayed emptying of the stomach) or uncontrolled narrow-angle glaucoma should not use Gelnique.

Christine P. Nguyen, MD, medical officer, division of reproductive and urological products, Center for Drug Evaluation and Research, FDA, Silver Spring, Maryland.

When a Hidden Infection Is the Culprit

Erno Daniel, MD, PhD, an internist and geriatrician in private practice at the Sansum Clinic in Santa Barbara, California. The author of Stealth Germs in Your Body *(Sterling), he lectures throughout the US on medical topics, including geriatrics and hidden infections.*

All of us think that we know the telltale symptoms of an infection. Depending on the part of the body that's affected, there might be redness, warmth, swelling and tenderness at the infection site—or whole-body symptoms, such as a fever and/or chills.

Little-known fact: Many infections cause subtle, if any, symptoms and often are misdiagnosed. This is particularly true of low-level, smoldering infections—due to bacteria or viruses, for example—that are now thought to be a largely unrecognized cause of several diseases, including some forms of arthritis, dementia, hearing loss and digestive problems.

STEALTH GERMS

Our bodies contain more microorganisms (microbes) than human cells. Although many of these microbes are harmless, others are disease-causing (pathogenic). Our immune systems generally keep these harmful microbes in check, but mild infections still can be carried in the body—even when our immunity is strong—and persist for decades. These hidden infections can irritate and damage tissues throughout the body.

Example: Peptic ulcers were once thought to be caused by such factors as spicy foods or stress. It wasn't until the 1980s that researchers proved that the vast majority of these ulcers were caused by a bacterium, *Helicobacter pylori* (H. pylori), and could be treated with antibiotic therapy.

Conditions that can be caused by a hidden infection…

ARTHRITIS

People who develop joint pain after about age 50 usually assume that it is age-related arthritis. But pain and swelling in the joints also may be a sign of infection.

Suspect infection if: Joint pain (which may shift from joint to joint) develops after a flulike illness. Swelling and fatigue as well as fever also may occur.

Possible cause: Lyme arthritis. This form of arthritis can affect people who have untreated, late-stage Lyme disease and typically occurs months after a bite from an infected tick. Without treatment, the pain can persist for years, sometimes with periods of remission.

What to do: The *enzyme-linked immunosorbent assay* (ELISA) test shows the presence or absence of antibodies to *Borrelia burgdorferi,* the bacterium that causes Lyme disease. The Western blot test is performed to confirm a diagnosis of Lyme disease.

Lyme arthritis is more likely to occur in areas of the US where the so-called deer tick is prevalent, including the Northeastern, North-Central and Pacific states.

Lyme disease is readily treated with oral antibiotics—usually *doxycycline* (Vibramycin) or *amoxicillin* (Amoxil)—typically taken for 14 to 21 days. For Lyme arthritis, your doctor may recommend a longer course of antibiotic treatment (typically 30 to 60 days). If the infection is more severe (or has persisted for months or longer), intravenous antibiotics may be needed.

DEMENTIA

Older adults who experience gradual mental decline are often assumed to have Alzheimer's disease. But some forms of more rapidly progressive dementia can be caused by exposure to harmful microorganisms.

Suspect infection if: Rapidly progressive memory loss, confusion or other cognitive disorders occur along with gastrointestinal (GI) symptoms, such as persistent diarrhea and/or unexplained weight loss.

Possible cause: *Tropheryma whippelii*, a bacterium that can cause a long-term infection, damages the intestine and spreads to other areas of the body (including the brain, where it can impair mental functions). The infection, known as Whipple's disease, can be treated.

Unfortunately, doctors don't tend to look for Whipple's disease, because it is rare and the same GI symptoms can be caused by medications—including *cholinesterase inhibitors*, such as *donepezil* (Aricept) and *rivastigmine* (Exelon)—that are used to treat Alzheimer's.

What to do: If you or a loved one has been diagnosed with dementia and has the symptoms described above, ask the doctor if Whipple's disease could be the cause. It's diagnosed with a small-intestine biopsy and can be treated with antibiotics—typically intravenous *ceftriaxone* (Rocephin) for two weeks, followed by long-term use of oral *trimethoprim-sulfamethoxazole* (Septra) to fully eradicate the bacterium from the brain.

HEARING LOSS

Most cases of gradual hearing loss are idiopathic—that is, there isn't a known cause. However, hearing loss that occurs suddenly might be due to a virus.

Suspect infection if: You wake up one morning and have virtually no hearing in one ear.

Possible cause: Certain herpes viruses can damage the nerves that control hearing, a condition known as sudden sensorineural hearing loss. (Often the virus has been dormant in the body for a long time and is activated for unknown reasons.)

What to do: The herpes viruses associated with hearing loss can be detected with blood tests and treated with antiviral drugs, such as *valacyclovir* (Valtrex) or *acyclovir* (Zovirax), along with corticosteroids (such as *prednisone*). These drugs usually are taken for up to 10 days. Most patients will start to recover their hearing within a few days.

These herpes viruses also can cause vertigo, characterized by spinning dizziness. If you suddenly develop this symptom, ask your doctor if antiviral therapy would be appropriate.

IRRITABLE BOWEL SYNDROME

Irritable bowel syndrome (IBS) is among the most common digestive complaints, causing unpredictable episodes of diarrhea, gas, bloating and other symptoms in up to one in every five Americans at some point in their lives. The underlying cause isn't known.

Suspect infection if: You've gone camping or have traveled to parts of the world with poor sanitation. Contaminated food and/or water may contain organisms that cause persistent intestinal discomfort. In the US, these organisms are sometimes found on unwashed produce and in water from wells and streams.

Possible cause: *Giardia lamblia,* a common organism that can rapidly multiply in the first section of the small intestine (*duodenum*) and cause mild, but persistent, gassiness and loose stools.

What to do: The infection, known as giardiasis, is diagnosed by testing stool samples, sometimes collected over several days. Either of two antibiotics, *metronidazole* (Flagyl) or *tinidazole* (Tindamax), is usually taken for three to five days.

Important: Avoid alcohol when using these drugs (and for three days afterward)—the combination can cause severe nausea, vomiting or cramps.

SENSITIVE STOMACH

If you get an upset stomach when you drink alcohol, eat spicy foods or take aspirin, your doctor may have told you that you have inflammation in the lining of the stomach (gastritis)—and to avoid these or other stomach "irritants."

Suspect infection if: Your stomach problems "came out of the blue"—and persist even after eliminating irritating foods from your diet and/or taking acid blockers, such as *ranitidine* (Zantac) or *omeprazole* (Prilosec).

Possible cause: H. pylori, which causes most ulcers, can burrow into the stomach lining, leading to irritation and inflammation.

What to do: Ask your doctor for a breath or stool test to check for H. pylori. If the bacterium is present, a one-week course of treatment—usually metronidazole, amoxicillin and *bismuth subsalicylate* (the active ingredient in Pepto-Bismol)—should eliminate the infection.

The Secret to Being a Great Caregiver

Vicki Rackner, MD, a board-certified surgeon based on Mercer Island, Washington, and founder of the Caregiver Club (*www.thecaregiverclub.com*), an Internet-based community for caregivers and their loved ones. She is the author of *Caregiving Without Regrets* (Medical Bridges).

If you've ever taken care of a person who is seriously ill, you know how stressful it can be.

What you may not know: There are greater risks to the caregiver's health than previously recognized.

Troubling research finding: Caregivers are 63% more likely to die within a four-year period than people without this extra burden, according to a study published in *The Journal of the American Medical Association.*

Compared with non-caregivers, people who provide care to a loved one tend to exercise less and eat less nutritiously and are at much higher risk for physical exhaustion and depression.

CARING FOR TWO

Family members are responsible for about 80% of the elder care in the US. To meet this challenge, caregivers must care not only for a loved one (and, in many cases, other members of their family), but also maintain their own physical and emotional well-being.

As a medical doctor and longtime advocate for caregivers, I know how crucial it is to tend to your own needs while caring for a loved one. *My advice…*

•**Know what you can—and cannot—change.** Every caregiver wants to create a different reality and to "fix" things. If you're caring for a stroke patient or someone with Alzheimer's disease, for example, some part of you will think that you can prevent the person from getting worse just by working harder. That's simply not true.

There are some things that we can't change. People who think that they can change the natural course of aging or disease are the ones who are most vulnerable to self-recrimination, depression and even alcoholism or drug addiction. You can make a loved one happier by engaging him/her in conversation or planning activities he enjoys—but remember that you cannot change the overall course of his disease.

My advice: Understand that caregiving is usually a long-term process and identify not only what's important but what's possible.

Example: Suppose you're caring for someone who is disabled by rheumatoid arthritis. He won't care if the house is perfectly clean. What's likely to matter are the more personal things, such as preparing a favorite food or giving an affectionate touch. You've fulfilled your job every time you create one of these special moments.

•**Learn the "51% Rule."** Most caregivers will do anything for their loved one. They prepare meals, go to doctor appointments, get medications, change linens and clean the house—and then, when they're ready to collapse, there's always something else that needs to be done. This approach doesn't work.

Most caregiving situations require more work than a full-time job. All too often, people strive to be a "super caregiver"…to do everything perfectly, setting aside their own needs. It's not uncommon for caregivers to wind up in the hospital themselves—or, worse, to die before their loved ones.

My advice: Follow the "51% rule"—accept that you will make mistakes and will disappoint your loved one at times (maybe even half the time). You will have to make choices and decisions that are in the best interests of your loved one but may make him unhappy. You may even lose your patience at times. Treat your loved one with respect, compassion and kindness, but accept that you will fall short of perfection as a caregiver.

Important: People who become martyrs while caregiving invariably burn out. They also tend to become worse caregivers because they don't have the emotional reserves to stay focused.

•**Get—and give—help.** A lot of caregivers don't realize that accepting help from others is one of the best gifts you can give those who are closest to you.

For people who feel guilty accepting help without returning the favor, bartering is a great solution. We all have activities that we enjoy and activities that we don't. Suppose you hate doing laundry but love walking the dog—and one of your friends is great with laundry but dreads going for walks. You can help each other.

My advice: Consider forming a caregivers' bartering community. It might include neighbors or people from your church or synagogue. Or you could post an announcement on the bulletin board at your local health food store or doctor's office to recruit people in similar situations who will trade chores, such as yard work or grocery shopping.

It's easier to ask for help if you know that you will pay back the favor in your own way—especially if it's an activity you enjoy.

■ **More from Dr. Rackner…**

To Help Your Loved One…

With caregiving, not all issues have clear-cut solutions. *Here's my advice for navigating some of the trickier challenges…*

•**Reluctance to talk about health problems.** As a caregiver, you most likely already know—or will learn—intimate details about your loved one's health that the ill person may be reluctant to share.

Example: Many older adults won't discuss bodily functions with their doctors.

My advice: You might say, "Don't you think we should talk to the doctor about this issue? If you want, I'll bring it up so that you don't have to." Most patients will say, "Okay."

•**A doctor's disregard for quality-of-life issues.** I knew a woman who took her elderly father to the doctor because his knee was hurting. The doctor glanced at the knee—then sent them home with a prescription for blood pressure medicine.

The doctor was worried about this patient's high blood pressure because it raised the man's risk for stroke and heart attack. A "simple" bad knee didn't concern the doctor, even though it was preventing this patient from doing the things he enjoyed.

My advice: Sit down with the person you're caring for and make a list before each doctor visit and include not only the key issues, including drug side effects, the presence of pain or other symptoms, but also your loved one's mood and lifestyle issues, such as his level of social and physical activity. If the doctor won't take the time to discuss all your concerns, consider finding another doctor.

_____

Asthma, Allergy & Autoimmune Disorders

Allergies Can Dampen Your Sex Life

Having allergies can take a toll on your sex life, new research now shows. When polled, 83% of people with *allergic rhinitis* said it affected their sexual activity at least sometimes, with approximately 17% of those affected saying their allergies nearly always got in the way of a satisfying sex life.

"I was kind of surprised that it made that much of a difference," said study author Michael Benninger, MD, chairman of the Head and Neck Institute at the Cleveland Clinic in Ohio.

Commercials for allergy-relief products tend to focus on helping people get back to enjoying an active lifestyle, such as taking their kids to the park, Dr. Benninger said. Rarely is there mention of sex lives, and that could be because it's an area that has been studied so little, he noted.

ALLERGIC RHINITIS

Allergic rhinitis, also called hay fever, affects 10% to 40% of the US population, according to the researchers. Symptoms include a runny nose, congestion and sinus pressure. Those affected are reacting to indoor or airborne allergens, such as pollens and dust mites.

STUDY DETAILS

The researchers polled about 700 people, roughly half with allergic rhinitis, asking questions about sexual function, sleep and fatigue. The participants averaged in their late 30s to mid-40s, and those with allergic rhinitis were not being treated for their allergies.

About 17% of those with allergic rhinitis said they always or almost always noticed an adverse impact on their sex life. Those affected

Michael Benninger, MD, otolaryngologist and chairman, Head and Neck Institute, Cleveland Clinic.

Clifford Bassett, MD, clinical assistant professor, medicine, State University of New York Health Sciences Center, and clinical instructor, New York University School of Medicine, New York City and medical director, Allergy & Asthma Care of New York, *www.nyc-allergist.com.*

Allergy and Asthma Proceedings.

by allergic rhinitis were also more likely to have sleep problems than those without allergies.

The study was published in *Allergy and Asthma Proceedings*.

POSSIBLE EXPLANATION

Exactly why the allergies affect sexual functioning isn't certain, but Dr. Benninger suspects that the runny nose, itchy eyes and other symptoms can make a person feel less than sexy.

The study definitely sheds light on a new area, said Clifford Bassett, MD, a clinical assistant professor of medicine at the State University of New York Health Sciences Center and a clinical instructor at New York University School of Medicine. "Sexual function is not something typically evaluated [with allergies]," he said.

But the finding makes sense to Dr. Bassett, based on what patients report to him. "If people have a runny, drippy nose and feel unsexy, they might be embarrassed by what would be normal intimate contact," he said.

EXPERT ADVICE

But the condition can be treated, both Dr. Bassett and Dr. Benninger stressed. From over-the-counter nasal sprays to prescription or over-the-counter antihistamines and prescription intranasal steroids, there are plenty of options that minimize uncomfortable symptoms. The trick is finding what regimen works best for each individual.

The message to allergy sufferers, Dr. Benninger said, is not to confine lovemaking to times when their symptoms aren't so bad but to seek treatment that can help them feel better much of the time. Paying attention to allergy triggers and, for instance, closing bedroom windows so pollen levels are at a minimum can help, too.

Bassett also said he hopes the study will wake up those with allergy symptoms whose sex life is less than ideal. "I think it's essential for patients to realize that help is out there," he said.

info For more on allergies, visit the Web site of the American Academy of Family Physicians, *http://familydoctor.org*. Under "Conditions A to Z," choose "Allergies."

Day Care May Not Shield Kids From Asthma, Allergies

Johan C. de Jongste, MD, PhD, professor, pediatric respiratory medicine, Erasmus University Medical Center–Sophia Children's Hospital, Rotterdam, the Netherlands.

John Heffner, MD, chair of medical education, Providence Health & Services, Portland, Oregon, and past president, American Thoracic Society.

American Journal of Respiratory and Critical Care Medicine.

Early day care, so the story goes, exposes kids to more germs and illnesses at a young age, thereby protecting them from asthma and allergies later on. Scientists call it the "hygiene hypothesis," but a new study casts doubt on whether early infections have an effect on asthma and allergy rates.

CHILDHOOD ASTHMA RATES INCREASING

An unexplained increase in asthma among children in both industrialized countries and developing nations has scientists searching for ways to reduce the disease. In the United States, asthma affects nearly 5 million children and is the most common serious chronic childhood disease, according to the American Academy of Allergy, Asthma & Immunology.

STUDY FINDINGS

Dutch researchers followed more than 3,600 children from birth through age 8, noting their day care use and health problems, such as wheezing. Those who started day care early were twice as likely to experience wheezing in their first year as those who didn't attend day care.

By age 5, however, the early day care kids—who started from birth to age 2—had less wheezing than the kids who didn't go, the researchers found.

But three years later, the discrepancy disappeared. "We found no evidence for any protection for asthma or allergy at 8 years," said Johan C. de Jongste, MD, PhD, professor of pediatric respiratory medicine at Erasmus University Medical Center in the Netherlands, who led the study.

The children had an increase in airway symptoms until age 4, an overall decrease from age 4 to 8, but no protection at age 8 compared with to those who weren't in day care.

Assessments included blood tests to measure *IgE*, antibodies typically elevated in a person with allergies and lung function tests. The researchers also examined annual parental reports that asked about symptoms and controlled for such factors as a mother's allergies.

Would the results for Dutch children hold in the United States? "The study population was a reasonable reflection of the Dutch general population, including rural and urban areas; in other words, white children with a western European lifestyle," said Dr. de Jongste. "This should not be very different for US children who live under comparable conditions."

CONCLUSION

Early exposure to germs and other organisms does cause more symptoms early in a child's life, but may not be counterbalanced by health benefits later on, as previous studies suggested. The study was published in the *American Journal of Respiratory and Critical Care Medicine.*

EXPERT COMMENTARY

The study is considered a "landmark investigation" by John Heffner, MD, past president of the American Thoracic Society. Dr. Heffner said that the investigation "is the first to follow children prospectively from birth to 8 years and assess the effect of day care enrollment on both asthma symptoms and immunologic evidence of allergic disease.

"This study provides strong evidence that enrollment in day care provides no protection against asthma and cannot be promoted as a public health strategy to decrease asthma prevalence," Dr. Heffner added.

Dr. de Jongste said parents should consider day care for many other reasons, however. "Day care may serve many purposes, including social contacts and enabling both parents to work," he said.

info To learn more about childhood asthma, visit the Web site of the American Academy of Allergy, Asthma & Immunology, *www.aaaai.org/.* Under "Patients & Consumers," search "childhood asthma."

Is Swimming Bad for Your Lungs?

Alfred Bernard, PhD, professor, toxicology and research director, Catholic University of Louvain, Brussels, Belgium.
Jennifer Appleyard, MD, chief, allergy and immunology, St. John Hospital and Medical Center, Detroit, Michigan.
Pediatrics online.

Swimming in pools disinfected with chlorine may increase the odds that a child will develop asthma or allergies, new research suggests.

The study, published in *Pediatrics,* found that teenagers who spent more than 1,000 hours swimming in chlorinated pools, either indoors or outdoors, had more than eight times the risk of having asthma than did teens who primarily swam in pools using a copper-silver disinfecting method.

"When used properly, [chlorine] is an efficient and safe disinfectant for swimming pools. However, when too much chlorine is added to water or builds up in the air of indoor pools, there is unavoidably some irritation of the organs of the bather in contact with the water and air," said lead author Alfred Bernard, PhD, a professor of toxicology and research director at Catholic University of Louvain in Brussels, Belgium. "There is now increasing evidence that these irritating effects may be detrimental to the airways of regular swimmers, especially the children, who are the most vulnerable and the most frequent attendees of chlorinated pools."

BACKGROUND

More than 17 million people in the United States have asthma, according to the American Academy of Allergy, Asthma & Immunology. Symptoms of the disease include wheezing, shortness of breath and coughing. The airway disease can be triggered by a number of factors, such as cold air, exercise and chemical irritants. While chlorine has long been known to be an airway irritant and potential trigger of asthma, particularly in indoor pools, Dr. Bernard's study suggests that chlorinated pools might play a role in the development of asthma and allergy.

STUDY DETAILS

The study included 847 Belgian teenagers between the ages of 13 and 18. All had attended indoor or outdoor swimming pools, but at various rates of attendance. One hundred and fourteen children mainly attended pools that were kept clean with a copper-silver disinfectant, rather than chlorine. The remainder primarily attended pools disinfected with chlorine.

The number of children who ever had asthma went up in proportion to their chlorinated pool exposure. Teens who swam for 100 to 500 hours in chlorinated pools had an 80% increased risk of having asthma, while those who logged 500 to 1,000 hours had just over twice the risk. When teens spend more than 1,000 hours swimming in chlorinated water, the risk of ever having had asthma nearly quadrupled. The risk of currently having asthma was more than eight times higher in the group with more than 1,000 hours in chlorinated pools compared with those who were rarely in chlorinated water, according to the study.

The risk of allergies also increased significantly when adolescents spent more than 100 hours swimming in chlorinated pools. In fact, the risk of hay fever and other allergies more than doubled with significant chlorinated pool exposure.

EXPERT ADVICE

Jennifer Appleyard, MD, chief of allergy and immunology at St. John Hospital and Medical Center in Detroit, said this study highlights the fact that "asthma and allergies are caused by a multitude of different factors, and chlorine may have a potential effect. But, this is a very preliminary study, and we don't yet know what the whole picture is."

She said that she wouldn't advise parents to stop taking their kids swimming, even if they have asthma already. "If your kids have asthma and you know chlorine is a trigger, it's a good idea to try to limit their exposure, but you can't exclude your child from everything and every potential trigger. You have to let them be kids."

If you know your child is bothered by chlorine exposure, and he has an event such as a birthday party that he really wants to attend,

discuss it with your child's doctor to find out the best way to manage the exposure.

Dr. Bernard said that if you have a backyard pool, you should use as little chlorine as you can to safely disinfect the pool. He said that many people overchlorinate their pools to get clear blue water. But, he said, "chlorine is a disinfectant, not a cleaning agent."

info For more about asthma triggers and controlling asthma, visit the Centers for Disease Control and Prevention Web site, *www.cdc.gov/asthma.*

The Dirt on Dust Mites

Matthew J. Colloff, PhD, senior research scientist, CSIRO Entomology, Canberra, Australia, and author of *Dust Mites* (CSIRO).

It's not just your imagination—allergies have been on the rise. Epidemiological data show that your children are likely to have more allergies than you, and their children to have more yet…and this doesn't just include those who are allergic to peanuts. Dust mites have become a common cause of year-round allergy symptoms, with one study reporting that 51% of children tested positive for dust mite allergies, compared with just 39% of their parents.

Dust mites are common—in fact, nearly ubiquitous. These unwelcome houseguests can be found everywhere—they were even detected on the Mir Space Station. Unless your furnishings are brand-new, you can be fairly certain that some are living in your mattress, carpet and living room couch. Expert Matthew J. Colloff, PhD, author of *Dust Mites,* a book that delivers all the dirt on these nasty little creatures—including where they live, why people are allergic to them and, most important, how to get rid of them—helped explain the implications.

Dust mites cause damage way out of proportion to their microscopic size. At least 100 million people worldwide suffer from sneezing, runny noses, asthma, skin rashes and other reactions to these mighty mites. Relatives of the spider, dust mites thrive in warm, dark and humid conditions, burrowing deep into rugs, upholstered furniture, bedding, mattresses, box springs and stuffed animals. They feed on the shedded skin of humans and pets and on bacteria and molds—all common components of house dust.

DISGUSTING THINGS IN DUST

In fact, it's not house dust that most people are allergic to, but rather what dust mites have contributed to it. Specifically, dust mite allergies are immune-system reactions to the various dust mite proteins—including in their feces and in the decaying bits of dead dust mites. *Dr. Colloff explains…*

•**For people with hay fever or allergic rhinitis,** the immune reaction to dust mites is likely to present as inflammation in their nasal passages, triggering symptoms such as sneezing, congestion, a runny nose, red and watery eyes, itchy nose and roof of the mouth or throat, coughing and facial pressure or pain.

•**If you have asthma,** exposure to the mites may produce inflammation and contraction of the airways of your lungs, leading to wheezing, shortness of breath and chest tightening.

•**If you are prone to skin rashes,** your encounter with dust mites might bring on an inflammatory skin reaction, such as eczema.

DECLARE WAR ON DUST MITES

For people with severe allergies, drugs may be essential (especially for people with asthma), but avoiding the mite allergens can prevent symptoms from occurring in the first place. The best strategy is to declare war on house dust and the critters that feast on it. Keep your home clean and dust-free, and do whatever you can to keep humidity low. The most critical room of all is your bedroom. Specifically, focus on your bed, which—with its mattress, box spring, pillows and cozy quilt or duvet—provides an ideal nesting place for literally millions of microscopic pests.

DEBUG YOUR BEDDING

Dr. Colloff has developed a "flexible, simple, inexpensive and integrated dust mite control strategy." *Depending on how aggressive you want or need to be, Dr. Colloff advises…*

•**Encase your bed and its components in microporous (or semipermeable) covers,** which discourage dust mites from colonization. This type of bedding—allergy pillows, pillow covers, mattress covers, duvet covers, etc.—ranges widely in price (from $50 to several hundred dollars for a mattress cover, for instance) and is readily available online if you can't find it in local stores.

•**A more moderate strategy is to strip your bed daily.** Also helpful is to open doors and windows to thoroughly air the room.

•**At the very least, consider washing bedding in hot water (at least 130°F) at least once a month.**

Note: There are allergy-relief laundry soaps/detergents that work in cold water. It's also great to dry items outdoors, in direct sunlight, which dehydrates and kills dust mites.

FLOORS & FURNITURE

To deal with dust mites in rugs and upholstery, Dr. Colloff recommends…

•**Removing carpeting and rugs from bedrooms**—this is the most aggressive strategy.

•**Vacuuming carpets, upholstered furniture and curtains every week,** using a device with a double-layered microfilter bag or a HEPA (high-efficiency particulate air) filter. This is a less extreme plan.

•**Regularly steam-cleaning rugs, upholstered furniture and mattresses** with equipment that heats water to at least 212°F, to help ensure removal of dust and dust mites.

Note: These strategies were adapted from Dr. Colloff's *Dust Mites.*

A NOTE OF CAUTION

Many people assume that they are allergic to dust mites, observes Dr. Colloff, but this is not always the case. Before you invest significant time and money to control dust mites, see an allergist to make sure you actually are allergic to them. If you are, then take aggressive steps to eliminate them to the greatest extent possible from your home.

■ ■ ■ ■

Tasty Way to Fight Allergies

In a recent study, it was found that people who ate seven ounces of broccoli sprouts daily for three days had up to a 200% increase in the production of antioxidant enzymes in the nasal passages. The antioxidants help fight the inflammation that contributes to allergy symptoms. Broccoli sprouts are very high in sulforaphane, which starts a process that leads to the antioxidant increase.

Marc A. Riedl, MD, researcher, department of medicine, section of clinical immunology and allergy, University of California, Los Angeles, and coauthor of a study published in *Clinical Immunology*.

Superfoods for Super Allergy Relief

Leo Galland, MD, director, Foundation for Integrated Medicine in New York City. An internist, he treats many patients with chronic allergies and specializes in integrating nutrition and herbs with conventional medicine. Dr. Galland is a recipient of the Linus Pauling award and author of *The Fat Resistance Diet* (Broadway) and *Power Healing* (Random House). *www.mdheal.org.*

The right foods can help relieve allergies to dust, pollen, mold and other spores in the air—easing symptoms that include sneezing, stuffy nose and wheezing.

Recent finding: Allergy symptoms are less common on the rural Greek island of Crete than elsewhere in Greece, even though there's no shortage of allergens blowing around. According to a study published in *Thorax,* the people of Crete can thank their diet. Researchers tested 690 island children for airborne allergies and asked their parents to answer questions about their children's diets and symptoms. Eighty percent of the children ate fruit at least twice a day, and 68% ate vegetables that often. Those who ate more nuts, grapes, oranges, apples and tomatoes—the main local products—had fewer allergy symptoms than those who ate less.

Allergy symptoms occur when an overactive immune system responds to harmless substances as if they could cause disease. Inflammation is an early step in the immune response. Most of the foods that relieve allergies are ones that are anti-inflammatory, modulating the immune system response.

FOODS THAT FIGHT ALLERGIES

The following foods can help in the battle against airborne allergies…

•**Fruits high in vitamin C, an antioxidant, may help reduce inflammation.** Year-round, eat two pieces of fruit daily. When you're especially congested, choose from these twice a day—an orange, one cup of strawberries, an apple, one cup of grapes or a medium-sized wedge of watermelon.

Bonus: The skins of red grapes are loaded with the antioxidant resveratrol and were found to relieve wheezing in the Crete study.

•**Nuts, especially almonds, hazelnuts and peanuts, are a good source of vitamin E,** which helps minimize inflammation. Eat a single one-ounce serving of any of these nuts daily year-round to help prevent symptoms. If you do have symptoms, increase the servings—try two tablespoons of peanut butter and one ounce each of hazelnuts and almonds a day.

•**Cold-water fish (wild salmon, mackerel, trout, herring and sardines), as well as walnuts and flaxseed, contain omega-3 fatty acids,** which help fight inflammation. Eat at least two servings of cold-water fish each week year-round and three servings during the seasons when you experience airborne allergies. Also have 12 walnuts and one tablespoon of ground flaxseed a day.

•**Oysters, shrimp and crab, as well as legumes, whole grains and tofu, are all high in zinc,** which has antibacterial and antiviral effects that provide relief for immune systems overtaxed by fighting allergies. Have six oysters, six shrimp or a few crabs every week, and twice that when your allergies bother you. Also have one serving of whole grains and one of beans or tofu a day.

•**Tea, whether green, white or black, is full of flavonoids,** plant compounds that reduce inflammation. Tea also increases proteins in the body that fight infection, again relieving an overtaxed immune system. Enjoy one cup daily, and increase to two when your allergies are a problem.

Helpful: Drink your tea first thing in the morning with lemon and honey to stimulate the cilia—the tiny hairs in the nose that sweep pollen and dust out of the way.

• **Horseradish, hot mustard, fennel, anise and sage also stimulate the cilia and act as natural decongestants.** Add a dash to food whenever possible.

FOODS TO AVOID ALL YEAR

If you experience congestion or other symptoms year-round, ask an allergist to conduct a skin test to identify allergies to dust, mold and foods. *Then consider the following changes in your daily diet…*

• **Mold and yeast in food can aggravate an allergy to mold in the air.** If you're allergic to mold, avoid foods that contain yeast, such as bread and baked goods (unless they are labeled "yeast free")…wine, beer and spirits… fermented foods, such as sauerkraut and cider… foods that tend to get moldy, such as cheese and mushrooms…vinegar and sauces that contain vinegar, such as mayonnaise, barbecue sauce, mustard and salad dressing.

Helpful: Use lemon juice and spices in dressings instead.

• **Milk and dairy products, such as yogurt, butter and ice cream, could be making you feel worse** if you have a congested nose year-round, a symptom typically caused by an allergy to dust. One explanation is that casein, the protein in milk, can promote the formation of mucus. Although there isn't strong science showing that milk aggravates congestion, it's worth experimenting by cutting dairy from your diet for at least two weeks. If your allergies improve when you avoid dairy products, eliminate dairy year-round. You will then need to take a calcium supplement, usually 1,000 milligrams (mg) a day, to compensate for the decreased calcium intake that accompanies a dairy-free diet.

• **Soy, corn and wheat.** Soy, including soy milk, tofu, soybean oil, edamame and soy sauce, may aggravate chronic congestion, according to

clinical observation. Even if you don't appear allergic to soy on a skin-prick test, experiment by eliminating soy from your diet for at least two weeks.

The same is true of corn (including cornflakes, corn chips and corn oil) and wheat (including all breads and baked goods unless they are marked "wheat-free" or "gluten-free"). If you find that your symptoms are alleviated when you stop eating any of these foods, eliminate them year-round.

■ ■ ■ ■

Allergies May Reduce Cancer Risk

Cancers of the mouth, throat, digestive tract, colon, bladder, uterus, cervix, lung and skin were less common among allergy sufferers.

Theory: Symptoms such as sneezing, coughing and tearing eyes help the body expel environmental toxins that can trigger abnormal cell growth. More research is needed to see if allergy patients would benefit from discontinuing symptom-suppressing medication.

Paul Sherman, PhD, professor of neurobiology and behavior, Cornell University, Ithaca, New York, and leader of an analysis of 646 studies.

Get Rid of Canker Sores Once and for All

Jamison Starbuck, ND, naturopathic physician in family practice in Missoula, Montana. She is past president of the American Association of Naturopathic Physicians and a contributing editor to The Alternative Advisor: The Complete Guide to Natural Therapies and Alternative Treatments *(Time Life).*

At first glance, canker sores seem like a trivial complaint. These small sores inside the mouth aren't life-threatening or contagious. They don't leave a scar and usually go away within a week. What's the big deal? The problem is that many people have recurrent canker sores that occur several times a month. Because the nerves in the mouth are so sensitive, canker sores, which occur on the tongue, inside the cheek and/or behind the lips, cause a lot of pain. If you have recurrent canker sores, it can be extremely painful to eat—or even speak. Unlike cold sores, which are triggered by the herpes simplex virus and can be treated with antiviral medications, most canker sores result from a localized immune reaction brought on by stress, a food allergy, nutritional problems or trauma, such as biting your tongue or lip. *If you have recurrent canker sores…*

•**Consider allergy testing.** You may develop a canker sore because your mouth becomes irritated within a matter of hours of eating a highly acidic meal that includes tomatoes, citrus or chocolate—or after drinking coffee, black tea or carbonated beverages. With a food allergy, the reaction may not occur for several hours—or it may be immediate. If you get recurrent canker sores, it's wise to get an *immunoglobulin G* (IgG) food allergy blood test to identify the specific foods that weaken your immune system and trigger an allergic reaction. If it's not convenient for you to get allergy testing, try avoiding the most common offending foods—one at a time for one week each—to identify those that trigger an allergic reaction in you. In my practice, wheat, garlic, nuts, soy and citrus are the most frequent allergens among canker sore sufferers.

•**Check for a nutritional deficiency.** If you have a deficiency of vitamin B-12, the B vitamin folic acid or iron, you are likely to develop recurrent canker sores. Even if you already take a daily multivitamin, you can safely add 600 micrograms (mcg) in supplemental folic acid and an 800-mcg supplement of vitamin B-12 daily. Try these supplements for one month to see whether they are effective.

Caution: Be sure to get your iron levels tested if you suspect an iron deficiency. Taking an iron supplement unnecessarily can lead to liver damage.

•**Take precautions if you're under stress.** Stress leads to canker sores because it reduces digestive function, decreases immune health and increases inflammation. If you are prone to canker sores, add more bland foods, such as brown rice, baked potatoes, lightly steamed vegetables, poultry and fish, to your diet when you're under stress. Bland foods are easier to digest and less likely to irritate the mouth and digestive tract.

•**Use herbal remedies.** If you develop a canker sore, you can speed healing by taking two slippery elm capsules every four hours on an empty stomach. In addition, drink three cups of licorice root tea daily. Both these herbs moisten and soothe the mucous membranes of the mouth and digestive tract.

Caution: if you have high blood pressure, avoid licorice—which can adversely affect blood pressure in some people.

The Folic Acid–Asthma Link

University of Adelaide news release.

Children born to women who take folic acid in late pregnancy are at increased risk for asthma, Australian researchers say.

THE STUDY

The University of Adelaide study included more than 500 women whose diet and supplement intake were assessed during pregnancy. The women's children were checked for asthma at age 3.5 years and at 5.5 years. Asthma was found in 11.6% of children at 3.5 years and in 11.8% of children at 5.5 years.

"In our study, supplemental folic acid in late pregnancy was associated with an increased risk of asthma in children, but there was no evidence to suggest any adverse effects if supplements were taken in early pregnancy," said Michael Davies, MD, an associate professor at the university's Robinson Institute. The researchers also said they found no association between asthma and dietary folate, which is found in green, leafy vegetables, certain fruits and nuts.

FOLIC ACID RECOMMENDATIONS

Pregnant women are advised to take a supplemental dose of 400 micrograms (mcg) of folic acid per day in the month before and during the first trimester of pregnancy to reduce the risk of neural tube birth defects.

"Our study supports these guidelines, as we found no increased risk of asthma if folic acid supplements were taken in pre- or early pregnancy," Dr. Davies said. "However, these guidelines may need to be expanded to include recommendations about avoiding use of high-dose supplemental folic acid in late pregnancy."

The study was published in the *American Journal of Epidemiology.*

info For information about childhood asthma, visit The Nemours Foundation Web site, *http://kidshealth.org/parent,* and type "asthma basics" into the search box.

The Pill May Ease Asthma

Piush Mandhane, MD, PhD, assistant professor, pediatric pulmonology, University of Alberta, Canada.
Jennifer Appleyard, MD, chief, allergy and immunology, St. John Hospital and Medical Center, Detroit, Michigan.
Chest.

Women with asthma may notice that their asthma symptoms get worse at certain times of the month. Now, a new study confirms that fluctuating female hormone levels appear to affect airway inflammation, but oral contraceptives might help ease those changes.

In women who were not using birth control pills, the study found that increased levels of estrogen were associated with decreased levels of exhaled nitric oxide—indicating decreased airway inflammation. In these same women, increased levels of progesterone were associated with increased levels of exhaled nitric oxide, indicating increased airway inflammation.

However, birth control pills lessen dramatic hormone fluctuations, and researchers didn't find differences in asthma symptoms throughout the month for women who took them.

FIRST STUDY ON HORMONES AND ASTHMA

Because many women report a change in asthma symptoms related to menstrual cycles, it's often assumed that there is an association, said the study's lead author Piush Mandhane, MD, PhD, an assistant professor of pediatric pulmonology at the University of Alberta in Canada. But, he said, the relationship between hormonal fluctuations and asthma symptoms hasn't been well studied.

"This study is a first step in looking at the relationship between hormones and asthma," said Dr. Mandhane. The findings might be of use in managing asthma among premenopausal women, the researchers said.

Results of the study were published in the journal *Chest.*

STUDY DETAILS

The study included 17 women. Eight were on birth control pills that contained estrogen and progesterone. The average age of the women using oral contraceptives was 25.5, while the average age of the women not taking birth control pills was 37.5.

Three of the women in the group not on birth control reported experiencing menstrual-cycle–related asthma prior to the study, while just one woman in the birth control group did.

The researchers gathered daily information about symptoms and conducted blood tests to measure estrogen and progesterone levels, performed *spirometry* (a lung function test) and took measurements of exhaled nitric oxide. They also conducted allergy tests, via skin pricks every other day.

They found that women who didn't take birth control pills had an average exhaled nitric oxide level of 48.2 parts per billion (ppb), while those on oral contraceptives had an average level of 27 ppb. In women who weren't taking oral contraceptives, an increase in estrogen was associated with a decrease in exhaled nitric oxide, while each increase in progesterone was associated with an increase in exhaled nitric oxide. That means when progesterone levels are elevated (before menstruation), asthma symptoms are likely to be worse.

Progesterone increases also aggravated allergy symptoms—with more severe allergic reactions evident on skin prick tests when progesterone levels were elevated.

The researchers didn't find any statistically significant differences in allergic reactions during the month for women on birth control pills.

THEORY

Dr. Mandhane said that "birth control works by flattening out the fluctuations in hormone levels," and that's likely why there weren't many differences in asthma symptoms for women taking birth control pills.

"Hormones do play a role," said Dr. Mandhane, "and women need to be aware that there's a potential relationship between their asthma symptoms and their menstrual cycles."

EXPERT REACTION

Jennifer Appleyard, MD, chief of allergy and immunology at St. John Hospital and Medical Center in Detroit, said that this study "lends credence to the fact that asthma is affected by hormones. This is definitely not something women should just write off. It's not just all in their minds."

But she also pointed out that this was a small study, and that the women in each group were very different from each other. "There were a lot of older women in one group who took more asthma medication. It's not really comparing apples to apples," she said.

Because birth control pills can have some serious side effects, Dr. Appleyard said she would not advise someone to go on oral contraceptives just to help manage her asthma. However, if a woman notices a difference in her symptoms throughout her menstrual cycle, she may want to talk to her doctor about increasing her asthma medications during that particular time in her cycle, she said.

info To learn more about asthma, visit the Web site of the US National Heart, Lung, and Blood Institute, *www.nhlbi.nih.gov,* and search "What is asthma?"

■ ■ ■ ■

Tai Chi Helps Control Asthma

When 17 asthma patients took classes in tai chi (an ancient Chinese practice that coordinates breathing and slow body movements) once weekly for six weeks and performed daily exercises for 30 minutes using audiovisual aids at home, patients showed significant improvements in asthma control and reduced their use of short-acting asthma relief medication.

Theory: Tai chi strengthens the respiratory muscles.

If you have asthma: Check for tai chi classes at your local community center or health club.

Sumalee Kiatboonsri, MD, professor of medicine, division of pulmonary and critical care medicine, Ramathibodi Hospital, Bangkok, Thailand.

Wider Waist Boosts Asthma Risk

Alejandro Arroliga, MD, pulmonolgist and chairman, medicine, Scott & White Memorial Hospital and Clinic, Temple, Texas.

Julie Von Behren, MPH, research associate, Northern California Cancer Center, Berkeley.

Thorax online.

Women with extra fat around their waists are more likely to develop asthma, even if they aren't overweight, a new study finds.

The California Teachers Study of more than 88,000 women found the same association between obesity and increased incidence of asthma that has been seen in other research, according to the report in the journal *Thorax*.

However, it also found an increased incidence of asthma among women with a larger waist size, even if they were of normal weight.

STUDY DETAILS

Using the standard designations of "obese" for a woman with a body mass index (BMI) of 30 or higher and "extremely obese" for a body mass index (BMI) of 40 or higher, the study found a doubled incidence of asthma among the obese women and a more than tripled incidence among the extremely obese.

The study also uncovered a 37% increased incidence of asthma among women with a waist circumference of 88 centimeters—about 35 inches—even if they were not overweight.

Other studies have documented the overall association between obesity and asthma, said Alejandro Arroliga, MD, a pulmonologist and chairman of medicine at the Scott & White Memorial Hospital and Clinic in Temple, Texas. "This is one of the biggest, with more than 88,000 women. It's huge," he said.

POSSIBLE EXPLANATIONS

While the study was not designed to determine why the location of body fat could play a role in development of asthma, "waist size can be an indicator of the type of body fat," explained study author Julie Von Behren, MPH, a research associate at the Northern California Cancer Center. "Abdominal fat is visceral fat, which is more biologically active. It has been linked to diabetes and heart disease."

Fat around the waist "could be acting in some inflammatory way," she said.

That is a plausible, though unproven, explanation, said Dr. Arroliga. "We know that obesity can cause an inflammatory state," Dr. Arroliga said. "Markers of inflammation are increased in obesity."

While one conventional explanation is that body fat puts a squeeze on airways, some previous studies have pointed toward the composition of body fat as a possible element in asthma risk, he said.

"But it is still unclear why there is this association," Dr. Arroliga said. "The biological explanation lags behind the epidemiological evidence."

ADVICE

Whatever the reason, the association with asthma provides another reason not to put on extra weight, Von Behren said.

info To learn more about asthma, visit the US National Library of Medicine Web site, *www.nlm.nih.gov/medlineplus*. Under "Health Topics," choose "A" and click on "Asthma."

Asthma Patients Neglect Flu Shots

People with asthma are at higher risk for influenza complications, such as pneumonia, than people without asthma, according to a recent study.

In a survey of 173,000 adults, researchers found that only 33.9% of asthma patients ages 18 to 49 and 54.7% of asthma patients ages 50 to 64 got annual influenza vaccinations (compared with 28.8% of adults ages 18 to 64 without asthma).

If you have asthma: Regardless of your age, get all flu vaccinations—including the new H1N1 vaccine—recommended by your doctor.

Gary L. Euler, PhD, epidemiologist, National Center for Immunization and Respiratory Diseases, Centers for Disease Control and Prevention, Atlanta.

Teen Obesity Raises MS Risk in Women

Kassandra Munger, ScD, research associate, department of nutrition, Harvard School of Public Health, Boston.
John Richert, MD, executive vice president, Research and Clinical Programs, National Multiple Sclerosis Society, New York City.
Neurology.

While there are plenty of good reasons to avoid obesity in your teens, a new study now suggests that extra weight in adolescence may increase your risk of *multiple sclerosis* (MS) later.

Reporting in the journal *Neurology*, Harvard researchers found that being obese at age 18 more than doubles a woman's risk for developing MS later in life, compared with her slimmer peers.

"This is one more study that shows obesity leads to another unhealthy outcome, and obesity during adolescence may be critical in determining MS risk," said study author Kassandra Munger, ScD, a research associate at the Harvard School of Public Health in Boston.

MULTIPLE SCLEROSIS

Multiple sclerosis is a chronic disease of the central nervous system, according to the National Multiple Sclerosis Society. While the exact cause of the disease is unknown, scientists believe it's an autoimmune disease. That means the body's immune system mistakenly targets its own cells. In the case of MS, the immune system destroys myelin, a fatty substance that covers and protects nerve fibers, according to the MS society.

THE STUDY

The current study examined more than 238,000 women between 1976 and 2002. The women were between the ages of 25 and 55 at the start of the study.

Body mass index (BMI) was calculated using information given by the women about their height and weight when they were 18, and at the start of the study. A BMI of 18.5 to 24.9 is considered a healthy weight, according to the US Centers for Disease Control and Prevention, while 25 to 29.9 is overweight and 30 or higher is obese.

The women were also asked to look at pictures of nine different body silhouettes that ranged in size from very thin to extremely obese, and to identify which silhouette most closely matched hers at ages 5, 10 and 20.

STUDY FINDINGS

Women who were obese at age 18 had a 2.25 times greater risk for developing MS, according to the study. Being overweight seemed to increase the risk slightly, but not to a level that was statistically significant, Dr. Munger noted.

A large body silhouette at age 20 increased the risk for MS by 96%, the researchers found. A large body size at age 5 or 10 was not associated with an increased risk for MS, provided that the woman had slimmed down by age 20.

POSSIBLE EXPLANATIONS

Although this study wasn't designed to find the reason behind the increase, Dr. Munger said that people who are obese may have lower circulating levels of vitamin D, and low vitamin D levels have been suspected of playing a role in the development of MS. Another possibility, suggested Dr. Munger, is that fat tissue secretes a lot of substances that can affect the immune system.

EXPERT COMMENTARY

"We're beginning now to get clues about things that might predispose a person to MS," said John Richert, MD, executive vice president of research and clinical programs at the National Multiple Sclerosis Society. "Up until recently, we've looked at MS as a disease for which the onset can't be controlled, and though it's still mostly that way, maybe there are circumstances where people might be able to lower their risk a little bit. If all the incoming data [from this and other studies] is correct, not smoking and maintaining an ideal weight might lower the risk of MS."

But, of the current study, he added, "As with so many interesting observations, this study raises a lot more questions than it answers."

Dr. Munger noted that the study was done solely in women, so the results may not hold true for men. And, additionally, she said, the study participants were almost all white, so it's not clear if this association would hold up for other races.

info To learn more about potential causes of MS, visit the Web site of the National Multiple Sclerosis Society, *www.nationalmssociety. org,* and click on "About MS."

New Drugs Key to Living Well with MS

Patricia K. Coyle, MD, professor and acting chair of the department of neurology at Stony Brook University Medical Center, and director of the Stony Brook Multiple Sclerosis Comprehensive Care Center.

The term *multiple sclerosis* (MS) conjures up frightening images of life in a wheelchair—but thanks to recent advances, an MS diagnosis no longer means that disability is inevitable. This is especially good news for women, given that MS is two to three times more common in women than men.

It is now possible to detect MS earlier…begin effective treatment just about as soon as symptoms appear…and slow the disease's progression. Yet despite this encouraging news, MS often goes undiagnosed for months or years—narrowing the window of opportunity that early treatment provides.

What you must know to protect yourself...

MS EXPLAINED

With MS, the immune system's white blood cells mistakenly attack the myelin (nerve fibers' protective coating) and nerve fibers themselves in the brain, spinal cord and optic nerves. This impairs the nerves' ability to transmit messages.

Women's greater vulnerability to MS may be related to hormones. MS typically strikes young adults, but it can appear as late as in one's 70s. People of northern European descent are more genetically predisposed to MS. Parents, siblings and children of MS patients have a 2% to 5% chance of developing it, too. Genes alone don't bring on the disease, however. Something in the environment—such as exposure to the Epstein-Barr virus (which causes mononucleosis) or vitamin-D deficiency at a young age—seems to help trigger MS.

DIAGNOSIS DIFFICULTIES

MS diagnosis often is delayed because the first symptoms can be vague. Patients tend to attribute them to a minor problem, such as a pinched nerve...doctors may mistake MS for spinal disk disease, vitamin B-12 deficiency or anxiety.

Any of the symptoms below merit a call to the doctor. If MS is suspected, a neurologist or MS center can run tests.

Referrals to a specialist: National Multiple Sclerosis Society, 800-344-4867, *www.national mssociety.org*...Consortium of MS Centers, 201-487-1050, *www.mscare.org*.

Initial symptoms...

- **Clumsiness, loss of balance**
- **Double vision, blurred vision**
- **Eye pain, facial pain**
- **Numb face, limbs or torso**
- **Shocklike sensations upon bending the neck**
- **Stiffness, muscle spasms**
- **Weakness, extreme fatigue.**

Later symptoms...

- **Bladder or bowel incontinence**
- **Difficulty becoming sexually aroused or climaxing**
- **Paralysis, typically in the legs**
- **Poor concentration and memory**
- **Speech or swallowing problems.**

Diagnosis is based on a patient's medical history, a neurological exam and magnetic resonance imaging (MRI) to check for damaged tissue in the brain and spinal cord. *There are four types of MS...*

- **Relapsing-remitting MS,** which affects about 85% of patients, is characterized by sudden flare-ups (relapses) of symptoms followed by periods of improvement, during which patients are stable.

- **Primary progressive MS** accounts for about 10% of MS cases. Symptoms worsen progressively from onset with no improvement.

- **Progressive-relapsing MS,** which affects about 5% of patients, involves steady worsening of symptoms from onset, plus later flare-ups.

- **Secondary progressive MS** refers to relapsing-remitting MS that transitions to slow worsening. Patients get increasingly disabled instead of stabilizing between flare-ups.

MS is rarely fatal. Except when vital brain stem functions (such as breathing and heart rate) are affected or the disease has led to severe disability, most patients have a near-normal life expectancy.

MS TREATMENT TODAY

New disease-modifying therapy (DMT) drugs are key to treatment. Starting a DMT soon after MS develops can lower the risk for long-term disability...cut the number of relapses...and lessen symptom severity during flare-ups. DMTs cannot reverse existing damage but can forestall future damage and significantly reduce the likelihood that relapsing MS will transition to progressive MS. For patients who have had MS for years, DMTs also are helpful so long as relapses are still occurring.

Each MS medication has its own pros and cons, so doctors work with each individual patient to determine the optimal treatment. *Options...*

- ***Glatiramer*** (Copaxone) and ***interferon betas*** (Avonex, Betaseron, Rebif) are DMTs that reduce nervous system inflammation and protect nerve cells. These drugs are given by self-injection once or more weekly.

•**Natalizumab** (Tysabri), a monthly DMT given by intravenous infusion (IV drip) at an infusion center, targets errant white blood cells.

•**Mitoxantrone** (Novantrone), an intravenous chemotherapy drug, suppresses the immune system.

•**Prescription steroids** are used during flare-ups to calm symptoms.

Natural therapies also ease MS symptoms. *Examples...*

•**Dietary changes.** MS patients may benefit from eating less saturated fat and more vitamin B-12 (found in dairy foods, eggs, meat, poultry and shellfish)...vitamin D (found in dairy foods and fish)...omega-3 fatty acids (found in fatty fish, cod liver oil and flaxseed oil)...and omega-6 fatty acids (found in safflower seed oil and sunflower oil). If blood tests show a deficiency, supplements may be recommended.

•**Exercise.** Aerobics are known to help reduce fatigue, stress and incontinence...stretching eases stiffness.

Recommended: Yoga, tai chi, aquatics.

•**Acupuncture.** For many patients, this eases pain, numbness, spasms and incontinence.

•**Massage.** This may reduce pain, stiffness and spasticity.

On the horizon: Though still a long way off, novel therapies—such as oral DMTs and a DNA vaccine to treat MS—hold some promise that, in the future, MS may become a thing of the past.

■ ■ ■ ■

Home-Based Psoriasis Treatment

In a three-year study of 196 adults with the skin disease psoriasis, patients received ultraviolet B therapy at a hospital two to three times weekly or self-administered the therapy at home with a phototherapy machine.

Result: Home and hospital phototherapy were equally safe and effective, and the home therapy group reported greater satisfaction.

If you suffer from psoriasis: Ask your doctor about using home-based phototherapy.

Mayke B.G. Koek, research fellow, department of dermatology, University Medical Center Utrecht, the Netherlands.

■ ■ ■ ■

Ease Arthritis with Dental Floss

In a study of 40 patients with gum disease and moderate or severe rheumatoid arthritis (RA), those who received periodontal treatment had improvement in arthritis symptoms (such as pain and swollen joints) with the greatest improvement seen in patients who also took arthritis medications known as anti-TNF (tumor necrosis factor) drugs, such as *etanercept* (Enbrel) or *infliximab* (Remicade).

If you have RA or are at risk (due to family history): Be sure to brush your teeth twice daily, floss once daily and see your dentist at least twice a year.

Nabil Bissada, DDS, chairman, department of periodontics, Case Western Reserve University School of Dental Medicine, Cleveland.

The Most Underdiagnosed Condition in the US— Do You Have It?

Peter H.R. Green, MD, director of the Celiac Disease Center at Columbia University and professor of clinical medicine at Columbia University College of Physicians and Surgeons, both in New York City. Dr. Green is coauthor of *Celiac Disease: A Hidden Epidemic* (HarperCollins). *www.CeliacDiseaseCenter.org.*

Celiac disease is the most underdiagnosed autoimmune condition in the US. This gastrointestinal disorder affects one in every 100 Americans—yet only about 3% of those afflicted get properly diagnosed and treated. It takes 11 years, on average, from the time symptoms appear until the diagnosis is made. In the interim, as the disease progresses, patients grow increasingly at risk for complications that can harm their bones, blood and nervous system ...or even lead to cancer.

Women are twice as likely as men to have celiac disease. Contrary to what many doctors believe, it can develop at any time, even among seniors.

New finding: Celiac disease is now four times as common as it was 50 years ago, tests of old blood samples show.

CONFOUNDING SYMPTOMS

When a person who has celiac disease consumes gluten—a protein in wheat, rye, barley and triticale (a wheat-rye hybrid)—her immune system attacks the protein. This inflames and damages the intestinal lining and interferes with absorption of nutrients. *The person may develop…*

•**Classic, overt symptoms.** Typically, celiac disease causes severe chronic or recurrent diarrhea. Poor nutrient absorption leads to weight loss, smelly stools, gassiness and/or weakness. Many doctors, mistaking these symptoms for irritable bowel syndrome or inflammatory bowel disease, advise eating more high-fiber grains—which only makes patients sicker.

•**Silent symptoms.** When there is no diarrhea, it's called silent celiac disease. In some silent cases, there are no symptoms at all. In others, atypical symptoms—abdominal pain, migraines, numbness or pain in hands and feet—lead to various wrong diagnoses. Silent celiac disease nonetheless continues to cause intestinal damage.

•**Skin symptoms.** *Dermatitis herpetiformis* (DH) is a chronic itchy, blistery rash. Only people with celiac disease get DH—but the vast majority of DH patients do not develop intestinal symptoms. Consequently, they often are misdiagnosed with eczema, psoriasis or "nerves."

Untreated, celiac disease creates an ever-increasing risk of developing very serious complications, such as osteoporosis, anemia, infertility, neurological problems (poor balance, seizures, dementia) and/or various cancers (melanoma, lymphoma). A missed diagnosis also represents a missed opportunity to watch for other autoimmune disorders that often go hand-in-hand with celiac disease, including thyroid disease, rheumatoid arthritis and *alopecia areata* (patchy hair loss).

GETTING DIAGNOSED AT LAST

Celiac disease is genetic—you cannot get it by eating too much gluten. The genes can "express" themselves at any point in life, and the disease is never outgrown.

Vital: Get tested if you experience any of the following…

•**Possible celiac symptoms.**

•**A family history of the disease.** Almost 10% of family members of celiac patients also have it, even if they have no symptoms.

•**Type 1 diabetes.** Genetic factors link this autoimmune disorder to an increased risk for celiac disease.

•**Down syndrome.** Again, there appears to be a genetic link.

Celiac disease usually can be diagnosed with blood tests for certain antibodies. A biopsy of tissue from the small intestine then is needed to confirm the diagnosis. If a patient has skin symptoms, a skin biopsy that confirms the DH rash also confirms the celiac diagnosis.

Sometimes nutritionists or naturopaths will recommend that patients adopt the gluten-free diet used to control celiac disease—but without first confirming the diagnosis with a blood test or biopsy.

Problem: Starting a gluten-free diet before you complete the diagnostic tests will yield a false-negative result. If you do not actually have celiac disease, you subject yourself to needless limitations…you incur the extra cost of buying gluten-free foods…and your diet may lack adequate fiber.

THE DIET SOLUTION

Currently there are no drugs or supplements available to treat celiac disease. However, following a strict gluten-free diet can work wonders at alleviating celiac symptoms.

Important: If tests confirm celiac disease, the diet is essential even if you have no symptoms—otherwise, intestinal damage continues.

The diet can be tricky because gluten is in all foods that contain wheat, rye, barley and triticale. What's more, gluten grains have many aliases.

Example: Bulgur, couscous, dinkle, durum, einkorn, emmer, fu, graham, kamut, matzah, mir, seitan, semolina and spelt all are wheat products. Avoid oats, too—these often get tainted from being processed in proximity to gluten grains—unless labeled "gluten-free."

Unexpected: Gluten may be found in processed luncheon meat, imitation seafood, canned soup, frozen entrées, soy sauce, beer, medications, supplements and lipsticks.

Adhering to a gluten-free diet is easier than it used to be because all products with wheat now must be labeled as such. Though products containing gluten-grain–derived ingredients are not all necessarily labeled that way, requirements for allowing a food to be labeled gluten-free have become stricter. Now, gluten-free breads, cereals, pastas and other foods are sold in supermarkets and health food stores. Do be sure to get enough fiber from gluten-free grains and other sources.

After adopting a gluten-free diet, some patients see radical improvement within weeks... for others, it takes months or longer. If improvement is slow, your gastroenterologist should investigate possible underlying conditions (such as infection or hormonal problems) that can exacerbate celiac symptoms.

Information: Contact the American Celiac Disease Alliance (703-622-3331, *www.american celiac.org*)...Celiac Disease Foundation (818-990-2354, *www.celiac.org*)...Celiac Sprue Association/USA (877-272-4272, *www.csaceliacs.org*).

Breast Cancer Treatment

Soy Foods Good Medicine for Breast Cancer Survivors

Regular, moderate consumption of soy foods can help lower the risk for death and cancer recurrence in women who've had breast cancer, new research shows.

What's more, the association between soy and a reduced risk of death held true even for women with estrogen receptor-positive cancers and women taking the breast cancer medication *tamoxifen* (Nolvadex), according to the study published in *The Journal of the American Medical Association*.

"We found that women with a history of breast cancer who consumed moderate amounts of soy food were doing better in terms of prognosis. They had reduced mortality and reduced recurrence," said study author Xiao Ou Shu, MD, PhD, a professor of medicine and a cancer

epidemiologist at Vanderbilt University Medical Center in Nashville, Tennessee.

SOY'S EFFECT ON ESTROGEN

There has been some concern that soy might increase the risk of breast cancer or worsen the prognosis for women already diagnosed with the disease because soy is what's known as a phytoestrogen. That means that it can act like a weak form of estrogen in the body.

However, it appears those concerns may have been unfounded because Dr. Shu and her colleagues found that soy actually reduces the availability of naturally occurring estrogen by binding to its receptors.

"In our study, we found that soy food has a very similar effect to tamoxifen," said Dr. Shu. Tamoxifen is a drug that blocks the action of estrogen in the body, which can be helpful for treating cancers that are fueled by estrogen.

Xiao Ou Shu, MD, PhD, professor, medicine, and cancer epidemiologist, Vanderbilt University Medical Center, Nashville, Tennessee.

Gina Villani, MD, chief, division of hematology/oncology, the Brooklyn Hospital Center, New York City.
The Journal of the American Medical Association.

THE STUDY

Dr. Shu's study included just over 5,000 Chinese women who had been previously diagnosed with breast cancer between 2002 and 2006. The women were aged 20 to 75, with the majority of women between the ages of 40 and 60 at the time of diagnosis.

The researchers collected information on cancer diagnosis and treatment, lifestyle factors (including diet) and disease progression at six months after diagnosis, and then again at 18, 36 and 60 months after diagnosis.

Women who had the highest intake of soy (more than 15.3 grams [g] a day) had a 29% reduced risk for death and a 32% decrease in the risk for cancer recurrence compared with those who ate less than 5.3 g of soy per day.

"There was a linear response, and we found the higher the intake, the lower the mortality, up to 11 grams of soy protein," Dr. Shu said, adding that after 11 g daily the benefit leveled off but didn't decline.

Eleven grams of soy translates to about one-fourth of a cup of tofu each day, she said.

NATURAL VS. PROCESSED SOY

Both Dr. Shu and Gina Villani, MD, chief of hematology/oncology at The Brooklyn Hospital Center in New York City, said it's important to note that Chinese women tend to get their soy from natural sources, such as tofu, edamame or unsweetened soy milk, instead of the processed types of soy foods that many Americans eat, such as sweetened, flavored soy milk or soy-based protein bars.

"The take-home lesson is that whole foods are what we need to eat more of," said Dr. Villani. "Try to stay away from the processed stuff. Don't bulk up on soy milk or soy candy bars."

Dr. Shu also pointed out that Chinese women might be replacing unhealthier food choices, such as red meat, with soy. In an accompanying editorial in the same issue of the journal, experts from the US National Cancer Institute noted that the average daily soy intake for people living in China makes up 10% or more of their daily protein intake.

Both Dr. Shu and Dr. Villani advise against loading up on soy supplements, as these haven't been proven to be beneficial, and Dr. Villani said it's unclear if such high levels of soy could cause harm.

And, Dr. Villani added, "supplements don't replace food. We haven't even begun to understand the interactions between nutrients in food and the body. Soy as a bean may react different than soy from a candy bar in the body."

"Soy food intake has been shown to reduce the risk of breast cancer, and it may have cardiovascular benefit, so overall, whether or not you have cancer, soy could be very beneficial to you and could become an important component of a healthy diet," Dr. Shu said. "But try to get it in natural sources, not from processed food."

info For more on soy, visit the US National Library of Medicine Web site, *www.med lineplus.gov.* Click on "Medical Encyclopedia," then under "S," click on "Soy."

Important Breast Cancer Update

Robert Smith, PhD, director of cancer screening for the American Cancer Society, *www.cancer.org*, and an adjunct professor of epidemiology at the Rollins School of Public Health at Emory University in Atlanta.

When the US Preventive Services Task Force (USPSTF) recently issued updated recommendations for less frequent breast cancer screening than has been previously used for many women, it sparked an immediate controversy.

The debate focused mainly on two of the USPSTF's recommendations—that there is insufficient evidence to support routine mammography for women ages 40 to 49 with an average risk for breast cancer...and that women ages 50 to 74 with an average risk should undergo screening mammography only every two years (biennial).* For women age 75 and older, the USPSTF concluded that there was insufficient

*To read a summary of the USPSTF's new recommendations (including a clarification of the task force's intent), go to the Web site of the Agency for Health Care Research and Quality, *www.ahrq.gov/clinic/Uspstf/uspsbrca.htm.*

evidence to advise for or against breast cancer screening.

Many doctors disagreed with the new recommendations, claiming that reducing the frequency of mammography would increase deaths from the disease.

How can women make the best choices for themselves?

Here are some important details that weren't widely reported in the press—and what you need to know about breast cancer tests besides mammography...

WHY THE CONTROVERSY?

The USPSTF is an independent panel of doctors and scientists that bases its recommendations on an analysis of the benefits and harms associated with preventive services such as screening for the early detection of various diseases.

In reviewing the evidence for breast cancer screening, the USPSTF analyzed several studies and mathematical simulations of women undergoing regular mammography screening. The task force found that while most of the studies did show a greater benefit with annual versus biennial mammography—as many as one-third of cancers would be missed with biennial versus annual screening—the harms, including false-positive test results, inconvenience, anxiety and unnecessary biopsies of noncancerous abnormalities, were judged to outweigh the benefits.

Doctors who object to the USPSTF's recommendations argue that although the majority of women will experience a false-positive test result for breast cancer at some point in their lives (resulting in a follow-up mammogram, ultrasound or, less often, a biopsy), the risk is worth the potential benefit of detecting a malignancy earlier. That's why the American Cancer Society (ACS), the American College of Obstetricians and Gynecologists and several other groups believe that the guidelines that existed prior to the USPSTF's updated recommendations should continue to be followed.**

For most women, this means that yearly mammography should begin at age 40 and continue as long as the woman is in good health. Women

**To read the ACS's guidelines for breast cancer screening, go to the ACS Web site, *www.cancer.org.*

of any age who are at increased risk for breast cancer (due to such risk factors as a family or personal history of the disease) should talk to their doctors about the appropriate age and frequency for screening.

How can medical experts interpret the data so differently?

The ACS, in particular, analyzed the same data reviewed by the USPSTF but also looked at supplemental data because some of the trials examined by the USPSTF screened women with procedures that are no longer used today, such as single-view mammography. The more recent data studied by the ACS found that when women in their 40s were screened annually with high-quality mammography, there were two to three times fewer breast cancer deaths than what the USPSTF estimated.

OTHER IMPORTANT TESTS

What you should know about other tools that can be used in addition to mammograms to help detect breast malignancies—and the ACS's position on each...

•**Magnetic resonance imaging** (MRI) uses a magnet and computer technology to create highly detailed images of the breast without exposing the patient to radiation.

Women at high risk for breast cancer—such as those who have a known BRCA1 or BRCA2 gene mutation...a first-degree relative (mother, sister or daughter) with a BRCA1 or BRCA2 gene mutation...or a history of radiation treatments to the chest for childhood cancer—should get an annual MRI plus mammography.

Women who are at moderately increased risk—a personal or family history of breast cancer or other breast conditions, such as extremely dense breasts—should talk with their doctors about the benefits and risks of adding MRI screening to their yearly mammography.

•**Ultrasound** produces an image by bouncing nonradiation-producing, ultra-high frequency sound waves off of breast tissue.

Ultrasound is mainly used in women with unusually dense breast tissue to help determine whether a questionable image on a mammogram is a noncancerous, liquid-filled cyst or a solid mass that might be a cancerous tumor.

•**Breast self-exam** (BSE) involves a woman inspecting her own breasts for changes, such as hard lumps or thickening. Most women do not perform frequent BSEs, or they use poor technique (such as failing to inspect the entire breast).

Since BSE has not been found to reduce deaths due to breast cancer, women should consider this an optional technique. (For advice on the proper way to perform a BSE, go to *www.cancer.org* and type "breast self-exam" in the search field.)

Women should always be attentive to the look (color, size and shape) and feel of their breasts while changing clothes or showering and report any changes to their physicians right away.

•**Digital mammography** uses a computer so the image can be sharpened for greater clarity.

Digital mammography has been shown to be equal to—not better than—film mammography in detecting cancers in most women. For premenopausal women and women with dense breasts, however, digital mammography appears to provide more accurate results. And it may be able to reduce the rate of false-positives.

The latest statistics indicate that more than half the breast-imaging facilities in the US now have digital technology. For postmenopausal women, either technology is acceptable.

■ ■ ■ ■

Will My Breasts Hurt If I Have Cancer?

It would be good if pain were the first sign of breast cancer, because that would help us catch it earlier. However, malignant breast lumps usually are painless in the early stages. Rarely, a woman reports a tugging or pulling sensation in a breast and then a biopsy reveals cancer—but we seldom do biopsies based on breast pain. Usually the pain has some benign cause, such as cyclical hormonal changes, pulled ligaments or tenderness related to fibrocystic lumpiness. Discomfort that occurs in both breasts or at the same time every month is highly unlikely to signal cancer.

Cystic pain prevention: Try taking evening primrose oil capsules at 1,500 milligrams (mg) twice daily and consider giving up caffeine.

Benjamin O. Anderson, MD, professor and director, University of Washington Breast Health Clinic, and chair and director, Breast Health Global Initiative, both in Seattle.

■ ■ ■ ■

Better Mammograms

When scheduling a mammogram, ask if the imaging center's accreditation is current. The federal Mammography Quality Standards Act (MQSA) passed in 1992 requires imaging centers that provide mammograms to have their equipment inspected annually to ensure that it meets the act's stringent criteria. Faulty mammography equipment can produce inaccurate test results.

Joseph Daniels, MBA, RT (radiological technologist), imaging director, Baylor Regional Medical Center, Plano, Texas.

■ ■ ■ ■

Synthetic Hormone Replacement Warning

Almost three in every 100 women taking synthetic hormone replacement therapy (HRT) whose breasts became tender during the first year of the therapy developed breast cancer, say researchers at University of California at Los Angeles, who analyzed data on more than 16,000 women who took estrogen-plus progestin as part of the Women's Health Initiative study. If you are on synthetic HRT, speak to a holistic physician about switching to a bio-identical hormone, especially if you experience breast tenderness.

Mark A. Stengler, NMD, naturopathic medical doctor in private practice, La Jolla, California…adjunct associate clinical professor at the National College of Natural Medicine, Portland, Oregon…author of many books, including The Natural Physician's Healing Therapies and coauthor of Prescription for Natural Cures (both from Bottom Line Books)… and author of the Bottom Line/Natural Healing newsletter

Preventive Mastectomy May Not Be Needed

European Breast Cancer Conference news release.

Removing a breast after the other breast has been treated for breast cancer does not improve the odds that women with two genetic mutations will be free of disease or live longer, new research has found.

Women with the mutations—which affect the genes known as *BRCA1* and *BRCA2*—have a much higher risk for developing cancer. Some women choose to have their breasts removed as a preventive measure, called a preventive mastectomy, even without a cancer diagnosis.

STUDY DETAILS

Annette Heemskerk-Gerritsen, a graduate student at Erasmus Medical Centre in Rotterdam, the Netherlands, and her colleagues studied 390 women who had the mutation and had developed cancer in one breast. Of the group, 138 had remaining breast tissue removed as a preventive measure.

The recurrence and survival rates between the two groups of women were similar, the study found.

The study results were presented at the European Breast Cancer Conference in Barcelona, Spain.

IMPLICATION

"We hope that our findings will provide additional information to improve the counseling of breast cancer patients considering mastectomy for risk reduction by emphasizing that the gain that may be obtained by this radical surgery is mainly in respect of reducing the risk of cancer in the opposite breast," said Heemskerk-Gerritsen. "As yet, we have found no benefits with respect to disease-free and overall survival."

info For more information about BRCA1 and BRCA2 mutations, visit the Web site of the US National Cancer Institute, *www.cancer.gov.* Under "Cancer Topics," choose "Breast Cancer," then type "BRCA" in the search box.

Should You Be Screened For Breast Cancer Genes?

Julia A. Smith, MD, PhD, clinical assistant professor in the departments of medicine and oncology at New York University...director, NYU Cancer Institute Breast Cancer Screening and Prevention Program...and director, Lynne Cohen Breast Cancer Preventive Care Program at NYU Cancer Institute, all in New York City.

If your family tree includes one or more relatives with a history of breast cancer, you probably know that you could be at increased risk for the disease, too.

Reason: About 5% to 10% of breast cancer cases are due to inherited genetic mutations. Women who carry one of these altered genes are at least five times more likely than average to develop breast cancer. They also are at increased risk for ovarian cancer.

A blood test can reveal whether you have one of the genes linked to breast cancer. Why might you want to know? Because learning that you do not have the gene reduces anxiety...and if you do have the gene, you can consider the options for lowering your risk.

Reassuring: By law, health insurance companies can no longer deny coverage or charge higher premiums based on a person's genetic predisposition for developing a certain disease in the future...and employers cannot use genetic information when making decisions about hiring, promoting or firing personnel.

FAMILY HISTORY

A first-degree relative is your parent, sibling or offspring. A second-degree relative is your grandparent, grandchild, half-sibling, uncle, aunt, nephew or niece. *Consider genetic testing if you have or had any of the following...*

•**A personal history of breast cancer or a biopsy that showed benign changes** (such as *atypical ductal hyperplasia* or *lobular carcinoma in situ*), especially by age 50.

•**A first-degree relative who had breast cancer by age 50 or tested positive for a breast cancer gene.**

•**Three or more first- or second-degree relatives with breast cancer,** regardless of age.

•**A first-degree relative who has ovarian cancer.**

•**A first- or second-degree relative with cancer in both breasts…or with breast and ovarian cancer.**

•**A first- or second-degree male relative who had breast cancer.**

•**One first-degree relative or two second-degree relatives who had breast or ovarian cancer** if you are of Ashkenazi Jewish, Dutch, Icelandic or Norwegian descent.

HOW TO GET TESTED

These days, most major hospitals have genetic testing programs.

Recommended: Consult a medical or surgical oncologist—a cancer specialist who can evaluate your overall risk, perform the test, discuss results, advise you on risk reduction and provide individualized follow-up care.

Referrals: National Cancer Institute, 800-422-6237, *www.cancer.gov/search/geneticsservices.*

The doctor takes a complete family history to help you assess the advisability of testing. If you decide to go ahead, blood is drawn for analysis. Typically it takes several weeks to get test results.

The test looks at genes that belong to a class called *tumor suppressors*, whose role is to prevent uncontrolled cell growth. Most inherited breast cancers result from harmful alterations of the *BRCA1* and *BRCA2* genes. There are more than a half dozen other gene mutations linked to increased risk for a hereditary cancer syndrome, which can be assessed and tested for separately. In rare cases, a person carries more than one of the gene mutations linked to breast cancer.

Blood is sent to a lab for DNA sequencing (a description of the order of the chemical building blocks in a given stretch of DNA). If a patient's history suggests that it is necessary to sequence only a small number of specific sites on the gene, the test costs about $400. To sequence the entire BRCA1 and BRCA2 genes costs about $3,100.

Insurance may cover the cost. If you have Medicaid, contact your state Medicaid program—some states cover breast cancer genetic analysis for qualifying individuals.

Or: Contact the nonprofit Susan G. Komen for the Cure (877-465-6636, *www.Komen.org*), which can help you find ways to cover the cost.

WHAT YOUR RESULTS MEAN

Of course you'll feel relieved if your test reveals no mutated breast cancer gene.

But remember: You may have one of the other, less common hereditary cancer syndromes or a genetic mutation as yet unidentified, or you may develop a noninherited form of breast cancer—so it's still important to have regular mammograms and pelvic exams.

If it turns out that you do carry a mutated breast cancer gene, this does not mean that breast cancer is definitely in your future. Women with such a gene have about a 40% to 85% lifetime risk of developing breast cancer and a 15% to 40% risk for ovarian cancer. They also may be at increased risk for cancer of the pancreas or colon and/or for melanoma.

Let this information empower you to take steps to minimize your risk. *Your doctor can help you decide which of the following options might be right for you…*

•**Increased surveillance.** Additional and more frequent screening tests cannot alter your risk for getting breast cancer, but they can help detect a malignancy early, when it may be most treatable. Each year, get a mammogram and breast ultrasound together…get an MRI six months later. You also may be advised to have a *transvaginal ultrasound* and *CA-125* blood test periodically, which may help screen for ovarian cancer.

•**Lifestyle changes.** Do aerobic exercise for at least 20 minutes three or more times each week. Limit alcohol consumption to no more than three glasses of wine weekly. Don't smoke. Maintain a healthful diet, and work with a dietitian to lose weight if necessary. Do not take menopausal hormone therapy—it increases risk.

•**Chemoprevention.** The oral drugs *tamoxifen* and *raloxifene* block the effects of estrogen on breast tissue.

Encouraging: Among pre- and postmenopausal women at increased risk, tamoxifen reduces the likelihood of invasive breast cancer by 49%…raloxifene's protective effects are similar for women past menopause. Typically the drug is taken once daily for five years.

Important: Work with your doctor to weigh the advantages against the disadvantages. Possible side effects include hot flashes, leg cramps, joint pain and increased risk for blood clots and/or uterine cancer.

•**Prophylactic bilateral (double) mastectomy.** This surgical procedure removes as much breast tissue as possible. It reduces a woman's risk by more than 95% (though not 100%, since some breast tissue cells may remain). It can be combined with surgical reconstruction of the breast.

•**Prophylactic bilateral salpingo-oophorectomy.** Surgical removal of ovaries and Fallopian tubes lowers breast cancer risk in premenopausal women by about 50% because it greatly reduces hormone production. It also reduces ovarian cancer risk by 93%. (There is still a small risk for an ovarian cancer variant that arises in the abdominal lining.) This option should be discussed with a doctor who understands the risks and knows your family-planning goals.

•**Consider joining a clinical trial.** You may learn of ways to reduce risk…have access to experimental therapies…and help uncover knowledge that may protect women in the future.

Contact: National Cancer Institute (800-422-6237, *http://www.ClinicalTrials.gov*)…Society for Women's Health Research (202-223-8224, *www.womancando.org*)…NYU Cancer Institute Breast Cancer Screening and Prevention Program (212-731-5452).

Best Ways to Get Through a Breast Biopsy

Janet K. Baum, MD, and Elvira Lang, MD, both associate professors of radiology at Harvard Medical School in Boston. Dr. Baum is director of breast imaging at Cambridge Health Alliance and author of numerous studies on breast imaging. Dr. Lang is coauthor of *Patient Sedation Without Medication* (Trafford), and founder and president of Hypnalgesics (*www.hypnalgesics.com*).

A woman finds a lump in her breast. After a mammogram and ultrasound, her radiologist says that the only way to determine if it's cancer is to do a biopsy (removal and analysis of a small tissue sample).

Or: After a routine mammogram, a woman with lumpy breasts is informed that suspicious-looking calcifications have appeared. Again, a biopsy is recommended.

Such scenarios are common. Each year in the US, more than 1.6 million breast biopsies are done. But that's small comfort when you need a biopsy—because the situation naturally provokes a lot of anxiety.

Recent study: Women waiting for breast biopsy results have levels of the stress hormone cortisol equal to those of women actually diagnosed with breast cancer. The flood of cortisol can impair immune function.

Reassuring: Only about 20% of breast biopsies turn out to reveal cancer…and knowing what to expect helps ease stress.

WHAT TO DO FIRST

From your primary care doctor or gynecologist, get a referral to a breast radiologist, a doctor who specializes in breast imaging and biopsies.

Best: Ask any breast radiologist you are considering if he/she is a member of the Society of Breast Imaging or is affiliated with a facility certified as a Breast Imaging Center of Excellence by the American College of Radiology. These credentials indicate adherence to high standards.

Ask the breast radiologist about various biopsy techniques (see below). The technique used depends on the location and size of the lump, how suspicious the area looks and other factors.

Concern: A national panel of experts recently concluded that nonsurgical needle biopsy should be the "gold standard" for initial diagnosis of breast abnormalities—yet about 35% of initial breast biopsies in the US still are done using more invasive open surgery.

Recent study: Patients who received guidance in self-hypnotic relaxation before and during their breast biopsies experienced significantly less emotional distress and less physical discomfort. Ask your doctor if the biopsy facility provides procedure hypnosis…or consult a hypnotherapy professional for instruction and/ or an audiotape you can listen to during your procedure.

Referrals to a hypnotist: American Society of Clinical Hypnosis, 630-980-4740, *www.asch. net.*

NONSURGICAL BIOPSY

Percutaneous (through the skin) needle biopsy usually is done at a doctor's office or breast-imaging center. Often an imaging technique, such as mammography, MRI or ultrasound, is used to pinpoint the area to be biopsied. Typically, an injection of local anesthesia is given… the procedure requires no stitches…and there is little or no scarring. Sometimes a tiny metal clip is left in the breast to mark the biopsy site for future reference—in case surgery is needed to remove a malignancy, for instance, or to show that a particular benign cyst has been tested. *Options…*

•**Fine needle biopsy.** Using a fine needle with a hollow center, the doctor withdraws a sample of cells. The least invasive biopsy procedure, this takes a few minutes, and results may be available within hours.

But: It is appropriate only in limited cases, such as when a palpable (easily felt) mass is present…and there is a significant risk for false-negative results because with the small sample, cancerous cells may be missed.

•**Core needle biopsy.** A thicker hollow needle is inserted one or more times to extract samples of breast tissue. This type of biopsy is appropriate in most cases and takes about 20 to 30 minutes. It is more accurate than fine needle biopsy because actual breast tissue (not just a sample of cells) is examined.

With vacuum-assisted core needle biopsy, a needle is inserted through a very small incision, then a tiny vacuum and cutting device extracts breast tissue samples. This takes 20 to 60 minutes and may be used when larger samples are needed.

Recovery: After a needle biopsy, use ice packs as directed by your doctor to minimize discomfort, swelling and bruising. You may take nonprescription *acetaminophen* (Tylenol). Keep the area dry and avoid strenuous activity for 24 to 48 hours.

SURGICAL BIOPSY

This procedure may be warranted when a needle biopsy is inconclusive or the suspicious area is not accessible with a needle biopsy. Generally there is some scarring.

Often the procedure involves a breast radiologist, who uses imaging tests to locate and mark (with a tiny wire) the precise area to be biopsied… and a surgeon, who does the surgery.

Best: Ask your doctor for a referral to a surgeon whose practice consists primarily of breast procedures or who has completed a fellowship in breast surgery.

A surgical biopsy usually is done in a surgical center or a hospital outpatient department using local anesthesia plus sedation (to make you drowsy). If you take a blood thinner, such as aspirin or *warfarin* (Coumadin), ask your doctor about temporarily discontinuing it before surgery to avoid excess bleeding.

How it is done: Using a scalpel, the surgeon cuts through the skin. With an incisional biopsy, just a portion of the suspicious tissue is removed. This gives the best cosmetic results—which is important, considering that the majority of breast biopsies turn out to be benign. With an excisional biopsy, the goal is to remove all abnormal tissue, which may reduce the odds of needing additional surgery if cancer is diagnosed. Stitches are used to close the incision.

Recovery: You may be told to rest for one to two days and avoid strenuous activity for two weeks. Your doctor may prescribe pain medication. See your doctor as directed for your post-operative check.

Pros and cons: This is the surest way to get a definitive diagnosis, with the smallest risk for a false-negative result.

But: Compared with needle biopsy, a surgical biopsy involves more discomfort, more scarring and a higher risk for complications.

GETTING THE RESULTS

Ask the doctor who performs your biopsy when and by whom—the radiologist, surgeon or primary care doctor—you will be given your results. On average, it takes two to five days to analyze the tissue.

This waiting period can be very stressful.

To reduce anxiety: Express your emotions—confide in loved ones, write in a journal. Keeping fears and feelings pent up increases stress and lowers immune response.

If results are negative…

•**Ask your doctor when you should repeat imaging tests**—in a few weeks, a few months or a year.

•**Discuss your breast cancer risk factors**—menstrual history, family history, breast density, radiation exposure, alcohol use—and ask if you should see a breast specialist or genetic counselor.

•**Tell your doctor right away if you notice changes in your breasts.**

If results are positive…

•**Find out if more tests are needed to determine the cancer's stage.**

•**Get a referral to an oncologist.**

•**Research treatment options.** Treatment decisions do not need to be made all at once—but having a sense of what lies ahead can make the process more manageable.

■ ■ ■ ■

Test Reduces Need for Breast Biopsies

After a suspicious mass is detected in the breast through mammography or an MRI, patients typically are sent for an ultrasound. An *elastogram*, which looks at the stiffness of tissue, can be taken at the same time.

Benign (noncancerous) masses tend to measure smaller on elastograms in comparison with the standard ultrasound image…suspicious ones usually are larger.

Not all offices that do ultrasounds offer elastograms—ask your doctor.

Stamatia V. Destounis, MD, diagnostic radiologist at Elizabeth Wende Breast Care, LLC, Rochester, New York, and leader of a study of 193 patients who underwent elastograms and ultrasounds.

Acupuncture Brings Relief to Breast Cancer Patients

Eleanor M. Walker, MD, division director of breast services, department of radiation oncology, Henry Ford Hospital, Detroit.
Jay Brooks, MD, chairman, hematology/oncology, Ochsner Health System, Baton Rouge.
Journal of Clinical Oncology online.

Acupuncture is just as good as standard medication to ease hot flashes and other uncomfortable symptoms in women undergoing breast cancer treatment, according to a new study.

And as an added bonus, the needle treatment may boost the patient's sex drive and contribute to clearer thinking.

BACKGROUND

Prior studies have shown that acupuncture can reduce hot flashes in postmenopausal women without breast cancer.

All of these studies, however, compared acupuncture to sham acupuncture, not to commonly used drugs, noted Eleanor Walker, MD, division director of breast services in the department of radiation oncology at Henry Ford Hospital in Detroit, and lead author of the new study. This is the first randomized controlled study to compare acupuncture to medication.

Many women with breast cancer receive anti-estrogen hormone therapy, usually for as long as five years, in addition to other treatments.

Although hormone therapy is effective in reducing tumor recurrence, it does cause hot flashes and night sweats.

The antidepressant *venlafaxine* (Effexor) is the most commonly used therapy for relieving these symptoms, but the drug brings its own side effects, namely dry mouth, reduced appetite, nausea and constipation.

"We need something that's accessible that doesn't add adverse effects," Dr. Walker said.

ACUPUNCTURE STUDY

For this study, 50 women with breast cancer were randomly assigned to receive 12 weeks of acupuncture (twice a week for four weeks, then once a week) or daily Effexor. They were followed for a year.

THE RESULTS

Initially, both groups of women experienced similar reductions (about 50%) in hot flashes and depression, with an overall improvement in quality of life.

But the acupuncture benefits were longer lived. After two weeks, women taking the antidepressant saw a resurgence in hot flashes, while women in the acupuncture arm continued to experience fewer adverse effects.

About 25% of women receiving acupuncture also reported more interest in sex while many also reported more energy and clearer thinking.

The study was published in the *Journal of Clinical Oncology.*

IMPLICATION FOR
THE FUTURE

"I think the data shows you that acupuncture is a good option for these patients [and] it has no side effects," said Dr. Walker.

"The issue most of the time is the cost of it and whether insurance companies will pay for it," Dr. Walker said. Additional studies also need to look at how often women would need booster acupuncture to minimize their symptoms.

EXPERT REACTION

"It's provocative but the problem is it's a small number of patients and, having participated in research trials in vasomotor symptoms [hot flashes, night sweats, etc.] in women, it's a field that has a large placebo effect," said Jay Brooks, MD, chairman of hematology/oncology at Ochsner Health System in Baton Rouge. "It needs to have a bigger trial."

info For more on breast cancer treatments, visit the Web site of the National Cancer Institute, *www.cancer.gov/cancertopics/treatment/breast.*

■ ■ ■ ■

Yoga Helps Cancer Patients

In a 10-week study of 44 women with breast cancer, half the women took a weekly 75-minute gentle yoga class, while the others did not practice yoga.

Result: The yoga group reported a 50% drop, on average, in depression symptoms (such as hopelessness), less fatigue and better sleep, while the nonyoga group reported no significant change in symptoms.

If you are undergoing treatment for breast cancer: Ask your doctor about taking a gentle yoga class.

Suzanne Danhauer, PhD, assistant professor, department of internal medicine, Wake Forest University School of Medicine, Winston-Salem, North Carolina.

■ ■ ■ ■

New Breast Cancer Weapon?

In laboratory studies using breast cancer cells, researchers have found that the dietary supplement bitter melon reduced the growth and division of cancer cells and caused the cells to die more quickly. More research is needed.

Cancer Research, 615 Chestnut Street, Philadelphia, Pennsylvania.

Antidepressant Lowers Effectiveness of Breast Cancer Drugs

David Juurlink, MD, PhD, division head, clinical pharmacology and toxicology, Sunnybrook Health Sciences Center, Toronto.

Frank Andersohn, MD, senior research associate, Institute for Social Medicine, Epidemiology, and Health Economics, Charité University Medical Center, Berlin.

Harold J. Burstein, MD, PhD, clinical investigator, breast oncology center, Dana-Farber Cancer Institute, Brigham and Women's Hospital, and associate professor, medicine, Harvard Medical School, Boston.

BMJ (*British Medical Journal* online).

Women with breast cancer who take both *tamoxifen* (Nolvadex), an antiestrogen drug used to treat breast cancer, and the antidepressant *paroxetine* (Paxil) may increase their risk of dying because Paxil reduces tamoxifen's effectiveness, Canadian researchers report.

"Paxil can deprive women of the benefit of tamoxifen, especially when it is used in combination with tamoxifen for a long time," said lead researcher David Juurlink, MD, PhD, division head of clinical pharmacology and toxicology at Sunnybrook Health Sciences Center in Toronto.

"Patients who are on tamoxifen and who require an antidepressant should probably be given something different," he added.

The report was published in *BMJ*, the online edition of the *British Medical Journal*.

THE STUDY

Dr. Juurlink's group looked at the medical records of 2,430 women with breast cancer who began taking tamoxifen between 1993 and 2005. About 30% of the women were also taking an antidepressant, Paxil being the most common. Antidepressants are often prescribed to reduce hot flashes associated with tamoxifen in addition to easing symptoms of depression.

Paxil plus tamoxifen was linked to an increased risk of dying from breast cancer, and the risk increased with the amount of time the drugs were taken together, the researchers found.

Taking Paxil for 41% of the time that tamoxifen was also taken resulted in one extra death from breast cancer within five years of stopping tamoxifen among every 20 women taking the drugs simultaneously, Dr. Juurlink's team estimated. The more time the drugs were taken together, the greater the risk, they added.

EXPLANATION

Paxil is a *selective serotonin reuptake inhibitor* (SSRI) that significantly inhibits an enzyme called *cytochrome P450 2D6*, which is needed to metabolize tamoxifen into its active form. But this dampening effect was not seen with certain other SSRIs evaluated, including *citalopram* (Celexa) and *venlafaxine* (Effexor), the researchers said.

SSRIs inhibit 2D6 to varying degrees, the authors said, noting Paxil is "exceptionally potent" in that respect.

WHAT TO DO

Patients taking Paxil and tamoxifen should talk with their doctors about changing their antidepressant, Dr. Juurlink said. But he advised against abruptly discontinuing Paxil.

"There is a very real danger to stopping Paxil suddenly. There is a well-described withdrawal syndrome and the risk of depression becoming more severe," he said.

In addition, any transition to another antidepressant should be done gradually over several weeks, he said.

EXPERT COMMENTARY

Frank Andersohn, MD, a senior research associate at the Institute for Social Medicine, Epidemiology, and Health Economics at Charité University Medical Center in Berlin, Germany, and author of an accompanying journal editorial, said that "physicians should be aware that paroxetine and other strong 2D6-inhibiting drugs should be avoided in women treated with tamoxifen."

Fluoxetine (Prozac) is also a strong 2D6 inhibitor, the authors noted.

Another expert, Harold J. Burstein, MD, PhD, clinical investigator in the breast oncology center at Dana-Farber Cancer Institute, Brigham and Women's Hospital in Boston, said this paper adds to the substantial literature suggesting that drugs that affect the metabolism of tamoxifen might affect breast cancer outcomes for women taking the drug.

INTERPRETING THE RESULTS

While the results should not alarm patients currently taking SSRIs, they do suggest that patients on tamoxifen who also need SSRIs should probably seek out agents such as Effexor in preference to Prozac or Paxil," said Dr. Burstein.

"The findings are also a reminder that each drug that a patient takes should be thought through carefully," said Dr. Burstein.

info For more information on drug interactions, visit the Drug Digest Web site at *www.drugdigest.org* and click on "Check Interactions."

■ ■ ■ ■

Grapefruit May Be Linked To Cancer

Women who ate the equivalent of half a grapefruit every other day had a 30% increase in breast cancer risk.

Possible reason: The compound in grapefruit that changes blood levels of some drugs also may increase estrogen levels. More research is needed—but women at high risk for breast cancer may want to avoid grapefruit. Other citrus fruits appear to be safe.

Kristine R. Monroe, PhD, assistant professor, department of preventive medicine, University of Southern California, Los Angeles, and lead author of a study of 46,080 postmenopausal women, published in *British Journal of Cancer*.

■ ■ ■ ■

Bean that Fights Breast Cancer

Women who ate one-half cup of lentils at least twice a week were 24% less likely to develop breast cancer, compared with women who ate the same amount of lentils less than once a month or not at all.

Theory: Lentils' protective effects may be due to particular types of *phytochemicals*. One-half cup of lentils has 9 grams (g) of protein, 8 g of fiber, 3 milligrams of iron and only 115 calories. And they are inexpensive. Add lentils while cooking soups and whole grains, and use cooked lentils in salads.

Clement A. Adebamowo, MD, ScD, professor, department of epidemiology and preventive medicine, Institute of Human Virology, member of the Greenebaum Cancer Center, School of Medicine, University of Maryland, Baltimore, and coauthor of a study of 90,630 women, published in *International Journal of Cancer*.

■ ■ ■ ■

Women with Migraines Have Lower Breast Cancer Risk

Pre- and postmenopausal women who have a history of migraines have a 26% lower risk for breast cancer. Researchers aren't sure what the connection is, but both migraines and breast cancer are affected by the body's estrogen levels.

UC Berkeley Wellness Letter, 500 Fifth Ave., New York City 10110.

Cancer Breakthroughs

Soft Drinks May Raise Pancreatic Cancer Risk

People who down two or more soft drinks a week may have double the risk of developing deadly pancreatic cancer, compared with non-soda drinkers, new research suggests.

The overall number of people developing the malignancy remains low, with the US National Cancer Institute (NCI) estimating 42,470 new cases last year. However, it is among the most aggressive cancers, and the fourth leading cause of cancer death.

"Soft drinks are linked with a higher risk of pancreatic cancer," said Noel T. Mueller, MPH, lead author of a study appearing in *Cancer Epidemiology, Biomarkers & Prevention.* "We can't speculate too much on the mechanism because this is an observational study, but the increased risk may be working through effects of the hormone insulin."

THE STUDY

The study was a collaboration between the University of Minnesota and National University of Singapore. Mueller, formerly at Minnesota, has since joined Georgetown University Medical Center in Washington, DC, as a research associate.

The analysis involved more than 60,000 middle-aged or older Chinese Singaporeans. Researchers calculated how much juice and soda the participants drank on average and followed them for 14 years to see how many developed cancer of the pancreas.

Those who drank two or more sodas a week were 87% more likely to develop this kind of tumor than individuals who didn't consume any soda.

Noel T. Mueller, MPH, research associate, Georgetown University Medical Center, Washington, DC.

Eric Jacobs, PhD, strategic director, pharmacoepidemiology, American Cancer Society.

Colin D. Weekes, MD, PhD, assistant professor of medicine, University of Colorado-Denver.

Richard Adamson, senior scientific consultant to the American Beverage Association and former scientific director and director of cancer etiology of the National Cancer Institute.

Cancer Epidemiology, Biomarkers & Prevention.

Although the study didn't differentiate between regular and diet soda, it was conducted in Singapore, where most soda consumed is regular, Mueller said.

Researchers found no link between juice consumption and cancer risk, perhaps because fruit juice has less effect than sugary sodas on glucose and insulin levels, the authors noted.

Previous research in US and European populations has suggested an association between sweetened sodas and juices and pancreatic cancer. This is the first study to examine the association in an Asian population, although the authors feel the findings can be extrapolated to Western nations.

"We feel that these findings may be generalizable to other Western countries," said Mueller. Genetically Singaporeans are very different from Caucasians; however, their lifestyle, including a tendency to eat fast food, is similar to Western countries.

THEORY

Type 2 diabetes, a disorder of blood sugar levels and insulin underactivity, has also tentatively been linked to pancreatic cancer.

The researchers speculate that elevated blood sugar levels associated with soda drinking and the associated increase in insulin levels prompt pancreatic cells to divide abnormally.

"Drinking sugar-sweetened soft drinks has been linked to weight gain, obesity and diabetes. Both obesity and diabetes are associated with higher risk of pancreatic cancer, one of the leading causes of cancer death in the United States," said Eric Jacobs, PhD, strategic director of pharmacoepidemiology at the American Cancer Society.

EXPERT REACTION

"The study was well designed but smaller than some previous studies that did not find a link between sugar-sweetened soft drinks and pancreatic cancer," noted Dr. Jacobs. "Direct evidence linking sugar-sweetened soft drinks to pancreatic cancer remains limited."

And adult soda drinkers may also engage in other lifestyle habits, such as smoking, which could contribute to the elevated risk.

"It's an interesting finding but if you look at the people who had the high soft drink intake,

they also had other issues that may also predispose you to pancreatic cancer," said Colin D. Weekes, MD, PhD, assistant professor of medicine at the University of Colorado-Denver. "It's hard to make any true associations from this. We could argue that smoking could be the issue here and not the soda intake."

SOFT DRINK INDUSTRY REACTION

"The [study] authors are skipping several steps in trying to connect soft drinks with pancreatic cancer, including an allegation regarding an increase in insulin production," said Richard Adamson, a consultant to the American Beverage Association and former scientific director of the NCI.

"You can be a healthy person and enjoy soft drinks. The key to a healthy lifestyle is balance—eating a variety of foods and beverages in moderation along with getting regular physical activity," Adamson added.

LIMIT SOFT DRINK INTAKE

"The bottom line is that limiting consumption of sugar-sweetened soft drinks can help in maintaining a healthy weight, which in turn will reduce risk of many types of cancer and other serious diseases," Dr. Jacobs said.

info To learn more about pancreatic cancer, visit the Pancreatica Web site, *www.pan creatica.org*.

■ ■ ■ ■

Hot Tea Danger

In a study of 871 men and women, those who drank very hot tea (158°F or higher) several times a day were eight times more likely to develop cancer of the esophagus (the muscular tube that leads from the throat to the stomach) than those who drank warm or lukewarm tea. (The boiling point of water is 212°F.)

Theory: Very hot liquids can damage cells in the lining of the esophagus, potentially leading to cancer.

Self-defense: Before drinking tea or any other hot beverage, wait at least four minutes for the beverage to cool after being poured.

Reza Malekzadeh, MD, professor and director, Digestive Disease Research Center, Tehran University of Medical Sciences, Iran.

■ ■ ■ ■

Pomegranate Juice May Slow Prostate Cancer

In a study of 48 men who had undergone surgery or radiation therapy for prostate cancer, those who drank eight ounces of pomegranate juice daily for six years prolonged their "doubling time" from 15 months to 54 months. Doubling time is the amount of time it takes for levels of *prostate-specific antigen* (PSA) to double—a sign of prostate cancer progression.

Theory: The juice's antioxidants and/or anti-inflammatory substances may help slow cancer progression.

Allan J. Pantuck, MD, associate professor of urology, University of California, Los Angeles.

Java and Jogging Fight Prostate Cancer

Kathryn M. Wilson, PhD, research fellow, epidemiology, Harvard School of Public Health, Boston.

Stacey A. Kenfield, ScD, research associate, Harvard School of Public Health, Boston.

American Association for Cancer Research's Frontiers in Cancer Prevention Research Conference, Houston.

Having a few more cups of coffee and running that extra mile each day can reduce a man's risk of dying of prostate cancer, two studies indicate. The case for coffee and physical activity as prostate cancer preventatives is far from proven, but research reported at an American Association for Cancer Research meeting in Houston shows a clear association with both daily activities.

COFFEE STUDY

Data on the nearly 50,000 men in the study showed how common a diagnosis of prostate cancer has become since widespread screening began. In the 20 years from 1986 to 2006, 4,975 cases of prostate cancer were diagnosed, affecting just about 10% of the men in the study.

But only 846 of those cancers were life-threatening, because they had spread beyond the prostate gland or were growing aggressively, according to Kathryn M. Wilson, PhD, a research fellow in epidemiology at the Harvard School of Public Health, and lead author of the report. And while the study found just a weak relationship between consumption of six or more cups of coffee a day and a reduced risk of all forms of prostate cancer (down about 19%), the reduction for the aggressive form was much more marked—41%.

And there was a clear relationship between the amount of coffee consumed and prostate cancer risk. Dr. Wilson said, "The more coffee you drank, the more effect we saw."

The caffeine in coffee doesn't seem to be the link, since the same reduction was seen for consumption of decaffeinated coffee, she said. Instead, "it has something to do with insulin and glucose metabolism," Dr. Wilson said. "A number of studies have found that coffee is associated with a reduced risk of diabetes.

"I wouldn't recommend that people change their coffee-drinking habits based on this study," said Dr. Wilson. "But if you like coffee, there is no compelling reason to cut back at this point."

EXERCISE STUDY

The other study, by Stacey A. Kenfield, ScD, a research associate at the Harvard School of Public Health, looked at the levels of physical activity among 2,686 men who were diagnosed with prostate cancer. It found, as many other studies have, that exercise is good for overall health, with a 35% lower death rate for men who reported three or more hours a week of vigorous physical activity, such as jogging, biking, swimming or playing tennis.

The death rate from prostate cancer for men who exercised vigorously was 12% lower than for those who didn't—a figure that did not quite reach the level of statistical significance because the numbers were small, Kenfield went on to explain.

Nevertheless, "this is the first study to show an effect of physical activity not only on overall survival, but particularly on prostate cancer survival," she said.

It's already well-known how physical activity reduces overall mortality, Kenfield said. "It affects immune function and reduces inflammation, among the major processes involved.

But it's not clear yet how it is related to prostate cancer and survival."

info For more information on prostate cancer, visit the Web site of the Prostate Cancer Foundation, *www.prostatecancerfoundation.org.*

■ ■ ■ ■

Coffee Lowers Cancer Risk Up to 25%

Women who consumed at least two cups of caffeinated coffee daily were 22% less likely to develop cancer of the endometrium (uterine lining) than women who drank one cup or less per day…among those who drank four or more cups daily, risk decreased by 25%. (Decaffeinated coffee was not studied.) For overweight and obese women, who typically are at highest risk for endometrial cancer, coffee's benefits were greatest.

Theory: Coffee and/or caffeine has beneficial effects on blood sugar, fat cells and estrogen, all of which play a role in endometrial cancer.

Best: Have several cups of coffee daily—preferably before mid-afternoon so that the caffeine won't interfere with sleep.

Emilie Friberg, PhD, nutritional epidemiologist, National Institute of Environmental Medicine, Karolinska Institute, Stockholm, Sweden, and leader of a study of 60,634 women.

■ ■ ■ ■

Eat More Fish to Fight Cancer

Studies have shown that when intake of omega-3 fatty acids (found in fish) is low compared with intake of omega-6 fatty acids (found in processed foods), prostate cancer risk increases. Now, analysis of the Shanghai Women's Health Study data has found that those with the highest ratio of omega-6 to omega-3 have a 95% increased risk of developing colorectal cancer. Both men and women can benefit from eating more fish and less processed food.

H.J. Murff, et al., "A Prospective Study of Dietary Polyunsaturated Fatty Acids and Colorectal Cancer Risk in Chinese Women," *Cancer Epidemiology, Biomarkers and Prevention.*

Spices that Cut Cancer Risk

Food Safety Consortium news release

Researchers report that adding certain spices to your burgers before tossing them on the grill will not only add to the flavor of the meat, but can also cut the risk of cancer long associated with the cooking of beef.

STUDY DETAILS

Heterocyclic amines (HCAs) are cancer-causing compounds that are produced when foods such as beef are barbecued, grilled, broiled or fried.

"Cooked beef tends to develop more HCAs than other kinds of cooked meats, such as pork and chicken," noted Kansas State University (KSU) food chemistry professor J. Scott Smith, PhD. Cooked beef patties appear to have the highest cancer-causing activity and may be the most important source of HCAs in the human diet, Dr. Smith added.

Dr. Smith and his colleagues at KSU looked into the HCA-inhibiting potential of six spices: cumin, coriander seeds, galangal, fingerroot, rosemary and turmeric.

They found that three spices in particular—fingerroot (Chinese ginger), rosemary and turmeric—seem to direct the greatest amount of antioxidant activity towards preventing the formation of HCAs.

Specifically, the three spices appeared to cut back on HCA production by upwards of 40%, the team observed, thereby likely reducing the HCA-associated risk for developing colorectal, stomach, lung, pancreatic, mammary and prostate cancers.

GRILLING WITH SPICES

The authors suggested that consumers integrate these spices into their menus when appropriate, noting that some, such as rosemary, come in an extract form that has demonstrated HCA inhibition of 61% to 79%.

They pointed out that spicing allows for the sort of high-temperature cooking (above 352°F) that is typically recommended for safe grilling, while at the same time blocking the increased

HCA production that is known to occur when the flames intensify.

Dr. Smith and his team plan further research to see what other marinades and powders might do by way of HCA curtailment—they noted that earlier work has shown that marinating steaks with particular herbs and spices effectively lowers HCA production.

info For more grilling safety tips, visit the US Department of Agriculture's Food Safety and Inspection Web site, *www.fsis.usda.gov*, and type "barbecue food" into the search box.

Top 10 Anticancer Foods And Supplements

Mark A. Stengler, NMD, naturopathic medical director in private practice, La Jolla, California…adjunct associate clinical professor at the National College of Natural Medicine, Portland, Oregon…author of many books, including *The Natural Physician's Healing Therapies* and coauthor of *Prescription for Natural Cures* (both from Bottom Line Books)…and author of the *Bottom Line/Natural Healing* newsletter.

If you are confused about whether certain vitamins, supplements or foods can prevent cancer, you're not alone. The results of several recent studies have been conflicting and perplexing—which is why this topic has raised questions for consumers as well as members of the health-care and research communities.

What you need to know: Cancer is not a single disease, and it can have many different causes. That makes it virtually impossible for any one nutrient to protect against all types of cancer. In fact, studying whether single nutrients reduce the risk for cancer often is like looking for a magic bullet—more wishful thinking than good science.

Nothing can absolutely guarantee that you'll remain cancer free. However, good nutrition and a healthful overall lifestyle—not smoking, not abusing alcohol, limiting exposure to pollutants, eliminating food additives, exercising and controlling stress—can lower your odds of developing cancer. Here are my top five foods and top five supplements that definitely can lower your long-term risk of getting cancer.

MY TOP ANTICANCER FOODS

Consume a diet that emphasizes a variety of fresh, natural and minimally processed foods. Include a selection of vegetables, some fruits (such as berries and kiwifruit), fish, chicken (free-range or organic), legumes, nuts and modest amounts of healthful starches (such as sweet potatoes and whole grains). Eat healthfully—and you will lay the foundation for everything else that you can do to lower your long-term risk for cancer.

My favorite anticancer foods…

•**Broccoli.** Cruciferous vegetables are my top anticancer food, and broccoli heads the list. It is rich in *sulforaphane*, an antioxidant that helps the liver break down and destroy cancer-causing toxins. Sulforaphane also increases the activity of liver enzymes that help to get cancerous substances out of the body. (Sulforaphane is available as a supplement, although I recommend people get this phytonutrient through food.) Even better, broccoli sprouts contain 50 times more sulforaphane than that found in regular broccoli. A product called BroccoSprouts is available at select supermarkets (877-747-1277, *www.broccosprouts.com*). Broccoli sprouts also have been shown to fight *H. pylori*, a type of bacteria believed to cause stomach cancer.

Advice: Eat one-half cup of raw or lightly steamed broccoli daily. (Boiling reduces its nutritional value.) Add some broccoli sprouts to your salads or sandwiches.

•**Tomatoes.** This fruit is rich in lycopene, the antioxidant that gives tomatoes their red color. Studies have found that tomatoes reduce the risk for prostate cancer—and also might reduce the risk for lung and stomach cancers.

Advice: Consume cooked tomatoes or tomato sauce. Lycopene is best absorbed from cooked tomatoes because cooking breaks down the fiber in the tomatoes. A little fat (e.g., olive oil) also enhances absorption. Include one serving of tomato sauce (one-half cup) in your diet several times a week. Watermelon and guava also contain a lot of lycopene.

•**Cold-water fish.** Salmon, sardines and trout are rich in healthy omega-3 fats—specifically *eicosapentaenoic acid* (EPA) and *docosahexaenoic acid* (DHA). EPA and DHA have potent anti-inflammatory benefits. Low intake of these fats appears to be a factor in breast, colon, pancreatic and stomach cancers.

Advice: Eat cold-water fish at least once or twice a week, or take a fish oil supplement daily that contains 1 gram of EPA and DHA. Or consider using krill oil, a type of fish oil from shrimp-like crustaceans.

•**Garlic.** Slice or dice a garlic clove, and a relatively inert compound called *allicin* undergoes an amazing cascade of chemical changes. Nearly all allicin-generated compounds function as antioxidants that prevent the types of cell mutations that give rise to cancer. Evidence suggests that garlic might help protect against cancers of the colon, prostate, esophagus, larynx, ovaries and kidneys.

Advice: Consume garlic regularly. Because chopping and cooking garlic seem to increase its biological activity, sauté or bake it rather than eating it whole or raw. There is no recommended serving size for garlic, but the more you consume, the better.

•**Spinach.** Spinach and other "greens," such as chard and collard greens, are rich in antioxidants that protect cells from the type of damage that can create cancerous mutations. One study published in *Journal of Agricultural and Food Chemistry* gave spinach the top "bioactivity index" ranking of vegetables for its ability to protect against cancer.

Advice: Eat spinach and other greens daily. You can make spinach salads or 50/50 lettuce and spinach salads, or gently sauté spinach. A single serving is equivalent to one cup of raw or one-half cup of cooked spinach or greens.

MY TOP ANTICANCER SUPPLEMENTS

Research on the role of individual supplements in reducing cancer risk has been especially confusing. Taking all evidence into account, I'm convinced that these five supplements have clear benefits…

•**Vitamin D.** If you were to take just one immune-enhancing supplement to lower your long-term risk for cancer, vitamin D would be the one to choose. More than 60 studies have found that high levels of vitamin D offer broad protection against many types of cancer. A recent German study reported that people with low vitamin D levels were one-third more likely to die of any type of cancer.

Advice: Take at least 1,000 international units (IU) of vitamin D-3 daily. Vitamin D-3, with its slightly different molecular structure than D-2, is a more bioactive form of the vitamin, which means that the body can use it more readily. Take 2,000 IU if you don't get much sun or have a dark complexion. (Dark skin absorbs less of the rays necessary for conversion to vitamin D.)

Best: Have your blood tested to determine how much vitamin D you need.

•**Vitamin K.** Two recent studies have shown an unexpected benefit of vitamin K—that it reduces the odds of developing breast and liver cancers.

Possible mechanism: Vitamin K activates *osteocalcin,* a protein involved in making strong bones. Recent research found that osteocalcin also may function as an anticancer nutrient.

Advice: Take 300 micrograms (mcg) of either vitamin K-1 or vitamin K-2, the forms most often studied.

Caution: Vitamin K may increase blood clotting. Do not take vitamin K if you also are taking blood-thinning medication unless you are being monitored by a doctor.

•**Selenium.** This essential dietary mineral forms part of *glutathione peroxidase,* an antioxidant enzyme that helps the liver break down cancer-causing toxins. A study published in *The Journal of the American Medical Association* found that 200 mcg daily of selenium led to significant reductions in the risk for prostate, colon and lung cancers within just a few years.

Advice: Take 200 mcg daily. Don't take a higher dose (which could be toxic) without the supervision of a nutrition-oriented doctor.

•**Coenzyme Q10 (CoQ10).** I believe that modest amounts of this vitamin-like nutrient may reduce an individual's general risk for cancer. Studies have shown that large amounts of CoQ10 can inhibit the spread of breast cancer and boost immunity…and may have benefits in other types of cancer as well. A recent study of women with breast cancer who were on the drug *tamoxifen* found that a combination of 100 milligrams (mg) of CoQ10 daily and vitamins B-2 (10 mg) and B-3 (50 mg) boosted the activity of enzymes that can repair genes.

Advice: Take 100 mg daily. If you already have been treated for cancer, take 300 mg daily.

•**Lycopene.** This antioxidant helps prevent cell damage. Several small studies have shown that lycopene supplements can reduce the size of prostate tumors and their tendency to spread. They also can lower levels of *prostate-specific antigen* (PSA), a common marker of prostate cancer risk.

Advice: For prostate cancer prevention and for men with elevated PSA levels, I recommend taking 5 mg to 10 mg of lycopene daily, even if you eat lycopene-rich foods. If you have been diagnosed with prostate cancer, discuss taking 30 mg daily with your physician. Use tomato-based (not synthetic) lycopene, which contains other beneficial antioxidants.

Note: Some multivitamins may contain these nutrients but not in the amounts recommended for cancer prevention. Check the label of your multivitamin, and add to it, based on the recommendations above.

■ ■ ■ ■

New Study Proves Antioxidants Don't Raise Melanoma Risk

A recent study of 13,017 people suggested that supplementing with vitamins C and E, beta-carotene, selenium and zinc quadrupled women's risk for melanoma skin cancer.

Update: In a new study of 69,671 people, these antioxidant supplements did not increase melanoma risk.

Explanation: The smaller study did not adequately adjust for some risk factors, such as number of moles, sunburn history, hair color and family history of skin cancer.

Maryam M. Asgari, MD, MPH, dermatologist and research scientist, Kaiser Permanente Northern California, Oakland, and leader of a two-year study.

Novel Drug Combats Advanced Melanoma

Steven O'Day, MD, chief, research, and director, melanoma program, The Angeles Clinic and Research Institute, Los Angeles.
Timothy Turnham, PhD, executive director, Melanoma Research Foundation, Washington, DC.
New England Journal of Medicine online.
American Society of Clinical Oncology annual meeting, Chicago.

Scientists say that a new drug to treat melanoma, the first in its class, improved survival by 68% in patients whose disease had spread (metastasized) from the skin to other parts of the body.

This is big news in the field of melanoma research, where survival rates have refused to budge, despite numerous efforts to come up with an effective treatment for the increasingly common and fatal skin cancer over the past three decades.

"The last time a drug was approved for metastatic melanoma was 12 years ago, and 85% of people who take that drug have no benefit, so finding another drug that is going to have an impact, and even a bigger impact than what's out there now, is a major improvement for patients," said Timothy Turnham, PhD, executive director of the Melanoma Research Foundation in Washington, DC.

Both the incidence of metastatic melanoma and the death rate have risen during the past 30 years, and patients with advanced disease typically have limited treatment options.

HOW NEW MELANOMA DRUG WORKS

The drug, *ipilimumab*, is the first in a new class of targeted T-cell antibodies, with potential applications for other cancers as well.

"Ipilimumab is a *human monoclonal antibody* directed against *CTLA-4*, which is on the surface of T-cells [which fight infection]," explained lead study author Steven O'Day, MD, director of the melanoma program at the Angeles Clinic and Research Institute in Los Angeles. "CTL is a very important brake on the immune system, so by blocking this brake with ipilimumab, it accelerates and potentiates the T-cells. And by doing that they become activated and can go out and kill the cancer. This drug is targeting not the tumor directly, but rather turning the T-cells on by blocking their brakes and allowing the T-cells to do their work, which is very different from chemotherapy and other targeted therapies directed at cancer cells."

STUDY DETAILS

For this study, 676 patients at 125 centers around the world were randomly assigned to one of three treatment groups: ipilimumab plus *gp100*, a peptide vaccine that has shown some benefit in melanoma cases; ipilimumab on its own; or gp100 alone. All participants had stage 3 or 4 melanoma, and had been previously treated.

Those in both the combination arm and the ipilimumab-alone arm lived a median of 10 months vs. 6.4 months in the gp100-alone arm, a 68% increase in survival time.

"This is important because this is a disease where the average survival is six to nine months, so an increase on average by an additional four months is a very large difference in this population," Dr. O'Day said. "Even more importantly than the median survival are the one- and two-year landmark survivals, which were nearly doubled in the two ipilimumab arms, going from 25% to 46 percent% at one year and 14% to 24% at two years."

Fourteen of the patients (2.1%) died because of reactions to the treatment, seven of those from immune system problems.

The findings were reported simultaneously at the annual meeting of the American Society of Clinical Oncology (ASCO) in Chicago and in an online issue of the *New England Journal of Medicine*.

The drug was developed and the study funded by Bristol-Myers Squibb and Medarex.

IMPLICATIONS

It's not entirely clear at this point which patients will benefit most but, Dr. Turnham pointed out, a large proportion of patients benefited from this therapy, whereas other therapies help only 5% to 15% of patients with metastatic melanoma.

The drug has not yet received approval from the US Food and Drug Administration, but it is available at many medical centers and some patients may be able to get access to it, Dr. O'Day said.

info The Skin Cancer Foundation Web site, *www. skincancer.org/Melanoma/*, has more information on melanoma.

Harvard University News Release: Cancer Vaccine Shows Promise

Harvard University news release.

A cancer vaccine delivered in a fingernail-size implant eliminated melanoma tumors in mice, a new study reports.

The method uses polymer disks, 8.5 millimeters in diameter, which are loaded with tumor-specific antigens and implanted under the skin to reprogram the immune system to attack tumors. The Harvard University scientists who developed the implant predicted that it would be more effective and easier to use than other cancer vaccines currently in clinical trials.

HOW THE VACCINE WORKS

"Inserted anywhere under the skin—much like the implantable contraceptives that can be placed in a woman's arm—the implants activate an immune response that destroys tumor cells," said David J. Mooney, PhD, a bioengineering professor at Harvard.

The disks release *cytokines*, which are powerful recruiters of immune-system messengers called *dendritic cells*. The cells are able to enter the implant, where they're exposed to antigens specific to the type of tumor being targeted in a particular individual. The dendritic cells then "report" to nearby lymph nodes, where they tell immune system T cells to seek and destroy tumor cells.

Because the method targets only tumor cells, there is no damage to healthy tissue, like there is with chemotherapy, the researchers noted.

The successful test results with mice are reported in the journal *Science Translational Medicine*.

info For more on cancer vaccines, visit the Web site of the US National Cancer Institute, *www.cancer.gov*. Under "Cancer Topics," click on "NCI Fact Sheets" and type "cancer vaccines" in the search box.

■ ■ ■ ■

Better Skin Cancer Prevention—Full Body Exams

Researchers who analyzed 126 cases of melanoma (the most serious type of skin cancer) found that dermatologists had identified 56.3% of the cases during full-body exams of patients who had sought treatment for other reasons. Melanomas detected by doctors were caught at earlier, more treatable stages than those found during patient self-exams.

If you are at increased risk for skin cancer (due to many moles and/or fair skin, or a personal or family history), see your dermatologist annually for a skin exam. Also be sure to perform self-exams monthly.

Jonathan Kantor, MD, dermatologist, North Florida Dermatology Associates, Jacksonville.

■ ■ ■ ■

Broccoli Sprouts May Protect Against Stomach Cancer

When 48 adults infected with the bacterium *Helicobacter pylori* (H. pylori)—a major cause of stomach cancer—ate about 2.5 ounces daily of fresh broccoli sprouts or alfalfa sprouts for eight weeks, H. pylori levels were significantly lower in the broccoli sprouts group but were unchanged in the alfalfa group.

Theory: The protective effects may be due to *sulforaphane*, a compound produced by broccoli plants to defend against predators. Broccoli sprouts are available at health food stores and online.

Jed Fahey, ScD, faculty research associate, department of pharmacology, Johns Hopkins School of Medicine, Baltimore.

■ ■ ■ ■

Calcium: the Anticancer Supplement

In a seven-year study of more than 490,000 adults, women who consumed the most calcium (1,881 milligrams [mg] daily, on average) were 23% less likely to develop cancers of the digestive system (such as colorectal or stomach cancer) than those who consumed the least calcium. Men had a slightly different outcome. Those who consumed the most calcium (1,530 mg daily, on average) had a 16% lower risk.

Self-defense: Aim to eat several servings daily of calcium-rich foods (such as low-fat dairy products, leafy green vegetables, navy beans and calcium-fortified orange juice) and/or take a calcium supplement.

Yikyung Park, ScD, staff scientist, National Cancer Institute, Bethesda, Maryland.

How Gender Affects Your Cancer Risk

Otis W. Brawley, MD, a practicing medical oncologist in Atlanta and chief medical officer of the American Cancer Society, www.cancer.org. Previously he was professor of hematology and medical oncology at the Emory University School of Medicine, also in Atlanta.

Beyond the gender-specific cancers, such as prostate and ovarian, most people assume that other malignancies affect men and women equally—but that's not true.

Recent development: Researchers are increasingly identifying gender-related differences in genes, environmental exposures and behavioral factors that may affect cancer growth and help in detection and treatment.

BLADDER CANCER

In the US, bladder cancer is expected to strike about 53,000 men and 18,000 women this year. The increased risk among men is mainly due to environmental factors, including smoking (more men smoke) and job-related exposure to toxins—especially in the processing industries, such as textile, metal, rubber and printing, which often use heavy metals and other carcinogens. When such carcinogens are inhaled, they pass into the urine where they can lead to cancer in the bladder. The inhalation of carcinogens while smoking cigarettes also increases bladder cancer risk, as does exposure to secondhand smoke.

While men have greater average exposure to such carcinogens, their risk also is higher because they urinate less often, on average, than women (seven times daily rather than eight), exposing the bladder to potential carcinogens longer.

Self-defense for men and women: Don't smoke. If you have symptoms of bladder cancer, such as blood in your urine, see your doctor. If you're at increased risk for bladder cancer due to your job, ask your doctor about one of several new tumor marker tests that can help identify bladder cancer early. Drinking water (about 50 ounces daily) also has been shown to reduce bladder cancer risk.

COLORECTAL CANCER

This year, colorectal cancer is expected to strike about 76,000 men and about 71,000 women in the US. Studies show that hormone replacement therapy significantly lowers menopausal women's risk for colorectal cancer—so younger women's higher estrogen levels also may have a protective effect.

A person's average bowel transit time—the time it takes food to pass through the digestive tract—also seems to play a role over several decades. Women, being smaller on average, have shorter intestines, reducing transit time. A diet high in fruits and vegetables cuts transit time. Women average three-and-one-half to four daily servings of fruits and veggies, while men average two to two-and-one-half.

Self-defense for men and women: Starting at age 50, get checked regularly for precancerous polyps with a colonoscopy (examination of the colon using a lighted, flexible tube) or, in some cases, flexible sigmoidoscopy (a similar procedure that examines the lower one-third of the colon). Follow your doctor's advice on the frequency of these tests.

ESOPHAGEAL CANCER

One of the primary risk factors for esophageal cancer is chronic acid reflux—also known as *gastroesophageal reflux disease* (GERD). With

GERD, the esophagus is repeatedly exposed to acidic stomach contents, which can cause cellular changes in the esophageal lining that may lead to cancer.

In the US, esophageal cancer is expected to affect about 13,000 men and about 3,500 women this year.

The main reason: Men are much more likely than women to have GERD—and related risk factors, such as drinking alcohol excessively, which increases stomach acid production...and having big bellies, which increase pressure on the stomach contents.

Self-defense for men and women: Drink in moderation (up to one drink daily if you're a woman...up to two drinks daily if you're a man) and lose weight, if necessary. If you have chronic acid reflux (common symptoms include burning in the throat, chronic cough or chronic hoarseness), seek medical treatment, such as prescription medication, to reduce symptoms.

LIVER CANCER

This year, liver cancer is expected to affect about 16,000 men and 6,000 women in the US. Men are more likely than women to develop and die from liver cancer, largely because men are at greater risk for cirrhosis—the main risk factor for this type of malignancy. Men also have higher rates of hepatitis B and hepatitis C, both of which can cause cirrhosis. Twice as many men as women drink alcohol excessively, which also increases cirrhosis risk.

Self-defense for men and women: Drink moderately (as described earlier)...avoid hepatitis by protecting yourself against infected blood and body fluids by practicing safe sex and making sure that any nail salons you visit use sterilized manicure tools...and know hepatitis B and C symptoms (brief, flulike illness, nausea, vomiting and diarrhea, loss of appetite, abdominal pain and jaundice) so you can get treatment if you become infected.

LUNG CANCER

Lung cancer—the deadliest of all malignancies—is expected to strike about 116,000 men and approximately 103,000 women in the US this year.

Statistics show that women are more likely to be among the 10% of lung cancer patients who never smoked. Although exposure to secondhand smoke and other carcinogens (such as asbestos and radon) play a role in lung cancer, women's risk for this disease may be influenced by estrogen, which some studies indicate can fuel lung tumor growth. Hormone replacement therapy, for example, has been shown to increase risk of dying from lung cancer, particularly among female smokers. Even so, women have better survival rates than men for all types and stages of lung cancer.

Groundbreaking research: The role of estrogen is being investigated in studies under way at the University of Pittsburgh and the University of California, Los Angeles. Specifically, researchers are studying whether women with lung cancer fare better when given the estrogen-blocking drug *fulvestrant* (Faslodex) in addition to the lung cancer drug *erlotinib* (Tarceva).

Self-defense for men and women: Do not smoke, and avoid secondhand smoke, radon and asbestos whenever possible.

MELANOMA

Melanoma, the most dangerous form of skin cancer, is more common among women than men under age 40...occurs equally in both sexes between ages 40 and 50...and strikes significantly more men than women after age 50.

Some research theorizes that estrogen may account for the difference in melanoma rates in men and women. In total, about 30,000 women and 39,000 men in the US are predicted to develop melanoma this year.

Important new study finding: Researchers at New York University Langone Medical Center found that women under age 40 diagnosed with melanoma were much more likely to have a variation in a potentially cancer-promoting gene called *MDM2*. Besides offering an explanation for melanoma's prevalence in younger women, the discovery suggests that screening for this variation with a blood test may help identify women at risk and increase early detection of melanoma while it is most treatable.

Self-defense for men and women: Undergo yearly skin exams by a dermatologist, and perform self-exams in front of a mirror to identify changes in size, shape or color of existing moles and to check for new moles, spots or freckles that look unusual.

How a Top Brain Doc Protects His Own Brain From Cancer

Keith Black, MD, chairman of the department of neurosurgery and director of Maxine Dunitz Neurosurgical Institute at Cedars-Sinai Medical Center, Los Angeles. A former professor of neurosurgery at UCLA, he was named the Ruth and Raymond Stotter chair in the department of surgery and was head of the UCLA Comprehensive Brain Tumor Program. He is author, with Arnold Mann, of *Brain Surgeon: A Doctor's Inspiring Encounters with Mortality and Miracles* (Wellness Central).

A large study that examined data over a 20-year period found that the incidence of brain tumors had increased by 200% in older adults. In people age 19 years and younger, brain tumors now are the second most common cause of cancer deaths after leukemia. But is brain cancer really on the rise—or simply more likely to be detected? A noted expert explains the latest research—and tells what he does to protect his own brain...

IS THE INCREASE REAL?

CT scans are an important tool for diagnosing brain tumors. Before they were introduced in the 1970s, many patients with tumors might have been misdiagnosed as having strokes or other neurological diseases. The increased use of CT scans—along with MRIs and brain biopsies—may have caused an apparent increase in brain tumors.

Using research that took into account better imaging technology, scientists at the National Brain Tumor Registry concluded that the incidence of new tumors has remained stable. The National Cancer Institute Brain Tumor Study actually found a slight decrease in the incidence of brain tumors between 1990 and 2002.

However, the data is murky. There does appear to be an increase in brain tumors in some populations, but it still is unclear if this is due to better diagnostic tests or other factors.

We know that secondary brain tumors (those that originate in other parts of the body before spreading to the brain) are about five times more common than primary tumors (ones that originate in the brain and tend to stay in the brain)—in part, because many people with cancer now are living long enough for the cancer to spread to the brain.

About 30% of those who die from breast cancer are later found to have evidence of brain cancer. With lung cancer, about 60% will be found at autopsy to have had the cancer spread to the brain.

REDUCE THE RISK

Primary brain cancers are relatively rare, accounting for about 2% of all cancers. Each year, about 19,000 Americans are diagnosed with a primary brain cancer. Sadly, only about one-third of patients with brain or other nervous system cancers survive more than five years.

Brain tumors are difficult to treat. Surgery isn't always possible or effective, because these tumors tend to grow rapidly and invade large areas of brain tissue. Unlike other blood vessels in the body, those in the brain are selective in what they allow to pass. This so-called blood-brain barrier makes it difficult to deliver chemotherapeutic drugs to brain tumors.

The causes of brain cancer are largely unknown, but there are some clear risk factors…

•**Dental X-rays.** Most dentists routinely use X-rays during checkups.

The danger: Radiation scatters and can potentially irradiate—and damage—brain cells. Even low-dose X-rays may increase the risk for *gliomas* (a type of brain tumor) and *meningiomas* (tumors that develop in the membranes that cover the brain and spinal cord).

I tell my dentist, flat-out, that I don't want X-rays. An occasional X-ray probably isn't harmful, but no one should get them routinely.

•**Air pollution.** At Cedars-Sinai, we're doing a study now to look at the association between air pollution and brain cancers. We see molecular changes in the brains of rats after three months of exposure to air pollution that are similar to the changes we see just prior to the development of brain cancer.

•**Electromagnetic radiation from cell phones, cellular antennas and the like.** A Swedish study found that the risk for brain cancer is 250% higher in those who used a cell phone for up to an hour a day for 10 years.

This is controversial. Other, shorter-term studies have found no risk from cell-phone use. But we know that it typically takes 20 to 30 years before toxic exposures lead to cancer. Cell phones haven't been around long enough to know what the long-term consequences might be.

My advice: Use a wireless earpiece when talking on a cell phone. If you don't use an earpiece, hold the phone as far away from your head as possible. The amount of radiation that reaches the brain drops significantly with distance.

Caution: Children have thinner skulls than adults. It's easier for electromagnetic radiation from cell phones to penetrate a child's skull and reach the brain. It's possible that even low levels of electromagnetic radiation can produce cancer-causing changes in brain cells. Children and young adults should always use an earpiece.

•**Hot dogs and other processed meats** usually contain nitrites, substances that have been linked with brain tumors. I like a hot dog as much as anyone, but moderation is important. Also, whenever possible, buy nitrite-free hot dogs, bacon and other processed meats.

•**Heating plastic in the microwave.** There isn't direct evidence that using plastic containers in the microwave can increase brain tumors, but we know that the *vinyl chloride* in some plastics is a risk factor. Personally, I don't use plastic containers or cover foods with plastic wrap in the microwave.

Pregnant women should be especially careful. We've found in animal studies that adult females exposed to vinyl chloride or other carcinogens might not develop brain tumors themselves, but their offspring face a much higher risk.

■ ■ ■ ■

Cancer Linked to CT Scans

Computed tomography (CT) scans can be extremely valuable, but they expose patients to high radiation levels.

Self-defense: If your doctor recommends a CT scan, find out why and whether there are other ways to get the same information, such as ultrasound, MRI or watchful waiting.

Rita F. Redberg, MD, MSc, editor of *Archives of Internal Medicine* and a cardiologist in the department of medicine at University of California, San Francisco.

HPV: The Killer that No One Talks About

Diane M. Harper, MD, MPH, vice-chair for research and a professor in the departments of community and family medicine, obstetrics and gynecology and bioinformatics and personalized medicine at the University of Missouri-Kansas City School of Medicine. She is one of the country's leading experts on human papillomavirus (HPV).

When Farrah Fawcett died, few reporters thought to ask what may have led to the 62-year-old actress's deadly case of anal cancer.

Little-known fact: The majority of anal and cervical cancers—and most cancers affecting the penis and oral cavity (mouth, throat and sinus cavities)—are linked to the *human papillomavirus* (HPV), the most common sexually transmitted infection in the US.

Each year, about 5,000 Americans are diagnosed with anal cancer...approximately 11,000 women are found to have cervical cancer...an estimated 1,500 American men are diagnosed with penile cancer...and some 34,000 Americans are found to have oral cancer.

Why you should be informed about HPV: Even if you've been in a monogamous sexual relationship for years, you may unknowingly be carrying the potentially deadly virus. At least half of all sexually active men and women in the US will be infected with HPV at some point in their lives, and an estimated 20 million Americans are currently carrying the virus.

CANCER-CAUSING HPVS

There are more than 100 strains of viruses in the papilloma family. HPV is a well-known cause of warts on the genitals and elsewhere on the body (such as on the hands or feet). Two strains of HPV—known as type 6 and type 11—lead to genital warts, while more than 30 strains can cause warts on other parts of the body.

Important: Even though genital warts may be emotionally disturbing, they do not turn into cancer.

All the remaining types of HPV have cancer-causing (oncogenic) potential. Of the high-risk strains, two—known as type 16 and type 18—account for about 70% of all cases of cervical cancer, as well as most cases of anal cancer. These strains of HPV also can infect the penis, the vagina and the mouth.

A HIDDEN THREAT

Infections due to cancer-causing strains of HPV usually go undetected because they do not cause warts or any other signs or symptoms.

Both women and men who are infected can unknowingly transmit the virus—usually during sexual encounters (vaginal, anal or oral sex). The virus enters the body through cuts or tiny tears in the outer layer of the skin in the vagina, cervix, penis, anus and mouth. Because HPV is spread through skin-to-skin contact, it's possible that kissing is another route of transmission, but the virus is usually transmitted sexually.

The good news is that the body's immune system effectively eliminates the cancer-causing virus in about 90% of HPV infections—usually within two years. When the virus stays in the body beyond two years, it is considered chronic, and the risk for cancer of the genitals, cervix, anus or oral cavity rises.

ARE YOU AT RISK?

Most HPV infections are transmitted through sexual activity, but about 10% to 15% of the population become infected via nonsexual sources that have not yet been identified. In general, the risk for HPV infection is higher for people with impaired immunity—for example, anyone undergoing chemotherapy or those with diabetes or an autoimmune disease, such as lupus or rheumatoid arthritis, and for people who have many sexual partners or who use devices that cause tears (even very tiny ones) in the skin of the genitals, anus or mouth.

Startling new finding: A common ingredient in many vaginal spermicides, *nonoxynol-9,* triples a woman's risk for HPV infection. It damages the lining of the vagina and makes it easier for the virus to enter through the skin.

TESTING AND DIAGNOSIS

Precancerous changes to cells in the cervix can be detected by a Pap smear—named after physician Georgios Papanikolaou, who invented the test. If a woman's Pap results are described as atypical, she is advised to undergo a test that checks for one or more of 13 cancer-causing HPV types.

New finding: A study of 130,000 women published in *The New England Journal of Medicine* found that a test used to check for HPV could replace the Pap test at some point. Women who got the HPV test were 37% less likely to die due to cervical cancer than those who received Pap tests, suggesting that the HPV test identifies cervical cancer sooner than a Pap test.

THE HPV VACCINE

Gardasil, a vaccine that prevents infection from four strains of HPV—the high-cancer-risk types 16 and 18, as well as the genital wart–causing 6 and 11—was approved by the FDA in 2006.

How it's used: The Centers for Disease Control and Prevention (CDC) recommends Gardasil for girls/young women ages nine through 26.

Latest development: A controversial new study published in *The Journal of the American Medical Association* found some serious adverse effects, including death, after Gardasil use. Discuss the risks and benefits of the vaccine with your physician.

OTHER PREVENTIVE STEPS

Using a condom reduces—but does not eliminate—risk for HPV infection in women and men. This is because the virus can occur in areas that aren't covered by a condom, and it can be spread by hand-to-mouth contact. Being in a mutually monogamous relationship with someone who has had few or no previous partners also curbs risk.

To protect yourself: Women are advised to have Pap tests to identify cervical cell changes—every three years if the last test results were normal. If abnormal, an annual Pap test is recommended until the results are normal for three consecutive years.

Women who use spermicides that contain nonoxynol-9 (including male condoms that use this ingredient) to prevent pregnancy should consider switching from this form of birth control to some other method, such as oral contraceptives or cervical caps. Both men and women should ask for an oral cancer check during each dental visit. And men should regularly check for signs of penile cancer, such as visible bumps or ulcers.

Oral Cancer... Few Know About It, Many Get It

Michael A. Kahn, DDS, professor and chairman of the department of oral and maxillofacial pathology at Tufts University School of Dental Medicine...professor in the department of pathology, Tufts University School of Medicine...and laboratory director of Tufts Oral Pathology Services (TOPS), all in Boston. Dr. Kahn has published more than 80 articles and abstracts in professional journals.

Has your dentist ever performed an exam to detect oral cancer? Your answer is likely to be no.

In one survey, only 15% of respondents said they were aware that their dentist had performed such an exam. Informal polling of dental professionals shows that the percentage probably is accurate, with only about one in five saying that they consistently conduct the exam.

That's a mouthful of bad news...

Every year, more than 34,000 Americans are diagnosed with oral cancer, and more than 8,000 people die every year from the disease—a death rate higher than that of other cancers routinely featured in the news, such as cervical cancer and melanoma.

Oral cancer affects the oral cavity—the inside of the mouth, the tongue and the back of the mouth (*oropharynx*), where the tongue is attached to the throat. When oral cancer is detected in its earliest stages, the survival rate after five years is 80% to 90%. But when it advances undetected—even for a few months—the five-year survival rate drops to 55%. Unfortunately, the majority of cases of oral cancer are diagnosed when they are advanced.

How to protect yourself...

RISK FACTORS

Three out of four people diagnosed with oral cancer are regular users of tobacco products. Cigarettes, cigars, pipes and chewing tobacco damage the DNA of cells in the oral cavity—which is why tobacco use is the leading cause of oral cancer. However, there are other risk factors as well. *These include...*

•**Alcohol.** Heavy alcohol use (five or more weekly drinks for men and three or more for women) is associated with oral cancer. Also, years of tobacco and alcohol use increase your risk for oral cancer more than tobacco use alone. That's because *aldehyde*, a compound in alcohol, boosts the absorption of cancer-causing substances in tobacco.

Mouthwash update: Although a few studies have pointed to a possible link between the alcohol in mouthwash and oral cancer, it is not a proven risk factor. Nevertheless, I advise my patients to use a nonalcohol mouthwash with the ADA seal of approval.

•**Oral infection with HPV (human papilloma virus).** HPV consists of more than 100 strains and is the cause of warts of all types, including genital warts. A longtime (five- to 10-year) infection in the oral cavity with the strain HPV-16 or HPV-18 has been linked to oral cancer at the base of the tongue as well as on the oropharynx.

The most common source of transmission for this infection is probably oral sex, and HPV-16 can infect the oral cavity without a history of multiple oral sex partners. Recent research suggests that it even is transmissible via open-mouth kissing.

•**Age.** About 95% of oral cancers are in people over 40 years old. The average age of diagnosis is 60.

•**Male.** Men are twice as likely to develop oral cancer. However, women now are smoking and drinking more than they used to—the rate of male-to-female oral cancer patients was six to one in 1950, and it is now two to one.

•**Family history.** If a parent or sibling developed oral cancer, you are more likely to develop it, too.

DENTAL AND SELF-EXAMS

Oral cancer starts as precancer—an area of abnormal cell maturation called *dysplasia*. It appears as a small white or red plaque or patch that is slightly elevated.

A thorough exam for oral cancer by a dentist or hygienist checks for signs of precancer on all the soft tissues inside the mouth—the roof...the floor...inside the lips...inside the cheeks...on the top, sides and bottom of the tongue...and at the back of the mouth, using a tongue depressor.

You should receive the exam at least twice a year, at your regular cleaning.

If you don't think the dentist or hygienist conducted the exam—ask. You might say, "You've probably already done it and I didn't realize it, but did you look today to make sure that I don't have anything that looks like a precancer in my mouth?"

Smart idea: If you have one or more of the risk factors for oral cancer, conduct a self-exam once a month. Using a hand mirror and flashlight, examine the inside of your mouth. If you see a slightly raised red or white patch, check for it again in two weeks. If it still is present, see your dentist immediately.

TREATMENT

If there is an area inside your mouth that the dentist cannot identify as normal and that looks like precancer, a biopsy (tissue sample) should be taken by your dentist from the area and examined under a microscope.

If the biopsy reveals abnormal cells—either a dysplasia or cancer—the area should be surgically excised.

Treatment for advanced oral cancer often is disfiguring and disabling, affecting food intake and speech. In many cases, significant areas of the oral cavity (such as the tongue) and surrounding areas (such as the jaw) are cut out. Your surgeon may recommend reconstructive surgery to restore the appearance of your face or help you regain the ability to talk and eat. The surgeon may transplant grafts of skin, muscle or bone from other parts of your body to reconstruct your face.

Radiation is used to help prevent the spread and recurrence of the disease. Chemotherapy is not a standard treatment for oral cancer, but it may be used when conventional treatment has failed to control the cancer.

Seemingly Harmless Symptoms that May Be Red Flags for Cancer

Amy P. Abernethy, MD, program director of the Duke Cancer Care Research Program and associate director of the Cancer Control Program at the Duke Comprehensive Cancer Center, both in Durham, North Carolina. Dr. Abernethy is also an associate professor of medicine in the division of medical oncology at the Duke University Medical Center.

If you are one of the estimated 1.5 million people in the US who will be told "you have cancer" this year, much of your medical fate will depend on how advanced the malignancy is when it is diagnosed.

When cancer is caught early—before the abnormal cells multiply and spread—the odds of defeating the disease improve dramatically.

Problem: Because cancer is tricky—early symptoms most often (but not always) are painless, and they often mimic common noncancerous conditions—many people ignore red flags that could help them get an early diagnosis.

For the best possible chance of beating cancer: Be alert for subtle symptoms of the disease. Here are nine such cancer symptoms that you should never ignore—and how to distinguish them from more benign causes.*

1. Difficulty swallowing. When you swallow, you've probably had the uncomfortable or painful experience of food getting "stuck"—for example, high in the esophagus or in the middle of the upper chest.

It may be cancer if: You have this sensation all or most times that you eat, and it's usually not painful. Difficulty swallowing is common in people with esophageal or stomach cancer and may be a sign that a tumor is obstructing the esophagus or that inflammation and scarring have narrowed the opening. Inflammation can

*Important: If you have a troubling symptom that is not listed in this article, see your doctor.

be a precursor to cancer and also can indicate that a malignant tumor has irritated surrounding healthy tissue.

Because difficulty swallowing evolves slowly, many people adjust the way they eat, taking smaller bites, chewing longer and perhaps even switching to a diet that is mostly liquid. If eating becomes difficult—for any reason—see a doctor.

2. Excessive bleeding and/or unexplained bruising. Leukemia causes a shortage of blood platelets (cellular elements responsible for clotting), which results in easy and excessive bleeding and unexplained bruising. (Normal bleeding, such as that caused by a cut, should stop after application of direct pressure.)

It may be cancer if: You have an unusual number of unexplained nosebleeds (for example, not due to dry air, a common trigger) and/or develop unexplained bruises (a change in frequency or severity from the norm) that tend to be painful when touched, dark purple and large (the size of a fist or bigger).

Important: Bleeding gums may be a sign of poor dental care or a serious medical problem, such as leukemia. If brushing causes bleeding, see your dentist for an evaluation to determine the cause.

3. Exhaustion. Everyone gets tired, but extreme fatigue due to cancer is quite different. Although all cancers can cause fatigue, this symptom is most common with colon cancer, leukemia and other cancers that may cause anemia.

It may be cancer if: For no apparent reason, you experience overwhelming and debilitating fatigue similar to that caused by the flu.

Important: Fatigue due to cancer is sometimes mistaken for depression.

Key difference: A person with depression often lacks the will and desire to perform daily activities, while a person with cancer-related fatigue wants to stay active but lacks the physical ability to do so.

4. Fever and night sweats. The presence of cancer causes a storm of chemical processes as the body ramps up its immune defenses to fight cancer cells. Fever is one indication that your immune system is fending off an illness, such as a cold or the flu, or even cancer.

It may be cancer if: You have fevers (typically 100°F or higher) that come and go over a period of days or weeks. Cancer-related fevers occur most often at night—often along with drenching night sweats.

Important: Menopausal women often have hot flashes that may lead to night sweats—but sweats due to menopause also occur during the day. Anyone who experiences night sweats—including menopausal women who have night sweats but no daytime hot flashes—should see a doctor.

5. Lumps. Any new, firm, painless lump that is growing in size or that is bigger than a nickel should be immediately examined by a doctor. Worrisome lumps typically feel firmer than the tip of your nose, while spongy or painful lumps are less of a concern. Lumps can be caused by several types of cancer, including breast, testicular and throat malignancies, and melanoma (skin cancer).

The immune response launched by your body when it is fighting a serious disease—including cancer—may lead to enlarged lymph nodes (the small filtering structures that help prevent foreign particles from entering the bloodstream). Painful and/or swollen lymph nodes are common signs of infection and usually return to normal size within a few days of the infection resolving.

It may be cancer if: Enlarged lymph nodes do not return to normal size and/or have the characteristics described above.

Helpful: Lymph nodes can be found throughout the body, but enlarged ones are easiest to feel behind the neck (at the base of the skull or behind the ears)…in the armpit…in the groin (at the junction of the torso and leg)…in the hollowed space above the collarbone (clavicle)…in back of the knee…and at the crook of the elbow.

6. Persistent cough. Longtime smokers get used to coughing, so they tend not to notice this important symptom of lung cancer. Nonsmokers can experience persistent cough as well, which also can be a symptom of other cancers, including malignancies of the throat and esophagus.

It may be cancer if: You have a cough—with or without breathlessness—that persists for longer than one month. Coughing up blood also can be a cancer symptom.

7. Skin changes. Most people know that changes in a mole can be a sign of skin cancer. But the moles that are most prone to cancerous changes are the type that are flat (as opposed to raised or bumpy in shape).

It may be cancer if: You have a mole that becomes darker…changes color…changes shape (especially in an asymmetrical pattern)…or grows larger. Guidelines recommend seeing a doctor if you have a mole that grows larger than a pencil eraser, but don't wait to see your doctor if you have a mole that undergoes any of the changes described above.

Important: A sore that doesn't heal also can be skin cancer. (In healthy people, most superficial wounds heal within days.)

8. Stumbles or falls. If you suddenly become "clumsy," it may signal a neurological problem, such as nerve damage from diabetes or multiple sclerosis, or it could be a sign of a brain tumor.

It may be cancer if: Your clumsiness is accompanied by confusion, difficulty concentrating and an inability to move your arms and/or legs. Although paralysis is an obvious sign that something is wrong, it is rarely the first sign of a brain tumor. Check with your doctor immediately if your body's basic functions change in any way.

9. Unexplained weight loss. If you experience significant weight loss (about 10 pounds or more of your body weight) that is not a result of an intentional weight-loss regimen, it often is a symptom of a potentially serious medical condition, such as cancer or depression.

It may be cancer if: Weight loss is due to a reduced appetite. Always see your doctor promptly if you experience unexplained weight loss.

■ ■ ■ ■

New Therapy Saves Esophagus

Esophageal cancer is usually treated by removing the esophagus (swallowing tube). Patients spend a week in the hospital, have a 50% rate of postsurgical complications and face lifelong dietary restrictions.

New: With outpatient *endoscopic mucosal resection,* a scope inserted into the esophagus shaves off cancer cells...patients can eat full meals within days. Both procedures have similar five-year survival rates.

G.A. Prasad, MD, consultant, division of gastroenterology and hepatology, Mayo Clinic, Rochester, Minnesota, and leader of a study of 178 early-stage esophageal cancer patients.

New Procedure Helps Prevent Esophageal Cancer

Joel E. Richter, MD, chair of the department of medicine at the Digestive Disease Center at Temple University.
Michael S. Smith, MD, director of the Esophageal Program at the Temple University School of Medicine Digestive Disease Center.

While there is no such thing as a good cancer, there are some that are particularly lethal. Esophageal cancer is one of the lethal ones, and it's not as rare as it used to be. The National Cancer Institute estimates that this year alone there will be more than 16,000 new cases and more than 14,000 deaths from it. There is, however, a bit of positive news about a less drastic treatment called *radiofrequency ablation* (RFA). The procedure appears helpful in eradicating a certain kind of tissue damage (called Barrett's esophagus) thought to be a precursor to esophageal cancer.

WHAT IS BARRETT'S ESOPHAGUS?

Barrett's esophagus refers to a type of damaged esophageal tissue thought to often develop from repeated exposure to stomach acids in people who have chronic *gastroesophageal reflux disease* (GERD).

Joel E. Richter, MD, chair of the department of medicine at the Digestive Disease Center at Temple University in Philadelphia, provided some insight into the new treatment. He explained that until recently the "gold standard" treatment for patients with high-grade dysplastic Barrett's esophagus and esophageal cancer was surgery that completely removed the esophagus. While this may be one way of solving the

problem, it's a drastic step that also is associated with a wide range of debilitating complications and a high mortality rate that, depending on the hospital, ranges from 7.5% to 29%.

NEW TREATMENT EFFECTIVE, LESS TRAUMATIC

All that explains why there is great enthusiasm about this less invasive but apparently effective treatment, which has few side effects. Radiofrequency ablation (RFA) is an outpatient endoscopic procedure performed under mild sedation in which the doctor (usually a gastroenterologist) uses a tiny camera to guide wires and a device through the esophagus, where it will heat up the water inside the Barrett's cells and cause them to die.

Though the procedure is fairly new, thus far complications of RFA are very rare. According to Barrx Medical, manufacturer of the technology used for RFA, of the 13,663 procedures performed last year, only 22 serious adverse events were reported (0.16%). While some people experienced post-op chest pain and other mild, transient side effects (such as fever, discomfort with swallowing, sore throat), many have no significant complaints at all, Dr. Richter said.

RFA IS VERY EFFECTIVE

The effectiveness of RFA was demonstrated in a recent study published in *The New England Journal of Medicine.* Researchers divided 127 patients with dysplastic Barrett's esophagus into two groups—one group received RFA and the other received a "sham" (control) procedure. The condition was eradicated in fully 90% of patients with low-grade dysplasia and 81% of those with high-grade dysplasia, compared with 2% of those in the control group. Moreover, patients in the ablation group had less disease progression (3.6% versus 16.3%) and fewer cancers (1.2% versus 9.3%) compared with the control group.

Michael S. Smith, MD, director of the Esophageal Program at the Temple University School of Medicine Digestive Disease Center, is cautiously enthusiastic about RFA. "RFA has become the new gold standard," he said, noting, however, that as yet there is no long-term data on efficacy, though results thus far look promising. "It's useful, easy to use and has few side effects." Most of the studies have focused on patients with high-grade dysplasia, so Dr. Smith said that "it is too soon to tell if RFA will be appropriate for the vast majority of people with Barrett's esophagus or for those with low-grade dysplasia." Cautioning that more research on short- and long-term efficacy is needed, Dr. Smith pointed out that at present, RFA is performed at only a few academic centers by top gastroenterologists. "When it goes out into the wider community, it has the potential for misuse, which may lead to more side effects and complications," he said.

In the meantime, patients of Barrett's esophagus may want to consider RFA. Dr. Smith recommends getting the treatment done at a center of excellence where many RFA procedures have been done. "The more experience the endoscopist has with different patients, the more likely he/she will be able to successfully customize a treatment plan for you," he explained, adding that it is fine to use the Internet to find physicians who offer RFA, "but I believe the most important step is to schedule a face-to-face consultation so you can make sure you are comfortable with the doctor that will be performing your procedure."

Controlling Incurable Cancer

Richard C. Frank, MD, director of cancer research at the Whittingham Cancer Center at Norwalk Hospital in Norwalk, Connecticut. He is the author of *Fighting Cancer with Knowledge and Hope—A Guide for Patients, Families, and Health Care Providers* (Yale University).

Receiving a diagnosis of cancer is always frightening, but it can be devastating if you're told that the condition is "incurable." For all cancers combined, about two-thirds of patients will be cured (have no evidence of disease five years after being diagnosed). However, many people are diagnosed when a cancer is at an advanced stage, when it has spread (*metastasized*) beyond its original site to other areas of the body. At that point, a patient typically will be told that the cancer is "stage four"—and not curable.

Latest development: Thanks to the ongoing development of sophisticated new treatments, many cancers that are labeled as incurable can now at least be controlled for several years as chronic conditions.

TREATING INCURABLE CANCER

When diagnosed with an incurable cancer, a patient should ask his/her oncologist to clearly explain the cancer type…the extent of its spread in the body…the average prognosis (assessment of the future course of the disease)…as well as treatment options—both "standard" therapies that are widely available and "experimental" ones that are being tested in clinical trials. It's also a good idea to obtain a second opinion from another oncologist, especially if the center where the patient will receive care does not offer clinical trials.

One man's story: I once treated an active 60-year-old man diagnosed with gallbladder cancer that had spread to his liver. His surgeon had told him that the tumors in his liver could not be removed and that he had six months to live. Undaunted, the patient began chemotherapy and his cancer responded well. He continues to receive periodic chemotherapy treatments and now is a still-active 65-year-old.

Many individuals are living with "incurable" cancer—often significantly better and longer than they ever expected. Although advanced cancers still claim the lives of patients, a variety of new therapies now offer real hope for many.

Example: A woman with metastatic breast cancer may receive one of seven hormone-blocking drugs that can be used to fight the spread of the disease. When one stops working, another can be tried. At the same time, she has more than 10 chemotherapy drugs that can be used singly or in combination.

We also have smarter ways of administering cancer treatments that are more effective and less toxic, including using smaller doses of chemotherapy but at more frequent intervals. This approach is less harmful to noncancerous tissues (so that the nausea and weakness caused by chemotherapy is generally much milder than it otherwise would be) but equally effective against the cancer itself.

In addition, "targeted" therapies have been developed that block specific pathways of cancer growth. These therapies, which may be given alone or in combination with chemotherapy, often have fewer side effects than chemotherapy.

Examples: Rituximab (Rituxan) for the treatment of lymphoma…*trastuzumab* (Herceptin) for breast cancer…*erlotinib* (Tarceva) for lung cancer…and *sunitinib* (Sutent) and *sorafenib* (Nexavar) for kidney cancer. *How to get the best possible results in cancer treatment…*

•**Remember that every cancer is unique.** Two people diagnosed with exactly the same cancer will almost certainly experience their disease differently. Their cancers will grow at different rates and respond differently to various treatments.

In formulating a patient's plan, an oncologist will consider a number of factors, including the aggressiveness of the cancer…the health and age of the patient…the side effects associated with a specific treatment…the availability of clinical trials…and the patient's wishes.

My advice: Understand that the treatment of an incurable cancer often continues for the life of the patient (with occasional breaks), so there's no way your doctor can predict at the onset of your disease which sequence of cancer treatments will work best. For each patient, the treatment strategy often is a "work in progress."

•**Make sure you have a good rapport with your oncologist.** Patients with incurable cancers see their oncologists often, and open communication is critical to successfully managing their cancers.

An oncologist should be empathetic, sincere and caring—and should take time to answer any questions the patient has. Oncologists also should provide a sense of hope—not false hope, but a realistic appreciation that people with chronic cancer are living longer than ever before and often much longer than predicted in the initial prognosis.

My advice: Be honest and direct with your oncologist about how you are coping with cancer and its treatment. This will help ensure that you receive the support you need—and the treatments that are best for you. If you don't communicate openly, there's no way your doc-

tor can know your state of mind or how cancer-fighting medicines are affecting your body.

•**Focus on quality of life.** When a person is living with a cancer that can be controlled but not cured, the ongoing treatments must be compatible with a reasonably good quality of life. The practice of using smaller doses of chemotherapy more frequently (often weekly) rather than larger doses every few weeks may not only reduce side effects, but also help maintain a patient's sense of well-being. Some patients can carry out all of their regular activities, while others will need to rest more and cut back on some responsibilities.

If it becomes apparent at some point that a cancer's growth cannot be controlled and that treatment is doing more harm than good, the patient may want to enroll in a hospice program, which focuses on comfort, control of pain and coming to terms with the end of life.

My advice: Find a treatment location that is near your work or home. Also, don't hesitate to get psychological support for yourself and your family. Free counseling services are available at most treatment centers and through organizations such as CancerCare (800-813-4673, *www.cancercare.org*).

Also helpful: Focus on yourself. Rest when you need to rest. When your energy is high, do the things that you want to do. Celebrate good results…laugh as often as possible. Surround yourself with friends and loved ones and tell them how they can help you—by assisting with household chores, for example.

■ ■ ■ ■

Could Stronger Muscles Help You Beat Cancer?

In a study of 250 obese people with lung or gastrointestinal cancer, those with normal muscle mass lived an average of 10 months longer than those who had *sarcopenia* (depleted muscle mass).

Theory: Muscle mass may play a role in the body's immune response to cancer.

If you have cancer: Get screened by your doctor for sarcopenia and discuss moderate strength training.

Carla Prado, PhD, researcher, department of oncology, University of Alberta, Cross Cancer Institute, Canada.

A Medicinal Mushroom For Cancer?

Mark A. Stengler, NMD, naturopathic medical doctor in private practice, La Jolla, California…adjunct associate clinical professor at the National College of Natural Medicine, Portland, Oregon…author of many books, including *The Natural Physician's Healing Therapies* and coauthor of *Prescription for Natural Cures* (both from Bottom Line Books)… and author of the *Bottom Line/Natural Healing* newsletter.

Researchers have been studying the health benefits of *Agaricus blazei* (A. blazei), an edible mushroom native to Brazil.

A. blazei appears to act as an antioxidant, to balance glucose within the body, prevent abnormal cell growth, bolster the immune system and attack existing tumor cells. Is it worth taking in supplement form?

HEALTH BENEFITS

Studies show the benefits of A. blazei for the following conditions…

•**Cancer.** In one study, patients with cervical, ovarian or endometrial cancer were treated with chemotherapy, plus either an oral A. blazei extract or a placebo. The activity of tumor-fighting cells was significantly higher in those taking A. blazei compared with those who took the placebo.

Most striking: Patients taking A. blazei also suffered fewer side effects of chemotherapy, including hair loss, weakness and decreased appetite.

•**Hepatitis C.** A study in *Japanese Pharmacology & Therapeutics* suggests that A. blazei extract may be effective in treating hepatitis C. In 80% of study participants, A. blazei extract appeared to reduce levels of the liver enzyme *gamma-glutamyl transpeptidase* (GGT), an indicator of liver damage.

MY ADVICE

For those with any type of cancer (particularly those noted above) or hepatitis C, I recommend 1,500 milligrams (mg) to 3,000 mg daily of A. blazei. Have your doctor determine the dose and monitor your response, including blood glucose levels. (A. blazei can improve insulin resistance, a condition in which the body doesn't use insulin properly.)

Caution: A. blazei should not be taken by anyone on immune-suppressing transplant medications—these patients do not want their immune system to reject the new organ. Avoid A. blazei if you have an autoimmune disease (such as rheumatoid arthritis) in which the immune system already is overactive.

Good choice: NutraceuticsRx AgariPure Agaricus Blazei Murrill Extract by American Nutrition (800-454-3724, *www.americannutrition.com*).

More from Dr. Mark Stengler…

Natural Way to Kill Cancer Cells

Most people have never heard of intravenous (IV) vitamin C, and yet it is one of the best alternative therapies to fight cancer. As most people know, vitamin C is an antioxidant with an immune-boosting effect. But when I—and a host of other natural physicians—administer it at very high doses, it plays an altogether different role, acting like a type of natural chemotherapy and killing cancer cells. When used in conjunction with regular chemotherapy, IV vitamin C works right alongside it, helping to kill cancer cells while also boosting the immune system and helping the body to rid itself of unwanted waste products.

At my clinic, I use IV vitamin C treatment for patients at all stages of cancer. All of these patients are also under the care of an oncologist. I give IV vitamin C to cancer patients at the outset of their treatment, to those who have tried conventional treatments to no avail and to those in remission who want an immune system boost. For patients with terminal disease, it helps to improve quality of life by increasing their energy and reducing nausea.

The use of vitamins in the treatment of cancer is controversial, extending back 40 years to when Nobel Laureate Linus Pauling, PhD, first proposed the use of high-dose vitamin C in the treatment of cancer. Many oncologists today remain skeptical about using any type of vitamin therapy in the treatment of cancer. Cancer specialists maintain that some types of chemotherapy and radiation kill cancer cells by generating large numbers of destructive free radicals. Because vitamin C is an antioxidant, they believe that it will neutralize these free radicals and reduce the effectiveness of chemotherapy and radiation.

I think this view is simplistic. At low doses (under 25 grams [g], or 25,000 milligrams [mg]), vitamin C's antioxidant properties do help to neutralize disease-causing free radicals. But at doses higher than 25 g, vitamin C has a pro-oxidant effect that exploits a weakness in the biochemistry of cancer cells and increases production of *hydrogen peroxide,* an acid that has been shown to kill cancer cells without harming healthy cells.

It's impossible to achieve the required high concentrations of vitamin C through oral supplements alone. The body regulates the amount of vitamin C that can be absorbed through the gut, and very large amounts of the vitamin will cause diarrhea. Intravenous vitamin C bypasses this problem because it goes directly into the bloodstream. I provide my patients with IV vitamin C in the office. They lie comfortably in a reclining chair during a one- to two-hour treatment session, at which time they receive doses of 30 g to 75 g of vitamin C.

PROMISING RESEARCH

The benefits of IV vitamin C for cancer patients has been demonstrated in studies, including those by researchers at the National Institutes of Health. Laboratory studies have shown that IV vitamin C kills cancer cells but not normal cells. Studies by physicians at University of Kansas Medical Center in Kansas City, for example, described two cases in which patients suffering from advanced ovarian cancer underwent surgery and then received chemotherapy and IV vitamin C. Three years after treatment, both women had no sign of disease, which is quite unusual, because the prognosis for ovarian cancer typically is quite poor. Other research has shown the benefit of this treatment for terminally ill patients. A Korean study found that a combination of IV and oral vitamin C improved quality of life, reducing nausea and increasing energy in terminally ill patients.

Most researchers agree that data from large clinical trials is needed. Several clinical trials currently are under way to assess the effect of IV vitamin C and other antioxidants on different types of cancers.

WHAT TO DO...

Many oncologists will not advocate vitamin therapy in any form.

My advice: While you're undergoing conventional therapy, look for a medical doctor or naturopathic physician experienced in IV therapies to work with your oncologist. You and your doctors can decide whether to administer IV vitamins during or immediately after receiving conventional therapies. Your doctor will determine the number of treatments you need. Some patients get one or two IV vitamin C infusions weekly for the first year after diagnosis and initial treatment for cancer, and then every other week for a few years to help prevent cancer cells from returning and to boost the immune system.

Large amounts of vitamin C are nontoxic and generally safe for everyone except those with kidney failure, who can't tolerate large amounts. In addition, a small percentage of people are deficient in the enzyme *glucose-6-phosphate dehydrogenase* (G6PD), which is needed to maintain normal red blood cells. Without this enzyme, large amounts of vitamin C can cause *hemolytic anemia,* a type of anemia that involves the abnormal breakdown of red blood cells. Before receiving IV vitamin C, ask your doctor to test you for this deficiency. If you have it, you should not have IV vitamin C.

Note that patients' response to cancer treatment of any kind varies, and no physician can ever know for certain how a tumor will respond to a specific treatment.

■ ■ ■ ■

Milk Thistle Protects Liver

Chemotherapy drugs can inflame the liver, forcing patients to reduce or halt cancer-fighting treatment.

Study: Leukemia patients undergoing chemo took a daily placebo or milk thistle extract. After 28 days, liver enzyme levels were better among milk thistle users than placebo users. Ask your oncologist about milk thistle.

Kara Kelly, MD, associate professor of clinical pediatrics, Columbia University Medical Center, New York City, and leader of a study of 50 pediatric cancer patients.

"Good" HDL Cholesterol Tied to Lower Cancer Risk

Richard Karas, MD, PhD, executive director, Tufts Medical Center Molecular Cardiology Research Institute, Boston.

Jennifer Robinson, MD, MPH, professor, epidemiology and medicine, University of Iowa College of Public Health, Iowa City.

Journal of the American College of Cardiology.

Higher blood levels of HDL cholesterol, the "good" kind that protects against heart disease, are also strongly associated with a lower risk of cancer, a new review of studies suggests.

STUDY DETAILS

"For about a 10-point increase of HDL, there is a reduced risk of cancer by about one third over an average follow-up of 4.5 years," said Richard Karas, MD, PhD, executive director of the Tufts Medical Center Molecular Cardiology Research Institute and lead author of a report in an issue of the *Journal of the American College of Cardiology.*

Those numbers come from an analysis of 24 randomized controlled trials that examined the effect that lowering levels of "bad" LDL cholesterol with cholesterol-lowering statin drugs had on heart disease. The review singled out trials that also recorded the incidence of cancer among the participants.

The researchers report a 36% lower cancer rate for every 10 milligrams per deciliter (mg/dl) higher level of HDL.

STUDY DOES NOT PROVE CAUSE AND EFFECT

But while the relationship between higher HDL and lower cancer risk was independent of other cancer risk factors, such as smoking, obesity and age, Dr. Karas was careful to say the study does not prove cause and effect.

"We can say that higher levels of HDL are associated with a lower risk of cancer, but we can't say that one causes the other," he said.

Exactly so, said Jennifer Robinson, MD, professor of epidemiology and medicine at the University of Iowa College of Public Health, who wrote an accompanying editorial. High HDL levels may simply be a marker of the kind of good traits that reduce both cardiovascular and cancer risk, she said.

"People have a lot of characteristics that are all kind of interrelated," she said. "They may not exercise, be obese and so on, and so have lower HDL than normal. The higher risk of cancer may have nothing to do with what HDL does."

HDL'S POTENTIAL ANTICANCER MECHANISMS

That's a real possibility, Dr. Karas said, but he also mentioned some possible physical mechanisms that might give HDL cholesterol anticancer activity.

"HDL alters the function of the immune system, which looks for abnormal cells that may be cancerous or precancerous and attacks them," he said. "It also has antioxidant properties, and there is a lot of interest in the role of antioxidants in reducing cancer risk."

HDL cholesterol also has anti-inflammatory activity, which might act against cancer, Dr. Karas said.

STUDIES NEEDED TO PROVE LINK

Dr. Karas's laboratory is "starting to think" about experiments to test these various theories, he said.

The only convincing proof would be a controlled trial testing whether medication that raises HDL levels reduces cancer incidence, Dr. Robinson said.

No such medication is now on the market (other than niacin, which has a minor effect in raising HDL levels), although several are being tested for their effect on heart disease, stroke and other cardiovascular problems.

"We actually don't know that something is causing [or preventing] a disease unless we do controlled trials," she said.

The researchers who conduct those studies should monitor cancer incidence as well as cardiovascular disease among the participants, Dr. Karas said.

The new study's finding that an appreciable effect on cancer was evident in just a few years "shows the importance in current studies to track cancer," he said. "Many don't."

KEEPING HDL LEVELS HIGH

Until the anticancer hypothesis is proved or disproved, Dr. Karas and Dr. Robinson said, the best thing to do is adopt the healthy lifestyle that can keep HDL cholesterol levels high—exercising regularly, eating a healthy diet, not smoking and consuming alcohol in moderation.

info To learn more about HDL, LDL "bad" cholesterol and other blood fats, visit the American Heart Association Web site, *www.heart.org* and search "Good vs. Bad Cholesterol."

Diabetes Update

No Fasting Needed for This Diabetes Test

In its new set of clinical guidelines, the American Diabetes Association is promoting a more prominent role for the hemoglobin A1C blood test in the diagnosis of type 2 diabetes and prediabetes.

ABOUT THE A1C BLOOD TEST

Long used in the management of diabetes, the A1C blood test measures average blood sugar levels for the previous two to three months. The new guidelines call for the diagnosis of type 2 diabetes at A1C levels above 6.5%, and prediabetes at A1C levels between 5.7% and 6.4%. Generally, people without diabetes have an A1C level of less than 5%.

"We've added a test that can make it easier to find out if you have diabetes," said Richard M. Bergenstal, MD, president of medicine and science for the American Diabetes Association (ADA).

The new guidelines were published in *Diabetes Care.*

Dr. Bergenstal said the A1C isn't necessarily superior to other methods used to detect type 2 diabetes and prediabetes, such as fasting blood sugar tests and the oral glucose tolerance test, but it is easier and more convenient for people because you don't have to fast before an A1C test.

In the past, the A1C wasn't recommended for use in the diagnosis of diabetes because the test wasn't standardized from lab to lab, according to the ADA. That means a reading of 6.5% at one lab could have been 6.3% at another. Now, the test is highly standardized, according to the ADA, making it a useful tool for detecting diabetes and prediabetes without the need for fasting.

"I think we may diagnose more people because the A1C is used a lot more now because of its convenience," Dr. Bergenstal said.

Richard M. Bergenstal, MD, president, medicine and science, American Diabetes Association.

Michael Bergman, MD, clinical professor of endocrinology, NYU Langone Medical Center, New York City.

Diabetes Care.

The A1C measures the percentage of hemoglobin (the main component of red blood cells) in the blood that is *glycated*. Glycated hemoglobin is hemoglobin that has a blood sugar molecule attached to it, which happens more frequently when blood sugar levels are higher than they should be.

This percentage gives the doctor an idea of what the patient's blood sugar levels have been for the past two to three months, which may help diagnose more people with type 2 diabetes and prediabetes sooner than they might have been in the past.

COMMENTARY FROM AN EXPERT

"This is a very practical, innovative concept," said Michael Bergman, MD, a clinical professor of endocrinology at the NYU Langone Medical Center in New York City.

"People don't need to be fasting for an A1C, and there are fewer variables that can affect the outcome of the A1C," Dr. Berman explained.

"I think diabetes is grossly underdiagnosed and prediabetes, even more so. It's a real problem, and these guidelines may help sensitize the medical community to it."

GET THE RIGHT TEST

Dr. Bergenstal said the ADA does recommend that A1C levels should be measured using a central lab, rather than a point-of-care A1C test. Like blood glucose monitors, some doctors' offices have A1C tests that can provide nearly instant A1C test results.

While these machines can be useful in the management of diabetes, the ADA is not recommending that they be used for the initial diagnosis of diabetes or prediabetes.

info To learn more about the hemoglobin A1C test, visit the Web site of the US National Library of Medicine, *www.nlm.nih.gov/medlineplus*, and search "hbA1C."

■ ■ ■ ■

Gum Disease? It Could Mean Diabetes

Researchers at New York University College of Nursing found that 93% of Americans with periodontal disease were at high risk for diabetes. In contrast, a far smaller proportion of people without gum disease—about 63%—were at risk for diabetes. If you have periodontal disease, get it treated—and be sure that you are tested for diabetes.

Mark A. Stengler, NMD, naturopathic medical doctor in private practice, La Jolla, California...adjunct associate clinical professor at the National College of Natural Medicine, Portland, Oregon...author of many books, including The Natural Physician's Healing Therapies and coauthor of Prescription for Natural Cures (both from Bottom Line Books)... and author of the Bottom Line/Natural Healing newsletter.

Surprising Symptoms of Prediabetes

Frederic J. Vagnini, MD, a cardiovascular surgeon and medical director of the Heart, Diabetes & Weight Loss Centers of New York in New York City. He is coauthor of The Weight Loss Plan for Beating Diabetes (Fair Winds).

One of the best ways to prevent diabetes is to spot blood sugar (glucose) problems before the full-blown disease develops. But most people don't realize that diabetes—and its precursor, prediabetes—can cause no symptoms at all or a wide range of symptoms that often are misinterpreted.

Common mistake: Because diabetes is strongly linked to excess body weight, many people who are a normal weight assume that they won't develop the disease. But that's not always true. About 15% of people who are diagnosed with diabetes are not overweight. And paradoxically, even weight loss can be a symptom of this complex disorder in people (normal weight or overweight) who have uncontrolled high glucose levels.

Shocking new finding: The Centers for Disease Control and Prevention now estimates that 40% of Americans ages 40 to 74 have prediabetes, and nearly two out of three Americans over age 65 have prediabetes or diabetes—most likely due to the increasing numbers of people who are overweight and inactive, both of which boost diabetes risk.

However, most primary care doctors aren't diagnosing and treating prediabetes early enough in their patients—often because they fail to order the necessary screening tests (see page 90). And because the symptoms of prediabetes can be subtle, especially in its early stages, most people are not reporting potential red flags to their doctors.

Fortunately, prediabetes can virtually always be prevented from progressing to diabetes if the condition is identified and treated in its early stages (by following a healthful diet, exercising regularly and taking nutritional supplements and medications, if necessary).

WHAT IS PREDIABETES?

Prediabetes occurs when the body's cells no longer respond correctly to insulin, a hormone that regulates blood sugar. With prediabetes, blood sugar levels are higher than normal but not high enough to warrant a diagnosis of diabetes.

RED FLAGS FOR DIABETES

•**Being overweight** (defined as having a body mass index, or BMI, of 25 or higher) is perhaps the best-known risk factor for diabetes.* The more excess body weight you have, the more resistant your cells become to the blood sugar–regulating effects of the hormone insulin, ultimately causing blood glucose levels to rise.

Greatest danger: Abdominal fat, in particular, further boosts diabetes risk. That's because belly (visceral) fat hinders the processing of insulin. The single biggest risk factor for prediabetes is having a waistline of 40 inches or more if you're a man….or 35 inches or more if you're a woman. *Lesser-known red flags for prediabetes (and diabetes)—if you have one of these symptoms, see your doctor…*

•**Increased thirst and need to urinate.** Because excess blood glucose draws water from the body's tissues, people with elevated blood glucose levels feel thirsty much of the time. Even when they drink fluids, their thirst is rarely quenched. Therefore, they drink even more, causing them to urinate more often than is normal for them.

•**Unexplained weight loss.** While being overweight is a significant risk factor for pre-

*For a BMI calculator, go to the Web site of the National Heart, Lung and Blood Institute, *www.nhlbisupport.com/bmi.*

diabetes, the condition also can paradoxically lead to unexplained weight loss resulting from a lack of energy supply to the body's cells and a loss of glucose-related calories due to excessive urination.

•**Dry, itchy skin.** Excess blood glucose also draws moisture from the skin, leaving it dry and prone to itching and cracking—especially on the legs, feet and elbows.

•**Blurred vision.** When excess blood glucose draws fluids from the body, this can dehydrate the lenses of the eyes, making it difficult to focus properly.

•**Slow-healing cuts, sores or bruises and frequent infections.** For unknown reasons, excess blood glucose appears to interfere with the body's healing processes and its ability to fight off infection. In particular, women with prediabetes and diabetes are prone to urinary tract and vaginal infections.

•**Red, swollen and tender gums.** Because the body's ability to heal can be compromised by prediabetes, gum inflammation, involving red, swollen, tender and/or bleeding gums, may develop.

•**Persistent feelings of hunger.** When the body's cells don't get enough glucose due to prediabetes, the cells send signals to the brain that are interpreted as hunger, typically about one hour after consuming a meal.

•**Lack of energy.** Because their cells are starved of energy-boosting glucose, people with prediabetes tend to tire quickly after even mild physical effort. Dehydration due to excess blood glucose also can contribute to fatigue.

•**Falling asleep after eating.** An hour or so after eating, our digestive systems convert the food we've eaten into glucose. In people with prediabetes, the process is exaggerated—blood glucose levels spike, triggering a surge of insulin as the body attempts to stabilize high glucose levels. This insulin surge is ineffective in lowering blood glucose, causing the person to become drowsy. If you feel sleepy after meals, it can be a sign that your blood glucose levels are riding this prediabetic roller coaster.

•**Moodiness and irritability.** Lack of energy production in your cells, together with sharp rises and dips in blood glucose levels, can trigger feelings of restlessness, irritability and exaggerated emotional responses to stress.

•Tingling or numbness in the hands and feet. Excess blood glucose can damage small blood vessels feeding the body's peripheral nerves, often causing tingling, loss of sensation or burning pain in the hands, arms, legs or feet.

•Loss of sex drive and erectile dysfunction in men. Prediabetes is associated with low testosterone in men, which often reduces libido. In addition, glucose-related damage to the body's small blood vessels often impairs the ability of prediabetic men to have an erection.

■ **More from Dr. Vagnini…**

Three Key Diabetes Tests

If you suspect that you may have prediabetes, ask your doctor to order the following tests…

•Fasting blood glucose. This traditional blood test for diabetes is usually part of a standard physical. Until recently, a result over 125 mg/dL was considered a sign of diabetes, while 100 mg/dL to 125 milligrams per deciliter (mg/dL) indicated prediabetes.

New finding: Standard guidelines established by the American Diabetes Association have not changed, but recent data suggest that a person who has a fasting blood glucose reading over 90 mg/dL should be evaluated by a physician.

•Hemoglobin A1C. This blood test, also included in many annual checkups, measures the average blood glucose level over a two- to three-month period. An A1C result of 4.5% to 5.9% is considered normal…6% to 6.5% indicates prediabetes…and two separate readings of 6.5% or above indicate diabetes.

New danger level: Standard guidelines still use 6% as the lower end of the prediabetes range, but recent data suggest that results as low as 5.6% or 5.7% may signal prediabetes.

•Oral glucose tolerance test. Administered over two hours in your doctor's office, this test can spot problems with blood-sugar regulation that may not show up in the other tests. For the oral glucose tolerance test, blood levels of glucose are checked immediately before drinking a premixed glucose formula and two hours afterward.

A result of 140 mg/dL to 159 mg/dL is a sign of increased risk for diabetes…160 mg/dL to 200 mg/dL indicates high risk for diabetes…and over 200 mg/dL signals full-blown diabetes. Also ask your doctor to measure your insulin levels—insulin fluctuations can be an even earlier predictor of prediabetes than the tests described above.

Getting the Most from Your Metformin

Kaiser Permanente news release.

If people with diabetes start the drug metformin early—within three months of diagnosis—it appears the drug will remain effective longer, a new study finds.

"This study suggests that to gain full benefit from metformin, patients should start taking it as soon as they find out they have diabetes," said lead author Jonathan B. Brown, PhD, an investigator with the Kaiser Permanente Center for Health Research in Portland, Oregon.

ABOUT METFORMIN

Metformin, a generic drug, treats type 2 diabetes by helping the body control blood-sugar levels. Unfortunately, most people are forced to turn to other medications after a while because metformin stops working. These other drugs can be more expensive and can boost the risk for weight gain.

STUDY DETAILS

The study, which followed nearly 1,800 people with diabetes for up to five years, found that the drug took longer to fail in people who began taking it within three months of being diagnosed with diabetes.

In them, it failed at a rate of 12% a year. For those who began taking metformin a year or two after diagnosis, it failed at a rate of 21.4% a year.

The study was published in *Diabetes Care*.

IMPLICATIONS

"We believe that starting the drug early preserves the body's own ability to control blood sugar, which in turn prevents the long-term complications of diabetes, like heart disease, kidney failure and blindness," said study coauthor Gregory A. Nichols, PhD, an investigator with the Kaiser center. "The American Diabetes Association recommends that patients start taking metformin and make lifestyle changes as soon as they are diagnosed. This study provides more evidence to back up that recommendation."

info For more information on diabetes treatments, visit the Web site *www.diabetes health.com.*

Avandia Access Allowed But with Severe Restrictions, Says FDA

Alan Kadish, MD, president and CEO, Touro College, New York City.
Kirk Garratt, MD, clinical director of interventional cardiovascular research, Lenox Hill Hospital, New York City.
The New York Times.
Associated Press.
Ellen Strahlman, MD, chief medical officer, Glaxo-SmithKline, prepared statement.

The controversial diabetes drug *rosiglitazone* (Avandia) does raise the risk of heart attack more than other medications of its kind but should stay on the market with tightened controls, recommended a US government advisory panel.

BACKGROUND

The Food and Drug Administration committee had been meeting intensively, hearing differing opinions not only from outside experts and pharmaceutical representatives but also from within the FDA itself.

The safety of the blood-sugar-lowering drug Avandia, part of the *thiazolidinedione* family, has been in question for years.

In 2005, the FDA asked GlaxoSmithKline, the company that makes Avandia, to conduct a meta-analysis of all its clinical trials on the drug.

The analysis, which did show an increased risk for heart attack, was submitted to the FDA the following year. The FDA then did its own analysis while a number of other trials came out also showing signs of heart problems.

In November of 2007, the FDA added a boxed warning to the drug saying that there was a potential risk of more heart problems, such as heart attack, with Avandia. The expert panel focused much of its attention on the results of the highly publicized trial RECORD (Rosiglitazone Evaluated for Cardiac Outcomes and Regulation of Glycemia in Diabetes), announced in June of 2009. The trial found that Avandia significantly raises the risk of heart failure (and bone fractures) though not cardiovascular disease or death.

Both Avandia and its sister medication, *pioglitazone* (Actos), which is made by Takeda, came with warnings regarding heart failure when they were first approved.

The drama intensified considerably just before the advisory meeting began when an FDA official posted statements on the agency's web site questioning the design and interpretation of the pivotal RECORD trial.

Then a *New York Times* report said that Glaxo knew more than a decade ago that Avandia caused an increased risk of heart problems but covered up the information.

Glaxo, in a prepared statement, said that, "The RECORD study was conducted according to good clinical practices and the data are reliable. RECORD demonstrated that Avandia was not associated with an overall increase in cardiovascular hospitalization or cardiovascular death compared with [diabetes drugs] metformin and sulfonylureas."

EXPERT PANEL RECOMMENDATION

By a complex series of votes, the 33-member panel of experts rejected the option that the FDA remove Avandia from the market for safety reasons.

The series of votes started, according to the Times, with 18 members of the panel voting that Avandia might up the risk of heart attack, six saying they weren't concerned about a raised risk, and nine saying they were unsure.

On their second vote, however, only one member of the committee thought that Avandia increased the risk of death when compared with older medicines, 20 said it did not increase the risk of death, and 12 remained unsure.

The panel seemed more decided when comparing Avandia's safety risks to Actos. Twenty panel members voted that Avandia was more likely to cause heart attack than Actos, four voted that it was no more likely to do so, and eight said they did not know, the Associated Press reported.

And on the key vote, the decision on Avandia's future, 12 members voted for pulling the drug, 17 voted for new warning label revisions or restrictions on use, and three voted that no changes were needed.

Update: In the fall of 2010, the FDA responded to the panel's recommendation by severely restricting access to Avandia.

EXPERT REACTION

"I don't think there's any question that the use of the drug will decrease and that both physicians and patients will look at the warning very carefully before prescribing Avandia, although that assumes that the final FDA ruling will follow the panel's recommendation," said Alan Kadish, MD, president and CEO of Touro College, after the votes.

The outcome, he added, was not a surprise. "I expected the vote to be split, and it was split in even more complex ways than one might have imagined. The panel did the best they could with data that weren't completely conclusive, that suggested an increased risk but didn't make it clear how much that increased risk was," he said.

And he explained, "The majority of the panel didn't feel the increased risk was enough to summarily remove a drug that hundreds of thousands of people are taking successfully."

A second heart expert agreed.

"I didn't think that the evidence was yet compelling enough to withdraw the product from the market," said Kirk Garratt, MD, clinical director of interventional cardiovascular research at Lenox Hill Hospital in New York City. "It sounds like they're going to add some new warnings regarding the risk, and that seems like an appropriate step."

And such a step will likely decrease the use of Avandia, anyway, Dr. Garratt added. "Use went down pretty sharply after criticism started to fly and the presence of new boxed warnings will further depress the prevalence of this product in the marketplace," he said.

But Dr. Garratt also said he didn't think the experts' votes would end the controversy over Avandia.

"There is so much dissent within the FDA about the appropriate action to take with this drug that I can't imagine this will be the final word," he said. "Also, we've got an alternative product [Actos] that seems to be essentially as effective at controlling diabetes but hasn't been linked to the cardiovascular risks."

GLAXO REACTION

In a statement released after the vote, Ellen Strahlman, MD, chief medical officer at GlaxoSmithKline, said, "Following today's recommendations, we will, of course, continue to work with the FDA in the best interest of diabetes patients....Patients taking Avandia should speak with their physician about their treatment and any questions they may have regarding the safety of the medicine."

Caution! Blood Sugar That's Too Low Can Cause Serious Accidents

Donald A. Redelmeier, MD, professor, medicine, and director, clinical epidemiology unit, University of Toronto, Ontario, Canada.

Luigi F. Meneghini, MD, MBA, associate professor, clinical medicine, and director, clinical operations, division of endocrinology, diabetes and metabolism, University of Miami Miller School of Medicine, Miami.

PLoS Medicine online.

People with diabetes who keep their blood sugar tightly controlled run the risk of having traffic accidents due to low blood sugar, Canadian researchers report.

DIABETES AND DRIVING

Controlling blood sugar is the cornerstone of managing diabetes. By keeping blood sugar under control, people with diabetes can ward off many of the complications associated with the condition, including heart and kidney disease. However, blood sugar that is too low—known as *hypoglycemia*—can cause dizziness and loss of consciousness, the researchers say.

"Diabetes is a common disease that may impair an adult's ability to drive," said lead researcher Donald A. Redelmeier, MD, a professor of medicine at the University of Toronto.

Worldwide, Dr. Redelmeier said, people with diabetes are required to produce proof of good blood-sugar control to keep their driver's license. The United States, United Kingdom, Canada, Germany, Holland, Australia and other countries all have such laws, but they're "based on theory rather than science," he said.

And contrary to the prevailing theory, people with good blood-sugar control were found to have a higher risk for crashing, Dr. Redelmeier said of his study's results. The risk was substantial, accounting for almost 50% of the accidents, he said.

The accidents were mostly related to severe hypoglycemia in association with strict blood sugar control, he noted. The findings were published in *PLoS Medicine*.

STUDY DETAILS

For the study, Dr. Redelmeier's team collected data on 795 drivers with diabetes. They found that one in 14 of the drivers had been involved in car accidents. Those with low blood sugar were more likely to have had an accident than were people with diabetes whose blood sugar was not as well controlled.

Moreover, the risk for having a car accident increased fourfold if the person had a history of hypoglycemia, the researchers found.

IMPLICATIONS

"This finding calls into question laws that restrict driver's licenses on the basis of this measure of diabetes control," Dr. Redelmeier said.

The study could be the first step in getting driving laws changed, he added. His research group, Dr. Redelmeier said, was the first to identify driving and talking on cell phones as a hazard, which led to laws restricting the use of cell phones while driving.

EXPERT ADVICE

Luigi F. Meneghini, MD, an associate professor of clinical medicine and director of clinical operations for the division of endocrinology, diabetes and metabolism at the University of Miami Miller School of Medicine, agreed that the study "brings up the risk of driving while you have diabetes."

People taking medication to lower their blood sugar need to be aware of any symptoms of an oncoming hypoglycemic episode, Dr. Meneghini said. And older people, who he said often aren't aware that a hypoglycemic episode is starting, should check their blood sugar more often.

"They should certainly check their blood sugar before they get into a car," he said. "If they have low blood sugar, treat the low blood sugar and wait until their blood sugar is in a safe range before getting behind the wheel."

Dr. Redelmeier said he advises people with diabetes not to drive if they feel dizzy or have other symptoms of hypoglycemia. In addition, he urges people to always have food available to boost their blood sugar should a hypoglycemic episode start.

"If you had a hypoglycemic episode yesterday, you should be wary of driving a car tomorrow," Dr. Redelmeier said.

Seek Support to Survive Diabetes

Paul Ciechanowski, MD, MPH, associate professor, psychiatry and behavioral sciences, program director, Psychosomatic Medicine Fellowship, University of Washington School of Medicine; program director, CHAMMP Training Institute, Harborview Medical Center; affiliate investigator, Group Health Research Institute; and CEO/founder, Samepage (health-care communications), Seattle.

Vasudevan A. Raghavan, MBBS, MD, director, cardiometabolic and lipid clinic and medical weight management service, division of endocrinology, Scott & White Healthcare, Temple, Texas.

Diabetes Care.

People with diabetes do much better, in terms of survival, if they can turn to others for support in times of need, new research suggests.

The study found that those who are more independent and feel they don't need help from others have a 33% increased risk of dying over a five-year period.

"These are self-reliant, pull-yourself-up-by-your-bootstraps self-starters and go-getters. But, in the health-care setting with a chronic illness, what is normally an advantage can become a liability over time," said Paul Ciechanowski, MD, an associate professor in the department of psychiatry and behavioral sciences at the University of Washington School of Medicine.

"Day-in, day-out, when you have the mortgage to pay, the kids to get to soccer, work deadlines, medications to take and refill, exercise that needs to be done, healthy food that needs to be cooked, and doctors' appointments, it all starts to break down if you're trying to do it all on your own," he said.

BACKGROUND

Previous research has found that people who have chronic illnesses, including diabetes, who lack a good support system are more likely to die, according to background information in the study.

Dr. Ciechanowski and his colleagues wanted to expand on past research and see what effect personality type had on the risk of mortality in the presence of chronic illness.

STUDY DETAILS

The researchers recruited 3,535 nondepressed adults with either type 1 or type 2 diabetes. They found that 53.8% of the study participants had an interactive relationship style, meaning that they had a greater propensity to reach out to others, according to the study. The remainder—46.2%—had an independent relationship style. These people have difficulty reaching out to others and may have a hard time trusting other people, the study found.

The death rate for those in the interactive group was 29 per 1,000 individuals, compared with 39 per 1,000 in the independent group. That means independent people have a 33% increased risk of death, according to the study.

Results of the study were published in *Diabetes Care*.

EXPERT COMMENTARY

"Much of this study is quite intuitive," said Vasudevan Raghavan, MBBS, MD, director of the cardiometabolic and lipid clinic, and the medi-

cal weight management service at Scott & White Healthcare in Temple, Texas. "Having a support system provides additional incentive to do the right thing. For example, if you have a mother who visits or calls frequently, she may remind you to get to your doctor's appointment and refill your medication, which prompts you to do it."

Dr. Raghavan said one finding that was particularly telling was that even though people with an interactive style had a higher body mass index (BMI), they still had a lower risk of death. BMI is a measurement of body fat that takes into account a person's height and weight. Normally, a higher BMI in people with diabetes would tend to be associated with a higher risk of death.

Unfortunately, Dr. Raghavan said, "you can't provide a social prescription. You can't mandate that people reach out to or live with others."

HELPFUL STRATEGIES

Both Dr. Ciechanowski and Dr. Raghavan said these findings should prompt doctors to try to consider a person's relationship style in treatment.

"We need to develop different approaches for people who aren't able to collaborate. Often, they'd love extra help, but are afraid to reach out," said Dr. Ciechanowski. Possible options are e-mails, telephone calls or appointments with other health-care professionals, he said.

info To learn more about the people who should be part of your health-care team, visit the Web site of the American Diabetes Association, *www.diabetes.org*, and search "health-care team."

Easy Ways to Control Your Blood Sugar

Stanley Mirsky, MD, associate clinical professor at Mount Sinai School of Medicine and founder of the Stanley Mirsky MD Diabetes Education Unit at the Mount Sinai Metabolism Institute, both in New York City. Dr. Mirsky is coauthor, with Joan Rattner Heilman, of Diabetes Survival Guide (Ballantine).

From the time you wake up until you go to bed, it is essential to keep your blood sugar as stable as possible if you have diabetes. Over time, uncontrolled elevated blood sugar harms the blood vessels, kidneys, eyes and nerves, increasing the risk for heart attack, stroke, kidney failure, blindness and tissue damage that can require limb amputation.

Recent finding: Diabetes is also linked to dementia.

Despite these dangers, scarcely half of the 23 million Americans who have been diagnosed with diabetes have their disease under control. If you're struggling, you can significantly improve your blood sugar control by eating the right foods and doing the right things at the right times of day.

THROUGHOUT THE DAY

It is key to eat foods that digest slowly, so blood sugar remains relatively stable...and avoid foods that are digested quickly, triggering rapid blood sugar spikes. This also helps control weight—an important factor because excess weight contributes to diabetes complications. *Guidelines...*

•**Have 40 grams (g) to 50 g of carbohydrates at each meal.** Stick with mostly complex carbs (whole grains, vegetables, nuts)...limit refined carbs (cakes, white pasta). Check labels!

•**Avoid foods with more than 10 g of sugar per serving.**

•**Have some lean protein every day—**chicken, fish, lean beef, low-fat dairy, eggs, tofu. Most people get enough protein, so you do not need protein with each meal unless your doctor recommends this.

•**Limit starches** (corn, peas, potatoes, sweet potatoes) to one serving per meal.

•**Limit fruit to two servings per day.** A serving equals one small handheld fruit (peach, plum)...half an apple or half a banana...12 grapes...one cup of strawberries...or one-half cup of blueberries, raspberries or diced fruit (such as melon). Avoid pineapples and dried fruits, which are high in sugar.

AT WAKE-UP TIME

Test your blood sugar before breakfast. If it is high, you may have eaten too many carbohydrates too close to bedtime the night before. Or your levels may have fallen too low during the night, so your liver released more glucose (sugar), causing a blood sugar "rebound." Talk to your doctor—you may need to adjust your medication dosage and/or timing.

AT BREAKFAST

The morning meal helps get your metabolism running efficiently, so don't skip it.

Ideal: One or two slices of whole-grain bread with a butter substitute that contains cholesterol-lowering plant sterols, such as Smart Balance or Promise Activ...plus a two-egg vegetable omelet. It is fine to use whole eggs—but if you have high cholesterol, make your omelet with egg whites instead and limit egg yolks to two per week.

Another good choice: One cup of unsweetened or lightly sweetened whole-grain cereal that contains no more than 25 g of carbohydrates per cup, such as Cheerios or Product 19...plus one-half cup of blueberries and one cup of low-fat milk. Don't be fooled into thinking that high-fiber necessarily equals healthful—you still must check labels to see if the food is too high in carbs.

Your doctor may advise you to take a dose of diabetes medication right before breakfast.

Also: If you have diabetic nerve damage, take 100 micrograms of vitamin B-1 daily. If you take blood pressure medication, morning is the best time because blood pressure typically is higher during the day than at night. If you plan to drive, test your blood sugar before leaving home.

IN MIDMORNING

A midmorning snack generally is not necessary unless your doctor advises you to have one (for instance, due to the type of insulin you are on). However, if you start to feel weak or dizzy, have a snack that provides no more than 10 g of carbohydrates—for instance, a small tangerine, half a banana or two graham cracker squares.

AT LUNCH

Good choices include a sandwich, such as turkey, lettuce and tomato on whole-wheat bread...or sushi with rice (preferably brown).

Common mistakes: Eating too much (especially at restaurants)...choosing a fruit plate (too much sugar and no protein)...overdoing it on chips or condiments (which can be high in fat or sugar).

IN MIDAFTERNOON

Again, have a snack only if you feel weak or your doctor recommends it, and limit yourself to no more than 10 g of carbs.

Good choices: About 15 pistachios...10 almonds...or one-third of an ounce of whole-grain crackers.

AT DINNER

Check your blood sugar before dinner. If you are on oral diabetes medication, take it just before your meal.

Dinner should include four ounces of lean protein...several generous servings of vegetables...and one serving of a starch. Have a green salad, but skip the high-carb, high-fat dressings. Instead, drizzle greens with lemon juice, balsamic vinegar, safflower oil and/or olive oil.

Limit: One alcoholic drink daily, consumed with a meal. Opt for five ounces of wine...12 ounces of a low-carb beer, such as Miller Lite... or one ounce of distilled liquor (Scotch, vodka). Avoid mixed drinks, which often are high in carbs.

Dessert options: A scoop of low-carb, no-sugar-added ice cream...berries...two Lorna Doone cookies...or three Social Tea Biscuits.

IN THE EVENING

This is the best time to exercise to maximize muscle cells' absorption of glucose. Strength training and stretching are good, but aerobic exercise is most important because it increases insulin sensitivity (cells' ability to respond to insulin) for up to 14 hours. Each week, aim for two-and-a-half hours of moderate-intensity aerobic exercise, such as walking...or one-and-a-half hours of strenuous activity. For blood sugar control, 30-minute workouts generally are most effective. As part of your exercise regimen, consider tai chi. In one study, diabetes patients who did this martial art significantly lowered their blood sugar levels.

Caution: Ask your doctor before starting an exercise program. Test blood sugar before each workout. If it is below 100 milligrams per deciliter (mg/dL), have a snack before exercising. Do not work out when your blood sugar is higher than 250 mg/dL—when blood sugar is this high, exercise may elevate it even further. If you have retinopathy (damaged blood vessels in the retina), to protect vision, do not lift weights above eye level.

AT BEDTIME

If you are on long-acting insulin, a bedtime injection controls nighttime glucose levels. If you take cholesterol-lowering medication, do so now—it is most effective at night. Test your blood sugar at bedtime. If it is somewhat elevated (but not above 250 mg/dL), lower it with 10 minutes of moderate exercise, unless exercise interferes with sleep.

Insomnia doesn't raise blood sugar, but the stress it creates can.

To promote sleep: Turn off the cell phone, TV and computer at least 30 minutes before bedtime so your mind can quiet down. Take a warm bath (checking your feet for wounds or signs of infection, because diabetes often damages nerves in the feet) an hour or more before bedtime.

Have you been told that you snore? Diabetes patients are prone to sleep apnea (repeated halts in breathing during sleep), which contributes to poor blood sugar control. Do you frequently get up at night to urinate? It could be a sign that your medication needs adjusting. If you have either symptom, tell your doctor.

■ ■ ■ ■

Tai Chi Lowers Blood Sugar

In a six-month study of 62 people with diabetes, those who practiced the Chinese martial art tai chi weekly (two supervised sessions and three at home) significantly reduced their blood sugar levels compared with those who did not practice tai chi.

Theory: Tai chi coordinates breathing with slow, gentle movements, which may improve insulin sensitivity.

To find a tai chi class near you: Consult *www.taichiforhealth.com* and click on "Find a Class."

Beverly Roberts, PhD, RN, professor for teaching and research, University of Florida College of Nursing, Gainesville.

■ ■ ■ ■

Control Blood Sugar with Tea

When researchers compared concentrations of *polysaccharides* (a type of carbohydrate) in black, green and oolong teas, the polysaccharides in black tea were the best blood sugar (glucose) inhibitors.

Theory: Polysaccharides in black tea block an enzyme that converts starch into glucose. If you have diabetes or prediabetes: Consider drinking three cups of black tea daily to better control blood sugar.

Haixia Chen, PhD, associate professor, School of Pharmaceutical Science and Technology, Tianjin University, Tianjin, China.

Drop Pounds and Blood Sugar—with Vinegar

Mark A. Stengler, NMD, naturopathic medical doctor in private practice, La Jolla, California…adjunct associate clinical professor at the National College of Natural Medicine, Portland, Oregon…author of many books, including *The Natural Physician's Healing Therapies* and coauthor of *Prescription for Natural Cures* (both from Bottom Line Books)… and author of the *Bottom Line/Natural Healing* newsletter.

Vinegar has been used as a folk medicine for such things as headaches and indigestion. Now several studies reinforce its benefit for weight management and blood sugar control. Researchers believe that it is the acetic acid in any type of vinegar (apple cider, balsamic, white or red wine) that produces this effect, interfering with enzymes involved in the digestion of carbohydrates and those that alter glucose metabolism (so that insulin does not spike).

One recent study found that mice fed a high-fat diet—and given acetic acid—developed up to 10% less body fat than those not given acetic acid. Another study found that having small amounts of vinegar at bedtime seemed to reduce waking blood glucose levels in people.

More studies need to be done on vinegar, but it does seem that people can benefit from sprinkling vinegar on salads…adding a teaspoon to marinades…and adding a few drops to mustard.

For blood sugar balance (for those with diabetes or on diabetes medication) or weight loss, dilute one to two tablespoons (some people start with teaspoons) in an equal amount of water—and drink it at the beginning of a meal.

■ ■ ■ ■

Attention Women: Diabetes Linked to Irregular Heartbeat

When 34,744 adults were followed for an average of 7.2 years, women with diabetes were 26% more likely to develop *atrial fibrillation* (irregular heartbeat) than women without diabetes. No such association was found in men, but past research has shown an increased risk for heart disease in general in both men and women with diabetes.

If you have diabetes: Ask your doctor to closely monitor your cardiovascular health.

Gregory A. Nichols, PhD, investigator, Kaiser Permanente Center for Health Research, Portland, Oregon.

When Heart Surgery Is NOT the Answer

William E. Boden, MD, FACC, clinical chief, division of cardiovascular medicine, professor of medicine and preventive medicine, University at Buffalo Schools of Medicine & Public Health, medical director, cardiovascular services, Kaleida Health chief of cardiology, Buffalo General and Millard Fillmore Hospitals, Buffalo, New York.

If you have diabetes and heart disease—and many Americans do, or will, since the two tend to go hand in hand—it is important to be aware of special considerations regarding your treatment, especially when it comes to invasive heart procedures.

A LANDMARK STUDY

Surprisingly, there is no clear consensus on how to treat diabetic patients with heart disease. That, coupled with concern about the exorbitant cost of treating diabetes (it now accounts for one out of every five federal health-care dollars spent), led researchers to undertake the Bypass Angioplasty Revascularization Investigation

(BARI 2D) trial, which is a comparative effectiveness study of two different treatments for diabetic patients with heart disease.

In the five-year randomized, clinical trial of 2,368 diabetics with heart disease at 49 sites in six countries, researchers compared optimal medical therapy (medications and lifestyle counseling) with the same plus surgery to see which worked best in preventing a cardiovascular event and/or early death. These patients were generally considered to be at low risk for heart attack and stroke based on the extent of their coronary artery disease and symptoms, such as their degree of angina (chest pain), when the study began. The "optimal medical therapy" (medications such as beta-blockers and statins, for example) was given to all participants to control blood pressure and cholesterol, and participants were also counseled, as appropriate, to quit smoking and/or lose weight, noted William E. Boden, MD, FACC, clinical chief of the division of cardiovascular medicine and professor of medicine and preventive medicine at the University at Buffalo Schools of Medicine & Public Health.

For the group that received medical therapy plus surgery, half the participants were randomly assigned to either undergo *stent angioplasty* or *coronary-artery bypass grafting* (CABG).

Over the five-year period following the intervention, Dr. Boden and his colleagues found that…

•**There was little or no difference in outcome between those who underwent angioplasty versus only optimal medical therapy**—angioplasty patients had a 10.8% death rate, compared with a 10.2% death rate among those on optimal medical therapy.

•**In the bypass group—which included individuals with more severe heart disease—surgery was more effective than optimal medical therapy.** Bypass recipients had a 22.4% chance of having a heart attack or stroke or dying in the next five years, compared with 30.5% of participants who only took medications.

These results were published in *The New England Journal of Medicine.*

HIGH TECH IS NOT ALWAYS THE ANSWER

We're often inclined to believe that high-tech devices and interventions are superior, Dr. Boden observed. This is not always the case —sometimes conservative medical therapy is more effective, since it is less invasive and therefore less dangerous, and it costs less, too. The BARI 2D results confirm that intensive medical (nonsurgical) therapy can be an effective first line of treatment for diabetics with heart disease, particularly for those with less severe disease.

Secret to Preventing Serious Bone Infections

George Cierny, MD, and Doreen DiPasquale, MD, physician-partners at REOrthopaedics in San Diego. Dr. Cierny is an international lecturer in orthopedic surgery who has published more than 100 scientific papers and book chapters in the field of musculoskeletal pathology and infection. Dr. DiPasquale, an orthopedic surgeon, is former residency program director at George Washington University in Washington, DC, and National Naval Medical Center in Bethesda, Maryland.

When most people think of bone problems, broken bones and osteoporosis (reduced bone density and strength) come to mind. But our bones also can be the site of infections that can sometimes go unrecognized for months or even years.

This is especially the case if the only symptoms of bone infection (a condition known as *osteomyelitis*) are ones that are commonly mistaken for common health problems, such as ordinary back pain or fatigue. *What you need to know…*

ARE YOU AT RISK?

Older adults (age 70 and older), people with diabetes or arthritis and anyone with a weakened immune system (due to chronic disease, such as cancer, for example) are among those at greatest risk for osteomyelitis.

Anyone who has an artificial joint (such as a total hip replacement or total knee replacement) or metal implants attached to a bone also is at increased risk for osteomyelitis and should discuss the use of antibiotics before any type of surgery, including routine dental and oral surgery. Bacteria in the mouth can enter the bloodstream and cause a bone infection.

TYPES OF BONE INFECTIONS

Before the advent of joint-replacement surgery, most bone infections were caused by injuries that expose the bone to bacteria in the environment (such as those caused by a car accident) or a broken bone…or an infection elsewhere in the body, such as pneumonia or a urinary tract infection, that spreads to the bone through the bloodstream.

Now: About half the cases of osteomyelitis are complications of surgery in which large metal implants are used to stabilize or replace bones and joints (such as in the hip or knee).

Osteomyelitis is divided into three main categories, depending on the origin of the infection…

•**Blood-borne osteomyelitis** occurs when bacteria that originate elsewhere in the body migrate to and infect bone. People with osteoarthritis or rheumatoid arthritis are prone to blood-borne infections in their affected joints due to injury to cells in the lining of the joints that normally prevent bacteria from entering the bloodstream.

•**Contiguous-focus osteomyelitis** occurs when organisms—usually bacteria, but sometimes fungi—infect bone tissue. These cases usually occur in people with diabetes, who often develop pressure sores on the soles of their feet or buttocks due to poor circulation and impaired immunity.

•**Post-traumatic osteomyelitis.** Trauma or surgery to a bone and/or surrounding tissue can open the area to bacteria and other microbes. The use of prosthetic joints, surgical screws, pins or plates also makes it easier for bacteria to enter and infect the bone.

Important: Any of the three types of bone infections described above can lead to chronic osteomyelitis, an initially low-grade infection that can persist for months or even years with few or no symptoms. Eventually it gets severe enough to literally destroy bone. Left untreated, the body part with the affected bone may have to be amputated.

DIFFICULT TO DIAGNOSE

When osteomyelitis first develops (acute osteomyelitis), the symptoms—such as pain, swelling and tenderness—are usually the same as those caused by other infections.

If the initial infection is subtle (low-grade) or doesn't resolve completely with treatment, it can result in chronic osteomyelitis. In this case, you may have no symptoms or symptoms that are nonspecific. For example, someone who has had surgery might blame discomfort on delayed recovery, not realizing that what they have is a bone infection.

Surprising finding: When we studied the histories of more than 2,000 osteomyelitis patients, we found that most of those with chronic infections had relatively little pain from the infection itself. About 28% of those who required surgery for infection had normal white blood cell counts—suggesting that, over time, the body adjusts to lingering infections.

If a doctor suspects that you may have osteomyelitis because of chronic pain…swelling…possibly fever…fatigue…or other symptoms, he/she will usually order special laboratory tests that detect the formation of antibodies. If the results indicate the presence of infection, he may then order an X-ray or magnetic resonance imaging (MRI) scan. These and other imaging tests can readily detect damaged bone tissue and reveal the presence of infection.

BEST TREATMENT OPTIONS

About 60% to 70% of people with acute osteomyelitis can be cured with antibiotics (or antifungal agents, if a fungal infection is present) if treatment begins early enough to prevent the infection from becoming chronic. In these cases, patients exhibit symptoms…test positive for infection…and readily respond to drug treatments. Most patients can be cured with a four- to six-week course of antibiotics. Fungal infections are more resistant to treatment—antifungal drugs may be needed for several months.

For chronic osteomyelitis, surgical *debridement* (the removal of damaged tissue and bone using such instruments as a scalpel or scissors) usually is necessary.

Reasons: Damaged bone can lose its blood supply and remain in the body as "dead bone"—

without living cells or circulation. Such infections are invulnerable to the effects of antibiotics.

After debridement, the surgeon may insert a slow-release antibiotic depot, a small pouch that releases the antibiotic for up to a month. This approach can increase drug concentrations up to 100 times more than oral antibiotic therapy.

Even with these treatments, in people with chronic osteomyelitis who are otherwise healthy, up to 6% may require a second or even a third operation to cure the infection. In people with diabetes or other disorders, the percentage may be as high as 25%.

To improve your chances of a full recovery from chronic osteomyelitis: Eat well, maintain healthy blood sugar levels, stay active after treatment (to promote blood circulation, prevent blood clots and help maintain an appetite) and don't use tobacco products.

Good News for Anyone with Diabetic Retinopathy

Mark A. Stengler, NMD, naturopathic medical doctor in private practice, La Jolla, California...adjunct associate clinical professor at the National College of Natural Medicine, Portland, Oregon...author of many books, including *The Natural Physician's Healing Therapies* and coauthor of *Prescription for Natural Cures* (both from Bottom Line Books)... and author of the *Bottom Line/Natural Healing* newsletter.

Pycnogenol (pronounced pic-noj-en-all), an extract from the bark of the French maritime pine, is known to improve cir-

culation, reduce swelling and ease asthma. Now Italian researchers have found another use for it—it helps patients with diabetes who are in the early stages of diabetic retinopathy, a complication of diabetes in which the retina becomes damaged, resulting in vision impairment, including blurred vision, seeing dark spots, impaired night vision, reduced color perception and eventually blindness.

All people with diabetes are at risk for diabetic retinopathy—and it's estimated that as many as 80% of people with diabetes for 10 years or more will have this complication.

Participants in the Italian study had been diagnosed with type 2 diabetes for four years, and their diabetes was well-controlled by diet and oral medication. Study participants had early stage retinopathy and moderately impaired vision. After two months of treatment, the patients given Pycnogenol had less retinal swelling as measured by ultrasound testing. Most important, their vision was significantly improved. This was especially noticeable because the vision of those in the control group did not improve.

My view: If you have type 1 or 2 diabetes, undergo a comprehensive eye exam at least once a year. If retinopathy is detected, it would be wise to supplement with Pycnogenol (150 milligrams daily). Because retinopathy among diabetes patients is so prevalent, I recommend this amount to all my patients with diabetes to protect their vision. Pycnogenol has a blood-thinning effect, so people who take blood-thinning medication, such as warfarin, should use it only while being monitored by a doctor.

Drug News

Lower Heart Attack and Stroke Risk by 60%

Giving daily doses of a statin that lowers cholesterol and an ACE inhibitor (medication that lowers blood pressure) to people at high risk for a heart attack or stroke reduced their incidence of these conditions by more than 60% in two years, researchers report.

People in the study all had diabetes or a history of cardiovascular disease, but the drug regimen probably could provide similar benefits to anyone vulnerable to cardiovascular trouble because of obesity, high blood pressure or simply age, said R. James Dudl, MD, diabetes clinic lead at the Kaiser Permanente Care Management Institute in Oakland, California, and lead author of a report in the *American Journal of Managed Care.*

The study was based on a model that assumed that high blood cholesterol and high blood pressure were each responsible for about 25% of cardiovascular risk, Dr. Dudl said.

"We hypothesized that while there were different mechanisms, the effects are additive," Dr. Dudl said. "Our model showed a potential 71% drop in cardiovascular risk."

STUDY DETAILS

The study included 170,024 members of the Kaiser Permanente health plan in California, all ages 55 or older. They were divided into three groups: 21,292 who took the bundled drugs (the two drugs provided at a discounted cost) more than half the time during the two-year study, 47,262 who took the drug bundle less than half the time and 101,464 who took neither or just one drug during the study.

Their use of the medications was determined by monitoring their prescription refill records. Participants were also advised to take low-dose

R. James Dudl, MD, diabetes clinic lead, Kaiser Permanente Care Management Institute, Oakland, California.

Michael A. Blazing, MD, associate professor, medicine/cardiology, Duke University, Durham, North Carolina.
American Journal of Managed Care.

aspirin daily, but their use of that medication was not monitored for the study.

STUDY RESULTS

After taking the drugs for two years, the rate of heart attacks and strokes in the next year was reduced by 26 per 1,000 people among those in the high-use group and 15 per 1,000 people in the middle-use group, compared with those in the no-use or just one drug group, the study found.

"This was accomplished by using three inexpensive, well-proven medications that don't have significant side effects," Dr. Dudl said.

The ACE inhibitor used in the study was *lisinopril* (Prinivil, Zestril), given at 20 milligrams (mg) a day, and the statin was *lovastatin* (Altoprev, Mevacor), given at 40 mg daily, but any combination of drugs in the two families could be used, Dr. Dudl said.

IMPLICATIONS

"We went for people with the highest risk, but the program could benefit anybody with atherosclerosis caused by any mechanism, particularly high blood pressure," explained Dr. Dudl. Atherosclerosis is the hardening of arteries that can lead to a heart attack, stroke or other cardiovascular problem.

EXPERT COMMENTARY

Michael A. Blazing, MD, an associate professor of medicine and cardiology at Duke University, said that the study confirms in one large sweep what has been seen in smaller studies of individual preventive drug treatments.

"The key is bundling the drugs and the distribution system," Dr. Blazing said. "Much of the effect is due to getting the drugs to the population that needs them. What they are doing is validating the bits and pieces that have been shown in different studies in different ways. They are also validating the work that shows that individuals who stay on these drugs do better."

info To learn more about risk factors for coronary heart disease, visit the Web site of the American Heart Association, *www.heart.org*, and search "heart disease risk factors."

■ ■ ■ ■

Dangerous Drug Still Sold in US

Meridia (chemical name *sibutramine*) has been banned in Europe because it can cause heart attacks and strokes in people with high blood pressure or heart disease. Meridia is still sold in the US, but it should not be used by people with a history of heart disease, stroke, irregular heartbeat, heart failure, peripheral artery disease or uncontrolled hypertension. Ask your doctor for details.

US Food and Drug Administration, Washington, DC. *www.fda.gov.*

■ ■ ■ ■

Dry Mouth Alert

About 91% of 483 dentists recently surveyed said that patients complaining of dry mouth (*xerostomia*) often take prescription and over-the-counter (OTC) drugs—such as antidepressants, painkillers and antihistamines—that can cause the condition. Symptoms include stringy or foamy saliva and tongue irritation. Reduced saliva often leads to gum disease, tooth decay and even tooth loss.

If you suffer from dry mouth: Ask your doctor about switching to medications that don't cause dry mouth. Also avoid alcohol and caffeine…try an OTC saliva substitute (such as Biotene or Oasis)…and see your dentist twice a year.

Raymond K. Martin, DDS, dentist in private practice, Mansfield, Massachusetts.

Finally! Effective Treatment for Those With Scleroderma

Hospital for Special Surgery news release.

A new study suggests that the cancer drug *imatinib mesylate* (Gleevec) may benefit people with *scleroderma*, a chronic connective tissue disease.

BACKGROUND

No effective treatment currently exists for scleroderma, which affects the skin, blood vessels and often muscles and joints, as well as the gastrointestinal tract, kidneys, heart and lungs. About 300,000 people in the United States have scleroderma, which typically strikes people between the ages of 30 and 50, according to the Scleroderma Foundation.

Gleevec is currently approved in the United States to treat two types of cancer—*chronic myeloid leukemia* and *gastrointestinal stromal tumor.*

THE STUDY

The study included 30 patients with diffuse scleroderma, a widespread, severe form of the disease. They took 400 milligrams of Gleevec a day and were evaluated monthly for 12 months during treatment and were seen for follow-up three months after they stopped taking the drug.

The researchers assessed the effectiveness of the drug treatment by using a tool called the *modified Rodnan skin score*, a measure of how much skin is affected by the disease.

"The skin score seems to be a very good marker of disease status and most scleroderma trials use this as an outcome measure," said study leader Robert Spiera, MD, an associate attending rheumatologist at the Hospital for Special Surgery and an associate professor at Weill Cornell Medical College. They also used two tests to measure patients' lung function. Lung disease is one of the main causes of death in scleroderma patients.

PROMISING RESULTS

Interim findings showed a 23% improvement in skin scores and a 9.6% to 18% improvement in lung function tests.

"The lung function data was really exciting," Dr. Spiera said. "In patients with scleroderma, you usually see lung function tests getting worse over time, and if doctors try a therapy for a year and a patient doesn't get any worse, we get pretty excited. What is amazing to me in this study is that we actually saw improvements in both lung function tests."

The interim results were presented at the American College of Rheumatology annual meeting in Philadelphia. The study received funding and donated drugs from Novartis, which makes Gleevec.

info For more on scleroderma, visit the Web site of the US National Institute of Arthritis and Musculoskeletal and Skin Diseases, *www.niams.nih.gov*, and search "fast facts about scleroderma."

First Ever Drug to Stop Premature Ejaculation

Sciele Pharma Inc. news release.

A spray touted as the first potential treatment for premature ejaculation (PE) has proved effective in a second study, according to the company that developed it.

BACKGROUND

Premature ejaculation affects about one-third of US men aged 18 to 59, which means it's twice as common as erectile dysfunction. No prescription treatments are approved in the United States to treat PE.

THE STUDY

PSD502—which combines the drugs *lidocaine* and *prilocaine*—is sprayed on the head of the penis before intercourse.

The study of men in Canada, Poland and the United States found that those treated with the spray five minutes before intercourse were able to delay ejaculation up to five times longer than those who used a placebo. In addition, men who used the spray and their partners reported improved sexual satisfaction.

The findings, presented recently at the annual meeting of the Sexual Medicine Society of North America, are consistent with those from a previous trial in Europe, according to San Diego-based Sciele Pharma Inc.

"Premature ejaculation can have a powerful negative impact on the emotional and sexual lives of men and their partners," said Stanley E. Althof, PhD, of the Center for Marital and Sexual Health of South Florida. "Recently, the international sexual health community agreed that PE should be defined as ejaculation occurring within approximately one minute of penetration that causes the patient distress. Now we need to work to develop treatments, and these encouraging results with PSD502 seem to be a step in the right direction."

Sciele Pharma plans to seek US Food and Drug Administration approval of the spray.

info To learn more about premature ejaculation, visit the Web site of the American Academy of Family Physicians, *http://familydoctor.org*, and search "premature ejaculation."

New Treatment Works for Alcoholics With Depression

American Psychiatric Association news release.

Combined treatment with the antidepressant *sertraline* (Zoloft) and the alcoholism drug *naltrexone* (ReVia) improves the likelihood that people with both major depression and alcohol dependence will be able to stop drinking, US researchers report.

STUDY FINDINGS

The 14-week study of 170 patients found that 54% of those who received the combined treatment were able to stop drinking, compared with 21% to 28% of patients who received a placebo, sertraline only, or naltrexone only.

The patients who received the combined treatment also went for a longer period of time before they started drinking again—61 days compared with 15 days for patients in the other groups.

The study was published in *The American Journal of Psychiatry*.

IMPLICATIONS

The findings may prove an important advance in the treatment of patients with alcohol dependence and depression, said the University of Pennsylvania researchers who conducted the study.

"When depression and alcohol dependence occur together, each condition has a negative

influence on the outcome of the other, so not only does this pairing of illnesses affect a lot of patients, it also makes the individual disorders worse," said study author Helen Pettinati, PhD. "Combining sertraline and naltrexone could be a practical approach for these patients because both have [US Food and Drug Administration] approval."

info For more information about treatment of alcohol use disorders, visit the American Psychological Association's Web site, *www.apa.org,* and search "alcohol disorders."

Real Relief for Shingles

The FDA has approved Qutenza, a prescription skin patch containing high-dose capsaicin (8%), to treat *postherpetic neuralgia* (chronic pain after a shingles attack).

Recent study: After 402 adults with postherpetic neuralgia wore the patch for one hour, 40% reported a decrease in pain lasting up to 12 weeks—much longer than the over-the-counter capsaicin cream that is currently used.

If you have postherpetic neuralgia: Ask your doctor about Qutenza.

Miroslav Backonja, MD, professor of neurology, anesthesiology and rehabilitation, University of Wisconsin School of Medicine and Public Health, Madison.

New Treatment for COPD

The FDA has approved *tiotropium bromide* inhalation powder (Spiriva HandiHaler) to reduce "exacerbations" (episodes of worsening or new symptoms, such as cough, wheezing or difficulty breathing, lasting three or more days) in patients with chronic obstructive pulmonary disease (COPD), a group of lung diseases that includes emphysema and/or chronic bronchitis.

If you suffer from COPD: Ask your doctor whether once-daily Spiriva is appropriate for you. The current COPD treatment, *fluticasone* and *salmeterol* oral inhalation (Advair), is usually taken twice daily.

Brenda Stodart, PharmD, Division of Drug Information, FDA, Silver Spring, Maryland.

■ ■ ■ ■

New Drug Eases Rheumatoid Arthritis Where Others Fail

Anew drug called Actemra (*tocilizumab*) may help patients with moderate-to-severe rheumatoid arthritis (RA) who have not done well with previous drugs. Most other RA drugs—such as Enbrel, Humira and Remicade—are TNF inhibitors. They block the activity of *tumor necrosis factor*, which promotes the inflammation that causes many symptoms. Actemra blocks the *interleukin-6* (IL-6) receptor, also associated with inflammation.

Beth L. Jonas, MD, rheumatologist and director, Rheumatology Fellowship Training Program, Thurston Arthritis Research Center, University of North Carolina at Chapel Hill.

New Drug May Prevent Fractures, Cancer and More

Steven R. Cummings, MD, professor emeritus, former director, San Francisco Coordinating Center, University of California, San Francisco.
Carolyn Becker, MD, associate professor, medicine, Harvard Medical School and Brigham and Women's Hospital, Boston.
The New England Journal of Medicine.

Anew drug to fight osteoporosis, the bone condition associated with aging and debilitating fractures, reduces the risk of fractures and the risk of some breast cancers, heart disease and stroke, according to a new study.

But, like other anti-osteoporosis drugs already on the market, the drug—called *lasofoxifene*—also boosts the risk of blood clots, the researchers found. Lasofoxifene (the drug's proposed brand name is Fablyn) is not yet approved by the US Food and Drug Administration.

ABOUT THE DRUG

The new drug is in a class of medications known as *selective estrogen-receptor modulators* (SERM), which act like estrogen in some tissues but anti-estrogen in others. "They act like estrogens when binding to bone cells and don't act like estrogen in the breast [thus not 'feeding' any cancers of the breast]," said lead study author Steven R. Cummings, MD.

Another SERM, already on the market, is *raloxifene* (Evista).

THE STUDY

For the study, Dr. Cummings, professor emeritus and former director of the San Francisco Coordinating Center at the University of California, San Francisco, and his team assigned 8,556 women with osteoporosis, ages 59 to 80, to take a daily dose of the drug (either 0.25 milligrams [mg] or 0.5 mg a day) or a placebo for five years. All had a bone mineral density T score of –2.5, which is considered osteoporosis.

In the study, the researchers found that lasofoxifene "reduces the risk of all fractures (spinal and elsewhere), breast cancer, heart disease and stroke," said Dr. Cummings. "Breast cancer by more than half, nonspinal fractures by about a quarter, which is similar to what other drugs have done, stroke and heart disease by a quarter to a third."

The results he cites are all for the higher dose, 0.5 mg a day, when compared with placebo. The higher dose worked better, they found, and is the dose planned for clinical use.

SIDE EFFECTS

When Dr. Cummings looked at adverse events during the follow-up, he found deaths were comparable in the high-dose and placebo group (73 and 65), but more deaths occurred in the low-dose group (90) from any cause.

More women taking the drug developed lung cancer, too—28 compared with four in the placebo group. Dr. Cummings said that may be related to chance. Further studies should help explain this link.

Blood clot risk more than doubled on the drug, they found, a risk similar to what is found with estrogen and other SERMs, although the absolute risk was still small.

The study was published in *The New England Journal of Medicine*.

IMPLICATIONS FOR THE FUTURE

Overall, lasofoxifene looks good, according to Dr. Cummings.

But Carolyn Becker, MD, associate professor or medicine at Harvard Medical School, is taking a wait-and-see approach. "It may turn out to be a dynamite drug, but it's not anything I would rush in to use as a clinician," she said. "There are too many unknowns."

"The big news for osteoporosis is that lasofoxifene also prevents the fractures that cause most of the disability," Dr. Cummings said, referring to nonspinal fractures such as hip, upper arm and pelvis.

But Dr. Becker pointed out that this effect did not kick in until five years, and the absolute risk reductions were small.

ADVICE

Women with osteoporosis should first consider drugs known as *bisphosphonates* (Fosamax and others), Dr. Cummings said, turning to SERM drugs if they are considered at higher risk.

Dr. Cummings has reported receiving consulting fees from pharmaceutical companies including Pfizer, which is developing Fablyn. Dr. Becker reports no such consulting fees.

info To learn more about medications for osteoporosis, visit the Web site of the National Osteoporosis Foundation, *www.nof. org*. Click on "Patient Info" and then choose "Medications & Osteoporosis."

■ ■ ■ ■

Beat Osteoporosis Now!

Osteoporosis patients received one annual dose of intravenous *zoledronic acid* (Reclast)...daily injections of *teriparatide* (Forteo)...or both.

After one year: Lumbar spine bone mass increased by 7.51% in the combination group, 7.05% in the teriparatide group and 4.37% in the zoledronic acid group.

Best: Discuss osteoporosis treatment options with your doctor—the drugs can have unwanted side effects.

Kenneth Saag, MD, MSc, professor of medicine, University of Alabama, Birmingham, and investigator of a study of 388 postmenopausal osteoporosis patients.

■ ■ ■ ■

Pricey Osteoporosis Drug No Better than Cheaper Generics

The medicine *ibandronate* (Boniva) can be taken monthly. Other cheaper drugs in the same class, called *bisphosphonates*, must be taken weekly or daily. But they all are about equally effective at preventing bone fractures—and Boniva costs 10 times as much as *alendronate* (Fosamax). Ask your doctor to consider price when prescribing an osteoporosis medication for you.

Consumer Reports, 101 Truman Ave., Yonkers, New York 10703.

The Amazing Power of Aspirin

Randall S. Stafford, MD, PhD, medical director of Stanford Prevention Research Center, director of the Program on Prevention and Outcomes Practices at the Stanford Prevention Research Center and associate professor of medicine at Stanford University. Dr. Stafford is author or coauthor of more than 110 scientific papers in leading medical journals. He is on the advisory panel of experts of "Aspirin Talks," an educational campaign from the American College of Preventive Medicine.

It costs pennies a pill—but for heart disease and stroke, the number-one and number-three killers of Americans, aspirin can be just as powerfully preventive as more expensive medications, such as cholesterol-lowering statins.

Two-thirds of people at high risk for heart attack and stroke don't take aspirin daily—leading to an estimated yearly death toll of 45,000 people who might have lived if they had taken a low-dose aspirin every day. And recent evidence shows that aspirin also plays a role in fighting colon cancer and possibly other diseases...

PROTECTING DISEASED ARTERIES

If you've had a heart attack, taking aspirin daily reduces your risk for a second attack by 23%. If you have angina—chest pain that signals serious heart disease—daily aspirin reduces heart attack risk by 51%. Type 2 diabetes—which damages arteries, increasing risk for heart attack and stroke—is another reason for daily aspirin. Taking aspirin if you have diagnosed heart disease or are at high risk for heart disease due to type 2 diabetes is called secondary prevention—it's too late to prevent the problem, but you're controlling it.

What to do: If you have heart disease or type 2 diabetes, talk to your doctor about aspirin therapy. The recommended dosage for secondary prevention is 81 milligrams (mg) daily, or one "baby aspirin." There continues to be debate about whether 162 mg daily may be more protective for some people with heart disease or diabetes—ask your doctor.

PREVENTING HEART ATTACK

In March 2009, the US Preventive Services Task Force (USPSTF) recommended the daily use of aspirin for primary prevention—preventing heart attack and stroke in people who don't have diagnosed cardiovascular disease.

Because older age is a risk factor for heart attacks and strokes, the recommendation included all men between the ages of 45 and 79 and all women between the ages of 55 and 79.

Among these groups, the USPSTF said to use aspirin for primary prevention only in cases in which the benefits are likely to outweigh the risks. When aspirin blocks the production of blood-clotting *thromboxane*, it increases the risk for internal bleeding.

The benefits of taking aspirin are likely to be greater than the risks in those with an elevated risk for heart attack and stroke. These risk factors include high total cholesterol, lower than normal HDL (good) cholesterol, high blood pressure, smoking and older age.

Factors that may indicate aspirin is too risky for you include…

•**Recent bleeding from a stomach ulcer or hemorrhagic stroke,** caused by a ruptured blood vessel

•**History of gastrointestinal (GI) bleeding** caused by other nonsteroidal anti-inflammatory drugs (NSAIDs)

•**Taking an anti-inflammatory corticosteroid,** such as *prednisone*

•**Rheumatoid arthritis.**

AGE 80 OR OLDER

The USPSTF didn't include a recommendation for people age 80 or older, because there's not enough scientific evidence to know whether aspirin protects this age group. However, your risk for heart attack and stroke increases with age, so those over 80 are likely to benefit from aspirin, but they also are more likely to have GI or brain bleeding.

What to do: If you're 80 or older, ask your doctor about taking aspirin. You probably shouldn't take it if you have a history of GI bleeding or falls (a head injury is more likely to cause hemorrhagic stroke in someone taking aspirin).

COLON CANCER

A study by researchers at Harvard Medical School published in *The Journal of the American Medical Association* showed that people with colorectal cancer who began taking aspirin regularly after diagnosis had a 29% lower risk of dying from the disease than those who never used aspirin. Researchers also found that those who used aspirin regularly before their diagnosis had a 61% lower risk of dying from the disease. Aspirin reduces inflammation, which may play a role in the progress of colon cancer.

What to do: If you've been diagnosed with colorectal cancer, talk to your doctor about taking aspirin. There is not enough scientific evidence to justify taking aspirin to prevent colorectal cancer.

USING ASPIRIN WISELY

•**Don't worry about the formulation.** In most cases, aspirin doesn't cause GI bleeding because it irritates your GI tract—the bleeding is caused by a systemic effect on COX (see the explanation that follows). That means enteric-coated tablets don't decrease the risk for GI bleeding.

•**Be cautious of blood-thinning supplements.** Fish oil and the herb ginkgo biloba also affect platelets, increasing the risk for internal bleeding. If you're taking aspirin, talk to your doctor about whether it's safe to be taking those supplements.

•**Don't take aspirin and another NSAID at the same time.** Recent research shows that NSAIDs, such as *ibuprofen* and *naproxen* (Aleve, Naprosyn), interfere with aspirin's ability to affect COX. If you take another NSAID, take it four to six hours before or after taking aspirin.

•**Think twice about stopping aspirin before surgery.** Surgeons often ask patients to stop taking aspirin about two weeks before surgery. But if you take aspirin for secondary prevention, the risk for a heart attack may outweigh the risk for additional bleeding during surgery. Ask your physician.

•**If you think you're having a heart attack, call 911 immediately and take aspirin.** Chew an uncoated full-strength (325-mg) aspirin right away. Taking aspirin once a day for the next month can reduce the risk for death by 23% and may significantly reduce damage to the heart.

■ **Also from Randall S. Stafford, MD, PhD...**

How Aspirin Works

Aspirin is *acetylsalicylic acid*—a compound that blocks the action of *cyclooxygenases* (COX), enzymes that are found in every cell.

COX help manufacture *prostaglandins*, hormones that are involved in pain, fever and inflammation. COX also help produce *thromboxane*, which allows cells in the bloodstream called platelets to stick together, forming blood clots.

By impeding prostaglandins, aspirin lowers fever, relieves acute pain such as headache, and eases the soreness that accompanies inflammation. By reducing thromboxane, aspirin helps stop the formation of blood clots, reducing the risk for a heart attack and stroke.

■ ■ ■ ■

Ouch! Naproxen Raises Ulcer Risk

In a new study of 56,515 adults, those who took low-dose (500 milligrams daily) *naproxen* (Aleve)—a nonsteroidal anti-inflammatory drug—were 2.5 times more likely to be hospitalized due to complications from gastric or intestinal ulcers (such as stomach bleeding) than those who did not take the drug.

If you take over-the-counter naproxen: Do so sparingly. If your doctor prescribes naproxen, ask whether you should also take a drug, such as *esomeprazole* (Nexium) or *omeprazole* (Prilosec), to reduce ulcer complications.

Gurkipal Singh, MD, adjunct clinical professor of gastroenterology and hepatology, Stanford University, Palo Alto, California.

■ ■ ■ ■

Stomach-Acid Drugs Raise Food-Poisoning Risk

Medicines that lower production of stomach acid, such as Prevacid and Prilosec, can increase food-poisoning risk by reducing the acid that is the body's natural defense.

Self-defense: If you use these drugs, be especially careful when handling raw meat and poultry, and avoid foods associated with food poisoning, such as raw oysters, raw eggs and unpasteurized milk.

Leo Galland, MD, internist, director, Foundation for Integrated Medicine, New York City. His latest book is *The Fat Resistance Diet* (Broadway). *www.fatresistance diet.com*. Dr. Galland is a recipient of the Linus Pawling award.

Timing Is Everything...

William J.M. Hrushesky, MD, principal investigator at the Chronobiology and Oncology Research Laboratory at the Dorn Research Institute VA Medical Center in Columbia, South Carolina. He also is a professor of cell development and biology at the University of South Carolina School of Medicine in Columbia and the author of *Circadian Cancer Therapy* (CRC).

Few doctors talk to their patients about the best time of day to take medication or undergo surgery, but it can make a big difference. *Examples...*

If you have high blood pressure, it's usually best to take slow-release medication at bedtime. For osteoarthritis, your pain reliever needs to work hardest in the afternoon. Why does the timing matter?

Virtually every bodily function—including blood pressure, heart rate and body temperature—is influenced by our circadian (24-hour) clocks. External factors, such as seasonal rhythms, also play a role in certain medical conditions.

For optimal results when treating…

HIGH BLOOD PRESSURE

There are both daily and seasonal fluctuations in blood pressure. It's normal for systolic pressure (top number) to drop several points during the warm months, then to rise again in winter. Cold weather is thought to trigger the release of substances known as *catecholamines*, which may raise blood pressure.

Most people experience a sharp rise (about 10 to 25 points, systolic) in blood pressure when they first get up in the morning—this contributes to the morning peak in heart attacks.

Research shows that heart attacks are 40% to 50% more likely to occur during the first six hours after a person awakens than later in the day or during sleep. Blood pressure declines at night and reaches its lowest level during sleep.

With standard treatments for high blood pressure, a patient might experience consistent reductions in pressure, including during times when the reduction isn't needed.

For best results: Ask your doctor about taking a drug that works in sync with the daily rhythms of your blood pressure. For example, the calcium channel blocker *verapamil* (such as Verelan PM) and timed-release *diltiazem* (Cardizem LA)…as well as the beta-blocker *propranolol* (InnoPran XL) are all designed to be taken at bedtime.

With each of these slow-release, long-acting drugs, none of the active ingredient is released during the first four hours. Most of the drug effects occur between 6 am and noon, when blood pressure tends to be most elevated.

OSTEOARTHRITIS

Caused by inflammation due to wear and tear on the joints, osteoarthritis is almost always more painful late in the day after a full day of activity using damaged joints. A nonsteroidal anti-inflammatory drug (NSAID), such as *ibuprofen* (Advil), is the most commonly recommended pain reliever with significant anti-inflammatory properties.

For best results: Ask your doctor about taking a dose at noon…again in the afternoon…and at bedtime. This schedule allows drug levels to peak at about the same time that the symptoms are flaring.

Helpful: To help reduce the risk for NSAID side effects, such as gastrointestinal bleeding and ulcer, take each NSAID dose with food. Long-term use of NSAIDs has been linked to increased risk for heart attack, stroke and kidney disease, so if you regularly take an NSAID, discuss these potential risks with your physician. Also ask about taking occasional NSAID "drug holidays" (stopping use of the drug for a day or so each week). Do not discontinue any other drug without asking your doctor.

RHEUMATOID ARTHRITIS

NSAIDs also reduce pain caused by rheumatoid arthritis, an autoimmune disease in which the body's immune system "attacks" joints. This type of arthritis tends to hurt more in the morning. After the hormone cortisol, which suppresses the immune system, peaks at about 4 a.m. each day, the immune system reactivates, inflaming joints by 8 a.m. to 10 a.m.

For best results: Take your regular pain reliever dose at bedtime to help reduce morning pain and stiffness associated with rheumatoid arthritis. Taking the medication at night means that the drug reaches effective levels while you sleep, which helps reduce pain when you awaken. Keep another dose on your nightstand to take before getting up in the morning if necessary. Eat a few crackers first to help prevent stomach distress.

DIABETES

Physiological reactions that are more detrimental at night than in the morning are believed to play a role in both type 2 diabetes and metabolic syndrome—a constellation of conditions that includes insulin resistance (in which the body's cells don't use insulin properly), abdominal obesity, high blood pressure and elevated LDL "bad" cholesterol.

The body produces and uses insulin most effectively in the daytime hours and its metabolism is most active during the day. The liver, pancreas and muscles are better able to utilize blood sugar (glucose) and burn calories when metabolism is high. Because metabolism slows at night, someone who eats a lot of snack foods, for example, at night will be unable to efficiently remove the resulting glucose and fats from the blood. Over time, this can cause a chronic rise in insulin and cholesterol and may lead to metabolic syndrome.

For best results: People with metabolic syndrome or diabetes (or those who are at increased risk for either condition due to obesity or high blood pressure) should synchronize their meals with their metabolic rhythms. Consume most of your calories early in the day. Eat a relatively light supper—for example, a piece of fish, a green salad and vegetables—preferably at least a few hours before going to bed. Diabetes drugs, such as insulin, should be taken in anticipation of daytime calories and carbohydrates.

CANCER

Research has identified ways in which the circadian rhythm affects the toxicity and effectiveness of cancer treatments. *For example...*

•**Chemotherapy.** In an important study involving patients with colon cancer, researchers found a measurable response rate of more than 50% in those treated at an optimal time, compared with only 32% in those treated at other times. Patients in both groups were given exactly the same drug and the same dose. The only difference was the timing of treatment.

What accounts for this difference? All cells undergo replication, repair and *apoptosis* (cell death) at predictable times of day. By pinpointing these times, doctors can deliver chemotherapeutic drugs when cancer cells are most vulnerable—and when healthy cells are more resistant to toxic effects.

For best results: Discuss the optimal timing of your chemotherapy with your oncologist, who will determine this, in part, based on the anticancer drugs used.

•**Cancer surgery.** Several different studies have found that the timing of cancer surgery can significantly affect outcomes in women.

For example, research has found that performing breast cancer surgery in women shortly after ovulation can improve the cure frequency

between two and two-and-a-half times. The reason may be that elevated progesterone (which coincides with ovulation) may inhibit the production of enzymes that facilitate the *metastasis* (spread) of cancer.

Conversely, during the first half of the menstrual cycle (the *follicular phase*), there may be an increase in *angiogenesis*, the growth of blood vessels that supply tumors. There also may be delays in cancer-cell death or changes in immune activity.

For best results: If you are a woman facing cancer surgery, discuss its timing within your menstrual cycle with your doctor. The optimal timing depends on the type of cancer and the individual patient.

■ ■ ■ ■

Never Use a Spoon to Measure Meds

Mayo Clinic study participants were asked to pour one teaspoon of cold medicine into ordinary kitchen spoons. They either under- or overpoured mainly because kitchen spoons hold more or less than an official-sized teaspoon.

Best: Use a measuring cap or a dosing spoon when administering medication.

Mark A. Stengler, NMD, naturopathic medical doctor in private practice, La Jolla, California...adjunct associate clinical professor at the National College of Natural Medicine, Portland, Oregon...author of many books, including *The Natural Physician's Healing Therapies* and coauthor of *Prescription for Natural Cures* (both from Bottom Line Books)... and author of the *Bottom Line/Natural Healing* newsletter.

■ ■ ■ ■

Where to Put Your Patch

For the medication in a transdermal patch to work effectively, you must periodically alter the site. Where you place it and how often you move it depend on the particular drug being used. Each of the eight or so skin-patch medications on the market has its own specific guidelines, so be sure to read the instructions carefully and discuss correct usage with your doctor or pharmacist. You also must refer to the instructions if your patch becomes loose, falls off or is cut or punctured—otherwise, you may receive too small or too large a dose of medication.

Jack M. Rosenberg, PharmD, PhD, professor of pharmacy practice and pharmacology, Long Island University, Brooklyn, New York.

■ ■ ■ ■

FDA Warns Against Two Zicam Nasal Products

More than 100 people have reported losing their sense of smell after using intranasal zinc products. The FDA advises consumers to stop using and discard Zicam Cold Remedy Swabs (regular and kids size) and Zicam Cold Remedy Nasal Gel. The warning did not involve zinc taken orally.

For refunds: Contact Zicam, 877-942-2626, *www.zicam.com/refunds.*

Siobhan DeLancey, MPH, press officer, US Food and Drug Administration, Silver Spring, Maryland.

Are You Taking a Drug That Isn't FDA-Approved For Your Illness?

G. Caleb Alexander, MD, MS, assistant professor, department of medicine, University of Chicago, Chicago, and adjunct research associate, department of pharmacy practice, University of Illinois at Chicago School of Pharmacy.

Are the drugs your doctor is prescribing safe and effective? Who knows? In a recent survey by researchers at the University of Virginia, the University of Chicago and the University of Illinois at Chicago, almost half of physicians who responded mistakenly believed that at least one use of a drug listed in the survey was FDA-approved, when in fact, it wasn't. So-called off-label prescribing is both legal and common—but this survey's findings may mean that doctors are prescribing drugs when there is insufficient evidence of their efficacy and safety for a specific purpose.

CONFUSION IS COMMON

University of Chicago lead researcher G. Caleb Alexander, MD, MS, and his colleagues conducted

a national random-sample survey of doctors. A total of 1,199 physicians (599 primary care doctors and 600 psychiatrists) were sent questionnaires and nearly half responded. They were asked about 22 drug-indication pairs (i.e., particular drugs prescribed for particular conditions) and correctly identified the FDA-approved indications of just over half the drug-indication pairs. They misidentified the FDA-approval status of the rest of the drug uses examined—and that may lead them to prescribing that puts patients at serious risk. *For example...*

●**Nearly one in five thought *quetiapine* (Seroquel) was FDA-approved for dementia and agitation,** when in fact the drug carries a strong "black box" warning that it is dangerous for elderly people with dementia.

●**One in three who prescribed *lorazepam* (Ativan) for chronic anxiety** incorrectly believed that it was FDA-approved for this purpose—in truth, the FDA advises against using it for anxiety, because it is a strong drug with a high risk of addiction.

Dr. Alexander said that there are many reasons why doctors may not be fully aware of the FDA-label status. "The amount of information that physicians must master is vast, the evidence base is constantly changing, and some would argue that physicians should focus on the evidence and not the FDA label," he noted. "In addition, some of the drug uses that we examined may have been ones that were actually promoted by the pharmaceutical industry, which leads to confusion on the part of physicians regarding the FDA-approval status."

This is dangerous territory. "The results indicate an urgent need for more effective ways to inform physicians about the level of evidence supporting off-label drug use—especially for common off-label uses that are ineffective or carry unacceptable risks of harm," warns Dr. Alexander. These findings were published online in *Pharmacoepidemiology and Drug Safety.*

REVIEW YOUR MEDICATIONS

Off-label prescribing can allow physicians to anticipate valuable new drug uses before formal FDA approval and also can offer an alternative to patients who do not respond to standard treatments. At the bare minimum, however, doctors should know whether they are writing a prescription for an approved condition or an off-label use—in the latter case, it would be best if the prescription were then subject to added scrutiny before it was written. Physicians should carefully consider the safety and effectiveness off-label, especially as compared with approved medications.

Dr. Alexander explains what steps consumers can take to make sure that doctors prescribe the most appropriate medications, whether approved or off-label. He advises consumers to ask questions about drugs their doctors prescribe—their FDA-approval status, the scientific evidence to support their use, risks and benefits, side effects, potential drug and food interactions, dosage, cost, etc. Since there may not be time to discuss every drug at each doctor visit, Dr. Alexander notes that these questions are most important for treatments that are new on the market. It's also a good idea to do your own research to ensure that you are as educated as possible. You have a right to know all about the medications you take so you can work with your doctors to determine those that are safest and most effective in meeting your individual health-care needs.

Emotional Well-Being

Severely Depressed Gain Most from Antidepressants

ntidepressants seem to be most effective for the people with the most severe symptoms of depression, new research suggests.

Individuals with mild-to-moderate symptoms may fare no better on antidepressants than on a placebo, say the authors of a new analysis published in *The Journal of the American Medical Association*.

But the findings are not actually that surprising, said one expert, and don't necessarily mean that people with mild-to-moderate depression should not try antidepressants.

PREVIOUS ANTIDEPRESSANT STUDY

The findings follow on the heels of another study, published in the *Archives of General Psychiatry,* reporting that one in five US adults fails to get minimum guideline-recommended treatment for depression, and even fewer receive optimal care in minority populations such as Mexican Americans.

NEW STUDY

The authors of the more recent study reviewed results from six previously completed large, randomized and placebo-controlled trials looking at major and minor depression.

Virtually no difference was noted between placebo and medication effects in people with mild-to-moderate depression. But as depression severity increased, so did the drug benefits.

According to the study authors, most studies showing a benefit to antidepressants focus on more severely depressed individuals.

IMPLICATION

They suggested that patients and health-care providers should be aware that antidepressant therapy might not be as beneficial in people with milder forms of the condition.

Gregory Asnis, MD, director, anxiety and depression program, Montefiore Medical Center, New York City. *The Journal of the American Medical Association.*

Many of the study authors reported receiving funding from different pharmaceutical companies, although the National Institute of Mental Health funded this study.

EXPERT COMMENTARY

"I'm not sure this is a finding that's counter to giving medication to people with depression that's mild to moderate," said Gregory Asnis, MD, director of the anxiety and depression program at Montefiore Medical Center in New York City.

Even the placebo group showed a response and, over time, the placebo effect tends to wear off, Dr. Asnis explained, whereas true drug responders continue to benefit, a difference that might not be evident in the time periods involved in the study.

"The bottom line is even though the benefits of a drug compared with placebo may be most demonstrated in severely ill people, one question is what happens in time," he said.

info To learn more about antidepressants, visit the Web site of the National Institute of Mental Health, *www.nimh.nih.gov,* and search "What medications are used to treat depression."

■ ■ ■ ■

88% of People Don't Get the Needed Treatment

An estimated 5% of Americans suffer from persistent depression or anxiety disorders. Among this group, only 12% got both medication and counseling—the appropriate care for these conditions.

Best: If you feel depressed or anxious for more than two weeks, make sure to see a mental health professional.

Alexander S. Young, MD, professor of psychiatry, University of California, Los Angeles and leader of a study of 1,642 people with mood disorders.

■ ■ ■ ■

Depression–Migraine Connection

Twenty-five percent of people who have migraines also suffer from depression—versus only 13% of people who do not get

migraines. Migraines are known to have a strong genetic basis—which may be linked to the genetic tendency to develop clinical depression.

Best: Migraine sufferers should discuss any signs of depression with their doctors.

Gisela M. Terwindt, MD, PhD, assistant professor, neurology, Leiden University Medical Centre, the Netherlands, and coauthor of a study of 2,652 people, including 360 with migraines, published in *Neurology.*

Depression Can Make Pain Worse

Elsevier news release.

Being depressed can make real physical pain feel worse, British researchers have found.

Noting that pain and depression often occur at the same time, the current observation blends two competing schools of thought, in which some believe that pain is "all in the head" while others contend that pain is "all in the body."

THE STUDY

To see how pain and depression might intersect, the research team—led by the University of Oxford's Chantal Berna, MD—used brain imaging to conduct pain tests on healthy participants who were induced to feel sad.

A depressed mood appeared to affect brain nerve circuitry responsible for emotion, resulting in a stronger perception of pain, according to the report published in Biological Psychiatry.

"When the healthy people were made sad by negative thoughts and depressing music, we found that their brains processed pain more emotionally, which lead to them finding the pain more unpleasant," Dr. Berna said.

THEORY ON PAIN/DEPRESSION LINK

Dr. Berna's team theorized that one's ability to control the negative emotions linked to pain are short-circuited by depression, leading to a bigger punch when pain hits. In other words, depression may not only be a consequence of being in pain. It might actually exacerbate pain, making it worse than it would be for those in a positive frame of mind.

"Our research suggests depressed mood leads to maladaptive changes in brain function associated with pain, and that depressed mood itself could be a target for treatment by medicines or psychotherapy in this context," Dr. Berna explained.

TREATING PAIN IN DEPRESSED PEOPLE

Following this line of research, the next step would be to study patients with chronic pain, because they often also suffer from depression, the researchers noted. The goal would be to find ways to more effectively treat the millions of people worldwide who experience chronic pain and depression, the authors explained.

info For more on pain and depression, visit the National Pain Foundation Web site, *www.nationalpainfoundation.org*. Type "pain and depression" into the search box.

■ ■ ■ ■

Eat to Beat Depression

Spanish researchers have found that depression was almost 30% less likely to occur in those who best adhered to a Mediterranean-style diet. The same inflammation that occurs in those with heart disease affects those with depression, the researchers believe.

Also postulated: Olive oil enhances the amount of *serotonin*, the neurotransmitter in the brain associated with feelings of well-being.

Diet details: *www.mayoclinic.com* (search for "Mediterranean diet").

Mark A. Stengler, NMD, naturopathic medical doctor in private practice, La Jolla, California…adjunct associate clinical professor at the National College of Natural Medicine, Portland, Oregon…author of many books, including *The Natural Physician's Healing Therapies* and coauthor of *Prescription for Natural Cures* (both from Bottom Line Books)… and author of the *Bottom Line/Natural Healing* newsletter.

■ **Also from Mark Stengler, NMD…**

Fish Oil Works as Well as Drugs

Results of the largest-ever trial of omega-3 supplements for depression, the Omega-3D Trial, found that fish oil supplements (1,050

milligrams, or mg, daily of *eicosapentaenoic acid*, or EPA) improved depression symptoms as much as is reported by those taking prescription drugs—particularly those with major depression who did not also have an anxiety disorder. Speak to a physician about switching from a prescription medication to fish oil that has at least 1,050 mg of EPA, the component that helps depression. The amount of *docosahexaenoic acid* (DHA) doesn't affect depression.

Nondrug Alternatives to Antidepressants

James S. Gordon, MD, founder and director of the Center for Mind–Body Medicine, *www.cmbm.org*, and a clinical professor in the departments of psychiatry and family medicine at the Georgetown University School of Medicine, both in Washington, DC. He is the former chairman of the White House Commission on Complementary and Alternative Medicine Policy and the author of *Unstuck: Your Guide to the Seven-Stage Journey Out of Depression* (Penguin).

If you suffer from depression and seek treatment from a conventional psychiatrist or general practice physician, odds are you will receive a prescription for an antidepressant.

However, your doctor most likely will not tell you about any of the research showing that these drugs may be less effective than we've been led to believe.

Important recent finding: After analyzing published and unpublished data, researchers reported in the journal *Public Library of Science—Medicine* that four widely prescribed antidepressants—*fluoxetine* (Prozac), *venlafaxine* (Effexor), *paroxetine* (Paxil) and *nefazodone* (Serzone)—were no more effective in treating most forms of depression than placebos. Only when used to treat patients who were "very severely depressed" were the drugs more effective than placebos.

Also, it's widely known that many antidepressants can cause side effects, such as headache, weight gain and erectile dysfunction, but many people are unaware that discontinuing these drugs can lead to irritability, sweating, diarrhea and other symptoms.

Caution: Never stop taking an antidepressant without the supervision of a doctor.

OVERLOOKED CAUSES

I see depression as often being a "wakeup call" that a person's life is out of balance. However, it also can be a red flag for an undetected physical illness, so see a primary care physician if you suffer from a low mood that lasts for more than two weeks.

Serious conditions such as diabetes, heart disease, thyroid problems and cancer are widely known to affect mood, but other physical causes of depression often are missed. *Among them...*

•**Small intestine bacterial overgrowth.** Researchers and clinicians have discovered that gastrointestinal problems are sometimes associated with depression. "Friendly" bacteria, which can be reduced by stress, help control harmful bacteria and may improve mood by enhancing absorption of nutrients.

If you have flatulence, diarrhea or abdominal pain along with a low mood, try taking probiotic capsules daily containing 2 billion to 3 billion *lactobacillus* and *bifidus* organisms. Probiotics can be taken indefinitely to replenish the healthful bacteria in your gut.

•**Chronic yeast overgrowth.** Prolonged use of certain drugs, such as antibiotics, and compromised immunity (due to cancer therapy, for example) often lead to yeast infections.

If you have symptoms of a yeast infection, such as itching or rash on the vagina or penis ...or white patches in the mouth (thrush), ask your doctor about testing for this type of infection. If the results are positive, your doctor will probably prescribe an antifungal drug, such as *fluconazole* (Diflucan).

Also, consider following a yeast-free diet (no fermented products, such as wine, certain cheeses and soy sauce...or sugary foods—all of which are believed to promote yeast growth).

MY NONDRUG APPROACH

Any practice that boosts mood—including exercise, meditation, acupuncture and psychotherapy—can effect lasting, positive changes in the brain. Such changes include increases in certain brain chemicals (such as *serotonin* and *norepinephrine*) and positive alterations in brain physiology associated with optimism and happiness.

Even when an antidepressant seems to help, it may be masking your symptoms and should be used, in my opinion, only as an adjunct to a comprehensive program including the strategies described below.

In my 40 years of practice, hundreds of my patients have experienced significant and long-lasting relief from depression after following a nondrug approach.

Important: In rare cases, I do recommend antidepressant medication to my patients in life-threatening emergencies and when nondrug approaches have been tried unsuccessfully.

But to uncover and truly heal many of the underlying causes of depression, I recommend whenever possible working with a psychotherapist or physician who uses a nondrug approach, including...

•**"Calming" tool.** A calming tool (such as slow, deep breathing) not only lowers levels of the depression-promoting stress hormone cortisol, but also reduces blood pressure and heart rate. You can perform slow, deep breathing on a daily schedule (start with three to five minutes per session, three to five times daily) and also use it whenever you feel agitated or overwhelmed.

What to do: Sit quietly in a comfortable chair and breathe slowly and deeply, in through your nose and out through your mouth. Let your belly be soft, repeating "soft" to yourself as you breathe in and "belly" as you exhale.

•**Energizing exercise.** Traditional forms of aerobic exercise, such as walking, jogging or cycling, have been shown to improve mood for some depressed people as well as, or better than, antidepressants.

I often also prescribe "energizing" exercise, which helps move you out of the lethargy that so often accompanies depression. This may include yoga or a sequence of shaking and dancing. Yoga allows the body to relax and emotions to be released as you stretch...vigorous shaking breaks up stress-induced physical and emotional patterns...and dancing allows your body to move freely.

What to do: Try moving your body freely to any rhythmic music that you enjoy for five to 10 minutes daily. Even those with physical limitations, such as people who are bedridden, can move at their own pace and capacity.

Helpful: Prepare your own CD or tape with five to 10 minutes of fast, rhythmic music for shaking. It may seem silly at first, but shake from your feet up through your slightly bent knees to your shoulders and head. Follow with a minute or two of silence, during which you can relax and be aware of your body and your breath. Continue with three to five minutes of movement to rhythmic music that you love.

Also helpful: Do not perform these exercises within two hours of bed. The best time is first thing in the morning or early evening. Build up to 20 minutes a day.

•**Light therapy.** Seasonal affective disorder (SAD) is widely recognized but still tends to be overlooked by doctors who treat people with depression. If your spirits decline in the winter (when most people get less sun exposure) and improve when the days lengthen, consider sitting in front of a light box that supplies 10,000 lux of full-spectrum light (that simulates natural light) for 30 minutes every morning. Light boxes are available at *www.sunbox.com* (800-548-3968) and *www.fullspectrumsolutions.com* (888-574-7014).

•**Vitamin D.** Many people who are depressed have nutritional deficiencies that contribute to their low mood. In addition to taking a multivitamin and multimineral supplement, it's important that you get enough vitamin D. It is produced in the body as a result of sun exposure, but there is increasing evidence that low levels of this vitamin are often present in people who suffer from depression. However, many physicians are unaware of this.

Ask your doctor for a blood test to check your vitamin D level. Depending on the results, he/she may prescribe a dose that is significantly higher (for example, 2,000 international units daily) than the dose provided in a multivitamin.

•**Omega-3 fatty acids.** Numerous studies have linked high dietary intake of omega-3s with decreased incidence of depression—and shown a direct positive effect of omega-3 supplements on depression. In addition to increasing your intake of omega-3–rich fish (such as salmon, sardines and mackerel), I suggest taking supplements totaling about 3,000 mg of omega-3s daily, divided in two equal doses.

Caution: A dose this high may have a blood-thinning effect, so consult your doctor if you take a blood-thinning drug.

Money Can't Buy Happiness...but Psychotherapy Can

University of Warwick news release.

Psychological therapy may be much more effective at making people happy than getting a raise or winning a lottery prize, suggests an English study.

THE STUDY

Researchers analyzed data on thousands of people who provided information about their mental well-being and found that the increase in happiness from a four-month course of therapy (at a cost of about $1,300) was so significant that it would take a pay raise of more than $41,542 to achieve an equal boost in well-being.

That suggests that therapy could be as much as 32 times more cost-effective at improving well-being than simply getting more money, the researchers said.

The study was published online in the journal *Health Economics, Policy and Law.*

IMPLICATION

"We have shown that psychological therapy could be much more cost effective than financial compensation at alleviating psychological distress," said study author Chris Boyce, PhD, of the University of Warwick. "This is not only important in courts of law, where huge financial rewards are the default way in which pain and suffering are compensated, but has wider implications for public health and well-being.

"Often the importance of money for improving our well-being and bringing greater happiness is vastly overvalued in our societies," Dr. Boyce explained. The benefits of having good mental health, on the other hand, are often not fully appreciated and people do not realize the powerful effect that psychological therapy can have on improving our well-being, he added.

info To learn more about emotional health, visit the American Academy of Family Physicians Web site, *http://familydoctor.org*, and search "keeping your emotional health."

■ ■ ■ ■

Pumpkin Seeds Boost Mood

Like chocolate, pumpkin seeds are a good source of the amino acid *tryptophan,* which improves mood—but pumpkin seeds don't have the sugar that chocolate does, and one ounce of pumpkin seeds contains about half the daily requirement of magnesium, which strengthens bones. Sprinkle toasted seeds on soups and salads, or put raw, unsalted seeds on the tops of muffins before baking.

Melina B. Jampolis, MD, physician nutrition specialist, San Francisco, and author of The Busy Person's Guide to Permanent Weight Loss *(Thomas Nelson).* www.DrMelina.com.

■ ■ ■ ■

Watch for Warning Signs of Suicide

Rates of suicide are increasing among both men and women ages 40 to 64. The current economic malaise could be a contributing factor.

Warning signs: Acting highly pessimistic, hopeless or angry…increasing alcohol or drug use …making impulsive, out-of-character decisions …getting rid of previously prized possessions… talking about wanting to die…withdrawing from friends, family and society…mood changes. If you notice any of these warning signs in someone you know, contact a mental health professional or call 800-273-TALK, a free 24-hour hotline sponsored by the Substance Abuse and Mental Health Services Administration.

Holly Wilcox, PhD, assistant professor of psychiatry and public health, Johns Hopkins School of Medicine, Baltimore, and coauthor of a study published in American Journal of Preventive Medicine.

■ ■ ■ ■

DHEA Helps You Cope with Stress

Soldiers who had higher levels of the hormone *dehydroepiandrosterone* (DHEA) were better able to cope with extreme stress than those who had less of the hormone, say researchers at Yale University and the Veterans Administration National Center for Post-Traumatic Stress Disorder. DHEA is secreted by the adrenal glands in response to stress. Have a blood test to measure DHEA. If levels are low, both men and women can work with a holistic physician to supplement.

C.A. Morgan III, et al., "Relationships Among Plasma Dehydroepiandrosterone and Dehydroepiandrosterone Sulfate, Cortisol, Symptoms of Dissociation, and Objective Performance in Humans Exposed to Underwater Navigation Stress," Biological Psychiatry.

■ ■ ■ ■

Breathing Trick Reduces Stress

Close your eyes, take in a deep breath while thinking the word *calm*, then exhale while thinking the word *down*. Repeat several times— giving yourself the message to calm down.

Prevention, 33 E. Minor St., Emmaus, Pennsylvania 18098.

IBS Breakthroughs

Brian E. Lacy, MD, PhD, associate professor of medicine at Dartmouth Medical School in Hanover, New Hampshire, and director of the gastrointestinal motility laboratory at Dartmouth–Hitchcock Medical Center in Lebanon, New Hampshire. He is the author of *Making Sense of IBS* (Johns Hopkins).

If you're among the estimated one in six American adults who suffers from chronic abdominal pain or discomfort due to irritable bowel syndrome (IBS), you know that effective, long-lasting treatment remains elusive.

Good news: The American College of Gastroenterology recently published a review of the most effective treatments, including dietary approaches, nondrug therapies and medications, that should finally give relief to people with IBS.

DO YOU HAVE IBS?

With IBS, the nerves that control the gastrointestinal tract are hypersensitive—that is, sensations that other people wouldn't notice, including those produced by the ordinary process of digestion, are amplified and often painful.

Research has shown that many times IBS begins after a severe bout of digestive upset caused by a bacterial or viral infection, such as "stomach flu" or "traveler's diarrhea"—perhaps because such infections temporarily or permanently affect nerves in the gastrointestinal tract.

What most people don't know: Researchers have found that people with a history of abuse (physical, emotional or sexual) are at heightened risk for IBS—probably due to stress on the intestinal nervous system.

Diagnosis of IBS can be tricky because symptoms, including abdominal pain, bloating and troublesome bowel patterns (frequent or persistent bouts of diarrhea, constipation or both, generally occurring at least three days a month), often wax and wane in severity. So-called "flares" (episodes of severe symptoms) may occur weeks, months—or even years—apart.

IBS symptoms that may be missed: Mucus in the stool or straining during, or a feeling of incomplete evacuation after, a bowel movement.

If you think you may have IBS: See your primary care doctor. IBS almost always can be identified with a standard history and physical exam.

WHEN FOOD IS THE TRIGGER

Lactose intolerance (the inability to digest dairy sugar) can lead to misdiagnosis because its classic symptoms—bloating and diarrhea—mimic those caused by IBS.

My advice: If your digestive problems seem to worsen when you consume dairy products, follow an elimination diet.

What to do: Go without all dairy products for seven to 10 days—and slowly reintroduce each type of dairy product, such as yogurt or cheese, to see how much you can tolerate before symptoms return.

IBS food triggers that often are overlooked—try the elimination diet (as described above) with each…

•**Soft drinks and other high-fructose drinks and foods.** Fructose—a sugar commonly added to carbonated soft drinks and sports drinks and naturally occurring in fruit juices and high-sugar fruits (such as dried fruits)—can cause bloating, gas and diarrhea in people with IBS.

•**Caffeine.** It stimulates the digestive tract and may cause cramps and more frequent bowel movements in people with IBS.

THE FIBER FACTOR

For many people with IBS—especially those with recurrent constipation—adequate fiber intake (25 milligrams [mg] to 30 mg per day) helps relieve symptoms. If you are not consuming this much fiber, increase your intake of fruits and whole grains or take a fiber supplement containing *psyllium* (such as Metamucil or Konsyl).

Fiber-rich foods I recommend most often: Raspberries, artichokes, green peas, almonds, oatmeal, oat bran and whole-grain bread.

Important: IBS patients who have recurrent diarrhea should limit fiber intake to about 10 grams daily and avoid leafy greens and cruciferous vegetables (such as cauliflower) because high-fiber foods can worsen symptoms in these patients.

BEST ALTERNATIVE APPROACHES

If dietary changes (described above) do not relieve IBS symptoms, there is credible scientific evidence to support the use of two natural remedies for IBS…

•**Peppermint oil.** In enteric-coated capsule form, peppermint oil appears to relax smooth muscle in the gastrointestinal tract and therefore reduce IBS abdominal pain caused by muscle spasms. For dosage, follow label instructions.

•**Probiotics.** Probiotics augment the "friendly" bacteria in the large intestine. Probiotic dietary supplements containing the *Bifidobacterium* species are worth trying when bloating and diarrhea are prominent. Look for probiotic supplements providing at least 100 million colony-forming units per dose. Be patient—it may take up to three months to produce substantial benefits.

BEST IBS MEDICATIONS

If your IBS persists, there are medication options for…

•**Diarrhea.** Try an antidiarrheal medication, such as the over-the-counter (OTC) product *loperamide* (Imodium) or the prescription drug *diphenoxylate* and *atropine* (Lomotil). For diarrhea and abdominal pain, consider adding a low-dose of a tricyclic antidepressant, such as *imipramine* (Tofranil) or *amitriptyline* (Elavil). These antidepressants may affect how the brain interprets pain.

•**Pain and bloating.** A tricyclic antidepressant often reduces discomfort and other symptoms, including diarrhea, pain and bloating, to a tolerable level. If the drug causes side effects, such as dry mouth or dizziness, a *selective serotonin reuptake inhibitor* (SSRI), such as *citalopram* (Celexa) or *fluoxetine* (Prozac), can be used, but there is less proof that SSRIs are effective for IBS symptoms.

•**Constipation.** If you're consuming adequate levels of fiber (described earlier) but still have constipation, you may want to try an OTC laxative, such as *polyethylene glycol* (Miralax) or Milk of Magnesia for seven to 14 days. (See your doctor if symptoms persist after that trial period.) For more extended periods of treatment, the prescription medication *lubiprostone* (Amitiza) has been shown to be effective for IBS with constipation.

■ ■ ■ ■

Click Your Way to a Great Night's Sleep

For five weeks, 118 adults with chronic insomnia received either no treatment or online cognitive behavioral therapy (CBT), which included multiple strategies, such as modifying anxiety-provoking thoughts about sleep.

Result: 81% of the CBT participants reported at least mild improvement in sleep, and 35% of participants rated their insomnia as much or very much improved.

Theory: CBT teaches strategies for coping with worries and an overactive mind.

If you suffer from chronic insomnia: Ask your doctor about CBT. Online insomnia treatment is available at *http://healthcoach.myselfhelp. com* for $20 a month. Click on "Sleep better."

Norah Vincent, PhD, associate professor, department of clinical health psychology, University of Manitoba, Winnipeg, Canada.

■ ■ ■ ■

Better Sleep, Better Marriage

When 29 couples were tracked for seven days, the women's negative feelings about interactions with their partners during the day were associated with poor sleep that night for themselves and their partners. For men, poor sleep was associated with negative feelings about interactions with their partners the next day.

Theory: Daytime interactions both affect—and are affected by—sleep quality.

Self-defense: Avoid disputes on days when you or your partner have not slept well the night before.

Brant Hasler, PhD, postdoctoral fellow, department of psychiatry, University of Pittsburgh Medical School, Pittsburgh.

■ ■ ■ ■

Breaking Up Is Hard On Your Health

Compared with married people, middle-aged divorced or widowed people had 20% more chronic health conditions (including heart disease, diabetes and cancer)…those who had divorced and remarried had 12% more chronic conditions.

Implication: Some health problems may reflect stressors, such as a divorce or death of a spouse.

Linda J. Waite, PhD, director, Center on Demography and Economies of Aging, National Opinion Research Center, University of Chicago, and coauthor of a study of 8,652 people ages 51 to 61.

■ ■ ■ ■

Kiss to Lower Stress

When couples kiss, it sets off a multitude of chemical reactions, including a reduction in levels of the stress hormone cortisol.

Also effective: Holding hands while talking together.

Wendy L. Hill, PhD, professor of psychology, Lafayette College, Easton, Pennsylvania, and her student Carey Wilson, author of a thesis on kissing.

Make Kindness Contagious!

Proceedings of the National Academy of Sciences news release.

Acts of kindness spread rapidly, and it takes only a few people acting cooperatively to influence dozens of others, US researchers report.

THE STUDY

When study participants played a game in which they had an opportunity to cooperate with one another, people who received a donation of money were more likely to donate money to other people in future games.

This generated a domino effect in which one person's generosity spread to three other people and then to nine people that those three people interacted with, and then on to many others as the experiment progressed, said the researchers at the University of California, San Diego, and Harvard Medical School.

IMPLICATIONS

This spirit of generosity persists in people who've experienced it.

"You don't go back to being your 'old selfish self,'" said study coauthor James H. Fowler, PhD, an associate professor in the political science department at UC San Diego and Calit2's Center for Wireless and Population Health Studies. He is also coauthor of *Connected: The Surprising Power of Our Social Networks and How They Shape Our Lives* (Little, Brown).

"Though the multiplier in the real world may be higher or lower than what we've found in the lab, personally it's very exciting to learn that kindness spreads to people I don't know or have never met. We have direct experience of giving and seeing people's immediate reactions, but we don't typically see how our generosity cascades through the social network to affect the lives of dozens or maybe hundreds of other people," Dr. Fowler said.

The study was published in the *Proceedings of the National Academy of Sciences*.

info For information on other issues relating to social psychology, visit the Social Psychology Network Web site, *www.socialpsychology.org*.

Smile! You'll Live Longer

Ernest L. Abel, PhD, professor, obstetrics and gynecology and psychology, Wayne State University, Detroit.
Sonja Lyubomirsky, PhD, professor, psychology, University of California, Riverside, and author of *The How of Happiness* (Penguin).
Psychological Science Online First.

If you're always the one in the photo flashing the biggest smile, a new study suggests your odds of living to a ripe old age may be increased.

Researchers from Wayne State University in Detroit evaluated the photographs of 230 Major League Baseball players who started playing before 1950, rating their smiles as nonexistent to full.

"People who had the most intense smiles lived the longest," said Ernest L. Abel, PhD, a professor of obstetrics and gynecology and of psychology at Wayne State.

"The more intense smile, we infer, indicates an underlying happiness, if you will, a more positive attitude," he said. "It's hard to fake an intense smile."

STUDY DETAILS

The researchers gathered other information potentially linked with longevity from a long-standing database on the players, such as college attendance, marital status, birth year and body mass index, an indicator of body fatness calculated from a person's weight and height.

They asked reviewers who didn't know the study's purpose to rate the player's smiles as a 1, 2 or 3, with 1 being no smile, 2 a partial, and 3, a broad full smile, the kind that makes your eyes crinkle.

As of June 1, 2009, all but 46 of the baseball players had died. Researchers looked back to see if the smile intensity in photos was linked with longer life. It was.

On average, the longevity of the nonsmilers was 72.9 years, 75 years for the partial smilers and 79.9 years for the big smilers.

The big smilers had what is known as a Duchenne smile, named after the French neurologist who discovered it. Cheeks and the corners of the mouth are raised, and crows-feet wrinkles appear around the eyes.

After Dr. Abel and his team controlled for variables such as marital status, birth year and body mass index, they found that the smile–longevity link still held. Those with the biggest smile were half as likely to die in a given year than the nonsmilers. The new research builds on previous studies that linked smile intensity in childhood and college yearbook photos with marriage stability or life satisfaction later.

The study was published in *Psychological Science Online First*.

EXPERT REACTION

The study findings make sense to Sonja Lyubomirsky, PhD, a professor of psychology at the University of California, Riverside, and a happiness researcher who wrote *The How of Happiness* (Penguin). "Most likely, the smiles are an indicator of the baseball players' dispositions," she said. The smiles could be reflecting happiness, optimism or resilience, she said.

Experts already have found those who are happier tend to live longer, she said. While it hasn't been proven to be cause-and-effect, she said, evidence is accumulating that happiness as a trait "does predispose people to live longer," she said.

GRIN AND LIVE LONGER

So if you're a sourpuss who scowls at the camera, can grinning help you take a better picture and improve your life expectancy?

That's difficult to say, as it's way beyond the scope of the study. But it may not hurt. According to Dr. Lyubomirsky, "Darwin was the first to suggest that the outward manifestation of an emotion will intensify it."

info For more information about happiness research, visit the Web site of the American Psychological Association, *www.apa.org*. Click on "Psychology Topics" and choose "Emotional Health."

The Healing Power Of Compassion

Charles Raison, MD, clinical director, Mind–Body Program, Emory University School of Medicine…and former Tibetan Buddhist monk Geshe Lobsang Tenzin Negi, PhD, senior lecturer, Emory University, and spiritual director, Drepung Loseling Monastery, all in Atlanta.

Thinking empathetically about other people improves your own health, research shows. Regularly meditating on the well-being of others reduces your body's inflammatory responses to stress—and that lowers your risk for heart disease, diabetes, dementia and other stress-related health problems.

The goal of compassion meditation is to reshape your responses to other people by concentrating on the interconnectedness of every human being.

It's easy: Try the following technique for 10 minutes a day, three to four times per week.

•**Week One.** Sit comfortably, eyes closed, breathing deeply. Think about a time when you were kind to another person—for instance, helping a loved one through a crisis or simply holding a door for a stranger. Recognize your great capacity for goodness. For the last few minutes of your meditation, repeat, "May I be free from suffering…may I find the sources of happiness."

•**Week Two.** Repeat the same exercise, this time building compassion toward a loved one. Think about someone close to you—your mother, daughter, dear friend—and focus on what a blessing she is in your life. Then think about any suffering she is experiencing…and what you can do to ease her pain.

Recite: "May she be free from suffering…may she find the sources of happiness."

• **Week Three.** Think about someone with whom you have only a minor connection—a bus driver, a waiter at your favorite café. How is he a blessing in your life? How might he be suffering? How can you ease his pain (for instance, with a smile and a sincere word of thanks)? Conclude with the recitation.

• **Week Four.** Focus on someone you dislike—a whiny neighbor, a critical cousin. Identify blessings, perhaps as lessons you have learned about being patient or not judging others. Consider how the person may suffer…for instance, from being a quitter or having few friends. Finish with the recitation.

• **Moving Ahead.** Continue to practice several times weekly, incorporating all four types of compassion into your meditation.

Six Ways to Overcome Chronic Illness

Brenda Stockdale, director of mind–body medicine for Georgia Cancer Treatment Center. She completed clinical training at Harvard Medical School's mind–body medicine program and is the author of *You Can Beat the Odds—Surprising Factors Behind Chronic Illness and Cancer* (Sentient).

Scientists have long known that our genes play a role in determining whether we develop various medical conditions ranging from cancer and heart disease to diabetes and dementia.

What's new: Researchers are now discovering that certain genes must be "expressed" (activated) in order to trigger their ability to cause diseases. One of the most significant findings in the emerging field of *epigenetics* (the study of gene expression) is the degree to which the environment—including what we eat and how we respond to stress—affects our genetics. The unchecked flow of stress hormones can lead to inflammation and deregulate immune function,

increasing the likelihood that inborn genetic vulnerabilities to disease will be activated.

Important new finding: People with a 10-year history of workplace stress had five times the incidence of colorectal cancer as people with less job stress. Besides the link to increased cancer risk, stress also has been shown to make cancer patients less responsive to treatment.

If you have any chronic medical condition, here are some important ways to increase your odds of overcoming your illness—or at least keep it in check…

• **Take control.** Researchers who study "survivors"—people who remain healthy after stressful life events that make others sick—have found that one of several traits that they all share is a feeling of being in control of their own lives.

Helpful: To start taking better control of your life, draw a circle and divide it into your various daily activities. Next, identify which activities energize you and which leave you feeling depleted. Then look for ways to spend more time on the former and less on the latter. If certain friends or relatives drain you, modify or limit your time with them. If your job has stressful elements, work on solutions.

• **Commit…to yourself.** Another survivor trait pinpointed by research is a strong commitment to self.

To cultivate this trait, try this exercise: Sit quietly and breathe deeply. Consider all that your lungs, internal organs, muscles, bones and five senses allow you to do.

Then ask yourself: "Is there something special I can do for my body to help it heal more completely?"

This could include steps to improve your nutrition, exercise or lifestyle—or any action that would make your body's job easier.

• **Don't forget your childhood.** In a large study sponsored by the federal Centers for Disease Control and Prevention, childhood physical, sexual or emotional abuse was the single most predictive factor of chronic illness in adulthood. While you can't undo the past, several studies show that disclosing and working through troubling childhood experiences can lead to health benefits, such as a reduction in harmful levels of stress hormones.

Consider talking to a psychotherapist or mental health counselor and/or writing about these experiences.

Helpful: Expressive writing (a form of writing that focuses on feelings) has been found to improve both physical and psychological health. For those who have undergone traumatic experiences, this type of writing has been shown to have a number of benefits, including a reduction in posttraumatic stress disorder symptoms.

•**Make sure you have a confidant.** Just as toxic relationships can be damaging, positive relationships benefit your health.

In one Harvard study of 56,000 subjects, those without at least one confidant had the worst health. If you feel your social network could be stronger, consider inviting more potential friends into your life…joining a support group (such as one that focuses on a medical condition)…and/or seeing a therapist or counselor (who can provide support and perhaps help improve your relationship skills).

•**Find a bigger purpose.** Research shows that helping people—by doing some form of public service, for example—reduces illness and mortality.

Studies also have found that spirituality and belief in something greater than oneself is linked to increased longevity.

•**Embrace stillness.** A regular habit of quieting yourself is important. This can be achieved through meditation, which can take many forms.

Examples: Repeating a calming phrase, such as "In this moment, all is well" or "I am safe and secure"…breathing deeply while sitting quietly…or taking walks in nature can be considered meditation.

A 19-year study found that people who meditated regularly had 30% fewer heart attacks and 49% less risk of dying from cancer over a 7.6-year period than those who didn't meditate regularly—perhaps due to reduced levels of disease-promoting stress hormones.

Deepak Chopra on How to Create a New You

Deepak Chopra, MD, fellow of the American College of Physicians, member of the American Association of Clinical Endocrinologists, adjunct professor at Kellogg School of Management, Evanston, Illinois, and senior scientist with The Gallup Organization. His most recent best-seller is *Reinventing the Body, Resurrecting the Soul: How to Create a New You* (Harmony).

Anything is possible—but we reject certain alternatives without a second thought. We've convinced ourselves—or social conditioning has convinced us—that rejecting these options is necessary or proper.

Examples: An unemployed office worker might automatically reject a blue-collar job…a retiree might automatically decide he's too old to go on a backpacking trip in the mountains.

We need to dislodge our negative beliefs if we wish to weigh all of our options, overcome the power of "no" and elevate our lives to a higher level. *Here, the negative beliefs that are holding us back and what to do…*

Negative belief: **We're stuck with our habits.** A habit is simply a shortcut imprinted on the brain. We cook our eggs the same way every morning or sit in front of the television every evening because we have done this so many times that we now do it without making a conscious choice.

A habit is just a choice that is ingrained for practical purposes, but the fact that our habits have become ingrained does not mean that we cannot pursue alternatives.

What keeps us trapped is the "spell of no." We voluntarily renounce the power to change, while at the same time blaming our bad habits as if they have an independent will. The spell that our habits hold over us is one that we have created and thus one that we can break.

What to do: Examine your unwanted habits objectively, as if they belonged to someone else. Ask yourself why you have chosen a bad habit. Search for a hidden benefit that it provides. Does this habit make you feel like a victim, a convenient way to avoid taking responsibility for your problems?

Spend six weeks doing what you want to do, rather than what your habit encourages you to. After six weeks, the new way of doing things will be imprinted on your brain in place of the old habit.

***Negative belief:* Our obsessions are not really obsessions.** People tend to believe the term "obsessive" applies only to those with mental disorders. We certainly don't consider ourselves obsessive. In truth, many of us are obsessive—we simply chose to overlook our obsessions, because we believe that the things we obsess about are things that deserve this much time and energy.

Examples: Obsessions that people tend to view as positive include obsessions with health and safety...career or income...religion...their children's success...or a political or charitable cause.

There might be positive aspects to these obsessions, but having any obsession robs us of our ability to make objective choices—automatically saying yes to spending our time and resources on an obsession means automatically saying no to alternatives. This blunts our ability to evolve and get the most from our lives.

What to do: Stop taking pride in your consistency or single-mindedness even in pursuit of a good cause. Engage in activities that reduce your stress levels, such as meditation or hobbies. Relaxed minds are more open to new alternatives.

***Negative belief:* Our fears are valid because they seem valid to us.** External threats aren't what make the world seem unsafe—it's the concerns and beliefs that we project onto every situation that create our fears. If we worry about crime, then everyone we pass on the street becomes a potential mugger. If we're afraid of heights, then even a small stepladder may seem too dangerous to climb.

Our fears deny us our most basic freedom, the freedom to feel safe in the world. They encourage us to reject possibilities that deserve our consideration by making them seem too risky. Some threats are real, but our fears don't

help us identify these. Our fears deprive us of our ability to rationally evaluate dangers.

What to do: Don't try to fight your fears at times when you feel afraid—that's when fears are most powerful. At these times, just remind yourself that fear is a passing emotion that soon will be released. Later, when you are calm, recall the fear for objective examination. With long-standing fears, remind yourself that the fact that you have worried about something for years does not mean that this thing is especially dangerous—it just means that your mind has had a lot of time to blow it out of proportion.

Show yourself compassion about your fears. Fear is not a sign of weakness. It can and does affect everyone.

***Negative belief:* People don't change.** Most of us think this from time to time when those close to us chronically repeat mistakes or misbehavior. Yet paradoxically, most of us believe that we, personally, are capable of change and growth. We cannot have it both ways—if we are capable of change, then other people must be, too.

In fact, not only are people capable of change, we all change all the time. When we think, *People don't change*, we're just giving in to resignation and defeatism. Thinking in this way could dissuade us—and those around us—from attempting positive growth in the future.

What to do: View yourself as in a perpetual state of change. Search for options for anything in your life that seems fixed and unchangeable. Don't listen to naysayers when you attempt change—their warnings and criticisms are rooted in defeatism, not reality. Encourage attempts to change by others, particularly when these changes are new and fragile.

Example: If a seemingly stingy friend finally offers to pick up a small check, don't make a joke or belittle the effort. Choose to view this person as generous and offer a heartfelt thanks. Your positive reaction could reinforce your friend's attempt to change and encourage greater generosity in the future.

***Negative belief:* "Bad" thoughts are forbidden and dangerous.** Many of us waste energy repressing thoughts that we wish we didn't have. These "bad" thoughts might be feelings of jealousy, rage, lust or a desire for vengeance. Trouble is, repressing thoughts doesn't make them go away—it allows them to grow.

Viewing some of our own thoughts as bad also encourages us to divide ourselves into a good side and a bad side, creating an inner struggle that we can never win.

The truth is, we all have thoughts that we wish we didn't have. That doesn't mean we're bad people, as long as we don't act on these thoughts.

What to do: Understand that it is not in our power to stop "bad" thoughts. It is in our power to let these thoughts pass rather than repress them or act on them. Don't believe that the thoughts drifting through your mind define who you are—these thoughts are not you.

Never condemn anyone for his/her thoughts, including yourself. Give up the impossible goal of totally controlling your mind.

■ ■ ■ ■

Change Your Attitude, Live Longer

Researchers who analyzed data that measured attitudes and perspectives of about 100,000 women (age 50 or older) found that those who were "cynically hostile"—highly mistrustful and resentful of others—were 16% more likely to die from any cause during the eight-year study period than those who were the least cynically hostile.

Theory: Negative attitudes may contribute to high blood pressure, heart disease and other health problems.

If you tend to be cynical and mistrustful: In addition to eating well and exercising, consider extending your social network…and, if necessary, talk with a therapist to help change your thinking.

Hilary A. Tindle, MD, assistant professor of medicine, University of Pittsburgh School of Medicine, Pennsylvania.

What to Do When You're Really, Really Mad

Judy Kuriansky, PhD, clinical psychologist and sex therapist on the adjunct faculty of Columbia University Teachers College in New York City. She is author of six books, including *The Complete Idiot's Guide to a Healthy Relationship* (Alpha). *www.DrJudy.com.*

Occasionally we all get angry—at other people, at events, at ourselves. But frequent or intense fury can strain the heart, unleash harmful stress hormones and ruin relationships. *To control anger…*

•**Interrupt the feeling.** Distract yourself with an activity that you enjoy (taking a walk, watering plants).

Or: Cover your face gently with your hands to block stimuli, then breathe deeply, inhaling through your nose and exhaling through your mouth.

•**Explode—alone.** Downloading ire onto others makes them resentful. Go somewhere private to scream or pound pillows. Once composed, calmly state what you want ("I need you to clean up this mess").

•**Channel anger constructively.** When mad at yourself ("My clothes don't fit!"), adopt an action plan (such as joining a gym). If your blood boils at someone's incompetence, take more control—of your finances, for instance, if your accountant made a mistake.

•**Explore anger's root.** If you often feel that other people fall short, you need to lower your standards. When feelings get bruised, seek an explanation ("You didn't call—is everything OK?") instead of taking it personally. Is fury triggered by a memory? Dwelling on the past wastes energy better spent on activities that help you—and others—feel good.

■ More from Judy Kuriansky, PhD…

Secret to Telling Grown Kids About Your Past

As your family matures, you may feel inclined to treat grown offspring as friends and share more openly about your own past.

Revelations can bring you closer—or drive you apart. *For a good outcome, ask yourself...*

•**What is the motivation?** Are you looking for acceptance (for instance, by explaining that you dropped out of school to help at home after your father abandoned the family)? Hoping to warn them against making the mistakes you made (such as buying a house you couldn't afford, then having to scrape for years to get by)? These are good reasons to share your experiences.

But: If you're motivated by vengeance or bitterness ("My dad was cruel, so he deserved to have his next marriage fail"), keep quiet.

•**Is this information helpful?** Grown children do have a right to know about inherited factors that might affect their own futures, such as a family history of mental illness or addiction. Also speak up if you suspect your children of subconsciously copying damaging behaviors (verbal abuse, infidelity) that were part of their childhood household environment.

•**What's the reaction?** Stop talking if you sense discomfort or resentment. Don't be disappointed—once your child has a chance to process uncomfortable emotions, he/she may feel ready to hear about your past.

Family Health

Research Explains Sudden Infant Death Syndrome

Lack of the brain chemical *serotonin* may be crucial to sudden infant death syndrome (SIDS), new research finds.

Babies who died of SIDS had significantly lower levels of serotonin—an important regulator of involuntary functions, such as breathing and heart rate—compared with babies who died of other causes, the study found. This finding may eventually lead to a test that could screen newborns to spot those most vulnerable to SIDS.

Results of the study have been published in *The Journal of the American Medical Association.*

SOME BACKGROUND ON SIDS

SIDS involves the sudden, unexplained death of an infant less than one year of age, according to background information in the study. Although the rate of SIDS has decreased in the United States—largely as a result of a national Back-to-Sleep campaign that encouraged parents to put babies to sleep on their backs—one out of every 2,000 American babies is still dying of SIDS, the authors note.

Researchers have long suspected that a lack of serotonin, an important neurotransmitter in the brain, may be a factor in SIDS deaths. Neurotransmitters are chemicals that transmit messages from one brain cell to another. Experts have theorized that a lack of serotonin affects the way a baby responds to a loss of oxygen and a buildup of carbon dioxide while sleeping. In babies with a normally functioning system, the lack of oxygen would cause them to awaken and turn their head to get fresh oxygen.

Hannah C. Kinney, MD, neuropathologist, Children's Hospital Boston, and professor, pathology, Harvard Medical School, Boston.

Raymond Pitetti, MD, associate director, emergency medicine, Children's Hospital of Pittsburgh.

The Journal of the American Medical Association.

In babies who die of SIDS, this important protective mechanism is either underdeveloped or lacking, and they don't awaken. That may be one reason why the Back-to-Sleep campaign was so successful in reducing SIDS. By putting babies to sleep on their backs and taking soft, fluffy bedding out of the crib, parents are taking away environmental stressors that may contribute to SIDS, the researchers said.

THE STUDY

In the current study, senior author Hannah C. Kinney, MD, a neuropathologist at Children's Hospital Boston, and her colleagues measured levels of serotonin and *tryptophan hydroxylase 2* (TPH2) in 35 babies who died from SIDS and in 12 babies who died of other, known causes. TPH2 is an enzyme that helps make serotonin. In the group of babies who had died of other causes, the researchers included infants who had experienced oxygen deprivation near death to rule out that factor as a cause of lower serotonin levels.

They found that serotonin levels were 26% lower and TPH2 levels were 22% lower in babies who died of SIDS compared with babies who died of other causes.

IMPLICATIONS

"This study is confirming that SIDS is a serotonin problem, and we're getting closer to the fundamental mechanism behind SIDS," said Dr. Kinney, also a professor of pathology at Harvard Medical School. "The goal is to develop a test to identify which babies are at risk, and then to find a drug that might be able to help them through the critical period. But these are long-term goals."

"This study is getting close to the underlying mechanism," said Raymond Pitetti, MD, associate director of emergency medicine at Children's Hospital of Pittsburgh.

"The goal would be to develop screening tests so we can identify someone who might need a monitor or to be more closely watched," he said.

ADVICE FOR PREVENTING SIDS

In the meantime, he and Dr. Kinney advised parents to continue to put their babies to sleep on their back, to avoid soft bedding, to ensure adequate ventilation in the room where the baby sleeps and maybe even add a ceiling fan to the room. Some research has suggested that putting babies to bed with a pacifier in the mouth may help prevent SIDS, too.

"The most important thing for parents to know is that SIDS is a biological problem. It's a disease process, and right now, there's no way to identify it in advance," said Dr. Kinney. That is why it's so important to take away any environmental challenges, like soft bedding and sleeping on the stomach, she added.

info To learn more about preventing SIDS, visit the American Lung Association Web site, *www.lungusa.org*, and search "preventing SIDS."

■ ■ ■ ■

Don't Let Newborns Sleep in Car Seats

Blood oxygen levels were significantly lower after healthy two-day-old infants sat in car seats for 60 minutes than when the infants lay in cribs.

Reason: An upright position leads to partial obstruction of the upper airway.

Lesson: A car seat is essential for travel safety but should never substitute for a crib. On long car trips, stop frequently to give your baby a break from the car seat.

Lilijana Kornhauser Cerar, MD, head of the neonatal intensive care unit, University Medical Centre, Ljubljana, Slovenia, and leader of a study of 200 infants.

Autism Rates Higher in Children with Older Moms

Janie Shelton, doctoral student, University of California, Davis.
Geraldine Dawson, PhD, chief science officer, Autism Speaks, New York City.
Autism Research.

Older moms are more likely to have a child with autism than women who give birth at a younger age, new research shows.

ABOUT AUTISM

Autism is a developmental disorder that causes problems with social and communications skills and repetitive or restrictive behaviors. Because the condition has a wide range of symptoms and degrees of severity, autism is now called *autism spectrum disorders*. About one in 110 children in the United States has such a disorder, according to the US Centers for Disease Control and Prevention.

In this study, autism was defined as a diagnosis of full-syndrome autism. The study was conducted at a California Regional Center where children receive autism-related services.

THE STUDY

Researchers from University of California, Davis, looked at records for the nearly 5 million births in California between 1990 and 1999, a decade in which diagnoses of autism increased 600% statewide.

A woman's risk of having a child diagnosed with autism rose by 18% for each five-year increment in her age, according to the study. That means that a woman who gave birth at age 40 or older had a more than 50% greater chance of having a child with autism than a woman who gave birth between 25 and 29, and a 77% greater chance of having a child with autism than a woman who gave birth before the age of 25.

While previous research has shown that older dads are more likely to have a child with autism, this study found no such link between autism and paternal age, with one exception—older men who had children with much younger women. Men over 40 who had a child with a woman under 30 had a nearly 60% increased risk of having a child diagnosed with autism compared with men ages 25 to 29 who fathered a child with a young woman.

Among mothers over 30, the increased risk associated with having a baby with a man older than 40 dissipated.

The study was published in the journal *Autism Research*.

PUTTING THE FINDINGS IN CONTEXT

In California, women having babies after the age of age 40 increased by 300% between 1982 and 2004, the researchers noted. Still, they stressed that the rise in women over 40 having babies probably accounted for less than 5% of the statewide surge in autism cases noted in 1990s.

"Advancing maternal age is contributing only a very small proportion of the increase in autism cases," said study author Janie Shelton, a UC Davis doctoral student.

Geraldine Dawson, PhD, chief science officer for Autism Speaks, praised researchers for using such a large database to uncover the impact each parent's age can have on autism risk. But she also urged older mothers not to worry about this finding unnecessarily.

"We need to look at this finding in context," Dr. Dawson said. "This study is important, but we are not going to find one factor that can explain this dramatic increase in the prevalence of autism. We are going to find multiple factors, and advanced maternal age appears to be one of them."

PATERNAL AGE AND RISK FOR AUTISM

The new research contradicts an earlier study out of Israel that found the children of men over age 40 were at higher risk of autism. In that study, fathers over 40 were six times more likely than fathers under 30 to have a child with autism.

But subsequent studies did not confirm those findings. The Israeli study included only four women over age 40 whose children had autism—too small for an accurate analysis, Shelton said. The new California study included more than 12,000 cases of autism, and 501 women who gave birth after age 40 and whose children were diagnosed with autism.

Researchers do not know why their study found that children with an older father but relatively young mother were more apt to develop autism, but they suspect it's more than a statistical blip. "We feel it's indicative of some underlying biological process," Shelton said.

Mothers under age 30 have only a minimal age-related risk of having a child with autism, Shelton noted. It's possible that the impact of the father's age is more pronounced when dad is older and mom is much younger, whereas the risk conferred by older mothers "drowns out" any age-linked risk from fathers.

EXPERT COMMENTARY

The findings are not that surprising, given what's known about advancing maternal age on other birth-related conditions, Dr. Dawson said. Previous research has shown that older moms are at higher risk of miscarriage or delivering low birth-weight babies, and of having babies with chromosomal aberrations such as Down syndrome and congenital anomalies.

"We've known for a long time that advanced parental age is associated with changes in the DNA, more chromosomal abnormalities and more birth complications," Dr. Dawson said. "Still, overall the risk [for any one couple] is small."

info For more information on autism, visit the Web site of Autism Speaks, *www. autismspeaks.org.*

■ ■ ■ ■

New Pregnancy Weight-Gain Guidelines

When expectant moms gain too little or too much, babies and mothers are at increased risk for health problems. Institute of Medicine (IOM) guidelines, which now include a weight-gain range for obese women, are based on body mass index (BMI).

Best: If you started pregnancy underweight (with a BMI of less than 18.5), aim to gain 28 to 40 pounds…normal weight (BMI 18.5 to 24.9), gain 25 to 35 pounds…overweight (BMI 25 to 29.9), gain 15 to 25 pounds…obese (BMI 30 or higher), gain 11 to 20 pounds. With twins, recommended weight gain is higher—see *www.iom.edu.*

For a BMI calculator: *www.nhlbisupport. com/bmi.*

Anna Maria Siega-Riz, PhD, RD, professor of nutrition and epidemiology, University of North Carolina, Chapel Hill, and IOM guidelines coauthor.

■ ■ ■ ■

Probiotics Reduce Belly Fat

Pregnant women took either placebos or daily supplements of probiotics (beneficial bacteria) from the first trimester until up to six months postpartum. At 12 months postpartum, 43% of the placebo users—but just 25% of probiotics users—had central obesity (waist

measuring more than 31.5 inches). Ask your obstetrician about probiotics.

Kirsi Laitinen, PhD, adjunct professor of clinical nutrition, University of Turku, Finland, and leader of a study of 256 pregnant women.

■ ■ ■ ■

Treating Mild Gestational Diabetes Is Best

Experts disagree on whether to treat pregnant women who develop mild gestational diabetes, although the condition can cause babies to grow very large.

New finding: Compared with untreated mothers with gestational diabetes, those who were treated (with diet, blood sugar monitoring and/or insulin) were significantly less likely to have a large baby or require cesarean delivery… their babies were less likely to suffer shoulder injuries during vaginal delivery.

Mark B. Landon, MD, professor, department of obstetrics and gynecology, Ohio State University College of Medicine, Columbus, and leader of a study of 958 women.

Women Born Early More Apt to Have Preterm Baby

Siladitya Bhattacharya, MD, professor, reproductive medicine, Aberdeen Maternity Hospital and University of Aberdeen, Scotland.
William H. Barth Jr., MD, chief, maternal-fetal medicine, Massachusetts General Hospital, Boston.
Obstetrics & Gynecology.

Women who were born early are themselves more likely to give birth to a baby who isn't full-term, a new study suggests.

The same finding applies to women who weren't born early but had one or more siblings who were born preterm, according to a team of Scottish researchers.

STUDY DETAILS

"There was a suspicion that preterm birth might be linked with previous experience of preterm birth in the family," said Siladitya Bhattacharya,

MD, senior author of the study and a professor of reproductive medicine at Aberdeen Maternity Hospital, in Aberdeen.

So Dr. Bhattacharya and his team of researchers evaluated 22,343 pregnancies in Scotland that occurred among 13,845 daughters born to 11,576 different mothers, spanning a period of 60 years.

When the researchers looked at women who had been born preterm (single deliveries, not multiple births) and were pregnant for the first time, they found a higher risk for early birth compared with those not born preterm.

"The mums who themselves were born preterm are 60% more likely to have a preterm baby themselves in their first pregnancy," Dr. Bhattacharya said.

That risk for early birth declined slightly, to about 50%, for preterm women experiencing a second or subsequent pregnancy, he said.

Preterm was considered any birth that occurred at 24 to 37 weeks of gestation. Preterm birth is the leading cause of death and illness of newborns in the developed world, accounting for 60% of deaths and serious complications after delivery, according to the study.

The findings were published in *Obstetrics & Gynecology*.

EXPERT REACTION

William H. Barth Jr., MD, chief of maternal-fetal medicine at Massachusetts General Hospital, who wrote an accompanying editorial in the journal, said the new study is useful because it confirms earlier research.

But he does not expect the new results to change medical practice at this time. He pointed out some limitations to the study, including that all participants lived in Scotland, making the sample very homogeneous.

The potential for a preterm birth based just on the mother being born preterm or having a sibling born early doesn't call for therapies currently used to prevent preterm births, such as the use of the female hormone progesterone, Dr. Barth wrote in the journal.

More will be learned about the risk for preterm birth in coming years, he wrote, because genetic research focused on families with a tendency for preterm birth should yield more insights.

WHAT YOU CAN DO

Dr. Bhattacharya said his new research suggests that if women know they were born early—or that their mother gave birth to a sibling early—they would be well-advised to pass along to their obstetrician or midwife this "extra bit of information."

The health-care provider could then decide whether more frequent prenatal visits or other special attention or treatment would be needed, he said.

info To learn more about preventing preterm birth, visit the March of Dimes Web site, *www.marchofdimes.com*, and type "prematurity" into the search box.

■ ■ ■ ■

Endometriosis Boosts Risk for Preterm Birth

Pregnant women previously diagnosed with *endometriosis*—in which uterine lining tissue grows outside the womb—had a 33% increased risk for premature delivery. If you have endometriosis, see a maternal-fetal specialist for prenatal care.

Olof Stephansson, MD, PhD, obstetrics consultant, Karolinska University Hospital and Institute, Stockholm, Sweden, and leader of an analysis of data on 1.4 million women.

Study Suggests Higher Cancer Rate Among IVF Babies

Bengt Kallen, MD, PhD, professor emeritus, embryology, Tornblad Institute, University of Lund, Sweden.

David Cohen, MD, chief, reproductive medicine, and associate professor, obstetrics and gynecology, University of Chicago.

Edward Illions, MD, reproductive endocrinologist, Montefiore Medical Center, New York City, and Montefiore Institute for Reproductive Medicine, Hartsdale, New York. *Pediatrics*.

Children conceived using *in vitro fertilization* have a higher risk of developing cancer than do children who were conceived naturally, new research shows.

ABOUT IN VITRO FERTILIZATION

In vitro fertilization (IVF) is an assisted reproduction technology. Using eggs harvested from the prospective mother and sperm given by the prospective father, doctors can create human embryos that are then implanted into the mother's uterus.

Babies born using this technology are known to have an increased risk of birth defects and of birth complications, such as preterm birth. Previous research has also suggested that children born through this method of conception may also have an increased risk of cancer.

STUDY DETAILS

Using the Swedish Medical Birth Register, the researchers gathered information on nearly 27,000 children who were born after being conceived with IVF in Sweden from 1982 through 2005.

When they looked at the number of children who had cancer, they found that 53 IVF children had developed cancer compared with the expected rate of 38 cases of cancer in non-IVF children.

While the risk for cancer was increased by 42% for Swedish youngsters conceived with IVF, the absolute risk of cancer was still quite low.

"We found a roughly 50% increased risk for cancer in the IVF children, which means that if the risk without IVF is two per 1,000, it increases to three per 1,000 after IVF," explained study author Bengt Kallen, MD, PhD, a professor emeritus in embryology at the Tornblad Institute at the University of Lund in Sweden.

Other factors appeared to influence the risk of cancer as well. Children born before 37 weeks' gestation and those with a low birth weight, respiratory problems or a low Apgar score (a test given at birth to assess a newborn's health), had higher rates of cancer.

A mother's age, weight, smoking status and the number of miscarriages she'd already had didn't appear to affect a child's cancer risk. A multiple birth pregnancy also didn't appear to affect the risk of cancer.

Cancers of the blood, such as acute lymphoblastic leukemia, were the most common, affecting 18 children. The next most common were cancers of the eye or central nervous system, affecting 17 children.

The findings were published in *Pediatrics*.

EXPERT COMMENTARY

Although it's not clear what's to blame for the increase, the study authors think it's unlikely that IVF is at the root of the increased risk of cancer.

"This study is interesting and thought-provoking, and it adds to our growing knowledge of potential IVF consequences," said David Cohen, MD, chief of reproductive medicine at the University of Chicago.

"But, it's difficult to think what the biological plausibility would be. If it were something that occurs during the in vitro process or some substance in the media used, I would think that it would cause a much higher number of cancers. This may just be a statistical oddity," he added.

"This is the largest study that I'm aware of, and it does suggest an increased risk of childhood cancers ... but it doesn't really delineate whether it's the IVF process or the patient selection. Is this increase due to the procedure, or is it secondary due to a difference in the patient population?" said Edward Illions, MD, a reproductive endocrinology specialist at the Montefiore Medical Center in New York City and the Montefiore Institute for Reproductive Medicine in Hartsdale, New York.

The three experts do not believe these findings will have a significant influence on a couple's decision to have the IVF procedure.

"The absolute risk is so small that it will hardly influence the decision to get an IVF," Dr. Kallen said.

"This adds more information to the [pre-IVF] counseling session, but I don't think it will change the decision. The absolute risk is still well less than 1%," said Dr. Cohen.

info To learn more about in vitro fertilization, visit the Web site of the American Pregnancy Association, *www.americanpregnancy.org/ infertility/ivf.html.*

Sugar Before Shots Helps Infants Tolerate Pain

BMJ (*British Medical Journal*) news release.

A sugar solution appears to help babies tolerate immunizations and get through the pain, researchers have found.

The approach works so well that a new report is recommending that doctors and nurses consider giving a sweet solution to babies before immunization in children one month to one year old.

BACKGROUND

Previous research has shown that a small amount of sucrose or glucose—a few drops to half a teaspoon—in a solution can reduce pain.

NEW RESEARCH FINDINGS

In the new report, published in *Archives of Disease in Childhood*, researchers from Canada, Australia and Brazil reviewed findings from 14 studies that examined 1,674 injections given to children one year or younger.

In 13 of the studies, babies who were given a bit of sugary solution—compared with those given water or nothing—were found to cry less after immunization. Babies given 30% glucose in the solution were about half as likely to cry, the study found.

EXPERT ADVICE

"Health-care professionals responsible for administering immunizations should consider using sucrose or glucose during painful procedures," study author Denise Harrison, RN, PhD, of the Hospital for Sick Children in Toronto, and her colleagues concluded. "This information is important for health-care professionals working with infants in both inpatient and outpatient settings, as sweet solutions are readily available, have a very short onset of time to analgesia, are inexpensive and are easy to administer."

info For more information on immunization, visit the Web site of the Centers for Disease Control and Prevention, *http://cdc.gov*, and search "vaccines."

Are Antibiotics Making Your Child Sick?

BMJ (*British Medical Journal* online) news release.

R epeated use of antibiotics to treat acute ear infections in young children increases the risk for recurrent ear infections by 20%, according to researchers in the Netherlands who called for more prudent use of antibiotics in young children.

The researchers found that 63% of children given the antibiotic *amoxicillin* (Amoxil) experienced a recurrent ear infection within three years, compared with 43% of children given a placebo at the time of their initial infection.

STUDY DETAILS

The finding came from a survey of parents of 168 children, 6 months to 2 years old, who took part in a study on the use of antibiotics to treat ear infections. The study results were published in *BMJ*.

In the group given amoxicillin, 47 out of 75 of the children had at least one recurrent ear infection, compared with only 37 of 86 children in the placebo group.

POSSIBLE EXPLANATION

The higher recurrence rate among children who took amoxicillin could be due to a weakening of their body's natural immune response as a result of taking an antibiotic at the initial stage of infection, the researchers said. Antibiotic use in such cases may cause an "unfavorable shift" toward the growth of resistant bacteria.

Antibiotics may reduce the length and severity of the initial ear infection, but may also result in a higher number of recurrent infections and antibiotic resistance, the researchers stated. Because of this, they said, doctors need to be careful in their use of antibiotics in children with ear infections.

info To learn more about treating ear infections, visit the Web site of the American Academy of Pediatrics, *www.healthychildren. org*, and search "acute ear infection."

Tabs on Beverage Cans Still Risky for Kids

Radiological Society of North America news release.

Tabs on beverage cans—the kind that stay attached once a can is opened—still pose a danger to children, who can swallow the tabs and damage their digestive tract, according to a new study.

About three decades ago, beverage makers starting using what they call stay-tabs instead of pull-tabs, which were believed to pose a hazard for children who swallowed them and for anyone who stepped on them. But the new finding raises "the possibility that the redesign of beverage cans may not have reduced the number of ingestions," said Lane F. Donnelly, MD, radiologist-in-chief and director of biodiagnostics at Cincinnati Children's Hospital Medical Center and the study's lead author.

Swallowing objects, particularly those with sharp edges, can cause injury to the gastrointestinal tract, sometimes requiring surgery.

THE STUDY EXPLAINED

The study identified 19 youths who had accidentally swallowed a stay-tab and were treated at Cincinnati Children's Hospital between 1993 and 2009. Their average age was 8, but most were teenagers. Only four were younger than age 5.

"It is unusual that the majority of cases occurred among teenagers since foreign body ingestion typically occurs in infants and toddlers," Dr. Donnelly said.

Surgery was required in just a few of the 19 cases, the study reported.

A major challenge for doctors in such cases, Dr. Donnelly said, is that the beverage can tabs are difficult to see on X-rays.

Of the 19 cases in the study, only four of the stay-tabs were visible on X-rays. In each of those four cases, the tab was located in the stomach.

IMPLICATIONS FOR THE FUTURE

"Clinicians and radiologists should be aware that this does occur," Dr. Donnelly said. "Not seeing the tab on the X-ray does not mean it was not swallowed."

He said the findings call into question the current design of beverage cans.

"The identification of 19 ingested stay-tabs at a single children's hospital suggests that such occurrences are not uncommon," Dr. Donnelly said.

The study was presented at the annual meeting of the Radiological Society of North America in Chicago.

info For more about swallowing a foreign object, visit the US National Library of Medicine Web site, *www.nlm.nih.gov/medline plus*, and search "foreign object—inhaled or swallowed."

Simple Test Reveals Sleep Apnea in Kids

American Thoracic Society news release.

A simple urine test could be developed to detect whether a child has *obstructive sleep apnea* (OSA), US researchers say.

OSA, a potentially serious disorder, occurs when throat muscles intermittently relax and block the airway during sleep. An estimated 3% of children younger than age 9 have OSA, which can lead to cognitive, behavioral, cardiovascular and metabolic problems.

Such a test "would alleviate the need for costly and inconvenient sleep studies in children who snore, only about 20% to 30% of whom actually have OSA," said David Gozal, MD, a professor and chairman of pediatrics at the University of Chicago.

THE STUDY EXPLAINED

He and his colleagues studied 90 children referred to a sleep clinic for evaluation of breathing problems during sleep, and 30 children who didn't snore. All the children underwent standard overnight sleep tests. Urine samples were collected the morning after the sleep tests.

After screening hundreds of proteins in the children's urine, the researchers found that the expression of a number of the proteins was different in children with OSA than in those with habitual snoring or healthy, non-snoring children.

The finding was reported in the *American Journal of Respiratory and Critical Care Medicine.*

IMPLICATION

"It was rather unexpected that the urine would provide us with the ability to identify OSA," Dr. Gozal said.

"However, the field of biomarkers is one that is under marked expansion, and this certainly opens the way for possible simple diagnostic screening methods in the future," Dr. Gozal said.

"We wish to validate these findings in urine samples from many children from laboratories around the country and to develop a simple test that can be done in the physician office or by the parents," Dr. Gozal said.

info For more about sleep apnea in children, visit the Web site of the Nemours Foundation, *http://kidshealth.org/parent*, and search "apnea."

Helping Your Anxious Child

Anxiety affects up to one-fifth of children in the US but often is not recognized—and delays in diagnosis and treatment can lead to depression and substance abuse.

A recent study suggests weekly family sessions of cognitive behavioral therapy may prevent children from developing the same problems with anxiety that their parents struggle with.

Parents should seek help if they notice early signs of anxiety in children, such as physical complaints with no medical cause, avoidance of daily activities and too much worry.

Resources to find cognitive behavioral therapists: Anxiety Disorders Association of America (*www.adaa.org*)...Association for Behavioral and Cognitive Therapies (*www.abct. org*)...Academy of Cognitive Therapy (*www. AcademyOfCT.org*).

Golda Ginsburg, PhD, child psychologist, Johns Hopkins Children's Center, Baltimore, and leader of a study of 40 children, published in *Journal of Consulting and Clinical Psychology.*

Protect the Family From the Flu— No Vaccine Needed

Mark A. Stengler, NMD, naturopathic medical doctor in private practice, La Jolla, California...adjunct associate clinical professor at the National College of Natural Medicine, Portland, Oregon...author of many books, including *The Natural Physician's Healing Therapies* and coauthor of *Prescription for Natural Cures* (both from Bottom Line Books)... and author of the *Bottom Line/Natural Healing* newsletter.

I have developed a flu-prevention protocol that I believe can lower your risk of contracting the H1N1 flu and other flu strains this winter. It also can reduce the severity of your illness if you do get sick.

First question: When my patients ask me if they should get either flu vaccine, I tell them that my family and I, and many of my patients, are not planning to get them. And I don't recommend that other healthy people get them either. I have several concerns about flu vaccines—namely, that we don't know the long-term impact of using them...many contain a mercury-based preservative (mercury is known to suppress the immune system)...and some people develop a flulike illness after receiving the vaccine. The truth is that the vaccines' effectiveness is, at best, hit or miss. However, the regular seasonal flu vaccine (mercury-free is best) should be considered for those who are over age 65...suffer from chronic pulmonary or cardiovascular disease...are nursing home residents...have a weakened immune system from chronic disease, such as cancer...or are pregnant. I don't recommend the H1N1 vaccine for anyone, because far too little is known about it and its long-term side effects.

What everyone needs when combatting the flu is a strong immune system. The natural therapies I recommend can enhance and fine-tune your immune system. People who take these supplements, eat a healthful diet, get some exercise and sleep for at least seven hours a night have more protection against the flu than they would get from the flu vaccine.

MY FLU-PROTECTION PROTOCOL

My protocol results in a tremendous boost for the immune system. Begin this protection protocol in October—and continue it through April.

•**Influenzinum.** At the heart of my special flu-protection program is Influenzinum, a homeopathic remedy that is a safe alternative to conventional flu shots. I have recommended it to my patients for 15 years—with good results. Influenzinum has been prescribed by homeopathic physicians for the last 150 years and is reported to have protected people against the Spanish flu of 1918. It contains a homeopathic preparation of the flu virus that is made each year based on the predicted flu strains. In 1998, the French Society of Homeopathy concluded a 10-year survey of 23 homeopathic doctors and their use of Influenzinum for flu prevention in 453 patients.

Result: Only 10% of those patients developed the flu.

Action plan: Follow label instructions. Adults and children (age six and older) should take one dose (at least two pellets or a small vial of several pellets) of a 9C potency once a week for four weeks…wait a month…and then take a fifth dose. (For infants starting as young as one day old, crush one pellet and place on the tongue.) Many health food stores carry Influenzinum. One good brand is made by Homeopathic Educational Services (510-649-0294, *www.homeopathic.com*).

•**Vitamin D.** Studies show that vitamin D protects against upper respiratory infections and can enhance the body's production of *cathelicidin*, a germ-killing compound.

Action plan: Adults and teenagers take 2,000 international units (IU) of vitamin D-3 daily and children (as young as one day old and up to 12 years old) 1,000 IU. Increase this amount to 5,000 IU daily for adults and 2,000 IU for children during peak flu season (January through March).

•**N-acetylcysteine (NAC).** Italian researchers found that seniors who took this antioxidant had virtually no flu symptoms, even though testing showed that they were infected, whereas people taking placebos in the same study suffered the brunt of flu symptoms. Research supports NAC's pulmonary benefits.

Action plan: Adults and teenagers take 1,000 milligrams (mg) of NAC daily and children (age six to 12 years old) take 500 mg daily. At the first sign of symptoms, immediately increase the amount to 4,000 mg daily (1,500 mg daily for children) and continue until symptoms are gone.

IF YOU DO GET THE FLU

To treat the flu, use the remedies just described and add the ones below to your regimen. Take them for as long as symptoms last, unless otherwise indicated. These supplements are safe, in these amounts, for everyone.

Take for the first two days only…

•**Oscillococcinum.** This homeopathic remedy is made from animal organ–derived ingredients that provide natural immunity to the flu virus. It can ease flu symptoms if taken within 48 hours after they start.

Action plan: Follow label directions for use, beginning on the first day of a cold or flu.

Take for as long as symptoms last…

•**Lomatium.** This herbal remedy (*Lomatium dissectum*) was used by Native Americans to treat respiratory infections. It has well-documented antimicrobial properties.

Action plan: Look for an alcohol- or glycerin-based tincture of lomatium. Follow label directions for use.

Note: Lomatium may amplify the effect of blood-thinning medications, so check with your doctor first if you are taking *warfarin* or any other blood-thinning medication. If you develop a rash or nausea, stop taking it.

•**Elderberry** (*Sambucus nigra L.*) was also used medicinally by Native Americans. Studies show that it significantly improves flu symptoms within two to four days.

Action plan: My favorite elderberry product is Sambucol syrup, available at drugstores (*www.sambucolusa.com* for a store locator). Follow label directions.

■ ■ ■ ■

Cold and Flu Season Etiquette

If you are worried about shaking hands, shrug your shoulders with one palm up and say "Flu" or "Swine flu," to show that you are concerned about health. If you would rather not hug someone who is about to hug you, put your hands on the top or sides of his shoulders instead of wrapping them around his back. Carry tissues when flying. If a seatmate sounds ill, offer a tissue to hint that you want to avoid his/her germs. Also bring hand sanitizer and use it often.

Anna Post, etiquette expert, the Emily Post Institute, Burlington, Vermont. *www.EmilyPost.com*.

■ ■ ■ ■

New Tool Available for Flu Self-Diagnosis

If you are feeling ill, go to *www.flu.gov/evaluation*. There you can answer a few questions, and the site will tell you if you should seek medical help or if bed rest and plenty of fluids are best.

Important: If you are unsure, talk to your doctor. The site also features a flu vaccination locator and information about H1N1 flu and seasonal flu.

Christopher Cox, spokesperson, Centers for Disease Control and Prevention, Atlanta.

■ ■ ■ ■

Ahhh! Hot Drinks Ease Cold Symptoms

Thirty people with cold symptoms rated their symptoms before and after drinking an apple and black currant drink, either hot or at room temperature.

Finding: Both beverage temperatures relieved sneezing, runny nose and cough, but only the hot drinks improved sore throat, fatigue and chills. The researchers speculate that any hot fruit drink would be effective.

Theory: Hot, flavorful liquids promote salivation and mucous secretions, which lubricate and soothe the throat and nose.

Ronald Eccles, PhD, director, Common Cold Centre, Cardiff University, Cardiff, Wales.

■ ■ ■ ■

Signs that the Flu Is Getting Worse

Take note of these symptoms: trouble breathing, severe coughing, drinking much less than usual, less frequent urination and extreme irritability are all signs that your flu is getting worse. See your doctor if these symptoms develop. If a child gets the flu, seems to recover and symptoms reappear, that could indicate complications, such as bacterial pneumonia—contact your pediatrician.

William Schaffner, MD, professor and chairman of the department of preventive medicine and professor of medicine in the division of infectious diseases, Vanderbilt University School of Medicine, Nashville, and vice president of the National Foundation for Infectious Diseases.

Beyond Lyme Disease— More Reasons to Steer Clear of Ticks

Robert T. Schoen, MD, a clinical professor of medicine at Yale University School of Medicine, former director of the Lyme Disease Clinic at Yale University Medical Center and an internist and rheumatologist at New Haven Rheumatology, all in New Haven. He has published numerous medical journal articles on tick-borne illness.

Lyme disease is the most common illness caused by ticks and among the most feared—especially in Northeastern, North-Central and Pacific Coast states, where most cases occur.

But ticks that can cause lesser-known illnesses are found in virtually all parts of the US, and they are most active May through September in most regions.

You're at greater risk for all tick-borne illnesses if you live in areas populated by animals, including deer, that can carry ticks or if you spend a good amount of time outdoors—gardening, doing yard work or hiking, for example. In some cases, outdoor animals, such as dogs and horses, also can carry disease-causing ticks.

Important: If you are bitten by a tick and develop symptoms (such as fever, chills and muscle aches), see your primary care physician. If possible, save the tick to show to your doctor, who can send the tick to a laboratory to identify it.

Some tick-borne illnesses you should know about…

BABESIOSIS

This disease occurs mainly in Northeastern, upper Midwestern and Northwestern states. The parasite that causes babesiosis is usually spread by the black-legged tick (commonly referred to as the deer tick), which also transmits Lyme disease. The disease tends to be most serious in older adults and people whose immune systems are compromised as a result of taking immunosuppressive drugs or undergoing cancer treatment. Life-threatening complications of babesiosis include kidney failure, liver problems and low blood pressure.

Main symptoms: Fever, fatigue and flulike symptoms. Chills, in which the entire body shakes, may occur.

Diagnosis: Patients may have anemia or other blood abnormalities, which can be detected via routine laboratory tests. Diagnosis is usually based on examination of a blood smear to identify the presence of parasites.

Treatment: Mildly ill patients may require no treatment. Those with more serious symptoms often are given a combination of antibiotics, such as *clindamycin* (Cleocin) or *azithromycin* (Zithromax), plus an antiparasitic drug, such as *atovaquone* (Mepron).

EHRLICHIOSIS

This bacterial infection is transmitted primarily by the Lone Star tick in the Mid-Atlantic, South-Central and Southeastern US. Although some people experience serious illness, most get only a mild-to-moderate infection, while some are symptom-free. However, the disease can be fatal—most often in older adults or people with compromised immunity.

Main symptoms: Fever, headache, body aches, nausea and other flulike symptoms.

Diagnosis: A special blood test can detect the bacterium that causes the disease. Some patients also will have low platelet and white blood cell counts and elevated levels of liver enzymes.

Treatment: A *tetracycline* antibiotic such as *doxycycline* (Vibramycin) taken for seven to 10 days.

ROCKY MOUNTAIN SPOTTED FEVER

First identified in the Rocky Mountain region, Rocky Mountain spotted fever (RMSF) has spread into other areas, including the Southeastern, Pacific and South Central regions of the US. RMSF, which is the most severe tick-borne illness, can be spread by the Rocky Mountain wood tick, the Lone Star tick and even the common dog tick. The mortality rate in untreated cases of RMSF is 20% to 25%—often due to *myocarditis* (infection of the heart).

Main symptoms: Most often, patients have a fever and headache and also may develop a mottled rash that starts on the wrists, forearms or ankles and may spread to the palms of the hands or soles of the feet. Nausea, body aches and extreme fatigue also may occur.

Diagnosis: A blood test that detects the bacterium that causes RMSF.

Treatment: Doxycycline or another tetracycline antibiotic taken for one week to 10 days.

Important: Patients who develop the symptoms described above should seek treatment as quickly as possible.

TICK-BORNE RELAPSING FEVER

Without treatment, this disease is fatal in about 5% to 10% of cases, usually due to liver failure and/or severe bleeding. Some patients die even with treatment. Fortunately, tick-borne relapsing fever (TBRF) is rare, with only about 25 cases reported in the US each year. TBRF is transmitted by a family of ticks known as soft ticks. Most cases occur in the Western US, particularly in people who have spent time in rustic cabins at high elevations, which tend to attract rodents that may carry soft ticks.

Caution: While most tick-borne infections occur when a tick has remained attached to a human for a day or more, patients can get infected with TBRF within one hour of a tick attaching to the skin.

Main symptoms: Sudden high fever with chills, body aches, headache and sweats. Within about three days, the patient's body temperature usually drops, but extreme sweats can occur. The fever typically recurs.

Diagnosis: There isn't a definitive test for TBRF. Characteristic symptoms include dehydration, an enlarged liver and spleen, and *jaundice* (a yellowing of the skin).

Treatment: A tetracycline antibiotic taken for a week to 10 days.

■ **More from Dr. Schoen...**

Our Best Tick Tips

When spending time outdoors, consider using a tick repellent that contains 20% to 30% DEET on your skin and clothing. Check yourself (and your pets) thoroughly for ticks after spending time in wooded and/or grassy areas.

Important: Some ticks are smaller than the head of a pin, so you must look very carefully. Use a magnifying glass, if necessary.

To remove a tick: Using pointed tweezers, grab the tick near its head and as close to your skin as possible, and pull it out. Don't use your bare hands. Remove as much of the tick as you can, being careful not to squeeze its body, which could introduce fluid from the tick into the skin. If any fragments remain in the skin, leave them there—they will work themselves out. Such fragments do not increase risk for infection.

■ ■ ■ ■

Teach Children How to Avoid Dog Bites

Children who experience dog bites and are the most seriously injured are under age seven. Teach children to avoid dog bites by showing them proper behavior and explaining basic rules: Never approach a dog you do not know or one that is alone, without an owner nearby. Ask the owner's permission before petting a dog. Do not go near a dog that is sleeping, eating, nursing

puppies or playing with a bone or toy. Do not tease a dog in any way—the dog may not realize that you are being playful.

American Humane Society recommendations, published in Dog Fancy.

Diseases You Can Get From Your Pets

Jon Geller, veterinarian at Veterinary Emergency Hospital, Fort Collins, Colorado. Dr. Geller writes for numerous pet magazines and answers dog owners' questions online at www.dogchannel.com.

In recent years, the drug-resistant bacteria *methicillin-resistant Staphylococcus aureus* (MRSA), which used to be found exclusively in humans, has turned up in pets. Humans can acquire MRSA (often pronounced "mersa") during a hospital stay, then pass it on to their pets, where it can live for several months before being passed back to humans that have close contact with the pets. Dogs and cats both appear to be potential carriers of the bacteria, which can cause severe skin infections, pneumonia and even death in both humans and pets. For protection, always wash your hands after handling a pet, and don't let a pet lick your face. Take your pet to the vet if he/she has any sign of a skin infection.

Other diseases that you can get from your pets...

DOGS

•**Roundworms.** *Toxocariasis* is an infection acquired from the roundworm parasite that lives in the feces of infected dogs. Roundworm eggs find their way into the soil and can be ingested after gardening in infected soil or petting a dog that has been rolling around on the ground. Once ingested, the eggs develop into worms that migrate around the human body. Roundworm infections are more common in arid areas, where the eggs can survive in soil for years.

Human symptoms: Mild infections may not cause symptoms. More serious infections may cause abdominal pain, cough, fever, itchy skin and shortness of breath.

Human treatment: Antiparasitic drugs.

Dog symptoms: Diarrhea, weight loss.

Dog treatment: Deworming medication.

Prevention: Wash hands thoroughly after working in the garden or petting your dog.

•**Hookworms** are in the feces of infected dogs. Hookworm larva can penetrate the skin and develop into worms that tunnel under the skin, creating itchy red tracks.

Human symptoms: Itching, rash, abdominal pain, diarrhea, loss of appetite.

Human treatment: Antiparasitic drugs.

Dog symptoms: Diarrhea, weight loss.

Dog treatment: Deworming medication.

Prevention: Avoid bare-skin contact with soil or beaches where dogs may have defecated.

•**Leptospirosis** is a bacterial infection that affects the urinary tracts of dogs and other animals that acquire the infection through their noses or mouths after spending time in habitats shared by raccoons and other wildlife. Humans acquire it when an open sore or mucous membrane comes in contact with the bacteria.

Human symptoms: Some infected people have no symptoms. Others have high fever, severe headache, chills, vomiting and sometimes jaundice.

Human treatment: Antibiotics.

Dog symptoms: Lethargy, loss of appetite, jaundice.

Dog treatment: Fluids and antibiotics.

Prevention: Wear gloves when working around soil or a habitat shared with raccoons. Avoid swimming or wading in water that might be contaminated with animal urine.

CATS

•**Ringworm** is not a worm but a fungal infection named for the circular rash it causes on humans. Ringworm is transmitted via direct contact with an infected animal's skin or fur.

Human symptoms: Ring-shaped rash that is reddish and often itchy.

Human treatment: Antifungal ointment.

Cat symptoms: Fur thinning and loss.

Cat treatment: Antifungal ointment.

Prevention: Keep your cat inside to minimize the risk for skin parasites.

•**Toxoplasmosis.** Some cats shed a potentially infectious organism in their feces that can be particularly dangerous if ingested by pregnant women and people with compromised immune systems. Cats typically become infected when they eat infected prey, such as mice or birds. Humans can accidentally ingest the parasites after cleaning out a litter box.

Human symptoms: Most people never develop symptoms. Those who do may have headache, fever, fatigue, body aches.

Human treatment: Certain medications can reduce the severity.

Cat symptoms: Often no signs.

Cat treatment: Antibiotics.

Prevention: Pregnant women should avoid cleaning litter boxes. Keep your cat indoors.

•**Cat scratch fever.** This is a bacterial disease caused by *Bartonella henselae.* The organism usually is carried by fleas that live on the cat.

Human symptoms: Swollen lymph nodes, fever and malaise.

Human treatment: Antibiotics.

Cat symptoms: Most cats don't show any signs of illness.

Cat treatment: Flea medication.

Prevention: Promptly wash and disinfect any cat scratches.

BIRDS

•**Psittacosis.** Some birds carry bacteria that cause a bacterial respiratory infection in humans, acquired when they inhale dried secretions from infected birds.

Human symptoms: Fever, chills, headache, muscle aches and dry cough.

Human treatment: Antibiotics.

Bird symptoms: Typically no symptoms, though some birds show signs of respiratory illness, such as lethargy and discharge from eyes and nasal airways.

Bird treatment: Antibiotics.

Prevention: Use extreme care in handling any pet bird showing signs of respiratory illness.

■ ■ ■ ■

Family Dinners— More than Just a Meal

Teens who have dinner with their families at least five times a week are less likely to abuse alcohol and/or drugs than teens who have dinner with their families three or fewer times a week. Teens who are less involved with their families are twice as likely to use tobacco or marijuana…more than one-and-a-half times more likely to use alcohol…and twice as likely to try drugs.

"The Importance of Family Dinners V," a report by the National Center on Addiction and Substance Abuse at Columbia University, New York City. *www.casacolumbia.org*.

■ ■ ■ ■

How to Keep Your Teen Driver Safe

Teens with their own cars are more likely to get into accidents than teens who share a car with a family member.

Recent finding: 25% of teens who had their own vehicles had been involved in crashes, compared with only 11% of those who shared a car. Traffic crashes are the leading cause of death for US teens, resulting in more than 5,000 deaths each year.

Best: Discuss driving privileges with your teen. Set clear rules, and monitor teens' whereabouts. Teens who said their parents did this in a supportive, noncontrolling way were half as likely to crash, compared with teens who said their parents were uninvolved.

Flaura Koplin Winston, MD, PhD, scientific director of the Center for Injury Research and Prevention, Children's Hospital of Philadelphia, and leader of a study of 5,500 teenagers, funded by State Farm Insurance Co. and published in *Pediatrics*.

■ ■ ■ ■

Is TV Keeping You Awake?

When researchers analyzed lifestyle surveys completed by 21,475 Americans, they found that television viewing was the most common activity in the two hours before bedtime.

Concern: Watching television before bedtime often causes people to stay up later—potentially reducing sleep time, which raises risk for obesity and other health problems.

Self-defense: Limit your TV viewing time to allow for seven to eight hours of sleep nightly.

Mathias Basner, MD, assistant professor of sleep and chronobiology in psychiatry, University of Pennsylvania School of Medicine, Philadelphia. His study appeared in the journal *Sleep*.

How to Handle a Hard-of-Hearing Husband

Adrienne Rubinstein, PhD, professor and codirector of the clinical doctoral program in audiology, Brooklyn College, New York. She has taught audiology for more than 25 years and has done extensive research on hearing aids.

You feel annoyed as you beseech your partner to turn down the TV…frustrated at constantly having to repeat yourself…isolated when he skips social events because he can't follow the conversation. The obvious solution is for him to wear a hearing aid—but he's likely to refuse.

Three-quarters of adults with impaired hearing don't even own a hearing aid. Hearing loss is an emotional issue, and your husband may not be aware of his true concerns. To help him overcome reluctance, be sensitive to his real objections. *What you should know and do if he believes…*

•**"I can hear just fine."** Gradual hearing loss often goes unnoticed. In private, gently point out instances in which he misunderstood someone's words and express concern for his safety—for instance, if he can't hear a car honk. Suggest an exam with an audiologist (his doctor can provide a referral)…or download the at-home test uHear to an iPhone (visit *www. Unitron.com*, and click on "Hearing Loss," then "Assessment" and then "test yourself").

•**"If people didn't mutter, I wouldn't have a problem."** Acknowledge that people sometimes mutter, but say that a person with good hearing generally understands mutterings. Tell him you'll speak clearly yourself, but note that he can't control every situation and that speaking loudly can be taxing to others.

•**"A hearing aid will make me look old."** While some people view hearing aids as signs of age-related decline, the inability to follow a conversation is more conspicuous and may be mistaken for mental decline. Besides, some new aids are not noticeable.

•**"It's too expensive."** Features that minimize feedback (annoying whistling) and voice distortion—formerly available only in top models—are now included in aids that cost only about $1,500. Some insurance policies provide partial coverage (Medicare does not). For a 47-page pamphlet, "Your Guide to Financial Assistance for Hearing Aids," contact the Better

Hearing Institute (202-449-1100), or download it from their Web site, *www.BetterHearing.org.*

•**"It's uncomfortable."** If he owns an older hearing aid, explain that new models are much more comfortable. Any new aid should be custom-fitted by an audiologist...and he should return for adjustments, if needed.

•**"Those things don't work."** If he has a hearing aid but says it doesn't help, try replacing the battery and brushing earwax out of the mold and tubing. If he has hearing loss in both ears, he'll hear best with two aids.

•**"Hearing aids aren't worth the trouble."** He may not realize the full consequences of his hearing loss. Gently explain that other people may avoid speaking to him...that he no longer enjoys music or parties...and that you miss his company and conversation.

Heart Disease

New, Easy-to-Manage Blood Thinner Could Replace Warfarin

A new blood thinner known as *dabigatran etexilate* may be just as effective in preventing dangerous venous clots as an old standby, *warfarin* (Coumadin), but much easier for doctors and patients to manage, a recent study finds.

Dabigatran is marketed as Pradax in Canada and Pradaxa in Europe. It is not yet approved for use in the United States.

NEW DRUG FOUND EFFECTIVE AND EASIER TO USE

The study, published online in *The New England Journal of Medicine*, follows on the heels of two other promising reports presented at the American Heart Association (AHA) meeting in Orlando, Florida. Those studies found that dabigatran appeared safe and effective in preventing blood clots when patients were treated for *acute coronary syndrome*, a cluster of symptoms that might indicate a heart attack. It was also found superior to warfarin in preventing strokes in patients with the irregular heartbeat known as *atrial fibrillation*.

In the new trial, warfarin and dabigatran seemed to perform equally well in helping patients with potentially dangerous clots in their veins avoid a subsequent clot or death over the next six months.

But it is in its ease of use that the newer drug appears to outshine warfarin, the authors of this latest study say.

Doctors have for years been looking for a safe alternative to warfarin, which is notoriously difficult to manage.

Jonas Oldgren, MD, chief physician, cardiology, Uppsala University Hospital, Uppsala, Sweden.

Bernard Gersh, MD, professor, medicine, Mayo Clinic College of Medicine, Rochester, Minnesota.

The New England Journal of Medicine online.

American Heart Association annual meeting, Orlando, Florida.

"For patients and health-care providers, dabigatran is a far more convenient drug than warfarin because it has no known interactions with foods and minimal interactions with other drugs and therefore does not require routine blood-coagulation testing," according to the international team of researchers led by Sam Schulman, MD, of McMaster University and the Henderson Research Center in Hamilton, Ontario, Canada.

BLOOD CLOT STUDY

In the prospective trial, which was funded by dabigatran's maker, Boehringer Ingelheim, nearly 1,300 patients who had experienced a *venous thromboembolism* (VTE) received 150 milligrams of dabigatran in pill form twice a day. VTE is a blood clot that typically originates in the deep veins of the legs, and then travels to the lungs. Another group of nearly 1,300 patients was given warfarin, adjusted in dose to suit their particular needs.

Six months after the therapies began, 30 patients on dabigatran experienced another VTE compared with 27 patients on warfarin, for a 0.4% difference in risk, the authors reported. Side effects such as major or minor bleeding were similar between the two groups, with slightly more bleeding events occurring in those on warfarin.

Based on the results, the authors concluded that, "a fixed dose of dabigatran is as effective as warfarin, has a safety profile that is similar to that of warfarin, and does not require laboratory monitoring."

ACUTE CORONARY SYNDROME STUDY

Those optimistic findings echo those from a study presented at the AHA meeting that involved more than 1,800 patients in 24 countries with acute coronary syndrome. Patients received one of four doses of dabigatran or a placebo on top of aspirin and the blood thinner *clopidogrel* (Plavix).

The study found dabigatran safe in preventing blood clots in these heart patients. Researchers also saw reductions in mortality, nonfatal heart attack and stroke, although the trial was not specifically designed to look at effectiveness.

"Dabigatran seems to be safe on top of dual antiplatelet therapy [meaning aspirin and Plavix]," said study author Jonas Oldgren, MD,

chief physician in the department of cardiology at Uppsala University Hospital in Uppsala, Sweden. "It has already been shown to have superior efficacy compared with warfarin."

ABNORMAL HEART RHYTHM STUDY

And another trial, also presented at the AHA meeting, demonstrated that dabigatran outperformed warfarin in preventing strokes in patients with atrial fibrillation.

EXPERT REACTION

"Dabigatran appears to be superior to warfarin in terms of safety and more effective as well. This is the first alternative to warfarin that could signal a changing of the guard," said Bernard Gersh, MD, a professor of medicine at the Mayo Clinic College of Medicine in Rochester, Minnesota. "I think there are still questions that need to be answered, but it's fair to say that warfarin has been around for many, many years and everybody hates warfarin. Patients hate warfarin. Doctors hate warfarin. It's not the most convenient drug, but it's effective and it is cheap.

"It's premature to say that a drug like dabigatran will take the place of warfarin," Dr. Gersh added. "There will be a lot of discussion about cost and convenience. It's a twice-daily dose and there are some questions about a possible higher rate of heart attack. I don't think this is truly resolved yet, but I think we can say that for the first time we have seen a drug that certainly has the potential to be an alternative to warfarin, and maybe even superior."

info For more information on blood thinners, visit the American Heart Association Web site, *www.heart.org*, and search "anticoagulant drugs."

Stem Cells Pump Up Damaged Hearts

Rush University Medical Center news release.

Adult stem cells appear to help repair heart attack damage, a new study shows.

The preliminary study of 53 patients found that stem cells from donor bone marrow promoted the growth of new blood vessels in heart tissue damaged by heart attack.

STUDY DETAILS

The patients received the stem cell injections within 10 days of having a heart attack. During follow-up, they were compared with patients who had received a placebo injection.

After six months, those who got the stem cells were four times more likely to be better off overall, pumped more blood with each heartbeat, and had one-quarter as many irregular heartbeats, when compared to the placebo group. There also were no serious side effects with the stem cell treatment, according to the report published in the *Journal of the American College of Cardiology*.

IMPLICATIONS

This is the strongest evidence so far that adult stem cells can repair heart attack damage, the Rush University Medical Center researchers said. It had been believed that only embryonic stem cells could turn into heart or other organ cells.

"The results point to a promising new treatment for heart attack patients that could reduce [death] and lessen the need for heart transplants," said Gary Schaer, MD, director of the Rush Cardiac Catheterization Laboratory.

info For more information about heart attack, visit the Web site of the US National Heart, Lung, and Blood Institute, *www. nhlbi.nih.gov*, and search "heart attack."

A Doctor's Own Cardiac Comeback Plan

Marc Wallack, MD, chief of surgery at Metropolitan Hospital in New York City and vice-chair of the department of surgery at New York Medical College, Valhalla. He is author, with his wife, Jamie Colby, of the new book *Back to Life After a Heart Crisis: A Doctor and His Wife Share Their 8-Step Cardiac Comeback Plan* (Avery). *www.back tolifethebook.com*.

In 2002, Marc Wallack, a surgeon, started having chest pains while jogging. Though heart disease runs in his family—his father and paternal grandfather died of heart attacks—

he thought he had heartburn and took antacids. After four days of "heartburn," he finally saw a doctor and learned that all of his coronary arteries were 95% blocked. He needed bypass surgery to survive.

The operation was a success, but Dr. Wallack, then in his 50s, found that his life had changed dramatically. He was afraid to fall asleep at night because he was worried that he wouldn't wake up again. He wondered if his heart could withstand exercise or sex.

What Dr. Wallack realized is that while surgery and cardiac rehabilitation keep patients alive, they don't necessarily help them live. *Here, he shares his eight steps to a complete recovery, physically and mentally...*

***Step 1:* Get sleep.** The majority of patients who undergo heart-related procedures sleep poorly following their procedures. Nearly half experience some degree of insomnia for eight weeks or more. Even when patients think they sleep soundly, they often have little or no rapid-eye movement (REM) or slow-wave sleep, both of which are critical for recovery.

Nighttime fears—particularly of death and disability—are extremely common in heart patients. The resulting sleep disturbances increase the risk for subsequent heart disease.

I used prescription sleep medications for about three months before I was able to sleep most nights without them. New generations of medications, such as *eszopiclone* (Lunesta) and *zolpidem* (Ambien), are extremely safe (though carry some risk for dependency).

I also discovered that I felt calmer and slept better when there was static noise in the background. I used a white noise machine. Or you can use a fan, and there are Internet sites that play white noise through the computer.

Example: *www.simplynoise.com*.

In addition, I slept with the blinds open so that I could see the lights outside (I live in New York City)—it made me feel alive.

***Step 2:* Overcome depression.** Nearly one in three heart attack survivors experiences post-surgical depression, in part because microclots can travel to the brain and cause mood changes. According to researchers at University of Maryland and Columbia University Medical Center, patients who were depressed after cardiac surgery were twice as likely to die from heart problems within seven years, compared with those who were not depressed.

Talk therapy, sometimes combined with antidepressants, can help patients get past their depression and regain a sense of balance. One study found that patients who attended group therapy after heart surgery and/or a heart attack had a 60% lower rate of rehospitalization than those who didn't get therapy.

Step 3: **Get back into the world.** It can take months or longer to recover from major surgery. Patients are weak and disoriented. They often are reluctant to leave home, even after their doctors say it's OK to do so, because they're afraid of falling or that they'll somehow damage their hearts.

Getting out of the house is a major step in recovery. Everyone needs sunlight, fresh air and a change of scenery. Even gentle exercise, such as walking to a corner store, can alleviate depression and improve your motivation to recover. Bring a friend or family member if you're not sure of your ability to get around on your own. Eventually work up to driving and going out by yourself to build your confidence.

Step 4: **Optimize doctor visits.** Patients who have had heart surgery initially have numerous postsurgical doctor visits. These often are stressful because patients fear that they might hear bad news. The anxiety surrounding these visits can undermine the patient's confidence and make him feel more like a patient than a person. To counteract that, my wife and I turned a doctor visit into an outing. We would go out to breakfast or lunch first. (I tried to make my appointments for first thing in the morning or the first appointment after lunch so that I wouldn't have to wait long for the doctor.)

Helpful: Bring someone with you when you see a doctor or undergo tests. Your mind can go blank when you're the patient, so you need someone who can listen carefully, take notes and ask questions.

For further peace of mind, ask your cardiologist what's the best way to contact him/her. Get the names and contact information for key people in the office, such as the nurse practitioner. You need to know who to call or e-mail if, for example, you notice that your heart is beating faster than usual.

Step 5: **Make love again.** After the first few months of recovery, ask your doctor if it's OK for you to have sex. Heart patients often worry that the exertion of sex will strain their hearts. Not true. The odds of having a heart attack during sex, even if you already have had a heart attack, are typically about 20 in one million. Less than 1% of patients who die of a heart attack do so during sex.

Step 6: **Eat for recovery.** I advise most postsurgical patients to eat small meals frequently. The lingering effects of anesthesia can make people feel nauseous and reluctant to eat. Pain medications often inhibit appetite. So does prolonged bed rest and postsurgical fatigue.

My story: Every time I ate, I worried that the food would instantly clog my arteries or cause a clot to form. This wasn't rational, and it made it difficult for me to gain weight and recover my strength after surgery.

I found that smoothies were ideal.

I made them with low-fat yogurt, skim milk, fruit and ice. They didn't upset my stomach, and the more I ate, the more I wanted to eat.

Step 7: **Prepare for career issues.** After my surgery, I was surprised to discover that some of my colleagues were vying for my job. When you go back to work, don't talk much about your health history, and don't let people see you taking your medicine.

But ask your boss or human resources representative for accommodations, such as time off for rehab three times a week or the OK to take a 15-minute nap every day. Chronic work stress doubles the odds of experiencing a second heart attack within six years. Give yourself time to get back into the groove.

Step 8: **Set an exercise goal.** Regular exercise improves cholesterol, lowers blood pressure and reduces stress. Just as important, it gives you a goal. People need strong goals to get through the grueling months of rehabilitation.

My goal was to run another marathon after I recovered. This gave me the internal strength to try to get better even when I was so weak that I could only take a few steps. I did run a marathon in November 2005, a little more than three years after my surgery.

Develop an exercise program with a rehabilitation expert who can work with you for the first few months (this typically is covered by insurance). Your first exercise goal might be to build up enough strength so that you can comfortably walk up and down stairs or to work in the yard without fatigue. No matter what you hope to achieve, the best way to get there is to move your body again.

■ ■ ■ ■

Secret to Better Bypass Surgery

Bypass surgery using a heart-lung machine is better than off-pump surgery for low- to medium-risk patients. On-pump surgery uses a heart-lung machine to take over blood circulation. A new method of doing bypass surgery on a still-beating heart was developed in the 1990s. Now a study shows that one year after surgery, about 10% of patients getting the off-pump procedure needed a repeat operation, had a heart attack or died, compared with 7.4% of those who underwent operations using heart-lung machines.

Frederick L. Grover, MD, staff cardiothoracic surgeon at Denver VA Medical Center and chair, department of surgery, University of Colorado at Denver Medical Center, Aurora. He is a coprincipal investigator of a seven-year study of 2,203 bypass-surgery patients.

■ ■ ■ ■

Best Way to Perform CPR

In a study of 506 cardiac arrest patients, researchers analyzed the effectiveness of chest compressions given during *cardiopulmonary resuscitation* (CPR) prior to the use of a defibrillator to restore normal heart rhythm.

Result: Patients' survival rates were highest when study subjects administered continuous chest compressions with the fewest interruptions possible until emergency rescuers arrived.

Theory: Chest compressions prepare the heart to start its own rhythm when a defibrillator delivers a shock. The American Heart Association recommends giving 100 chest compressions per minute.

James M. Christenson, MD, clinical professor of emergency medicine, University of British Columbia, Vancouver, Canada.

■ ■ ■ ■

How to Double CPR Success

According to a recent study, the odds of surviving cardiac arrest outside of a hospital were 5% without CPR...6% with standard CPR (alternating chest compressions and mouth-to-mouth breaths)...and 11% with continuous compressions without mouth-to-mouth. If someone needs CPR, call 911 and perform continuous chest compressions until help arrives.

Gordon A. Ewy, MD, director, University of Arizona Sarver Heart Center, Tucson, and presenter of an analysis of 4,850 cardiac arrest cases.

Chest Pains—What They Mean...What to Do

Albert J. Miller, MD, recently retired professor of clinical medicine (cardiology) at Northwestern University's Feinberg School of Medicine and a clinical cardiologist at Northwestern Memorial Hospital, both in Chicago. He is the author of *Chest Pain—When & When Not to Worry* (Self-help Success). He has authored or coauthored more than 120 medical journal articles on cardiovascular disease.

Virtually everyone feels chest pain at some point—and for good reason. Any of the organs in the chest, as well as the chest wall itself, can cause pain.

While severe pain is clearly something that you should pay close attention to, lesser degrees of pain also can indicate trouble. Surprisingly, mild chest pain can signal a heart attack, while some severe pains may not always be serious (such as pains due to sore muscles).

Your health—and, in some cases, your life—depends on knowing when chest pain indicates a serious condition that needs immediate attention.

Important: If you experience any feeling in your chest that's new or that you don't understand—especially if it persists—consult a doctor.

Some possible causes of chest pain—and what each may mean…

IT'S THE HEART!

•**Heart attack.** Typical symptoms are pressure, squeezing or heaviness behind the breastbone in the center of your chest, often associated with nausea, sweating, light-headedness or shortness of breath.

This could signal a heart attack, caused when blood flow to the heart is cut off by a blood clot in a coronary artery. Many people mistakenly think the heart is located on the left side of the chest (because they feel their heartbeat there), but it's actually in the center—so pain in the mid-chest should be taken seriously.

What you may not know: It's common to have a history of milder chest pain in the center of the chest preceding (by up to two weeks in some cases) the more severe pain of a heart attack. Pain from a heart attack also can radiate to one or both shoulders and arms (especially the left) or to the neck or jaw.

If you suffer mid-chest pain, call 911 and get to a hospital emergency department as quickly as possible! Do not wait to see if the pain goes away. Prompt treatment will minimize damage to your heart muscle and may save your life.

•**Stable angina pectoris.** Typical symptoms are crushing pain or mild to moderate squeezing, tightness or heaviness in the middle of the chest brought on by physical exertion, emotional stress or cold weather—all of which can increase the work of the heart. Pain is relieved by rest and usually lasts five minutes or less.

The pain of angina pectoris indicates insufficient blood flow to the heart muscle, usually due to partial blockages from fatty deposits that narrow one or more coronary arteries. While this pain isn't a medical emergency like a heart attack, it's a sign that you need to schedule a doctor visit.

•**Unstable angina pectoris.** Typical symptoms are unexplained pain (not necessarily severe) in the middle of the chest, tightness, constriction, squeezing or heaviness…and/or pain in the neck, left shoulder or left arm. These symptoms persist and/or may occur while you're at rest or awaken you at night.

Associated with significantly impaired blood flow to the heart muscle, unstable angina pectoris frequently indicates an impending heart attack. If you experience these symptoms, go to a hospital emergency department immediately.

THE HEART IS NOT THE CULPRIT

•**Lung condition.** Typical symptoms are sharp pain in either side of the chest, made worse by breathing.

This may indicate a lung problem such as pneumonia…*pleurisy* (inflammation of the surface lining of a lung)…or a blood clot that formed elsewhere (usually in a leg vein), broke off and traveled to the lungs. A pulmonary blood clot is life-threatening and requires hospitalization and treatment.

•**Aortic dissection.** A typical symptom is a usually excruciating, tearing pain in the chest or between the shoulder blades.

This pain arises from "dissection" of the aorta (the large artery that carries blood from the left ventricle to the rest of the body) and occurs when blood from the aorta burrows between the layers of its wall. This condition is a major emergency requiring immediate medical care.

LESS SERIOUS CHEST PAINS

•**Acid reflux.** Typical symptoms include a burning discomfort in the middle of the chest that may radiate to the throat, usually after eating spicy food or drinking alcohol or coffee. Acid reflux (in which stomach contents wash up into the esophagus) is not an emergency but warrants treatment if it is recurrent.

•**Musculoskeletal problem.** Typical symptoms include pain in the chest, shoulder or upper back that is aggravated by specific movements, such as reaching for an object or putting an item on a high shelf.

These pains are typically due to a musculoskeletal problem, such as a strained muscle or tendon or arthritis. Each merits medical attention, but none is a serious health threat.

Important: Sharp, shooting pains in the chest that last just a few seconds also can be musculoskeletal in origin. These transitory pains are usually insignificant.

•**Neck problem.** Typical symptoms include pain on the side of the neck and/or across the right or left shoulder, and sometimes also in the upper chest on the same side of the affected shoulder.

This can be caused by a ruptured spinal disk in the neck. Treatment depends on the severity of the problem.

•**Panic attack.** Typical symptoms include breathing problems (such as shortness of breath or hyperventilation), perhaps accompanied by chest discomfort. These symptoms should be evaluated by a doctor.

■ ■ ■ ■

Heart Attack Symptoms Can Be The Same in Men and Women

It is commonly believed that men and women experience different heart attack symptoms. Canadian researchers tested this perception in a small study. They found that men and women were equally likely to report chest discomfort, shortness of breath, nausea and clammy skin before a heart attack. Women were more likely also to report pain in the throat, jaw and neck. If you experience any of these symptoms, seek medical attention immediately.

M.H. Mackay, et al., "Gender Differences in Reported Symptoms of Acute Coronary Syndromes," *Canadian Journal of Cardiology* (2009).

Why People Faint...and Why You Should Never Ignore It

Lewis A. Lipsitz, MD, a professor of medicine at Harvard Medical School, vice president for academic medicine and co-director of the Institute for Aging Research at Hebrew SeniorLife in Boston. He is the chief of the gerontology division at Beth Israel Deaconess Medical Center, also in Boston.

Even though some people faint for seemingly harmless reasons, such as the sight of blood, there are several potential causes. This temporary loss of consciousness that lasts no more than a few minutes can occur any time the brain isn't getting enough oxygen-rich blood.

What you need to know about the most common causes of *syncope* (pronounced "SIN ko PEE"), the medical term for fainting...

•**Heart conditions.** *Arrhythmias,* in which the heart beats too fast (*tachycardia*), too slow (*bradycardia*) or in an irregular pattern, cause fainting in up to 12% of older adults who suffer from syncope. With an arrhythmia, ineffective pumping of blood can result in an insufficient amount of blood going to the brain.

Typical treatment: Medication to help control the underlying heart condition.

•**Medications.** Certain drugs, such as medications for high blood pressure, heart failure, depression and Parkinson's disease, can cause fainting, especially when you first start taking them and/or if the dosage is too high. Men who take excessive doses of medication for an enlarged prostate, such as *tamsulosin* (Flomax), also may faint.

Typical treatment: Your doctor may lower the dosage or prescribe a different medication. Never stop taking a prescription drug without speaking to your physician.

•**Orthostatic (postural) hypotension (low blood pressure).** Sitting or lying down causes blood to pool in the legs. When you stand, blood vessels normally constrict in response to this postural change, ensuring that your brain continues to get enough blood. But in people with orthostatic hypotension, this mechanism is defective.

Typical treatment: Drinking enough water (which increases blood volume and prevents dehydration)...avoiding alcohol (which is dehydrating)...and wearing support hose (to prevent blood from pooling in the legs). Some people may be prescribed *fludrocortisone* (Florinef) to increase blood volume (including that to the brain) and *midodrine* (ProAmitine) to constrict blood vessels.

•**Postprandial hypotension.** After a meal (postprandial), blood pools in the intestines, thus reducing blood flow to the brain. In healthy people, the body responds by increasing heart rate and constricting blood vessels to maintain normal blood pressure. This mechanism fails in people with postprandial hypotension.

Typical treatment: Eat smaller, more frequent meals with fewer carbohydrates.

•**Vasovagal syncope.** This type of fainting, which can be triggered by emotional distress, exertion (such as straining on the toilet), heat or the sight of blood, leads to an exaggerated bodily process. The heart rate slows and blood vessels in the legs widen, allowing blood to pool in the legs. This lowers blood pressure, reduces blood flow to the brain and can result in fainting.

In some people, vasovagal syncope results from overly sensitive reflexes involved in swallowing, urinating or defecating. Vasovagal syncope also can occur in people who have a condition known as *carotid sinus hypersensitivity*, which causes fainting when excess pressure is placed on the carotid (neck) artery—for example, when a shirt collar is too tight.

Typical treatment: Avoiding situations that trigger vasovagal syncope. In people with swallowing syncope, eating smaller, more frequent meals can help. Men should sit on the toilet while urinating if they have this form of syncope. Adding more fiber to your diet helps prevent constipation.

•**Illnesses.** People with anemia may be more prone to fainting if they bleed excessively (due to an injury, for example), because blood loss can trigger a sharp drop in blood pressure. Hypoglycemia (low blood sugar), which can occur in people with or without diabetes, also can lead to fainting.

Typical treatment: People who have anemia should see their doctors regularly for treatment and monitoring of the condition. People with diabetes should control their blood sugar levels.

IDENTIFYING THE CAUSE

Syncope is sometimes misattributed to a stroke, brain tumor or seizure—all of which can cause loss of consciousness. But strokes, tumors and seizures are more apt to also cause slurred speech and/or vision loss. According to a recent study, doctors often rush to perform costly heart tests, such as cardiac enzyme tests, which measure possible heart damage, while overlooking much less expensive postural blood pressure testing.

Simple test: When assuming a standing position after lying down, you may have orthostatic hypotension if systolic (top number) blood pressure drops by more than 20 points or if systolic pressure drops below 100.

Another important tool: The tilt table test. For this test, you lie down and are strapped to a table, which is then tilted to raise the upper body to simulate what happens when you go from a lying to a standing position. Your body's response to the change in position may indicate whether you have orthostatic hypotension.

The tilt table test may be used in addition to postural blood pressure testing (mentioned above).

If your doctor suspects that your fainting is due to a heart problem, you may receive an *electrocardiogram* (which measures electrical activity of the heart) and an *echocardiogram* (a type of ultrasound test that helps detect abnormalities in heart rate or rhythm).

■ **More from Dr. Lipsitz...**

If You or Someone Else Faints

If you're feeling faint, lie or sit down immediately. If you're sitting, put your head between your knees to help restore blood flow to your brain. *If someone else faints...*

•**Get the person into a supine position (lying down with the face up).** Raise the legs so they're higher than the head to bring blood back to the heart and head.

•**Check the person's breathing.** If breathing has stopped, call 911 and perform cardiopulmonary resuscitation (CPR)—about 100 uninterrupted chest compressions per minute.

The 15-Minute Heart Cure

John M. Kennedy, MD, medical director of preventive cardiology and wellness at Marina Del Rey Hospital, California. He is on the board of directors for the American Heart Association and is coauthor, with Jason Jennings, of *The 15 Minute Heart Cure: The Natural Way to Release Stress and Heal Your Heart in Just Minutes a Day* (Wiley). *www.the15MinuteHeartCure.com.*

Most people know that smoking, high cholesterol and high blood pressure are among the main risk factors for heart disease. Few of us realize that daily stress is another key risk factor. It can damage the heart and arteries even in people who are otherwise healthy.

Recent finding: A University of Southern California study that looked at 735 patients for more than 12 years found that chronic stress and anxiety were better predictors of future cardiovascular events (such as a heart attack) than other risk factors. The researchers estimate that those who reduce or stabilize their stress levels are 50% to 60% less likely to have a heart attack than those who experience increasing stress.

TOXIC OVER TIME

Researchers have known for a long time that sudden traumatic events can trigger heart problems. Three years after the 9/11 terrorist attacks, for example, study participants—most of whom watched the attacks on live television—were questioned about their stress levels. Those who still were severely stressed were 53% more likely to have heart problems, and twice as likely to develop high blood pressure, as those with lower stress levels.

It appears that even "normal" stress—financial pressures or an unhappy job situation—is dangerous when it continues for a long time. It's estimated that more than 75% of visits to primary care physicians are linked to disorders that are stress-related.

What happens: Chronic stress increases vascular resistance, the main cause of high blood pressure. It increases the activity of platelets, cell-like structures in blood that clump together and trigger most heart attacks. It increases levels of cortisol, adrenaline and other stress hormones and can contribute to arterial inflammation.

Doctors have been slow to acknowledge stress as a major cardiovascular risk factor. This is partly because stress (like pain) is subjective and highly individual—it's difficult to quantify, because everyone has different stress triggers and experiences stress differently. One lawyer might thrive on hectic 16-hour days, while another might react with high anxiety.

Stress can't be directly measured, but tests show its toxic effects. When laboratory subjects who are asked to count backward from 100 by eights get increasingly frustrated, there is a corresponding increase in their heart rate, adrenaline and substances linked to inflammation, such as C-reactive protein and *interleukins*.

STRESS REDUCTION WORKS

We can only partly control our emotional environments—stress-causing events can't always be avoided. But we can greatly change the ways in which we react to stress. People who do this can significantly lower their cardiovascular risks.

In one study, patients with heart disease were divided into three groups and followed for up to five years. Those in one group practiced stress reduction. Those in the other groups were treated either with an exercise program or with standard medical care. (The standard-care group maintained their regular medical regimen and did not participate in an exercise or stress-management program.)

Only 10% of those in the stress-control group had a subsequent heart attack or required bypass surgery or angioplasty, compared with 21% in the exercise group and 30% in the medical-care group.

BREATHE

The traditional techniques for reducing stress, such as yoga, are helpful but typically too complicated and time-consuming for most people. My colleagues and I have developed a simpler approach that anyone can do in about 15 minutes a day. It goes by the acronym B-R-E-A-T-H-E, which stands for Begin, Relax, Envision, Apply, Treat, Heal and End.

•**Begin.** Pick a time of day when you won't be interrupted for 15 minutes. Find a comfortable location. Many patients use their bedrooms, but any quiet, private place will work.

•**Relax.** This phase of the exercise is meant to elicit the relaxation response, a physiological process that reduces stress hormones, slows electrical activity in the brain and reduces inflammation.

Sit or lie quietly. Focus so completely on your breathing that there isn't room in your mind for anything else. Inhale slowly and deeply through your nose. Then exhale just as slowly through your mouth. Each inhalation and exhalation should take about seven seconds.

Repeat the breathing cycle seven times. You'll know you're ready to go to the next step when your body is so relaxed that it feels as if all of your weight is supported by the chair or bed rather than by your muscles.

•**Envision.** Spend a few minutes imagining that every part of your heart—the arteries, muscles, valves and the electrical system—is strong and healthy. Form a mental picture (it doesn't have to be anatomically accurate) of the heart pumping blood and sending nourishment throughout your body. Hold this image in your mind for several minutes.

Studies using positron emission tomography (PET) scans show that people who imagine that they are performing an action activate the same part of the brain that is involved when they actually do that action. Imagining a healthy heart literally can make the heart healthier.

•**Apply.** It's up to you when (and how often) you perform this relaxation exercise. Most people can find 15 minutes a day to take a mental break from stress to keep their hearts healthy. Others also use this technique when they notice that their stress levels are rising.

During a hectic day at work, for example, you might take a break for 15 minutes to calm down with conscious breathing and visualization.

•**Treat and heal.** I encourage patients to embrace the pleasurable aspects of this exercise. Don't consider it a chore. It's more like a spa treatment than a physical workout.

The healing aspect can be strongly motivating, particularly if you already have a history of heart disease. Every time you do this exercise, you are strengthening the neural networks that connect the heart and brain. This can lead to a decrease in heart arrhythmias (irregularities), an increase in immune-cell activity and even better sleep.

•**End.** Finish each relaxation session by making a mental checklist of what you have achieved. You have imagined that your heart and arteries are healthy. You have reduced stress hormones, and you are feeling more relaxed and energized than you did before.

The results are long-lasting. People who practice this for a few weeks will find themselves dealing with unexpected stressful events productively and in a calm, focused manner.

■ ■ ■ ■

Go to Bed! (It's Good for Your Heart)

In a study of 251 healthy men, those who typically went to bed after midnight were more likely to have arterial stiffening, an early stage of *atherosclerosis* (hardening of the arteries)—a heart disease risk factor.

Theory: A late bedtime may promote insulin resistance (a condition in which the body is less able to respond to insulin), which can lead to atherosclerosis and heart disease.

Yu Misao, MD, PhD, chief researcher, laboratory of disease prevention, department of medicine, Misao Health Clinic, Gifu, Japan.

Beware! This Supplement May Be Bad for Your Heart

University of Warwick news release.

Taking selenium supplements could boost your cholesterol levels and increase your risk of heart disease, English researchers suggest.

Selenium—a trace essential mineral with antioxidant properties—is found in meat, vegetables and seafood. Some people also take selenium supplements because they believe the mineral will reduce the risk for cancer and other diseases.

STUDY FINDINGS

University of Warwick researchers examined the link between levels of selenium in the blood and fats in the blood in 1,042 people, ages 19 to 64. The study found that participants with blood levels of selenium higher than 1.20 micromoles per liter (µmol/L) had an 8% higher average total cholesterol level and 10% higher non-HDL cholesterol levels (LDL "bad" cholesterol and other cholesterol levels that help predict risk for heart attack), compared with those with the lowest selenium blood levels. Of the participants with the highest selenium levels, 48.2% said they took dietary supplements.

The study was published in *The Journal of Nutrition.*

IMPLICATIONS

Although high selenium levels were not exclusively caused by taking dietary supplements, the findings are cause for concern because the use of selenium dietary supplements is increasing, said study leader Saverio Stranges, MD, PhD.

"This use has spread despite the lack of definitive evidence on selenium supplements efficacy for cancer and other chronic disease prevention. The cholesterol increases we identified may have important implications for public health. In fact, such a difference could translate into a large number of premature deaths from coronary heart disease," Dr. Stranges said.

ADVICE

"We believe that the widespread use of selenium supplements, or of any other strategy that artificially increases selenium above the level required, is unwarranted at the present time," said Dr. Stranges. "Further research is needed to examine the full range of health effects of increased selenium, whether beneficial or detrimental."

info The Web site of the US National Institutes of Health's Office of Dietary Supplements has more information about selenium at *http://ods.od.nih.gov.* Search "selenium."

Heart Supplements that Can Save Your Life

Dennis Goodman, MD, clinical associate professor of medicine at New York University School of Medicine in New York City and at the University of California in San Diego. Dr. Goodman also is director of integrative medicine at New York Medical Associates, a group private practice in New York City. He is board certified in internal medicine, cardiology, interventional cardiology, critical care, clinical lipidology and holistic (integrative) medicine. *www.dennisgoodmanmd.com.*

One of the most common reasons that people take nutritional supplements is to improve their heart health.

Problem: Very few cardiologists are aware of the ways in which heart supplements work synergistically—that is, by taking carefully selected supplements in combinations, you will heighten the effectiveness of each one. Over the past 22 years, I have treated thousands of heart patients with this approach.

What you need to know to make the most of your nondrug regimen for better heart health…*

THE ESSENTIAL THREE

There are three daily supplements that I recommend to anyone who is concerned about heart health…

•**Fish oil** capsules primarily lower harmful blood fats known as triglycerides but also have a mild blood pressure–lowering effect.

Typical dose: 1 gram (g) total of the omega-3 fatty acids *eicosapentaenoic acid* (EPA) and *docosahexaenoic acid* (DHA) for blood pressure benefits. To reduce triglyceride levels, the typical daily dose is 2 g to 4 g total of EPA and DHA.

Caution: Fish oil can increase bleeding risk, so talk to your doctor if you take a blood thinner, such as *warfarin* (Coumadin).

•**CoQ10** helps enhance energy production in cells and inhibits blood clot formation.

Typical dose: 50 milligrams (mg) to 100 mg per day. CoQ10, which is commonly taken with the classic HDL-boosting treatment niacin (vitamin B-3), also helps minimize side effects, such as muscle weakness, in people taking cholesterol-lowering statin drugs.

•**Red yeast rice** is an extract of red yeast that is fermented on rice and is available in tablet, capsule, powder and liquid form. Long used by the Chinese, it mimics the action of cholesterol-lowering statin drugs.

Typical dose: 600 mg twice daily.

Red yeast rice is often used in combination with plant *sterols,* naturally occurring chemical compounds found in small amounts in fruits, vegetables and nuts…and added to food products, including butter substitutes, such as Promise activ and Benecol spreads.

Typical dose: About 400 mg daily of plant sterols.

*To find a doctor to oversee your heart-health supplement regimen, consult the American Board of Integrative Holistic Medicine, *www.holisticboard.org.*

Also important: Low levels of vitamin D (below 15 nanograms per milliliter) have been linked to a 62% increase, on average, in heart attack risk.

Typical dose: 5,000 international units (IU) of vitamin D-3 per day for those who are deficient in the vitamin…at least 1,000 IU daily for all other adults.

BETTER BLOOD PRESSURE CONTROL

The heart-friendly properties of fish oil are so well-documented that the American Heart Association endorses its use (by eating fatty fish at least twice weekly and/or taking fish oil capsules).

To enhance fish oil's blood pressure–lowering effect, ask your doctor about adding…

•**L-arginine.** This amino acid boosts the body's production of the chemical compound nitric oxide, which causes the blood vessels to dilate, thereby lowering blood pressure.

Typical dose: 150 mg daily.

L-arginine is also used to treat erectile dysfunction and *claudication* (impeded blood flow in the extremities) and has a mild and beneficial HDL-boosting effect.

Caution: L-arginine should not be taken by children or pregnant or nursing women, or by anyone with genital *herpes*—it can stimulate activity of the herpes virus. Possible side effects include indigestion, nausea and headache.

•**Lycopene.** This *phytochemical* is found in tomatoes—especially processed tomato sauce—watermelon, pink grapefruit, red bell peppers and papaya. I usually recommend that patients try L-arginine first, then add lycopene, if necessary, for blood pressure reduction.

Research conducted at Ben-Gurion University in Israel has shown that lycopene lowers systolic (top number) blood pressure by up to 10 points and diastolic (bottom number) by up to four points.

A potent antioxidant, lycopene is also thought to have potential cancer-preventive effects, but this has not been proven.

Typical dose: 10 mg daily.

In rare cases, lycopene supplements can cause diarrhea and/or nausea. Because tomatoes and other acidic foods can aggravate ulcer pain, people with stomach ulcers should consult their doctors before consuming tomatoes and tomato-based products regularly.

BOOST HDL CHOLESTEROL

In addition to taking CoQ10 and niacin, ask your doctor about trying…

•**Policosanol.** This plant-wax derivative has been found to boost HDL levels by more than 7%. The research on policosanol is considered controversial by some, but I have found it to be an effective HDL booster in my practice.

Typical dose: 10 mg daily.

There is also some evidence that policosanol may have LDL- and triglyceride-lowering benefits. There are no known side effects associated with policosanol.

Bonus: Used together, CoQ10, niacin and policosanol will allow you to raise your HDL levels while taking much lower doses of niacin (about 20 mg daily). A lower niacin dose reduces the risk for facial flushing, a common side effect in people who take the vitamin.

REDUCE LDL CHOLESTEROL

Red yeast rice extract and plant sterols (both described earlier) are well-known natural methods of lowering LDL cholesterol levels.

To lower your LDL cholesterol further, ask your doctor about adding policosanol (described earlier), along with…

•**Pantethine.** This is a more biologically active form of *pantothenic acid* (vitamin B-5).

Typical dose: 600 mg daily.

Numerous small studies have found that pantethine significantly lowers LDL cholesterol and triglycerides.

•**Grape seed extract.** This antioxidant-rich substance reduces the blood's tendency to clot and helps lower blood pressure by boosting levels of the chemical compound nitric oxide found in the body. Some research shows that grape seed extract also reduces LDL cholesterol.

Typical dose: 200 mg daily.

In addition, studies suggest that grape seed extract helps protect against Alzheimer's disease.

Caution: Because grape seed extract has a blood-thinning effect, it should not be taken by anyone who uses warfarin or other blood-thinning medications or supplements.

■ **More from Dr. Goodman...**

Best Nutrients for Heart Health

Food is our best source of nutrients. That's because food sources offer a variety of minerals, vitamins and antioxidants that work synergistically to boost the nutritional value of each. *I urge all of my patients to get ample amounts of the following heart-healthy nutrients from food...*

•**Antioxidants,** which help prevent plaque formation on the walls of your arteries. Good sources are pomegranate, blueberries, and fruits and vegetables in general.

•**Magnesium,** which helps regulate blood pressure and stabilize heart rhythm. Good sources are dark green, leafy vegetables...soy beans...almonds...cashews...black-eyed peas...and peanut butter.

•**Potassium,** which helps regulate blood pressure and heart function. Good sources are apricots, cantaloupe, melons, kiwi, oranges (and orange juice), bananas, lima beans, tomatoes, prunes, avocados...as well as meat, fish and poultry.

Caution: If you have kidney disease, consult your doctor before consuming potassium-rich foods.

Foods that Lower Risk For Heart Disease

American Heart Association news releases.

Eating plenty of potassium-rich foods, such as leafy greens, potatoes and bananas, may reduce the risk of stroke and coronary artery disease, say Italian researchers.

POTASSIUM STUDY

The new analysis was based on 10 studies published between 1966 and 2009 that included nearly 280,000 adults. During follow-ups that ranged from five to 19 years, there were more than 5,500 strokes and nearly 3,100 coronary heart disease events, the investigators found.

Higher potassium intake was associated with a 19% lower risk for stroke and an 8% lower risk for coronary heart disease. The findings support global recommendations for people to increase their consumption of potassium-rich foods in order to prevent vascular disease, said Pasquale Strazzullo, MD, of the University of Naples, and colleagues.

Other foods high in potassium include soybeans, apricots, avocados, plain nonfat yogurt, prune juice, and dried beans and peas.

The findings were presented at the American Heart Association's Nutrition, Physical Activity and Metabolism conference in San Francisco.

RAW FRUITS AND VEGETABLES STUDY

Another study presented at the meeting found that a diet high in raw fruits and vegetables might help protect against stroke.

Researchers examined the incidence of stroke among more than 20,000 men and women, ages 20 to 65, who were free of cardiovascular disease at the start of the study. During 10 years of follow-up, there were 233 strokes among the participants.

After they adjusted for a number of factors, the researchers found that people with a high intake (more than 9 ounces per day) of raw fruits and vegetables were 36% less likely to suffer a stroke than those with a low intake (less than 3.2 ounces per day) of raw fruits and vegetables.

However, there was no association between stroke risk and a high intake (more than 8 ounces per day) or low intake (less than 3.9 ounces per day) of processed fruits and vegetables, said Linda Oude Griep of Wageningen University in the Netherlands.

info For more information about potassium, visit the US National Library of Medicine Web site, *www.nlm.nih.gov/medlineplus,* and search "potassium in diet."

■ ■ ■ ■

Eat Nuts to Beat Heart Disease

A recent study of women who have type-2 diabetes (which puts them at high risk for heart disease) found that those who ate five or more servings a week of nuts or peanut butter had a 44% lower risk for heart disease than those who rarely or never ate these foods.

Theory: Monounsaturated fat in nuts reduces cholesterol and inflammation.

Best: At least five times weekly, have one ounce of nuts or one tablespoon of peanut butter.

Frank Hu, MD, PhD, professor of nutrition and epidemiology, Harvard School of Public Health, Boston, and lead author of a 22-year study of 6,309 women.

Yummy Way to Lower Blood Pressure!

European Heart Journal news release.

Just one small square of chocolate a day might help lower your blood pressure and reduce your risk for heart disease.

THE STUDY

After analyzing the diet and health habits of 19,357 people between the ages of 35 and 65 for at least 10 years, German researchers found that those who ate the most chocolate (an average of 7.5 grams [g], or 0.3 ounces, a day) had lower blood pressure and were 39% less likely to have a heart attack than those who ate the least amount of chocolate (an average of 1.7 g, or 0.06 ounces, a day).

"To put that in terms of absolute risk, if people in the group eating the least amount of chocolate [of whom 219 per 10,000 had a heart attack or stroke] increased their chocolate intake by 6 g [0.2 ounces] a day, 85 fewer heart attacks and strokes per 10,000 people could be expected to occur over a period of about 10 years," said study leader Brian Buijsse, PhD, a nutritional epidemiologist at the German Institute of Human Nutrition. The study was published online in *European Heart Journal.*

"If the 39% lower risk is generalized to the general population, the number of avoidable heart attacks and strokes could be higher because the absolute risk in the general population is higher," he said.

Six grams of chocolate is equivalent to about one small square of a 100-g (3.5-ounce) bar, the researchers said.

IMPORTANT ADVICE

But Dr. Buijsse cautioned that eating chocolate shouldn't increase a person's overall intake of calories or reduce the consumption of healthy foods.

Small amounts of chocolate may help to prevent heart disease, but only if it replaces other high-calorie foods, such as snacks, in order to keep body weight stable, he said.

info For more information on preventing heart disease, heart attack and stroke, visit the Web site of the American Heart Association, *www.heart.org,* and search "ABCs of preventing heart disease."

The Hidden Key to Heart Health Even Doctors Overlook

Gerald M. Lemole, MD, a professor of surgery at Jefferson Medical College, Thomas Jefferson University in Philadelphia, and medical director of the Preventive Medicine and Rehabilitation Center and Center for Integrative Health in Wilmington, Delaware. Dr. Lemole is the author of *The Healing Diet: A Total Health Program to Purify Your Lymph System and Reduce the Risk of Heart Disease* (William Morrow & Company). He has authored or coauthored 150 scientific papers on cardiovascular medicine.

We're all familiar with the circulatory system that transports oxygen-rich blood to the tissues of the body, including the heart. But there's another major system that is largely overlooked by patients—and doctors—when it comes to heart health.

The lymphatic system, which is widely known for its ability to help our bodies fight infection, may have a much greater impact on the heart than previously recognized. The lymphatic system is a network of vessels, nodes and fluid (lymph) that helps the body fight infection. As lymph seeps through the bloodstream, it passes through the nodes located throughout the body. Toxins are filtered out before the cleansed fluid is returned to the bloodstream.

New thinking: Most scientists agree that low-level, chronic inflammation can be a significant underlying cause of heart disease.

Some now believe that impaired lymph circulation may be what allows inflammatory substances to irritate blood vessel walls and promote *atherosclerosis* (fatty buildup in the arteries). Impaired lymph flow also can cause cholesterol to remain longer inside blood vessel walls, which contributes to the formation of plaque and increases risk for heart attack and stroke.

The lymphatic hypothesis of cardiovascular disease isn't widely embraced by mainstream physicians, but it's supported by several laboratory studies.

A leading proponent of this hypothesis is Gerald M. Lemole, MD, a heart surgeon who worked closely with the cardiac-surgery pioneers Michael DeBakey, MD, and Denton Cooley, MD, and was a member of the surgical team that performed the first successful heart transplant in the US, in 1968. Since then, Dr. Lemole has performed or overseen close to 20,000 cardiac-surgery procedures.

Dr. Lemole spoke recently about the ways in which the lymphatic system may affect heart health.

SLUGGISH LYMPH FLOW

Our bodies contain more lymph than blood, and we have more miles of lymph vessels than blood vessels. Normally, all of the lymph in the body circulates through the lymphatic system about once every two days. This turnover means that inflammatory *cytokines* and other irritating substances are swept out of circulation and to the liver for disposal—ideally, before these substances are able to damage adjoining arterial linings.

Stress, poor diet and a sedentary lifestyle impair lymph drainage. Because these lifestyle factors are so prevalent in the US, many Americans are thought to have "lymph stasis," in which lymph flow is slower than normal.

In people who have lymph stasis, pools of lymph essentially stagnate. Irritating substances suspended in lymph have more time to damage nearby blood vessels, which is thought to contribute to the buildup of LDL "bad" cholesterol and other substances that promote atherosclerosis.

Even though lymph flow in humans has been measured only in research settings, cardiac surgeons have long noted that atherosclerosis develops mostly in blood vessels on the surface of the heart. In this area, lymph flow is relatively weak. Atherosclerosis usually doesn't occur in deeper coronary tissues, where the beating of the heart presses against lymph ducts and promotes rapid lymph drainage.

While the blood circulatory system is largely powered by the heart, the lymphatic system depends mainly on muscle and respiratory movements to supply the pressure changes that are needed for lymph circulation. In addition, the flow of lymph is thought to be enhanced by antioxidants (such as those in green tea) that dilate lymph vessels.

TO KEEP LYMPH MOVING

Even though the link between lymph and cardiovascular disease still is theoretical, it may be possible to reduce the risk for heart disease by up to 30% by enhancing lymph circulation—in part because the same things that promote lymph circulation (regular exercise, stress management and a healthful diet) also can help lower blood pressure, inflammation and other proven cardiovascular risk factors. *Actions you can take...*

•**Go for brisk walks.** Muscle movements from walking or other forms of exercise press against the lymph ducts and increase circulation. For example, a daily walk (about 20 to 30 minutes) can double or triple lymph flow.

This may be one reason why people who exercise tend to have lower cholesterol and better immunity than those who are sedentary.

My advice: When performing exercise (such as walking), open your arms as wide as you can and then bring them back together in front of your body (roughly in sync with your breathing). This arm movement opens the chest cavity and allows the lungs to expand more fully, which enhances lymph circulation.

•**Practice deep breathing.** It's the best way to promote lymph circulation in the heart. Taking deep breaths produces pressure in the chest cavity, which makes it easier for lymph to flow through tissues in the heart. Deep breaths also massage the thoracic duct (which carries lymph through the chest and into the bloodstream) and promote better lymph circulation.

My advice: Set aside about 10 minutes a day for deep breathing. Take slow, deep breaths, exhaling completely at the conclusion of each one. You can combine deep breathing with walking and/or other forms of exercise.

Helpful: To ensure proper movement of the diaphragm, make sure that your posture is erect when performing deep breathing, whether you are sitting or standing.

•**Try Daflon-500.** This supplement is marketed under brand names such as Detralex and Arvenum 500. It is available online and in some health food stores. Originally designed to improve damaged blood vessels in patients with hemorrhoids as well as other venous disorders, such as leg cramps, the supplement contains *bioflavonoids,* plant chemicals that promote lymph flow.

My advice: If you are at high risk for cardiovascular disease, ask your doctor about trying Daflon-500. Follow the label directions—the usual dose is 500 milligrams (mg), two to three times daily.

•**Drink green tea.** The flavonoids in green tea promote *peristalsis* (contractions) of the lymph ducts. The same chemicals inhibit the activation of the inflammatory cytokines that are closely linked to heart disease.

My advice: Drink three or more cups of green tea daily—the amount shown to confer the most benefit. Water (six to eight glasses daily, between meals) also helps promote lymph flow.

•**Get regular massages.*** The lymph ducts that are located in deeper tissues get a natural massage every time you breathe or move your muscles. However, those closer to the surface

Caution: If you have scar tissue due to an injury or surgery or if you have recently received radiation treatments, ask your doctor if massage is safe for you.

may not receive enough muscle pressure for optimal lymph circulation.

My advice: Get a massage from a massage therapist or a friend or your spouse at least once a month to keep lymph moving.

Best: A lymphatic massage, a specialized form of massage that promotes lymph circulation.

Also helpful: Take a few minutes every day to rub your neck, shoulders, chest, etc. Exert enough pressure to compress the muscles, which will stimulate lymph flow.

Simple Stretch Test that Could Save Your Life

American Physiological Society news release.

Sit on the floor and reach for your toes. If you can get your fingers past them and you're 40 or older, that could be a sign that your arteries are flexible, researchers say.

In an unusual finding, new research suggests that flexibility, as defined by how far you can reach while sitting down with legs stretched out in front of you, may be linked to the stiffness of your arteries. It's known that arterial stiffness can often precede life-threatening cardiovascular disease.

"Our findings have potentially important clinical implications because trunk flexibility can be easily evaluated," said study coauthor Kenta Yamamoto, PhD, of the University of North Texas and the National Institute of Health and Nutrition in Japan. "This simple test might help to prevent age-related arterial stiffening."

THE STUDY

In the study, 526 nonsmoking adults, ages 20 to 83, who were not obese, participated in a test that measured how far they could reach while sitting with legs extended.

The researchers also tested the participants' blood pressure and took other measurements regarding their cardiovascular systems and their endurance.

The study authors found that more flexibility was linked with less arterial stiffness, but only in middle-aged and older participants.

The findings were published in the *American Journal of Physiology—Heart and Circulatory Physiology*.

POSSIBLE EXPLANATION

Researchers don't know why flexibility might be linked to arteries. One theory is that people who are more flexible do stretching exercises that help slow down stiffening of the arteries.

However, it's not clear if there's a direct cause-and-effect relationship between greater flexibility and less arterial stiffness, the study authors added.

IMPLICATION

"Together with our results, these findings suggest a possibility that improving flexibility induced by the stretching exercise may be capable of modifying age-related arterial stiffening in middle-aged and older adults," Dr. Yamamoto said. "We believe that flexibility exercise, such as stretching, yoga and Pilates, should be integrated as a new recommendation into the known cardiovascular benefits of regular exercise."

info To learn more about heart disease, visit the Web site of the US Centers for Disease Control and Prevention, *www.cdc.gov/heartdisease*.

■ ■ ■ ■

Meditation Lowers Heart Disease Risk by 47%

Patients with coronary heart disease practiced transcendental meditation for 20 minutes twice a day for five years, on average…or got instruction in heart-protecting diet and exercise habits. Meditators were 47% less likely than nonmeditators to have a heart attack or stroke, or to die.

Information: *www.TM.org.*

Robert Schneider, MD, director, Institute for Natural Medicine and Prevention, Maharishi University of Management, Fairfield, Iowa, and leader of a study of 201 heart patients.

■ ■ ■ ■

Surprising Sign of Heart Disease in Men

Top way for men to prevent and reverse sexual dysfunction is the same way to reduce heart disease risk. Erectile dysfunction (ED) results from diminished blood flow and can be an early warning sign for heart disease. Men who have ED are 80% more likely to develop heart disease than other men.

Self-defense: Exercise regularly, eat a healthful diet and maintain a healthy weight. Keep blood pressure, cholesterol and blood sugar under control.

Joshua Green, MD, urologist specializing in male sexual dysfunction and infertility, and medical director, Urology Treatment Center of Southwest Florida, Sarasota, and clinical assistant professor of medicine, Florida State University, Sarasota.

■ ■ ■ ■

Good News! Sex Lowers Risk for Heart Disease

Men who have sex once a month or less are approximately 50% more likely to suffer cardiovascular events, such as heart attack, stroke or heart failure, than men who have sex at least twice a week. Further research is needed. The frequency of sex may simply indicate a man's overall health. In the meantime, men should discuss with their doctors any sexual problems.

Susan A. Hall, PhD, research scientist, department of epidemiology, New England Research Institutes, Watertown, Massachusetts, and lead author of a study of 1,165 men, published in *The American Journal of Cardiology*.

■ ■ ■ ■

Cheer Up—It Helps Your Heart

In a study of 1,017 heart disease patients, those who were depressed were 31% more likely to have a heart attack, heart failure (insufficient pumping action of the heart), a stroke or to die over a five-year period.

If you have heart disease: The American Heart Association recommends that you get routinely screened for depression.

Mary Whooley, MD, physician investigator, Veterans Affairs Medical Center, San Francisco.

■ ■ ■ ■

Chickpeas Curb Cholesterol

A recent study followed 45 adults with high total cholesterol levels (250 milligrams per deciliter, on average) who ate at least 25 ounces (about three cups) of canned chickpeas (garbanzo beans) weekly for 12 weeks.

Result: The participants' total cholesterol levels dropped by 7.7 points, on average.

Theory: Chickpeas are high in fiber and polyunsaturated fats, which help reduce total cholesterol when they replace saturated fats.

Self-defense: Enjoy chickpeas in salads, hummus and other dishes.

J.K. Pittaway, researcher and lecturer in health and biomedical science, University of Tasmania, Launceston, Tasmania, Australia.

When "Good" Cholesterol Isn't So Good

Steven Jones, MD, assistant professor of medicine and cardiology at Johns Hopkins University and director of inpatient cardiology at Johns Hopkins Hospital, both in Baltimore. He has presented several scientific papers on lipid research and is coauthor of a recent article in *The American Journal of Cardiology.*

For years, we've heard about two forms of cholesterol—the "bad" low-density lipoprotein (LDL) and the "good" high-density lipoprotein (HDL). Higher levels of HDL cholesterol—50 milligrams per deciliter (mg/dL) or above—are considered desirable because this form of cholesterol has long been associated with the cleanup of *lipids* (blood fats) from the arteries.

THE ROLE OF LDL

Even though lipids are generally perceived as harmful, they play an essential role in cellular functions.

Here's how: Cholesterol and *triglycerides* (a type of blood fat) are transported by lipoproteins (complex particles consisting of proteins and lipids) to the body's tissues, where they reinforce cell membranes and aid in the synthesis of hormones and other substances.

However, once these useful lipids are stripped away from the transporting lipoproteins, the leftover portion is known as low-density lipoprotein (LDL)—and it can be harmful. LDL cholesterol can accumulate in artery walls and initiate changes that can lead to heart disease.*

New thinking: HDL cholesterol readings that appear on blood tests may not always be a good indicator of a person's heart disease risk after all. In fact, some people with lower HDL cholesterol actually can be at lower risk than those with very high HDL numbers.

Why is this so? Most people don't realize that unwanted cholesterol is removed from the arteries through a process known as *reverse cholesterol transport.*

Cutting-edge research: The HDL that is measured on standard cholesterol tests does not necessarily indicate the efficiency of the reverse transport mechanism, researchers now are discovering. This means that some people with very high HDL, for example, could have inefficient disposal of unwanted cholesterol.

Result: Excess lipids remaining in the arteries and an increased risk for heart disease.

Bottom line: High HDL generally confers protection—but only when it accompanies a robust transport mechanism.

IDENTIFYING HEART DISEASE RISK WITH GREATER ACCURACY

Routine cholesterol testing remains the mainstay of heart disease risk assessment, along with consideration of known cardiovascular risk factors, such as smoking, high blood pressure, family history and diet. Combined, these conventional risk factors identify most patients who are at risk for heart and vascular diseases.

*LDL cholesterol levels of 100–129 mg/dL are generally considered optimal for healthy adults…below 100 mg/dL is typically recommended for people at risk for heart disease (due to such factors as smoking and high blood pressure).

Problem: About half of all heart attacks occur in people with so-called normal cholesterol levels.

Solution: There now are additional cholesterol tests that measure different types of LDL and HDL cholesterol, which may identify some people at risk for heart disease who are missed by conventional cholesterol testing and assessment of risk-factors. These blood tests, which typically are covered by insurance, may give a more accurate assessment of your heart disease risk, when combined with standard measures.

You may want to ask your doctor about getting advanced tests, such as…

•**Lp(a).** Lipoprotein (a) is a small cholesterol particle that readily penetrates the artery wall, accelerating plaque formation. Lp(a) is associated with increased heart attack risk in most people.

•**Markers of abnormal LDL particle size, density or number.** Tests measuring these markers can help assess cardiovascular disease risk. For some patients, measurement of *apolipoprotein B* (another lipoprotein) levels may better represent the number of particles that cause *atherosclerosis* (fatty buildup in the arteries).

LOWERING YOUR RISK

Although it's important to know your cholesterol levels, lifestyle changes and other strategies are crucial for reducing heart disease risk. *They include…*

•**A Mediterranean-style diet,** which emphasizes fruits, vegetables, fish, whole grains and the use of olive oil as the main vegetable fat—and includes only small amounts of meat and saturated fats—is associated with very low cardiovascular disease risk.

•**Regular exercise can increase HDL by up to 10%**—and the weight loss that accompanies exercise can produce an additional 20% to 30% increase.

•**Omega-3 fatty acids,** taken either by prescription or as high-dose fish oil, can lower triglycerides (a type of blood fat) by about 40%. This treatment often is combined with other lipid-lowering drugs under the care of a physician.

•**Statin drugs, such as *simvastatin* (Zocor), *lovastatin* (Mevacor) and *atorvastatin* (Lipitor),** which work primarily by lowering LDL cholesterol as well as inflammation, are among the most effective ways to lower cardiovascular risk. In general, every 1% reduction in LDL reduces the risk for heart attack by 1%.

•**Niacin.** *Nicotinic acid,* a form of niacin, has long been known to raise HDL by up to 30%.

But the real benefit of niacin now is thought to be due to improvements in reverse transport and its additional ability to lower levels of triglycerides and LDL. Niacin also makes LDL particles less toxic to the arteries by favorably changing the chemical properties of LDL and HDL—and is used to lower Lp(a) levels.

Caution: Because improper use of niacin can cause serious liver damage, it should be taken only in prescription form under a doctor's supervision.

Amazing! Laughter Lowers Cholesterol

Lee Berk, MPH, DrPH, associate professor of Allied Health and Pathology, Schools of Allied Health Professions and Medicine, Loma Linda University, Loma Linda, California.

Laughter is great medicine…it's not just a platitude. Nor should this come as a surprise, since previous studies regarding laughter have noted its impact on cardiovascular risk, blood pressure and stress. The latest finding is that it even can lower cholesterol.

In research presented at a meeting of The American Physiological Society, 20 high-risk diabetes patients who had both hypertension and high cholesterol were divided into two groups. One group received standard pharmaceutical treatments for diabetes (Metformin, Actos, and Glipizide, etc.), hypertension (ACE inhibitors) and high cholesterol (statin drugs), while the second group received the same medication, but also were instructed to watch 30 minutes a day of humorous videos. Since different people find different things funny, participants were able to select their own.

LAUGHING ALL THE WAY
TO GOOD HEALTH

By the end of the second month, the benefits were already evident. By the end of one year, the laughter group had increased their "good" cholesterol by 26% (compared with 3% for the control group) while also decreasing C-reactive protein, an inflammatory marker, by 66% (versus 26% in the control group). In addition, over the course of the year-long study, only one patient in the laughter group suffered a heart attack—compared with three in the control group.

"The benefits we see with laughter are very similar to what we see with moderate exercise," noted researchers Lee Berk, DrPH, of Loma Linda University and Stanley Tan, MD, PhD, of Oak Crest Research Institute. Dr. Berk has even coined a term—Laughercise—to describe the benefits of therapeutic laughter. This newest finding builds upon previous research by the same team in which laughter was found to boost blood flow to the heart. Dr. Berk told me that further studies are planned to determine how long this positive effect will last.

HEALING POWER OF LAUGHTER

How much laughter does Dr. Berk recommend? It's "all new stuff—we're still learning how to measure and what to measure relative to the positive emotion and experience of Laughercise," he said. However, he added, "it's clear that the repetitive use of laughter produces physiological changes that lower stress hormones, increase endorphins, and—in our studies—lower risk factors for heart disease, including inflammation and cholesterol."

Medical Newsmakers

Vaccines *Not* Linked to Autism? Journal Retracts Study

The prestigious British medical journal *The Lancet* formally retracted a highly controversial study that had linked the measles, mumps and rubella (MMR) vaccine to autism and gastrointestinal problems.

The original article, published on February 28, 1998, set off a worldwide furor, with many researchers condemning it as shoddy science. But parents of children with autism rallied around the main researcher, Andrew Wakefield, MD, of Great Britain, to condemn vaccines.

The result: Vaccination rates in both the United States and Britain plummeted while new cases of measles rose.

Ten of Dr. Wakefield's 13 coauthors renounced the study's conclusions several years ago, and *The Lancet* had previously said it should never have published the research.

"We fully retract this paper from the published record," the journal's editors said in a statement.

ABOUT AUTISM

Autism is a complex developmental disability that causes problems with social interaction and communication. Because the condition has a wide range of symptoms and severity, it is called *autism spectrum disorders*. According to a recent report, one in every 110 children in the United States has been diagnosed with an autism spectrum disorder. The number of 8-year-old children diagnosed with autism jumped

Gwen Wurm, MD, assistant professor, pediatrics, University of Miami Miller School of Medicine.

Paul A. Offit, MD, director, Vaccine Education Center, and chief, infectious diseases, Children's Hospital of Philadelphia.

Robert Frenck, MD, professor of pediatrics, division of infectious diseases, Cincinnati Children's Hospital Medical Center.

Geraldine Dawson, PhD, chief science officer, Autism Speaks.

The Lancet online.

BMJ (*British Medical Journal* online) statement.

an average of 57% between 2002 and 2006. This rise is part of a trend predating the 1980s, when autism was still considered rare. Previously, the national estimate was that one in 150 children had autism.

DETAILS OF THE RULING

The United Kingdom General Medical Council, a regulatory body, ruled that Dr. Wakefield had violated a number of ethical codes while doing the autism research. Among other things, he apparently paid his son's friends $8 to let him draw blood and showed "callous disregard" for children in carrying out various tests, including spinal taps, according to published reports.

According to *Time* magazine, Dr. Wakefield, speaking from Austin, Texas, where he heads an autism research center, called the panel's ruling "unfounded and unjust."

Since the publication of Dr. Wakefield's original research, a number of large studies have failed to replicate the findings and have concluded that the MMR vaccine is safe.

And a US court ruled a year ago that there is no scientific evidence that childhood vaccines, such as the measles, mumps and rubella vaccine, caused autism in children. Parents of children with autism had been seeking compensation from a federal fund.

EXPERT REACTION

The retraction came a day before a competing British medical journal, *BMJ* (*British Medical Journal*), was to publish a commentary urging *The Lancet* to retract the study, according to the Associated Press.

BMJ welcomed news of the retraction.

"This will help to restore faith in this globally important vaccine and the integrity of the scientific literature," said Fiona Godlee, MD, editor of *BMJ*.

Pediatricians in the United States also applauded the retraction.

"We clearly welcome this—this is another statement that the original studies done by Wakefield do not hold up to expert scrutiny," said Gwen Wurm, MD, an assistant professor of pediatrics at the University of Miami Miller School of Medicine. "Measles still affects over 10 million people a year and is one of the major causes of vaccine-preventable deaths. The MMR vaccine is safe.

Over 25 studies have refuted the connection. The largest one, a wonderfully done epidemiologic study, was conducted in Denmark on more than 500,000 children. It found absolutely no difference in the rate of autism in children who got the vaccine compared with children who did not get the vaccine," said Dr. Wurm.

Paul A. Offit, MD, director of the Vaccine Education Center and chief of infectious diseases at the Children's Hospital of Philadelphia, said, "Wakefield had a hypothesis that MMR [vaccine] causes autism. That hypothesis was wrong. Study after study has shown it was wrong.

"The paper should never have been published, and it did a lot of harm. Hundreds of people in England were hospitalized and four children died of measles because parents thought MMR caused autism. Will those children get their lives back? It's too little, too late," Dr. Offit said.

Robert Frenck, MD, professor of pediatrics in the division of infectious diseases at Cincinnati Children's Hospital Medical Center, said, "This [retraction] further supports the position that there has not been any correlation with autism and vaccines or any constituents of vaccines. Autism is a terrible disorder and pediatricians want to find and eliminate the cause, but vaccines aren't the cause and by spending time and money looking at vaccines, it takes resources away from finding the actual cause."

Autism Speaks, a leading advocacy group, said the discrediting of the vaccine research won't hinder its efforts to search for a cure for the disorder. "We are committed to funding science that is rigorous and stands up to independent scrutiny in order to ensure that families and individuals with autism, and practitioners, can rely on scientific findings with confidence," said Geraldine Dawson, PhD, chief science officer of the organization.

info For more information on autism spectrum disorders, visit the Web site of the Centers for Disease Control and Prevention, *www.cdc.gov/ncbddd/autism/index.html.*

Oh No! Air Pollution May Cause Appendicitis

Gilaad G. Kaplan, MD, assistant professor of medicine, division of gastroenterology, University of Calgary, Alberta.
F. Paul Buckley III, MD, assistant professor of surgery, Texas A&M Health Science Center College of Medicine, and surgeon, Scott & White Healthcare-Round Rock, Texas.
Canadian Medical Association Journal.

Air pollution is already linked to respiratory and cardiovascular ills, and now researchers say the dirty air you breathe may also contribute to appendicitis.

Authors of a new study published in the *Canadian Medical Association Journal* found that cases of appendicitis go up when the air is dirtier.

"This makes us think about the underlying cause of appendicitis that could potentially be linked to air pollution," said Gilaad G. Kaplan, MD, senior author of the study and assistant professor of medicine in the division of gastroenterology at the University of Calgary in Alberta. "Air pollution is a modifiable risk factor. If these findings are confirmed and we are able to legislate better air pollution control, cleaner air, then potentially we could prevent more cases of appendicitis."

But at this early point in the research, the implications are not so clear-cut, warned another expert.

"It's provocative, but there's a huge difference between correlating any number of factors with a disease and proving that any of these factors might actually cause a disease, and this study fails to show causation," said F. Paul Buckley III, MD, assistant professor of surgery at the Texas A&M Health Science Center College of Medicine and a surgeon at Scott & White Healthcare-Round Rock in Texas.

BACKGROUND

No one really knows why appendicitis, or swelling and infection of the appendix, occurs.

Appendicitis cases rose significantly in the late 19th century and early 20th century, as industrialization took hold. Cases declined in the middle and later parts of the last century, at about the time clean air legislation gained headway. Meanwhile, countries that are just now industrializing have increasing rates of the condition, the study authors stated.

A prevailing theory is that appendicitis occurs when the opening to the appendix, a pouch-like organ attached to the large intestine, gets blocked. Specifically, some experts believe that lower fiber intake among citizens of industrialized countries leads to obstruction of the appendix by the stool.

But that doesn't explain the decreased incidence of appendicitis in the second half of the 20th century, Dr. Kaplan said.

THE STUDY

Dr. Kaplan and his colleagues looked at more than 5,000 adults who were hospitalized in Calgary with appendicitis during a period of more than six years. This data was cross-referenced with an analysis of air pollutants the week prior to the admissions.

"We found that individuals were more likely to come in with appendicitis in weeks with higher concentrations of air pollutants, specifically ozone and nitrogen dioxide," Dr. Kaplan said.

More appendicitis admissions took place during Canada's warmest months (April through September, when people are more likely to be outdoors), and men seemed more likely to be affected by air pollutants than women. It's unclear why this gender difference exists, the researchers said.

POSSIBLE EXPLANATION

Dr. Kaplan theorizes that inflammation may explain the link—if it proves to exist—between air quality and appendicitis.

"It's speculative, but air pollution might be driving inflammation which triggers appendicitis," he said. "We're a few steps away before we can make that statement. We need to confirm and replicate these findings."

Dr. Kaplan and his coauthors plan more studies in multiple cities in Canada.

info For more information on appendicitis, visit the Web site of the US National Library of Medicine's online encyclopedia, MedlinePlus, at *www.nlm.nih.gov/medlineplus* under the "Encyclopedia" tab, choose "A" and then "Appendicitis."

Early Morning Colonoscopies Find 27% More Polyps

University of California, Los Angeles, news release.

Early morning colonoscopies detect more polyps than colon cancer screenings done later in the day, and the number of polyps found decreases by the hour as the day progresses, a new study has found.

Removing polyps is believed to reduce the risk of colon cancer by 60% to 90%.

THE STUDY

Researchers from the University of California, Los Angeles, analyzed data on 477 people who had colonoscopies in a one-year span at a Veterans Affairs hospital. Colonoscopies that started at 8:30 a.m. or earlier detected 27% more polyps per patient than colonoscopies performed at a later time, according to the study.

POSSIBLE EXPLANATIONS

The improved rate in the early morning may be due to better bowel preparation the night before, according to the researchers. They also suggested that doctor fatigue might also play a role in declining detection as the day wears on.

IMPLICATIONS

"We may find that setting a cap on the duration of endoscopic work shifts or other types of adjustments may be helpful," said Brennan M.R. Spiegel, MD, director of the UCLA/Veterans Affairs Center for Outcomes Research and Education and a coauthor of the study.

ADVICE

Dr. Spiegel emphasized that colonoscopy is an effective way to screen for colon cancer at any time of the day and said that people should not worry about getting early morning procedures. The most important thing was to get one.

"The impact of appointment time for any individual is very, very small," Dr. Spiegel said. "Patients should feel confident that colonoscopy is helpful regardless of time of day and should be more focused on the quality and experience of their doctor rather than on the time of their appointment."

The study was published in *Clinical Gastroenterology and Hepatology*.

info For more information about colonoscopy, visit the Web site of the US National Institute of Diabetes and Digestive and Kidney Diseases, *http://digestive.niddk.nih.gov,* and search "colonoscopy."

Why You Must Detox Your Body and Brain Now!

Mark Hyman, MD, founder of the UltraWellness Center in Lenox, Massachusetts, and editor of the journal *Alternative Therapies in Health and Medicine*. He is the author of several best-selling books, including *UltraMetabolism* (Atria) and *The UltraMind Solution* (Scribner). *www.Ultra Wellness.com.*

Toxic metals are pervasive in our environment. Mercury is in the fish we eat, the vaccines we receive and the fillings in our teeth. Lead belches from coal-burning factories, and the residue of old leaded gasoline and paint remains in our soil and groundwater. Aluminum appears in medications that we swallow and personal-care products that we put on our skin.

These toxic metals can build up in the brain and body—and create big problems. *Examples...*

•**Mercury** is linked to dementia, depression, high blood pressure, autism and attention disorders. It disrupts hormones, mitochondria (the energy-producing parts of cells) and dopamine (a mood-affecting brain chemical). A large study of American women of childbearing age showed that 8% had toxic levels of mercury in the blood.

•**Lead** exposure has been shown to lead to depression, schizophrenia, reduced cognitive function, behavioral problems, heart attack, stroke and death.

Estimated: Nearly 40% of Americans have lead levels that are high enough to cause health problems.

•**Aluminum** exposure may be linked to increased risk for breast cancer and/or Alzheimer's disease.

New concern: Many people lack a gene called *GSTM1* that appears to be key for proper functioning of the body's own natural detoxification mechanisms. This may explain at least in part why some people develop the chronic health problems linked to heavy metals while others who are similarly exposed do not.

To protect yourself, follow a dual strategy that maximizes your body's ability to rid itself of toxins and minimizes future toxic exposure.

TO BOOST DETOX POWER

•**Maximize glutathione production.** The body's most important natural detoxifier is the amino acid–based antioxidant glutathione. It contains sulfur, which is like flypaper—toxins stick to it, then are excreted via urine and stool.

To increase your glutathione levels, eat plenty of foods that contain sulfur.

Examples: Garlic, onions and radishes… cruciferous vegetables (bok choy, broccoli, cauliflower)…and egg yolks.

•**Take detox supplements.** Each day, take a multivitamin and follow this metal-chelating regimen—500 milligrams (mg) to 1,000 mg of vitamin C…10 mg to 30 mg of zinc…and 100 micrograms (mcg) to 200 mcg of selenium.*

Also consider supplementing with any or all of the following glutathione building blocks— *N-acetylcysteine* (NAC) at 500 mg to 1,000 mg twice daily…milk thistle extract at 175 mg twice daily…and *alpha-lipoic acid* at 100 mg to 200 mg twice daily.

•**Sweat out toxins.** Take a dry-heat sauna or moist-heat steam bath, or soak in a hot bathtub five or so times per week, starting with 10-minute sessions and gradually increasing to 30 minutes. Drink 16 ounces of water before and after each session to help flush out toxins…shower with soap afterward to rinse toxins from your skin.

Cautions: If you take medication or have a chronic medical condition, get your doctor's okay first. If you are pregnant, do not use a sauna or steam bath or soak in a hot bathtub.

•**Fill your plate with colors.** Richly pigmented foods generally are high in *phytonu-trients*, plant compounds that help boost your body's own detoxification pathways. The more colorful your diet, the more different types of phytonutrients you get.

Simple: Each day, eat something red or purple (berries, pomegranate, red peppers)…yellow or orange (cantaloupe, sweet potatoes, yellow beans)…and dark green (collard greens, kale, spinach).

Best: Buy organic to limit exposure to chemical fertilizers and pesticides.

•**Get your metal levels measured,** especially if you have any symptoms of possible metal toxicity, such as unexplained fatigue, memory loss or depression. But don't rely on blood tests, which show what's happening in your bloodstream only at the moment.

More accurate: You swallow a chelating agent (which binds to heavy metals), then your urine is tested for toxins.

To find a doctor who performs this test, contact the Institute for Functional Medicine (800-228-0622, *www.functionalmedicine.org*). If your metal levels are high, the doctor can prescribe an oral chelating drug, such as *dimercaptosuccinic acid* (DMSA), to pull out metals.

TO REDUCE METAL EXPOSURE

•**Eat smaller fish.** Metal contamination is common in large fish (tuna, shark, swordfish, tilefish, sea bass) and river fish—so avoid eating these. Instead, to get omega-3 fatty acids that protect the heart and brain function, stick to fish small enough to fit whole in your frying pan—catfish, flounder, herring, mackerel, fresh or frozen sardines, shrimp and other shellfish.

Even small fish are not entirely free of toxic metals, however—so eat no more than two six-ounce servings per week. The limits apply to farm-raised fish, too, as these may be contaminated by their feed.

•**Drink only filtered water.** Economical faucet-mounted water filters, such as those from Brita or Pur, can reduce metal levels. Even more effective is a reverse osmosis filter installed under the sink. Avoid bottled water in plastic bottles—though probably free of metals, it may contain chemical contaminants from plastic, such as *phthalates*.

Guideline: Drink at least six to eight full glasses of filtered water daily to maximize the excretion of toxins.

• **Choose metal-free drugstore products.** Avoid underarm products and antacids that have any form of aluminum on the ingredients list… and contact lens fluid with *thimerosol,* a mercury-based preservative. Cosmetics can contain metals, too—for instance, some lipsticks have trace amounts of lead, so opt for chemical-free cosmetics (see *www.safecosmetics.org*). Limit use of *acetaminophen* (Tylenol), which depletes your stores of glutathione, to no more than twice weekly.

• **Consult a biological dentist.** Even though mercury-containing silver amalgam fillings are banned in some European countries, they still are used routinely in the US, and the American Dental Association continues to maintain that such fillings are not hazardous.

However: Some studies show that mercury migrates through the teeth into the bloodstream…and amalgam fillings are considered toxic waste when removed from the body.

Prudent: If you need a new filling, get one made of composite resin or another mercury-free material. If you have a chronic unexplained illness or if testing shows that your mercury levels are high, consider having your old amalgam fillings removed and replaced with a safer material. For this, consult a biological dentist—this type of professional is trained in the techniques required to remove amalgam safely.

Referrals: International Academy of Oral Medicine and Toxicology, 863-420-6373, *www.iaomt.org*.

■ ■ ■ ■

Eye Test for Alzheimer's?

A simple, noninvasive test that measures damage to cells in the retina of the eye can reveal stages of cell death in the brain. The technique will be tested in human trials later this year and could allow doctors to diagnose and treat Alzheimer's at an earlier stage.

Cell Death & Disease.

■ ■ ■ ■

Cancer vs. Alzheimer's

People with Alzheimer's disease may be less likely to get cancer, and cancer patients appear to have a lower risk for Alzheimer's disease. The currently unexplained link between the two diseases could lead to future treatments.

Neurology.

FDA Approves Vaccine For Advanced Prostate Cancer

J. Leonard Lichtenfeld, MD, deputy chief medical officer, American Cancer Society.
Mark S. Soloway, MD, professor and chair of urology, University of Miami Miller School of Medicine.
US Food and Drug Administration news release.

The US Food and Drug Administration granted approval to Provenge, a therapeutic vaccine aimed at preventing the spread of prostate cancer in men with an advanced form of the disease.

The new approval is limited to "the treatment of asymptomatic or minimally symptomatic prostate cancer that has spread to other parts of the body and is resistant to standard hormone treatment," the FDA said.

ABOUT PROSTATE CANCER

According to American Cancer Society estimates, more than 192,000 new cases of prostate cancer are diagnosed in the United States each year, and 27,360 men die from the disease.

Prostate cancer is the most common form of cancer diagnosed in American men, after skin cancer. More than 2 million American men who have had prostate cancer at some point are still alive today. The death rate is going down, and the disease is being found earlier, according to the cancer society.

HOW THE VACCINE WORKS

Provenge is a therapeutic (not preventative) vaccine that is made from the patient's own white blood cells. Once removed from the patient, the cells are treated and placed back into the patient. These treated cells then cause an immune response, which in turn kills cancer cells, while leaving normal cells unharmed.

According to the FDA, Provenge is given intravenously in a three-dose schedule delivered at two-week intervals.

The vaccine was developed by Seattle-based Dendreon Corp., which conducted initial studies among men with advanced prostate cancer who had already failed standard hormone treatment. Among these men, Provenge extended life by an average of 4.5 months, although some patients saw their lives extended by two to three years. The only side effects were mild flulike symptoms, according to the study results.

The FDA noted that in one study, men taking Provenge had a slightly higher risk for cerebrovascular events, such as stroke, with 3.5% of those taking Provenge suffering such events versus 2.6% of those who did not take the drug.

In 2007, an FDA advisory panel recommended that the agency approve Provenge, but at the time the FDA said more data was needed before it would approve the vaccine.

IMPLICATIONS

"The availability of Provenge provides a new treatment option for men with advanced prostate cancer, who currently have limited effective therapies available," said Karen Midthun, MD, acting director of the FDA's Center for Biologics Evaluation and Research.

Experts say the vaccines approval could be a milestone against the disease and cancer in general.

Provenge appears to extend survival in men with advanced prostate cancer, and it does so without the serious side effects associated with chemotherapy, radiation and hormone therapy.

"It is certainly exciting to see a drug that has made it this far," said J. Leonard Lichtenfeld, MD, deputy chief medical officer of the American Cancer Society.

The vaccine is not aimed at preventing prostate cancer in men who have not developed the disease, and it is far from a cure for those who have it, Dr. Lichtenfeld stressed. "Provenge represents a modest advance in survival for patients with advanced prostate cancer, but the drug doesn't delay the progression of the disease," he said.

Still, it might prove possible to use Provenge in the earlier stages of prostate cancer, where it might be even more effective, Dr. Lichtenfeld said. "The hope is if a vaccine is effective in late-stage disease that it is going to be even more effective in the earlier treatment of that same disease," he said.

But that benefit would have to be shown in clinical trials, Dr. Lichtenfeld said. "It will represent a new treatment option. It will have a modest impact on prostate cancer survival, but it is small changes in treatments that add up to a major improvement over time. So I wouldn't be discouraged by what is a small increment in survival."

EXPERT REACTION

Mark S. Soloway, MD, professor and chair of urology at the University of Miami Miller School of Medicine, said, "We certainly need the opportunity for our patients to have alternatives."

The big question, according to Dr. Soloway, is when do you use Provenge? Whether it should be used before chemotherapy or hormone therapy isn't clear, he said.

"There are problems with Provenge," Dr. Soloway said. "One is that it's very cumbersome, because patients have to provide their white cells, and I think that's on a regular basis. And two, it's likely to be very expensive." Costs are expected to total $75,000 for the full regimen, experts say.

Dr. Soloway agreed that Provenge might also be useful in earlier-stage prostate cancer, but studies are needed to prove that.

However, "once it's approved, it's on the market, and with proper informed consent you can use it for localized [early stage] prostate cancer. Whether insurance companies will pay for it is also not known," Dr. Soloway said.

Other new drugs to treat prostate cancer, such as *abiraterone,* which prevents the production of the male hormone testosterone, are on the horizon and will compete with Provenge for new treatment regimens, he added.

info For more on prostate cancer, visit the Web site of the American Cancer Society, *www.cancer.org.* Under "Learn About Cancer," choose "prostate cancer."

Freezing Cancer Cells to Kill Them

Peter J. Littrup, MD, vice-chair for radiology research and director of interventional radiology, Barbara Ann Karmanos Cancer Institute, and professor of radiology, urology and radiation oncology, Wayne State University School of Medicine, both in Detroit. Dr. Littrup is a founder of theAmerican Cancer Society's National Prostate Cancer Detection Project.

Most of the promising new cancer treatments are complicated and hard to understand for those of us who don't have advanced degrees in chemistry, but here's one that's quite simple and effective—killing cancer cells by freezing them. Called *cryotherapy*, the technique has been in use for decades for some very specific problems (for instance, a type of prostate surgery), but recently, more precise technology has brought it to a new level. This led some doctors to ask, why can't we do this elsewhere in the body? It turns out that they can, and that may be very good news for some cancer patients.

We're at a tipping point with cryotherapy, said Peter Littrup, MD, vice-chair for radiology research and director of interventional radiology at the Barbara Ann Karmanos Cancer Institute in Detroit. In this country, 120 hospitals now use cryotherapy to treat cancer, though it still has far to go before it becomes a standard of care. *He discussed some of the exciting new developments...*

COLD KILLS CANCER CELLS

Many cancers that once required extensive open surgery now can be treated with this type of "thin needle surgery." Cryotherapy (also known as *cryosurgery* or *cryoablation*) uses extreme cold generated by liquid nitrogen or argon gas to destroy abnormal tissue. The procedure is far safer, less painful and easier to recover from than heat ablation techniques that burn the tumor and/or open surgery.

Dr. Littrup said that today's extremely thin "cryoprobes" (needlelike tubes that deliver the freezing gas) are so small that they can be inserted through tiny pencil-point-sized nicks in the skin. New imaging technology lets doctors target tumors with great accuracy, providing a better road map for treatment, as Dr. Littrup puts it.

Here's how a cryotherapy procedure works: The patient is lightly sedated. Using guided imaging such as ultrasound, computed tomography (CT) or magnetic resonance imaging (MRI), the radiologist inserts the cryoprobes at carefully selected locations within a tumor, where they deliver freezing gas that causes a ball of ice crystals to gradually develop around the probes.

In this way, cancerous tissue is frozen and destroyed with minimal harm to nearby healthy tissue. When it thaws, the tissue is naturally and safely absorbed by the body and may initiate an immune response.

Cryotherapy can be safely repeated as often as necessary to local tumors and can be combined with standard surgery, chemotherapy, radiation and hormone therapy and potentially immune therapy.

WHO CAN BE HELPED BY CRYOTHERAPY?

Cryotherapy has become a primary treatment for some types of cancer (specifically prostate, liver and renal cell carcinoma, which is a type of kidney cancer, and also breast and bone tumors) and may someday provide a treatment option for cancers that are inoperable or that fail to respond to standard treatment. It is helpful as a localized treatment for elderly patients and cancer patients who also have medical problems such as heart disease but who aren't healthy enough to undergo the rigors of more dramatic surgery.

Dr. Littrup summarized the advantages of cryotherapy...

•**Excellent visualization and targeting of a tumor,** which is a distinct benefit compared with heat ablation techniques. Imaging techniques now provide doctors with a superb picture of the ice treatment zone during and after the procedure.

With three-dimensional breast MRI imaging, for example, interventional radiologists can see and measure a tumor in the breast, then insert probes accordingly and monitor how the resulting "ice ball" grows and destroys the cancer.

•**Fewer side effects.** Because it is minimally invasive, cryotherapy largely eliminates the bleeding and pain associated with surgery. The tiny incision has less chance of infection.

•**Shorter recovery time.** Cryotherapy is usually an outpatient procedure, and patients heal faster with minimal scarring and may even return to normal activities the next day.

•**At $10,000 to $15,000 or so per procedure, it is less expensive than many other cancer therapies** (chemotherapy can cost double or more per month), but it is considered experimental—Medicare covers it, but not all insurance carriers will.

Another limitation is that little is known about the long-term effectiveness—it's hard to tell whether all cells are destroyed and there is concern that it may miss microscopic cells that can't be seen with imaging techniques. (This is also quite true of heat ablation and surgical treatments.) And there's some danger of collateral damage to the surrounding area if it is not adequately protected.

THE FUTURE OF CRYOTHERAPY

Be aware that this cutting-edge treatment is still new in cancer treatment and not widely available. Additional large-scale, multicenter studies are needed to confirm its long-term effectiveness in controlling cancer and improving survival.

You can find a board-certified interventional radiologist (the type of doctor who performs cryotherapy) in your area at the Web site of the Society of Interventional Radiology (*http://doctor-finder.sirweb.org*).

If you have cancer, cryotherapy may well be a promising treatment option to explore with your physician.

Breakthrough Discoveries from a Nobel Prize Winner

Carol Greider, PhD, the Daniel Nathans Professor and director of molecular biology and genetics in the Institute for Basic Biomedical Sciences at the Johns Hopkins School of Medicine and one of the winners of the 2009 Nobel Prize in Physiology or Medicine for her discovery of *telomerase*, an enzyme that maintains the length and integrity of chromosome ends.

More often than not, medical breakthroughs require years—if not decades—of arduous research.

Carol Greider, PhD, one of the 2009 winners of the Nobel Prize in Medicine, explained how her years of scientific research may affect our ability to fight life-threatening diseases, such as cancer, and treat age-related illnesses, soon after the award was announced.

The research conducted by Dr. Greider, director of molecular biology and genetics in the Johns Hopkins Institute for Basic Biomedical Sciences, advances our understanding of the intricate functions of human chromosomes. These strands of gene-carrying DNA, which are found in the nucleus of every human cell, control the life-giving processes of cellular division and replication.

In 1984, Dr. Greider played a key role in the discovery of *telomerase*, an enzyme that maintains the length of structures, known as *telomeres*, that keep chromosomes intact—much the same way a plastic tip at the end of a shoelace stops it from unraveling. Without telomerase, telomeres would shorten every time a cell divides, leading to the death of the cell.

These discoveries, made by Dr. Greider and two of her colleagues with whom she shared the 2009 Nobel Prize in Medicine, have led to new areas of investigation into controlling cancer (cancer cells may depend on telomerase to divide)...treating age-related diseases (telomeres shorten with age)...and understanding several genetic diseases (caused by dysfunctional telomerase and telomeres).

For insights into the ways that these discoveries may affect human health, Dr. Greider answered these questions...

•**Which diseases are believed to be caused by shorter telomeres?** Telomerase and telomeres may play a role in several genetic disorders. For example, research at Johns Hopkins has shown that genetic mutations in telomerase may contribute to the development of a progressive and often fatal lung disease called idiopathic pulmonary fibrosis, which afflicts approximately 50,000 Americans.

A similar mutation may cause *dyskeratosis congenita*, a disorder in which the bone marrow fails to manufacture healthy blood cells, usually leading to severe skin, nail, oral and lung problems and premature aging.

•**Why is it important to study these less well-known diseases?** Studying patients with telomere-related genetic disorders will help us treat those diseases and understand the consequences of shorter telomere length in everyone. That's important, because there is a wide variability in telomere length among the general population, with many individuals having shorter telomeres.

Research has linked shorter telomere length to an increased risk for coronary artery disease and heart attacks...and to a shorter life span.

As our scientific and medical understanding of these links increases, shorter telomere length may become a recognized risk factor for a variety of diseases and a target for treatment.

•**What, specifically, is the role of telomeres and telomerase in the battle against cancer?** In the cancer cell, division and replication is not a healthy, regulated function but an uncontrolled disease.

Scientists think that experimenting with telomerase and telomeres—even experimentally shortening telomeres—may have unexpected and positive effects in cancer treatment.

In my laboratory, for example, we bred mice to have nonoperating telomerase and then mated them with mice bred to develop *Burkitt's lymphoma*, a fast-growing and deadly cancer of the white blood cells.

The first generation of those mice, which developed lymphoma in seven months, had cancer cells containing long telomeres. But by the fifth generation, telomeres in the cancer cells had shortened—and that generation of mice did not develop lymphoma.

Upon investigation, we found that the mice had started to form microtumors in their lymph nodes, but the cancer cells didn't continue to divide.

This study and others have provided the evidence for researchers to begin human trials.

However, cancer is not one disease but many different conditions—and telomerase inhibitors may not work against every cancer.

A recent study in the journal *Lancet Oncology* showed that lifestyle factors may increase telomerase activity in people with cancer. What can we learn from that research? Elizabeth Blackburn, PhD, with whom I shared the Nobel Prize, participated in research on 30 men with prostate cancer.

It showed that three months of intensive lifestyle changes, such as a low-fat, plant-based diet, moderate exercise, stress management and social support, increased telomerase activity by almost 30% in a type of immune cell. This increases the cell's ability to maintain telomere length, which may provide protection against cancer progression.

Dr. Blackburn and the other researchers note that this was a small study and a preliminary finding and is not evidence that lifestyle changes affect telomerase or that increasing telomerase affects cancer. This interesting study is the basis for future research but not yet applicable for practical recommendations about lifestyle changes and telomerase levels.

•**How should people regard supplements or other products that purport to increase telomere length and extend life?** At present, there is no scientific evidence showing that any supplement or nutritional factor can reliably increase the length of telomeres. Until such evidence is produced, I think people should be wary of such supplements and products.

Health Alert: Regenerative Medicine Could Save Your Life

Anthony Atala, MD, director of the Institute for Regenerative Medicine and chair of the department of urology at Wake Forest University Baptist Medical Center in Winston-Salem, North Carolina. He also is the author or editor of eight books, including *Principles of Regenerative Medicine* (Academic Press) and the author of more than 250 medical journal articles.

If you heard about scientists growing body parts in a laboratory, you might assume that it's something out of science fiction. But such "regenerative medicine" is now occurring—and it will undoubtedly play an important role in the future of medical care.

Landmark breakthrough: Nine children and teenagers with a congenital defect that prevented their bladders from functioning properly received regenerated (laboratory-grown) bladders beginning in 1998. They have been followed for an average of seven years, and their bladders are continuing to function.

Anthony Atala, MD, director of Wake Forest University's Institute for Regenerative Medicine, one of the country's leading regenerative medicine research facilities, answered questions about this cutting-edge medical therapy.

•**Where are we in the development of regenerative medicine?** Much of the existing research has been conducted on animals, such as mice and rats. But we also know that there is a constant "turnover" of cells in the human body—that is, the growth of new cells and the regeneration of tissue after injury.

For example, if a person's liver is damaged in a car accident and half of the organ must be surgically removed, the liver can regenerate. If you take an X-ray of the same patient nine months later, the liver is fully regrown. Since we know that many parts of the human body are able to regenerate, our goal is to enhance that function to treat certain injuries and diseases.

•**What is unique about regenerative medicine's capacity for healing?** Because the damaged or diseased body part is completely replaced, it has the potential to cure rather than manage illness. Regenerative medicine also will help solve organ shortages—the lengthy waiting period for a transplantable organ, such as a kidney, liver or heart, that sometimes ends in the patient's death if an organ does not become available. And because regenerated organs can be grown from a patient's own cells, there is less risk for organ rejection, a significant problem in transplants.

•**Besides accident victims, what types of patients could potentially benefit most from regenerative medicine?** People with diabetes or·kidney, liver or heart failure are among the prime candidates. Others include patients who need replacement bone, muscle, ligament and tendon during surgery, and burn patients who don't have enough healthy skin for grafting.

•**How exactly are new organs and body tissues grown?** Many methods are being tested and developed, but the most commonly used technique has already been utilized to create implantable bladders in humans (described earlier). This method is also being used in the laboratory to grow other organs, such as kidneys and livers, and structures, including the esophagus, blood vessels and heart valves.

For the regenerated bladders, the first step involved taking a small tissue sample—about half the size of a postage stamp—from the diseased organ. Cells from the sample were mixed with growth factors (naturally occurring substances capable of stimulating cell growth and reproduction) so that the cells would multiply in the lab.

Those cells were then layered onto a scaffold-like structure (or mold) that had the same shape as the diseased organ and was made out of materials that are compatible with the human body.

The cell-covered scaffold was then placed in an ovenlike device or incubator that reproduced the conditions inside the human body—the same temperature and the same combination and concentration of biological elements. After approximately six to eight weeks, the cells had grown into tissue and the regenerated organ was ready to be implanted. It was removed from the incubator and placed in the patient by suturing it to the diseased organ. The scaffolding gradually degraded, and the new tissue integrated with the body.

•**How is regenerative medicine currently being used?** The process I just described was used to create the implantable bladders for children and teenagers with stiff, poorly functioning bladders. Previously, this defect was fixed by using a section of intestine to fashion a pouch to hold urine. But because intestinal tissue is not designed for such a use—but rather to absorb and excrete waste—this procedure increased the risk for osteoporosis, kidney stones and cancer. The recipients of the regenerated bladders have fully functioning bladders without the side effects produced by the old procedure.

Clinical trials focusing on implantable bladder technology are now being conducted at about 10 US research centers. The next step will be to make the technology available for widespread use.

In another case, cells from ear cartilage were used to formulate an injectable gel to repair the bladder sphincter in women with a type of severe stress incontinence called *intrinsic sphincter deficiency*. This single injection was far more effective in producing continence than the existing procedure, which involves repeatedly injecting collagen (derived from cow carcasses) into the neck of the bladder.

•**What are the greatest challenges scientists face in the development of regenerated organs and tissue?** The least difficult processes involve flat organs, such as the skin and cartilage in some areas of the body. The next level of difficulty is a hollow organ, such as the bladder or stomach, which consists of many different cell types and must "respond" on demand (for example, the bladder must expand to hold urine, and the stomach expands when food is consumed).

The most difficult is a solid organ, such as a kidney or heart, which has the greatest number of cells and requires the most blood supply. Ensuring that a regenerated organ has a sufficient blood supply is a major challenge.

•**Which human organs and tissues are being studied most for regeneration?** At Wake Forest Institute, scientists are working on the regeneration of more than 20 different types of organs and tissues. For example, blood vessels for heart bypass surgery (which now are harvested from leg veins) and heart valves (which are currently replaced with the heart valves of pigs) are being engineered.

To treat battlefield injuries, we're developing new skin to repair burns and heal wounds without scarring. Meanwhile, attempts are being made to replace a human ear, engineer new muscle and grow fingers and limbs. Cellular therapies, such as the creation of cells from the pancreas that produce insulin to treat diabetes and the production of red blood cells to treat anemia, also are being investigated in the lab.

An exciting development in this area is the recent discovery of a new source of stem cells from amniotic fluid and placental tissue—a readily available, fast-growing stem cell that we have used in the laboratory to create muscle, bone, fat, blood vessel, nerve and liver cells. A "bank" of such cells could provide 99% of the US population with perfect genetic matches for organ transplantation.

•**You haven't mentioned lungs or eyes— are there any developments happening there?** Yes. The Wake Forest laboratory is currently involved in efforts to engineer lung tissues and cornea tissues.

•**How close are we to actually deriving the benefits of such treatments?** Most of the developments in regenerative medicine are not yet ready for clinical use, but there may well be applicable results, such as engineered heart valves and blood vessels, during the next decade.

■ ■ ■ ■

Blue to the Rescue?

Brilliant Blue, a food additive used to color foods such as blue M&Ms and Gatorade, interferes with the molecular events that cause spinal cord damage hours after an initial injury. This animal study finding may lead to new treatments for spinal cord injuries.

University of Rochester Medical Center.

■ ■ ■ ■

Clothes that Block Sun

When researchers dyed lightweight cotton fabrics different shades of blue, red and yellow and measured the amount of ultraviolet

(UV) radiation that penetrated them, they found that darker, color-intense blue and red hues blocked more harmful UV rays than lighter yellow hues. This confirms past research that shows that dark colors such as black block harmful UV rays.

To protect skin from sun damage: Wear darker blue and red cottons.

Ascension Riva, PhD, engineer, Institute of Textile Research of Terrassa, Technical University of Catalonia, Barcelona, Spain.

Vaginal Gel Cuts Risk of HIV Infection, Study Shows

Salim S. Abdool Karim, MD, PhD, director, Centre for the AIDS Programme of Research in South Africa (CAPRISA), and pro vice-chancellor (research), University of KwaZulu-Natal, South Africa.

Quarraisha Abdool Karim, PhD, associate director, CAPRISA, and associate professor, epidemiology, Columbia University Mailman School of Public Health, New York City.

Kevin Fenton, MD, PhD, director, National Center for HIV/AIDS, Viral Hepatitis, STD, and TB Prevention, US Centers for Disease Control and Prevention, Atlanta.

Science.

A vaginal gel applied consistently before and after sex reduced the risk of HIV infection by more than half, according to a study presented at the International AIDS Conference in Vienna.

The gel contains *tenofovir* (Viread), an antiretroviral drug used to treat HIV/AIDS.

"If this was implemented and women in the general population used it in the same way as we observed in the trial, it could avert 1.3 million infections over the next 20 years," said study coauthor Salim S. Abdool Karim, MD, PhD. The report also appears in *Science.*

BACKGROUND

Nearly three-quarters of AIDS cases worldwide are in Africa, especially sub-Saharan Africa. Women represent about half of all HIV infections globally; young women are particularly at risk.

So far, trials of *microbicides*—compounds to be applied to the vagina or rectum to prevent infection with sexually transmitted diseases (STDs)—have been disappointing.

Eleven trials in the past 15 years have shown no change or even sometimes an increase in transmission rates, said study coauthor Quarraisha Abdool Karim, PhD, associate director of the Centre for the AIDS Programme of Research in South Africa (CAPRISA) and an associate professor of epidemiology at the Columbia University Mailman School of Public Health in New York City.

Dr. Quarraisha Abdool Karim and Dr. Salim S. Abdool Karim, who is director of CAPRISA and pro vice-chancellor (research) at the University of KwaZulu-Natal in South Africa, are married.

THE STUDY

For this study, nearly 900 HIV-negative women, ages 18 to 40, in urban and rural KwaZulu-Natal, South Africa, an epicenter of the AIDS epidemic, were randomized to take the Viread gel or a placebo gel.

Participants were told to administer two doses of the gel: one within 12 hours before sex and one within 12 hours after sex.

The trial lasted almost three years.

Overall, the gel reduced HIV infection by 39%. But in women who had high adherence (using the gel more than 80% of the time), the risk reduction was 54%, compared with women in the placebo group.

"Without this gel, for every 100 women we may see 10 women being infected in a year," said Dr. Salim S. Abdool Karim. "With this gel, we would see only six women being infected."

The gel also reduced the risk of contracting genital herpes by 51%, a factor that could slow the spread of HIV even further, given that people with genital herpes have double the risk of getting HIV, said Dr. Salim S. Abdool Karim.

The gel appeared to be less effective after 18 months. "We think the diminishing protection is largely due to diminished adherence," said Dr. Salim S. Abdool Karim, although this is not proven.

Despite these promising results, the gel still needs to be further researched, licensed and approved and is not likely to be available to women at clinics any time within the next year or two, said Dr. Salim S. Abdool Karim.

EXPERT REACTION

"The CAPRISA microbicide trial results are an exciting step forward for HIV prevention. While these findings may need to be confirmed by other research to meet requirements for licensure by [the US Food and Drug Administration] and other regulatory bodies throughout the world, they suggest that we could soon have a new method to help reduce the heavy toll of HIV among women around the world," said . Kevin Fenton, MD, PhD, director of the National Center for HIV/AIDS, Viral Hepatitis, STD, and TB Prevention at the US Centers for Disease Control and Prevention.

"Women represent the majority of new HIV infections globally, and urgently need methods they can control to protect themselves from infection. It is also very encouraging that the study found that the microbicide significantly reduced the risk of genital herpes [HSV-2], which is common in developing countries and in the United States, and facilitates HIV transmission," Dr. Fenton added.

MARKETING THE GEL

In their quest to get the gel on the market and widely used, the researchers will be enlisting the help of marketers.

"This is simply a cylindrical white plastic tube. You can't get anything more unattractive," said Dr. Salim S. Abdool Karim. "Even Coke would have gone bankrupt if they had adopted this approach to their marketing. We only made this gel for the study. I think the future is going to involve making this gel sexy, making this gel something that is part-and-parcel of the sex act, that enhances sex." Attractive packaging could lead more people to use it, and to use it a higher percentage of the time, he added.

info For more on HIV/AIDS, visit *www.aids. gov,* the official US Government Web site managed by the US Department of Health and Human Services.

Amazing Contact Lens Advancement Helps Blind See

Nick Di Girolamo, PhD, Senior Research Fellow NHM-RC, Director of Ocular Research Centre for Infection and Inflammation Research, School of Medical Sciences, University of New South Wales, Australia.

Contact lenses have been used to correct vision for a long time—but what if you could wear one that would actually help heal blindness? This kind of healing contact lens is exactly what researchers at the University of New South Wales in Sydney, Australia, have created to restore vision to three legally blind patients who had damaged corneas. What's really intriguing is that the researchers used stem cells from the patients' own eyes as part of the healing process.

STEM CELLS FOR EYE REPAIR

Yes, stem cells are what did the trick. The cornea is constantly replenished from a bank of stem cells. In each of these patients, however, that bank had been depleted or damaged.

The researchers began by taking a small tissue biopsy of the cornea that contained stem cells from each patient's healthy eye, plus a blood sample that was used to create a serum to nourish the stem cells. The cells were placed on a therapeutic contact lens and immersed in the serum, taking about 10 days to grow sufficiently to cover the lens. A surgeon then scraped each patient's cornea to remove abnormal cells, after which the lens was placed on the damaged eye in a procedure that took about a half hour. The lens remained in place for two weeks, during which time the stem cells transferred to the damaged cornea, eventually creating a healthy corneal surface. Vision improved for all three patients, one of whom even went from being legally blind to passing a vision test for a driver's license. Since the technique is new, there is no long-term experience to know if the change is permanent, but the effects in this study have thus far lasted beyond the eight to 13 months of follow-up.

EASY TO EXPAND UPON

One really exciting aspect of this particular course of treatment is that it is actually very low-tech and therefore easy for physicians to learn and perform, said Nick Di Girolamo, PhD, director of ocular research at the University of New South Wales and lead researcher in this project. "The simplicity of this technique means that it can ultimately be performed anywhere in the world," he said, "providing it is performed under sterile conditions by an experienced ophthalmic surgeon with proper facilities to culture cells." The cells and serum are the patient's own, so there's no need for immunosuppressive drugs, and the procedure itself is quick, so there is minimal time in the hospital.

Keep in mind that this treatment is still very, very new—only those three patients have had it so far. Much more research and follow-up need to be done before it can be used everywhere. Still, for the millions who suffer from cornea-related vision loss, this research could make the future look bright, indeed.

Life-Saving Tattoos

Saleh Aldasouqi, MD, director, Cape Diabetes and Endocrinology, Saint Francis Medical Center, Cape Girardeau, Missouri.

Never say never...even when it comes to getting a tattoo. In a new trend, some people are getting tattoos with a greater purpose than honoring their latest love interest or mother—they're sporting tattoos identifying that they have a dangerous medical condition in order to boost likelihood they'll get the right treatment in a life-threatening emergency.

"Like it or not, this is something people are doing," diabetes expert Saleh Aldasouqi, MD, reported at the recent annual meeting of the American Association of Clinical Endocrinologists. It's better for doctors to be in on the plan, he pointed out, so they can help patients get their "tats" done safely.

WHY DO IT?

This idea makes a strange sort of sense, especially for people with life-threatening problems such as severe allergies or diabetes. Dr. Aldasouqi said he has a patient who got a medical tattoo because the medical alert bracelets he'd worn for years often broke. Others are concerned about problems that might make it impossible to communicate in an emergency.

Dr. Aldasouqi said that he has seen some tattoos that are quite attractive. Some people choose the six-point asterisk-like Star of Life symbol that is the universal medical logo for emergency medical services, along with information identifying their condition—such as "diabetes," "steroid dependency" or "allergic to penicillin."

SAFE TATTOOING

If you are interested in getting a medical tattoo, check with your local city, county or state health department for licensing and regulations for tattoo parlors. You can also learn more at *www.cdc.gov/features/bodyart/.* When and if you do so, keep in mind that this is a situation in which you should also pay attention to the special precautions people with chronic medical problems need to follow anyway—for instance, if you have diabetes, make sure your blood sugar is well-controlled to avoid problems with healing and local infections. Dr. Aldasouqi suggested that an ideal location for a medical tattoo is on the right wrist, since emergency personnel are trained to check a patient's pulse there.

Why I Love Lasers to Zap Fat

Mark A. Stengler, NMD, naturopathic medical doctor in private practice, La Jolla, California...adjunct associate clinical professor at the National College of Natural Medicine, Portland, Oregon...author of many books, including The Natural Physician's Healing Therapies and coauthor of Prescription for Natural Cures (both from Bottom Line Books)...and author of the Bottom Line/Natural Healing newsletter.

How can I get rid of this belly fat?" That is the question countless patients ask when they come to my clinic. My answer to that question (as you might expect) is a healthful diet, an exercise program and some hormone balancing. But as I have observed from countless patients, losing weight in these ways is not easy. So before you schedule that tummy tuck or sign up with some gimmicky program that promises to take inches off your abdomen and waist, find out about a new alternative…

It is a low-level laser treatment (LLLT) called Zerona that is currently awaiting FDA approval for body contouring, although it has been tested and used by physicians since 2008. (There are other LLLT devices made by other companies. Zerona is the one I am most familiar with.) The procedure is performed by holistic physicians, plastic surgeons and some dermatologists.

Are you wondering why I recommend a laser therapy for fat reduction? Because aside from diet and exercise, it is one of the most noninvasive therapies for eliminating fat cells—and I believe that there's nothing wrong with using technology to help make things easier. This type of laser therapy does not involve surgery or anesthesia—and there are no wounds and no pain. I recommend it for people who are five pounds to 25 pounds overweight, who really want to lose that fat and who haven't been able to do it.

WHAT IS A LOW-LEVEL LASER?

One of the reasons I like LLLT is that the energy output of the laser is extremely low, only about 1/1,000 as intense as the lasers used to perform other procedures, such as those to eliminate age spots and skin blemishes. Known as cold laser technology (because it isn't hot and doesn't burn the skin), Zerona involves a focused light that penetrates below the skin, stimulating receptors inside individual cells. In the case of fat cells, the laser emulsifies some of the fat that they contain, allowing it to move into the surrounding extracellular fluid. From there, the liquefied fat is absorbed into the lymph nodes and eventually released as fatty acids into the bloodstream, where it is eliminated as waste. Unlike liposuction, the cosmetic surgical procedure that removes excess fat from the body, LLLT doesn't eliminate fat cells. LLLT patients retain all the fat cells that they started with—the cells simply contain less fat. And the

body uses its own detoxification process to rid itself of the contents of the fat cells.

In a study conducted by Erchonia Medical, the manufacturer of the Zerona laser, and published in the peer-reviewed journal *Lasers in Surgery and Medicine*, researchers found that volunteers treated for two weeks with the laser lost about 0.7 inches from each thigh…0.98 inches across the waist…and 1.05 inches across the hips. The weight loss can be long term if patients continue to maintain a healthful diet and exercise program. If they don't, of course, the weight loss is not permanent.

Thomas Barnes, MD, a cosmetic surgeon in Newport Beach, California, who uses Zerona to treat patients provided more details on how the technique works. Dr. Barnes also serves as a consultant to Santa Barbara Medical Innovators (SBMI), the company that distributes the Zerona laser.

LOSING INCHES OF FAT IN WEEKS

The Zerona device consists of five individual lasers, each mounted on a slowly revolving platform that allows the laser light to reach a relatively large surface area. During each treatment, the lasers are beamed from the waistline down to the middle of the thighs, first on the front of the body for 20 minutes and then on the back of the body for 20 minutes. Because the energy level is low, patients don't feel anything.

Although this approach is designed to reduce the fat content of areas directly exposed to the laser light, Dr. Barnes has found that the laser produces a systemic effect, draining fat from adjacent cells that aren't directly under the laser beams.

Example: A laser pointed at the torso can remove fat around the arms. For this reason, Dr. Barnes takes additional before—and after—measurements of his patients' upper arms, neck and upper abdomen. While results vary, he reports an average circumference reduction of one inch per measurement area.

Patients undergo a 40-minute session every other day for 14 days. This sequence is necessary because pores in fat cells (which are opened by the laser) begin to close after 72 hours. The treatment works best for those who want to lose areas of fat and for those who need motivation to spur on their weight-loss efforts. It is not for obese patients, who usually need to lose several inches of waist circumference.

Dr. Barnes also advises patients to drink eight glasses of water and walk for 30 to 60 minutes every day.

One of Dr. Barnes' patients, a 50-year-old woman who had been unable to lose fat in her midsection despite ongoing dieting, lost an average of 1.875 inches from her hips, waist, thighs and knees. Another patient, a woman of 35, lost an average of one inch from these areas.

SBMI reports that more than 15,000 patients have been treated with the laser over the last year. The cost for a full treatment regimen of six sessions is about $2,500. It is not covered by insurance.

ADDITIONAL HEALTH BENEFITS

Liposuction carries significant risk for complications (such as bruising, swelling and tissue damage), but LLLT has never been associated with any adverse effects. There also appear to be benefits associated with emptying fatty acids from the fat cells. The study published in Lasers in Surgery and Medicine found that those who had LLLT had significant reductions in total cholesterol and triglycerides.

LLLT is available around the country. To find a physician or other health-care provider in your area who offers Zerona treatments, visit *www.findzerona.com*.

The Awesome Healing Power of Leeches and Maggots

Ronald A. Sherman, MD, board chair, BioTherapeutics, Education & Research Foundation, *www.bterfoundation.org*.

As the saying goes, you have to take the bad with the good. A case in point is ancient healing. Not all the medicinal techniques handed down over time are as appealing as, say, honey or ginger. Ancient healers used some nasty-sounding treatments that have also withstood the test of time...including

leeches and maggots. You may be surprised to learn that these critters are still in use today—not only in so-called natural medicine circles, but also in some very cutting-edge and contemporary medical settings, such as the operating room. In many cases leeches and maggots are as good—or better than—more modern medical treatments. They're even regulated by the FDA as medical devices and often covered by medical insurance.

LEECH THERAPY

There is some evidence that the medicinal use of leeches—a kind of segmented worm that feeds on blood—dates as far back as ancient Egypt. Their natural ability to draw blood makes leeches useful in a number of medical situations, so much so that researchers continue to search for new ways that leech therapy can be applied to 21st-century medicine.

The saliva of leeches contains a unique mix of substances that serve as anticoagulants, *vasodilators* and anesthetics. These let the leech attach and feed without drawing the attention of the host, so the blood keeps flowing freely. This can be helpful to certain patients—particularly those who have recently had reconstructive surgery or limbs or appendages reattached. Why? A common complication following limb-reattachment surgery is blood that pools in the limb. Because it takes time for the minuscule veins that carry blood away from the limbs to heal after a reattachment surgery, this accumulation of blood creates pressure that could lead to tissue damage and, often, ultimately to the loss of the limb. Leeches are a solution to that problem. "Decompressing the appendage by draining venous blood with leeches for a few days, until the venous drainage system can reconnect itself, often saves the transplant," explains Ronald A. Sherman, MD, board chair of the BioTherapeutics Education & Research Foundation (*www.bterfoundation.org*).

Also, at Beth Israel Medical Center's Department of Integrative Medicine in New York City, doctors are utilizing leech therapy for some patients with osteoarthritis of the knee. The treatment involves attaching several leeches to the affected knee and allowing them to feed until they drop off (which takes an hour or two). One treatment is all it takes—the benefits of the therapy for knee pain and mobility can last for three to 12 months.

Of course, the leeches used for medical purposes are not simply plucked from the wild. The species of leech (*Hirudo medicinalis*) used for medical purposes is bred and processed to comply with FDA regulations.

LARVAL THERAPY—MAGGOTS

Similarly, physicians and researchers are looking to the effectiveness of larval treatment —that is, the use of medical-grade maggots—for treatment of problematic wounds such as diabetic foot ulcers, pressure ulcers (bed sores) and gangrene. The maggots excrete enzymes that dissolve the dead tissue, disinfect the wound and help speed healing. The maggots used for this purpose are first sterilized to kill microorganisms and are contained under a specially designed dressing.

SOUND GOOD TO YOU?

Do most people find the idea of treatment with leeches and maggots (collectively and somewhat more comfortably known as "biotherapy") repulsive, or are they open to it? Dr. Sherman's answer, while graphic, made a great deal of sense. "Most people do not have open, draining, stinking, gangrenous wounds that have prevented them from working, walking and socializing and maybe even put them at risk of losing their limbs," he said. "If you ask people who have these types of wounds and who need those types of treatments, you will find that they're not against it. They can weigh the benefits against the true risks of continued gangrene or surgery." Such patients are usually willing—and able—to overcome their squeamishness about a treatment that is proven to be so beneficial.

■ ■ ■ ■

Text Messages Can Make You Healthier

A University of California, Davis, study found that participants who received a daily cellphone text message reminding them to apply sunscreen did so 56% of the time. Those who did not get a reminder used sunscreen only 30% of the time. Send a loved one text reminders urging him/her to exercise or take supplements.

Mark A. Stengler, NMD, naturopathic medical doctor in private practice, La Jolla, California...adjunct associate clinical professor at the National College of Natural Medicine, Portland, Oregon...author of many books, including *The Natural Physician's Healing Therapies* and coauthor of *Prescription for Natural Cures* (both from Bottom Line Books)...and author of the *Bottom Line/Natural Healing* newsletter.

Natural Remedies

Worried About Alzheimer's? Forget Ginkgo, Study Says

Many older adults consume *ginkgo biloba,* hoping to keep their minds sharp, but a new study finds that the herbal product doesn't stave off cognitive decline.

"Measuring the effect of ginkgo in a big trial in older people, we didn't see any effect of the drug on slowing down or delaying normal age-related changes of cognition," said lead researcher Steven T. DeKosky, MD, vice president and dean of the University of Virginia School of Medicine in Charlottesville.

"If you are older and thinking 'I'll try ginkgo to preserve brain health,' we have no evidence that it is useful," he said. "I won't take it anymore."

The report, published in *The Journal of the American Medical Association,* supports the findings of earlier, smaller studies.

THE STUDY

To evaluate ginkgo's effect on cognitive decline, Dr. DeKosky's group looked at data on 3,069 community-dwelling adults, ages 72 to 96. The participants, who were generally healthy when the study began, took 120 milligrams of ginkgo or placebo twice a day. They were routinely tested for cognitive abilities.

Over more than six years of follow-up, the researchers found no evidence that ginkgo delayed or prevented normal declines in memory, language, attention, or executive functions,

Steven T. DeKosky, MD, vice president and dean, University of Virginia School of Medicine, Charlottesville.

Mark Blumenthal, founder and executive director, American Botanical Council, Austin, Texas.

Douglas MacKay, ND, vice president of scientific and regulatory affairs, Council for Responsible Nutrition, Washington, DC.

Lon S. Schneider, MD, director, State of California Alzheimer's Disease Research and Clinical Center at the University of Southern California, Los Angeles.

The Journal of the American Medical Association.

such as anticipating outcomes and adapting to changing situations and thinking abstractly.

These results remained the same regardless of sex, age, race or education, the researchers noted.

However, ginkgo was safe and no serious side effects were noted, Dr. DeKosky added. "The good news is it appeared that it was fairly safe; the bad news was it didn't seem to do anything at least as far as trying to slow down the cognitive changes of aging."

Earlier results from the same study found that ginkgo did not prevent or slow the development of Alzheimer's or other dementias, Dr. DeKosky said.

EXPERT REACTION

"There are many significant limitations of this study," said Mark Blumenthal, founder and executive director of the American Botanical Council. "First, the data being published this week are drawn from a previous clinical trial which was not designed to determine the decline in cognition. Second, about 40% of the subjects dropped out over the six-year duration of the trial; the statistics reported in the study include the dropouts for which no final data are available. Further, the subjects in the study were not monitored for certain cognitive parameters until several years after the trial began, creating difficulty in determining accurately whether they experienced a decline in cognition or not. Also, the age of the subjects is quite advanced, at an average of 79 years at the beginning of the trial. This age group is not typical of the age of both healthy people and those with mild cognitive impairment who use ginkgo for improving mental performance."

Another group, the Council for Responsible Nutrition (CRN), which represents the dietary supplement industry, also had reservations about the study.

Douglas MacKay, ND, CRN's vice president of scientific and regulatory affairs, said that "there is a large body of previously published evidence, as well as ongoing trials, which suggest that ginkgo biloba is effective for helping to im-

prove cognitive impairment in older adults." He added that, "as a former practicing naturopathic doctor, I have had the benefit of working with patients and have seen firsthand how ginkgo biloba can be effective in improving cognitive function."

Ginkgo biloba is believed to have antioxidant and anti-inflammatory properties that protect cell membranes and help govern the workings of *neurotransmitters,* which are the brain's chemical messengers.

Lon S. Schneider, MD, director of the state of California's Alzheimer's Disease Research and Clinical Center at the University of Southern California, Los Angeles, said that these findings were "straightforward and expected."

No measurable effect from ginkgo is seen on cognition, Dr. Schneider said. "Regardless of whether people say 'I take it and I feel better,' you just don't see an effect," he said.

Still, Dr. Schneider won't object if someone wants to try it. "It is not in my position to deflate hope," he said. "If someone really feels they need to take this and they need to try it, well go ahead and do it. But their expectations should be realistic, and if they don't experience anything, then they probably should stop."

info For more information on ginkgo biloba, visit the Web site of the National Center for Complementary and Alternative Medicine, *http://nccam.nih.gov/health/ginkgo/.*

Listen Up! Music Can Ease Anxiety

Group Health Cooperative news release.

Massage can reduce anxiety, but no better than a cheaper approach—simply relaxing while listening to soft, soothing music.

MASSAGE VS. MUSIC

A new study shows that patients, on average, had half the symptoms of anxiety three months after getting a series of 10 hour-long massages. But researchers were surprised to find that massages didn't reduce anxiety any more than lying down and listening to enjoyable music.

The study is the first to examine the effectiveness of massage as a treatment for patients with generalized anxiety disorder, which is characterized by chronic anxiety and excessive and often irrational worry about everyday things.

STUDY DETAILS

The researchers randomly assigned 68 patients with anxiety to one of three treatments. Some received 10 one-hour massages as music played, while others breathed deeply while lying down and listening to music. Patients in a third group had their arms and legs wrapped with heating pads and warm towels as they listened to music.

After treatment ended, all three groups reported a 40% decrease in symptoms of anxiety. The groups showed the same level of relief (about a 50% decrease) after three months also.

The findings were published in the journal *Depression and Anxiety*.

IMPLICATIONS

"We were surprised to find that the benefits of massage were no greater than those of the same number of sessions of…listening to relaxing music," said Karen J. Sherman, PhD, MPH, a senior investigator at Group Health Research Institute. "This suggests that the benefits of massage may be due to a generalized relaxation response.

"Treatment in a relaxing room is much less expensive than the other treatments [massage or thermotherapy], so it might be the most cost-effective option for people with generalized anxiety disorder who want to try a relaxation-oriented complementary medicine therapy," Dr. Sherman said.

info For more on generalized anxiety disorder, visit the Web site of the National Institute of Mental Health, *www.nimh.nih.gov/health*. Click on "Anxiety Disorders" and then choose "Generalized Anxiety Disorders."

New Way to Boost Memory, Ease Anxiety, Erase Pain

Paul G. Swingle, PhD, RPsych, registered psychologist board-certified in biofeedback and neurotherapy and author of *Biofeedback for the Brain* (Rutgers University). Formerly a professor of psychology at the University of Ottawa in Canada, he currently is in private practice in Vancouver, British Columbia. *www.SwingleAndAssociates.com*.

Imagine finding relief from medical or psychological problems by changing the way your brain works. You can—with *neurofeedback*, a type of biofeedback in which you learn to control brain-wave activity. As brain function improves, symptoms associated with inefficient brain function also improve. Even physical pain is eased, because pain management has a psychological component—and there are no drug side effects to worry about.

Neurofeedback helps…

- **Age-related cognitive decline**
- **Alcohol and drug cravings**
- **Anxiety**
- **Attention disorders** (such as ADD and ADHD)
- **Brain damage from head injury**
- **Depression**
- **Epilepsy, seizures**
- **Fibromyalgia**
- **Migraine**
- **Posttraumatic stress**
- **Sleep problems**
- **Stroke effects**

How it works: The brain produces electrical signals in the form of waves that correspond to specific mental states. Neurofeedback boosts your ability to produce particular brain waves that have specific desired effects. The process is painless and noninvasive.

You don't even have to be ill or in pain to reap the advantages. Many healthy executives, musicians and athletes use neurofeedback to sharpen the mind, ease stage fright or just perform at their peak.

USEFUL TO YOU?

To explore whether neurofeedback can help you, consult a neurotherapist—a specially trained psychologist, psychiatrist, naturopathic doctor, medical doctor, chiropractor or other health-care professional.

Recommended: Choose one who is certified in neurofeedback by the Biofeedback Certification Institute of America (866-908-8713, *www.bcia.org*).

At your initial diagnostic meeting, the neurotherapist uses an *electroencephalogram* (EEG) machine to map your brain-wave activity. For relatively straightforward problems, such as depression or sleep disorders, or in cases where the goal is simply to maximize cognitive performance, several electrodes (sensors) are dabbed with conductive gel and attached to specific spots on your head. For complex problems, such as traumatic brain injury or epilepsy, you wear a close-fitting cap with 19 sensors.

These sensors, connected with wires to a computer, measure electrical impulses produced by your brain. The practitioner reads these impulses while your eyes are open, while your eyes are shut and while you are reading—because some abnormalities are apparent only under certain circumstances.

Example: With one form of attention deficit disorder, brain waves look normal when the mind is not challenged—but when given a task, such as reading, the brain produces a wave that is not conducive to concentrating.

Your brain map is compared with internationally recognized reference data showing which brain patterns are normal under which circumstances. This identifies areas of the brain that are functioning abnormally or suboptimally. These areas are then targeted for treatment.

DURING A TREATMENT SESSION

A typical treatment session lasts about 50 minutes. The practitioner places an electrode at the spot where your brain needs to become more or less active when producing a specific frequency. The electrode is connected to a computer that gives you feedback. When you succeed in altering your brain waves to the target frequency, the computer produces a special sound or visual cue.

At first, achieving this is a matter of trial and error—more the result of passively observing the mental and physical states that seem to work rather than actively trying to think or do something specific.

For instance, if you're trying to create alpha waves to ease anxiety, you may notice that the tone sounded when you closed your eyes and pictured a ship sailing into the horizon but not when you imagined yourself in a meadow. With practice, your brain learns to regulate these brain waves.

The severity of the problem determines the length of treatment. Some people have 10 to 30 weekly sessions…others come three times a week for up to 100 sessions.

A follow-up session assures that the brain wave change is stable. Some people get "tune-ups"—many older clients come four times a year to adjust the frequencies associated with mental focus.

Cost varies but typically runs about $100 per session. Insurance sometimes covers these treatments.

Recommended: Neurofeedback is a complementary therapy, best used in conjunction with psychotherapy, physical therapy, nutritional counseling, medical care or other treatment.

For instance: Neurofeedback can ease cravings for alcohol or drugs—but a person with a substance use disorder also needs counseling to learn how to create a new social environment that does not include drinking or drugs.

Important: Inform your medical doctor and other health-care providers before beginning neurofeedback (as you should with any new treatment) to make sure that none of your therapies conflict.

The Most Powerful Brain-Building Nutrients and Herbs

Maoshing Ni ("Dr. Mao"), PhD, DOM (doctor of oriental medicine), LAc (licensed acupuncturist), chancellor and cofounder of Yo San University in Los Angeles, and codirector of Tao of Wellness, a clinic in Santa Monica, California. He is author of 12 books, including *Second Spring: Dr. Mao's Hundreds of Natural Secrets for Women to Revitalize and Regenerate at Any Age* (Free Press). *www.taoofwellness.com.*

You open your cupboard but then can't recall what you wanted…you're introducing two friends and suddenly draw a blank on one's name.

Such instances of "brain fog" are common, but they are not an inevitable part of aging. Many people remain remarkably sharp all their lives—and the right nutritional strategies can help you be one of them.

Cognitive declines can result from hormonal changes and reductions in *neurotransmitters,* chemicals that help brain cells communicate with each other. Increasing your intake of certain nutrients helps balance hormones and protect neurotransmitters. *You can get these nutrients from…*

•**Foods.** Eating brain-boosting foods is an ideal way to get needed nutrients.

Reasons: The body is designed to absorb nutrients from foods rather than from isolated or manufactured chemicals (such as in supplements)…and foods contain complementary components that enhance nutrient absorption.

•**Herbs.** The healthful aromatic oils are most active when herbs are fresh, but dried herbs also will do.

•**Supplements.** These are an option if you cannot find the foods that provide certain nutrients, or if you need specific nutrients in quantities beyond what you typically get from food. Unless otherwise noted, the following supplements generally are safe, have few side effects and may be used indefinitely. All are sold at health food stores.

Important: Ask your doctor before supplementing, especially if you have a health condition…use medication…or are pregnant or breast-feeding. To reduce the risk for interactions, do not take supplements within 30 minutes of medication…and limit your use of these supplements to any four of the following.

NUTRIENTS YOUR MIND NEEDS

For the foods recommended below, one serving equals four ounces of meat, poultry, fish, or soy products…eight ounces of milk…two ounces of nuts…two eggs (with yolks)…one-half cup of vegetables or fruit…and one cup of leafy greens.

•**Choline.** The neurotransmitter *acetylcholine* plays a key role in learning and memory. Choline is a precursor to acetylcholine that is produced in the liver. Production of choline declines with age, as does the body's ability to efficiently use the choline that remains.

Brain boost: Eat one or more servings daily of choline-rich broccoli, cauliflower, eggs, kidney beans, navy beans, liver, milk or peanuts.

Supplement option: 1,200 milligrams (mg) daily.

•**DMAE** (*2-dimethylaminoethanol*). The body uses fatty acids to create brain cells and neurotransmitters. DMAE, a chemical in fatty acids, helps produce acetylcholine.

Brain boost: Have two servings weekly of DMAE-rich anchovies or sardines. If fresh fish is not available, have canned water-packed sardines or anchovies and rinse before eating to reduce salt.

Supplement option: 500 mg twice daily after meals.

•**L-carnitine.** Mitochondria are the engines of cells. The amino acid L-carnitine transports fatty acids to mitochondria for use as fuel and provides nutrients to brain cells.

Brain boost: Have two weekly servings of lamb or poultry, which are rich in L-carnitine.

Supplement option: 500 mg to 1,000 mg before breakfast and again in the afternoon.

•**Vitamin B-12.** This is key to red blood cell formation and nerve cell health. The body's ability to absorb vitamin B-12 diminishes with age—about 10% to 15% of people over age 60 are deficient in it.

Brain boost: Have two servings weekly of beef or lamb…halibut, salmon, sardines or sea bass…eggs…or vitamin B-12–enriched soybean products (miso, tempeh).

Supplement option: 500 micrograms (mcg) to 1,000 mcg daily.

THE MOST HELPFUL HERBS

An easy way to get the benefits of mind-sharpening herbs is to brew them into a tisane, or herbal infusion—more commonly called herbal tea.

To brew: Pour eight ounces of very hot water over one heaping tablespoon of fresh herbs or one teaspoon of dried herbs. Steep for five minutes, strain and drink.

Convenient: To reduce the number of cups needed to meet the daily recommendations below, brew two or more herbs together.

•**Chinese club moss.** This herb contains the chemical *huperzine A*, which helps conserve acetylcholine.

Brain boost: Drink one to two cups of Chinese club moss tea each day.

Supplement option: 50 mcg of huperzine A twice daily (discontinue if supplements cause gastric upset or hyperactivity).

•**Ginkgo biloba.** This herb increases blood flow to the brain's tiny capillaries and combats DNA damage caused by free radicals.

Caution: Do not use ginkgo if you take blood-thinning medication, such as *warfarin* (Coumadin).

Brain boost: Drink three cups of ginkgo tea daily.

Supplement option: 120 mg daily.

•**Kitchen herbs.** Oregano, peppermint, rosemary and sage have oils that may increase blood flow in the brain and/or support neurotransmitters, promoting alertness.

Brain boost: Use any or all of these herbs to brew a cup of tea for a pick-me-up in the morning and again in the afternoon.

Also: Use herbs liberally when cooking.

Supplement option: About 150 mg each of any or all of these herbs daily. They can be taken alone or in combination.

•**Mugwort (wormwood).** This herb improves circulation, aiding delivery of nutrients to brain cells.

Brain boost: Twice a week, drink one cup of mugwort tea…add a half-dozen leaves of fresh mugwort to salad…or sauté leaves with garlic or onions.

Supplement option: 300 mg daily.

Caution: Avoid mugwort during pregnancy—it may stimulate uterine contractions.

•**Don't forget green tea.** Strictly speaking, an herb is a flowering plant whose stem aboveground does not become woody. In that sense, the leaf of the *Camellia sinensis* shrub—otherwise known as tea—is not an herb. Yet green tea (which is less oxidized than black) is so helpful that it must be listed among the top brain boosters.

Along with antioxidant *polyphenols*, green tea provides the amino acid *theanine*, which stimulates calming alpha brain waves and improves concentration. Green tea also has been linked to a reduced risk for Alzheimer's disease.

To brew: Pour eight ounces of very hot water over one teaspoon of loose, fresh green tea leaves (or a tea bag if fresh is not available) and steep for three to five minutes. You needn't strain the tea. As you empty your cup, you can add more warm water to the remaining leaves—as long as the water turns green, the tea still contains polyphenols.

Brain boost: Drink three cups of green tea (caffeinated or decaffeinated) daily.

Supplement option: 350 mg of green tea extract daily.

Use "Common Scents" To Improve Your Mind And Mood

Alan Hirsch, MD, founder and neurological director of the Smell and Taste Treatment and Research Foundation and associate attending physician at Mercy Hopspital and Medical Center in Chicago. He has conducted more than 200 studies on smell and taste disorders and is the author of seven books, including *Life's a Smelling Success* (Authors of Unity) and *Sensa Weight-Loss Program* (Hilton). *www.SmellandTaste.org*.

Scents have subtle yet powerful effects on emotions—boosting confidence, easing stress, triggering fond memories and more. Here's how to use your sense of smell to manage your moods…and other people's, too!

•**Increase mental sharpness with fresh flowers.** When you need to focus—for instance, to memorize a speech or balance a checkbook—keep a vase of mixed fragrant flowers nearby. Take periodic breaks to consciously "stop and smell the roses."

For kids: This helps when doing homework or studying for a test.

•**Promote positive family interaction with garlic.** Serve garlic bread at dinner. In studies, this scent reduced negative dinnertime remarks by 22.7% and increased pleasantries by 7.4%. You don't even have to eat the bread to reap the benefits.

•**Feel younger with pink grapefruit.** To make others perceive you as youthful (so you feel that way, too), apply a grapefruit-scented or other citrusy body lotion or spray right after your shower.

Avoid: Lavender, which makes you seem granny-ish.

•**Feel more secure with baby powder.** Keep a small bottle or resealable plastic bag of baby powder in your purse or briefcase. Before heading into a challenging situation (a meeting with your ex, a job interview), open the container slightly and take a small whiff. Don't inhale too deeply—you may sneeze or get powder all over your face.

•**Curb food cravings with banana or peppermint.** You needn't eat a banana—just smell it (peeled or unpeeled).

Or: Place two drops of peppermint essential oil on a cotton ball, stick it in a plastic bag and take a whiff…or try sugar-free peppermint gum or hard candy.

•**Combat claustrophobia with evergreens.** Keep a small vial of evergreen essential oil in your pocket or purse. When in a cramped space (an elevator, a crowd), hold the vial near your nose and inhale two or three times. Repeat every 10 minutes as needed.

•**Assuage anger with cucumber.** Hold a sliced cucumber one-half inch from your face and level with your lips…inhale deeply, continuing for several minutes. To reduce road rage, use a cucumber-melon air freshener in the car.

Avoid: Barbecuing or roasting meat when you're angry—the scent stirs up fiery feelings that heighten aggression.

•**Relax and wind down with lavender.** Lie down and place a lavender-scented eye pillow over your eyes…breathe slowly and deeply for several minutes.

Avoid: Jasmine, which promotes alertness.

•**Rev up a man's libido with pumpkin pie or black licorice.** Bake a pumpkin pie for maximum effect…or use a reed diffuser (a stick that wicks the aroma from a bottle of scented oil).

On a date: Nibble on black licorice.

Noteworthy: Perfume is only 3% effective at arousing a man's romantic feelings…versus 40% for pumpkin pie and 13% for licorice.

■ ■ ■ ■

Green Tea May Help Millions of Women

Green tea extract shows promise as a treatment for uterine fibroids, say US researchers who add they'll soon begin human trials of the therapy.

Uterine fibroids, which affect 40% of women of reproductive age, cause excessive vaginal bleeding, anemia, fatigue and lack of energy.

STUDY FINDINGS

Green tea extract can kill human *leiomyoma* (fibroid) cells in tissue cultures and can eradicate fibroid lesions in lab animals, according to Ayman Al-Hendy, MD, PhD, director of clinical research at Meharry Medical College in Nashville, Tennessee, and colleagues. Their findings were published in the *American Journal of Obstetrics & Gynecology.*

"If we can prove this compound is effective, millions of women can start self-treatment and self-management," said Dr. Al-Hendy.

He and his team are recruiting volunteers to take part in clinical trials.

info The US National Women's Health Information Center Web site has more about uterine fibroids at *http://womenshealth.gov.* Under "Health Topics," choose "Fact Sheets" and then "Uterine Fibroids."

Meharry Medical College news release.

Revolutionary Nutrient Therapy for Macular Degeneration

Mark A. Stengler, NMD, naturopathic medical doctor in private practice, La Jolla, California…adjunct associate clinical professor at the National College of Natural Medicine, Portland, Oregon…author of many books, including *The Natural Physician's Healing Therapies* and coauthor of *Prescription for Natural Cures* (both from Bottom Line Books)…and author of the *Bottom Line/Natural Healing* newsletter.

Imagine sitting back in a comfortable chair in your holistic physician's office and providing your body with such a boost of nutrients that you are able to see more clearly after the one-and-a-half-hour treatment session than you could before it. That was what happened to Lou, an 83-year-old patient who had *age-related macular degeneration* (AMD), a disease in which the macula (part of the retina) degenerates, causing vision loss. Lou had "wet" AMD, the more severe form of the disease in which abnormal blood vessels form, leaking fluid into the macula.

The treatment that helped Lou was intravenous (IV) nutrient therapy, a technique in which vitamins and other nutrients are delivered directly into the bloodstream in an IV solution, flooding the body's cells with higher levels of the nutrients than they would get from ingesting them. IV nutrient therapy can help both wet and "dry" AMD, a less severe form of the disease.

I use IV nutrient therapy to treat patients with chronic fatigue and heavy metal poisoning. IV nutrient therapy has been found to help viral hepatitis C…heart arrhythmias caused by nutritional imbalances…and neurological diseases, such as Parkinson's. AMD responds particularly well to IV nutrient therapy.

One of the leading practitioners of IV nutrient therapy in the country is Paul Anderson, ND, a professor of naturopathic medicine at Bastyr University near Seattle. He created the IV nutrient therapy for AMD. I trained with Dr. Anderson and now use his protocol with my patients. Dr. Anderson provided more information about this treatment…

HOW IT WORKS

The eyes' tissues are extremely responsive to nutrients—which is why holistic physicians tell their patients to take antioxidants such as lutein, which has been found to slow the progression of AMD. So just consider what nutrients can do for eye tissue when administered intravenously at up to 100 times the concentration of antioxidants taken orally. While there have been no studies yet on IV nutrient therapy for AMD, patients who have had the treatment report extremely positive results that include restoration of most—but not all—of the vision that had been lost. The therapy can be effective at stopping the disease from progressing further.

First, a patient is cleared for IV nutrient therapy based on a medical exam and blood tests to ensure that the liver and kidneys can handle the treatment. (Patients also are monitored throughout the treatment.) The infusion for AMD includes vitamin C (for its antioxidant properties) and selenium and zinc, chromium (an element that strengthens blood vessels) and l-carnitine (for its neuroprotective benefits). Dr. Anderson gives patients at least six infusions, usually two a week for the first three weeks. If the patient is age 75 or older or has advanced

AMD, he may recommend as many as 12 infusions. Each infusion takes about one-and-a-half to two hours and typically costs $150 to $200. Check to see if your insurance plan covers this type of treatment.

After a patient's nutrient levels have gotten this boost, the patient can maintain any improvement in vision by following a therapeutic regimen of oral supplements combined with a diet high in *flavonoids*, plant nutrients that have antioxidant properties. This regimen also can be used to help prevent AMD.

Flavonoids are important to eye health because they can neutralize inflammation in the eye. Foods high in flavonoids include beans (red kidney beans, pinto beans), dark-colored fruits (blueberries, cranberries, blackberries) and vegetables (cabbage, onions, parsley, tomatoes). Make these foods a regular part of your diet. *Recommended maintenance supplements include...*

•**A multivitamin** to ensure that patients get many vitamins and minerals that are in the IV treatment.

•**Fish oil that contains the omega-3 fatty acids DHA and EPA.** These help to maintain the healthy structure and function of ocular tissue and keep eye cell membranes fluid and flexible.

Dose: At least 1,000 milligrams (mg) to 2,000 mg daily. Some patients need even more.

•**Eye-health supplement.** These supplements contain nutrients that support eye health.

Brand to try: Eye-Vite (made by KAL and available at health food stores and online), which contains zinc, beta-carotene, vitamin E and bilberry fruit extract (a rich antioxidant) and other nutrients.

•**Lutein and zeaxanthin,** two carotenoids that benefit macular tissue. The best way to ensure that you get the appropriate amounts of carotenoids is to take them in supplement form.

Dose: 15 mg daily of lutein and 3 mg daily of zeaxanthin with a meal.

•**Taurine and l-carnitine.** These amino acids are beneficial to eye health because they help nerve tissue in the brain conduct impulses needed for vision.

Dose: 500 mg daily of taurine and 1,500 mg daily of l-carnitine.

A high-density bioflavonoid supplement. To ensure that you get enough flavonoids, it is recommended that you take a supplement such as Cruciferous Complete (made by Standard Process, 800-558-8740, *www.StandardProcess.com*), which contains phytochemicals from plants in the Brassica family (vegetables such as kale and brussels sprouts). These vegetables protect against free radicals (disease-causing molecules), help eye function and stimulate the body's cleansing systems. Follow label instructions.

When patients are properly screened for IV nutrient therapy by a physician trained in this treatment, IV therapy is safe. To locate a physician who administers IV nutrient therapy, contact International IV Nutritional Therapy for Physicians (503-805-3438, *www.IVNutritional Therapy.com*). This organization helps people find IV nutrient therapists in their areas.

Herbal Supplements: Lies the Medical Establishment Hopes You'll Believe

Mark A. Stengler, NMD, naturopathic medical doctor in private practice, La Jolla, California...adjunct associate clinical professor at the National College of Natural Medicine, Portland, Oregon...author of many books, including *The Natural Physician's Healing Therapies* and coauthor of *Prescription for Natural Cures* (both from Bottom Line Books)... and author of the *Bottom Line/Natural Healing* newsletter.

I like to expose some of the lies and half-truths about nutritional supplements, including vitamins. Herbal supplements also have gotten an undeserved bashing in recent years. Yet millions of people benefit from these safe natural remedies. Also, many prescription drugs are based on plant molecules. Herbs often work as well as, or better than, medications—and they are much gentler on the body.

Lie: St. John's wort doesn't help severe depression.

***Truth:* St John's wort works as well as drugs. Severe depression requires a higher dosage.**

Back in 2002, a study published in *The Journal of the American Medical Association* claimed that St. John's wort did not help severe depression, which is difficult to treat even with pharmaceutical drugs. As a result, many headlines stated that St. John's wort was ineffective for all types of depression. At that time, the herb was most often used to treat mild-to-moderate depression—it worked well, caused few side effects and was less expensive than antidepressants. Later, in 2008, an analysis of 29 studies in which St. John's wort was used to treat major depression was published in the Cochrane Database of Systematic Reviews. The article concluded that the herb worked just as well as drugs, although the dose to treat severe depression was higher than that needed to treat milder forms. Yet the impression left by the earlier study remained.

Note: St. John's wort should not be taken with an antidepressant or by women who are pregnant, breast-feeding or taking birth control pills.

Lie: Garlic supplements do not reduce blood pressure.

***Truth:* Studies show garlic works, but doctors typically don't prescribe it.**

There's evidence that garlic supplements can reduce blood pressure in people who have high blood pressure. Analyses of studies in *Annals of Pharmacotherapy* and *BMC Cardiovascular Disorders* confirmed that garlic lowered systolic blood pressure (the top number in a blood pressure reading) or both systolic and diastolic blood pressure (bottom number). Despite this evidence, conventional medical doctors typically don't prescribe garlic to lower blood pressure.

Brand to try: Kyolic Healthy Heart Formula 106, which provides 300 milligrams (mg) of aged garlic extract (800-421-2998, *www.kyolic.com*).

Lie: Echinacea does not help fight the common cold.

***Truth:* Studies show echinacea reduces the length of the colds, but dosages vary as does the strength of the products.**

An analysis of 14 studies published in *The Lancet Infectious Diseases* found that echinacea supplements reduced the risk of catching a cold by 58% and reduced the length of colds by 1.4 days, on average. This herb's effectiveness may be in question because not all echinacea products are of the same quality or strength, which means dosages vary.

Brand to try: Nature's Way Echinacea (call 801-489-1500 or try *www.naturesway.com* for a store locator).

Lie: Black cohosh makes breast cancer spread.

***Truth:* Black cohosh reduces levels of estrogen, the hormone that can cause cancer risk.**

Many women use this herb to reduce hot flashes. An old theory is that black cohosh contains weak estrogen-like plant compounds that attach to estrogen receptors on the surface of the cell that could raise the risk for breast cancer. Concern increased when research published in *Cancer Research* found that mice bred to develop aggressive breast cancer were more likely to have the cancer spread to their lungs when given this herb. Other studies published in *Maturitas* and *BMC Pharmacology* demonstrated that black cohosh reduces estrogen levels and does not contain phytoestrogens (estrogen-like plant compounds). Also, a National Institutes of Health–sponsored study published in *International Journal of Cancer* that compared the supplement use of women with and without breast cancer found that women who took black cohosh had a 61% lower risk for breast cancer. I believe that black cohosh is safe for all women, even those who have a history of breast cancer.

Lie: Saw palmetto is not effective for benign prostate enlargement.

***Truth:* Saw palmetto works as well as drugs to right mild-to-moderate BPH.**

Enlargement of the prostate gland, known as *benign prostatic hyperplasia* (BPH), commonly affects men age 50 and older. The main symptom is reduced or erratic urinary flow. One study found that saw palmetto did not help men who had severe BPH. But many other studies reviewed in the Cochrane Database of Systematic Reviews have found that it does help men with mild-to-moderate BPH, which is the more common condition. For men with this condition, saw palmetto works just as well as prescription drugs, with fewer side effects—and it is less expensive.

Half-truth: Licorice root raises blood pressure.

Truth: **Most licorice supplements are safe because the ingredient that causes high blood pressure has been removed.**

In very large amounts, licorice root can increase blood pressure and deplete potassium, so if you have heart disease, diabetes or high blood pressure, you should not have licorice root tea or black licorice candies frequently. But these warnings about licorice don't apply to people who don't have these conditions or to multi-ingredient formulas that contain very small amounts of the herb. Most licorice supplements, which help to improve digestion, heartburn and ulcers, are *deglycyrrhized,* which means that the sweet-tasting ingredient that raises blood pressure has been removed.

Lie: Ginseng increases blood pressure.

Truth: **Research published in Hypertension finds otherwise.**

Conventional medical physicians and organizations often advise patients who have high blood pressure against taking certain types of ginseng. Studies published in *Hypertension* found that different types of ginseng, including Asian ginseng (*Panax ginseng*), did not increase blood pressure—and a study published in *Annals of Pharmacotherapy* found that Panax ginseng actually reduced it. I believe that ginseng can safely be used by those with high blood pressure.

Harvard Doctor Wary About Herbal Supplements

JoAnn E. Manson, MD, DrPH, professor of medicine and women's health at Harvard Medical School and chief of the division of preventive medicine at Brigham and Women's Hospital, both in Boston. She is one of the lead investigators for two highly influential studies on women's health—the Harvard Nurses' Health Study and the Women's Health Initiative. Dr. Manson is the author, with Shari Bassuk, ScD, of *Hot Flashes, Hormones & Your Health* (McGraw-Hill).

Herbal supplements are taken by nearly 18% of US adults. *Despite this popularity, I have some concerns about their use…*

•**Research has yet to show whether many of these products have any clear benefit.** Few herbal products have been rigorously tested to determine whether they relieve symptoms or otherwise improve health. Many studies that have been done tended to be small and/or to have design flaws.

•**Labels can be misleading.** Half of herbal products sold online erroneously and illegally claim to prevent, treat, diagnose or cure specific diseases.

•**Supplements are subject to little regulatory oversight.** Those containing agents that were on the market before 1994 are exempt from FDA review…with newer agents, manufacturers must notify the FDA but need not wait for approval before selling products. Many manufacturers fail to report to the FDA any supplement-related adverse reactions.

•**Some products are contaminated with heavy metals or bacteria…or adulterated with controlled substances, such as stimulants.** Buying organic products may reduce, but is unlikely to eliminate, these risks.

Big concern: An estimated 40% to 70% of patients do not report their herbal supplement use to their doctors. This is a mistake because some herbs can confer serious health risks—for example, by thinning the blood or interacting with medications.

Self-defense: The following herbs are among the most widely used. If you choose to take them (or any herbal supplement), do so under guidance from a knowledgeable health-care practitioner.

•**Echinacea.** Some studies show that echinacea slightly shortens the duration of colds and flu, but results are inconsistent. There is limited evidence suggesting that the herb may help prevent colds and flu, though more research is needed.

Be aware: Echinacea may exacerbate asthma…people with ragweed allergy also may be allergic to echinacea.

•**Ginkgo biloba.** Users take this to protect memory.

But: A six-year clinical trial of more than 3,000 seniors found ginkgo no more effective than a placebo at reducing dementia risk.

Caution: Ginkgo can increase bleeding, which is risky if you take an anticoagulant, such as *clopidogrel* (Plavix) or *warfarin* (Coumadin)... use any nonsteroidal anti-inflammatory, such as *aspirin* or *ibuprofen* (Motrin)...have a bleeding disorder...or need surgery or a dental procedure, such as a tooth extraction.

• **St. John's wort.** Studies suggest that this eases symptoms of mild-to-moderate (but not severe) depression.

Risks: It reduces blood levels of cholesterol-lowering statin drugs and the blood pressure drug *verapamil* (Verelan). Taking St. John's wort with an antidepressant, such as *fluoxetine* (Prozac), may increase risk for *serotonin syndrome,* an excess of serotonin that can cause blood pressure changes, hallucinations and kidney damage.

If You Take Herbs... Read This Before You Have Surgery

David J. Rowe, MD, assistant professor in the department of plastic surgery at University Hospitals Case Medical Center in Cleveland.

Every patient is asked before surgery, "What medications do you take?" Yet 40% to 70% of patients do not report their use of herbal supplements—typically because they don't think of supplements as medication.

The concern: Though many herbs generally are safe, when you are undergoing or recovering from surgery—even a minor procedure—certain herbs can lead to potentially serious side effects, such as...

Bleeding problems: Some herbs thin the blood, possibly complicating surgery and delaying healing. *These include...*

• *Dong quai,* commonly used for menstrual cramps and menopausal symptoms.

• *Feverfew,* for arthritis and headache.

• *Garlic,* to stimulate the immune system.

• *Ginkgo biloba,* used for eye disorders, cognitive problems and vertigo.

• *Ginseng,* used for stress.

Cardiovascular side effects: Postoperative hypertension, heart palpitations or other serious heart problems may develop if you are taking...

• *Feverfew,* for arthritis and headache.

• *Garlic,* for immune-strengthening.

Drug interactions: The actions and side effects of drugs commonly given before, during or after surgery—such as *lidocaine* (an anesthetic) and *midazolam* (a sedative)—may be intensified by...

• *Echinacea,* for cold and flu.

• *Goldenseal,* taken to relieve digestive and respiratory problems.

Photosensitivity: If you have laser surgery, you may develop a severe light-sensitivity rash if you are taking...

• *Dong quai,* for menstrual and menopausal symptoms.

• *St. John's wort,* for anxiety.

Reaction to anesthesia: Herbs that prolong sedation include...

• *Kava,* a sedative.

• *St. John's wort,* for anxiety.

• *Valerian,* for insomnia.

Self-defense: Follow these steps...

• A month before any scheduled surgery, give your doctor a list of every supplement and medication that you take.

• Even if your doctor is not concerned, it is safest to discontinue all supplements at least two weeks before surgery.

• On the day of your operation, remind your surgeon about any recent supplement use—and also show your list to the anesthesiologist.

• Carry a personal health record that lists all supplements and drugs you take. If you need emergency surgery, doctors can take precautions.

• After surgery, wait until your doctor declares you sufficiently healed before you resume taking your supplements.

Exceptions: Though clinical research is limited, anecdotal evidence suggests that recovery may be hastened by...

• *Arnica,* used for pain and inflammation.

• *Bromelain,* an enzyme with analgesic and anti-inflammatory properties.

With your doctor's okay, consider taking arnica and/or bromelain (following dosage instructions on labels) starting the day after surgery.

■ ■ ■ ■

Anesthesiologist's Sore Throat Secret

A licorice gargle before surgery can reduce sore throat afterward. Patients who gargled with a licorice solution five minutes before an operation also had less postsurgical coughing. Sore throats and coughs are common after surgery involving general anesthesia with intubation. The licorice gargle is easy to make.

How to do it: Boil about one teaspoon of licorice powder in one-and-a-half cups of water, then filter. Gargle should stay at room temperature and be used within 24 hours. Licorice contains compounds with anti-inflammatory and anti-irritant effects. Ask your doctor for details.

Anil Agarwal, MD, department of anaesthesiology, Sanjay Gandhi Post Graduate Institute of Medical Sciences, Lucknow, India, and leader of a study published in *Anesthesia & Analgesia.*

Tai Chi May Relieve Knee Pain in Seniors

Arthritis Care & Research news release.

W ant to improve that osteoarthritis in your knee? New research suggests that regular tai chi exercise can reduce pain and help your knee function better. "Tai chi is a mind–body approach that appears to be a useful treatment for older adults with knee osteoarthritis," said Chenchen Wang, MD, coauthor of the study published in *Arthritis Care & Research.*

BACKGROUND

In the United States, an estimated 4.3 million adults over age 60 suffer from this form of arthri-

tis, which causes wearing of joint cartilage. As many as half of American adults may develop symptoms by age 85, the US Centers for Disease Control and Prevention reported recently. Tai chi consists of slow, rhythmic movements that promote balance, strength and flexibility. The study participants performed Yang style tai chi, the most commonly practiced form, which uses slow, evenly paced, flowing movements.

THE STUDY

Dr. Wang and colleagues from Tufts University School of Medicine recruited 40 patients, average age 65, who had been diagnosed with knee osteoarthritis. Half of the group took part in tai chi sessions for an hour, twice weekly over a period of three months. The tai chi session consisted of 10 minutes of self-massage and review of tai chi principles, a half hour of tai chi movement, 10 minutes of breathing exercises and 10 minutes of relaxation. The other participants took two 60-minute classes per week for three months and learned about issues such as diet and nutrition, and treatments for osteoarthritis. They also stretched for 20 minutes.

TAI CHI MOST EFFECTIVE

Those who practiced tai chi had significantly less knee pain than the other group and also reported less depression, more physical function and better overall health.

Seven Ways to Get Rid of Stiff, Achy Joints And Muscles

David G. Borenstein, MD, clinical professor of medicine at the George Washington University Medical Center, Washington, DC. He maintains a private practice at Arthritis and Rheumatism Associates in the Washington, DC, area, and is author of *Back in Control!* (M. Evans).

D o you hobble when you get out of bed or up from the couch? Do you have trouble tying your shoes or raising your arm high enough to reach a high shelf? You're probably experiencing an age-related decline in *elastin,* the protein that gives muscles, ligaments and tendons their elasticity.

It's normal to experience short-lived and intermittent stiffness, such as when you change position. It's also normal to be stiff for a few minutes when you get up in the morning.

Reason: The gel phenomenon. Fluids accumulate in and around joints when you sleep. This extra fluid volume, known as gelling, impairs muscle and joint movements until it dissipates with movement.

When to worry: Persistent stiffness…discomfort in the absence of movement…and/or pain or stiffness in multiple locations can indicate arthritis. Anyone who is always stiff should get checked by a rheumatologist.

MORE MOBILITY

Some people naturally produce high levels of elastin. They may retain full mobility throughout their lives. Most people, however, start experiencing a noticeable decline in elastin and an increase in stiffness in their 50s or 60s. Past injuries can be a factor. Someone who tore a hamstring while skiing, for example, will probably develop *fibrosis* (tissue scarring) that eventually will make him/her less flexible.

Everyone recognizes the muscle/joint pain that occurs from overuse—from working all day in the yard, for example, or from playing three hours of tennis when you usually stop at two. Most stiffness, however, is due to lack of use. A lack of exercise causes a decline in connective tissue flexibility.

To gain more flexibility, try any of the following options…

•**Yoga.** I recommend yoga because it's one of the more efficient stretching exercises. The graduated lessons (from novice to intermediate and advanced) allow people to improve their range of motion without risking overuse injuries. Yoga elongates and relaxes muscles and stimulates the flow of lubricating fluid in the joints. Most health clubs and recreation/senior centers offer yoga classes. A style known as hatha yoga is ideal because it emphasizes slow, gentle stretches, along with breathing and other relaxation techniques.

•**Bed stretches.** People who are stiff first thing in the morning might want to stretch for a few minutes before getting out of bed. This helps remove excess fluid from joints and can reduce morning aches and creakiness.

Example: Raise your arms overhead and toward the headboard—hold the stretch for about 10 seconds. Then extend your toes toward the footboard to stretch the feet and ankles. You also can clasp your hands under your knees, one at a time, and gently pull each toward your chest.

•**Weight training.** We lose about 1% to 2% of our muscle strength every year after about age 50. Declines in muscle strength increase the risk for joint damage and stiffness.

Self-test: Sit in a straight-backed chair, and try to stand up and sit down without using your arms. Most people can do it at least five times. If you can't do it even once, you need to build more muscle strength.

Work with a trainer to design an exercise regimen that strengthens your abdominals, back, chest, thighs, shoulders and hips.

Example: Wall squats to strengthen the thighs. Stand with your back against a wall, with your feet about two feet out from the wall and your arms extended in front of you. Bend your knees and slowly squat, keeping your back supported against the wall. Try to lower yourself until your thighs are parallel to the floor, then slowly return to a standing position.

•**New mattress.** Most mattresses wear out in about seven years—yet many people keep the same sagging mattress for decades. If you're waking up with back stiffness, you might need a new mattress. Look for a mattress that's moderately firm, with a thin pillowtop that allows you to sink in slightly.

Also important: A firm pillow that's just thick enough to hold your head in line with your spine. A lot of my patients with neck stiffness use extra-large pillows that push the head almost on top of the chest.

•**Glucosamine.** Derived from the shells of shellfish, this supplement is reputed to repair and strengthen cartilage. In Europe, where glucosamine is given by prescription, it's widely believed that glucosamine reduces hip and knee stiffness, but research has been mixed. Some studies, particularly those looking at arthritis and stiffness of the hands and spine, indicate that glucosamine is not effective for cartilage in these areas.

My advice: Take 1,500 milligrams (mg) of glucosamine daily for eight to 12 weeks. If your stiffness/pain does not improve by then, the supplements probably won't help you.

Caution: Check with your doctor before taking glucosamine if you are allergic to shellfish.

•**Fish oil.** Patients with joint stiffness from rheumatoid arthritis or other inflammatory conditions may improve when they take fish-oil supplements. Many studies have shown that fish's omega-3 fatty acids can reduce systemic inflammation. They're less likely to be effective for inflammation caused by osteoarthritis.

Dose: The standard advice is to take 1 gram (g) to 2 g daily. However, you might have to take 5 g or more to achieve significant benefits for inflammatory conditions. Side effects may include diarrhea and nausea.

•**Acetaminophen.** The painkiller acetaminophen is less likely than ibuprofen or aspirin to cause stomach upset, and it's just as effective in patients with noninflammatory pain and stiffness. Take 325 mg to 650 mg every four to six hours, but don't take it for more than 10 days unless directed by your doctor.

An extended-release formula, such as Tylenol Arthritis Pain, can be effective for morning stiffness. Take it when you go to bed. The drug stays active throughout the night and can help you move more easily first thing in the morning.

Natural Infection Fighters Beat Five Common Conditions

Steven Sandberg-Lewis, ND, a naturopathic physician and diplomate of the Homeopathic Academy of Naturopathic Physicians. He is a clinical professor of naturopathic medicine at the National College of Natural Medicine in Portland, Oregon, and leader of "The Functional Gastroenterology" seminar there.

Antibiotics enable millions of people to survive infections that used to be fatal. However, the widespread use of these drugs has increasingly led to antibiotic resistance—some harmful organisms can keep making people sick even when treated with the newest, most powerful antibiotics.

We tend to hear a lot about the overuse of antibiotics, but medications used to treat viruses and fungi also can be harmful.

For example, over-the-counter and prescription drugs used to treat yeast infections have the potential to cause side effects ranging from headache to seizures, while antiviral medications can lead to gastrointestinal problems, dizziness and difficulty breathing in those with lung disease. Overuse of prescription drugs to treat viruses or fungi, such as *oseltamivir* (Tamiflu) and *acyclovir* (Zovirax), also can lead to resistance to these medications.

Little-known fact: Because the immune system of a healthy adult is quite effective at eliminating many types of bacteria, viruses and fungi, many infections can be successfully treated with natural products that strengthen immunity and fight microorganisms.

Important: Always see a doctor if the affected area is becoming more inflamed…seems to be spreading…is accompanied by a fever…or is not improving.

Conditions that typically improve within 24 to 48 hours when treated with natural antimicrobial agents (unless indicated otherwise, all can be found in health food stores)…*

BRONCHITIS

Bronchitis is inflammation of the lining of the bronchial tubes, which carry air to the lungs. Acute bronchitis is usually due to a virus and often develops in conjunction with a cold or some other upper-respiratory tract ailment.

Natural treatment: Add 10 drops of liquid *allicin* (an active antibacterial and antiviral compound in garlic) to the reservoir of a portable nebulizer (a device that converts liquid into a fine mist that can be inhaled). Breathe the mist until all of the extract is gone. Repeat the treatment once or twice a day until the infection is gone.

*Caution: If you have an allergy to a particular natural substance (such as garlic), do not use a remedy that contains the substance.

Also helpful: Take eight 180-milligram (mg) capsules daily of Allimax, a brand of fresh-garlic supplement that can shorten the duration of the illness.

SORE THROAT

Most sore throats are caused by viruses, such as those that also cause the common cold or flu.

Natural treatment: Perform a yoga exercise known as the Lion Pose to increase blood and lymph circulation at the back of the tongue. This movement promotes the migration of immune cells to the area to help fight the infection.

What to do: Stick out your tongue as far as it will go, and hold it there for three to four seconds. Repeat the movement five or six times daily until your sore throat is gone.

Also helpful: Most people know that gargling with saltwater helps ease sore throat pain.

For better results: Add a few drops of bitter orange oil to a mixture of one-quarter teaspoon salt and one-half cup warm water to help kill bacteria, including some organisms that cause strep throat.

Important: Use a "bass voice" when you gargle the mixture (every few waking hours). The lower-pitched gargling sound causes more of the solution to get into the throat.

SINUSITIS

Infections of the sinus cavities typically cause headache, facial pain or pressure and a loss of smell and taste. Antibiotics can help in some cases, but most sinus infections are caused by organisms, such as viruses or fungi, that aren't killed by antibiotics.

Natural treatment: *N-acetyl-cysteine* (NAC), an amino acid that promotes the drainage of mucus and mobilizes infection-fighting white blood cells.

Typical dose: 600 mg, three times daily.

BLADDER INFECTION

Virtually every woman gets an occasional urinary tract infection (UTI), either in the urethra (the tube that allows urine to leave the body) and/or the bladder. Though relatively rare in men, UTIs become more common in those over age 50—a time when prostate enlargement tends to occur and can lead to an infection when urine fails to drain properly from the bladder. Antibiotics work for both women and men but often lead to yeast infections and other side effects.

Natural treatment: Unsweetened cranberry juice (one eight-ounce glass daily)** is widely used to help prevent UTIs. Cranberry contains *anthocyanidins,* compounds that are thought to help prevent *Escherichia coli* (E. coli), the cause of most UTIs, from adhering to tissues in the urinary tract.

For better results: Also take an herb called *uva ursi* (500 mg three to five times daily). If symptoms do not significantly improve within 24 hours, consult a physician before continuing this treatment.

Important: Drink a minimum of six glasses of water daily (in addition to the juice) until the infection is gone. It dilutes the concentration of bacteria in the bladder…reduces irritation…and helps flush out harmful organisms.

EAR INFECTION

Several studies in children show that most ear infections don't require antibiotics. It's likely that the same is true for adults, particularly for infections affecting the ear canal (swimmer's ear).

Natural treatment for swimmer's ear: Use a clean bulb syringe or eyedropper to administer three to five drops daily of a 50-50 mixture of distilled water and *hydrogen peroxide,* followed by three to five drops of a 50-50 solution of white vinegar and distilled water.

Also helpful: A combination supplement that includes echinacea, goldenseal and *berberis* (such as Source Naturals' Wellness Formula), along with a multisupplement containing *bioflavonoids,* zinc and vitamins C and A. Follow the dosage instructions on the label.

Important: Patients who get frequent ear infections should try eliminating dairy and bananas from their diet. These foods are believed to lead to the production of thicker-than-normal mucus that inhibits normal ear drainage.

**If you take *warfarin* (Coumadin), consult your doctor before drinking this amount of cranberry juice—the juice may increase the effects of blood-thinning medication.

■ ■ ■ ■

Natural Relief for Shingles

For a homeopathic remedy to help relieve the pain of shingles, try one of the following remedies (all sold in health food stores). If lesions have appeared on the face, take *Apis mellifica.* For shingles on the left side of your chest, use *Ranunculus bulbosus.* If lesions cause burning pain that eases with a warm compress, try *Arsenicum album.* Whichever remedy you use, take three 30C pellets twice a day for three days, dissolving pellets under your tongue. (Do not take within 30 minutes of meals.) If there's no improvement or you feel worse, discontinue use. For chronic or recurring shingles, see a homeopath.

Edward Shalts, MD, DHt (diplomate in homeotherapeutics), faculty member, Continuum Center for Health and Healing, Beth Israel Medical Center, New York City, and author of *Easy Homeopathy* (McGraw-Hill).

Best Ways to Avoid Painful Diverticulitis

Jamison Starbuck, ND, naturopathic physician in family practice Missoula, Montana. She is past president of the American Association of Naturopathic Physicians and a contributing editor to *The Alternative Advisor: The Complete Guide to Natural Therapies and Alternative Treatments* (Time Life).

If you're over age 60, your chances are fifty-fifty that you have *diverticulosis,* a condition marked by numerous small pouches (diverticula) in the wall of the colon.

Virtually everyone over age 80 is affected by the disease, and even 10% of people age 41 to 60 have it.

The good news is that the vast majority of people with diverticulosis are symptom-free. The condition becomes a problem only when one or more of these pouches get inflamed, becoming *diverticulitis*—due, for example, to weakening of the gastrointestinal wall and/or poor diet. With diverticulitis, you are likely to experience a sudden onset of pain and tenderness in the lower left abdomen. Diarrhea or constipation and a fever can also occur, as well as rectal bleeding. Fortunately, diet and lifestyle can significantly reduce the likelihood of diverticulosis turning into diverticulitis. *My advice…*

•**Eat the right foods.** We now know that the old notion that diverticulitis is caused by small, fibrous foods is simply not true. Many doctors had believed that certain foods, such as poppy seeds, lodged in the diverticula and became inflamed. However, an 18-year study published in the *Journal of the American Medical Association* conclusively showed that eating foods such as nuts, seeds or popcorn does not increase the risk for diverticulitis. In fact, a high-fiber diet, including fruit, vegetables, nuts and seeds, offers good nutrition and promotes regular bowel movements, both of which reduce the risk for diverticular disease.

•**Get vigorous exercise.** People who routinely run, hike, walk briskly, swim and/or do aerobics are significantly less at risk for diverticular problems than those who are sedentary—perhaps because vigorous exercise promotes circulation and helps fight constipation.

•**Try probiotics.** These "friendly" bacteria help keep colon inflammation at bay. Three times a week, eat eight ounces of plain yogurt with "live cultures" or take a probiotic supplement containing at least five billion units of *acidophilus* and 2.5 billion units of *bifidus.*

If you are diagnosed with diverticulitis…

•**Drink tea.** Most doctors recommend a liquid diet, including water, soup and juice, for three or four days. To reduce abdominal pain and speed healing, include tea made from peppermint, slippery elm and marshmallow root.

What to do: Blend equal parts by weight of each herb (chopped, shredded or powdered), and use two teaspoons of the mix per 10 ounces of boiling water. Have up to one quart of the tea daily.

•**Take Oregon grape root.** This herb has a sedating and antiseptic effect on the gastrointestinal tract and will ease cramping and reduce inflammation. Take 60 drops of Oregon grape root tincture in two ounces of water on an empty stomach, three times a day for up to seven days.

If you have abdominal pain and a fever of 101°F or higher, rectal bleeding…or even mild abdominal pain that lasts for more than two days, see your doctor—each could signal an ailment that needs medical attention.

Homeopathic Healing for Colds and Flu

Richard Mann, ND, chair of the department of homeopathic medicine at Bastyr University School of Naturopathic Medicine and a faculty member in clinical practice at Bastyr Center for Natural Health, both in Seattle. He is a diplomate of the Homeopathic Academy of Natural Physicians.

You may never have tried homeopathy, a form of alternative medicine that boosts the body's own healing responses. But if you get sick this winter, chances are that homeopathy can bring relief—if you pick the appropriate homeopathic remedy for your specific symptoms. *What you need to know…*

HOW HOMEOPATHY WORKS

Like vaccination, homeopathy seeks to stimulate the immune system. A vaccine contains a tiny amount of the pathogen that causes a certain disease.

Principle of homeopathy: Substances of plant, animal or mineral origin that can cause symptoms of disease also can cure symptoms when given in the form of very highly diluted remedies.

Homeopathy is not a one-size-fits-all therapy. Rather, the remedy must be carefully matched to a particular person's specific symptoms and his/her physical and mental reactions to these symptoms. This individualization makes it difficult to devise clinical studies that accurately reflect homeopathy's effectiveness.

What is known: For more than 200 years, homeopathy has helped people heal.

People who have colds or flu often respond to self-treatment using nonprescription homeopathic remedies sold in health food stores and online.

Key: Match the right remedy to your combination of symptoms.

What to do: Follow directions on product labels, taking 6C, 12C or 30C potency remedies. "C" stands for *centesimal* and indicates that one part of the active substance was mixed with 99 parts of alcohol…the numbers reflect how many times the mixture went through a dilution process. Paradoxically, the more dilute the potency, the greater the effect.

Remedies usually are sold as tiny pellets that dissolve under the tongue. Oils or other substances on your hands can inactivate pellets, so use a spoon to remove them from the container and place them in your mouth. Do not put anything else in your mouth for 30 minutes before or after taking a remedy.

Homeopathic remedies generally work quickly. *Unless otherwise directed by your practitioner or product labels, follow these instructions…*

• **If there is no change in symptoms after several hours, repeat the dose once more.** If symptoms still do not change after several hours, try a different homeopathic remedy that corresponds to your symptoms.

• **If you feel somewhat better after taking a homeopathic remedy,** repeat it at four-hour intervals until you feel significantly better, for a maximum of four doses in total.

• **Once you feel significantly better, do not take another dose.** If symptoms return, repeat dosing according to the instructions above.

When to seek help: In some cases, patients need prescription-potency homeopathic remedies and/or conventional medical treatment. *See a homeopathic physician or your primary care practitioner if…*

• **None of the remedies below seem appropriate for your specific symptoms.**

• **You have tried three or four of the homeopathic remedies below without result.**

• **You are over age 65 or have a chronic health problem.**

• **You are pregnant or breast-feeding.**

Important: The flu can be deadly, so if your symptoms are severe—for instance, you have a very high fever, have trouble breathing and/or feel extremely weak—seek immediate medical care.

THE RIGHT REMEDY FOR YOU

The following homeopathic remedies are among those most commonly indicated for colds or flu. Choose the remedy that most closely correlates to your symptoms.

•**Use *Arsenicum album* if you...**

• Have alternating chills and fever.

• Are thirsty and prefer warm drinks to cold ones.

• Have a runny nose or burning sensation in the nose.

• Feel extremely weak.

• Are anxious or restless.

• Feel worse from 10 p.m. to 3 a.m.

•**Use *Belladonna* if you...**

• Spike a sudden fever.

• Cough a lot.

• Have a hot, red face (though hands and feet may be cold).

• Have glassy eyes or dilated pupils.

• Have a throbbing headache.

• Cannot tolerate light.

• Feel slightly delirious.

•**Use *Gelsemium* if you...**

• Ache all over (particularly if this comes on gradually).

• Feel exhausted and weak.

• Have a trembling sensation running up and down the spine.

• Sneeze and/or have a runny nose.

• Develop a sore throat.

• Get dizzy.

• Feel apathetic or antisocial.

•**Use *Hepar sulphuricum* if you...**

• Have a thick nasal discharge.

• Develop a sore throat.

• Cannot tolerate cold drafts.

• Are extremely sensitive to touch.

• Perspire heavily.

• Feel bothered by everything and everybody.

•**Use *Nux vomica* if you...**

• Are shivering.

• Sneeze frequently or feel a tickle in the nose.

• Have a backache or headache.

• Have stomach cramps, nausea or difficulty moving your bowels.

• Get more congested at night.

• Have trouble sleeping.

• Are sensitive to noise.

• Feel irritable or anxious.

•**Use *Pulsatilla* if you...**

• Have had symptoms for several days.

• Have a thick green or yellow nasal discharge.

• Must blow your nose often.

• Have an upset stomach.

• Crave cool, fresh air.

• Feel worse at night.

• Feel weepy or want attention.

To find a homeopath: Contact the Homeopathic Academy of Naturopathic Physicians (206-941-4217, *www.hanp.net*) or the National Center for Homeopathy (703-548-7790, *www.national centerforhomeopathy.org*).

Seven Secrets for a Great Night's Sleep

Mark A. Stengler, NMD, naturopathic medical doctor in private practice, La Jolla, California...adjunct associate clinical professor at the National College of Natural Medicine, Portland, Oregon...author of many books, including *The Natural Physician's Healing Therapies* and coauthor of *Prescription for Natural Cures* (both from Bottom Line Books)... and author of the *Bottom Line/Natural Healing* newsletter.

Consistently getting a good night's sleep isn't a luxury—it's essential to your health. Insufficient sleep not only leaves you feeling tired and irritable but also weakens your immune system and puts you at risk for depression, weight gain and chronic headaches. To get the full health benefits of sleep, most adults should aim for at least seven hours of uninterrupted sleep a night.

Many of my patients have trouble sleeping. I often help them determine the nature of their sleep problem—and what might help.

Choose your specific sleep problem below—and try one solution at a time for up to two weeks. If the problem persists, try a second solution in combination with the first. (Don't try three solutions at once.) Once you find the remedies that work for you, you can use them indefinitely. Before starting, check to make sure that your sleep problem is not caused by any prescription medication you might be taking.

TROUBLE FALLING ASLEEP

For any reason when you first go to bed, try…

●**Sublingual melatonin.** Melatonin, the hormone produced in the pineal gland in the brain, helps to control sleep and wake cycles. Sublingual melatonin supplements (lozenges placed under the tongue) generally work better than either capsules or tablets. Start with 1.5 milligrams (mg) of sublingual melatonin, 30 to 45 minutes before bedtime. (If this doesn't help within three nights, try 3 mg.) Do not take melatonin if you are pregnant, breast-feeding or taking oral contraceptives.

If you have feelings of anxiety, depression or stress, start with…

●**5-Hydroxytryptophan (5-HTP).** The body uses this amino acid to manufacture the "good mood" neurotransmitter *serotonin*. Taking a 5-HTP supplement increases the body's serotonin production, promoting a sense of well-being and better resistance to stress. Start with 100 mg one hour before bedtime. (If symptoms don't improve within three nights, try 200 mg.) You shouldn't take 5-HTP if you are pregnant, breast-feeding or taking an antidepressant or antianxiety medication.

If 5-HTP doesn't help and you need a more aggressive approach to anxiety and depression, add…

●*SedaLin.* This formula, manufactured by Xymogen (health-care professionals can order it at 800-647-6100, *www.xymogen.com*), can help relax the nervous system. It contains *Magnolia officinali* extract, from the bark of a type of magnolia tree, to relieve anxiety…and *Ziziphus spinosa* extract from a shrub to treat irritability and insomnia. Take one capsule at bedtime for a minimum of two weeks to allow your hormone levels to adjust. (SedaLin also can be used on its own to relieve anxiety and nervousness during waking hours. Since its main role is to calm the nervous system, it won't make you drowsy.) It is not recommended for women who are pregnant or breast-feeding.

If you are over age 60, try…

●**Calcium and/or magnesium.** These supplements can help seniors, who are most likely to be deficient in these minerals, fall asleep by relaxing the nervous system. Take 500 mg of calcium with 250 mg of magnesium one hour before bedtime. Some people are helped by taking either the calcium or the magnesium alone. Find what works best for you.

If you are menopausal, try…

●**Natural progesterone.** This bioidentical hormone (not to be confused with the pharmaceutical *progestin*) has a natural sedating effect for women with sleep problems related to low progesterone.

Best: Have your hormone levels tested. If progesterone is low, apply a total of one-quarter to one-half teaspoon of progesterone cream to the inner forearm and wrist or the inner thighs 30 minutes before bedtime.

One over-the-counter brand to try: Emerita Pro-Gest (800-648-8211, *www.emerita. com*). For a stronger effect, take a progesterone capsule (100 mg to 150 mg), available by prescription.

WAKING IN THE NIGHT

If you have trouble getting back to sleep…

●**Eat a light snack before bedtime.** Some people wake up in the night because their blood sugar dips, triggering the adrenal glands to produce adrenaline—exactly what you don't want while sleeping.

Solution: Eat a small snack before bedtime, such as six ounces of organic yogurt.

If you consistently wake up between midnight and 2 a.m., try…

●**Balancing stress hormones.** Many people wake up in the wee hours and are unable to fall back to sleep quickly because of an imbalance in stress hormones. Melatonin can help. *In addition, try…*

●*Walking after dinner.* Exercise of any kind decreases the production of stress hormones. Exercise as early as possible in the evening, at least three hours before bedtime.

•*Listening to relaxing music.* One study showed that listening to relaxing music (such as classical) for 45 minutes before bedtime resulted in better-quality and longer sleep.

If you consistently wake up between 2 a.m. and 4 a.m., try...

•**Balancing other hormones.** Waking between 2 a.m. and 4 a.m. can be related to hormone imbalances, including estrogen deficiency in menopausal women (note that this is a different sleep problem than that caused by progesterone deficiency described above)...testosterone deficiency in men age 50 and older...and/or growth hormone deficiency in people age 60 or older. Have your hormone levels tested—and if they are low, get a prescription for a bioidentical hormone.

■ **More from Mark Stengler, NMD...**

Natural Stress Busters

When it comes to your health, getting a good night's sleep is just part of the equation. It's also important to maintain a calm, relaxed state during the day. This is not when people's stress levels can soar because of overloaded schedules. Stress is bad for your health. It can cause gastrointestinal problems... increase risk for cardiovascular disease...and weaken immune response. To stay on an even, upbeat course, I recommend several remedies. Use only one daytime remedy at a time—in conjunction with the sleep remedies (from the previous story) that work for you.

For ongoing stress or anxiety...

•**Calm Natural Mind.** Created by natural physician Hyla Cass, MD, this remedy contains *gamma aminobutyric acid* (GABA), which increases levels of the calming neurotransmitters *serotonin* and *dopamine,* and *L-theanine,* a substance in tea leaves that has been shown to increase brain waves associated with a relaxed state. Take as recommended on the label during stressful or anxious periods. It helps some people within a day or two. Try for at least five days, and see if you have any improvement. There are no side effects, and it is safe for everyone except those on antipsychotic medications. To order, call 866-778-2646, or visit *www.drcass.com* (and click on "Health Store").

For quick relief of bouts of anxiety...

•**Bach Flower Rescue Remedy.** If you find yourself in a stressful situation during the day, this homeopathic formula, available in health food stores, can provide relief in about 10 seconds to a few minutes. (It is not as strong or long-lasting as Calm Natural Mind, mentioned above.) Take four drops in a glass of water. It also can be a "back to sleep" aid when you wake up in the middle of the night.

For compulsive or extreme worrying or mind-racing...

•**Coffea cruda.** This is an excellent homeopathic calming therapy. Take two pellets of a 30C potency when your mind goes into overdrive. It's also a sleep aid when you can't sleep because of mind-racing.

■ **Also from Dr. Stengler...**

Quick Cures

For nosebleeds: Pinch the nose closed, and keep your head tilted downward (not back, which can cause choking). If you continue to bleed profusely from a nosebleed (or any other small wound), take the homeopathic remedy *Phosphorus* (dissolve two 30C pellets under the tongue) to cut down on bleeding time. Take five minutes after the bleeding begins. If bleeding continues, wait five minutes and take another dose.

For motion sickness: If you are prone to nausea and dizziness while riding in a car or on a boat, travel with the homeopathic remedy *Cocculus,* which is available at health food stores. It works very quickly. Dissolve two pellets of 30C potency under your tongue. Wait five minutes. If you don't feel better, take an additional two pellets of 30C potency. Breathing fresh air also will help you feel better.

For constipation: Try the herb senna (*Cassia senna*), which is a natural laxative. Take 500 mg in capsule form (standardized to 20–60 mg sennosides). Or drink one cup of senna tea. Do not use senna for long-term relief (more than one week) of constipation or if you are pregnant or have Crohn's disease or ulcerative colitis.

For headaches: Put your feet in a bucket of warm water and put an ice pack around your neck. The strategic use of heat and cold causes blood to move away from your head and toward your feet, relieving headache pain. It takes about five to 10 minutes for the pain to recede. This technique might not help people with poorly controlled diabetes or vascular disease who have diminished blood flow to the feet.

Natural Ways to Soothe a Dry, Itchy Scalp

Crystal Stelzer, an herbalist and adjunct faculty member in the department of botanical medicine at Bastyr University in Kenmore, Washington. She teaches classes in herbal medicine–making, nutrition and plant identification in the wild.

Are you scratching your head and wondering what's causing those icky flakes? It could be that your commercial hair-care products contain chemicals that are too harsh. *Take a natural approach…*

•**Try homemade herbal scalp treatments.** Prepare one of the following (ingredients are sold at health food stores and online), pour into a spray bottle and store in the refrigerator. Once or more per week, wet your hair and then apply four to eight ounces, massaging it into your scalp for several minutes. Wait 15 minutes, then shampoo. *Options for all hair types…*

For flare-ups: Tea tree oil. In a small bowl, combine eight ounces of water with 40 drops of tea tree oil (a natural antifungal and antiseptic).

Preventative: Burdock root and nettle. In a saucepan, mix one tablespoon of dried or three tablespoons of fresh, finely chopped burdock root (which supports oil glands and hair follicles) with two cups of water. Bring to a boil, reduce heat, cover and simmer 30 minutes. Remove from heat. Stir in one tablespoon of dried or three tablespoons of fresh, chopped nettle, an anti-inflammatory. (With fresh nettle, wear rubber gloves to avoid getting stung.) Let sit, covered, for 15 minutes. Strain through cheesecloth. Cool before using.

•**Buy gentle commercial products.** Choose shampoos, conditioners and styling products free of harsh or potentially toxic ingredients. Avoid *sodium lauryl sulfate* (a strong detergent), various *parabens* (preservatives) and *cocomide DEA* (a foaming agent).

Recommended: Products from Aubrey Organics (800-282-7394, *www.Aubrey-Organics. com*) or Giovanni Cosmetics (*www.Giovanni Cosmetics.com*).

•**Use henna instead of hair dyes (which contain chemicals that can irritate the scalp).** Made from a flowering plant, henna provides a reddish tint that blends with your natural color and lasts up to six weeks. Henna is best for brown or black hair (it can be used on blond or gray hair, but may turn light hair too orange).

To intensify color: Instead of mixing powdered henna with water, mix it with brewed coffee for a richer brown tint…with red wine for auburn highlights…or with beet juice to tone down henna's orange cast.

•**Nourish your scalp from the inside out.** Take a daily probiotic supplement that contains live *bifidobacterium* and *lactobacillus* to help balance the beneficial bacteria in your digestive tract.

Good brands: Enzymatic Therapy Pearls IC (800-783-2286, *www.EnzymaticTherapy.com*) and Sedona Labs i-Flora Multi-Probiotic (888-816-8804, *www.SedonaLabs.com*).

■ ■ ■ ■

Bleach Baths Ease Eczema

Twice weekly, eczema patients soaked for five to 10 minutes in a tub of water mixed with very diluted bleach. After three months, 67% showed improvement, compared with 15% of patients who bathed in plain water.

Theory: Bleach kills the staph bacteria that often accompany eczema and can cause painful lesions.

Safety: Use no more than one-half cup of bleach per 40 gallons of water…do not let bleach bathwater enter the eyes or mouth…never apply undiluted bleach to skin.

Amy Paller, MD, chair, dermatology department, Northwestern University Feinberg School of Medicine, Chicago, and leader of a study of 31 eczema patients.

■ ■ ■ ■

Fruit Conquers Jet Lag

Tart cherries—also known as sour cherries—have high levels of melatonin, which helps regulate your circadian rhythm and induce sleepiness.

Best: Have one-half cup of dried tart cherries (such as Montmorency) or two tablespoons of any cherry juice concentrate one hour before you wish to sleep on the plane and an hour before bedtime for the three days after you land.

Russel Reiter, PhD, professor of neuroendocrinology, University of Texas Health Science Center, San Antonio.

Kick the Habit— Naturally

Mark A. Stengler, NMD, naturopathic medical doctor in private practice, La Jolla, California…adjunct associate clinical professor at the National College of Natural Medicine, Portland, Oregon…author of many books, including *The Natural Physician's Healing Therapies* and coauthor of *Prescription for Natural Cures* (both from Bottom Line Books)… and author of the *Bottom Line/Natural Healing* newsletter.

Quitting smoking isn't easy. Fortunately, several safe, natural substances can help reduce your cravings. Use these remedies on their own or in conjunction with a smoking-cessation program. I recommend quitting cold turkey—with help from the first two remedies on this list.

•**St. John's wort.** Researchers at Roswell Park Cancer Institute Prevention Center in Buffalo found that 37.5% of participants in a cessation counseling program were smoke-free after taking this herb for 12 weeks, compared with 30.5% who were smoke-free after using prescription drugs. Look for a product standardized to 0.3% *hypericin.* Take 300 milligrams (mg) three times daily with food.

Best: Take it for four weeks before you stop smoking and then for another month. Don't use St. John's wort if you are also taking an antidepressant or an oral contraceptive.

•**Caladium seguinum.** This homeopathic remedy can reduce cigarette cravings. Take two pellets, 30C potency, daily for 10 days, beginning the day you quit.

If you still can't quit, add the two remedies below to your regimen—and take all four at once—until your cravings subside.

•**Herbal oat straw (Avena sativa).** This herb can calm the nervous system. Take 20 drops of a tincture in water or juice three times daily at any time of day.

•**5-hydroxytryptophan (5-HTP).** This amino acid that enhances mood is converted in the body to the neurotransmitter *serotonin.* It can help reduce the anxiety and irritability associated with nicotine withdrawal. Take 100 mg three times daily on an empty stomach. It is safe when used with St. John's wort, but do not use 5-HTP if you also are taking an antidepressant or medication for Parkinson's disease.

Helpful: Acupuncture can help to reduce cravings. Most qualified acupuncturists will know how to treat smokers who want to quit.

Try hard, and don't stop trying. It takes most smokers about three attempts at quitting before they succeed.

Smile! Acupuncture Eases Dentist Fears

Palle Rosted, MD, department of oncology, Weston Park Hospital, Sheffield, England.
Marshall H. Sager, DO, acupuncturist, Bala Cynwyd, Pennsylvania, and past president, American Academy of Medical Acupuncture.
Acupuncture in Medicine.

Fear of the dentist keeps many people from getting the dental care they need, but new research suggests that an ancient Chinese treatment—acupuncture—may provide quick relief.

BACKGROUND

One in 20 people suffer from *odontophobia*— severe anxiety about dentistry—and a third of all people say they have moderate anxiety when seeing the dentist, the researchers said.

"We can offer patients a safe, fast and cheap treatment for their odontophobia," said lead researcher Palle Rosted, MD, from the department of oncology at Weston Park Hospital in Sheffield, England.

Other available treatments, such as distraction, relaxation techniques, tranquilizers and sedation, can be time-consuming or have side effects, Dr. Rosted said. "Moreover, in some patients, the more traditional treatments are not sufficient. By offering acupuncture, the dentist has an extra tool in his bag," he said.

The report was published in *Acupuncture in Medicine.*

THE STUDY

For the study, Dr. Rosted's group tested acupuncture on 20 patients who had suffered from dental phobia for two to 30 years. Their average age was 40, and their anxiety was considered moderate to severe.

Their anxiety was checked before and after five minutes of acupuncture and rated, using the Back Anxiety Inventory (BAI) questionnaire. The acupuncture treatment, which involves inserting thin needles into specific body points, targeted two points on the top of the head.

THE RESULTS

The researchers found the average BAI score of 26.5 dropped to 11.5 after the acupuncture session. And all the patients were able to have their dental treatment.

Before trying acupuncture, only six patients could withstand any dental treatment at all, and even at that, just a partial visit that required a great deal of effort by both dentist and patient, Dr. Rosted noted.

"From a scientific point of view, we demonstrated that 70% of patients had an effect from the treatment," Dr. Rosted said. "From a practical point of view, and that is the important thing, we demonstrated that it was possible to carry out the planned dental treatment in all patients."

ADVANTAGES OF ACUPUNCTURE

Acupuncture, practiced in China for more than 2,000 years, is not a miracle treatment, Dr. Rosted said. "However, it has some advantages over other treatments. The treatment is safe, fast and cheap. In this study, the dentist could com-

mence the dental treatment five minutes after insertion of the five needles."

EXPERT COMMENTARY

Marshall H. Sager, DO, a past president of the American Academy of Medical Acupuncture and an acupuncturist in Bala Cynwyd, Pennsylvania, was optimistic about the findings. "I believe the results of this preliminary study are wide-ranging and should encompass investigation into the use of acupuncture for all preoperative anxiety," he said.

Evidence shows that acupuncture helps release endorphins, which act not only as painkillers but also as sedatives, said Dr. Sager. "These opiate-like hormones, manufactured in the body, contribute to natural feelings of well-being and modulate anxiety," he said.

"My experience emphatically demonstrates that, when I administer acupuncture to patients prior to surgery, I am able to decrease their preoperative stress levels, causing them to be more relaxed so that they require less anesthesia during the surgical procedure," Dr. Sager said.

info For more information on acupuncture, visit the Web site of the American Academy of Medical Acupuncture, *www.medical acupunture.org.*

■ ■ ■ ■

Acupuncture Helps Cancer Patients

Radiation for head or neck cancer can damage salivary glands, leading to severe dry mouth, loss of taste, difficulty swallowing, tooth decay and oral infections. Relief from medication lasts only a few hours and can cause sweating and slow heart rate.

Study: Patients who had completed radiation got twice-weekly acupuncture treatments for four weeks—and reported significant improvement in symptoms.

Referrals: American Association of Acupuncture and Oriental Medicine, 866-455-7999, *www.aaaomonline.org.*

M. Kay Garcia, DrPH, clinical nurse specialist and acupuncturist, Integrative Medicine Program, University of Texas M.D. Anderson Cancer Center, Houston, and leader of a study of 19 cancer patients.

Drug-Free Way to Ease Nausea

Lixing Lao, PhD, LAc, director of the Traditional Chinese Medicine Program in the Center for Integrative Medicine at University of Maryland School of Medicine.

It's common for people to suffer nausea after having surgery. This is uncomfortable in and of itself; it can also put strain on incisions and fresh sutures, and immobilize patients as well. Curiously, no matter how sophisticated and complex your surgical procedure may have been, there is a simple and drug-free antidote at hand: acupressure. There have been numerous studies on this in the last several years, and recently a Cochrane review confirmed that stimulating the wrist acupressure point significantly reduces the risk of postsurgery nausea and vomiting for many people.

The specific point is acupuncture/acupressure *Pericardium 6* (P6), which when stimulated releases several neurotransmitters, including *serotonin, dopamine* and *endorphins*, said Lixing Lao, PhD, licensed acupuncturist and director at the Center for Integrative Medicine at University of Maryland School of Medicine. These brain chemicals block nausea-producing ones. In a recent interview, Dr. Lao said that studies have shown this to be effective not only for nausea from surgeries, chemotherapy and radiation but also motion sickness and morning sickness.

HOW TO DO IT

Many studies have used acupuncture or acupressure, and some used wristbands with a button positioned to stimulate the P6 point, but it's also easy to ward off nausea using only the tip of your thumb, says Dr. Lao.

Here is how to find the correct point: Put your index and middle finger together and place them lengthwise across the inner wrist, just under the first crease of your palm. Press the midpoint between the two prominent tendons just below your fingers but a little closer to the body. Do this on both sides, alternating arms.

Dr. Lao says to start massaging the P6 point in any situation where you anticipate becoming nauseated. For example, if you have a tendency to get motion sickness, begin your massage as you get into the car and continue for a few minutes. If you start to become nauseated later, press and massage some more until nausea goes away. This doesn't work for everyone, but it won't take you long to find out if you are among the lucky, because when you find the right spot, you'll feel relief in minutes. Dr. Lao adds that the wristbands, available in pharmacies and department stores, are fine and very convenient—just be sure you place the button, and the tip of your thumb, on the correct spot so you can add some pressure of your own if necessary to get sufficient stimulation.

Nutrition, Diet & Fitness

Cut Your Cancer Risk With Pistachios

Eating pistachios every day might help you reduce your risk for lung cancer and other malignancies, according to a recent study.

Pistachios are a good source of a type of vitamin E called *gamma-tocopherol*.

"It is known that vitamin E provides a degree of protection against certain forms of cancer. Higher intakes of gamma-tocopherol...may reduce the risk of lung cancer," said Ladia M. Hernandez, RD, LD, a senior research dietitian at the University of Texas M.D. Anderson Cancer Center and a doctoral candidate at Texas Women's University, both in Houston.

THE STUDY

The study included 18 people who ate 68 grams (about 2 ounces or 117 kernels) of pistachios a day for four weeks and 18 people in a control group who did not add pistachios to their normal diet. Those in the pistachio group showed significantly higher blood levels of gamma-tocopherol during the study period than those who did not eat pistachios.

The findings were presented at a cancer prevention conference in Houston sponsored by the American Association for Cancer Research.

ADVICE

"Pistachios are one of those 'good-for-you' nuts, and two ounces per day could be incorporated into dietary strategies designed to reduce the risk of lung cancer without significant changes in body mass index," Hernandez said.

"Other foods that are a rich source of gamma-tocopherol include peanuts, pecans, walnuts, soybean and corn oils," she added.

info The Web site of the National Institutes of Health's Office of Dietary Supplements has more information about vitamin E at *http:// ods.od.nih.gov*. Under "Quick Links" choose "Dietary Supplement Fact Sheets," then scroll down to vitamin E.

American Association for Cancer Research news release.

■ ■ ■ ■

Urgent Update:
Folic Acid May
Increase Cancer Risk

Recent studies have shown that people who regularly consume large amounts of folic acid may increase their risk for several forms of cancer, including colorectal and prostate. The government-recommended tolerable upper limit is 1,000 micrograms (mcg) a day.

At risk: People who take in a lot without realizing it.

Example: A daily multivitamin with 400 mcg of folic acid…a B-complex supplement with another 400 mcg…cereal with 400 mcg to 800 mcg…and flour-based products with 100 mcg to 200 mcg.

Joel Mason, MD, director, Vitamins and Carcinogenesis Laboratory, Jean Mayer USDA Human Nutrition Research Center on Aging, Tufts University, Boston.

Foods that Help You
Get Through Chemo

Rebecca Katz, MS, visiting chef and nutrition educator at Commonweal's Cancer Help Program in Bolinas, California. She is founder of Inner Cook, a Bay Area culinary practice that works with cancer patients, and executive chef for the Center for Mind-Body Medicine's Food as Medicine and CancerGuides Professional Training Programs. She is author, with Mat Edelson, of *The Cancer-Fighting Kitchen: Nourishing, Big-Flavor Recipes for Cancer Treatment and Recovery* (Celestial Arts). *www. rebeccakatz.com.*

Some people experience virtually no side effects from cancer chemotherapy, but this is rare. Most patients report at least some problems, including nausea, fatigue and diarrhea during the treatment.

Reason: The drugs that are used in chemotherapy are designed to kill fast-growing cancer cells. But they also damage fast-growing healthy cells, particularly in the mouth, digestive tract and hair follicles.

Good nutrition is critical if you're undergoing chemotherapy. It's estimated that up to 80% of cancer patients are malnourished. People who eat well before and during chemotherapy tend to have fewer side effects. They also are more likely to complete the full course of therapy than those who are poorly nourished and may feel too sick to continue. *What to do…*

•**Load up on nutrient-rich foods.** In the weeks before chemotherapy, patients should emphasize nutrient-dense foods, such as whole grains, vegetables and legumes. The high nutrient load of a healthy diet helps strengthen healthy cells so that they're better able to withstand—and then recover from—the effects of chemotherapy. *Good choices…*

•**Dark leafy greens,** such as spinach, kale and Swiss chard. They're high in antioxidants, such as beta-carotene, *lutein* and other *phytonutrients.* These compounds help minimize the damaging effects of free radicals, tissue-damaging molecules that are produced in large amounts during chemotherapy. Kale is particularly good because it contains *indole-3-carbinol,* a compound that has anticancer properties.

•**Olive oil,** like green vegetables, is high in antioxidants. It's one of the best sources of *oleic acid*, an omega-9 fatty acid that strengthens cell membranes and improves the ability of the immune system to fight cancer cells. I like extra-virgin olive oil because it has been exposed to the least heat.

•**Garlic.** The National Cancer Institute reports that people who eat garlic regularly seem to have a lower risk for intestinal and other cancers, including breast cancer. The sulfur compounds that taste so strong in garlic, such as *allicin,* have strong antiviral and antibacterial effects—important for chemotherapy patients because they're susceptible to infection. In my recipes, I use fresh garlic. I smash it and let it sit for 10 minutes to allow the antiviral properties to become more accessible—then chop and cook. (To smash garlic, set the side of a chef's knife on the clove, place the heel of your hand on the flat side of the knife and apply pressure.)

•**Increase protein.** It's the main structural component of muscle and other tissues. People who undergo chemotherapy need large amounts of protein to repair tissue damage that occurs during the treatments.

Recommended: About 80 grams of protein daily. That's nearly double the amount that healthy adults need. Cancer patients who increase their protein about a week before chemotherapy, and continue to get extra protein afterward, recover more quickly. They also will have more energy and less fatigue.

Try this: Two or more daily smoothies (made in a blender with juice or milk, a variety of fresh fruits and ice, if you like) that are supplemented with a scoop of whey powder. The protein in whey is easily absorbed by the intestine. And most people can enjoy a nutrient-rich smoothie even when they have nausea or digestive problems related to chemotherapy.

•**Drink to reduce discomfort.** Stay hydrated both before and after chemotherapy sessions to reduce nausea. Drink liquids until your urine runs clear—if it has more than a hint of yellow, you need to drink more.

Helpful: Soups and broths provide water, as well as protein, minerals and vitamins.

•**Avoid your favorite foods two days before treatments.** It's common for chemotherapy patients to develop food aversions when they get nauseated from treatments and then to associate the nausea with certain foods. It's sad when people develop aversions and can never again enjoy their favorite foods.

•**Eat lightly and frequently.** People tend to experience more nausea when the stomach is empty. During and after "chemo days," keep something in your stomach all the time—but not too much. Patients do better when they have a light snack, such as sautéed vegetables or a bowl of broth, than when they go hungry or eat a lot at one sitting.

•**Treat with ginger.** When your stomach is upset, steep three slices of fresh ginger in a cup of simmering water for 10 minutes, then drink the tea. Or grate fresh ginger with a very fine grater, such as a Microplane, and put the shavings under your tongue. Ginger alleviates nausea almost instantly.

•**Overcome "metal mouth."** The drugs used in chemotherapy can damage the nerves that control the taste buds. Some people complain about a metallic taste in their mouths after treatments. Others notice that foods taste "flat" or that their mouths are extremely sensitive to hot or cold.

These changes, known as transient taste changes, usually disappear a few weeks (or, in some cases, months) after treatments, but they can make it difficult for people to eat in the meantime.

Helpful: The FASS method. It stands for Fat, Acid, Salt and Sweet. Most people will find that it's easier to enjoy their meals, and therefore ingest enough nutrients, when they combine one or more of these elements in every meal.

For fat, add more olive oil than usual to meals…lemons are a good source of acid…sea salt has less of a chemical aftertaste than regular salt…and maple syrup gives sweetness with more nutrients (including immune-building manganese and zinc) than table sugar.

•**Try kudzu root.** Used in a powder form to thicken sauces, puddings and other foods, it soothes the intestine and can help prevent diarrhea. You also can dissolve one teaspoon of kudzu root in one teaspoon of cold liquid and drink that. Drink after meals, as needed. Kudzu root is available in most health food stores.

•**Soothe mouth sores with soft, easy-to-eat foods, such as granitas** (similar to "Italian ices") or smoothies. The sores can be intensely painful, which makes it difficult to eat.

Recommended: Watermelon ice cubes. Purée watermelon, and put it in a tray to freeze. Then suck on the cubes. The cold acts like a topical anesthetic—you can numb the mouth before eating a regular meal. And the juice from the melon is just as hydrating as water but provides extra nutrients, including the antioxidant lycopene.

Food Combos that Supercharge Your Health

Joy Bauer, RD, CDN, author of several nutrition books, including *Joy's LIFE Diet: 4 Steps to Thin Forever* (Collins Living) and *Joy Bauer's Food Cures* (Rodale). Bauer is the nutrition expert for the *Today* show and has a private practice with offices in New York City and Westchester County, New York, *www.joybauer.com.*

Until recently, most nutrition research has focused on the health benefits of individual nutrients. For example, it's well-established that vitamin A is good for the eyes...calcium builds stronger bones...and zinc boosts immunity.

Now there is strong scientific evidence that nutrition is much more complex than that. When certain foods are combined, their nutritional value is much greater than when the foods are eaten individually.

That's why dietitians recommend eating a varied diet with plenty of fruits, vegetables, whole grains and low-fat proteins—the greater the variety, the better your chances of maximizing the health benefits of your food.

Latest development: Scientists are beginning to understand exactly which specific food combinations are the most effective in helping the body fight common ailments.

For example...

TO FIGHT ARTHRITIS

• **Combine carotenes and spices.** Carotenes are a group of powerful antioxidants that attack toxic, cell-damaging molecules known as free radicals.

In addition to beta-carotene, there are other carotenes, including *beta-cryptoxanthin,* which has been shown to fight rheumatoid arthritis and osteoarthritis.

Good sources of both beta-carotene and beta-cryptoxanthin: Winter squash (especially butternut), pumpkin, red bell peppers and carrots...apricots and watermelon.

The spices turmeric (with its antioxidant oil *curcumin*) and ginger contain *phytochemicals* that help suppress inflammatory reactions that can lead to arthritis. Turmeric is the bright yellow, dried spice found in curry powder. Ginger is available in powdered form as a spice and also as a fresh root.

My favorite arthritis-fighting combos: Curried butternut squash soup...pumpkin-ginger muffins...Asian ginger stir-fry with red bell peppers...and curried carrots.

TO FIGHT HEART PROBLEMS

• **Combine lycopene and monounsaturated fats.** Lycopene is a fat-soluble antioxidant that has been shown to reduce the risk for heart disease, perhaps by stopping the process that leads to *atherosclerosis* (fatty buildup in the arteries).

Good sources of lycopene: Tomatoes, red and pink grapefruit, watermelon and guava.

Helpful: Eat cooked tomatoes—they contain three to four times more lycopene than raw tomatoes.

Monounsaturated fats are believed to protect against heart disease and have a number of cardiovascular benefits. These healthful fats help the body absorb all fat-soluble nutrients, including lycopene.

Good sources of monounsaturated fats: Olive oil and canola oil...avocado...almonds, walnuts, peanuts and cashews.

My favorite heart-healthy combos: Roasted tomatoes with a touch of olive oil...any meal made with homemade or store-bought tomato sauce that contains olive oil...a salad of grapefruit and avocado...and turkey, avocado and tomato sandwiches.

TO FIGHT MEMORY LOSS

• **Combine folic acid and anthocyanins.** One of the B vitamins, folic acid (also known as folate) helps lower blood levels of the amino acid *homocysteine*—a process that research suggests may promote blood flow to the brain. Folic acid also enhances communication between brain chemicals known as *neurotransmitters.*

Good sources of folic acid: Fortified whole-grain breakfast cereals and oatmeal...green, leafy vegetables, bok choy and broccoli...oranges (or orange juice) and berries (such as strawberries and blackberries).

Anthocyanins are antioxidant phytochemicals that have been shown to not only help prevent memory loss but also improve failing memory.

Good sources of anthocyanins: Berries (especially blueberries—their antioxidant flavonols help protect against brain degeneration), red or black grapes...red or purple cabbage, beets, red onions and eggplant.

My favorite memory-enhancing combos: Folic acid–fortified breakfast cereal with berries...coleslaw with red cabbage and bok choy ...chicken-vegetable stir-fry with red onions and broccoli...and fruit salad with oranges and blueberries.

TO FIGHT FATIGUE

•**Combine iron and vitamin C.** Iron helps red blood cells carry oxygen throughout the body. Without enough iron, your cells can become starved for oxygen. This can lead to anemia, which causes listlessness, headache, irritability and general lack of energy.

Good sources of iron: Lean beef, turkey, chicken, lamb and pork...clams, oysters and shrimp...soybeans, chickpeas and lentils...spinach, asparagus and green, leafy vegetables.

Vitamin C is a powerful antioxidant, but most people don't realize that it can help fight fatigue brought on by iron-deficiency anemia by enhancing the body's ability to absorb iron.

By adding a food that contains significant amounts of vitamin C to a meal with an iron-rich food, your body will absorb up to three times more iron.

This is especially important for vegetarians, premenopausal women (who lose iron through menstruation) and people with a genetic predisposition to anemia (determined through blood tests).

Caution: People with *hemochromatosis*, a dangerous disorder that causes iron to build up in the blood, should not combine foods high in iron and vitamin C.

Good sources of vitamin C: Bell and hot chili peppers, broccoli and kale...tomatoes, mangoes, oranges (or orange juice), strawberries and pineapple.

My favorite fatigue-fighting combos: Spinach salad with mandarin oranges...bean chili (such as kidney, pinto or black bean) with crushed tomatoes...steak with sautéed broccoli...and chicken cacciatore with tomatoes and peppers.

TO FIGHT MOOD SWINGS

•**Combine soluble fiber and protein.** Mood swings often are caused by fluctuations in blood sugar (glucose).

Low-quality carbohydrates, such as white rice, white bread, cakes and soft drinks, cause blood sugar spikes that can lead to a sluggish, depressed feeling when they begin to plummet about one hour after consumption of such foods.

High-quality carbohydrates, such as vegetables, fruits and whole grains, contain soluble fiber that causes a slower, less dramatic rise in glucose.

Good sources of soluble fiber: Oatmeal... barley, lentils, beans (such as kidney, lima, pinto and black) and peas...apples (all types), raisins, oranges and bananas...cauliflower and sweet potatoes.

Protein is another natural blood sugar stabilizer—it helps slow the absorption of carbohydrates in your diet. Pairing protein with soluble fiber at every meal will help keep your blood sugar as steady as possible.

Good sources of lean protein: Turkey or chicken breast...fish (all types)...pork tenderloin...lean beef...egg whites...yogurt (low-fat or fat-free)...milk (low-fat or fat-free)...and beans (such as pinto and black).

My favorite mood-stabilizing combos: Three-bean turkey chili with pinto, black and kidney beans...plain, low-fat or fat-free yogurt with fresh fruit (such as berries or peaches)...pork tenderloin with sweet potatoes and cauliflower... hard-boiled eggs with turkey bacon and fruit... and oatmeal with a hard-boiled egg.

Stop Cooking the Health Out of Your Food

Richard E. Collins, MD, director of wellness at South Denver Cardiology Associates in Littleton, Colorado. He is board-certified in cardiology and internal medicine, performs cooking demonstrations nationwide and is author of *The Cooking Cardiologist* (Advanced Research) and *Cooking with Heart* (South Denver Cardiology Associates). *www.TheCookingCardiologist.com.*

Inflammation is the body's natural, temporary, healing response to infection or injury. But if the process fails to shut down when it should, inflammation becomes chronic—and tissues are injured by excess white blood cells and DNA-damaging free radicals.

Result: Elevated risk for heart disease, cancer, diabetes, osteoporosis, arthritis and other diseases.

Richard E. Collins, MD, "the cooking cardiologist," recently weighed in on how to prevent chronic inflammation.

His advice: Follow a diet that is rich in immune-strengthening nutrients…and use cooking techniques that neither destroy food's disease-fighting nutrients nor add inflammatory properties to it.

SMART WAYS WITH VEGETABLES

Deeply colored plant foods generally are rich in antioxidants that help combat inflammation by neutralizing free radicals.

Examples: Healthful *flavonoids* are prevalent in deep yellow to purple produce…carotenoids are found in yellow, orange, red and green vegetables.

Exceptions: Despite their light hue, garlic and onions are powerful antioxidants.

Unfortunately, these nutrients are easily lost.

For instance: Boiling or poaching vegetables causes nutrients to leach into the cooking water—and get tossed out when that potful of water is discarded. The high heat of frying causes a reaction between carbohydrates and amino acids, creating carcinogenic chemicals called *acrylamides*. And even when healthful food-preparation techniques are used, overcooking destroys nutrients. *Better…*

- **Microwave.** This uses minimal water and preserves flavor (so you won't be tempted to add butter or salt). Slightly moisten vegetables with water, cover and microwave just until crisp-tender.
- **Stir-fry.** In a preheated wok or sauté pan, cook vegetables over medium-high heat for a minute or two in a bit of low-sodium soy sauce.
- **Steam.** This beats boiling, but because steam envelops the food, some nutrients leach out. To "recycle" them, pour that bit of water from the steamer into any soup or sauce.
- **Stew.** Nutrients that leach from the vegetables aren't lost because they stay in the stew sauce.
- **Roast.** Set your oven to 350°F or lower to protect vegetables' nutrients and minimize acrylamides.

BEST METHODS FOR MEAT

When beef, pork, poultry or fish is roasted at 400°F or higher, grilled, broiled or fried, it triggers a chemical reaction that creates inflammatory *heterocyclic amines* (HCAs)—especially when food is exposed to direct flame and/or smoke. At least 17 HCAs are known carcinogens, linked to cancer of the breast, stomach, colon and/or pancreas.

Safest: Roast meat, poultry and fish at 350°F. Avoid overcooking—well-done meats may promote cancer. Also, be sure to avoid undercooking to prevent food poisoning.

If you love to grill: Buy a soapstone grilling stone, one-and-a-quarter inches thick and cut to half the size of your grill. (Stones are sold at kitchen-counter retail stores and at Dorado Soapstone, 888-500-1905, *www.DoradoSoapstone. com*). Place it on your grilling rack, then put your food on top of it. Soapstone heats well, doesn't dry out food and gives the flavor of grilling without exposing food to direct flames or smoke.

If you eat bacon: To minimize HCAs, cook bacon in the microwave and take care not to burn it.

THE RIGHT COOKING OILS

Do you cringe when the Food Network chefs sauté in unrefined extra-virgin olive oil? You should. This oil has a very low smoke point (the temperature at which a particular oil turns to smoke) of about 325°F—and when oil smokes, nutrients degrade and free radicals form.

Best: Sauté or stir-fry with refined canola oil, which has a high smoke point. Or use tea seed cooking oil (not tea tree oil)—its smoke point is about 485°F.

Try: Emerald Harvest (*www.Emerald-Harvest. com*) or Republic of Tea (800-298-4832, *www. RepublicofTea.com*).

Rule of thumb: If cooking oil starts to smoke, throw it out. Use a laser thermometer (sold at kitchenware stores) to instantly see oil temperature, so you'll know when to turn down the heat.

■ ■ ■ ■

Don't Chop Those Carrots

Cooking carrots whole before chopping them helps to retain their nutrients. Chopping before cooking increases the surface area of carrots, so more of the nutrients, including vitamin C, disappear into the water. Cooking carrots whole also keeps them tasty—80% of people preferred the flavor of carrots cooked whole over the flavor of ones chopped before cooking.

Kirsten Brandt, PhD, senior lecturer, department of food and rural development, School of Agriculture, Newcastle University, UK, and lead researcher of a study reported in Tufts University Health & Nutrition Letter.

■ ■ ■ ■

Delicious Flavor Without Salt

Limiting sodium often lowers high blood pressure and cardiovascular disease risk—but many Americans consume double the recommended limit, as much as 5 grams (g) per day.

Problem: Reducing salt can reduce a food's flavor, too.

New study: Participants reported that low-sodium foods prepared with a broth flavored with *karebushi* (dried bonito, a fish in the mackerel family) tasted better than other low-sodium foods.

Try it: Karebushi is sold as thin shaven flakes in Asian food stores and online. Add it to low-salt soups, sauces, rice and vegetables.

M. Manabe, PhD, associate professor, laboratory of cookery science, Doshisha Women's College of Liberal Arts, Kyoto, Japan, and leader of a study of 61 people.

■ ■ ■ ■

Eat Your Way to Great Hair

Protein—found in foods such as fish, meat, cheese, and cereals—helps build strong keratin, which makes up the outer layers of hair.

Also: Silica, commonly found in cucumbers, oats and rice, can boost hair growth. Vitamin C, found in citrus foods, such as oranges, lemons, limes, melons and berries, supports the body's effort to absorb protein and will keep hair follicles and blood vessels in the scalp healthy. Finally, eat salmon, carrots, egg yolks and sardines—the high amounts of vitamin B in these foods promote hair's growth and improve its texture.

Natural Health, 1000 American Media Way, Boca Raton, Florida 33464.

Hair Loss? Get to the Root Cause

Jamison Starbuck, ND, is a naturopathic physician in family practice in Missoula, Montana. She is past president of the American Association of Naturopathic Physicians and a contributing editor to *The Alternative Advisor: The Complete Guide to Natural Therapies and Alternative Treatments* (Time-Life).

Whether you're a man or a woman, if you notice that your hair is thinning or find clumps of hair in your comb, do not assume that it's an inevitable part of aging. While most of us have changes in hair-growth patterns usually beginning in our 50s and 60s, hair loss (*alopecia*) also can be a red flag for several treatable conditions such as hormone imbalances, thyroid disorders and nutritional deficiencies. Hair loss also can follow an illness that is accompanied by a prolonged high fever, radiation therapy for cancer—or even severe stress.

To determine the underlying cause of your hair loss, see your primary care physician. By examining your pattern of hair loss, he/she will gain clues to the type of alopecia you may have. For example, with *alopecia areata*, hair loss usually occurs in a sharply defined patch (which can appear anywhere on the scalp). With my patients, I usually also order blood tests for hormone levels (estrogen, progesterone and testosterone) and thyroid function. If hair loss is due to a hormone imbalance—including a thyroid deficiency—hair growth will generally occur within three months with the proper hormone replacement therapy. But remember that while you can improve hair growth with hormone supplementation, it's very unlikely that you'll restore your hair to the volume you had when you were in your 20s or 30s.

For people who experience any type of hair loss, it's especially important that they get adequate levels of B vitamins, zinc and fatty acids.

The daily regimen I recommend, taken until hair health improves: A B-complex vitamin that contains at least 75 milligrams (mg) each of vitamins B-1, B-2, B-3, B-5 and B-6, as well as 800 micrograms each of vitamin B-12 and folic acid...along with 2,000 mg of fish oil...and 45 mg of zinc.

The herb *gotu kola* also promotes normal hair growth and calms the nervous system. Take the herb in tincture form (one-quarter teaspoon in two ounces water) 15 minutes before or after eating, once daily. Gotu kola, taken until hair health is restored, is generally safe for adults (except for those with liver disease). Pregnant women should not take gotu kola. Check with your doctor if you want to take the herb for more than six weeks.

I also recommend using a shampoo that contains oil of rosemary to soothe the scalp and promote hair growth in people with hair loss. Rosemary is an herb that has a long history of use for hair and scalp health. (Such shampoos can be found online and in health food stores.) Also use a scalp rinse, which nourishes the scalp and hair follicles. My favorite is a rinse made of strong chamomile tea. Use six tea bags per quart of boiling water...steep, covered, for 10 minutes...then strain. The rinse can be stored in the refrigerator. Pour one cup (at room temperature) on your head, then massage it thoroughly throughout the scalp at the roots of your hair. Leave the rinse on for at least five minutes, then rinse off. Do this daily until your hair and scalp health is restored (usually within a month if the supplements described above are also used).

■ ■ ■ ■

High-Fiber Diet Warning

When 13 people with diabetes followed a high-fiber diet (50 grams [g] of fiber daily), they had significantly lower levels of urinary calcium—a possible risk factor for osteoporosis—than when following a moderate fiber diet (24 g daily).

Theory: Dietary fiber binds to calcium, reducing absorption.

Good rule of thumb: Eat a high-fiber diet—but include foods that are rich in both fiber and calcium, such as broccoli and figs.

Abhimanyu Garg, MD, chief, division of nutrition and metabolic diseases, University of Texas Southwestern Medical Center, Dallas.

The Real Secret to Strong Bones

Susan E. Brown, PhD, medical anthropologist, certified nutritionist and director, The Center for Better Bones and Better Bones Foundation, both in Syracuse, New York. She is author of *Better Bones, Better Body* (McGraw-Hill) and *The Acid-Alkaline Food Guide* (Square One). *www.BetterBones.com.*

Contrary to popular belief, the degenerative bone disease *osteoporosis* is not an inevitable result of aging.

New research: An important but overlooked cause of osteoporosis is an acid-forming diet.

Susan E. Brown, PhD, is author of *Better Bones, Better Body*. Her insights on this important research...

THE ACID/ALKALI BALANCE

For survival, the body must maintain a balance between acids and alkalis, with good health depending on slight alkalinity. If the body's alkali reserves run low—a condition called chronic low-grade *metabolic acidosis*—alkaline mineral compounds are drawn from bones to buffer excess acids in the blood. The immediate benefit is that the body's pH (a measure of acidity or alkalinity) is balanced. But over time, if bone mineral compounds are not replenished, osteoporosis develops.

Bone-depleting metabolic acidosis is easily reversible through diet. Yet the average American diet is woefully deficient in many of the nutrients needed to balance pH.

To protect bones: Follow the dietary suggestions that follow. It's generally best to get nutrients from food. However, to help ensure adequate intake, take a daily multivitamin/mineral plus the other supplements noted…and consider additional supplements as well.

Before you start: Gauge your pH with a urine test kit, such as those sold in some pharmacies…or use the Better Bones Alkaline for Life pH Test Kit. (*www.BetterBones.com,* click on "Visit Our Store," or call 877-207-0232). An ideal first morning urine pH is 6.5 to 7.5. The lower your pH is, the more helpful supplements may be. As with any supplement regimen, talk to your doctor before beginning.

BONE-SUPPORTIVE DIET
For a diet that builds bones…

•**Emphasize vegetables (particularly dark, leafy greens and root vegetables), fruits, nuts, seeds and spices**—these are alkalizing foods.

Daily targets: Eight servings of vegetables… three to four servings of fruit…two servings of nuts or seeds…and plentiful spices.

•**Consume meat, poultry, fish, dairy, eggs, legumes and whole grains in moderation**—they are acidifying.

Daily targets: One serving of meat, poultry or fish…one serving of eggs or legumes…one to two servings each of dairy and whole grains.

•**Minimize sugar, refined grains and processed foods**…limit coffee to two servings daily…limit alcohol to one serving daily. All these are very acidifying.

•**Fats neither increase nor decrease blood acidity**—but for overall health, keep fat intake moderate and opt for those that protect the heart, such as olive oil.

Important: It's not the acidity of a food itself that matters, but rather its metabolic effects. For instance, citrus fruits taste acidic, yet once metabolized, they are alkalizing.

MINERALS THAT BONES NEED MOST
Bone is composed of a living protein matrix of collagen upon which mineral crystals are deposited in a process called mineralization. *Key minerals, in order of importance…*

•**Potassium** neutralizes metabolic acids and reduces calcium loss.

Daily goal: 4,000 milligrams (mg) to 6,000 mg.

Sources: Avocados, baked potatoes, bananas, beet greens, cantaloupe, lima beans, sweet potatoes.

•**Magnesium** boosts absorption of calcium and production of the bone-preserving hormone *calcitonin.*

Daily goal: 400 mg to 800 mg.

Sources: Almonds, Brazil nuts, kelp, lentils, pumpkin seeds, soy, split peas, whole wheat, wild rice.

•**Calcium** gives bones strength.

Daily goal: 1,000 mg to 1,500 mg.

Sources: Amaranth flour, broccoli, canned sardines with bones, collards, dairy, kale, mustard greens, sesame seeds, spinach.

Also: Supplement daily, at a two-to-one ratio, with calcium citrate or calcium citrate malate plus magnesium—increasing calcium intake without also increasing magnesium can exacerbate asthma, arthritis and kidney stones.

•**Zinc** aids collagen production and calcium absorption.

Daily goal: 20 mg to 30 mg.

Sources: Alaskan king crab, cashews, kidney beans, meat, oysters, sesame seeds, wheat germ.

•**Manganese** helps form bone cartilage and collagen.

Daily goal: 10 mg to 15 mg.

Sources: Beets, blackberries, brown rice, loganberries, oats, peanuts, pineapple, rye, soy.

•**Copper** blocks bone breakdown and increases collagen formation.

Daily goal: 1 mg to 3 mg.

Sources: Barley, beans, chickpeas, eggplant, liver, molasses, summer squash.

•**Silica** increases collagen strength and bone calcification.

Daily goal: 30 mg to 50 mg.

Sources: Bananas, carrots, green beans, whole grains.

•**Boron** helps the body use calcium, magnesium and vitamin D.

Daily goal: 3 mg to 5 mg.

Sources: Almonds, avocados, black-eyed peas, cherries, grapes, tomatoes.

•**Strontium** promotes mineralization.

Daily goal: 3 mg to 20 mg.

Sources: Brazil nuts, legumes, root vegetables, whole grains.

VITAL VITAMINS

The following vitamins enhance bones' self-repair abilities…

•**Vitamin D** is essential because, without adequate amounts, you cannot absorb enough calcium. Many people do not get adequate vitamin D from sunlight. Vitamin D deficiency accounts for up to 50% of osteoporotic fractures.

Daily goal: 1,000 international units (IU) to 2,000 IU.

Best source: A daily supplement of *cholecalciferol* (vitamin D-3)—foods that contain vitamin D (fatty fish, fortified milk) do not provide enough and are acidifying.

•**Vitamins K-1 and K-2** boost bone matrix synthesis and bind calcium and phosphorous to bone.

Daily goal: 1,000 micrograms (mcg) of K-1 …and 90 mg to 180 mg of K-2.

Sources: Aged cheese, broccoli, Brussels sprouts, collard greens, kale, spinach, green tea.

If you supplement: For vitamin K-2, choose the MK-7 form.

Caution: Vitamin K can interfere with blood thinners, such as *warfarin* (Coumadin)—so talk to your doctor before altering vitamin K intake.

•**Vitamin C** aids collagen formation, stimulates bone-building cells and helps synthesize the adrenal hormones vital to postmenopausal bone health.

Daily goal: 500 mg to 2,000 mg.

Sources: Cantaloupe, kiwifruit, oranges, papaya, pink grapefruit, red peppers, strawberries.

•**Vitamins B-6, B-12 and folate** help eliminate homocysteine, an amino acid linked to fracture risk.

Daily goal: 25 mg to 50 mg of B-6…200 mcg to 800 mcg of B-12…800 mcg to 1,000 mcg of folate.

Sources: For vitamin B-6—avocados, bananas, brown rice, oats, turkey, walnuts. For B-12—beef, salmon, trout. For folate—asparagus, okra, peanuts, pinto beans.

•**Vitamin A** helps develop bone-building osteoblast cells.

Daily goal: 5,000 IU.

Sources: Carrots, collard greens, pumpkin, sweet potatoes.

If you supplement: Choose the form with beta-carotene.

■ ■ ■ ■

Wine Boosts Omega-3 Fatty Acids

Moderate wine consumption increases the body's levels of heart-healthy omega-3s. The increase was greater for wine drinkers than for those drinking other alcoholic beverages. This means components other than alcohol are likely responsible for the boost in omega-3s. The results apply only to moderate wine consumption—up to two glasses a day for men and one glass a day for women.

Romina di Giuseppe, doctor in food science and technology, researcher in nutritional epidemiology, Catholic University, Campobasso, Italy, and leader of a study of 1,604 people, published in *The American Journal of Clinical Nutrition.*

Healthiest Omega-3s for Your Money

JoAnn E. Manson, MD, DrPH, is a professor of medicine and women's health at Harvard Medical School and chief of the division of preventive medicine at Brigham and Women's Hospital, both in Boston. She is one of the lead investigators for two highly influential studies on women's health—the Harvard Nurses' Health Study and the Women's Health Initiative. Dr. Manson is the author, with Shari Bassuk, ScD, of *Hot Flashes, Hormones & Your Health* (McGraw-Hill).

Omega-3 fatty acids are not all created equal. *Eicosapentaenoic acid* (EPA) and *docosahexaenoic acid* (DHA) are found primarily in fish and so are called "marine" omega-3s. *Alpha-linolenic acid* (ALA) is found in plant sources such as flaxseed, walnuts, canola oil, soybean oil.

Evidence for health benefits is much stronger for EPA and DHA than for ALA. *The marine omega-3s appear to protect against...*

•**Heart attacks, stroke and cardiovascular death**—by reducing blood clotting, irregular heart rhythms, *triglycerides* (a blood fat) and perhaps arterial plaque.

•**Cognitive decline and depression**—by combating inflammation, improving function of nerve cell membranes and boosting brain chemicals that help nerve cells communicate.

•**Some types of arthritis and bowel disease**—by easing inflammation.

Bonus: Omega-3s may reduce menstrual cramps and menopausal hot flashes in some women.

How much do you need? Adults should eat dark oily fish (such as salmon, tuna, herring, sardines, trout or mackerel) at least twice per week. This provides 400 milligrams (mg) to 500 mg of combined EPA/DHA per day, on average.

If you have heart disease, get 1,000 mg of EPA/DHA daily...if you have high triglycerides, your doctor may recommend 2,000 mg to 4,000 mg daily.

It's hard to eat enough fish to meet the higher dosages, so consider supplements.

Advantage: Whereas fish may be contaminated with mercury and *polychlorinated biphenyls* (PCBs), *Consumer Reports* found that none of the 16 major fish oil brands tested contained significant amounts of these toxins.

Bonus: Fish oil may alleviate dry eyes and dry skin. *Keep in mind...*

•**Many fish oil capsules are only about 30% EPA/DHA**—so look for a product with more concentrated EPA/DHA.

If you have high triglycerides, ask your doctor for information about a new prescription fish oil supplement that has 840 mg of EPA/DHA per 1,000-mg capsule.

•**Fish oil can thin the blood and trigger excessive bleeding in some people**—so do not take more than 3,000 mg daily without your doctor's okay. Check with your doctor before taking any fish oil if you use medication that affects blood clotting, such as aspirin, *warfarin* (Coumadin) or *clopidogrel* (Plavix).

If you prefer not to consume fish products, get 1,000 mg to 2,000 mg of ALA per day from ground flaxseed, flaxseed oil supplements or other sources.

To avoid gastrointestinal upset, start at a low dose and gradually build up...and drink a glass of water with each dose.

Consult your doctor before taking high doses of flaxseed if you have a personal or family history of breast cancer or another hormone-sensitive condition—flaxseed contains substances that may have estrogen-like effects.

•**New study under way.** My colleagues and I have begun the first-ever large-scale clinical trial designed to provide a definitive picture of the benefits and risks of marine omega-3 supplementation for initially healthy men and women.

Tales About Supplements That Could Ruin Your Health

Mark A. Stengler, NMD, naturopathic medical doctor in private practice, La Jolla, California…adjunct associate clinical professor at the National College of Natural Medicine, Portland, Oregon…author of many books, including *The Natural Physician's Healing Therapies* and coauthor of *Prescription for Natural Cures* (both from Bottom Line Books)…and author of the *Bottom Line/Natural Healing* newsletter.

Over the past few years, it's become almost fashionable for scientists and journalists to attack vitamins and other nutritional therapies. This makes no sense to me, because there now is much research showing the benefits of nutritional supplements. These attacks do a great disservice to people who want to stay healthy. Since there are many misconceptions about nutritional supplements, I'm going to set the record straight about vitamins and nutrients.

Lie: Vitamin D is toxic at doses higher than 2,000 international units (IU) daily.

Truth: Doctors now agree that adults should take a minimum of 2,000 IU daily.

Most of the fears about high doses of vitamin D date back to a small 1984 study in India, in which doctors blamed high calcium levels on vitamin D. (Vitamin D promotes calcium absorption.) Other studies involving high levels of vitamin D did not show the same high calcium levels, but for some reason, the Indian study continues to be the basis for the toxicity level recommendations of the Food and Nutrition Board of the Institute of Medicine. The US government recommendations for 200 IU to 400 IU of vitamin D daily are woefully inadequate. Most Americans don't get enough vitamin D. Have your vitamin D levels checked. In addition to what you get from the sun and foods, children (from one day old up to 12 years old) should take a minimum of 1,000 IU daily (and 2,000 IU during winter). Adults should take 2,000 IU daily (5,000 IU during winter).

Lie: Vitamin E increases the risk for death.

Truth: The original research was based on flawed interpretation of the data.

At the heart of this falsehood is a 2005 *Annals of Internal Medicine* analysis that looked at 19 clinical trials in which participants who were chronically ill were given vitamin E and/or other supplements. The authors concluded that adults who took supplements of 400 IU or more daily of vitamin E were 6% more likely to die from any cause than those who did not take vitamin E supplements. However, the data also revealed that the increased risk for death was statistically significant only at a dose of 2,000 IU daily (not to mention that the study did not look at the vitamin's effect on healthy people). These results should hardly be interpreted as saying that vitamin E is a substance that the general population should avoid. Other research shows that vitamin E can help treat and prevent cardiovascular disease, blood clots and dementia. Take 200 IU daily of a mixed supplement that contains a full blend of the vitamin E components *tocopherols* and *tocotrienols*.

Half-truth: Antioxidants reduce the effectiveness of chemotherapy.

Truth: Research shows some antioxidants help. Ask a holistic oncologist what's best for you.

This statement is a half-truth because certain antioxidant supplements, such as green tea extract, may interfere with some types of chemotherapy and radiation treatment. However, the majority of studies on antioxidants and chemotherapy show that antioxidants don't interfere with these treatments. Several recent medical journal articles show that cancer patients taking high-dose antioxidants live longer, have less pain and have better quality of life than people who do not take these supplements. Some of the studies even show that antioxidants enhance the effectiveness of chemotherapy and radiation therapy.

I often recommend antioxidants, such as 200 milligrams (mg) to 300 mg of coenzyme Q10 (CoQ10), to my cancer patients.

Note: Some antioxidants may interfere with specific chemotherapy drugs. If you are undergoing chemotherapy, check with a holistic physician or oncologist about potential interactions and ask which antioxidants are right for you.

Half-truth: Beta-carotene increases the risk for lung cancer.

***Truth:* A sythetic form was studied; look for the natural form insead.**

This half-truth about beta-carotene stems from results of a Finnish study of male smokers who took a synthetic form of beta-carotene. (The researchers did not test the natural form.) The men had greater incidence of lung cancer with a 15% higher death rate than the men in the study who took vitamin E alone…both vitamin E and beta-carotene…or a placebo. It's unclear why these long-term smokers had a detrimental reaction to synthetic beta-carotene supplementation, but it doesn't make sense to rule out this antioxidant for use by the general population—especially since other studies have pointed out its benefits. For example, an 18-year study of American men found that beta-carotene was associated with reduced risk for age-related mental decline. Nutrients such as beta-carotene work best in their natural form, where complementary phytochemicals are present, so look for supplements made with natural beta-carotene (from *D. salina* algae).

Best: Take a mixed carotenoid complex, such as Natural Factors BetaCareAll (800-322-8704, *www.naturalfactors.com* for a store locator).

Lie: CoQ10 doesn't help the heart.

***Truth:* Hundreds of scientific papers say otherwise.**

The truth is that CoQ10 can reverse two of the deadliest types of heart disease—cardiomyopathy and heart failure. And yet most of my patients with cardiovascular disease tell me that their cardiologists never told them to take CoQ10. This has led me to believe that most mainstream cardiologists haven't read the hundreds of published scientific papers on it and remain oblivious to its benefits. For my patients with congestive heart failure, for example, I generally recommend 100 mg of CoQ10 three times daily taken with meals.

Half-truth: Vitamin C doesn't prevent colds.

***Truth:* Vitamin C prevents colds in some, reduces symptoms in most.**

Vitamin C seems to help prevent colds in some people and not others, but it pretty consistently reduces cold symptoms in people who do catch a cold. In one study, vitamin C significantly reduced the risk of catching a cold (by 50%!)

in people who subject their bodies to extreme physical stress, such as marathon runners and soldiers. Other reviews have found that vitamin C supplements can cut cold symptoms and duration by one-third. The dose is crucial—taking just a little doesn't help with a cold. When sick, take 2,000 mg to 6,000 mg daily. For prevention, especially during stressful periods, take 1,000 mg to 2,000 mg daily.

The Simple Supplement That May Prevent Killer Diseases

Joseph Maroon, MD, a professor of neurological surgery and Heindl Scholar in Neuroscience at the University of Pittsburgh School of Medicine and team neurosurgeon for the Pittsburgh Steelers. He is the author of *The Longevity Factor: How Resveratrol and Red Wine Activate Genes for a Longer and Healthier Life* (Atria). *www.josephmaroon.com*.

When it comes to "hot" supplements, *resveratrol* is high on the list. Multiple studies conducted on laboratory animals have demonstrated the highly beneficial effects of this *polyphenol* (a class of plant chemicals), which is found most abundantly in the skins of grapes and in red wine—and now is available in supplement form.

Key animal study findings: Resveratrol has been shown not only to enhance muscle strength and reduce fatigue, but also to help prevent heart disease, stroke, diabetes and cancer…clear away the toxic proteins that cause Alzheimer's disease…and even lengthen life span by 25%.

Can this substance do the same for humans?

AN IMPORTANT DISCOVERY

Resveratrol's emergence as an anti-aging and disease-fighting powerhouse began in the 1930s with a seemingly unrelated finding—that severe calorie restriction extended the lives of rodents by 40% to 50%.

It wasn't until the 1990s, however, that researchers at Harvard Medical School discovered the genetic basis for the beneficial effect of calorie restriction. Through various experiments in animal studies, calorie restriction was shown to trigger a kind of chain reaction that activates "survival genes" (*sirtuins*), which, in turn, energize an enzyme (SIR2) that stabilizes DNA. This process slows cellular aging. In further studies, researchers discovered that resveratrol is one of the most potent sources of the molecules that activate these survival genes.

CURRENT EVIDENCE

To further test resveratrol's benefits, researchers conducted other animal studies—this time without calorie restriction. Resveratrol and other polyphenols were found to increase the life span of fish by 60%...worms and flies by 30%...and mice by 25%—benefits attributed to improved cellular health.

Resveratrol-enhanced cells are believed to help fight...

•**Heart disease and stroke.** Resveratrol appears to decrease harmful inflammation, which contributes to cardiovascular disease.

Breakthrough research: A human study showed that drinking one-and-a-half glasses of red wine a day lowered, by 40%, levels of lipid peroxide, a by-product of inflammation that damages arteries. This and other health benefits are believed to be due to resveratrol and several other polyphenols in red wine.

Through various animal studies, resveratrol was shown to spark the production of the beneficial gas nitric oxide, which gives blood vessels more flexibility. Resveratrol also thins the blood, reducing the risk for an artery-clogging clot. In studies of animals with induced heart attacks, those given resveratrol had a significantly lower fatality rate. In similar studies on stroke, resveratrol prevented paralysis and limited brain injury in animals.

•**Cancer.** Eighteen different types of cancer—including lung, colon, skin, liver and pancreatic—have been markedly inhibited by resveratrol in laboratory studies using both animal and human cells.

•**Diabetes.** In animals, resveratrol helps normalize blood sugar (glucose) levels by moving glucose out of the bloodstream and into cells. Laboratory research also shows that resveratrol reduces diabetic neuropathy (nerve pain that often occurs in the legs and feet).

New finding: In a human study, a synthetic, resveratrol-like compound was shown to give people the same type of glucose control that resveratrol gives mice.

•**Alzheimer's disease.** In animal studies, resveratrol helps remove the amyloid-beta protein associated with Alzheimer's disease.

New finding: In a study of 90 healthy people, researchers at Marywood University in Scranton found that a supplement containing resveratrol and other polyphenols improved memory and sped up reaction time.

RESVERATROL SOURCES

Even though the preliminary research is promising, there is a caveat. You would have to drink up to 1,150 bottles of red wine daily to get the amount of resveratrol used in most animal studies.

Since that's not feasible, I recommend a more practical approach that includes two things—a regular diet of resveratrol- and polyphenol-rich foods (the resveratrol is far lower than the doses used in animal studies, but these foods contain other beneficial compounds that may enhance absorption of resveratrol from food and/or supplements)...and the use of a mixed polyphenol supplement or a resveratrol supplement.

That strategy—along with regular exercise and the health-promoting effects of close emotional ties with family and friends—is your best bet for fighting chronic disease and living longer. *My advice...*

•**Eat a polyphenol-rich diet.** Resveratrol is the superstar of polyphenols, but many scientists think that a combination of polyphenols—ingesting them together, as they are found in nature—is the best way to activate survival genes.

The foods richest in resveratrol and a variety of other polyphenols...

•**Red wine or red grape juice.** These are the top dietary sources of resveratrol. Important: Wine grapes with the most resveratrol include pinot noir, merlot, grenache, cabernet sauvignon and tempranillo. (These wines also deliver up to about 500 different polyphenols along with resveratrol.)

Suggested daily intake: Four to 16 ounces of red grape juice daily (be mindful of the sugar content). Up to 12 ounces of red wine daily for men…and no more than six ounces daily for women (the potential health benefit of daily wine consumption by women must be weighed against a possible increase in breast cancer risk).

•**Pomegranate juice.** It is a good source of resveratrol and many other antioxidants.

Suggested daily intake: Three to five ounces.

•**Dark chocolate.** It is a rich source of concentrated *flavonols,* a potent type of polyphenol. Select unsweetened or semisweetened varieties with at least 70% cocoa.

Suggested daily intake: One bite-sized square.

•**Green tea.** Green tea contains resveratrol and is rich in *epigallocatechin gallate* (EGCG) and other polyphenols.

Suggested daily intake: Three eight-ounce cups. Decaffeinated green tea contains EGCG but relatively little resveratrol.

•**Blueberries.** They are rich in *procyanidins* and other polyphenols.

Suggested daily intake: At least one cup (fresh or frozen).

•**Take a mixed-polyphenol supplement.** I recommend the mixed polyphenol supplement Vindure 900, a product developed by Vinomis Laboratories based on Harvard University research. Vindure is available from Vinomis Laboratories (877-484-6664, *www.vinomis.com*). Follow the dosage recommendation on the label.

Because resveratrol absorption is thought to be enhanced when combined with other natural polyphenols, a mixed-polyphenol supplement is best.

However, an alternative is to…

•**Take a resveratrol supplement.** There are more than 300 resveratrol-containing products now available. The best products are made with trans-resveratrol (the active form of the substance shown by professional testing to activate the sirtuin "survival genes")…and produced by manufacturers who comply with "Good Manufacturing Practices" (GMP), which ensures that the product contains no major contaminants.

My favorite resveratrol products are manufactured by…

•Longevinex, *www.longevinex.com*, 866-405-4000.

•RevGenetics, *www.myrevgenetics.com*, 888-738-4363.

Suggested intake for most resveratrol supplements: 250 milligrams (mg) to 500 mg daily.

Exciting New Health Benefits of CoQ10

Peter H. Langsjoen, MD, a cardiologist in private practice in Tyler, Texas, who specializes in noninvasive treatment. He is an active researcher and expert in the biomedical benefits of CoQ10. A fellow of the American College of Cardiology, Dr. Langsjoen was a founding member of the International Coenzyme Q10 Association, *www.icqa.org.*

Until recently, the dietary supplement *coenzyme Q10* (CoQ10) was recommended for people who wanted to avoid the side effects of cholesterol-lowering statin drugs, including muscle pain and weakness.

Now: Researchers are discovering that CoQ10 may confer a variety of other health benefits that are unrelated to statin use.

Peter H. Langsjoen, MD, a foremost CoQ10 expert, spoke recently about the latest developments in this research…*

WHAT IS COQ10?

CoQ10 is a vitamin-like substance that plays a key role in the production of energy in every cell in the body. Discovered in 1957, the substance is naturally present in such foods as organ meats (including cow's liver and kidney), and, in smaller amounts, in beef, sardines, mackerel and peanuts. Because CoQ10 appeared to be everywhere in the body—or "ubiquitous"—it was fittingly dubbed *ubiquinone.*

Without adequate levels of this substance, the body's organs and systems, including the immune system and nervous system, will not function optimally.

UNEXPECTED HEALTH BENEFITS

Increasing scientific evidence now offers support for the use of CoQ10 supplements to help treat…

*Dr. Langsjoen has no financial interest in any company that manufactures or sells CoQ10 supplements.

•**Heart disease.** CoQ10 is involved in creating 90% of cellular energy in the heart.

Research has shown that people with heart failure (inadequate pumping action of the heart) have lower blood levels of CoQ10, on average, than people without heart failure—and the lower the CoQ10 level, the worse the problem.

Recent research published in the journal *Biofactors* showed that the *ejection fraction* (the amount of blood pumped with each heartbeat) in heart failure patients who took CoQ10 supplements rose from an average of 22% to an average of 39% after six to 12 months.

Important: Because statin medications deplete the body's supply of CoQ10, ask your doctor about adding CoQ10 supplements (to help protect the heart and counteract statin-related side effects) to your regimen if you take one of these drugs.

•**High blood pressure.** CoQ10 can also help improve high blood pressure (hypertension). Studies have shown that about half of people using one or more drugs for high blood pressure can stop taking at least some of their medications after taking CoQ10 supplements for about five months.

•**Cholesterol.** CoQ10 also acts as a powerful antioxidant. It is transported in the blood (along with cholesterol and other fat-soluble nutrients) and helps protect cholesterol from damaging oxidation, which plays a role in *atherosclerosis* (fatty buildup in the arteries).

•**Fatigue.** Because CoQ10 is part of the body's energy-producing processes, it is particularly valuable in reducing fatigue—even among people with severe fatigue, including that caused by such conditions as chronic fatigue syndrome.

•**Migraines.** In one study, 32 people who took CoQ10 supplements for three months had only half their usual number of migraines.

•**Neurological disorders.** Some of the most promising recent research involves the ability of CoQ10 to slow the progression of degenerative neurological disorders, including Parkinson's disease, Alzheimer's disease and Huntington's disease (a genetic disorder).

HOW TO USE COQ10 SAFELY

People who eat organ meats at least once or twice weekly usually have healthy CoQ10 levels. But other adults can improve their blood levels of CoQ10 by taking supplements. Work with your doctor to find an optimal dose.

For best absorption, do not take more than 180 milligrams (mg) at one time. CoQ10 is fat-soluble (dissolves in fat), so it is best to take the supplement with meals that contain at least a little bit of fat (any type).

In some people, CoQ10 may cause temporary side effects, such as nausea and other gastrointestinal disorders…dizziness…insomnia…or headache. However, these side effects are rare. If you experience side effects, try a different CoQ10 formulation.

Caution: One case study suggested that CoQ10 may act like vitamin K, lessening the blood-thinning effect of *warfarin* (Coumadin). But a controlled trial subsequently found no such effects.

Nevertheless, people taking warfarin or any other blood-thinning medication should consult a doctor before taking a CoQ10 supplement. After a few weeks of taking CoQ10, anyone who uses a blood thinner should have his/her *prothrombin time* (a measure of clotting ability) checked.

Also important: Because CoQ10 may cause your blood pressure and/or blood sugar (glucose) level to gradually improve, your doctor may want to adjust the dosage of any medications you may be taking to control elevations of either.

FINDING THE BEST PRODUCT

One reliable producer of CoQ10 is the Japanese company Kaneka, which sells CoQ10 in the US under many different brand names, including Healthy Origins (888-228-6650, *www.healthy origins.com*) and Jarrow Formulas, available through Pro Vitaminas (800-510-6444, *www. provitaminas.com*). Kaneka uses a yeast fermentation process with 99.9% pure natural CoQ10.

In addition to CoQ10 supplements, you may see products labeled "ubiquinol." Ubiquinol is a more bioavailable (absorbable)—and more expensive—form of CoQ10. However, if you take CoQ10, your body will naturally convert it to ubiquinol. While most healthy adults readily absorb CoQ10, patients with advanced heart failure absorb ubiquinol about four times better than CoQ10.

If you purchase ubiquinol (not CoQ10), test it for freshness (in case it has deteriorated during storage or shipping).

What to do: Cut one capsule in half, and look at the color of the contents. Cream-colored is good—orange or brown means that the product has become oxidized.

Low-Fat Diets Actually Boost Your Mood

Ewald Horvath, MD, MS, professor, department of psychiatry, University of Miami Miller School of Medicine, Miami.

Grant D. Brinkworth, PhD, research scientist, Food and Nutritional Sciences, Commonwealth Scientific and Industrial Research Organisation, Adelaide, Australia.

Archives of Internal Medicine.

Both a high-fat, low-carbohydrate diet, such as the popular Atkins program, and a low-fat, high-carb diet appear to help people lose pounds over the course of a year.

But as for mood? Only the low-fat diets will result in long-term improvement in mood, according to a study published in the *Archives of Internal Medicine.*

People on both diets consumed roughly the same number of calories.

BACKGROUND

Ewald Horvath, MD, professor of psychiatry at the University of Miami Miller School of Medicine, said the study was the first "to show both long-term weight loss and improved mood."

Other studies have found short-term improvements in mood in people who lose weight on different diets. And the new study also found such improvements over the first eight weeks of dieting.

Few studies, however, have looked at long-term mood changes among people who lose weight.

Health organizations, such as the American Heart Association, tend to advocate higher-carb, low-fat diets. But many overweight and obese people are propelled toward the high-fat diet books, *Livin' La Vida Low-Carb, Good Calories, Bad Calories,* and others by Dr. Robert Atkins perhaps because of quick initial weight loss, Dr. Horvath said.

STUDY DETAILS

For the new study, 106 overweight and obese adults, who averaged 50 years old, were randomly assigned to one of two diets—a low-calorie, low-carb, high-fat plan or a high-carb, low-fat diet—for one year. Both eating programs restricted calories to about 1,433 to 1,672 a day.

A year later, average weight loss was about the same in each group: 30.2 pounds.

After the first eight weeks, participants in both groups showed mood improvements, but that lasted only in the low-fat group. After a year, the mood of those in the high-fat group returned to what it had been before they started dieting, the study found.

IMPLICATIONS

"The exact mechanism for the observed effects on mood still remains largely unknown," said study author Grant D. Brinkworth, PhD, a research scientist with the food and nutritional sciences division of the Commonwealth Scientific and Industrial Research Organisation in Adelaide, Australia.

More carbs can increase *serotonin* concentrations in the brain, whereas added fat and protein can reduce concentrations. Serotonin is a *neurotransmitter* involved in mood.

"Altered mood has been shown to influence interpersonal behavior and, therefore, the consumption of a very low-carbohydrate diet may have psychosocial consequences for interpersonal behavior and relationships," Dr. Brinkworth said. A recent review article suggested that one of the factors that may pose risk for poor long-term weight maintenance may be "eating in response to negative emotions and stress" he added.

"Therefore, since negative mood may promote overeating, this suggests that consumption of a very low-carbohydrate diet over an even longer period beyond one year may have implications for maintaining dietary habits and weight loss maintenance," Dr. Brinkworth said.

"Further, longer-term studies would be required to confirm this."

info For more on healthy eating, visit the Web site of the American Dietetic Association, *www.eatright.org*, and search "healthy eating."

Melt Away Abdominal Fat with Help from Your Hormones

Mark A. Stengler, NMD, naturopathic medical doctor in private practice, La Jolla, California...adjunct associate clinical professor at the National College of Natural Medicine, Portland, Oregon...author of many books, including *The Natural Physician's Healing Therapies* and coauthor of *Prescription for Natural Cures* (both from Bottom Line Books)...and author of the *Bottom Line/Natural Healing* newsletter.

The size of your waist is believed to be a better indicator of health problems than the number on the scale or your body mass index (BMI), a measure of weight relative to height.

It is far more healthful to have a "pear" body shape (fat stored around the hips, buttocks and thighs) than an "apple" shape (fat stored around the middle). Both men and women with apple shapes (men with waists of 40 inches or more and women with waists of 35 inches or more) are more likely to be insulin resistant—a condition in which the cells do not receive insulin properly and which often leads to diabetes—than those with smaller waists. In fact, research shows that having just an extra four inches around your waist increases your risk for heart failure by 15%. Belly fat is associated with a greater risk for stroke, and every additional two inches around the waist in men increases the risk for *deep-vein thrombosis* and *pulmonary embolism* (blockage of the main artery of the lungs) by 18%.

Why abdominal fat is so bad: This fat, also known as *visceral fat*, produces hormones that work against you in the following ways...

• **Releasing free fatty acids** (the breakdown product of fat cells that circulate in the bloodstream).

• **Decreasing insulin sensitivity** (the degree to which your cells recognize insulin and use it properly).

• **Increasing cytokines,** compounds that contribute to inflammation and insulin resistance, including *resistin*, another chemical that reduces insulin sensitivity.

• **Decreasing hormones such as leptin** that help regulate metabolism and appetite.

HELP IS ON THE WAY

Abdominal fat often is associated with hormonal imbalances, such as high insulin (yes, even insulin is a hormone)...high cortisol...and high estrogen. Once the vicious cycle of abdominal weight gain and hormonal imbalance begins, it is hard to stop—especially because each one causes the other.

I put those who are caught in this cycle on a hormone-balancing protocol that they follow for at least two months and up to six months. The results are impressive.

THE PROTOCOLS

If you are a man with a waist measurement of 40 inches or more or a woman with a waist of 35 inches or more, ask your doctor to test your levels of cortisol, insulin and estrogen.

Note: Excess estrogen is not just a female problem. While high levels most often occur in women younger than 45 and in postmenopausal women, they can appear in men as well, especially when made worse by the presence of environmental estrogens, compounds found in many plastic household products.

If you have excess estrogen...

High levels of estrogen, particularly combined with low levels of progesterone, can cause abdominal fat. When either a male or female patient has excess estrogen, especially in conjunction with low levels of progesterone (a condition called *estrogen dominance*), I recommend an estrogen detox program. This includes eating two to three daily servings of cruciferous vegetables (such as broccoli, cabbage, brussels sprouts, cauliflower and kale), which contain plant compounds called *indoles* that help regulate estrogen metabolism and can make estrogen less toxic.

Supplements that help include *indole-3-carbinol* and *diindolymethane* (DIM). These phytochemicals in supplement form are similar to those found in cruciferous vegetables. Patients take 300 milligrams (mg) to 400 mg daily of indole-3-carbinol and 200 mg to 400 mg of DIM daily. (I recommend both the food, for the fiber, and the supplements because it's difficult to get enough of these phytochemicals through food.) For women who are perimenopausal or menopausal (and some men with prostate problems) with this type of hormonal imbalance, I also may prescribe a bioidentical progesterone cream.

If you have insulin resistance…

Abdominal fat and insulin resistance often go together like the proverbial chicken and egg, and it isn't always easy to know which one was there first. Insulin resistance increases the chances of developing type 2 diabetes and cardiovascular disease. It can be effectively treated by eating a diet with high-fiber foods, including vegetables, legumes and grains. Regular exercise also helps keep insulin resistance under control. For my insulin-resistant patients, I also recommend PGX, a form of glucomannon fiber.

Brand to try: Natural Factors PGX Daily (800-322-8704, *www.naturalfactors.com* for a store locator).

Also helpful: *Chromium picolinate*, a trace mineral (start with 500 micrograms [mcg] daily and increase to 1,000 mcg daily, if needed), which can help balance blood sugar levels… and *resveratrol* (50 mg to 100 mg daily), which improves insulin resistance.

If you have high levels of *cortisol*…

Cortisol, the major stress hormone produced by the adrenal glands, can signal the body to store fat around the middle. For my patients whose blood tests reveal high cortisol levels, I prescribe a basic program of aerobic exercise (30 minutes daily of swimming, jogging, bicycling or walking)…strength training…stress reduction…and deep breathing, all of which have been found to lower cortisol levels. The herb *ashwagandha* also can help normalize blood cortisol levels.

Brand to try: Sensoril Ashwagandha made by Jarrow Formulas (310-204-6936, *www.jarrow.com* for a store locator). Take one 225-mg capsule daily. Women who are pregnant or breast-feeding should not take this herb.

Eat What You Want, Never Go Hungry and Still Lose Weight

Seth Roberts, PhD, professor emeritus of psychology at University of California, Berkeley, and professor of psychology at Tsinghua University in Beijing, China. Dr. Roberts is author of *The Shangri-La Diet: The No Hunger, Eat Anything Weight-Loss Plan* (Perigee) and serves on the editorial board of the journal *Nutrition. www.sethroberts.net.*

The Shangri-la Diet (named after the mythical utopia) is a simple, effective way to adjust your natural appetite-regulation system. You just consume two 100-calorie doses of flavorless foods per day.

How it works: Much as a thermostat maintains your house temperature at a set level, your body maintains a set point weight—the number it perceives as normal. Just as a thermostat turns a heater on and off, your body's weight-control system turns hunger on and off. If the set point is adjusted upward, your body tries to put on weight…and if the set point is adjusted downward, you naturally lose weight.

Theory: Your body regulates weight partly in response to the flavors of food. A food whose flavor is associated with calories raises your set point and increases your appetite later…a flavorless food lowers your set point and curbs appetite.

Typical result: Two 100-calorie doses of flavorless foods reduce your appetite so much that the next day you automatically consume 500 fewer calories than usual—without feeling hungry. *Flavorless foods that work best…*

•**Flavorless oil.** Choose extra-light olive oil or refined walnut oil. One dose equals one tablespoon.

•**Sugar water.** Strangely, your body doesn't count sweetness as a flavor. One dose equals two tablespoons of sugar mixed with one cup of water.

•**Daily doses.** To lose less than 20 pounds, consume one dose each of oil and sugar water daily. To lose more, double each dose. Appetite suppression usually begins within a day or so.

Essential: To prevent flavorless foods from becoming associated with other flavors, you must wait one hour after tasting anything else (including toothpaste or gum) before swallowing the oil or sugar water—then wait one hour more before eating again. Otherwise, the flavorless foods simply add to your total calorie intake without suppressing appetite at all.

Convenient: Schedule food-free intervals for mid-morning (between breakfast and lunch) and bedtime.

•**Troubleshooting.** If swallowing pure oil makes you gag, mix the oil with the sugar water, then divide into two doses. If you develop diarrhea, cut your oil dose in half for a few days. *If you have…*

•**Gallbladder problems**—take just one teaspoon of oil per dose…or use only the sugar water.

•**Diabetes and/or recurrent yeast infections**—use only the oil.

•**Reaching your goal.** Typically, people lose one to two pounds per week. Once you reach your target weight, reduce your dose of oil and/or sugar water to a level that allows you to maintain your weight loss. Don't stop altogether, or you may regain the weight.

■ ■ ■ ■

Diet that Reduces Need for Diabetes Meds

After four years of following a Mediterranean-style diet, 44% of patients who had been diagnosed with type 2 diabetes before initiating the diet required medication for their condition, compared with 70% of patients who followed a low-fat diet after diagnosis, say researchers from Second University of Naples, Italy. Both diets included about 30% of calories from fat,

although the fat in the Mediterranean-style diet was mainly from olive oil, whereas the low-fat diet included all types of fat.

Diet details: www.mayoclinic.com (search for "Mediterranean diet").

Mark A. Stengler, NMD, naturopathic medical doctor in private practice, La Jolla, California…adjunct associate clinical professor at the National College of Natural Medicine, Portland, Oregon…author of many books, including *The Natural Physician's Healing Therapies* and coauthor of *Prescription for Natural Cures* (both from Bottom Line Books)…and author of the *Bottom Line/Natural Healing* newsletter.

Delicious Secrets to a Longer Life

Wendy Kohatsu, MD, director of the Integrative Medicine Fellowship at the Santa Rosa Family Medicine Residency Program in Santa Rosa, California. Dr. Kohatsu is also a graduate of the Oregon Culinary Institute.

There is abundant scientific evidence on the health benefits of the so-called Mediterranean diet, which promotes the traditional eating habits of long-lived people in such countries as Greece and Italy.

Landmark research: Among the most compelling evidence is one long-term European study of healthy men and women ages 70 to 90.

It found that following the Mediterranean diet as part of an overall healthful lifestyle, including regular exercise, was associated with a more than 50% lower rate of death from all causes over a decade. Numerous studies have associated this type of eating with reduced risk for heart disease, cancer, cognitive decline, diabetes and obesity.

But many Americans are reluctant to try the Mediterranean diet for fear that it will be difficult or costly to follow because it emphasizes such foods as omega-3–rich fish, vegetables and nuts.

Surprising findings: Mediterranean eating does not increase food costs, according to a new study—and this style of eating need not be complicated.

Here, Wendy Kohatsu, MD, director of the Integrative Medicine Fellowship at the Santa Rosa Family Medicine Residency Program in Santa Rosa, California, and a chef who conducts cooking demonstrations for patients and doctors, advises on the best ways to incorporate Mediterranean eating habits into your diet.

EASY WAYS TO GET STARTED

To effectively tap into the Mediterranean diet's powerful health benefits, it's important to know exactly which foods should be eaten—and in what quantities.

Start by getting four to five daily servings of whole grains (one serving equals one-half cup of cooked quinoa, brown rice or whole-wheat pasta, for example, or one slice of whole-wheat bread) and two to three daily servings of low- or nonfat dairy products (such as yogurt, cottage cheese or milk), which are an important source of bone-protecting calcium. *In addition, be sure to consume...*

•**Oily fish.** This high-quality protein contains abundant omega-3 fatty acids, which help fight the inflammation that plays a role in cardiovascular disease, Alzheimer's disease and asthma.

Best choices: Follow the acronym SMASH—salmon (wild)...mackerel (Spanish, not king, which tends to have higher levels of mercury)...anchovies...sardines...and herring.

How much: Three ounces (the size of a deck of cards), twice a week.

Chef's secret: Drain canned sardines (the large size), grill briefly, sprinkle with fresh lemon juice and chopped parsley.

Beware: Some fish—such as shark, swordfish, golden bass (tilefish), king mackerel and albacore tuna—can be high in mercury. Avoid these. If you eat tuna, choose the "light" version, which contains less mercury than albacore tuna does.

If you don't like fish: Take a fish oil supplement (1,000 milligrams [mg] daily). Choose a brand that guarantees that no lead or mercury is present.

My favorite brands: Carlson's and Nordic Naturals.

Vegetarians can get omega-3s from flaxseed, walnuts or algae-derived *docosahexaenoic acid* (DHA) capsules (1,000 mg daily). However, non-fish food sources of omega-3s are largely in the form of *alpha-linolenic acid* (ALA), which is not as potent as the more biologically powerful fatty acids found in fish.

What most people don't know: A small but important study shows that eating oily fish with beans, such as lentils and chickpeas (also known as garbanzo beans), improves absorption of the iron found in beans.

•**Olive oil.** Olive oil contains about 77% healthful monounsaturated fats. Olive oil is also high in sterols, plant extracts that help reduce LDL "bad" cholesterol and increase HDL "good" cholesterol.

Best choice: Look for extra-virgin (or "first-press") olive oil. ("Extra virgin" means that the oil is derived from the first pressing of the olives and is the least processed)

How much: Use olive oil as your primary fat—in salad dressings, marinades and sautées. To minimize your total daily intake of fat, do not exceed 18 grams (g) to 20 g of saturated fat and 0 g of trans fat from all food sources.

Chef's secret: If you dislike the "grassy" taste of some extra-virgin olive oils, look for Spanish and Moroccan versions, which tend to be more mellow. One good choice is olive oil made from the *arbequina* olive, which has a buttery taste.

What most people don't know: Nutrients in extra-virgin olive oil may offer some pain-relieving qualities over the long term.

•**Nuts.** Like extra-virgin olive oil, nuts are high in healthful monounsaturated fats. In fact, a recent Spanish study found that a Mediterranean diet that included walnuts significantly lowered risk for heart disease.

What kinds: Besides walnuts, best choices include almonds and peanuts. Choose plain raw nuts—not salted or honey-roasted.

How much: One-quarter cup daily.

Beware: A quarter cup of nuts contains about 200 calories. Eat only a small handful daily—for example, about 23 almonds or 35 peanuts. If you're allergic to nuts, try pumpkin, sunflower or sesame seeds instead.

Chef's secret: Store nuts in your freezer to prevent them from going rancid.

•**Fruits and vegetables.** Many of the most healthful vegetables—including those of the *brassica* family, such as cabbage, kale, broccoli and cauliflower—originated in the Mediterranean area.

What kinds: Choose brightly colored fruit, such as citrus and berries, and vegetables, such as spinach, chard, watercress, beets, carrots and broccoli.

How much: Five to nine servings daily. (A serving is one-half cup of cooked vegetables, one cup of leafy greens, one medium orange or one-half cup of berries.)

Contrary to popular belief, frozen vegetables, which are often far less costly than fresh produce, are just as nutritious—if not more so because they're frozen at their peak level of freshness and don't spoil in the freezer.

Chef's secret: Cooking tomatoes in olive oil concentrates the tomatoes' levels of *lycopene*, a powerful antioxidant that has been associated with a decreased risk for prostate, lung and stomach cancers.

Junk Food "Addiction" May Be Real

Paul Kenny, PhD, associate professor, department of molecular therapeutics, Scripps Research Institute, Jupiter, Florida.
Pietro Cottone, PhD, assistant professor, pharmacology and psychiatry, and codirector, Laboratory of Addictive Disorders, Boston University School of Medicine, Boston.
Julio Licinio, MD, director, John Curtin School of Medicine Research, Australian National University, Canberra.
Nature Neuroscience.

Obese people often say they'd like to eat less but feel almost powerless to stop indulging, and now new research suggests that explanation might be all too true.

NEW STUDY

When researchers gave rats unlimited access to a calorie-laden diet of bacon, pound cake, candy bars and other junk food, the rats quickly gained a lot of weight. As they plumped up, eating became such a compulsion that they kept eating even when they knew they would receive an unpleasant electric shock to their foot if they did so.

Meanwhile, rats fed the human equivalent of a well-balanced, healthy diet—and given only limited access to the junk food—didn't gain much weight and knew enough to stop eating when they received the cue that a foot shock was imminent.

Even more startling, the researchers report, is that when they took away the junk food from the obese rats and replaced it with healthier chow, the obese rats went on something of a hunger strike. For two weeks, they refused to eat hardly anything at all.

"They went into voluntary starvation," said study author Paul Kenny, PhD, an associate professor at Scripps Research Institute in Jupiter, Florida.

The findings were originally published in *Nature Neuroscience.*

IMPLICATIONS

Researchers aren't certain if the results apply to people struggling with their weight. But they say it's possible that a diet heavy in highly rewarding foods—quite literally, sausages, cheesecake and other highly processed foods—might cause changes in the brain's reward system for satiety.

When that goes awry, the result is not only that people gain weight, but that they feel compelled to seek out more and more junk food.

LINK TO ADDICTION

When the researchers looked at the obese rats' brains, they noted there were declines in the *dopamine* D2 receptor that previous research has implicated in addiction to cocaine and heroin.

"A hallmark of drug addiction is that it leads to changes in how the brain's reward system works," Dr. Kenny said. "Addiction is a loaded term, but in this case, there is evidence of addiction-like adaptations."

When the researchers then artificially suppressed the receptor using a virus in the brains of other rats, those rats started eating junk food compulsively.

"What we think is happening is that, as you become obese over a period of time, the D2 receptors go down, which plays a major role in becoming a compulsive eater," Dr. Kenny said, noting there are almost certainly other factors at play as well.

There also could be something in the accumulated fat itself that alters the brain's reward threshold, setting up a "vicious cycle" of overeating yet not feeling satisfied, said Pietro Cottone, PhD, codirector of the Laboratory of Addictive Disorders at Boston University School of Medicine.

PREVIOUS STUDY ON DIET AND ADDICTION

An earlier study by Dr. Cottone and his colleagues suggested that weaning rats off a high-calorie diet might lead to similar, though not identical, effects in the brain as withdrawing from drugs and alcohol.

In that study, researchers gave rats a regular diet for five days and then switched them to a chocolate-flavored food that was high in sugar. When deprived of the sugary food, they showed signs of anxiety and their brains acted as if they were withdrawing from alcohol or drugs. The study was published in the *Proceedings of the National Academy of Sciences*.

EXPERT COMMENTARY

Julio Licinio, MD, director of the John Curtin School of Medicine Research at the Australian National University, called the study answers "one of the many missing pieces in the puzzle of obesity and addiction.

"Now that it is clear that areas of the brain involved in addiction and also involved in obesity, the next question is: Why do those areas become deregulated in some people, but not in others?" Dr. Licinio asked. "And importantly, why do some people who have a biological tendency towards addiction go to drugs, while others go to alcohol, and others go to food?"

info The US Centers for Disease Control and Prevention Web site, *www.cdc.gov/obesity*, has more information about obesity.

■ ■ ■ ■

Reduce Blood Sugar With Beans

Beans can help lower blood sugar and insulin levels, reducing diabetes risk.

Recommended: Eat at least one-half cup of beans per day. Garbanzo beans, also called chickpeas, have the biggest effect on blood sugar levels.

Analysis of 41 clinical trials, most focusing on people with diabetes, reported in *UC Berkeley Wellness Letter*, 500 Fifth Avenue, New York City 10010.

Are Hidden Sweeteners Killing You?

Nancy Appleton, PhD, a clinical nutritionist in San Diego. She is author, with G.N. Jacobs, of *Suicide by Sugar: A Startling Look at Our #1 National Addiction* (Square One). *www.NancyAppletonbooks.wordpress.com*.

The phrase "addictive white powder" probably makes you think of illegal drugs. Add sugar to that addictive group. Americans consume vast quantities—and suffer withdrawal symptoms when they don't get it. In fact, animal studies indicate that sugar is more addictive than cocaine.

Excess sugar has been linked to obesity, cancer, diabetes and dementia. *What to do...*

SUGAR, SUGAR EVERYWHERE

In the US, the average person consumes about 142 pounds of sugar each year, the equivalent of 48 teaspoons a day. Of that amount, 74 pounds is "added" sugar—about 23 teaspoons every day. Added sugars are defined as those sugars added to foods and beverages during processing or home preparation as opposed to sugars that occur naturally.

People who want to cut back on sweeteners usually start with the sugar bowl. They spoon less sugar on their breakfast cereal, for example, or use a sugar substitute in their coffee.

•**This doesn't help very much.** The vast majority of added sugar in the diet comes from packaged foods, including foods that we think are healthful.

For example, eight ounces of one brand of sweetened apple yogurt contains 44 grams of sugar, according to the nutrition facts label. Four grams equals one teaspoon, so that's 11 teaspoons of sugar. (You cannot tell from the label how much sugar is from the yogurt, how much is from the apples and how much is added sugar.)

Most of the added sugar that we consume comes from regular soft drinks (there are about 10 teaspoons of sugar in 12 ounces of nondiet soda), candy, pies, cookies, cakes, fruit drinks and milk-based desserts and products (ice cream, sweetened yogurt).

If you look carefully at ingredients labels, which list ingredients in order of quantity, you will see that the first two or three ingredients often are forms of sugar, but many have innocuous-sounding names, such as barley malt, *galactose* and agave nectar. Other forms of sugar include honey, maple syrup, corn syrup, corn sweetener, *dextrine*, rice syrup, glucose, *sucrose* and *dextrose*.

DANGEROUS IMBALANCE

The difference between sickness and health lies in the body's ability to maintain homeostasis, the proper balance and performance of all of the internal functions. Excess sugar disturbs this balance by impairing immunity, disrupting the production and release of hormones and creating an acidic internal environment.

It's not healthy to maintain a highly acidic state. The body tries to offset this by making itself more alkaline. It does this, in part, by removing calcium and other minerals from the bones.

Result: People who eat too much sugar experience disruptions in insulin and other hormones. They have an elevated risk for osteoporosis due to calcium depletion. They also tend to have elevated levels of cholesterol and *triglycerides* (blood fats), which increase the risk for heart disease.

BREAK THE CYCLE

A sweet tooth is not the same as a sugar addiction. We're genetically programmed to enjoy sweets on occasion. It becomes an addiction when sweet foods make you crave even more

sugar and your consumption increases over time...you experience withdrawal (in the form of mood changes, such as irritability or feeling "down") when you briefly go without sugar...and you experience intense cravings when sweet foods aren't available.

Sugar, like drugs and alcohol, is addictive because it briefly elevates levels of *serotonin*, a neurotransmitter that produces positive feelings. When a sugar addict doesn't eat sugar, serotonin declines to low levels. This makes the person feel worse than before. He/she then eats more sugar to try to feel better—and the vicious cycle goes on.

For the best chance of breaking a sugar addiction, you need to ease out of it. This usually is more effective than going cold turkey. Once you've given up sugar entirely and the addiction is past, you'll be able to enjoy small amounts of sugar if you choose, although some people find that they lose their taste for it. *How to break the habit...*

Divide sugar from all sources in half. Do this for one week.

Examples: If you've been drinking two soft drinks a day, cut back to one. Eat half as much dessert. Eat a breakfast cereal that has only half as much sugar as your usual brand, or mix a low-sugar brand in with your higher-sugar brand.

• **Limit yourself to one sweet bite.** The second week, allow yourself to have only one taste of only one very sweet food daily. Then push the dish away. This might be ice cream, sweetened cereal or a breakfast muffin. That small "hit" of sugar will prevent serotonin from dropping too low, too fast. This is important because low serotonin can make you feel so poorly, physically and emotionally, that you'll want to self-medicate with more sugar.

After about two weeks with little or no sugar, your internal chemistry, including levels of serotonin and other neurotransmitters, will stabilize at a healthier level.

• **Eat fresh fruits and vegetables.** These foods help restore the body's natural acid–alkaline balance. This will help reduce sugar cravings and promote better digestion. Be sure to substitute fresh fruits for juices. Whole fruit is better because the fiber slows the absorption of sugars into the bloodstream. The fiber also is filling, which is why few people will sit down and eat four oranges—the number you would need to squeeze to get one eight-ounce glass of juice.

Helpful: All fruits are healthful, but melons and berries have less sugar than other fruits.

■ ■ ■ ■

Warning: We're No Longer Sweet on Agave

The latest "natural" sugar alternative—agave syrup—is no healthier than refined sugar. Agave syrup is being touted as healthier than sugar and used in an increasing number of foods and beverages.

But: With 20 calories per teaspoon, it has more calories than table sugar (16 calories per teaspoon). It contains up to 90% fructose, depending on how it is processed—substantially more fructose than in high-fructose corn syrup. Agave syrup is marketed as "diabetic friendly," but there are no studies to support that it is safe for people with diabetes. Some studies even suggest that large amounts of fructose can increase diabetes risk and have other harmful effects on the heart and the liver.

UC Berkeley Wellness Letter, 500 Fifth Ave., New York City 10110.

Stevia—the Healthy "Sugar"

Mark A. Stengler, NMD, naturopathic medical doctor in private practice, La Jolla, California…adjunct associate clinical professor at the National College of Natural Medicine, Portland, Oregon…author of many books, including *The Natural Physician's Healing Therapies* and coauthor of *Prescription for Natural Cures* (both from Bottom Line Books)…and author of the *Bottom Line/Natural Healing* newsletter.

Are you wondering whether stevia, the natural, virtually calorie-free sweetener, is safe to use? Until recently, the Food and Drug Administration (FDA) allowed stevia to be labeled only as a dietary supplement—not

as a sweetener—pending further research. And now stevia is cropping up everywhere—as a sweetener (marketed under brand names such as Sweetleaf, Truvia and PureVia)…as an additive in candies…in yogurt…and in soft drinks, such as Sprite Green made by Coca-Cola and Trop50, from Tropicana, a PepsiCo subsidiary. It's no wonder that people have questions.

That the FDA has given stevia the go-ahead is a good thing, but I wonder why it took so long.

Stevia has been used in the natural-medicine community for several decades. (I've been using it to sweeten beverages and shakes for the past 20 years.)

WHAT IS STEVIA?

An herb in the chrysanthemum family, *Stevia rebaudiana*, as the species is known, grows wild in Paraguay and Brazil. Its extract is 200 to 300 times sweeter than sugar. For centuries, it was used in South America in medicinal teas and as a sweetener. In Japan, stevia has been safely used since the early 1970s as an alternative to sugar and artificial sweeteners.

Coca-Cola and a manufacturing company then teamed up to develop products using a stevia extract as a sweetener. Later, the FDA approved the use of *rebaudioside A* (Reb A), an extract of the stevia leaf, as a sweetener, giving it "generally recognized as safe" (GRAS) status, a designation for substances or chemicals that are added to foods that are considered safe by experts. I don't think it's a coincidence that in previous years, the FDA didn't think there was enough research to give stevia a nod as a sweetener, but then when the soft drink giants got behind the herb, the FDA did as well.

HEALTH BENEFITS

In studies, stevia was found to lower blood pressure in people with mild hypertension and to reduce blood glucose levels in patients with type 2 diabetes, although the amount of stevia used in the studies was higher than the amount most people use when sweetening beverages. Also, an extract from stevia leaves was found to contain antioxidant *polyphenols* (free radical–reducing compounds found in plants), including *quercitrin*, *apigenin* and *kaempferol*, which may protect against DNA damage. People who use stevia as a sweetener will get small amounts of these antioxidants. Studies have shown that stevia does not negatively affect reproductive health, as was previously believed.

MY ADVICE

Because stevia does not affect glucose levels, it is a good choice for people with diabetes. Because it is practically calorie free, it's a healthful alternative to sugar for people with weight problems—or for anyone who uses artificial sweeteners, which have been linked to health problems, such as headaches, diarrhea, seizures and even cancer.

Stevia, which can have a licorice-like aftertaste, is available in liquid, powder and tablet form.

Advantage: You can also bake with it. Follow the conversion instructions on the label of products that contain stevia powder.

Studies Prove Exercise Is The Best "Drug" Ever

James O. Hill, PhD, professor, pediatrics, and director, Center for Human Nutrition, University of Colorado at Denver.
Qi Sun, MD, ScD, research fellow, department of nutrition, Harvard School of Public Health, Boston.
Archives of Internal Medicine.

Just in case the world needed more evidence on the matter, along come four new studies verifying that exercise is indeed good for you, even critical if you plan to survive to a vigorous, hardy and tough-boned old age.

All four studies were published in the same issue of the *Archives of Internal Medicine.*

"Every bit of information [already] suggests that being active is the healthier way and being inactive is the abnormal, unhealthy way," said James O. Hill, PhD, professor of pediatrics and director of the Center for Human Nutrition at the University of Colorado at Denver. "Exercise is better than any drug or anything else we have for aging. There's no downside. If this were a drug, it would be the safest, most effective drug in the universe."

STUDY #1: MODERATE EXERCISE

The first study, based on data from the Nurses' Health Study in the United States, found that women who were more physically active during middle age were more likely to be "successful survivors" by the time they reach age 70.

Even walking and other moderate-intensity exercises lowered the risk for chronic diseases, heart trouble and cognitive impairment, the study found. That's good news for women intimidated by activities such as tennis or running.

"In terms of magnitude, walking and other moderate activities were almost equivalent to the benefit gained from more vigorous physical activity," said study lead author Qi Sun, MD, ScD, a research fellow in the department of nutrition at the Harvard School of Public Health in Boston, adding that this finding was somewhat surprising.

STUDY #2: INTENSE EXERCISE

The second study, also focusing on women, found that those who participated in a higher intensity exercise program four days a week had stronger bones and less chance of falling than women who were in a "well-being" program that included relaxation, along with flexibility, endurance and balance.

The ramped-up exercise program did not, however, reduce the risk of heart disease, said the German researchers.

STUDY #3: COGNITIVE BENEFITS

Another study out of Germany found more evidence that exercise—either moderate or high-intensity—reduced the risk for cognitive impairment in men and women over the age of 55 over a two-year follow-up period.

STUDY #4: RESISTANCE TRAINING

And, finally, researchers in British Columbia, Canada, reported that women who practiced resistance training either once or twice a week had improved cognitive skills, but only in the areas of attention and conflict resolution, compared with women who focused on balance and toning activities.

The resistance training, which included leg presses on a resistance machine, had the added benefit of strengthening the quadriceps.

Surprisingly, women performing resistance training also experienced reductions in brain volume, a phenomenon normally linked with poorer cognitive function. This paradox needs more study, the study authors said.

BOTTOM LINE

Experts pointed out that nearly all physical ailments in later life result at least partly from lack of physical activity.

Meanwhile, exercise has been shown to improve arthritis, osteoporosis, heart disease, lung disease, cancer and many more woes.

"The bottom line," said Dr. Sun, "is that, no matter what, if you can you should do some physical activity."

info For more on exercise and physical activity, visit the Web site of the US National Institute on Aging, *www.nia.nih.gov,* and search "exercise guide."

The Longer You Sit, the Shorter Your Life Span

Alpa Patel, PhD, epidemiologist, American Cancer Society, Atlanta.
Jay Brooks, MD, chairman, hematology/oncology, Ochsner Health System, Baton Rouge, Louisiana.
American Journal of Epidemiology.

The more Americans engage in one of their favorite pastimes—sitting around—the shorter their average life span, a new study suggests.

The effect remained even after researchers factored out obesity or the level of daily physical activity people were engaged in, according to a study of more than 120,000 American adults.

BACKGROUND

The salutary effect of exercise on being overweight or obese, rates of which are at an all-time high, have been well documented.

But according to background information in the study, which was published in the *American Journal of Epidemiology,* the effects of sitting per se are less well-studied. Although several studies have found a link between sitting time and obesity, type 2 diabetes, heart disease risk, and

unhealthy diets in children, few had examined sitting and "total mortality," researchers noted.

THE STUDY

The authors of the study analyzed responses from questionnaires filled out by 123,216 people (53,440 men and 69,776 women) with no history of disease who were participating in the Cancer Prevention II study conducted by the American Cancer Society.

Participants were followed for 14 years.

THE RESULTS

In the study, people were more likely to die of heart disease than cancer. After adjusting for a number of risk factors, including body mass index (BMI)—a measurement of body fat based on height and weight—and smoking, women who spent six hours a day sitting had a 37% increased risk of dying versus those who spent less than three hours a day on their bottoms. For men the increased risk was 17%.

Exercise, even a little per day, did tend to lower the mortality risk tied to sitting, the team noted. However, sitting's influence on death risk remained significant even when activity was factored in.

On the other hand, people who sat a lot and did not exercise or stay active had an even higher mortality risk: 94% for women and 48% for men.

POSSIBLE EXPLANATIONS

Study lead author Alpa Patel, PhD, an epidemiologist with the American Cancer Society, said that the obvious reason for the connection is that "the more time you spend sitting, the less total energy expended and you can have consequences such as weight gain and increased obesity." And that affects your metabolism as well as risk factors for various diseases, she said.

But there could be other biological factors beyond simply getting fatter that explain the link.

There's a burgeoning literature evolving around "inactivity physiology," Dr. Patel said. When muscles, especially those in the legs, are "sitting," they stimulate or suppress various hormones which then affect triglycerides, cholesterol and other markers for heart and other diseases, she explained.

It's just one more reason to "get up and walk," said Jay Brooks, MD, chairman of hematology/oncology at Ochsner Health System in Baton Rouge, Louisiana. "The message here is like everything in your life. People need to recognize that the things you do every day have consequences. And if you're in a job that does require sitting, that's fine, but any time you can expend energy is good. That's the key."

info For more about the healthy effects of exercise, visit the Web site of the National Cancer Institute, *www.cancer.gov*, and type "exercise" into the search box.

The Key to Strong Bones and Muscles

Vikram Khanna, MHS, PA, clinical exercise specialist, health educator and chief executive officer of Galileo Health Partners, based in Ellicott City, Maryland. He is coauthor, with Henry Brinton, of Ten Commandments of Faith and Fitness: A Practical Guide for Health and Wellness (CSS). www.GalileoHealth.net.

No form of exercise is more essential to muscle and bone strength than strength training. Strength training involves lifting weights and/or using exercise bands or tubing. Strength training improves just about every measure of health, including the ability to stay active and independent in your later years.

Many people think that strengthening is less important than walking or other forms of aerobic exercise. Not true. Aerobic exercise is important, but people with weak muscles don't have enough strength to adequately work the cardiovascular system.

Other strength-training myths…

Myth: **I'll get too bulky if I lift weights.** Just about every woman with whom I've worked has said something like, "I don't want to look like Arnold Schwarzenegger."

You won't. That kind of physique is largely determined by testosterone. Few women produce enough testosterone to produce bulky muscles. For that matter, few men will ever look like Arnold in his heyday no matter how much they work out.

Genetics has more to do with bulking up than how much you lift. I'm a good example. I've been lifting weights for more than 30 years. I weigh 150 pounds, exactly the same as when I started.

When you start strength training, about 30% of the initial improvement occurs because of improved efficiency between your muscles and central nervous system. After that, your muscles start growing—but maximizing muscle size requires specific training, which most people don't need.

Myth: **Strength training takes too much time.** Actually, it's among the most efficient forms of exercise. People are told, for example, to walk or get other forms of aerobic exercise for at least 30 minutes most days of the week. With strength training, you need to spend only about 20 minutes twice a week.

Many of my clients are busy executives. I typically advise them to go to the gym, warm up with five to 10 minutes of light cardio work (such as walking or running on a treadmill) and then strength train for 15 to 20 minutes. That's long enough to work all of the main muscle groups.

Myth: **I can get just as strong with yoga or Pilates.** No, you can't. These activities are certainly beneficial, but they provide only light-to-moderate workouts. They're useful if you're just starting to exercise after being sedentary. After that, people tend to "top out" within a few months because the exertion levels don't change.

With strength training, you can constantly change the intensity of workouts by changing the weight and/or repetitions as your strength increases. People who lift weights can double their strength within a year.

Myth: **"Free weights," such as barbells, give a better workout than machines.** They give a different workout. When you lift a barbell or dumbbell, you have to balance the weight in multiple planes. For example, you not only have to lift the weight but also have to prevent it from swaying from front to back or from side to side. This brings additional muscle groups into play.

Weight machines allow you to lift in a more controlled manner. There's no side-to-side or front-to-back movement. There is less stress on the joints, which generally is preferable for older or less fit adults. The machines isolate particular muscle groups, which can give notable gains with less stress.

■ ■ ■ ■

Secret to Better Workouts

In a recent study, mental fatigue was shown to slow workout routines.

Finding: When 16 men and women watched a film or performed a difficult computer task for 90 minutes, then rode a stationary bicycle until the point of exhaustion, they grew tired 15% sooner, on average, after the computer task than after film watching.

Theory: Mental fatigue affects the brain's perception of physical effort.

Self-defense: Exercise at a time when you are not mentally fatigued.

Samuele Marcora, PhD, senior lecturer, exercise physiology, Bangor University, UK.

Four "Steps" to Improve Your Walking Program

Danny Dreyer, *www.chiwalking.com*, a walking and running coach and a nationally ranked ultramarathon runner. He is coauthor, with his wife, Katherine, of *Chi-Walking—Fitness Walking for Lifelong Health and Energy* (Fireside).

In the US, nearly 80 million adults call themselves walkers—and half of these people consider themselves "fitness" walkers.

Problem: Most people don't know how to walk correctly for optimal health benefits. As a result, the activity is more difficult and less enjoyable than it should be, and you are at greater risk for injury.

Solution: With ChiWalking*—which is based on the traditional Chinese concept of maximizing the flow of "chi" (life energy) throughout

*ChiWalking is a registered trademark of ChiLiving, Inc.

your body—you allow gravity to help move your body in a relaxed and balanced way. This approach releases tight joints so that you are able to walk longer and more easily with less stress on your body.

By following these principles, even avid walkers can improve their technique while still gaining all the health benefits of regular walking, including increased heart strength and blood flow…greater agility and flexibility…and proven reductions in risks for serious illnesses, including diabetes, Alzheimer's and some forms of cancer. *How to get started…*

PROPER WALKING POSTURE

To perform ChiWalking, you must first learn the proper posture so that your body is supported by your bones, ligaments and tendons rather than by muscles such as those in the low back and calves. This posture reduces the workload on these muscles, making your movements more energy efficient.

Step 1: Align your feet. Make sure your feet are hip-width apart and parallel. Soften your knees so they're not locked. If your feet naturally turn out, rotate each leg toward your centerline until each foot is pointing forward to reduce the risk for lower leg injuries.

Step 2: Align your upper body. Rest one hand on your belly button and the other just under your collarbone. Lift up your chest with your upper hand while pulling down your torso with your lower hand. This straightens your upper spine and opens up your chest, allowing you to breathe more fully.

Next, lift the forefinger of your upper hand straight up and rest your chin on it to align your neck with the rest of your posture.

Step 3: Level your pelvis. To do this, slightly lift your pubic bone by contracting your lower abdominal muscles (your waistband should be parallel to the ground). This stance prevents your pelvis from moving from side to side. Too much side-to-side movement can lead to hip *bursitis* (inflammation of small sacs of fibrous tissue called *bursae*) and *iliotibial* (IT) band syndrome, a painful tightening of the IT band that runs from the hip to just below the kneecap.

Step 4: Tilt your "statue." Most people tend to lean back when walking, with their shoulders slightly behind their hips. In ChiWalking, the shoulders are held directly over the hips.

Helpful: Imagine that your upper body is one solid unit, like a statue. Now tilt your statue one-quarter-inch forward. As you do this, you'll feel your abdominal muscles engage—signaling that you're using your abdominals to stabilize your posture.

Now stand still and memorize this stance. Return to this stance whenever you are standing or walking.

LET GRAVITY DO THE WORK

Now you're ready to begin ChiWalking. After assuming your walking posture, shift your weight onto one leg, leveling your pelvis. Next, extend your unsupported leg behind you at a comfortable distance, resting your entire foot on the ground. You should find yourself in this position at the end of each stride.

Now, walk by picking up your feet instead of pushing off with your rear leg. Keep your posture tall and your shoulders forward.

As you practice this technique, keep these points in mind...

•**Always lean forward** so you'll be drawn forward by gravity.

•**Keep your pelvis level,** and don't lead with your hips.

•**Keep your knees slightly bent.** Other important points...

•**Rather than swinging your arms forward, swing your elbows to the rear** as you walk to counterbalance your forward lean. Slightly curl your fingers (to relax the hands and wrists).

•**To speed up, bend your elbows more** and swing your arms faster.

DESIGN YOUR OWN PROGRAM

When creating a walking program, ask yourself: How many days would I like to walk each week? (My recommendation is to aim for at least three days a week and at least 30 minutes per walk.) What days work best for me? What time of day do I most enjoy walking? By answering these questions, you'll develop a walking schedule that's right for you.

YOUR WALKING "MENU"

For specific health benefits, try...

•**Cardio walk.** Warm up with 10 minutes of easy walking (at a leisurely pace), then alternate one minute of faster walking and one minute of somewhat slower walking for 10 to 15 minutes. Finish with 10 minutes of easy walking.

•**Calming walk.** Walk for 10 minutes at a very slow and relaxing pace, breathing out for six steps and in for six steps. (Breathe through your nose if possible.) Next, continue breathing this way as you visualize a waterfall flowing down your spine, washing all tension from your body. Hold this focus for 20 to 30 minutes. Finish by sitting silently for several minutes, watching the world go by.

•**Energizing walk.** Walk at a relaxed pace for five minutes. As you do, practice "belly breathing."

Here's how: Force all the air out of your lungs by pulling in your belly while blowing out through pursed lips, then relax your abdominals and allow your belly and then your chest to expand, filling your lungs from the bottom.

Continue belly breathing while visualizing a stream of energy rising up the back of your spine as you inhale...and the same stream flowing down the front of your spine as you exhale. Continue for 15 to 55 minutes, depending on how much energy you need. If you follow these steps properly, the longer you walk, the more energized you will become.

Weak Feet Wreak Havoc

Katy Bowman, MS, director, Restorative Exercise Institute, Ventura, California, *www.restorativeexercise.com.*

Our poor feet just don't get what they need to be healthy and happy—and you know who pays the price, don't you? According to Katy Bowman, MS, director of the Restorative Exercise Institute in Ventura,

California, modern life is hard on our feet. An astonishing 25% of the body's bones are in the feet, says Bowman, noting "every one of them has a job to do." We actually weaken our feet by wearing shoes—encasing them this way diminishes their natural strength and abilities. Walking on artificially flat surfaces does further damage, since the foot is deprived of the natural workout it is supposed to get from varying natural terrain. The result of all this is that we're no longer really using our feet, says Bowman. By midlife, most of us have lost not only muscle strength but also the fine motor skills that our feet need to properly support us. We end up using the ankle muscles instead and, in a vicious cycle, this further weakens foot muscles.

TEST YOUR FEET

Here is an easy way to test your foot muscle strength: Try to raise your big toe, by itself, and then the second toe with it. It sounds easier than it is—few are able to do more than lift the big toe slightly off the floor. When the foot is being used properly, however, all toes should retain their ability to move independently from the other four.

WALK THIS WAY

Foot problems start in your feet—your posture and style of walking play a role, too. You may never have noticed it but, if you are like many folks, you're likely walking with your feet slightly turned out, duck-fashion. This interferes with how the muscles and ligaments in the feet, knees and hips are supposed to work. Your feet should point straight ahead in the direction you are walking.

Try this: Find straight lines on the floor (a tile joint or wood slat works well), and line up the outside edges of both feet. Keeping that alignment, walk forward. As you try to adapt to this new gait, you may initially feel like you've become pigeon-toed and knock-kneed, but if you stay with it you'll soon notice how your hips are engaged and rotating smoothly—it all feels quite facile and natural.

STRAIGHTEN UP

When standing and walking, many people tuck their pelvises under, creating weak abdominal muscles—wearing elevated heels (men's shoes, too) further amplifies this effect. Coupled with the turned-out duck-walking style, this posture puts too much weight on the front of the feet, which is what creates bunions. Instead, the weight should be back over the heels and spread among four contact points.

Try this: Picture your foot as a rectangle with four corners. Now consciously distribute your weight equally to the inside of the heel… the outside of the heel…the ball of the foot… and just below the pinkie toe.

And here's an exercise that can help you identify a forward-thrusting pelvis and poor weight placement: Stand barefoot and move your hips back until they are over your ankles—when you do this correctly, you should be able to lift all 10 toes off the floor. Do this near a chair or wall in case you need support. Once you learn what this centered position feels like, try to achieve it regularly.

WHAT TO WEAR?

Bowman advises walking shoeless often, and when footwear is required urges selection of heels that are as flat as possible. She said that an elevation of even an inch or so puts too much weight on the ball of the foot—it's like walking downhill. In fact, she recommends shoes that draw your weight back, onto the heels, such as those made by Earth, Inc. (*www.earthfoot wear.com*). Arch supports may be helpful for people with very high or very low arches, but Bowman cautions that regular use weakens foot muscles.

Bowman is ardently against flip-flops—she says they force the wearer to scrunch the toes, which can cause hammer toes and also makes proper weight distribution (those four proper contact points) impossible. Nor does she favor the new types of workout shoes that rock the foot and purposely throw off the body's balance to make leg muscles work harder—including "FitFlops" and MBTs. She says the shape of the sole creates an unnatural gait pattern that can harm the feet, knees, hips and spine.

As for high heels on dress-up occasions, she suggests women bring heels to put on at the last minute. If you wear them regularly, she advises visiting the chiropractor or an osteopathic physician to get some special attention for your feet and *sacroiliac* joints, which will help to minimize the damage.

EASY STEPS TO FEEL-GOOD FEET

The real path to pain-free feet, however, involves giving them tender, loving care in the form of regular exercises that stretch, balance and strengthen their muscles, tendons and ligaments. Start by simply spreading and lifting your toes as often as possible. *Other easy exercises…*

•**Toe lifts.** While standing, lift your big toe alone, followed in succession by each of the remaining toes…repeat in the opposite direction, big toe last.

•**Toe tucks.** Stand with one foot flat on the floor and the other pointed slightly behind you, toes tucked under so that the tops of your toes are resting on the floor. This stretches your upper foot. (This won't be easy or comfortable at first.)

•**Arch support.** Stand erect, shift your weight to the outside of one of your soles, and lift that foot's ball and toes…slowly lower the ball of the foot without letting your arch collapse, and then relax your toes back to the ground.

•**Toe spacers.** Available at nail-care salons, online and in many stores, they fit between your toes and spread them. They may feel odd at first, but then are soothing. If you use them fairly often, such as while reading or watching TV, your toes will eventually relearn their normal spreading motion.

•**Barefoot walking.** Do this as often as you can.

And here are some fast fixes for feet that hurt…

•**For instant relief of aching feet, run your foot repeatedly over a tennis ball—**start while you are in a seated position and then slowly stand, increasing the weight on your foot.

•**Elevating tired, sore feet feels great, as does wrapping them in a warm, wet towel.**

•**A gentle foot massage or a session with a well-trained reflexologist** does wonders for the heart and sole.

The 10-Minute Total Body Workout

Sean Foy, MA, exercise physiologist and behavioral and nutritional coach in Placentia, California. He is founder and president of Personal Wellness Corporation, a consulting firm that provides health and fitness testing, education seminars and wellness programs to hospitals, Fortune 500 companies and other organizations. He is author of *The 10-Minute Total Body Breakthrough* (Workman). *www.4321Fitness.com.*

Most people think that they'll benefit from aerobic exercise only when they do it for 30 to 60 minutes most days of the week.

This is old thinking. You don't need extended workouts to strengthen muscles, increase cardiovascular fitness or lower your blood pressure, blood sugar and triglycerides. You can achieve these and other fitness benefits with 10 minutes of exercise a day.

The secret is High Energy Aerobic Training (HEAT), my take on high-intensity interval training.

HOW IT WORKS

For decades, trainers argued that effective aerobic exercise required elevating your heart rate to 65% to 80% of its maximum rate and keeping it there for 30 minutes or longer.

The problem with this approach—besides the fact that few people are willing to dedicate this much time to exercise—is that it's not as effective as higher-intensity movements. For example, high-intensity interval training has been shown to not only accelerate your metabolism during exercise but also long after the workout is over. Research shows exercise is most effective when it challenges muscles, including the heart and lungs, at higher levels of intensity.

With HEAT, you alternate intense 30-second bursts of exercise with 30-second periods of moderate exercise. This means that your muscles and organs are repeatedly pushed to their limits. But because the intense phase lasts only 30 seconds, it's achievable even for those who are new to exercise.

A study at the University of New South Wales and Garvan Institute found that overweight women who alternated high-intensity with moderate activity lost three times more weight than those who exercised at a continuous pace for twice as long. The HEAT method also improves levels of *lipids* (blood fats) and increases endurance.

THE EASY
4-3-2-1 PROGRAM

I developed a program that packs every type of beneficial exercise into one 10-minute session. It's called 4-3-2-1 because it includes four minutes of aerobic exercise…three minutes of resistance exercise (such as body-weight exercises)…two minutes of core strengthening…and one minute of stretching and deep breathing.

To keep time, you can use a large wall clock with a second hand…a wristwatch with a second hand…a digital sports watch…a stopwatch…or a cell phone with a stopwatch feature.

As you advance, you can repeat sections or the entire circuit. *For beginners, I recommend the following…*

4-MINUTES OF
AEROBIC TRAINING

•**Chair jogging.** Sit upright on the edge of a sturdy chair with your arms bent at a 90° angle. Warm up by gently moving your arms and legs as though jogging slowly, raising your knees as high as you comfortably can. Do this for 30 seconds. Next, bend forward slightly from the waist, and perform the same motion, but faster. Move as quickly as you comfortably can. Maintain this brisk pace for 30 seconds. Alternate between fast and slow "running" every 30 seconds for four minutes.

3-MINUTES OF
RESISTANCE TRAINING

•**Wall squat.** Lean your back against a wall with your feet hip-width apart and your arms at your sides. Walk your feet out from the wall two to three feet. Bend your knees slightly. Keeping your back against the wall, bend your knees more and slowly slide down. Go as low as you comfortably can, but not so far that your knees extend over your toes. Try to hold the squat for one minute. *Then, without resting, do a wall push-up…*

•**Wall push-up.** Face the wall. Place your hands against the wall, with your hands a little wider than shoulder-width apart. Walk your feet

back from the wall two to three feet. Rise onto the balls of your feet, and lean into the wall. With your knees slightly bent, lower your face and chest slowly toward the wall. Go as far as you comfortably can. Now press your hands into the wall to push yourself back to the starting position. Repeat as many times as you can in one minute. *Then, without resting, move on to a stationary lunge…*

•**Stationary lunge.** Stand straight (next to the wall or a chair for balance, just in case) with your arms hanging loosely at your sides. Step backward three to four feet with your left foot. Press into the floor with the heel of your right foot (in front) and the ball of your left foot (in back). Make sure that your weight is balanced. Bend both knees, lowering your right thigh until it's parallel to the floor. "Lunge" down as low as you can—but don't let your left knee rest on the floor. Hold for 30 seconds. Return to the starting position. Reverse the sequence, and repeat with the other leg, again holding for 30 seconds.

2-MINUTES OF CORE
STRENGTHENING

•**Chair plank.** Place your hands shoulder-width apart on the back of a sturdy chair, desk or table at waist level. Keep your feet close together, and lean forward. Imagine that you're a long, strong board that's leaning against a table. While holding this position and keeping your body straight, rise onto the balls of your feet, keeping your arms extended, elbows slightly bent. *Try to hold the position for one minute. Without resting, do a chair side bend…*

•**Chair side bend.** Sit upright on the edge of a sturdy chair, with your feet hip-width apart and your knees at a 90° angle. Let your arms hang down, with your hands below your waist. Slowly lean your upper body to the left, lowering your left hand toward the floor, while keeping your buttocks firmly in place. Lean as far as you comfortably can without raising your buttocks off the chair. As you lean, let your head move in alignment with your upper body. Tighten the abdominal muscles, and stay in the side-bend position for two seconds. Return to the starting position, then repeat on the other side. Repeat as often as you can in one minute.

1-MINUTE OF STRETCHING

• **Chair forward bend.** Begin the same way you did in the exercise above but with your feet about shoulder-width apart. This time, lower your arms so that they're between your thighs. Relax your shoulders. Bend forward from the waist. Lower your chin to your chest, and let your hands drop toward the floor. Let your weight pull your upper body toward the floor. Hold this position for 30 seconds, breathing deeply throughout the stretch. *Without resting, do a chair spinal twist...*

• **Chair spinal twist.** Stay in the same chair, with your feet hip-width apart. Cross your hands and arms over your chest. Twist your upper body to the left, rotating from the waist and allowing your head and shoulders to move as one unit. Rotate as far as you can without bouncing or straining. Try to hold the stretch for 15 seconds, breathing deeply. Then repeat the movement in the other direction.

■ ■ ■ ■

Put Sleep Apnea to Bed

In a study of 31 adults with moderate obstructive sleep apnea (OSA)—temporary cessation of breathing during sleep—about half the patients performed a daily regimen of tongue and throat exercises for three months, while the others underwent a sham treatment that included deep-breathing exercises.

Result: The exercise group had a 40% improvement, on average, in OSA symptoms, compared with virtually no changes in the sham therapy group.

Theory: The exercise regimen may reposition the *hyoid* bone at the base of the tongue, reducing OSA symptoms.

If you have been diagnosed with moderate OSA: Ask your doctor to refer you to a speech therapist for tongue and throat exercises.

Geraldo Lorenzi-Filho, MD, PhD, associate professor, Sleep Laboratory, pulmonary division, University of São Paulo, Brazil.

Pain Treatment

Breathe Easy—Sinus Surgery Works

Three-quarters of patients who have undergone surgery for stubborn sinusitis saw significant and lasting improvements in their quality of life, according to recent research.

Most of the remaining 25% also saw some improvement, just not as dramatic, said Timothy L. Smith, MD, lead author of a study appearing in the journal *Otolaryngology—Head and Neck Surgery*.

"Certainly this reinforces our belief that sinus surgery increases the quality of life of patients, and I see that clinically as well as scientifically," added Jordan S. Josephson, MD, a sinus and allergy specialist in private practice in New York City. "Previous studies have been single-center studies, and this is a bigger study using multiple centers and using a fairly large population, so it further says sinus surgery is a really good thing to do if you need it."

SURGERY FOR CHRONIC SINUSITUS

Chronic rhinosinusitis (CRS) affects a sizable minority—14% to 16%—of US residents. The condition, marked by symptoms such as sinus pain and pressure, headache, stuffy nose and sneezing, can compromise quality of life more than congestive heart failure, back pain or chronic obstructive pulmonary disease, the study authors said.

Endoscopic sinus surgery has been performed in the United States since the mid-1980s, said Dr. Smith, who is director of the Oregon Sinus Center at Oregon Health & Science University in Portland.

Timothy L. Smith, MD, professor and chief, division of rhinology and sinus surgery and director, Oregon Sinus Center at Oregon Health & Science University, Portland.

Jordan S. Josephson, MD, an ear, nose and throat specialist in private practice in New York City. He is director of the New York Nasal and Sinus Center and an attending physician at Manhattan Eye, Ear and Throat Hospital, both in New York City. He is author of *Sinus Relief Now* (Perigee). *www.drjjny.com.*

Otolaryngology—Head and Neck Surgery.

It's a minimally invasive type of surgery performed with a fiber-optic scope that goes into the nostril, then basically snips away abnormal and interfering tissue while leaving normal tissue behind, Dr. Smith explained.

STUDY DETAILS

Dr. Smith and his coauthors studied 302 patients with CRS from three academic medical centers, following them for an average of a year and a half after their surgery.

"These were patients who have chronic sinusitis so, by definition, they have at least three months of symptoms and they have evidence of an ongoing inflammation or infection of their nose and sinuses on either a CT scan or an examination of the nose and sinuses," Dr. Smith said.

Following the surgery, about 76% of patients had "clinically significant" improvement in quality of life, as measured by various validated scales.

Patients with worse disease at the outset seemed to fare the best after the procedure, as did those undergoing surgery for the first time. This second finding is probably explained by the fact that people going for second or further surgeries were probably sicker to begin with, Dr. Josephson said.

ADVICE

"I don't think it means everyone with CRS should consider surgery. They should try medical therapy, and if medical therapy fails and the surgeon feels that their problem can be helped by surgery, then surgery would be a good tool for them to use," Dr. Josephson said. "Some people with milder disease may even get cured. This is a wonderful renewed hope of feeling better."

info For more on sinusitis, visit the Web site of the US National Institute of Allergy and Infectious Diseases, *www3.niaid.nih.gov/topics/sinusitis/.*

■ **More from Jordan S. Josephson, MD...**

New Help for Chronic Sinus Infections

Chronic sinusitis is the most common long-term disease in the US. Even though more than half of all cases of sinusitis clear up on their own within two weeks, about 40 million Americans develop the chronic variety.

What happens: The sinuses, four pairs of cavities in the skull that filter and warm air as it passes through the nose on its way to the lungs, are lined with mucus-producing tissue. The tissue typically produces more than a quart of mucus a day, which drains through tiny holes into the back of the throat. When these holes are blocked, mucus can't drain properly. The holes often become blocked when the tissues swell during an allergy flare-up or an upper-respiratory infection.

Result: Facial pain, headache, fatigue, nasal and ear congestion, postnasal drip, cough, snoring, nosebleeds and a reduced sense of smell or taste, along with other coldlike symptoms. As mucus accumulates, it provides an optimal environment for bacterial or fungal growth. The resulting infection can further irritate and inflame sinus tissues.

DO ANTIBIOTICS WORK?

Sinusitis is defined as "chronic" when it lasts for more than four weeks or keeps coming back. For many patients, sinusitis is a lifelong disease. The symptoms may come and go, but the underlying problems persist. Patients need to manage it daily just as they would any other chronic disease, such as diabetes or arthritis. A total cure is unlikely—but with the right medical treatment, patients can expect a significant improvement in quality of life.

A short-term course of antibiotics usually will eliminate a case of acute sinusitis (assuming that the infection is bacterial), but this rarely works for chronic sinusitis.

Reason: Most cases are multifactorial. Patients with a bacterial infection might simultaneously harbor viruses or mold, organisms that aren't affected by antibiotics. A Mayo Clinic study found that 93% of all chronic sinus disease cases are caused by fungus (mold) found in the nasal passages. The mold can cause persistent infection. Even in the absence of infection, mold spores can stimulate an allergic reaction that causes persistent congestion.

Antibiotics can make a difference in patients with chronic sinusitis, but only when they are used for three to eight weeks. The same is true of anti-fungal sprays or oral drugs. Long-term therapy (up to three months) usually is required.

Recommended: Regardless of the underlying cause, most patients can get some relief with prescription steroid nasal sprays. Decongestants (oral or spray) also can be helpful but should not be used for more than 48 hours without your doctor's OK. Nasal irrigation is among the best ways to promote mucus drainage and relieve sinusitis symptoms.

DAILY CARE

Every patient with a history of chronic sinusitis needs to be alert to lifestyle factors that increase congestion and symptom flare-ups. *Important…*

•**Track your diet.** Even patients without clear-cut food allergies may find that they produce more mucus when they eat certain foods, such as dairy or foods with gluten or certain sugars, including high-fructose corn syrup. I advise them to keep a food diary for a month or more. Write down everything that you eat and drink, and make a note when your sinuses feel worse. When you suspect that a certain food is causing problems, give it up for a few weeks and see if you feel better.

•**Take control of allergies.** They are among the main triggers for sinusitis. When you have an allergy flare-up—whether from pollen, animal dander or anything else—treat it promptly with an antihistamine to keep mucus from building up.

•**Blow your nose gently.** Blow one nostril at a time. This is more effective than blowing both at once.

•**Clean your house and car.** Any area that's moist, such as the bathroom or under the refrigerator, can harbor mold spores that irritate sinus tissues. Clean these areas well with soap and water or a commercial mold-killing solution. Don't neglect your car. Cars trap humidity as well as heat, both of which encourage mold growth. Keep the seats and dashboard clean.

SINUS SURGERY

Some patients may require surgery to restore normal drainage. *Endoscopic sinus surgery* (sinoscopy) is now the standard approach. A thin tube is inserted through the nostrils. Surgical instruments are used to remove blockages and sometimes to remove bone to enlarge the sinus openings. The procedure is done in an operating-room setting. Typically, you are home that night and back to work the next day with minimal discomfort that rarely requires more than Tylenol.

Recently, surgeons have added *balloon sinuplasty* to the procedure. A guide wire is used to position a deflated balloon inside the sinus openings. Then the balloon is inflated, which enlarges the openings and promotes better drainage, without removing tissue. It is appropriate in only about 10% or fewer of total cases—usually those involving a less severe condition.

Important: Most patients improve significantly after surgery, but few achieve a total remission of symptoms. Most still will need occasional help from steroid nasal sprays, decongestants, etc.

NASAL CLEANSE

Irrigating the nose once or twice daily is among the best ways to improve sinus drainage. This helps relieve symptoms, and it also can prevent sinusitis from getting started.

A neti pot (available at most pharmacies and health food stores) is an effective irrigation tool. It's an ancient Indian device that has a tapered conical tip at the spout end. You also will need saline solution. You can buy prepared sterile saline from most pharmacies, but large quantities may require a prescription from your doctor (some insurance companies will cover this). Or you can make your own saline. Bring eight ounces of distilled water to a boil, add one-quarter teaspoon of salt to the water, and let the mixture cool to room temperature.

Fill the pot with the cooled saline. Tilt your head to one side, and gently insert the spout of the neti pot into the raised upper nostril. Continue to breathe through your mouth, and slowly pour the saline into your upper nostril. The saline should pour through the upper nostril and out the other lower nostril into the sink (you also can try this in the shower).

When you're done, compress one nostril at a time by placing pressure on it with your finger

243

and then blow your other nostril by exhaling firmly several times.

Then reverse the tilt of your head and repeat the process on the other side by pouring saline into the other nostril.

Say Good-Bye to Your Chronic Headaches

Alexander Mauskop, MD, neurologist and director of the New York Headache Center in New York City (*www.nyheadache.com*). He is the author of *What Your Doctor May Not Tell You About Migraines* (Warner).

Of all the medical conditions that send patients to their doctors, chronic headaches (including migraines) are among the least likely to be treated effectively.*

Problem: Most chronic headache sufferers would like to simply pop a pill to relieve their pain. Although there are many helpful medications, each can have side effects and is designed to *reduce* headache pain rather than *prevent* it.

Solution: After treating thousands of headache patients, I devised a natural "triple therapy" that helps prevent migraines from developing in the first place.

Latest development: Now that I've prescribed this therapy for more than 15 years, I have added other treatments that complement the original program.

What you need to know...

WHEN THE PAIN WON'T GO AWAY

Approximately 15 million Americans have chronic headaches (occurring on at least 15 days a month).

The most common forms, in order of prevalence, are tension-type headaches (head pain caused by tight muscles—for example, in the neck—often due to stress)...and migraines (throbbing head pain accompanied by other symptoms, such as nausea or dizziness, and sometimes preceded by light sensitivity and visual disturbance known as an "aura").

*To find a headache specialist or headache support group near you, contact the National Headache Foundation (888-643-5552, *www.headaches.org*).

MY NATURAL THERAPY

Doctors don't know the exact cause of migraines, but the most popular theory focuses on disturbances in the release of pain-modulating brain chemicals, including the neurotransmitter *serotonin*.

In reviewing the medical literature, I found several references to the mineral *magnesium*, which has been shown to prevent migraines by helping open up blood vessels in the brain. Studies indicate that half of all migraine sufferers are deficient in this mineral.

Within a short time, I also discovered several references that supported the use of *riboflavin* (vitamin B-2), which plays a role in energy production in brain cells...and the herb *feverfew*, which promotes the health of blood vessels.

My advice: Each day, take a total of 400 milligrams (mg) of magnesium (as magnesium oxide or in a chelated form—if one form causes diarrhea, try the other)...400 mg of riboflavin... and a total of 100 mg of feverfew, divided in two doses with meals. Many people take this therapy indefinitely. Ask your doctor about the appropriate duration of treatment for you.

Caution: Feverfew may interfere with your blood's ability to clot, so consult your doctor before taking this herb. Riboflavin may turn your urine bright yellow, but the change is harmless.

FOR EVEN MORE PAIN RELIEF

• **Coenzyme Q10 (CoQ10)** is a substance that, like riboflavin, is believed to fight migraines by boosting energy production in brain cells. Research has shown that 100 mg of CoQ10 three times a day reduces migraine frequency.

My advice: Take a total of 300 mg of CoQ10 daily, in one or two doses.

• **An extract from the root of the butterbur plant** is another supplement that has shown promise as a remedy for migraines. In one study, 75 mg of butterbur taken twice daily for four months helped reduce the frequency of migraine attacks.

Although the exact mechanism of action is unclear, the herb might help reduce inflammatory substances in the body that can trigger headaches.

Butterbur is sold in the US under the brand name Petadolex (888-301-1084, *www.petadolex.com*).

My advice: Take a total of 150 mg of butterbur daily, in one or two doses.

OTHER HELPFUL STRATEGIES

All the natural therapies described earlier help prevent migraines, but you're likely to achieve even better results if you adopt a "holistic" approach that includes the following steps. These strategies also help guard against chronic tension headaches but are overlooked by many doctors. *My advice…*

•**Get regular aerobic exercise.** Exercise supplies more blood to the brain and boosts levels of feel-good hormones known as *endorphins*, which help fight migraines. Physical activity also helps release muscle tension that contributes to tension-type headaches.

Scientific evidence: In data collected from 43,770 Swedes, men and women who regularly worked out were less likely to have migraines and recurring headaches than those who did not exercise.

Helpful: Do some type of moderately intense aerobic activity for at least 30 minutes five times a week.

•**Use relaxation techniques.** A mind–body approach, such as progressive muscle relaxation (deliberately tensing then releasing muscles from toe to head)…guided imagery (in which you create calm, peaceful images in your mind)…or breathing exercises (a method of slow inhalation and exhalation), can ease muscle tension and relax blood vessels to help prevent migraines and tension headaches.

Also helpful: Biofeedback, which involves learning to control such involuntary functions as skin temperature, heart rate or muscle tension while sensors are attached to the body, helps prevent migraines and tension headaches. Biofeedback usually can be learned in about eight sessions and should be practiced daily by migraine and tension headache sufferers. To find a biofeedback practitioner near you, consult the Biofeedback Certification Institute of America (866-908-8713, *www.bcia.org*).

•**Try acupuncture.** There's good evidence that this centuries-old needling technique can reduce the severity and frequency of migraines and tension headaches.** It typically requires at least 10 sessions to see benefits. Ask your health insurer whether acupuncture is covered. If not, each session, typically an hour long, will cost $50 to $100, depending on your location.

If you feel that you are developing a migraine or tension headache: Perform a simple *acupressure* treatment on yourself to help relieve headache pain.

What to do: Place your right thumb on the webbing at the base of your left thumb and index finger, and your right index finger on the palm side of this point. Gently squeeze and massage this area, using small circular motions, for one to two minutes. Repeat on the right hand.

**To find an acupuncturist near you, go to the National Certification Commission for Acupuncture and Oriental Medicine Web site (*www.nccaom.org*) and click on "Find a Practitioner."

Illustration by Shawn Banner.

■ ■ ■ ■

Oxygen Helps Cluster Headaches

Cluster headaches involve excruciating bouts of pain. *Sumatriptan* (Imitrex) injections can cause side effects (nausea, chest pain).

New finding: 78% of patients got adequate or complete pain relief, with no side effects, within 15 minutes of treatment with high-flow 100% oxygen delivered via a face mask…versus 20% relief with placebo (high-flow air). High-flow oxygen is available but underused—so talk to your neurologist.

Peter J. Goadsby, MD, PhD, neurologist and director, Headache Center, University of California, San Francisco, and coauthor of a study of 76 people.

■ ■ ■ ■

The Secret to Fewer Headaches

When combined with painkiller medication, acupuncture reduced the number of days people had migraine or tension headaches by 40% or more, compared with painkiller use alone.

Referrals: American Association of Acupuncture and Oriental Medicine, 866-455-7999, *www.aaaomonline.org.*

Klaus Linde, MD, senior researcher, Technical University of Munich, Germany, and lead author of two analyses of studies involving about 6,800 people.

No More Foot Pain!

Sherri Greene, DPM (doctor of podiatric medicine). She has practiced conventional and holistic podiatric medicine in New York City for the past 12 years. Her treatment modalities include reflexology, herbal medicine and essential oils. *www.drsherrigreen.com.*

Many people downplay the significance of foot problems. But that's a mistake. A foot problem may really mean that you have an undetected medical condition. For example, numb or painful feet can be a red flag for the damaged blood vessels and nerves that can occur with diabetes or peripheral arterial disease (a circulatory problem that causes reduced blood flow to the limbs). Foot problems also may be associated with seemingly unrelated ailments, such as hip or back pain.

An effective way to identify the root cause of foot pain is to take a whole-body (holistic) approach that often can replace conventional treatments.* *Holistic approaches to everyday foot problems...*

•**Go barefoot.** After spending day after day confined in tight or ill-fitting shoes, the muscles of the foot can weaken—the same way an arm loses muscle tone when encased in a cast. Going barefoot in your home allows your feet to stretch, strengthen and find their natural alignment.

Caution: People with diabetes should *never* go barefoot—this medical condition commonly causes nerve damage in the feet, which makes it difficult to feel cuts or other injuries. Also, do not walk barefoot on marble or other potentially slippery floors or if you have balance or vision problems. In all of these cases, wear sturdy slippers or similar footwear that protect your feet and provide good traction.

*To find a holistic podiatrist near you, consult TheHolisticOption.

•**"Open" your toes.** This gentle form of stretching can improve flexibility of the tendons, release tension and stimulate blood flow to the feet and the rest of the body.

It can help prevent foot ailments, such as *hammertoe* (in which the end of a toe curls downward) and *Morton's neuroma* (inflammation of a nerve between the toes that causes pain in the ball of the foot), and is useful for people suffering from painful foot conditions such as *plantar fasciitis* (described below).

What to do: Lace your fingers between each toe (imagine holding hands with your foot)...or use physical separators, such as pedicure toe dividers (available at drugstores) or gel-filled YogaToes (available at YogaPro, 877-964-2776, *www.yogapro.com*). Open your toes for five to 30 minutes at least five days per week.

Caution: People with rigid bunions should not use YogaToes—they may strain the ligaments and cause additional pain.

FOR COMMON FOOT PROBLEMS

If you suffer from frequent foot pain, you may have one of these common foot problems...

•**Bunion.** No one knows exactly what causes this swollen, painful outgrowth of bone at the base of the big toe. Heredity plays a role, but podiatrists also suspect excess body weight and ill-fitting shoes.

Conventional treatment: Store-bought or custom-fitted orthotic shoe inserts to help reduce pressure on the bunion...and/or surgery to correct the position of the toe.

Holistic therapy: To relieve inflammation, massage the foot with peppermint, lemongrass, wintergreen or lavender oil. To make your own massage oil, start with a half teaspoon of a "carrier," such as almond oil or vitamin E oil, and add two to three drops of the healing oil. Warm the oil mixture in the palm of your hand before massaging your feet for five to 10 minutes daily.

•**Plantar fasciitis.** This condition is inflammation of the thick band of tissue that connects the heel to the base of the toes. The pain—often excruciating—is most pronounced under the heel.

Anything that stresses the bottom of the foot can cause plantar fasciitis, including being overweight, suddenly increasing the amount of exercise you do or wearing shoes without arch support.

Conventional treatment: Cortisone injections to relieve inflammation…custom-fitted orthotic shoe inserts to more evenly distribute pressure on the foot.

Holistic therapy: Massage the arch of the foot by rolling a squash ball (a tennis ball is too large) on the floor from heel to toes. Use pressure that is firm enough to move the tissues without causing pain.

This massage reduces inflammation by moving accumulated acids out of tissues. Perform it daily until symptoms resolve. *For plantar fasciitis, also perform this stretch twice daily on a regular basis…*

What to do: Take one large step forward and bend your forward knee. Press the heel of the back leg onto the floor. Hold for 10 to 30 seconds, then switch leg positions. For added stretch, bend the back knee, as well.

Important: If your foot problems affect your ability to walk or don't heal or improve after two weeks of home care, see a podiatrist.

Illustration by Shawn Banner.

Glucosamine Ineffective For Some Low-Back Pain

Philip Wilkens, MChiro, research fellow, orthopedic department, University of Oslo, Norway.

Andrew L. Avins, MD, MPH, research scientist, Division of Research, Kaiser Permanente Northern California, professor of medicine, epidemiology & biostatistics, University of California, San Francisco.

Andrew Sherman, MD, associate professor and vice-chair, department of rehabilitation medicine, University of Miami Leonard M. Miller School of Medicine.

The Journal of the American Medical Association.

The popular supplement glucosamine offers little or no relief for sufferers of chronic lower back pain caused by osteoarthritis, a new study finds.

The Norwegian trial seems to be another knock against glucosamine, with other recent studies showing similar results.

BACKGROUND

Osteoarthritis affects more than 20 million Americans. That number is expected to increase, the researchers note. Glucosamine is a common over-the-counter treatment for osteoarthritis, even though its use has been controversial.

For example, a University of Pittsburgh study presented at a rheumatologists' meeting found the supplement did not prevent loss of cartilage in osteoarthritic knees, while studies published in *Arthritis & Rheumatism* and the *Annals of Internal Medicine* found glucosamine had little or no effect on arthritis of the knee and hips, respectively.

NEW STUDY FINDINGS

For the study, lead researcher Philip Wilkens, MChiro, a research fellow in the orthopedic department at the University of Oslo and his team randomly assigned 250 patients with chronic back pain and degenerative lumbar osteoarthritis to 1,500 milligrams (mg) daily of glucosamine or an inactive placebo.

The patients' pain was measured using the Roland Morris Disability Questionnaire at 6 weeks, then again at 3, 6 and 12 months. In addition, the researchers evaluated the patients' self-reported quality of life.

At the start of the 6-month trial, patients taking glucosamine scored 9.2 on the pain scale while the patients taking placebo scored 9.7, the researchers note. At the 6-month point, both groups scored 5.0, and after one year the glucosamine group scored 4.8 while the placebo group scored 5.5, Wilkens's group found.

However, the small differences in scores at six months or one year were not statistically significant, the researchers say. Nor were minor differences in quality of life between the two groups deemed significant.

The new report was published in *The Journal of the American Medical Association.*

IMPLICATIONS

The bottom line, according to Wilkens: "People with chronic low back pain and degenerative osteoarthritis will not benefit more from glucosamine than placebo for treating their back problem."

"The study answers the question: 'I have suffered low back pain for a long time (more than 6 months), will a 6-month intake of glucosamine help me?' "And the answer according to this study is no."

On the up side, "glucosamine appears safe to use," he added. "And more research is needed to answer if glucosamine is beneficial to prevent chronic low back pain or have benefits in longer term, like five to 10 years."

EXPERT COMMENTARY

Andrew L. Avins, MD, MPH, a scientist in the division of research at Kaiser Permanente Northern California and the author of an accompanying journal editorial, said that, "from a clinical standpoint, the study demonstrates that glucosamine does not appear to be better than placebo for patients with chronic low back pain and spinal arthritis."

However, the study found no ill effects from taking the supplement.

So, patients who take glucosamine and feel that it is helping them should be reassured that it's at least not harmful, said Dr. Avins, who is also professor of medicine, epidemiology & biostatistics at the University of California, San Francisco.

"The larger implications [of this study] are that we still know very little about how to help most patients with chronic low back pain, and we need much more careful, directed research to help make progress in providing relief to patients with back pain," he added.

Even though back pain is an incredibly important public health and quality of life problem, it suffers from insufficient attention and research funding, Dr. Avins believes. "In the US, we spend far more on treatments of little or questionable value than we spend on research to find effective therapies; it's a poor use of scarce health-care resources," he said.

Andrew Sherman, MD, an associate professor and vice-chair of the department of rehabilitation medicine at the University of Miami Leonard M. Miller School of Medicine, agreed that the findings should dissuade doctors from recommending glucosamine to patients with

back pain. However, he added "this [study] is not going to stop people from trying it," and the finding does not mean that glucosamine won't work for other forms of arthritis.

info For more information on arthritis, visit the Web site of the National Library of Medicine, *www.nlm.nih.gov/medlineplus/arthritis.html.*

■ ■ ■ ■

Yoga Better than Pills for Low-Back Pain

Patients with mild-to-moderate chronic low-back pain took 90-minute classes twice weekly of *Iyengar* yoga, doing 31 postures that relax and align the spine.

After 24 weeks: The yoga group reported significantly better function, mood and pain relief than patients who got standard care, including drugs.

Kimberly Williams, PhD, research assistant professor, department of community medicine, West Virginia University, Morgantown, and leader of a study of 90 people.

Real Relief for Back, Neck and Leg Pain

Mitchell Yass, physical therapist, founder and director of PT2 Physical Therapy & Personal Training in Farmingdale, New York, *www.mitchellyass.com.* He is author of *Overpower Pain: The Strength-Training Program that Stops Pain Without Drugs or Surgery* (Sentient).

Millions of people suffer from chronic back, neck and leg pain. Doctors are likely to diagnose arthritis or a disk problem—but in many cases, that diagnosis is wrong. In my work as a physical therapist, I've found that much of joint and muscle pain can instead be traced to muscle imbalances, created when one muscle group gets overworked and becomes thick and shortened. A muscle must be at optimal length to contract properly, so a disproportioned muscle is not only weak…but it also affects the opposite muscle, which compensates by becoming overly long.

These weak, imbalanced muscles pull nearby joints—and other muscles—out of alignment, and that can lead to painful irritation and inflammation. This commonly occurs with the thigh muscles, affecting the low back and knees, and the shoulder and upper back muscles, affecting the neck. By bringing these muscles back into balance, you can realign these joints and relieve chronic pain.

HOW TO GET RELIEF

To get help for the most common areas of pain, do either the lower-body or upper-body exercises given here two to three times a week, depending on your own area of pain.*

Or you can do all four exercises—to ensure that your posture will improve and that you will feel stronger and more agile. These exercises use hand weights and resistance bands, which are available at sporting-goods stores and on-line. Choose enough resistance so that your muscles feel tired after 10 repetitions.

LOW-BACK PAIN AND/OR KNEE PAIN

Doctors love to blame low-back pain on disk problems, but the real cause in most cases stems from the fact that we all work our front thigh muscles (*quadriceps*) much more than the backs of our thighs (*hamstrings*) and *gluteal* muscles (buttocks). As a result, the front thigh muscles get bigger and shorter. This pulls the front of the pelvis downward, causing the low back to arch. Over time, this causes the low-back muscles to become short and weak, leaving them susceptible to painful strains and spasms. Shortened quadriceps also lead to chronic knee pain because they pull up on the kneecap, causing friction between bone surfaces and inflammation in the knee joint.

Solution: Stretch your quadriceps and strengthen your hamstring and gluteal muscles. This will lengthen and strengthen your low-back muscles and take pressure off your knees.

To stretch quadriceps: First, loop a non-stretchy belt (such as one made of leather) around one ankle. Then lie flat on your back along the edge of a bed so that the leg with the belt looped around the ankle hangs off the bed.

*Always consult your doctor before starting any new exercise program.

The other leg should be bent with the foot flat on the mattress. Pull the belt in toward your buttocks so that your knee bends. Continue pulling until you feel a pleasant stretch in the front of your thigh. Hold for 20 to 30 seconds, release, then repeat the stretch two or three times.

To strengthen the hamstrings and gluteals: Holding a dumbbell in each hand, stand with your feet slightly wider than your shoulders, legs straight. (Practice your form first without dumbbells...then when you can do the exercise properly, add dumbbells heavy enough so that you feel the hamstrings working.) With palms facing your thighs, slowly run the dumbbell down the front of the legs, as far as the knee, the mid-shin or the ankle, until you feel a pleasant tension in your hamstrings. Keep your back straight and your head in line with your back. Slowly return to starting position. Do three sets of 10.

NECK PAIN AND HEADACHES

Most neck pain and stiffness occurs because the muscles in the chest, the front of the shoulders and the biceps become overworked and shortened. Meanwhile, their opposing muscles in the upper back and back of your shoulders become overstretched and weak, creating a stooped, "forward-shoulder" posture. This leaves the muscles that support the head too weak to do their job, causing neck pain and headaches.

Solution: Strengthen the muscles between your shoulder blades and your shoulder muscles (*posterior deltoids*). This will pull your shoulders back, shortening and strengthening the muscles that support your head.

To strengthen the muscles between the shoulder blades: Take a resistance band and make a knot in the middle. (Practice the move first without a band, and then choose a strong enough band.) Place the knot over the top of a door, then shut the door so the knot is trapped on the other side and the ends of

the band hang straight down like handles. Place a chair facing the door, close enough so that when sitting, you can take an end of the band in each hand with your arms straight out in front of you. Grab the ends of the band and, keeping your arms at shoulder height, bend your elbows and bring them straight back, so that your shoulder blades squeeze together. Return to starting position. Do three sets of 10.

To strengthen the posterior deltoids: Stand with your feet a little more than shoulder width apart, holding a dumbbell in each hand in front of your thighs. Bend your knees and elbows slightly. Slowly lift both arms out sideways until they are about six inches to the sides of your thighs. Stop at the point just before your shoulder blades start squeezing together. Return slowly to starting position. Do three sets of 10.

Illustrations by Shawn Banner.

Breakthrough Patches Relieve Pain Without Drugs

Mark A. Stengler, NMD, naturopathic medical doctor in private practice, La Jolla, California…adjunct associate clinical professor at the National College of Natural Medicine, Portland, Oregon…author of many books, including *The Natural Physician's Healing Therapies* and coauthor of *Prescription for Natural Cures* (both from Bottom Line Books)… and author of the *Bottom Line/Natural Healing* newsletter.

A few months ago, 70-year-old Louise, one of my patients, was in an automobile accident. She wasn't seriously injured, but her back hurt, so her husband took her to a hospital emergency room. She waited for an hour and a half to see a doctor, then gave up and went home. She called me to tell me what had happened. At length, we discussed the nature of her back pain, which sounded like muscle strain. We agreed that her injury was minor and there was no need for immediate medical attention. Relieved that her injury was not severe, Louise went on to mention a new kind of pain patch that she had heard about and recently purchased to ease the occasional ache or pain.

Louise and I had already had several discussions about these pain patches. Called IceWave patches, they were created by a company called LifeWave (*www.LifeWave.com*) for drug-free pain relief.

Patients always are bringing new and interesting products into my office for me to look over. Louise had brought the patches to me, as had several of my other patients, many of whom reported good results after using them.

Louise and I agreed that she should try the patches for her back pain. She called me a few days later—and reported that when she applied the patches to her back, she felt much better in 30 minutes. She continued using the patches during the next several days and went on to make a full recovery without flooding her body with pain medication.

Louise had a phenomenal response to the pain patches. I also have seen a very high percentage of people with arthritis and musculoskeletal problems who respond well to these patches. The patches seem most helpful when used by patients for pain and stiffness related to muscle trauma and for problems such as back spasms or a stiff neck.

INSIDE THE PATCH

There are many types of pain patches on the market. Most release a type of anesthetic into the skin that numbs the area. The IceWave patch is not a medicated patch that contains pain-relief drugs. It contains no medication, and its ingredients never cross the skin or enter the body. According to the manufacturer, the IceWave patches work by emitting energy frequencies that are stimulated by the body's heat. These frequencies, they say, affect the electromagnetic field of nearby cells, reducing pain and inflammation in much the same way that acupressure or acupuncture needles do when applied to various body parts. When the IceWave patches are placed over a painful body part, the area around the patches becomes several degrees cooler as measured by thermography, a type of infrared imaging technique. This indicates that the inflammatory response in that area is being inhibited.

I believe that there is more to learn about how these noninvasive, nonmedicinal patches do the job, but my patients have seen good results.

WHERE TO PLACE THEM

IceWave patches are used in pairs. One patch is placed on the point where the pain is most noticeable. The other is placed a few inches away from it—and is held in place for about 10 seconds to see if there is any noticeable relief. If not, the second patch is moved in a clockwise circle around the other patch (repeating the 10-second test) until the spot that brings maximum pain relief is located.

Some people don't experience any pain relief at all from IceWave patches.

Helpful: Drink plenty of water because being dehydrated seems to prevent the patches from working properly.

There are other ways to place the patches, depending on the nature of the pain. Knee pain, for example, can be treated by placing one patch on the left side of the knee and one on the right. If that doesn't work, the patches can be placed on the same side of the knee, a few inches apart from one another. If you have pain in two different parts of the body, four patches (two sets) can be used at the same time.

LifeWave recommends leaving the patches on for 12 hours, after which they should be discarded. It's generally recommended that users apply the patches in the morning and remove them before going to bed.

Some patients experience immediate relief, while others feel less pain after three to five days of using the patches. The manufacturer claims that the patches can be used safely for longer than five days, but if at any time you feel discomfort, remove them. The patches are non-toxic, and there are no reports of safety issues or side effects from them. The patches are not recommended for use by children or pregnant women, because they have not been tested in these populations.

The IceWave patches are sold through regional distributors and cannot be purchased from Life-Wave directly. To find a distributor in your area, call 866-420-6288 or go to *www.LifeWave.com*

(click on "Customer Service" at the bottom of the page).

I have no financial interest in this company or its products.

Trick Your Body into Healing Itself

Allan Magaziner, DO, director of Magaziner Center for Wellness in Cherry Hill, New Jersey, and a clinical instructor at University of Medicine and Dentistry of New Jersey in New Brunswick. *www.drmagaziner.com*.

A medical procedure that "tricks" the body into healing itself, *prolotherapy* treats acute or chronic pain from damaged ligaments, tendons and cartilage. Some studies show significant improvement in patients with injuries or arthritis, especially in the joints, back, neck or jaw. Prolotherapy is used as a first-line therapy or when other treatments fail.

• **How it works.** A physician injects a solution, typically of dextrose (a sugar) and lidocaine (an anesthetic), into the painful area. This provokes minor, temporary inflammation…causing the body to send more blood and nutrients to the spot…which hastens healing.

• **What to expect.** Each session lasts 15 to 30 minutes and includes from one to 20 injections, depending on the areas treated. Patients experience slight discomfort during injection and mild soreness for several days after. Minor pain might need one session…severe pain might require 10 sessions spread over several months.

Cost: $100 to $400 per session. Because prolotherapy is considered experimental, insurance seldom covers it.

• **Cautions.** Your doctor may advise you to temporarily reduce or discontinue use of anti-inflammatory drugs—aspirin, *ibuprofen* (Motrin), *naproxen* (Aleve)—while undergoing prolotherapy. *Acetaminophen* (Tylenol) is okay. If you take blood thinners or other drugs, tell your doctor—extra precautions may be warranted.

• **How to find a practitioner.** Prolotherapy should be administered by a physician trained in the procedure—preferably through the American

Association of Orthopaedic Medicine (800-992-2063, *www.aaomed.org*) or the Hackett Hemwall Foundation (*www.hacketthemwall.org*). Visit these Web sites for referrals.

Yes, You Can Conquer Nagging Pain for Good!

Bonnie Prudden, who helped create the President's Council on Youth Fitness in 1956 and has been one of the country's leading authorities on exercise therapy for more than five decades. In 2007, she received the Lifetime Achievement Award from the President's Council on Physical Fitness and Sports. Based in Tucson, Arizona, she is the author of 18 books, including *Pain Erasure: The Bonnie Prudden Way* (M. Evans).

Can you imagine living well into your 90s and being able to eliminate virtually all of the aches and pains that you may develop from time to time?

Ninety-six-year-old Bonnie Prudden, a longtime physical fitness advocate, stays pain free—even though she has arthritis that led to two hip replacements—by using a form of *myotherapy* ("myo" is Greek for muscle) that she developed more than 30 years ago.

Now: Tens of thousands of patients have successfully used this special form of myotherapy, which is designed to relieve "trigger points" (highly irritable spots in muscles) that develop throughout life due to a number of causes, such as falls, strains or disease.

By applying pressure to these sensitive areas and then slowly releasing it, it's possible to relax muscles that have gone into painful spasms, often in response to physical and/or emotional stress.

A simple process: Ask a partner (a spouse or friend, for example) to locate painful trigger points by applying his/her fingertips to parts of your body experiencing discomfort—or consult a practitioner trained in myotherapy.*

*To find a practitioner of Bonnie Prudden's myotherapy techniques, go to *www.bonnieprudden.com* or call 800-221-4634. If you are unable to find a practitioner near you, call local massage therapists and ask whether they are familiar with the techniques.

If you're working with a partner, let him know when a particular spot for each body area described in this article is tender.

Pressure should be applied for seven seconds (the optimal time determined by Prudden's research to release muscle tension) each time that your partner locates such a spot.

On a scale of one to 10, the pressure should be kept in the five- to seven-point range—uncomfortable but not intolerable.

The relaxed muscles are then gently stretched to help prevent new spasms.

If you prefer to treat yourself: Use a "bodo," a wooden dowel attached to a handle, and a lightweight, metal "shepherd's crook" to locate trigger points and apply pressure. Both tools are available at 800-221-4634, *www.bonnieprudden.com*.

For areas that are easy to reach, use the bodo to locate trigger points and then apply pressure to erase them. For spots that are difficult to reach, use the shepherd's crook (see photo at left) to find and apply pressure to trigger points.

As an alternative to the specially designed tools, you can use your fingers, knuckles or elbows on areas of the body that can be reached easily. Common types of pain that can be relieved by this method...**

SHOULDER PAIN

Finding the trigger point: Lie face down while your partner uses his elbow to gently apply pressure to trigger points that can hide along the top of the shoulders and in the upper back. If you are very small or slender, your partner can use his fingers instead of his elbow.

Place one of your arms across your back at the waist while your partner slides his fingers under your shoulder blade to search for and apply pressure to additional trigger points. Repeat the process on the opposite side.

While still lying face down, bend your elbows and rest your forehead on the backs of your hands. With his hands overlapped, your partner can gen-

**Check with your doctor before trying this therapy if you have a chronic medical condition or have suffered a recent injury.

tly move all 10 of his fingers along the top of the shoulder to locate additional trigger points.

Pain-erasing stretch: The "shrug" is a sequence of shoulder exercises performed four times after myotherapy and whenever shoulder tension builds.

From a standing or sitting position, round your back by dropping your head forward while bringing the backs of your arms together as close as possible in front of your body. Extend both arms back (with your thumbs leading) behind your body while tipping your head back and looking toward the ceiling.

Next, with both arms at your sides, raise your shoulders up to your earlobes, then press your shoulders down hard.

LOW-BACK PAIN

Finding the trigger point: Lie face down while your partner stands to your right and reaches across your body to place his elbow on your buttocks in the area where the left back pocket would appear on a pair of pants. For seven seconds, your partner should slowly apply pressure to each trigger point—not straight down but angled back toward himself.

Repeat on the other side. If the pressure causes slight discomfort, your partner has found the right spot! If not, your partner should move his elbow slightly and try the steps again. Two to three trigger points can typically be found on each buttock.

Pain-erasing stretch: Lie on your left side on a flat surface (such as a bed, table or the floor). Bend your right knee and pull it as close to your chest as possible.

Next, extend your right leg, keeping it aligned with the left leg and about eight inches above it.

Finally, lower the raised leg onto the resting one and relax for three seconds. Perform these steps four times on each leg.

HIP PAIN

Finding the trigger point: The trigger points for hip pain are often found in the gluteus medius, the muscle that runs along either side of the pelvis.

Lie on your side with your knees slightly bent. Using one elbow, your partner should scan for trigger points along the *gluteus medius* (in the hip area, roughly between the waist and the

bottom seam of your underpants) and apply pressure straight down at each sensitive spot for seven seconds.

The same process should be repeated on the opposite side of your body.

Pain-erasing stretch: Lie on your left side on a table with your right leg hanging off the side and positioned forward. Your partner should place one hand on top of your waist and the other hand on the knee of the dangling right leg.

This knee should be gently pressed down eight times. The stretch should be repeated on the opposite side.

■ ■ ■ ■

Chinese Herb Works Better than Meds for Rheumatoid Arthritis

Rheumatoid arthritis patients took 60 milligrams (mg) three times daily of an extract of the herb *Tripterygium wilfordii Hook F* (TwHF)…a control group took 1,000 mg twice daily (a typical dose) of the anti-inflammatory drug *sulfasalazine*. After 24 weeks, 65% of TwHF users and 33% of drug users had a 20% or greater improvement in symptoms.

But: Many TwHF products are not standardized for strength—they are best used under a doctor's guidance.

Raphaela Goldbach-Mansky, MD, MHS, former acting chief of translational autoinflammatory disease, National Institute of Arthritis and Musculoskeletal and Skin Diseases, Bethesda, Maryland, and leader of a study of 62 people.

Relieve—and Even Stop—Arthritis with Food

Peter Bales, MD, a board-certified orthopedic surgeon and member of the clinical staff in the department of orthopedic surgery at the University of California at Davis Health System. A research advocate for the Arthritis Foundation (*www.arthritis.org*), he is the author of *Osteoarthritis: Preventing and Healing Without Drugs* (Prometheus).

Osteoarthritis has long been considered a "wear-and-tear" disease associated with age-related changes that occur within cartilage and bone.

Now: A growing body of evidence shows that osteoarthritis may have a metabolic basis. Poor diet results in inflammatory changes and damage in cartilage cells, which in turn lead to cartilage breakdown and the development of osteoarthritis.

A recent increase in osteoarthritis cases corresponds to similar increases in diabetes and obesity, other conditions that can be fueled by poor nutrition. Dietary approaches can help prevent— or manage—all three of these conditions.

Key scientific evidence: A number of large studies, including many conducted in Europe as well as the US, suggest that a diet emphasizing plant foods and fish can support cartilage growth and impede its breakdown. People who combine an improved diet with certain supplements can reduce osteoarthritis symptoms— and possibly stop progression of the disease.

A SMARTER DIET

By choosing your foods carefully, you can significantly improve the pain and stiffness caused by osteoarthritis. *How to get started...*

•**Avoid acidic foods.** The typical American diet, with its processed foods, red meat and harmful trans-fatty acids, increases acidity in the body. A high-acid environment within the joints increases free radicals, corrosive molecules that both accelerate cartilage damage and inhibit the activity of cartilage-producing cells known as *chondrocytes.*

A Mediterranean diet, which includes generous amounts of fruits, vegetables, whole grains, olive oil and fish, is more alkaline. (The body requires a balance of acidity and alkalinity, as measured on the pH scale.) A predominantly alkaline body chemistry inhibits free radicals and reduces inflammation.

What to do: Eat a Mediterranean-style diet, including six servings daily of vegetables...three servings of fruit...and two tablespoons of olive oil. (The acids in fruits and vegetables included in this diet are easily neutralized in the body.) Other sources of healthful fats include olives, nuts (such as walnuts), canola oil and flaxseed oil or ground flaxseed.

Important: It can take 12 weeks or more to flush out acidic toxins and reduce arthritis symptoms after switching to an alkaline diet.

•**Limit your intake of sugary and processed foods.** Most Americans consume a lot of refined carbohydrates as well as sugary foods and soft drinks—all of which damage joints in several ways. For example, sugar causes an increase in *advanced glycation endproducts* (AGEs), protein molecules that bind to collagen (the connective tissue of cartilage and other tissues) and make it stiff and brittle. AGEs also appear to stimulate the production of cartilage-degrading enzymes.

What to do: Avoid processed foods, such as white flour (including cakes, cookies and crackers), white pasta and white rice, as well as soft drinks and fast food. Studies have shown that people who mainly eat foods in their whole, natural forms tend to have lower levels of AGEs and healthier cartilage.

Important: Small amounts of sugar—used to sweeten coffee or cereal, for example—will not significantly increase AGE levels.

•**Get more vitamin C.** More than 10 years ago, the Framingham study found that people who took large doses of vitamin C had a threefold reduction in the risk for osteoarthritis progression.

Vitamin C is an alkalinizing agent due to its anti-inflammatory and antioxidant properties. It blocks the inflammatory effects of free radicals. Vitamin C also decreases the formation of AGEs and reduces the chemical changes that cause cartilage breakdown.

What to do: Take a vitamin C supplement (1,000 milligrams, or mg, daily for the prevention of osteoarthritis...2,000 mg daily if you have osteoarthritis).* Also increase your intake of vitamin C–rich foods, such as sweet red peppers, strawberries and broccoli.

•**Drink green tea.** Green tea alone won't relieve osteoarthritis pain, but people who drink green tea and switch to a healthier diet may notice an additional improvement in symptoms. That's because green tea is among the

*Check with your doctor before taking any dietary supplements.

most potent sources of antioxidants, including *catechins*, substances that inhibit the activity of cartilage-degrading enzymes.

For osteoarthritis, drink one to two cups of green tea daily. (Check with your doctor first if you take any prescription drugs.)

•**Eat fish.** Eat five to six three-ounce servings of omega-3–rich fish (such as salmon, sardines and mackerel) weekly. Omega-3s in such fish help maintain the health of joint cartilage and help curb inflammation. If you would prefer to take a fish oil supplement rather than eat fish, see the recommendation below.

SUPPLEMENTS THAT HELP

Dietary changes are a first step to reducing osteoarthritis symptoms. However, the use of certain supplements also can be helpful.

•**Fish oil.** The two omega-3s in fish—*docosahexaenoic acid* (DHA) and *eicosapentaenoic acid* (EPA)—block chemical reactions in our cells that convert dietary fats into chemical messengers (such as *prostaglandins*), which affect the inflammatory status of our bodies. This is the same process that's inhibited by nonsteroidal anti-inflammatory drugs (NSAIDs), such as *ibuprofen* (Motrin).

What to do: If you find it difficult to eat the amount of omega-3–rich fish mentioned above, ask your doctor about taking fish oil supplements that supply a total of 1,600 mg of EPA and 800 mg of DHA daily. Look for a "pharmaceutical grade" fish oil product, such as Sealogix, available at FishOilRx.com, 888-966-3423, *www.fishoilrx.com*…or RxOmega-3 Factors at iherb.com, *www.iherb.com*.

If, after 12 weeks, you need more pain relief—or have a strong family history of osteoarthritis—add…

•**Glucosamine, chondroitin and MSM.** The most widely used supplements for osteoarthritis are *glucosamine* and *chondroitin*, taken singly or in combination. Most studies show that they work.

Better: A triple combination that contains *methylsulfonylmethane* (MSM) as well as glucosamine and chondroitin. MSM is a sulfur-containing compound that provides the raw material for cartilage regrowth. Glucosamine and chondroitin reduce osteoarthritis pain and have anti-inflammatory properties.

What to do: Take daily supplements of glucosamine (1,500 mg)…chondroitin (1,200 mg) …and MSM (1,500 mg).

Instead of—or in addition to—the fish oil and the triple combination, you may want to take…

•**SAMe.** Like MSM, *S-adenosylmethionine* (SAMe) is a sulfur-containing compound. It reduces the body's production of *TNF-alpha*, a substance that's involved in cartilage destruction. It also seems to increase cartilage production.

In one study, researchers compared SAMe to the prescription anti-inflammatory drug *celecoxib* (Celebrex). The study was double-blind (neither the patients nor the doctors knew who was getting which drug or supplement), and it continued for four months. Initially, patients taking the celecoxib reported fewer symptoms—but by the second month, there was no difference between the two groups.

Additional studies have found similar results. SAMe seems to work just as well as over-the-counter and/or prescription drugs for osteoarthritis, but it works more slowly. I advise patients that they'll need to take it for at least three months to see effects.

What to do: Start with 200 mg of SAMe daily and increase to 400 mg daily if necessary after a few weeks.

■ ■ ■ ■

Treat Gums to Ease Arthritis

Patients with rheumatoid arthritis and gum disease had tartar beneath gums scraped away so that gums could heal. After six weeks, patients had significantly less joint pain, stiffness and swelling. Patients whose gums were not treated did not improve. Reducing oral bacteria may ease inflammation elsewhere. See your dentist if gums bleed—and especially if joints ache, too.

Nabil Bissada, DDS, chair, department of periodontics, Case Western Reserve University School of Dental Medicine, Cleveland, and leader of a study of 40 people.

■ ■ ■ ■

Chronic Pain Linked to Low Vitamin D

Chronic pain is the leading cause of disability in the US. In a recent study, it was found that patients with low vitamin D levels required twice as much narcotic pain medication to manage symptoms as those with adequate levels.

Theory: Vitamin D deficiency leads to low bone density, which can create achy pain throughout the body.

Best: Ask your doctor about testing your blood level of vitamin D and supplementing if it is below 20 nanograms per milliliter.

Michael Turner, MD, department of physical medicine and rehabilitation, Mayo Clinic, Rochester, Minnesota, and lead author of a study of 267 people.

Nine Things Everyone Needs to Know About Painkillers

Marjory Abrams, publisher, *Bottom Line/Personal* newsletter, 281 Tresser Blvd., Stamford, Connecticut.

I recently heard Cynthia Kuhn, PhD, professor of pharmacology at Duke University Medical School, speak about the best prescribing practices for pain management.

Some people don't like the idea of taking painkillers—but Dr. Kuhn points out that severe unresolved pain can decrease immunity and slow healing…lead to sleep disorders, depression and anxiety…and rewire the nervous system to cause chronic pain. It is very important to work with your physician to understand the source of the pain and to explore the best strategies to treat the pain effectively. Dr. Kuhn advises moving up the "analgesic ladder" only if pain persists.

Step 1: **Use acetaminophen** (Tylenol) or a nonsteroidal anti-inflammatory (NSAID), such as aspirin, *ibuprofen* (Advil) or *naproxen* (Aleve). If the pain is not relieved by the highest recom-

mended dose, your physician may suggest moving up the ladder to…

Step 2: **A weak opioid,** such as *codeine, hydrocodone* or *tramadol* (Ultram) or a Step 1/ Step 2 combination drug for a stronger effect.

Examples: Percocet (acetaminophen plus *oxycodone*)…Vicodin (acetaminophen plus hydrocodone). If the pain continues, your physician may go to…

Step 3: **Stronger opioids,** such as *hydromorphone* (Dilaudid), *methadone, morphine* or higher-dose oxycodone (OxyContin).

To enhance pain relief, physicians may prescribe an adjuvant at any step on the ladder.

Examples: Certain antidepressants, such as *amitriptyline* (Elavil) and *duloxetine* (Cymbalta), and antiepileptic drugs, such as *gabapentin* (Neurontin).

While narcotic drugs are effective, they are addictive and an overdose can be lethal. *Precautions to take…*

• **Ask about side effects** so that you will know what to expect.

• **Tell your doctor if you have ever been addicted to drugs or alcohol.** Such a history increases the risk for opioid addiction and may influence which drug is prescribed.

• **Take the prescribed medication on a schedule** to prevent over- or under-dosing.

• **Never increase the dosage or frequency on your own.** Overdose deaths have risen dramatically due to patients taking narcotic drugs more frequently than prescribed.

• **Do not stop prescription painkillers abruptly.** Discuss with your doctor a plan for tapering off to minimize withdrawal symptoms.

• **Once the pain resolves, discard any unused prescription drugs** so that no one is tempted to take them in situations for which they have not been prescribed.

Nondrug treatments, such as exercise and deep breathing, also are critical to pain management. Certain types of pain (especially back pain) are not well-controlled with medication alone. Discuss all options with your doctor.

Ginkgo for Pain?

Neuropathic pain—in which nerves that are damaged send erroneous pain signals in response to harmless stimuli such as a light touch—is hard to treat. Common causes include diabetes and shingles. Among rats with neuropathic pain, those given a ginkgo biloba herbal extract showed significantly lower pain responses to cold and pressure than those given a placebo. Human studies are needed.

Hae-Jin Lee, MD, chief/professor of anesthesiology, Catholic University of Korea, Seoul, Republic of Korea, and leader of an animal study.

More Relief for Shingles Pain

A recent study followed 87 patients with shingles who took the painkiller *oxycodone* (Oxycontin)…the antiseizure drug *gabapentin* (Neurontin), also used to treat pain…or a placebo for 28 days. All patients also took the antiviral drug *famciclovir* (Famvir).

Result: The oxycodone group was more than twice as likely to experience at least a 30% decrease in pain, compared with the placebo group. The gabapentin group did not report a significant reduction in pain.

Caution: Oxycodone can be habit-forming and can cause such side effects as constipation, dizziness and nausea.

Robert Dworkin, PhD, director, Anesthesiology Clinical Research Center, University of Rochester Medical Center, New York.

Are Pain Medications Sapping Your Sex Life?

Most men and women taking opioids, such as *codeine*, *hydrocodone* (Vicodin), *morphine* and *oxycodone* (OxyContin, Percocet), show reductions in blood levels of *estradiol*, *testosterone* and related hormones.

Among the consequences: Patients may experience loss of libido, depression, decreased energy, mood disturbances, osteoporosis and/

or premature menopause. Once the opioid is stopped, hormone levels rebound.

Norman J. Marcus, MD, founder and medical director, Norman Marcus Pain Institute (*www.nmpi.com*), New York City, and a past president of American Academy of Pain Medicine. He is coauthor, with Jean S. Arbeiter, of *Freedom from Pain* (Fireside).

Natural Ways to Relieve and *Reverse* Fibromyalgia

Mark A. Stengler, NMD, naturopathic medical doctor in private practice, La Jolla, California…adjunct associate clinical professor at the National College of Natural Medicine, Portland, Oregon…author of many books, including *The Natural Physician's Healing Therapies* and coauthor of *Prescription for Natural Cures* (both from Bottom Line Books)… and author of the *Bottom Line/Natural Healing* newsletter.

Pain relief is critically important to the eight to 12 million Americans who suffer from *fibromyalgia*, a condition characterized by muscle pain and multiple spots on the body that are tender when touched. The pain wears down these patients…and they also must cope with insomnia and severe fatigue. Other symptoms include anxiety…depression…morning stiffness…headaches…abdominal pain…bloating…and constipation.

In the past, many in the medical community dismissed this condition as "all in their patients' heads"—and didn't believe that it was a real medical condition. I never agreed with that. Fibromyalgia is as real as the pain and discomfort it causes. A few years ago, the FDA approved a drug—*pregabalin* (Lyrica)—to specifically treat the condition. Studies show that this drug is not very effective. I believe that treating fibromyalgia with pharmaceutical drugs, such as Lyrica, or with antidepressants, which also are commonly prescribed, is not the best way for patients to get relief. These drugs have many side effects, including dizziness and coordination problems. I find that many fibromyalgia patients regain their health with natural remedies.

FINDING THE CAUSE

The exact cause of fibromyalgia is unknown. Many patients receive a diagnosis of fibromyalgia from their rheumatologists before coming to see me. Those most at risk are women…people who are 40 to 50 years old…and those with an autoimmune disease, such as lupus or rheumatoid arthritis. I always first test my female patients for hormone deficiencies or imbalances. The results often show low levels of *thyroid* activity…low *progesterone*…and not enough of the stress hormone *cortisol*. With men, I typically first look at thyroid and cortisol levels. Often, once the patient's underlying condition is treated, symptoms disappear completely or are greatly reduced.

NATURAL HELP

Several natural substances can relieve the symptoms of fibromyalgia and reverse the disease's progression. I have used supplements to treat several hundred patients with fibromyalgia. Most of them show signs of improvement within two to four weeks of treatment. After several months, they feel much better. Once they improve, some reduce their doses or no longer need supplements at all. My fibromyalgia patients take most (if not all) of the remedies recommended below. *These supplements help in the following ways…*

BOOST ENERGY

•**D-ribose.** This naturally occurring sugar found in all cells is essential for cellular energy production. A study in *The Journal of Alternative and Complementary Medicine* found that patients with fibromyalgia who took d-ribose had less pain and improved energy, sleep, mental clarity and overall well-being. Side effects are rare. Although it is a type of sugar, it is safe for people with type 2 diabetes.

Dose: Take 5 grams twice daily in powder form (mixed with water or juice). If taking d-ribose makes you feel light-headed, take it with meals.

•**Coenzyme Q10 (CoQ10).** The antioxidant can increase energy production in cells. CoQ10 is a mild blood thinner, so if you are on blood-thinning medication, consult your physician before taking it.

Dose: Take 200 milligrams (mg) to 300 mg daily with meals.

•**Acetyl-L-carnitine (ALC).** This nutrient can increase cellular energy production. A study published in *Clinical and Experimental Rheumatology* found that ALC was effective in treating fibromyalgia patients.

Dose: Take 500 mg daily on an empty stomach. Cut back on the dosage if it causes digestive upset.

BALANCE NEUROTRANSMITTERS

•**5-hydroxytryptophan (5-HTP).** This form of the amino acid *L-tryptophan* helps to produce *serotonin*. A study reported in *The Journal of International Medical Research* of 50 patients with fibromyalgia found that 5-HTP can improve pain, morning stiffness, insomnia, anxiety and fatigue.

Caution: 5-HTP should not be taken with any psychiatric medications, nor should it be taken by women who are pregnant or breast-feeding. Side effects are rare.

Dose: Take 100 mg three times daily—30 minutes or more apart from eating any food.

•**S-adenosylmethionine (SAMe).** Clinical studies show that SAMe can help adjust neurotransmitter balance, which in turn reduces the body's release of pain signals.

Caution: SAMe should not be taken if you are on any psychiatric medications. Take either 5-HTP or SAMe. 5-HTP is less expensive, so try it first.

Dose: Take 400 mg twice daily on an empty stomach.

IMPROVE SLEEP

•**Melatonin.** This naturally occurring hormone, derived from serotonin, helps ensure a good night's sleep, which is critical for fibromyalgia patients.

Dose: Start by taking 1 mg 30 minutes before bedtime. If that amount doesn't help you sleep, gradually increase to 3 mg.

RELAX MUSCLES

•**Magnesium.** Take 400 mg to 500 mg daily in two divided doses, with or without food. You can get this total amount from all of your supplement sources added together, including a multivitamin.

•**Vitamin D.** Studies show that people with low levels of vitamin D are at greater risk for fibromyalgia. Taking vitamin D can help relax tight muscles. Your doctor can administer a blood test to check your vitamin D level and to determine the exact dose you need. Most people take 1,000 international units (IU) to 2,000 IU daily.

EATING TO REDUCE PAIN

I recommend that fibromyalgia patients eat an anti-inflammatory diet because this type of diet also will reduce pain. It includes plenty of cold-water fish, such as salmon and sardines...lots of green, leafy and brightly colored vegetables... fruits (berries and apples) and generous amounts of spices with anti-inflammatory properties, such as turmeric, garlic, onions and ginger.

GET MOVING

Exercise can help fibromyalgia patients fight fatigue and pain. In early treatment stages, most people are physically unable to do much exercise because they are in a lot of pain. After that, I advise patients to start walking or using a stationary bike for 10 minutes daily.

REDUCE STRESS

If patients don't exercise, I urge them to find other ways to relax. Stress management is important for all my fibromyalgia patients. Some turn to meditation...prayer...or listening to soft music.

■ **More from Mark Stengler, NMD...**

Finally, Pain Relief Without Side Effects

As a naturopathic physician, I find there is nothing more satisfying than helping patients alleviate pain with natural pain relievers—especially since these have few of the adverse effects of pharmaceutical medications.

More than 30 million Americans take conventional painkillers daily for a variety of ailments, including arthritis, headaches, sore muscles and back or neck pain. While these drugs are good at temporarily relieving pain, they all have unhealthful side effects, particularly when used over time for chronic conditions. They can irritate the stomach, cause stomach and intestinal ulcers and increase heart disease risk.

Fortunately, there are natural pain relievers that work as well as, or better than, these drugs, and they are much gentler on your body. I prescribe the herbs described here for patients with a variety of ailments. I believe that they can help you, too.

Caution: Women who are pregnant or breast-feeding should not take these remedies, because they have not been studied in these populations.

Strategy: For chronic pain involving any of the conditions in the table that follows, take the first painkiller listed for that condition for four weeks. If you notice an improvement, stay with it. If not, try the next one (if there is one).

Try the following herbs—which are all available at health food stores or online—for the conditions listed...

DEVIL'S CLAW

Devil's claw (*Harpagophytum procumbens*), a shrub found in southern Africa, works similarly to many pharmaceutical pain relievers—by blocking the action of pain-promoting compounds in the body—but without damaging the digestive tract. In studies involving people with chronic low-back pain, devil's claw extract proved as effective as prescription pain relievers.

Dose: Devil's claw extract is available in capsules. Look for 1.5% to 2.0% *harpagoside*, one of the active ingredients. Take 1,000 milligrams (mg) three times daily of a standardized extract.

Recommended brand: Nature's Way Standardized Devil's Claw Extract (800-962-8873, *http://naturesway.com*). The only significant potential side effect is diarrhea.

CURCUMIN

Curcumin (*diferuloylmethane*), a constituent of turmeric, is the pigment compound that gives the spice its distinctive yellow coloring. In one study of rheumatoid arthritis patients, 1,200 mg daily of curcumin extract improved morning stiffness and joint swelling.

Dose: Take 500 mg of standardized turmeric extract (containing 90% to 95% curcumin) three times daily.

Recommended brands: New Chapter Turmericforce (800-543-7279, *www.newchapter. com*) and Life Extension Super Curcumin (888-771-3905, *www.lifeextensionvitamins.com*). It has blood-thinning properties, so do not take curcumin if you take blood-thinning drugs, such as warfarin, unless you are being monitored by a physician.

Avoid this: If you have gallstones, because curcumin can cause gallstones to block bile ducts.

WHITE WILLOW BARK

This pain reliever has anti-inflammatory and blood-thinning benefits similar to those of aspirin, but unlike aspirin, it doesn't appear to damage the stomach lining. For centuries, the bark of the white willow (*Salix alba*), a tree found in Europe and Asia, was noted for its pain-relieving qualities. Its active ingredient is *salicin*, which the body converts to *salicylic acid,* a close cousin to aspirin (*acetylsalicylic acid*).

Dose: Take 120 mg daily of white willow bark extract capsules. If this amount does not reduce pain, try 240 mg.

Recommended brand: Solaray White Willow Bark (*For information:* 800-579-4665).

Avoid this: If you have an aspirin allergy and for one week before undergoing surgery. White willow bark is a blood thinner, so take it only while being monitored by a physician if you take blood-thinning medication.

BOSWELLIA

Part of India's Ayurvedic healing tradition, boswellia (*Boswellia serrata*) comes from a tree found in India, Northern Africa and the Middle East. The tree yields a milky resin containing *boswellic acids*, substances that inhibit the body's synthesis of inflammatory *leukotrienes*. A study of patients with knee arthritis found that boswellia extract relieved pain and stiffness as well as daily doses of the prescription drug *valdecoxib* (Bextra). And boswellia's benefits persisted for one month longer than those of Bextra.

Dose: Take 750 mg of a standardized extract containing 60% to 65% boswellic acid two to three times daily for as long as symptoms last.

Recommended brand: Solgar Boswellia Resin Extract (877-765-4274, *www.solgar.com*). While generally safe, boswellia has been known to cause occasional mild digestive upset.

NATURAL PAIN RELIEVERS

Condition	Pain relievers to try*
Headache (tension or migraine)	White willow bark
Inflammatory bowel disease	Boswellia, curcumin
Low-back pain	Devil's claw, white willow bark, curcumin
Muscle aches and pain	White willow bark, curcumin
Menstrual pain	Boswellia, white willow bark, devil's claw
Osteoarthritis, rheumatoid arthritis	Boswellia, curcumin, devil's claw
Tendonitis	Devil's claw, curcumin, white willow bark

*Take the first painkiller listed for your condition for four weeks. If it doesn't work, try the next one (if there is one).

Love Conquers All—Even Pain, Study Suggests

Association for Psychological Science news release.

Thinking about a loved one might help reduce physical pain, according to researchers, who said their findings show the importance of social relationships and of staying emotionally connected.

THE STUDY

The University of California, Los Angeles, study included 25 young women who'd been in a good relationship with a boyfriend for more than six months. Moderately painful heat was applied to the women's forearms as they looked at photos of their boyfriend, a stranger and a chair.

"When the women were just looking at pictures of their partner, they actually reported less pain to heat stimuli than when they were looking at pictures of an object or pictures of a stranger," said study coauthor Naomi Eisenberger, PhD, an assistant professor of psychology and director of UCLA's Social and Affective Neuroscience Laboratory. "Thus, the mere reminder of one's partner through a simple photograph was capable of reducing pain.

"This changes our notion of how social support influences people," Dr. Eisenberger explained. "Typically, we think that in order for social support to make us feel good, it has to be the kind of support that is very responsive to our emotional needs. Here, however, we are seeing that just a photo of one's significant other can have the same effect."

In another experiment, the women reported less heat-related pain when they held the hand of their boyfriend, compared with when they held the hand of a stranger or held a squeeze ball.

"This study demonstrates how much of an impact our social ties can have on our experience and fits with other work emphasizing the importance of social support for physical and mental health," Dr. Eisenberger added.

The findings were published in the journal *Psychological Science.*

info To find a pain management professional, visit the American Academy of Pain Management, *www.aapainmanage.org.*

Use Your Brain to Ease Your Pain Without Pills

James N. Dillard, MD, DC, CAc, a board-certified physician, doctor of chiropractic and certified medical acupuncturist who pioneered the integrative model in pain medicine. He is author of *The Chronic Pain Solution: Your Personal Path to Pain Relief* (Bantam). Previously he was an assistant clinical professor at Columbia University College of Physicians and Surgeons and medical director of Columbia's Rosenthal Center for Complementary and Alternative Medicine, both in New York City. Dr. Dillard now maintains private practices in New York City and East Hampton, New York. *www.drdillard.com.*

More people are disabled by chronic pain than by diabetes, heart disease and cancer put together. An estimated 27% of US women (and 29% of men) suffer from debilitating pain, yet the problem remains vastly undertreated. Pain medications do not always bring sufficient relief—plus they can lead to side effects and/or addiction.

The good news: Like everything in your body, pain is affected by the workings of your mind. No matter what the cause of your pain, you can harness the power of your brain to reduce your suffering. *Here's how...*

Your limbic system, the more primitive part of your higher brain centers, controls your involuntary nervous system and emotions. Pain activates the limbic system, triggering the fight-or-flight response. As stress hormones are released, your heart beats faster, blood pressure soars, muscles tense...and various emotions are sparked, including anxiety, panic, anger and sadness. Normally, these responses are temporary—but with chronic pain, the stress of these intense reactions creates a downward spiral.

Example: The pain of chronic arthritis provokes a continuous release of stress hormones, leading to headaches and insomnia that exacerbate discomfort. As your body weakens, it produces fewer mood-boosting *endorphins.* Soon you're too tired and despondent to socialize, and the resulting isolation only makes you feel worse.

Helpful: If you learn to cultivate a sense of distance from your pain, you can mute the limbic system's response, reducing physical pain signals and easing the accompanying emotional suffering.

At least twice a day, go somewhere quiet and safe where you won't be disturbed...sit or lie in whatever position is most comfortable...and practice one or more of the techniques below for five to 15 minutes.

CALMING BREATH

Pain can take your breath away, triggering a pattern of shallow breathing that increases muscle tension and deprives cells of oxygen. Deep breathing—especially when combined with a meditative focus—helps by relaxing muscles, stimulating endorphins and reducing emotional distress.

Remember: For both of the deep-breathing techniques below, inhale slowly through your nose and then exhale slowly through your mouth. Clear your mind, and focus only on your breath. If other thoughts intrude, let them float away and refocus on your breath.

•**Flare-control breath.** This is particularly effective for pain flare-ups. As you inhale, notice your lungs filling with the vitality of your breath. Imagine your breath flowing to the area of your pain, bringing healing energy to this spot. As you exhale, imagine the pain flowing out of your body along with your breath.

•**Purifying breath.** This is especially helpful for easing troubling emotions that accompany pain. Picture your body surrounded by pure, white light.

Inhaling: Imagine this light being drawn into your lungs and then spreading until your whole body glows with healing light.

Exhaling: Picture a dark essence—representing fear, anger and sorrow—being expelled with your breath, leaving your body pain-free and your mind at ease.

HEALING IMAGERY

The guided imagery method quiets the nervous system by convincing your mind that it does not feel pain. *Close your eyes and imagine either of these...*

•**A place of peace.** Picture yourself in an ideal setting of your choosing—a favorite vacation spot, a mountaintop, a lush garden, a tranquil lake. Immerse yourself in this scene by imagining what you see (majestic trees, an azure sky)...feel (a soft breeze, the warm sun)...smell (a campfire, fresh lilacs)...hear (singing birds, rustling leaves)...and taste (the salty sea, a perfect strawberry). The more details you can conjure up, the more effective the imagery is.

•**Soothing hues.** Take a few deep breaths, then focus on your pain. Note its location and intensity...describe its qualities (aching, throbbing, burning). Think of a color that represents pain (black, purple, hot pink), and imagine that your painful area is suffused with that color. Now choose a healing hue (such as white, silver or pale blue), and imagine that it has the power to dissolve your pain. Visualize the healing color pouring onto the painful area and spreading out wider and wider, until the painful color completely disappears. In your mind's eye, let that healing color continue to pour out for as long as you want—you have an unlimited supply.

PAIN-RELIEVING ACUPRESSURE

Like acupuncture, acupressure is based on a principle of traditional Chinese medicine—that *chi* (energy) flows throughout the body along invisible channels called *meridians*, and that pain occurs when the chi becomes blocked or unbalanced. In terms of conventional Western medicine, the firm pressure applied during acupressure is thought to distract the nervous system, halting pain messages from traveling up the spinal cord to the brain.

The following techniques are particularly good for head, neck and shoulder pain, but they also ease the tension that pain elsewhere in the body can trigger in the neck area. Do each technique for several minutes per side.

•**Catwalk.** With your right hand, feel along the top of your left shoulder for any tender, tight or tense spot...then massage that area by "walking" your index, middle and ring fingers along it (like a cat kneading with its paws). Do this repeatedly and quickly—each finger press should last only about half a second. Repeat on the other side.

•**Thumb press.** Place your right hand behind your head, palm facing you and thumb pointing downward. With the pad of your thumb, press firmly into the base of your skull, working all the way across the right side and paying extra attention to any tight or tender spots. Repeat on the other side.

SOOTHING AROMATHERAPY

Certain scents can invigorate you when pain saps your energy...or calm you when pain leaves you tense or anxious. Aromatherapy also distracts your attention from pain and may relax muscles. Add a few drops of essential oil to a hot bath or sprinkle a few drops on a handkerchief that you hold near your nose (do not apply essential oil directly to skin).

Or: Smooth a scented lotion into your skin, especially on painful areas.

•**Invigorating scents.** Try cedar...eucalyptus...or peppermint (this one also eases the nausea that can accompany pain).

•**Calming scents.** Try bergamot...geranium...lavender...rose...or sandalwood.

■ ■ ■ ■

Mirror Therapy Blocks Phantom Pain

Patients often experience phantom pain after the amputation of a limb.

New therapy: Patients look at a mirror reflection of the healthy limb (the one not being amputated) prior to surgery, which tricks the brain into thinking that the damaged limb is still there and functioning properly.

Anesthesia & Analgesia.

■ ■ ■ ■

Cupping Eases Pain

Carpal tunnel syndrome involves irritation of a nerve running from forearm to hand, causing arm pain and finger numbness. With wet cupping, a practitioner makes small skin punctures, then applies heated glass cups to create suction.

Study: Among carpal tunnel patients, those who underwent cupping on the neck and shoulders reported significantly more improvement than those treated with heating pads.

Theory: Cupping stimulates blood and lymph flow, improving nerve function.

Referrals to practitioners: American Association of Acupuncture and Oriental Medicine, 866-455-7999, *www.aaaomonline.org.*

Andreas Michalsen, MD, professor of medicine, Charité Medical University, Berlin, Germany, and leader of a study of 52 people.

Savvy Consumer

Could Watching TV Kill You?

Every hour spent watching TV each day may increase your risk of an early death from cardiovascular disease by as much as 18%, Australian researchers say.

What's on the television is not the problem; it's the time spent sitting while watching.

"This research provides another clear link between too much sitting and death from disease," said lead researcher David Dunstan, PhD, head of the Physical Activity Laboratory at the Baker IDI Heart and Diabetes Institute in Victoria.

Although the study was done in Australia, the findings are applicable to Americans, Dr. Dunstan said. Average daily television watching is about three hours in Australia and the United Kingdom, and up to eight hours in the United States, where many people are either overweight or obese, he noted.

Dr. Dunstan pointed out that while obesity can add to these problems, even normal-weight people can have increases in blood sugar and cholesterol if they sit too much.

The report was published in *Circulation*.

STUDY DETAILS

For the study, Dr. Dunstan's team collected data on the lifestyles of 8,800 healthy men and women ages 25 and older. In addition to lifestyle habits, the researchers tested participants' cholesterol and blood sugar levels. Over more than six years of follow-up, 284 people died. Among these deaths, 87 were due to cardiovascular disease and 125 from cancer.

The participants were grouped into three TV-watching categories—those who watched less than two hours a day; those who watched two to four

David Dunstan, PhD, professor and head, Physical Activity Laboratory, Baker IDI Heart and Diabetes Institute, Victoria, Australia.

Gregg C. Fonarow, MD, professor, cardiology, University of California, Los Angeles.

David Bassett Jr., PhD, professor, health and exercise science, University of Tennessee, Knoxville.

Circulation online.

hours a day; and those who watched more than four hours a day.

The researchers found that every hour of daily TV watching increased the risk of dying from any cause by 11%. For cardiovascular diseases the increased risk was 18%, and for cancer it was 9%. Compared with those who watched less than two hours per day, those who watched TV for more than four hours each day had an 80% increased risk of dying early from cardiovascular disease and a 46% increased risk of dying from any cause.

The association between TV watching and death remained even when the researchers took into account risk factors for cardiovascular disease, such as smoking, high blood pressure, high cholesterol, unhealthy diet, excessive weight and exercise.

STRUCTURED EXERCISE DOES NOT OFFSET TV VIEWING

"What we are now starting to understand is that the risks associated with sedentary behavior are not necessarily offset by doing more exercise," Dr. Dunstan said.

"In other words, irrespective of how much exercise you do, if you sit watching television for four hours on a daily basis you still have a substantially increased risk of early death from all causes and a much greater risk of cardiovascular disease," he said.

The good news is research has shown that moving the muscles frequently throughout the day is one of the most effective ways of managing weight and protecting against disease, Dr. Dunstan added.

"We tend to underestimate the value of incidental, non-sweaty activity throughout the day when we are either not sleeping or exercising—the more you move, the greater the benefits for health," he noted.

EXPERT COMMENTARY

According to Gregg C. Fonarow, MD, a professor of cardiology at the University of California, Los Angeles, "regular exercise has been consistently demonstrated to result in improved cardiovascular health and lower risk of heart attacks, stroke, diabetes and premature death."

"Reducing time spent inactive may be of benefit in reducing the risk of cardiovascular disease and should be considered as part of a comprehensive approach to improve cardiovascular health," he added.

David Bassett Jr., PhD, a professor of health and exercise science at the University of Tennessee, said, "When one looks at time trends in physical activity over the past century, it is clear that people are doing more structured, purposeful exercise than before."

However, what has changed is that people are doing less walking, household chores and manual labor than in the past, he said. "We are also spending more time in sedentary activities like television watching, computer use and desk jobs," Dr. Bassett explained.

"This study adds to a growing body of evidence that the amount of time spent in sedentary activity, as distinct from the amount of time spent in purposeful exercise, can affect your health," he said.

info For information on the benefits of exercise, visit the Centers for Disease Control Web site, *www.cdc.gov*, and search "physical activity for everyone."

Clever Ways to Get Free Expert Medical Advice

Charles B. Inlander, a consumer advocate and healthcare consultant based in Fogelsville, Pennsylvania. He was founding president of People's Medical Society, a consumer health advocacy group active in the 1980s and 1990s. He is author of more than 20 books, including *Take This Book to the Hospital with You* (St. Martin's).

Even though there is an abundance of health information online, you may not find answers to specific questions related to your personal medical diagnosis or treatment. For those questions, you may want to speak to an expert other than your own doctor, who may not have the necessary expertise or latest information about your condition. The good news is that it's often easy to reach an expert—and, in many cases, that medical information is free!

Clever ways to get information from top-notch medical experts...

• **Contact a medical school.** Faculty members at medical schools, such as physicians and researchers, know about the latest treatments for rare or complicated medical problems and can be good sources of referrals to doctors and hospitals that specialize in your medical condition. Over the years, I have found it relatively easy to contact medical school faculty by phone. First, check the listings of medical schools at the Web site of the Association of American Medical Colleges, *www.aamc.org/medicalschools,* and look for the school closest to you (in case you need to meet directly with the expert). When you call a medical school, ask for the chairperson of the department most closely related to your medical condition—for example, cardiology or endocrinology.

Insider tip: When you call, don't go into detail about your medical condition. Instead, get right to your question. For example, you may ask, "Where would you recommend I get a second opinion for this problem?"...or "Is the treatment my doctor recommended the only option?"

• **Call a teaching hospital.** Because medical students are taught in these hospitals, the physicians who head the specialty departments are often considered leaders in their field. You can get a list of teaching hospitals in your area at *www.healthguideusa.org/teaching_hospitals. htm.* Follow the steps described above in contacting the specific person best able to help you. Because department heads typically have busy schedules, chances are you will have to leave a message.

Insider tip: Most of these doctors have private practices, so you should be prepared to schedule an appointment if you have a complicated question or problem. But if you are looking for a referral or source of information (such as studies) about a disease or treatment, the doctor or his/her staff often will get back to you with a suggestion at no charge.

• **Go to your insurance carrier.** You may be surprised to learn that your insurance company may have the answer to your medical question. If you have questions about your medical care, call your insurer's nurse/medical expert hotline. More and more insurance companies are putting in hotlines that allow you to speak to health-care practitioners directly. In addition, members of many health plans can discuss their medical conditions and treatment issues with experts such as nurses, respiratory therapists and dietitians, known as case managers or disease management specialists. Check to see if your insurer has such a program.

■ ■ ■ ■

Are Web Sites that Provide Doctor Ratings Reliable?

They can be—but it's important to check for clues to the Web site's objectivity. First, find out how a site determines the ratings. If doctors pay to be listed, the site won't be very objective. If a health insurance company sponsors the site, its ratings may be influenced by the reviewed doctors' fees. Next, examine the reviews themselves. If the ratings are anonymous, a spouse, a nurse or even the doctor might post a positive review, while a competitor could be behind a negative one. Still, it is possible to find useful information, such as how a doctor runs his/her practice. As these Web sites accumulate dozens or more ratings for each doctor, they will yield more reliable information about physicians. No Web sites give comprehensive information, but *www.ucomparehealthcare.com* and *www.vitals. com* provide a good start.

Trisha Torrey, patient empowerment guide at About.com and author, *You Bet Your Life! The 10 Mistakes Every Patient Makes* (Langdon Street).

Is Today's Medical Care Making You Sick?

Dennis Gottfried, MD, a Torrington, Connecticut–based general internist and associate professor of medicine at the University of Connecticut School of Medicine in Farmington. He is the author of *Too Much Medicine: A Doctor's Prescription for Better and More Affordable Health Care* (Paragon House).

With all the high-tech—and expensive—medical care available in the US, you may assume that Americans are among the healthiest people in the world. But that's not true.

Troubling fact: The US spends more than any other country (about 17% of its gross domestic product) on health care but ranks 12th (among 13 industrialized nations) in measures of overall health, such as life expectancy.

Dennis Gottfried, MD, who has extensively researched this subject and worked as a general practice physician for more than 25 years, provides an insider's perspective on what's wrong with our medical system—and advice on how we can protect ourselves.

•**Why is the US health-care system in such bad shape?** Medical practices and hospitals are designed to care for patients, but they're also businesses. Doctors are reimbursed by insurers for such services as medical procedures and surgeries that the doctors themselves recommend and order. As a result, many doctors order too many tests, perform too many procedures and prescribe too many medications. Some doctors also provide excessive medical care to protect themselves against malpractice lawsuits. Much of this is not in the best interests of the patient.

•**What role do patients play?** Often, patients go to their doctors asking for specific treatments they've heard about from friends, read about on the Internet or seen in a drug company or advocacy group ad on TV or in a magazine. Doctors want happy customers, so after a while it's easier to acquiesce than to argue. Americans are conditioned to believe that more is better, but that's not always the case. Sometimes it's worse.

•**How so?** All medical procedures and even some tests carry risks for side effects or complications. For example, *angioplasty,* which uses a catheter and balloon to open a narrowed artery—and is sometimes followed by the placement of a stent (a tube to keep it open)—carries risks for heart attack, blood clots, kidney problems or stroke.

Similarly, some degree of brain damage (loss of cognitive functions, such as memory or judgment, that can last up to 12 months) can occur with coronary bypass surgery.

Yet many of these patients' symptoms, especially those with *stable angina* (chest pain), could have been treated with medication that has far less risk for side effects. In many cases, patients don't really need the stent or the surgery.

•**Then why were these procedures performed?** To a large degree, doctors create their own demand. For example, Miami has a lot more cardiologists than the Minneapolis area. And recent research found that annual Medicare spending on health care for Miami seniors was nearly two-and-a-half times higher than it was for statistically matched older adults in Minneapolis. The Miami health-care costs included six-and-a-half times more visits to specialists, compared with Minneapolis health-care expenditures.

•**Do doctors create their own demand in other areas of medicine?** In general, more specialists mean more expensive health care—and poorer health.

We need specialists to have a good health-care system. But based on several studies, including research by investigators at Dartmouth Medical School, regions in the US that have a greater proportion of primary care physicians (such as family physicians and general internists) than specialists provide better care at lower costs.

However, in the US, medical students want to be specialists because they make more money and usually can arrange less demanding schedules than generalists. And there's more prestige—brain surgeons are referred to often for their intellectual abilities, but you never hear that about pediatricians, for example.

•**But don't specialists provide better care when treating serious conditions?** Not necessarily. Studies by Dartmouth Medical School researchers and others show that as you increase the number of specialists, health care improves—up to a point. Increasing the availability of primary care doctors is associated with lower costs and better health-care quality.

This occurs perhaps because the extra procedures specialists perform increase the odds that something will go wrong. Primary care doctors more often follow a "watchful waiting" philosophy. They put more emphasis on preventive medicine and may know the patient well enough to recognize when stress or other medical conditions are worsening symptoms.

•**Should we avoid consulting specialists?** Certainly not. Just don't see them unless you have to. Go to your primary care doctor first and rely on his/her judgment as to whether specialist care is needed.

When you do go to a specialist, choose a busy one. Because they typically have enough medically indicated work to do, they are less likely to recommend marginal or unnecessary procedures.

And whenever any doctor—generalist or specialist—recommends a procedure, don't be shy about asking, "Is it really necessary?"

This query is particularly important when elective procedures that may carry risks, such as most orthopedic surgery or elective cardiac surgery, are recommended. If you're not convinced, get another opinion.

•**Does the same advice apply to medication?** Yes. Medication can be effective and even lifesaving. For example, drugs for elevated cholesterol and high blood pressure have played a substantial role in preventing heart disease and stroke. If you need them, take them.

But just make sure you really need them. In general, weight loss, salt reduction and exercise should be given a chance before using drugs to reduce blood pressure. Type 2 diabetes is often treatable with diet and exercise alone, but doctors frequently skip this step.

Even if you take medication for a chronic illness, such as high blood pressure, heart disease or diabetes, you need to maintain a healthy lifestyle. Patients have responsibility for their own health. However, when doctors prescribe a medication, they don't always choose wisely among available drugs.

•**What do you mean?** Because drug companies market new drugs heavily to patients and doctors, many physicians opt for these expensive medications when older, cheaper generic alternatives would do just as well—if not better.

Only 10% of new drugs are really new—the rest are molecular variations on existing ones, which are more profitable for the manufacturers but no more effective.

One of my patients with *gastroesophageal reflux disease* (GERD) recently came in and asked for "the little purple pill" she saw advertised on TV. I explained that the generic heartburn drug I had prescribed was nearly identical, but she insisted. She was sufficiently impressed by the flashy graphics on the TV ad to pay substantially—out of pocket—for the medication.

•**Shouldn't patients have access to newer drugs if that's what they want?** Yes, but they need to understand that when a drug is approved, it has generally been tested on several thousand people. Serious problems often aren't discovered until it's been prescribed hundreds of thousands of times.

That's why the cholesterol drug *cerivastatin* (Baycol)…the diabetes medication *troglitazone* (Rezulin)…and the heartburn drug *cisapride* (Propulsid) are no longer available. Serious—sometimes deadly—side effects were discovered after the medications had been on the market for a while. Such side effects are unlikely with drugs that have been around for several years.

Cheaper drugs are sometimes more effective, too. Several large studies have shown that diuretics ("water pills")—among the oldest and cheapest drugs for high blood pressure—reduce heart failure and stroke more effectively than newer compounds.

If you have high blood pressure and your doctor isn't prescribing a diuretic, ask why. If you need two or more drugs (about 70% of the time, that's necessary), a diuretic usually should be one of them.

Mail Order or Drugstore? How to Choose…

Charles B. Inlander, a consumer advocate and health-care consultant based in Fogelsville, Pennsylvania. He was founding president of People's Medical Society, a consumer health advocacy group active in the 1980s and 1990s. He is the author of 20 books, including Take This Book to the Hospital with You: A Consumer Guide to Surviving Your Hospital Stay (St. Martin's).

Not long ago, I asked one of my good friends, who is a retired pharmacist, what he thought of mail-order pharmacies. Are they as reliable as my neighborhood pharmacy? And what about price? Here's what he said: "I get most of my prescriptions via mail order. But you must do your homework so you'll know how to best use a mail-order or local pharmacy."

Important pros and cons to help you decide when to use a mail-order or local pharmacy...

•**Neighborhood pharmacies.** If you are filling a onetime prescription, such as an antibiotic for an infection or a painkiller after recent surgery, your local pharmacy is the way to go.

Pros: Your prescription can often be filled while you wait, and you can speak face-to-face with a pharmacist when you pick up the prescription. Some pharmacies will deliver your medication to your home the day the prescription is filled, which is handy when you are ill or housebound.

Cons: Some pharmacies, especially small, "mom-and-pop"–type stores, will not accept your employer's or health plan's prescription drug insurance. Since many smaller pharmacies may not have the drugs your doctor ordered on their shelves, it may take a day or two to get them. Drugs at local pharmacies also are usually more costly than those bought via mail order, and many chain drugstores will not dispense a greater-than-30-day supply even if your doctor writes the prescription for 90 days. (This allows the pharmacy to collect a copay or dispensing fee each time you refill.)

•**Mail-order pharmacies.** They are ideal for medications you take on a regular basis.

Pros: Mail-order prices are usually lower than those charged by local or chain pharmacies because mail-order overhead is lower. Mail-order pharmacies routinely fill up to 90-day prescriptions with a onetime copay, saving you more money. Most major online pharmacies, such as Medco Health Solutions (*www.Medco.com*)... CVS's Caremark (*www.Caremark.com*)...and AARP's prescription discount program, Walgreen Health Initiatives (*www.WalgreensHealth. com*), have pharmacists available 24 hours a day to answer questions, so there's no waiting for information.

Cons: Mail-order pharmacies are not practical for drugs you need quickly, although some have overnight delivery options at a steep price. You must plan your refill orders well in advance

(typically 15 days before your prescription runs out). Also, if you need to speak to a pharmacist often, you'll likely get a different person each time you call.

Caution: Some online mail-order companies are bogus. For this reason, the FDA recommends buying only from US mail-order pharmacies that are licensed to sell in your state. Find your state board at the National Association of Boards of Pharmacy, *www.nabp.net*, and check out the mail-order company you want to use.

How to Travel Comfortably with a Chronic Illness

Marvin C. Cooper, MD, a New York City–based internist and hematologist who specializes in medical issues related to travel. He is an assistant clinical professor of medicine at the New York University School of Medicine, also in New York City. Dr. Cooper has lectured and published extensively on the topic of travel medicine.

The thought of taking a trip may be daunting if you have diabetes, heart disease, lung problems, arthritis or some other chronic medical condition.

Will I be uncomfortable or get sick during my trip? These common concerns can be easily managed—if you plan properly.*

Helpful: If you have diabetes, heart disease or another chronic condition, it's useful to wear a medical identification bracelet or necklace when you travel.**

DIABETES

If you have diabetes...

•**Talk to your doctor about antibiotics.** Traveler's diarrhea can be extremely dangerous for people with diabetes (due to disturbances in blood sugar levels), so your doctor may suggest that you start taking antibiotics before your

*To find a clinic near you that specializes in travel medicine, consult the International Society of Travel Medicine (ISTM). Go to the ISTM Web site at *www.istm.org* and click on "Global Travel Clinic Locator."

**These products are available at American Medical ID (800-363-5985, *www.AmericanMedical-id.com*), starting at about $30.

trip—or bring antibiotics with you—if you are going to a less developed location where the sanitation is poor.

Important: Ask your doctor if the antibiotic you are prescribed is location-specific. For example, *ciprofloxacin* (Cipro) may be fine if you are heading to Central or South America, but resistance to ciprofloxacin is high in Asia, so *azithromycin* (Zithromax) is preferable.

•**Review your insulin schedule.** If you are traveling north or south (so there are no time zone changes)—or traveling east or west through fewer than six time zones (typically the maximum time difference to which our bodies can adjust without causing significant problems)—there is no need to modify the timing of your insulin injections. But if you are crossing six or more time zones, discuss your insulin schedule with your doctor. Also, bring a glucometer with you so that you can check your blood sugar levels while traveling.

To avoid hassles at security: Before your trip, get a letter from your doctor stating that you must travel with a syringe or insulin pen. Otherwise, airport security officers might confiscate these items.

•**Be careful with food.** Obey the well-known axiom "if you can't cook it, boil it or peel it, leave it." Also take precautions with unpackaged loaves of bread to avoid bacteria from food servers' possibly unwashed hands. Just rip off the crust all the way around and consume only the doughy inside of the bread. Insist that your hot food be served steaming hot to help avoid dangerous pathogens and lower the risk for infections, which can worsen diabetes symptoms.

HEART DISEASE

If you have a heart condition, see your cardiologist before taking any long trips (lasting more than about eight hours) for personalized advice to help you avoid a heart attack, stroke or dangerous increase in blood pressure. *Also...*

•**Don't fly too soon after surgery.** Avoid air travel for at least two weeks following hospital discharge after chest surgery. During such surgery, air may be introduced into the chest to assist the surgeon. Any remaining air may expand in the body during flight, greatly increasing the risk of rupturing stitches.

•**Find a specialist.** Ask your physician to refer you to a doctor you can contact at your destination in case you have a heart problem. Be sure that you have up-to-date contact information for this doctor.

•**Prevent blood clots.** You may be advised by your physician to take an anticoagulant drug, such as *warfarin* (Coumadin) or *enoxaparin* (Lovenox), before your trip to help prevent blood clots. Also, move around the airplane cabin or train (or take breaks from car travel) as often as possible. While you're seated, move your legs often (by "walking in place" and flexing and rotating your ankles).

If you have a pacemaker, ask your doctor for a note that says you have the device—this prevents problems when passing through metal detectors at security.

LUNG PROBLEMS

If you have asthma or severe *chronic obstructive pulmonary disease* (COPD)—obstruction of the airways due to *emphysema* and/or chronic bronchitis...

•**Be aware of air quality.** Areas that have high levels of air pollution can create breathing difficulties for people with asthma. Anyone with severe COPD should avoid visiting any destination with an altitude that exceeds 7,500 feet to help prevent shortness of breath.

•**Ask your doctor about oxygen.** If you have COPD and are unable to climb one flight of stairs without suffering shortness of breath, you may need oxygen during a flight. When making your reservation, ask the airline to provide in-flight oxygen (you may need a note from your doctor). Call about 48 hours before your flight to confirm that oxygen will be provided. (Airline customers are prohibited from bringing their own on airplanes.) As soon as you are seated, ask for your oxygen—a small tank with a face mask attached—and use it throughout the flight. Don't wait to experience shortness of breath.

•**Bring inhalers on the plane.** If you have asthma, be sure to bring your inhalers and any other asthma medication with you on the airplane or any other form of transportation you may take.

OSTEOARTHRITIS OR RHEUMATOID ARTHRITIS

If you have osteoarthritis or rheumatoid arthritis…

•**Invest in high-quality rolling luggage.** If you lug heavy bags, you're likely to inflame your joints.

Helpful: Pay a skycap to assist you…and pay the airline's extra fees to check an extra bag rather than wrestle with bulky carry-ons.

Be sure to take anti-inflammatory medication with you in case you become achy.

Helpful: Take your arthritis medication in advance to prevent joint pain if physical exertion is required, such as when climbing up the stairway to a plane that is boarded from the tarmac…or when transferring from a cruise ship to a smaller boat for trips to ports of call.

•**Wear comfortable clothing and shoes.** Everyone's legs and feet swell in the pressurized cabins of airplanes—but if your joints are prone to inflammation, swelling may prove especially uncomfortable.

•**Move around as much as possible.** To reduce soreness, take frequent breaks if you're in a car, or walk around the train or airplane cabin once an hour. (See the suggestions mentioned earlier for moving your legs while seated.)

■ **More from Marvin Cooper, MD…**

Five Secrets of Healthy Travel

Some simple strategies can help keep you well (especially if you plan to fly). These steps are useful even if you don't have a chronic medical condition. *For example…*

•**Observe your seatmates.** High-efficiency particulate air (HEPA) filters on airplanes are costly to run, so they typically are not turned on until an airplane has reached a cruising altitude. Even with air filtration, if your airplane seatmate is coughing, sneezing or showing other signs of illness and the flight isn't full, ask the flight attendant to give you a new seat.

•**Drink water and try nasal gel.** The dry air on airplanes often makes people feel dehydrated because the mucous membranes become dry, scratchy and irritated.

Helpful: Drink a glass of water every hour, and consider putting a dab of Ayr Saline Nasal Gel or Rhinaris Saline Nasal Gel (found at drugstores) just inside your nostrils every few hours to help reduce discomfort.

•**Always carry hand cleaners.** Use an alcohol-based hand sanitizer when you're away from a sink.

•**Get up-to-date information on vaccines.** Don't rely on travel agents. Their information is frequently inaccurate or out of date. Instead, ask your doctor and/or check the recommendations at the Web site of the Centers for Disease Control and Prevention, *wwwn.cdc.gov/travel.*

•**Don't count on traveler's insurance.** These policies often have loopholes that exclude the very medical emergencies most likely to arise if you have a preexisting condition. Before buying such a policy, read every clause carefully.

How to Save Your Own Life If You Have Cancer

Mark R. Fesen, MD, oncologist, clinical assistant professor at University of Kansas Medical School, Kansas City, and a member of the department of oncology at Hutchinson Clinic, Hutchinson, Kansas. He has trained at the National Cancer Institute and is a Fellow of the American College of Physicians. He is author of *Surviving the Cancer System: An Empowering Guide to Taking Control of Your Care* (Amacom). *www.HutchClinic.com.*

Panic typically follows a cancer diagnosis. Few patients can think clearly about their choices. The usual response is to stop thinking and to let their doctors (or their loved ones) make decisions for them.

This is understandable—but it can be harmful to the patient. Even at the best hospitals, cancer care tends to be chaotic. The primary physician might not know what the oncologist is doing. The oncologist might not communicate with, or might disagree with, the surgeon or radiologist.

Here's how to take charge of your care…

271

UNDERSTAND YOUR PATHOLOGY REPORT

It contains critical information about the type of cancer you have and how advanced it is. These reports are based on the microscopic findings of a biopsy.

It's rare for a biopsy to be completely incorrect, but even slight points of confusion can lead to ineffective treatments.

Example: One of my cousins passed away after he was diagnosed with a spinal tumor. The pathology report said that the tumor originated in the large intestine. Years later, I reexamined the biopsy sample and discovered that what he really had was a lung cancer—which requires totally different treatments.

Get a copy of your report, and talk to your oncologist to find out what everything means. Does the report seem to waffle with words or phrases such as "ranging from" or "possible"? These indicate that there's uncertainty about the findings. You need to understand if the tumor is "aggressive" or "slow-changing," or whether the cells are "poorly differentiated" (which means it might be hard to identify the specific cancer).

Important: You may want to get a second pathology opinion, particularly if the diagnosis seems unusual for someone of your age or lifestyle.

CHOOSE YOUR ONCOLOGIST

The oncologist is the point person who will supervise—and, in many cases, determine—your treatments. You want someone who is more than just an expert. He/she should also be a good listener…understand your concerns about quality of life…and help you cope with the emotional upheaval. *To find such a person…*

•**Talk to people you know.** A good oncologist will have a reputation in the community for being helpful as well as knowledgeable. A doctor might be a world-class expert, but that won't help if he/she won't return phone calls or always shifts your care to an assistant.

•**Plan a tryout.** Before committing to one oncologist, schedule a tryout visit to decide if you can trust this person with your life.

Helpful: Listen for "we" statements, such as, "We need to treat this" or "We have to get these tests done." The use of "we" instead of "you" is a good clue that the doctor plans to be closely involved with your care.

BOND WITH YOUR DOCTOR

Cancer patients are understandably frightened, which can make them difficult and/or argumentative. Many oncologists avoid or even drop difficult patients. Be respectful and courteous. Try to get to know your oncologist and his/her staff. Whenever possible, meet with your oncologist face-to-face, rather than telephoning or e-mailing your concerns.

Just as you would expect your sister-in-law or trusted uncle to give you the real scoop, when you make the oncologist your friend, you may get a more complete opinion.

BRING A SECOND SET OF EARS

Whenever possible, bring a friend or family member every time you meet with the oncologist. Most patients are too anxious to concentrate on details, including information about follow-up tests, treatment plans, etc. A friend or relative can take notes for you and ask pertinent questions.

DECIDE WHERE YOU'LL GET THE BEST TREATMENT

It's usually advisable to go to a hospital or cancer center close to where you live. This is where you are at your most comfortable and where the emotional support of your family and friends is at its strongest. Also, complications, such as infections and blood clots, are common in cancer patients. You might need emergency care, and it's always preferable to see doctors who know your history.

In general, I advise patients to go to a major cancer center only if they already live near one of these institutions…have a rare cancer…or require specialized treatments or surgery that can be provided only by a leading institution. Patients who are candidates for research studies also may benefit by going to a major center.

LISTEN TO YOUR DOCTOR, NOT THE "BOARD"

In large cancer centers, patient treatments are routinely reviewed, and sometimes guided by, recommendations from a "tumor board." This is a weekly discussion group that may include surgeons, medical oncologists and radiation oncologists, among other specialists. You can and should receive a written copy of the board's opinions. Ask for a transcript.

The problem: A tumor board is a good source of second opinions and specialized knowledge, but most of the doctors who attend have never seen the individual patient and may not be aware of his/her unique circumstances.

Follow the treatment suggestions of the oncologist who has interviewed and examined you directly—even if his conclusions differ from those of the tumor board.

ASK ABOUT RESEARCH STUDIES

This is mainly an issue for patients who are getting treatment at major cancer centers (which focus on research) or those with rare or difficult-to-treat cancers. Clinical trials may offer patients the best treatment, but there's no guarantee of this. No one should delay mainstream treatment in hope of being accepted into a clinical trial.

Patients who are seriously ill can lose valuable time when they wait to be admitted into a study. Patients often think that getting into a study means that they're going to get a better drug or therapy. Not necessarily. I've seen many patients in these studies get worse because the "cutting-edge" treatment turned out to be inferior to the already available treatments.

Caution: If you're a candidate for studies, pick one carefully. Review the study and your circumstances with your doctor (not someone who is involved with the study). Patients who participate in clinical trials may be prohibited from participating in certain other clinical trials. Understand whether this applies to you before you sign up for any clinical trial.

Financial Aid for Cancer Patients

Deborah E. Hoffman, MSW, LCSW, associate director, Shapiro Center for Patients and Families, Dana-Farber Cancer Institute, Boston, Massachusetts.

What's scarier—dying of cancer or paying for cancer treatment? It sounds like the punch line to an unfunny joke, but in fact, Americans are divided about half and half when asked to answer that question, according to a recent survey commissioned by the Community Oncology Alliance (COA).

Even if you have what you consider to be good health insurance, the financial burden on cancer patients can be overwhelming, notes Deborah E. Hoffman, MSW, LCSW, associate director of the Shapiro Center for Patients and Families at Dana-Farber Cancer Institute (*www.dana-farber.org*) in Boston. Most insurance policies have significant limitations, yearly caps and lifetime maximum payouts that can create financial disaster. Even middle-class professionals are not immune from the pressure. Recently, three out of four Americans who filed for bankruptcy cited medical expenses as a key factor even though most had health insurance and were well-educated, owned homes and held good-paying jobs...and that number has been going up, not down.

However, there is help to be had. An increasing number of medical institutions are realizing that financial help for patients can be nearly as important as medical help. At Dana-Farber, for example, cancer patients are now offered free financial coaching from the Financial Planning Association of Massachusetts (*www.fpama.org*) to help figure out how to handle medical costs, debt and other issues.

ASK FOR HELP—IT'S AVAILABLE

While not every medical center is equipped to offer full-service counseling such as that offered by the Dana-Farber program, most do have specialists on hand to help you overcome the daunting financial obstacles that accompany cancer—a list of challenges that may include how to cover the cost of required treatment versus available coverage...unexpected out-of-pocket expenses, often including the need to travel some distance for treatment...how to afford complementary and alternative treatments that are often not covered by health insurance...lost income, etc. Though it can be difficult to focus on anything but how to get better, the best strategy is to begin looking at treatment costs as soon as you can after diagnosis—or ask a capable family member or friend to do so. *Follow these steps to help stay on top of cancer costs...*

•**Meet with your hospital's designated professional** (the title may be something like "financial information officer" or "resource specialist") to discuss your practical concerns. He/she will be familiar with what's available to help with your financial burden. It's important to neither overstate nor understate your financial health, as some assistance is based on need.

•**Ask your insurer to assign you to a case manager.** It's usually easier to call a particular person with your questions about billing and coverage than to shuttle from one person to another each time you call.

•**Learn the details of what your health plan will pay for and what it won't cover.** For example, take note of the amount of your deductible (what you must pay before your coverage kicks in)…the covered length of any hospital stays (some pay for only 30 days, others for more)…annual or lifetime coverage limits (most plans have such limits on what they pay toward treatment for specific health conditions)…copays (the cost you are expected to cover at each visit)…and whether or not you are covered by another policy, such as your spouse's, and if so what are the different percentages each insurer will cover.

•**Stay in close touch with your insurer.** Even if the firm denies a claim or says it will not cover a particular treatment, keep asking…and ask your doctor to call on your behalf, too. The first answer isn't always the final answer—for instance, if you've been denied coverage for a type of treatment, it may help if you're able to provide evidence from your physician that it is most effective for your type of cancer.

•**Explore supportive programs and possible no-cost services.** Depending on your income, you may be eligible for free or low-cost drugs from pharmaceutical companies or treatment from providers. Cancer institutes such as Dana-Farber also have access to donor funds to help strapped patients with hidden cancer costs, such as paying for transportation, gas, parking and meals associated with hospital visits. Also, many private and hospital foundations provide assistance with treatment costs as well. Ask your specialist to outline the possibilities.

•**For particular types of cancer,** these organizations may provide additional financial support…

The Leukemia & Lymphoma Society
800-955-4572
www.lls.org

The CancerCare Co-Payment Assistance Foundation
866-552-6729
www.CancerCareCopay.org

The HealthWell Foundation
800-675-8416
www.healthwellfoundation.org

•**Maintain your liquidity.** The standard financial advice to pay off credit card balances may not be the right path for those who have cancer. It's an expensive disease to treat, and during this time, it might make sense to make only minimum payments and keep higher credit lines available to pay bills.

•**See a financial professional.** A financial planner can assist you with matters like budgeting, debt management, estate planning and insurance. If you have extensive credit card debt, a credit counselor can help you bundle three or four credit card payments into one monthly amount and, depending on your circumstances, negotiate for smaller or suspended payments.

•**Get a patient advocate.** The nonprofit Patient Advocate Association (*www.patientadvocate.org* or 800-532-5274) offers case-management services free of charge to help resolve insurance and financial difficulties.

CPR a Must—Even from Untrained Bystanders

Thomas D. Rea, MD, associate professor, medicine, University of Washington, Seattle, and program medical director, King County Medic One, EMS Division, Kent, Washington.
Michael Sayre, MD, associate professor, emergency medicine, Ohio State University, Columbus.
Circulation online.

The risk that an untrained bystander can do harm by giving *cardiopulmonary resuscitation,* or CPR, to someone who collapses in public is almost vanishingly small, a new study indicates.

And so the dispatchers who send emergency medical help when 911 is called should routinely tell the caller to start CPR, said Thomas D. Rea, MD, an associate professor of medicine at the University of Washington, and lead author of a report in an online issue of *Circulation*.

"There have been concerns expressed by laypeople and dispatchers that doing CPR might cause damage," Dr. Rea said. "Our study shows that you can help the person at risk and the chances that you can injure someone who is not in cardiac arrest are very, very small, and those injuries are not serious."

THE STUDY

Dr. Rea and his colleagues used data on 1,700 adults who received CPR in the King County emergency response system in a 36-month period. Dr. Rea is program medical director of the King County program. Of those, 55% were in cardiac arrest and 45% were not. Nearly half of those not in cardiac arrest received CPR from bystanders.

The data showed minor problems—discomfort or injuries in 9% to 11% of cases—but only four fractures, three due to chest compressions administered during CPR, one from repositioning the individual for CPR.

And while this study did not measure the benefits of giving CPR even when it eventually turned out to be unnecessary, "many studies have shown that the odds of surviving cardiac arrest increase by 20, 30, 100 percent, depending on what study you look at, when CPR is given," Dr. Rea said.

IMPLICATION

"The key finding here is that when a well-meaning member of the general public starts CPR and the victim is not in cardiac arrest, it will probably cause no injury at all," said Michael Sayre, MD, an associate professor of emergency medicine at Ohio State University, and a spokesperson for the American Heart Association. "The study reassures me that rescuers are rarely going to do any kind of injury."

WHEN TO GIVE CPR

King County emergency dispatchers use a basic two-question format to determine whether CPR

should be started. They ask if the person conscious and if the person is breathing normally.

"If the answers are 'no,' the dispatcher tells the caller to 'get the victim on a hard surface, on his back, bare the chest, put the hands in the center of the chest right between the nipples and then start compressions of one to two inches, counting aloud,'" Dr. Rea said. The dispatcher counts along with the CPR giver, and the routine continues until the emergency response team arrives.

It can end sooner if the person getting CPR regains consciousness and tells the rescuer to stop.

There often is uncertainty at the caller's end of the telephone encounter, Dr. Sayre said. "I know there can be hesitation in terms of training and doing it in person. But this shows that evaluating the situation quickly and starting CPR will rarely do any harm."

info For more advice on when and how to give CPR, visit the special CPR section of the American Heart Association Web site, *http://handsonlycpr.org/*.

How to Tell Your MD You're Using Natural Treatment

Mark A. Stengler, NMD, naturopathic medical doctor in private practice, La Jolla, California…adjunct associate clinical professor at the National College of Natural Medicine, Portland, Oregon…author of many books, including *The Natural Physician's Healing Therapies* and coauthor of *Prescription for Natural Cures* (both from Bottom Line Books)… and author of the *Bottom Line/Natural Healing* newsletter.

Many Americans are using complementary and alternative medicine, but how many are actually talking to their MDs about it?

To help get the conversation started, I asked Hyla Cass, MD, author of *Supplement Your Prescription: What Your Doctor Doesn't Know About Nutrition* (*www.cassmd.com*) for her advice. *Dr. Cass, who uses an integrated approach in her practice in Pacific Palisades, California, suggests the following…*

•**Good starting point.** Tell your MD about any vitamins or supplements you are taking—because harmful interactions with prescription medications may occur. Then let your doctor know that you believe natural medicine to be an important part of your health care.

•**Have realistic expectations.** Most MDs are not trained in integrative medicine and will not be able to give you advice about natural treatments. Common response from supportive MDs: "I have no problem with that if it's working for you."

•**How to deal with a negative response.** If your MD refuses to talk to you about this or is abrupt or dismisses your comments, ask him/her to reconsider. Suggest that he speak directly to your naturopathic physician, if you have one.

•**Find a doctor open to natural treatments.** Consider an MD who practices functional medicine, a form of integrative medicine in which the functioning of the entire body is taken into account rather than just the symptoms. To find a doctor who specializes in functional medicine, contact the Institute for Functional Medicine (800-228-0622, *www.functionalmedicine.org*).

Don't Wait for Your Doctor to Make You Well

Charles B. Inlander, consumer advocate and health-care consultant based in Fogelsville, Pennysylvania. He was founding president of People's Medical Society, a consumer health advocacy group active in the 1980s and 1990s. He is the author of more than 20 books, including *Take This Book to the Hospital with You* (St. Martin's).

A recent study on the health of Americans was a real shocker. It turns out we are far less healthy today than we were 20 years ago, according to the findings published in the *American Journal of Medicine.* While most of us are living longer, we are getting more serious diseases that are directly related to our lifestyles.

Overall, Americans received a C minus on their lifestyle habits from the study's lead researcher, who also noted that there's a tendency to believe that just taking a pill for high blood pressure or elevated cholesterol will compensate for

a poor diet and lack of exercise. But the good news is that you can change your lifestyle fairly easily, and there are many free or low-cost resources that can help. *My advice...*

•**Get creative with exercise.** If you're not exercising, whatever your excuse may be, there's a solution. For example, my wife recognized that she has a hard time maintaining her enthusiasm for her daily walks, so she persuaded a group of her friends to start an informal walking club. They go out every day and motivate each other to stay active. Many large malls sponsor walking programs inside the mall that typically begin each day just before the stores open. (Contact the management office of your local mall to find out whether it offers a walking program.) Older adults can find exercise programs designed specifically for people with arthritis or other physical limitations by contacting their local Area Agency on Aging (find your county's agency in the phone book) or go to *www.eldercare.gov* for a list of agencies.

•**Get smarter about nutrition.** The first step toward improving your eating habits is to get sound nutritional advice geared to your age and your specific health profile, including foods that contain optimal levels of vitamins and minerals and that help maximize your immunity. Many large hospitals offer free nutrition classes as well as weight-loss programs. Helpful resources also can be found online, such as the Web site *www.healthcastle.com,* which is operated by registered dietitians...or *www.nutrition.gov* (sponsored by the US Department of Agriculture).

•**Don't be sidelined by a chronic health problem.** US Senator Arlen Specter, who is now 80 years old, plays a game of squash nearly every day and did so while twice being treated for cancer over a four-year period. If you have a chronic condition, such as heart disease, diabetes or cancer, it doesn't mean that you should turn into a couch potato. In addition to asking your doctor about activities that can help you stay in better shape, contact your local chapter of the American Heart Association (*www.heart.org*)...the American Diabetes Association (*www.diabetes.org*)...or the American Cancer Society (*www.cancer.org*) for information about local programs focusing on maintaining a healthy lifestyle, and check their Web sites for online resources.

Remember, there's no pill that can take charge of your health the way you can.

■ ■ ■ ■

Doctors Do Not Always Inform Patients of Abnormal Test Results

One of every 14 cases of abnormal test results were not reported to patients, says a Weill Cornell Medical College study that looked at 23 physician practices across the country. In some practices, the failure rate was zero, while in others it was as high as one in four. Call your doctor's office if you do not get test results within one week.

Mark A. Stengler, NMD, naturopathic medical doctor in private practice, La Jolla, California…adjunct associate clinical professor at the National College of Natural Medicine, Portland, Oregon…author of many books, including *The Natural Physician's Healing Therapies* and coauthor of *Prescription for Natural Cures* (both from Bottom Line Books)… and author of the *Bottom Line/Natural Healing* newsletter.

Medical Scams: How Some Doctors and Hospitals Threaten Your Well-Being

Evan S. Levine, MD, clinical assistant professor of medicine at Albert Einstein College of Medicine and a practicing internist and cardiologist at Montefiore Medical Center, both in New York City. He is the author of *What Your Doctor Won't (Or Can't) Tell You* (G.P. Putnam's Sons).

Even though the overwhelming majority of physicians are honest and hard-working and make medical recommendations based only on their patients' well-being, some doctors and hospitals allow their desire to turn a profit to interfere with good medical practices.

Evan S. Levine, MD, an internist and cardiologist at Montefiore Medical Center in New York City, has 18 years' experience as a physician and has done extensive research in the area of un-

scrupulous medical practices. *Dr. Levine advises medical consumers to beware of…*

***Scam:* Using bait-and-switch tactics to get new patients.** Sometimes a store will advertise a "hot" product for a rock-bottom price, but when you go to buy it, you're told that it's "sold out." This type of bait-and-switch tactic—advertising a great-sounding product that is available only in limited numbers—is used by some hospitals.

Example: You see an ad for an impressive new doctor who trained at the most prestigious institutions, but when you call to make an appointment, he/she is too busy to see you for six months. You get an appointment with his junior partner instead, and the big-name doctor has successfully attracted another patient to the hospital.

My advice: Do your research when looking for a new physician. Don't rely on advertising to find one. Get referrals from a doctor you've seen for a long time (if you have one) and/or family members and friends whose judgment you trust. Schedule a "get acquainted" meeting with the doctor to make sure that you like his demeanor and overall treatment philosophy. (Your insurance provider may cover such a visit.)

Also helpful: If you are diagnosed with a serious illness, such as cancer or Parkinson's disease, promptly see two physicians for an initial consultation—one who specializes in research on the condition and one involved in patient care.

This will greatly increase your odds of getting information on state-of-the-art treatments and the personal care you need. You can find a doctor who conducts research on a particular condition via an Internet search or by calling a local university-affiliated hospital and asking for such specialists.

Scam: Giving costly medical tests that patients don't really need. More and more internists and specialists, such as cardiologists, are performing costly medical tests in their offices to increase profits.

Example: *Computed tomography angiograms* (CTAs), which examine blood flow in the arteries. This noninvasive test can be useful in determining the extent and severity of suspected or existing coronary artery disease.

But some doctors tell patients who don't have heart disease symptoms, such as chest pain or shortness of breath, to get the test—even though the American College of Cardiology (ACC) does not recommend it in these cases.

The machine used to perform a CTA costs at least $1 million, so there's a financial incentive for these doctors to recommend the test even when it's not needed. Aside from the unnecessary expense for the patient, the radiation from this test is equivalent to having more than 100 chest X-rays.

My advice: Only a cardiologist should determine if you need a CTA, and it should be performed at an outpatient hospital center—not in his office.

To read the ACC's guidelines for this test: Go to *www.acc.org* and click on "Quality and Science," then "Appropriate Use Criteria."

Another red flag: Sonography machines in an internist's office. Sonograms should be performed under the supervision of a cardiologist or radiologist. Internists don't have the appropriate training.

Scam: **Pushing patients out of the hospital prematurely to boost profits.** Some hospitals strive to get patients checked out as quickly as possible to make room for more patients. That's because insurance companies typically pay set fees based on a patient's diagnosis rather than the length of hospital stays. Shorter stays mean more turnover—and more money.

Some hospital administrators pressure doctors to check out patients quickly, and some doctors may even get bonuses if their patients have short lengths of stay.

Where the danger is greatest: Beds in the intensive care unit (ICU) are far more costly than regular beds, so to make room, patients are sometimes sent out of the ICU too soon. If a loved one is moved from an ICU to an area with fewer monitors and nurses, it can be dangerous —or even deadly.

My advice: Speak up. If you think a loved one is too sick to leave the ICU or hospital, complain to the head nurse on the floor or to the hospital administrator or patient advocate. (Get the administrator's or patient advocate's phone number from the hospital's operator.)

Scam: **Prescribing expensive or unnecessary drugs.** Some doctors are swayed by perks (such as free meals) from drug companies and prescribe costly brand-name medications that are no better than generic alternatives.

Oncologists are one of the few types of physicians who can sell medication in their offices in addition to prescribing it. To increase his bottom line, an oncologist could recommend pricey chemotherapy that won't necessarily make you feel better or prolong your life.

My advice: If your doctor recommends a drug that he sells, ask if there are studies showing that the medication is more effective in treating your condition than other drugs.

If it's chemotherapy, ask if research has shown that the treatment prolongs life. And seek a second opinion from another oncologist—preferably one based at an academic center.

Are Sinus Rinses Sabotaging Your Nose?

Talal Nsouli, MD, clinical professor, pediatrics and allergy/immunology, Georgetown University School of Medicine, and director, Watergate & Burke Allergy & Asthma Centers, Washington, DC.

Michael J. Bergstein, MD, senior attending physician, Northern Westchester Hospital Center, Mt. Kisco, New York, and assistant clinical professor, otolaryngology, Mount Sinai School of Medicine, New York City.

Jordan S. Josephson, MD, sinus specialist, in private practice in New York City. He is director of the New York Nasal and Sinus Center and an attending physician at Manhattan Eye, Ear and Throat Hospital, both in New York City. He is author of *Sinus Relief Now* (Perigee). *www.drjjny.com.*

American College of Allergy, Asthma & Immunology annual meeting, Miami Beach.

Rinsing sinuses with a saline solution might have soothing short-term benefits, but it could actually make you more prone to infections in the long run by stripping your nose of critical immune soldiers.

"By washing the nose, we are removing the bad mucus but, unfortunately, we are also removing the good mucus that contains the antimicrobial agents as well," said Talal Nsouli, MD, lead author of new research on the issue. That can leave a person exposed to even more sinus infections.

Legions of people, according to the researchers, use nasal saline irrigation to treat sinus infections, despite lack of robust evidence to support its use.

THE STUDY

For the study, 68 people irrigated at least twice a day for one year, then discontinued the practice and were followed for the next year.

The rate of sinus infections decreased 62% once irrigation was stopped, the study found.

The research was presented in Miami Beach at the annual meeting of the American College of Allergy, Asthma & Immunology.

"People who were using nasal sinus irrigation were having an average of eight sinus infections a year," said Dr. Nsouli. They dropped to three per year once the irrigation was stopped. Dr. Nsouli is a clinical professor of pediatrics and allergy/immunology at Georgetown University School of Medicine and director of Watergate & Burke Allergy & Asthma Centers, in Washington, DC.

STUDY AUTHOR RECOMMENDATIONS

"The nasal secretions do contain immune elements that protect patients against infection," he explained. "Our first-line protection is the mucus that we have.

"Our recommendation is that patients should not use nasal saline on a regular basis, only when they have an infection," Dr. Nsouli said. "Long-term use was harmful and not helpful at all, and depleting the nose of its immune elements caused infections to occur on a chronic basis."

EXPERT REACTION

Michael J. Bergstein, MD, senior attending physician at Northern Westchester Hospital Center in Mt. Kisco, New York, agrees with Dr. Nsouli.

"There's a blanket of little, hairlike projections called cilia in the nose, and those cilia can be stunned if they're chronically bathed in hypertonic, which is excess salt, or hypo, which is too-little salt, rinses," he said. "Do not use nasal saline irrigation as a maintenance because you'll be altering the natural immune benefit that the sinuses have."

But Jordan S. Josephson, MD, a sinus specialist with Lenox Hill Hospital in New York City and author of *Sinus Relief Now,* offered a different view. "I totally, wholeheartedly disagree with the article," he said. "I think irrigation is a marvelous thing."

Though it's possible for irrigation to wash away protective cells along with the infection, the protective "mucous blanket" of the sinus passages re-forms and goes back to work, he said.

info For more information on sinus infection, visit the Web site of the US National Institute of Allergy and Infectious Diseases, *www3.niaid.nih.gov,* and search "sinusitis."

■ ■ ■ ■

The Right Amount of Salt Is Key to Good Sinus Irrigation

"The key to nasal irrigation is to get the salt concentration right," said Timothy McCall, MD, medical editor of *Yoga Journal* and author of *Yoga as Medicine: The Yogic Prescription for Health and Healing.* "Too little (*hypotonic*) or too much (*hypertonic*) salt is very irritating to lining of the nose. Using an isotonic solution (the same salt concentration as the normal cells of the body) is quite soothing to nasal mucosa," he added. "To make the solution, use between ⅛ to ¼ of a teaspoon of non-iodized table salt stirred into eight ounces of warm water."

Timothy McCall, MD, a board-certified internist in Oakland, California, medical editor of *Yoga Journal* and author of *Yoga as Medicine: The Yogic Prescription for Health and Healing* (Bantam). *www.drmccall.com.*

■ ■ ■ ■

Portable Generators Can Emit Dangerous Levels of Carbon Monoxide

These gasoline-powered generators are used to power homes during electrical outages. One generator can produce 100 times more carbon monoxide than that found in a car's exhaust. Carbon monoxide poisoning can cause headaches, shortness of breath, nausea, even death.

Self-defense: Place generators as far away from the home as possible and also away from windows. Don't run a generator in a garage or any other enclosed space.

Steven J. Emmerich, MS, researcher on air cleaners, indoor-air quality, ventilation and energy consumption, National Institute of Standards and Technology, Gaithersburg, Maryland. *www.NIST.gov.*

■ ■ ■ ■

A Breath of Fresh Air

Levels of ozone, a gas that contributes to air pollution, dropped about 33% faster in airtight chambers containing three common houseplants (snake plant, spider plant and devil's ivy) than they did in chambers without plants. Indoor sources of ozone—which can cause such health problems as impaired lung function—include laser printers, ultraviolet lights and even some electrostatic air-purification systems.

Theory: A detoxification process is triggered when plant leaves absorb pollutants.

Dennis Decoteau, PhD, professor of horticulture, Pennsylvania State University, University Park.

Everyday Hiding Places Of Dangerous Bacteria And Viruses

Elizabeth Scott, PhD, assistant professor of biology and codirector of the Center for Hygiene & Health in Home & Community at Simmons College in Boston. *www.simmons.edu/hygieneandhealth.* A member of the scientific advisory board of the International Forum on Home Hygiene, she is coauthor of *How to Prevent Food Poisoning: A Practical Guide to Safe Cooking, Eating and Food Handling* (Wiley).

After the recent flu pandemic, everyone knows that the virus that causes this illness is easily transmitted person to person. As a protective measure, even hand shaking and "cheek kissing" were temporarily banned in some churches, schools and other public places.

But the H1N1 and seasonal flu viruses can often be found in places that many people would never suspect. This is also true of other harmful microbes, such as *methicillin-resistant Staphylococcus aureus* (MRSA) bacteria, and bacteria, including *Escherichia coli* and *salmonella,* that cause foodborne illness.

What you may not know: It's been estimated that about one in three Americans are carriers (and transmitters) of staph bacteria—usually in amounts so small that no infection occurs in the carrier.

Since it's impossible to completely avoid dangerous microbes, one of the best ways to stay healthy is to be aware of germ "hot spots" —including ones that often are overlooked, such as...

•**Telephone receivers (and cell phones), TV remote controls, computer keyboards and copying machines.** Most of us know to wash our hands after touching public doorknobs or handrails, but we may not consider the microbes on telephone receivers (and cell phones), TV remote controls and computer keyboards in public places, at work or even in our own homes.

Other areas to be wary of include the control buttons on office copying machines, handles of communal coffeepots, elevator buttons and shared books or tools.

It's best to assume that any inanimate surface—such as Formica, stainless steel or paper —that could have been touched by another person may be infected with viruses or bacteria. If you touch your mouth, nose and/or eyes (the body's main entry points for infectious organisms) after touching the infected surface, you will be exposed to the germ.

Cold viruses and many bacterial infections are primarily transmitted by such surface contact. Flu viruses—including the H1N1 and seasonal flu—tend to be transmitted through the air (via coughs and sneezes) but also can be passed through surface contact.

What you may not know: Since bacteria and cold and flu viruses can survive for up to several days on inanimate surfaces, you can be exposed to germs long after the infected person has contaminated the area. Scientists have estimated that 80% of all human infections are transmitted via hand-to-hand or surface contact.

Self-defense: After touching inanimate surfaces (such as those described earlier) in a public place—or at home, if someone in your household is sick and you will likely be exposed—wash your hands thoroughly with plain soap for 20 seconds under running water. Then dry them thoroughly with a paper towel or air dryer. Or apply hand-sanitizing gel containing at least 62% alcohol, such as Purell Instant Hand Sanitizer or Germ-X, as soon as possible after touching such surfaces.

If someone in your home or office is sick: Each day, clean surfaces that are touched by others with a cleansing wipe or other product (such as those made by Lysol or Clorox) that is registered with the Environmental Protection Agency (EPA)—check the product label for an EPA registration number. This means the product can be used as a disinfectant. Or simply squirt alcohol-based hand sanitizer on a paper towel and wipe the surface.

Important: Use wipes and gels that kill bacteria and viruses. These broader-spectrum cleansers are sometimes labeled "antimicrobial"—not "antibacterial."

•**Paper money.** A Swiss study found that some strains of flu virus can survive on paper money for up to three days—and for up to 17 days when mixed with mucus.

In addition, a University of California researcher cultured 68 $1 bills and found that all but four had colonies of dangerous bacteria, including the variety that cause staph infections and pneumonia. Coins tend to have lower levels of bacteria and viruses—perhaps because they contain trace metals that help inhibit such microbes.

Self-defense: To reduce your exposure to germs, use credit or debit cards in place of paper currency as often as possible during daily transactions, and wash your hands with soap or use a hand sanitizer after touching paper money.

•**Doctors' waiting rooms.** Studies have found that germs are transmitted at a particularly high rate in the waiting areas of doctors' offices—especially by touching countertops, pens and even magazines.

Self-defense: As much as possible, avoid touching shared surfaces (such as those described above), and wash your hands immediately after your doctor visit.

If hand-washing is inconvenient, keep hand sanitizer in your pocket or purse and carry your own pen to sign papers at doctors' offices and stores.

•**Pets.** An increasing body of evidence shows that dogs—and cats, especially—carry MRSA bacteria. It's believed that these animals are exposed to the germs by human carriers and that the bacteria contaminate the animals' coats, skin and saliva, where it can then be transmitted to other animals and people. MRSA bacteria can, of course, infect humans, but it also can make cats and dogs sick.

Important new finding: A recent random study conducted at the University of Guelph in Canada found that 2% to 3% of dogs carry MRSA bacteria. Meanwhile, in a study of 35 homes, researchers at Simmons College in Boston found that people who have cats in their homes are eight times more likely to have MRSA bacteria on household surfaces than those without household cats.

Self-defense: Wash your hands or use a hand sanitizer after touching your pet…make sure any cuts or abrasions you have are covered with a bandage before touching an animal …do not let pets lick your face…wash pets' food and water bowls in a sink separate from the one used to prepare your own food…and wear gloves whenever touching an animal that has an open wound.

•**Microwave ovens, countertops and salt and pepper shakers.** Most of us know that we need to clean kitchen faucet handles and sinks, sponges and cutting boards to avoid exposure to foodborne microbes. However, some surfaces tend to be overlooked, such as microwave oven controls—which are touched frequently, often while users are handling raw food—and countertops, which are high-contact areas for raw food. Research shows that salt and pepper shakers also are likely to be contaminated.

Self-defense: Immediately after preparing any raw food—including fruit and vegetables as well as meat, fish or poultry—wipe down any surfaces you may touch (such as microwave controls, countertops and salt and pepper shakers) with antimicrobial cleanser, or use a mixture of one part household bleach diluted in 10 parts water. Apply the cleanser with paper towels or disposable rags. If you use sponges, put them in the dishwasher each time you run it—or rinse, then microwave them for one minute at high power several times a week. Do not place sponges that contain metal fibers in the microwave.

•**Bathroom sink handles.** In one survey of the homes of 30 adults with colds, bathroom sink handles were identified as the place most likely to harbor traces of cold virus.

Self-defense: If anyone in your family has a cold or flu—or any other respiratory, skin or gastrointestinal infection—clean bathroom sink handles (as well as other potentially contaminated objects, such as doorknobs and light switches) at least once daily with antimicrobial cleanser.

■ ■ ■ ■

Contamination Alert!

Campylobacter was found in 62% of fresh whole broilers...*salmonella* in 14%...and both types in 9%.

Also: Most of the bacteria found were resistant to at least one antibiotic. A recent test shows a modest improvement since 2007, when these pathogens were found in 80% of broilers, but findings suggest that most companies' safeguards are inadequate.

Cleanest brand-name chicken: Perdue—56% of Perdue chickens were free of bacteria.

Self-defense: Thaw chicken in a refrigerator, inside its package and on a plate...in a bowl filled with cold water (change water every 30 minutes)...or defrost it on a plate in a microwave. Never thaw it on a counter—even when the chicken's inside is frozen, the outside can provide a breeding ground for bacteria. Cook chicken to at least 165°F.

Urvashi Rangan, PhD, director of technical policy, Consumers Union, Yonkers, New York, and leader of a study of 382 chickens, published in *Consumer Reports.* *www.ConsumersUnion.org.*

■ ■ ■ ■

Better Burger Tips

An off-color, such as brown or gray, does not indicate *E. coli* or other bacteria. The interior of packaged meat may be grayish brown due to lack of oxygen. However, if all the meat has turned brown or gray, it may be beginning to spoil. No brands or sources are certain to be free of contamination, because bacteria are everywhere in the environment. But cooking ground meat to an internal temperature of 160°F will kill any E. coli present.

Larry Beuchat, PhD, Distinguished Research Professor at the Center for Food Safety in the College of Agricultural and Environmental Sciences, University of Georgia, Griffin.

Don't Let Food Manufacturers Trick You Into Eating More

David A. Kessler, MD, former head of the Food and Drug Administration and onetime dean of the Yale School of Medicine. A professor at the University of California, San Francisco, he is author of *The New York Times* best seller *The End of Overeating: Taking Control of the American Appetite* (Rodale).

Take a moment and think of a food that is irresistible to you. You probably can see it vividly in your mind's eye...and you even may start to salivate.

Chances are that the food you imagined is not a vegetable or fruit but rather a processed food made with a precise combination of ingredients that trigger repeated cravings similar to those of addicts who can't resist a drug or alcohol.

Can our taste buds really be so easily tricked by food manufacturers?

Absolutely, says David Kessler, MD, former head of the Food and Drug Administration. Dr. Kessler, who has extensively researched the eating habits of Americans, recently answered questions about the ways the food industry is controlling our appetites.

•**It's widely reported that about one-third of American adults weigh too much. Why has this occurred in the US?**

There should be a balance between the food we consume and the energy we expend. All the evidence says that it's the amount we eat that's gotten out of hand.

It's useful to note that in 1960, the average 40- to 49-year-old American woman weighed 142 pounds. By 2000, the average weight in that age group had jumped to 169 pounds. Research shows that also during this period, American adults were gaining more from ages 20 to 40. Instead of just a few pounds, the average man gained more than 12 pounds during these ages.

• Why are Americans now eating so much more?

While past generations ate most of their food at mealtimes, processed foods that are highly "palatable"—meaning that they stimulate the appetite and prompt us to eat more—are now available 24/7. With such ready access, it's become socially acceptable to eat these foods at any hour of the day. For many people, they're impossible to resist.

• Can't a person use willpower to resist such foods?

Not necessarily. It's not a question of people lacking self-control or being lazy. What's really happening is that their brain circuitry has been "hijacked."

Considerable animal and human research shows that foods are made palatable by three ingredients—fat, sugar and salt. Sugar is the main driver of food appeal. Fat and salt work synergistically with sugar.

Get the proportions right, and you hit what might be called the "blisspoint." Candy bars, buffalo wings, Big Macs, cheese fries—they all combine fat, sugar and salt. The "white chocolate mocha frappuccino" served at Starbucks is coffee diluted with a mix of sugar, fat and salt.

• How do these foods hijack our brain circuits?

Foods that taste good are reinforcing—that is, they keep us coming back for more. But highly palatable—or so-called "hyperpalatable"—foods do even more.

They stimulate brain circuits that release *dopamine*, the neurotransmitter that focuses attention and increases motivation. It can take only a single taste of a hyperpalatable food to set this process in motion.

After you've eaten such a food several times, you become more sensitive to cues surrounding the experience—for example, the sight of the wrapper and the name of the food arouses your memory of how it felt to eat the food and focuses your attention on getting it.

Each time you repeat the experience by eating the food, you strengthen the neural circuits involved, making yourself ever more sensitive to anticipation cues—literally rewiring your brain.

• What is the food industry's role in all this?

The basic business plan of the typical modern food company is to sell foods loaded with fat, sugar and salt.

Take buffalo wings—it's the fatty part of chicken, fried and refried and covered with red sauce that's full of salt and sugar. Fat on fat, on fat, on sugar and salt.

You'll find similar combinations in many appetizers, snacks and fast foods, such as chocolate-covered pretzels and cinnamon rolls.

"The three points of the compass" is what one high-level food industry executive calls sugar, fat and salt. "They make food compelling," he told me. "They make it indulgent. They make us want to eat more."

But it's easy for consumers to tell when a food is fatty, salty and sugary—it's not like the food industry can hide it.

Actually, experts in the food industry have found additional, sneakier ways to increase what they call the "craveability" of food products.

They've learned how to combine ingredients, including chemical enhancers (such as artificial sweeteners, hickory smoke flavor and cheese flavorings) to create a complex series of flavors and textures that magnify the sensory appeal.

Food manufacturers even have spent considerable effort making their creations easier to swallow. It used to be that the average bite of food in the American diet required 20 chews before swallowing—now it's only two or three chews.

As soon as that fleeting taste and oral stimulation fade, you reach for more. Through careful engineering by food companies, you're led to eat quickly enough to override your body's "I'm full" signals.

On top of that, incessant advertising adds pleasurable associations to the sensory experience—it pairs foods with images of parties, barbecues and friends having fun. The combined effect is very powerful.

People in the food industry would argue that they're just giving consumers what they want. But we now know this means excessively activating our brains to overeat—not what most consumers would want once they understood what was happening.

•Why not go on a diet?

Diets alone won't work, because they can't change the brain circuitry that's been created by all the food cues put forth by the food industry. You can try to fight these forces by depriving yourself—and you may even lose weight for 30, 60 or 90 days. But if you're still living in the same environment, you'll be surrounded by all the same food cues you've been trained to respond to.

You can keep foods full of sugar, fat and salt out of the house, but every time you walk down the street, you'll be bombarded. Sooner or later, you'll gain back the weight. A diet alone doesn't get at the root of the problem—the way your behavior has been shaped by changes in your brain circuitry.

•What can we do to defend ourselves?

Simply knowing that the food industry has created many of its products in a way that is calculated to take control of your eating behavior will go a long way toward helping you see hyperpalatable foods for what they are—which is not at all appealing.

When you're armed with this knowledge, you can take some concrete steps to replace one set of automatic behaviors with another set that is much more healthful.

For example, for people who are overweight and those who may not be overweight but want to avoid unhealthful processed foods, I suggest that they establish their own rules and enforce them ruthlessly. Identify the foods that you know are uncontrollably appealing and decide that they're absolutely off limits.

For a while at least, plan all your eating. Decide what you want to eat and when, and limit it to three meals a day, with a midmorning and midafternoon snack.

•What if I start to lose my resolve?

If you feel yourself slipping into a mental dialogue of "This looks great, but I know I shouldn't have it...maybe just this once..." then reframe your thoughts and remind yourself of your goals. Tell yourself, for example, "If I don't give in to my desire for this food, I'll feel a lot better about myself tomorrow."

Many of us have gotten so caught up by the stimulation of food that we have lost touch with how much we really need to eat to feel satisfied. How much will it take to keep you from getting hungry until the next meal? Try increasingly smaller portions—you may be surprised by what you find out.

■ ■ ■ ■

Deadly Labeling Loophole for Trans Fats

Products with less than 0.5 grams of trans fat per serving are allowed to list their trans fat content as zero.

Problem: If you eat more than one serving of a product that has a small amount of trans fat, you may consume a significant amount.

Self-defense: Look for the words "partially hydrogenated" on products' ingredient labels. This means that there is some trans fat present, even if the listed content is zero. Eat as little trans fat as possible, even if you cannot eliminate it from your diet completely.

UC Berkeley Wellness Letter, 500 Fifth Ave., New York City 10010.

■ ■ ■ ■

Getting Hooked on Fish Is Healthy for Most

Despite reports that farmed fish contain more contaminants than wild, both generally are safe and nutritious to eat.

But: Pregnant women, nursing mothers and young children should be careful about which fish they eat. See the list at *www.Fish4Health. net,* and click on "Wallet Card" for a printable card that you can carry when dining out.

Charles R. Santerre, PhD, professor of food toxicology, department of foods and nutrition, Purdue University, West Lafayette, Indiana.

Stroke Prevention & Recovery

Shingles Raises Stroke Risk 31%

dults with the skin disease shingles appear to be at an increased risk for stroke, especially when it affects the area around the eyes, researchers report.

Previous reports have linked shingles with stroke risk, but "the exact frequency and risk for these phenomena are still unknown," said study lead author Jiunn-Horng Kang, MD, a principal investigator in the Neuroscience Research Center of Taipei Medical University Hospital, Taiwan. His team published their findings in the journal *Stroke*.

ABOUT SHINGLES

Shingles is a painful skin rash resulting from infection by the *varicella-zoster virus*, the same virus that causes chicken pox. The virus remains in the body after recovery from chicken pox and can erupt again to cause shingles.

Shingles usually starts as a rash on one side of the face or body, and often causes pain, itching and tingling. Attacks can last for two to four weeks. The incidence of shingles increases with age, and the US Centers for Disease Control and Prevention recommends most people over age 60 be vaccinated against the virus, with the major exception being those with weakened immune systems.

THE STUDY

Dr. Kang and his colleagues studied data on 7,760 adult Taiwanese who were treated for shingles between 1997 and 2001. In the year after treatment, 133 of them, or 1.7%, had strokes. The incidence in a control group of 23,280 adults who were not treated for shingles was 1.3% (306 people).

Analysis of the data found that the risk of stroke in that one-year period was 31% higher in

Jiunn-Horng Kang, MD, principal investigator, Neuroscience Research Center, Taipei Medical University Hospital, Taiwan.

Daniel Lackland, MD, professor, epidemiology and medicine, Medical University of South Carolina, Charleston.

Stroke.

the shingles group. The incidence was dramatically higher for those with a shingles infection in or around the eye—nearly 4.3 times higher than in the control group.

Strokes can be ischemic, caused by a blood clot blocking a brain artery, or hemorrhagic, due to rupture of a blood vessel. The study found a 31% higher incidence of ischemic strokes, the most common kind, and a 2.79-times higher incidence of hemorrhagic stroke in the shingles group.

POSSIBLE CAUSE

"The major mechanism of our findings is that stroke results from herpes zoster virus-induced *vasculopathy* [blood vessel damage]," Dr. Kang said. "The vessel to the brain damaged by the virus could be *occluded* [blocked] or ruptured."

"However, several other factors could also be involved," he added.

ADVICE

No known treatment exists to reduce the apparent risk of stroke that results from shingles infection, Dr. Kang said. "Our interest and ongoing research are focused on whether early antiviral treatment for herpes zoster can reduce the risk of stroke," he said. Also, patients who have a shingles attack should be aware of the risk of stroke, and talk to their doctor about managing risk factors for stroke, such as hypertension, high cholesterol and diabetes, said Dr. Kang.

EXPERT REACTION

While there have been scattered reports about a possible association of shingles with stroke, "to my knowledge this is the first study to link shingles very specifically with stroke," said Daniel Lackland, MD, professor of epidemiology and medicine at the Medical University of South Carolina, and a spokesman for the American Stroke Association.

"It might be a little too early for a lot of clinical implications here," Dr. Lackland said. "But a physician who is treating someone with shingles should emphasize the importance of traditional risk factors for stroke, and let the patient know that your risk might be a little bit increased and you should pay more attention to high blood pressure, cholesterol and the like."

info For more information about shingles, visit the Web site of the US National Library of Medicine, *www.nlm.nih.gov/medline plus/shingles.html.*

■ ■ ■ ■

Better Stroke Risk Predictor

To determine which patients need drugs and/ or lifestyle changes to reduce stroke risk, doctors consider blood pressure, blood sugar, cholesterol, weight, exercise, cigarette use and family history.

New: Patients thought to be at intermediate risk for stroke were more accurately classified as high risk or low risk when assessment also included blood tests for two inflammation markers, *C-reactive protein* (CRP) and *lipoprotein-associated phospholipase A2* (Lp-PLA2).

Best: Ask your doctor whether you should have CRP and Lp-PLA2 measured.

Vijay Nambi, MD, cardiologist, Methodist DeBakey Heart and Vascular Center and Baylor College of Medicine, both in Houston, and lead author of a study of 949 people.

New Stroke Research Shakes Up Medical Establishment

Peter Rothwell, MD, PhD, professor, neurology, University of Oxford, England.

Philip B. Gorelick, MD, professor, neurology, and director, Center for Stroke Research, University of Illinois, Chicago.

The Lancet.
The Lancet Neurology.

Challenging established medical wisdom about blood pressure and stroke, new British research suggests that extremely variable blood pressure, and not just high blood pressure, can greatly increase a person's risk for stroke.

Peter Rothwell, MD, PhD, a professor of neurology at the University of Oxford, is the lead author of four papers published in the journals

The Lancet and *The Lancet Neurology*, which examined variable blood pressure and stroke risk.

STUDY ON VARIABLE BLOOD PRESSURE

One paper looked at high blood pressure and blood pressure variability in four groups of 2,000 people, each of who had minor strokes, known as *transient ischemic attacks* (TIAs), or "mini-strokes." These are warning signs of stroke risk.

They found that people with the greatest variation in systolic blood pressure (the top number in a blood pressure reading) over seven visits to their doctor were six times more likely to have a major stroke. People with the highest blood pressure readings were 15 times more likely to have a stroke.

IMPLICATIONS

Underdiagnosis and undertreatment of hypertension is a major problem, Dr. Rothwell said. "The new research shows that part of the problem is likely to have been underrecognition of the impact of variability in blood pressure on diagnosis in routine clinical practice in primary care. It shows that doctors have to make diagnoses on the basis of blood pressure measurements that vary substantially from visit to visit."

The message for doctors is that they have to change the way they view high blood pressure, he said.

"All current clinical guidelines encourage doctors to ignore variability and occasional high readings and to rely exclusively on the average blood pressure from multiple visits or 24-hour monitoring," Dr. Rothwell said. "The new research shows that increased variability in blood pressure, a high maximum blood pressure and episodic hypertension are associated with high risks of stroke and other vascular events, and emphasize that any comfort taken from the fact blood pressure is sometimes normal is false."

Variability can easily be measured when people visit their doctors, although "the fact that many people now monitor their blood pressure at home will be helpful in identifying variability," he said.

BEST MEDICATIONS FOR BLOOD PRESSURE VARIABILITY

Other papers by Dr. Rothwell and his colleagues indicated that doctors should consider blood pressure variability when they choose among the many drugs now prescribed to control high blood pressure. A meta-analysis of 389 controlled trials found that effects on blood pressure variability explained why some classes of blood pressure drugs were more effective than others in preventing stroke. Another paper looked at the greater effectiveness of *calcium channel blockers* and *thiazide diuretics* vs. *beta blockers* in reducing stroke risk.

The result: "Calcium channel blockers and thiazide diuretics reduce [blood pressure] variability and beta blockers increase it," Dr. Rothwell concluded.

He called for development of new drugs that would stabilize and lower blood pressure at the same time. "Drugs that reduced variability without reducing average blood pressure should still prevent stroke and would be likely to be helpful in patients who cannot tolerate reductions in their average blood pressure," Dr. Rothwell theorized.

EXPERT REACTION

"I think these findings are very important and very compelling, and may revolutionize how we treat blood pressure in the future," said Philip B. Gorelick, MD, director of the Center for Stroke Research at the University of Illinois, and a leading American expert on blood pressure and stroke. "They provide a very important foundation for change in future treatment."

Dr. Rothwell's findings already are starting to affect Dr. Gorelick's practice, he said.

"First, we may begin to screen patients with blood pressure measurements for variability to see if we can select for classes of drugs that reduce variability," Dr. Gorelick said. "And we can certainly adopt an at-home program to detect blood pressure variability, although within-visit variability seems to be a more important factor."

The findings may also affect the choice of the first drugs prescribed for blood pressure control, he said. "We would consider calcium channel blockers and diuretics for initial use," Dr. Gorelick said.

info For more on spotting and controlling high blood pressure, visit the American Heart Association Web site, *www.heart.org.* Click on "high blood pressure" under "Diseases & Conditions."

Hidden Stroke Risks Very Few Know

Steven R. Messé, MD, assistant professor of neurology and director of the vascular neurology fellowship at the Hospital of the University of Pennsylvania in Philadelphia. Board-certified in neurology and vascular neurology, he has published scientific papers in *Stroke, Neurology* and the *Journal of Neurology, Neurosurgery and Psychiatry.*

Many risk factors for stroke are well known. For example, high blood pressure (hypertension), elevated cholesterol, diabetes, inactivity, smoking, a prior stroke or "mini-stroke" (also called a *transient ischemic attack*, or TIA) or a family history of stroke all increase your odds of suffering this potentially devastating condition.

Of the nearly 800,000 Americans who suffer a stroke each year, about 87% have an ischemic stroke (a clot blocks blood flow to the brain) and 13% have a hemorrhagic stroke (a blood vessel in the brain ruptures). In the US, stroke is the number-three cause of death and a leading cause of disability—complications can include paralysis...weakness in an arm or leg...and/or speech problems.

What few people realize: There are many little-known risk factors for stroke, which also should be taken seriously, particularly if you have one or more of the risk factors mentioned above. Each additional risk factor increases your chance of having a stroke.

For example...

COLD WEATHER

High blood pressure can triple your risk for a stroke.

Recent development: A study of nearly 9,000 people found that cold weather raises blood pressure levels in people age 65 and older. One-third of those studied had hypertension in the winter, compared with about one-quarter during the summer.

Self-defense: If you have hypertension—a systolic (top number) reading of 140 millimeters of mercury (mmHg) or higher and/or diastolic (bottom number) of 90 mmHg or higher—consider taking your blood pressure every day during the winter (at the same time of day) with an at-home device. Follow the same advice if you have *prehypertension* (the stage before hypertension)—systolic reading of 120 mmHg to 139 mmHg and/or diastolic reading of 80 mmHg to 89 mmHg. If you have hypertension or prehypertension and your blood pressure rises in the winter, see your doctor.

SHINGLES

If you had chicken pox as a child, you're at risk for an outbreak of the same virus—a condition known as shingles—years later.

After a bout of chicken pox, the virus (*varicella-zoster*) becomes dormant in sensory nerves along the spinal cord or near the brain. With shingles, the virus reemerges, causing an often painful rash that typically wraps itself around the trunk from mid-back to one side of the chest. The trigger behind this reactivation is thought to be related to stress and suppression of the immune system.

New research: In a study of nearly 8,000 adults who had been treated for shingles and 23,000 who had not suffered the disease, the shingles patients were 31% more likely to have had a stroke in the year following the shingles outbreak. It's important to note that shingles often occurs in people who are already ill or have a suppressed immune system—factors that in themselves raise stroke risk.

Self-defense: There is not enough evidence to recommend that the shingles vaccine be given for stroke prevention. However, it's wise for older adults to receive the vaccine, since it's estimated that half of people who live to age 85 will suffer a shingles attack. If you have a history of shingles, follow your doctor's advice on stroke prevention, such as making lifestyle changes and taking medication to prevent or control hypertension, cholesterol levels and/or diabetes.

STRESS AND DEPRESSION

When researchers studied 600 people who had recently had a stroke and 600 people who hadn't, those who had experienced stress for one year or longer had a 3.5 times higher risk for ischemic stroke.

What happens: Unrelieved stress triggers the ongoing release of *cortisol,* a hormone that can over time raise blood pressure, destabilize blood sugar levels and increase inflammation—all of which can raise stroke risk.

Self-defense: Chronic stress is often linked to clinical depression. If you suspect that you may be depressed (symptoms include change in weight and/or sleep habits), see your doctor. He/she may prescribe an antidepressant and/or recommend *cognitive behavioral therapy* (CBT), which research shows is as effective as medication in reducing depression. Regular exercise, a healthful diet and sufficient sleep also help fight depression. If you are not depressed but regularly experience stress, follow the lifestyle changes described above.

MIGRAINE

People who suffer migraines with "auras" (visual disturbances such as jagged lines and flashes of light) have twice the risk for ischemic stroke as people without migraines, according to recent research. The increased risk is most apparent in women who smoke and take oral contraceptives.

Self-defense: If you suffer migraines with auras, discuss your stroke risk with your doctor.

CHIROPRACTIC ADJUSTMENT

Because chiropractic adjustments to the neck often involve physical manipulation of the cervical spine (neck region), neurologists and chiropractors have long debated whether such movements can lead to a rare form of ischemic stroke known as *vertebrobasilar artery* (VBA) stroke, which can be triggered by a tear in the vertebral arteries that run along the neck bones.

Latest research: A study of 818 people found that those under age 45 who had suffered VBA strokes and were hospitalized for that type of stroke were three times more likely to have seen a chiropractor or a primary care physician before the hospitalization than people without VBA strokes. In people over age 45, VBA stroke was associated with visits to primary care practitioners.

The researchers speculated that the visits to both practitioners occurred when people had symptoms of a VBA tear, such as neck pain or stiffness, but had not yet had a VBA stroke.

Self-defense: It is unlikely that a chiropractic adjustment of the neck will greatly increase your risk for a stroke. But since all medical treatments have some risks, you'll need to decide whether the benefits of a chiropractic manipulation of the neck outweigh the likely small risk for stroke.

Warning: You can cause a VBA tear by bending your head backward over a sink while having your hair washed at a hair salon. If you've had a previous stroke or TIA, do not put your head in this position. If you have no history of stroke, make sure your neck is resting comfortably and securely on a towel and not on the sink itself.

FAST FOOD

People living in neighborhoods with the most fast-food restaurants had a 13% higher risk for ischemic stroke, according to a new study. This research doesn't prove that fast food causes stroke but shows a statistical association between the two factors. However, there is proof that high levels of saturated fat and salt—both commonly found in several fast-food meals—increase stroke risk.

Self-defense: Limit your intake of fast foods. If you go to a fast-food restaurant, choose more healthful menu items, such as salads.

■ ■ ■ ■

Early Menopause May Raise Stroke Risk

When researchers followed 1,430 women for an average of 22 years, they found that those who experienced natural menopause (cessation of menstruation for one year) before age 42 were twice as likely to suffer strokes as women whose natural menopause occurred at a later age.

Theory: Decreased estrogen levels due to early menopause may affect the arteries, thus promoting cardiovascular disease.

If you experienced natural menopause before age 42: Tell your doctor and ask him/her to evaluate your stroke risk.

Lynda D. Lisabeth, PhD, assistant professor of epidemiology, University of Michigan, Ann Arbor.

Type of Migraine Can Double Your Stroke Risk

Markus Schurks, MD, division of preventive medicine, Brigham and Women's Hospital, Boston.
Elizabeth Loder, MD, MPH, chief, division of headache and pain, Brigham and Women's Hospital, and associate professor, neurology, Harvard Medical School, Boston.
Vincent Martin, MD, associate professor, medicine, University of Cincinnati, Ohio.
BMJ (*British Medical Journal*) online.

For people who suffer migraine headaches with aura—visual disturbances before or during the migraine—the risk for ischemic stroke is doubled, according to researchers. Being female, under age 45, smoking and using oral contraceptives that contain estrogen added to the risk.

ISCHEMIC STROKE AND MIGRAINE

Ischemic stroke is caused by a blockage in a blood vessel. The connection between migraine and stroke was already suspected. What was unknown was the extent of risk and who is most at risk, the researchers said.

Migraine headaches affect up to 20% of the population. Women are up to four times more likely than men to get migraines, and as many as one-third also experience an aura before or during a migraine.

STUDY DETAILS

For the study, lead researcher Markus Schurks, MD, from the division of preventive medicine at Brigham and Women's Hospital in Boston and colleagues analyzed nine studies concerning the association between migraine, with and without aura, and cardiovascular disease.

"Migraine with aura is associated with a two-fold increased risk for ischemic stroke compared with people without migraine, while migraine without aura does not appear to change the risk," said Dr. Schurks.

"The risk appears to be highest among women with migraine with aura who smoke and use oral contraceptives," Dr. Schurks said.

In contrast, migraine alone does not appear to alter the risk for heart attack and death from cardiovascular disease, he added.

"Considering the low absolute risk, there is no reason to panic, but modifiable risk factors such as smoking and oral contraceptive use should be considered," he said.

The report was published in the online edition of the *British Medical Journal*.

EXPERT ADVICE

"In the scheme of things, aura is just one among many potential risk factors for stroke, so it is important to put this in context," said Elizabeth Loder, MD, MPH, chief of the division of headache and pain at Brigham and Women's Hospital. "The risk of stroke for most people with migraine is low—stroke is an uncommon event—and so a doubling of that low baseline risk is not cause for alarm." "Although it's not a reason for panic, having aura is a reason to pay extra attention to other stroke risk factors that can be modified. These include high blood pressure, high cholesterol, smoking and use of estrogen-containing contraceptives."

According to Vincent Martin, MD, an associate professor of medicine at the University of Cincinnati, we have always known that the risk of stroke increased in patients with migraine, but this study clarifies which groups of migraine sufferers are at more risk.

"If you are a female and you've got migraine with aura, you really need to be careful about managing your risk factors for stroke, because your risk for stroke is increased," he said. Smoking and/or taking birth control pills just aren't a good idea for you if you suffer migraines, he added.

info For more information on migraine, visit the Web site of MAGNUM, the National Migraine Association, *www.migraines.org.*

■ ■ ■ ■

Good Night's Sleep Pumps Up Artery Health

In a recent study of 495 men and women, 27% of those who slept fewer than five hours nightly developed coronary artery calcification (hardening of the arteries) over a five-year period. The rate was 11% for those who slept five to seven hours...and 6% for those who slept more than seven hours.

Theory: People who get insufficient sleep may have a higher average blood pressure than people who get adequate sleep, raising the risk for artery calcification.

Self-defense: Aim to get at least six hours of uninterrupted sleep nightly.

Diane Lauderdale, PhD, associate professor of epidemiology, University of Chicago.

■ ■ ■ ■

Take Time for Tea And Lower Your Stroke Risk

People who drank at least three cups of green or black tea daily had 21% lower risk for stroke, compared with those who drank only one cup daily, according to a study review in *Stroke*.

Tea has protective antioxidant and anti-inflammatory properties that may reduce blood pressure, a main risk factor for stroke. Drinking at least three cups of green or black tea daily is safe for everyone (except children and women who are pregnant).

Mark A. Stengler, NMD, naturopathic medical doctor in private practice, La Jolla, California...adjunct associate clinical professor at the National College of Natural Medicine, Portland, Oregon...author of many books, including *The Natural Physician's Healing Therapies* and coauthor of *Prescription for Natural Cures* (both from Bottom Line Books)...and author of the *Bottom Line/Natural Healing* newsletter.

Attention Men: Great Way to Reduce Stroke Risk More than 60%

American Academy of Neurology news release.

Moderate-to-high-intensity exercise such as jogging, swimming or tennis may help reduce stroke risk in older men but not in women, researchers report.

Stroke is the leading cause of disability in the United States and the third leading cause of death. *Ischemic stroke*, the leading type of stroke, is caused by a blockage in a blood vessel.

THE STUDY

The nine-year study followed nearly 3,300 men and women, average age 69, who lived in New York City. During that time, there were 238 strokes among the participants. At the start of the study, 20% of the participants said they did regular moderate-to-high-intensity exercise, while 41% said they did no physical activity.

Men who did moderate-to-high-intensity exercise were 63% less likely to have a stroke than people who didn't exercise. Over five years, the baseline risk of ischemic stroke for all study participants was 4.3%—2.7% for those who did moderate-to-high-intensity exercise and 4.6% for those who didn't exercise.

The study was published in an issue of the journal *Neurology*.

IMPLICATIONS

"Taking part in moderate-to-heavy-intensity physical activity may be an important factor for preventing stroke," said study author Joshua Z. Willey, MD, of Columbia University Medical Center and NewYork-Presbyterian Hospital.

"A large percentage of the participants were not taking part in any physical activities. This may be true of many elderly people who live in cities. Identifying ways to improve physical activity among these people may be a key goal for public health," Dr. Willey said.

info The Web site of the US National Institute of Neurological Disorders and Stroke has more about stroke risk factors. Visit *www.ninds.nih.gov* and type "stroke risk factors" into the search box.

Happy Marriage Reduces Stroke Risk for Men

Uri Goldbourt, PhD, professor, epidemiology and preventive medicine, Tel Aviv University, Israel.

Daniel Lackland, PhD, professor and director, graduate training, Medical University of South Carolina, Charleston, and spokesperson, American Stroke Association.

American Stroke Association annual stroke conference, San Antonio, Texas.

Single or unhappily married men seem to run a greater risk of dying from a stroke than those in good marriages, a new Israeli study indicates.

STUDY FINDINGS

The study, which tracked more than 10,000 civil servants and municipal workers from 1963 to 1997, found that 8.4% of the single men died of strokes, compared with 7.1% of the married men. When age and known stroke risk factors, such as obesity, smoking and diabetes, were included in the analysis, single men had a 64% higher risk for fatal stroke than married men, according to a report presented at the American Stroke Association's annual stroke conference in San Antonio.

The study also asked men to evaluate the success of their marriages. The 3.6% of men who reported dissatisfaction with marriage also had a 64% higher risk of a fatal stroke, compared with those who considered their marriages to be very successful.

POSSIBLE EXPLANATIONS

"Maybe summoning help in the case of suspected stroke took longer among those who were unmarried," said study author Uri Goldbourt, PhD, a professor of epidemiology and preventive medicine at Tel Aviv University. "If that were true, perhaps the probability to survive a stroke would be lower among those living alone."

Dr. Goldbourt said he had no explanation for the effect of happiness on stroke mortality. "I had not expected that unsuccessful marriage would be of this statistical importance," he said.

But it's clear that a long, happy relationship is associated with a higher likelihood of taking the recommended measures against the known stroke risk factors, said Daniel Lackland, PhD, director of graduate training at the Medical University of South Carolina, and a spokesperson for the American Stroke Association.

"If you look at something like cigarette smoking, there is better support in quitting," Dr. Lackland said. "Weight loss is so much better when two people are involved."

A good marriage means "having the support that makes you more compliant with therapy," he said. "Also, you are more likely to go see a physician if you are not feeling well."

STROKE IN WOMEN

Dr. Goldbourt said he does not know of a similar study of women. "Certainly, such a study would be of great interest," he said.

"There are some suggestions that it is the same for women," Dr. Lackland said. "If you are in a good relationship, it goes both ways. Social support is better in a good relationship."

info To learn the risk factors for stroke, visit the Web site of the Centers for Disease Control and Prevention, *www.cdc.gov,* and search "stroke risk factors."

The Blood Pressure Problem Even Great Doctors Don't Detect

Zeenat Safdar, MD, associate director of the Pulmonary Hypertension Service and assistant professor of medicine at Baylor College of Medicine in Houston. She is board-certified in internal medicine and pulmonary disease and is author of numerous research articles on pulmonary hypertension and other lung conditions.

High blood pressure, or hypertension, is easy to detect. A cuff around your upper arm measures the pressure of the blood against the walls of the main arteries...high numbers signal a need for treatment to prevent heart and blood vessel damage.

But it is much more difficult to spot *pulmonary hypertension*, a disorder in which high blood pressure develops in the pulmonary arteries that carry blood from the heart to the lungs. It is a progressive and potentially deadly disease that can appear at any age and often goes undiagnosed for months or years.

For unknown reasons, pulmonary hypertension affects women two to four times more often than men. Sometimes the initial symptoms— shortness of breath, dizziness, fatigue—appear during pregnancy when the fetus puts stress on the woman's heart and lungs.

RECOGNIZING THE PROBLEM

Pulmonary hypertension develops when tiny arteries in the lungs become narrowed, stiffened or blocked due to cellular changes or scarring in the arteries' lining. As blood flow is constricted, pressure in the pulmonary arteries rises and blood backs up, forcing the heart to pump harder. *Symptoms include...*

- **Shortness of breath.**
- **Palpitations or racing heartbeat.**
- **Dizziness or light-headedness.**
- **Fatigue upon exertion.**
- **Swollen ankles, legs or belly.**
- **Bluish lips and skin.**

At first, symptoms occur only during exertion and often are misdiagnosed as asthma, anxiety or signs that a person is out of shape. As the disease progresses, symptoms become constant. The longer pulmonary hypertension goes untreated, the more damage is done. *Possible consequences...*

- **The heart's right ventricle (lower right chamber) becomes enlarged and thickened** as it attempts to increase its capacity to hold and pump blood. Eventually, heart failure develops when the heart can no longer pump blood efficiently enough to meet the body's needs.

- **An irregular heartbeat may develop,** increasing the risk for stroke or sudden cardiac death.

- **Blood clots may form** in the pulmonary (lungs') arteries...and/or there may be bleeding into the lungs. These conditions can be deadly.

Self-defense: If you experience any possible symptoms of pulmonary hypertension, inform your doctor immediately. With a stethoscope, an experienced physician can detect a telltale heart murmur, a consequence of the backflow of blood from the lungs. An *echocardiogram*

(ultrasound of the heart) and/or right heart catheterization (in which a catheter is inserted into a pulmonary artery to measure pressure) confirms the diagnosis.

Recommended: Have a pulmonologist or cardiologist oversee your treatment.

Referrals: Pulmonary Hypertension Association. Call 800-748-7274, or go to *www.phassociation.org* and click on "Find a Doctor."

LIFE AFTER DIAGNOSIS

Often the cause of pulmonary hypertension is unknown (though in some cases, there is a genetic link). It also can occur as a result of another medical problem, such as a congenital heart defect, *chronic obstructive pulmonary disease*, sleep apnea, a blood disorder, an autoimmune disorder or disease of the liver, kidney or thyroid.

For most patients, pulmonary hypertension can be controlled but not cured. *Some keys to treatment...*

LIFESTYLE

To ease symptoms and slow the disease's progress...

- **Reduce sodium intake** to no more than 1,500 milligrams (mg), about two-thirds of a teaspoon of salt per day. Salt increases blood volume, straining the heart.

- **Do not use a hot tub, sauna or steam bath** or take long, hot showers or baths. Doing so could lower blood pressure excessively, leading to fainting or even death.

- **With your doctor's okay, do moderate exercise** (walking, yoga, low-impact aerobics). To avoid serious increases in pulmonary artery pressure, refrain from strenuous aerobic activity and heavy lifting.

- **Stay away from secondhand smoke**—it can exacerbate your disease. If you smoke, quit now.

For help: Visit *www.smokefree.gov.*

- **Avoid high altitudes.** Thin air is harder to breathe.

- **No dietary supplements treat pulmonary hypertension**—but for overall immune support, consider asking your doctor about taking the amino acid *L-arginine.*

•**Avoid decongestants** that have *pseudo-ephedrine* or *phenylephrine*, which can narrow blood vessels.

•**Get a flu shot every year.** Also, get vaccinated against pneumonia (typically only one or two injections are needed) to minimize risk for respiratory infections that could worsen your condition.

•**Do not use oral contraceptives or estrogen therapy** because they may increase blood clot risk.

•**Maintain a normal weight.** If you notice a rapid weight gain (two pounds in a day or five pounds in a week), call your doctor—this could indicate a buildup of fluid caused by heart failure.

•**It is strongly advised that you not become pregnant** because there is a risk for death for both mother and baby. If you want a child or are already pregnant, it is vital to work closely with a pulmonary hypertension specialist.

MEDICATION

You may need to take one or more of the following…

•**Vasodilators** open blood vessels. These are inhaled every few hours…or are continuously injected through a catheter attached to a small wearable pump.

•**Endothelin receptor antagonists** help reverse the effects of a substance that narrows blood vessels.

•**Calcium channel blockers** relax blood vessel walls.

•**Diuretics** help rid the body of heart-straining excess fluid.

•**Anticoagulants** improve blood flow and reduce clotting risk.

•**Supplemental oxygen** may be needed occasionally or constantly.

Pulmonary hypertension medications can minimize the disease's consequences and ease symptoms—allowing you to live more actively and comfortably.

■ ■ ■ ■

Tasty Tea Lowers Blood Pressure

In a study of 65 adults with prehypertension or mild hypertension, those who drank hibiscus tea had a 7.2-point drop, on average, in systolic (top number) blood pressure, compared with a one-point drop, on average, in the placebo group.

Theory: Antioxidant flavonoids in hibiscus help lower blood pressure.

If you have been diagnosed with prehypertension or hypertension: Three cups daily of hibiscus tea may benefit you.

Diane L. McKay, PhD, assistant professor of nutrition, science and policy, Tufts University, Boston.

■ ■ ■ ■

"Beet" High Blood Pressure

In a study of 14 healthy adults, participants' blood pressures dropped by an average of 10.4 millimeters of mercury (mmHg) systolic (top number) and 8 mmHg diastolic (bottom number) within a few hours of drinking two cups of beet juice (the effect lasted up to 24 hours).

Theory: Bacteria on the tongue convert chemical compounds found in beet juice into nitrites, which help keep blood vessels healthy. (The beet juice used in the study was sweetened with apple juice.)

Amrita Ahluwalia, PhD, professor of vascular pharmacology, Barts and The London School of Medicine, UK.

■ ■ ■ ■

How Blood Pressure Affects Your Memory

Several studies have shown that high blood pressure is linked to increased risk for cognitive decline.

Recent finding: In a four-year study of 19,836 adults, those with a diastolic (bottom number) of 90 millimeters of mercury (mmHg) or higher were more likely to have impaired memory and cognition than those with normal readings.

Theory: Elevated diastolic pressure, in particular, weakens arteries in the brain, which may damage small areas of the brain.

If you have high blood pressure: Ask your doctor to recommend lifestyle changes (such as regular exercise and weight loss) and medication, if necessary.

Georgios Tsivgoulis, MD, adjunct assistant professor of neurology, University of Alabama, Birmingham.

Little-Known Cause Of Stroke, High Blood Pressure and Aneurysm

Jeffrey W. Olin, DO, professor of cardiology at the Mount Sinai School of Medicine and director of vascular medicine at the Zena and Michael A. Wiener Cardiovascular Institute and the Marie-Josée and Henry R. Kravis Center for Cardiovascular Health at Mount Sinai, all in New York City. He is a recipient of the Founders Award from the Fibromuscular Dysplasia Society of America for outstanding achievements in promoting research and awareness of FMD.

Most people have never heard of the blood vessel disorder known as *fibromuscular dysplasia* (FMD), but doctors now recognize that it can be a hidden cause of high blood pressure (hypertension), strokes and brain aneurysms (due to bulging in the wall of an artery in the brain).

Recent development: Once considered a rare condition, FMD now appears to be more common than previously thought, possibly affecting up to 5 million adults in the US.

What you need to know…

WHAT IS FMD?

In people with FMD, abnormal cell growth occurs on the walls of one or more arteries (blood vessels), typically in the carotid (neck) arteries (leading to the brain) and renal arteries (leading to the kidneys). The normally smooth artery wall develops bumps, often resulting in a "string of beads" that can be seen on imaging tests used to examine blood vessels, such as ultrasound, a *computed tomography angio-*gram (CTA) or *magnetic resonance angiogram* (MRA).

When cell growth becomes extensive, the artery narrows, disrupting blood flow and possibly resulting in hypertension, a stroke or an aneurysm. While *atherosclerosis*—fatty build-up in the arteries—occurs at the opening of a blood vessel, FMD occurs at the middle and end of a blood vessel.

ARE YOU AT RISK?

Though FMD typically strikes adults under age 50, doctors now are finding more and more previously undiagnosed cases in people age 60 and older—perhaps due to the increasing use of imaging tests. FMD often is diagnosed as a result of an incidental finding on an unrelated radiological test. In many of these cases, the patient has no symptoms of the disorder.

No one knows what causes FMD. Genetics may play a role, but not everyone with FMD has a relative with the disease. FMD occurs more often in women (about 85% of cases) than in men. Researchers suspect that a gene predisposes an individual to the condition and that the gene is expressed due to outside influences, such as hormones.

GETTING A PROPER DIAGNOSIS

FMD often goes undiagnosed because many doctors mistakenly believe that it is very rare. In fact, many medical schools don't even teach their students about FMD.

To complicate matters further, many people with FMD have no symptoms. When symptoms do occur, they are related to the arteries that are affected and the degree of narrowing that has developed.

Example: Since the majority of FMD cases occur in the arteries leading to the kidneys, high blood pressure may develop (due to narrowing of the renal arteries, which triggers a series of adverse effects). Abnormal kidney function and flank pain (occurring on one side of the body between the upper abdomen and the back) also can occur.

In about 25% to 30% of FMD patients, the disease affects the carotid arteries. In these people, symptoms may include severe and unrelenting headaches…dizziness…ringing in the ears (tinnitus)…and neck pain.

FMD in the carotid artery also may lead to a swishing sound in the ears…temporary or permanent loss of vision in one or both eyes… brain aneurysms…and *transient ischemic attacks* (TIAs)—or "mini-strokes"…as well as full-blown strokes.

Though less likely, FMD can affect the arteries supplying the liver, spleen and intestines, which may cause abdominal pain after eating, unexplained weight loss or gangrene of the bowel. If the arteries to the legs or arms are affected, pain or fatigue when using the affected limb can occur. In very rare cases, FMD may affect the coronary arteries in the heart, leading to angina (chest pain) or a heart attack.

Helpful: Regardless of your age, ask your doctor during all routine physicals to place a stethoscope on your neck and abdomen and listen for a *bruit*, a noise that indicates a narrowing of a blood vessel. If a bruit is heard, your doctor can follow up with the appropriate test, such as an ultrasound or CTA.

Important: Not all FMD patients have an audible bruit.

BEST TREATMENT OPTIONS

FMD has no cure. The goal is to improve blood flow in the affected artery. Treatment depends on which artery is narrowed and the severity of the symptoms. Medication that alleviates high blood pressure, such as an *angiotensin-converting enzyme* (ACE) inhibitor, may be prescribed. Many patients take daily aspirin to help prevent clots from forming, thus reducing stroke risk.

FMD patients who have "new-onset" hypertension may require *percutaneous transluminal renal angioplasty* (PTRA). This procedure (usually outpatient) involves inserting a catheter into the affected artery and inflating a small balloon to open the narrowed area.

Important finding: A study published in the *Journal of Vascular Surgery* showed that renal artery angioplasty reduced high blood pressure in 72% of the 29 FMD patients studied—and the reduction was still evident five years after the procedure.

FINDING THE RIGHT DOCTOR

If you have FMD—or suspect that you may—see a vascular specialist or a physician who is experienced in treating the organ affected by the disease.

For example: A *nephrologist* (kidney doctor) if FMD affects your renal arteries (or you are having kidney problems such as those described above)…or a neurologist if the carotid arteries are affected.

More from Dr. Olin…

Cutting-Edge Research on FMD

Several medical centers in the US, including the Mount Sinai Medical Center in New York City and the Cleveland Clinic, participate in an international registry of FMD patients to help scientists conduct cutting-edge research to unravel some of the mysteries of the disease.

If you or a family member has been diagnosed with FMD, contact the Fibromuscular Dysplasia Society of America (FMDSA), 888-709-7089, *www.fmdsa.org*, which can provide information about the registry closest to you.

How Kidney Disease Can Hurt Your Blood Vessels

Joseph A. Vassalotti, MD, associate clinical professor of medicine at the Mount Sinai School of Medicine and chief medical officer of the National Kidney Foundation, *www.kidney.org*, both in New York City. He is the lead author of "Screening Populations at Increased Risk of CKD," *American Journal of Kidney Disease*.

When Richard*, a 66-year-old retired engineer from New Jersey, was recently screened for kidney disease, he assumed that he was in good health. He had no symptoms, worked out four times a week and had no family history of kidney problems. When test results showed that he had kidney failure (that is, his kidneys were no longer able to perform normal functions, including the removal of waste products), Richard was shocked but relieved that he could begin his treatment

*The patient's last name has not been used to protect his identity.

immediately to help prevent further damage to his kidneys. *What you need to know...*

HIDDEN DANGERS OF CHRONIC KIDNEY DISEASE

When your kidneys function properly, they remove excess fluid, waste and minerals from the body. The kidneys manufacture hormones that encourage red blood cell production, strengthen bones and influence blood pressure. When the kidneys fail—a condition sometimes known as *end-stage renal disease*—you're at increased risk for complications such as anemia, weak bones and nerve damage.

What you may not know: Because chronic kidney disease (CKD)—gradual loss of kidney function—can damage blood vessels and organs, including the heart, it also increases the risk for heart and blood vessel disease.

Troubling trend: CKD is on the rise—due in large part to the surge in risk factors for CKD, such as high blood pressure (*hypertension*) and diabetes, according to a study in *The Journal of the American Medical Association*. In fact, CKD now affects 26 million Americans—roughly 13% of all American adults, according to the National Kidney Foundation.

Important new finding: Impaired kidney function in older adults also accelerates memory problems, according to a recent study published in *Neurology*.

ARE YOU AT RISK?

CKD is often a silent condition, especially in the early stages. One study found that only 12% of men and 6% of women with CKD had been diagnosed with the disorder.

Latest development: Researchers have linked diets that are high in sodium and artificially sweetened beverages to declines in kidney function.

If kidney failure goes undetected, it usually progresses, causing *uremia*, a group of symptoms that result from impurities in the blood that accumulate because of the kidneys' inability to excrete waste and water. *Symptoms of kidney failure (or CKD) include...*

•**Foamy urine** (resembling the foam on the surface of eggs as they are scrambled).

•**Swelling of the feet or ankles or around the eyes** (due to fluid retention).

•**Difficulty concentrating and doing simple calculations,** such as counting money.

•**Fatigue and trouble sleeping.**

•**Dry, itchy skin.**

•**Frequent urination** (more often than the norm for the individual)—especially at night—or decreased urine output.

Even if you have no symptoms (such as those described earlier), you should be screened for CKD if you...

•**Are over age 60.**

•**Have cardiovascular disease, high blood pressure, diabetes or a family history of kidney disease** (in a parent or sibling)—all increase risk for CKD.

•**Have an autoimmune disease, such as lupus, or a chronic infection, such as hepatitis B.** Autoimmune diseases and certain chronic infections can cause kidney disease that is related to the body's immune response.

THE TESTS YOU NEED

If you are at increased risk for CKD or have symptoms of kidney failure (as described earlier), ask your doctor to give you screening tests to measure...

•**Estimated glomerular filtration rate (eGFR).** This is determined with a blood test for *creatinine* (a by-product of normal muscle metabolism that is removed by the kidneys). The amount of creatinine indicates how well the kidneys are filtering blood. An eGFR below 60 milliliter per minute is considered abnormal.

•**Urinary albumin-to-creatinine ratio (UACR).** Albumin is a protein in the blood that passes through the kidneys' microscopic filtering units, known as *glomeruli*. When albumin is found in the urine, it means that the kidneys have been damaged and can no longer properly filter albumin—much like a coffee filter that leaks coffee grinds. A normal UACR is less than 30 milligrams per gram of creatinine. A reading above that level is considered high and possibly a sign of early kidney disease.

An abnormal result for either of these tests doesn't necessarily mean that you have CKD. But you should be tested again in about three months. If either of these tests still shows abnormalities at that time, you are diagnosed with CKD.

Both tests are relatively inexpensive and typically covered by health insurance—the blood tests for creatinine and albumin are $40 to $50 each.

HOW TO FIGHT CKD

High blood pressure and diabetes cause two-thirds of the cases of CKD. High blood pressure is harmful to the kidneys because it increases pressure on the walls of the blood vessels, including those in the kidneys.

When blood sugar levels rise too high in people with diabetes, the kidneys and other organs often are damaged. For these reasons, one of the best ways to guard against CKD is to avoid high blood pressure and diabetes.

If you are diagnosed with CKD, it's crucial to control the root cause. For example, people with CKD and hypertension need to get their blood pressure below 130/80 millimeters of mercury (typically through dietary changes, such as limiting sodium intake, and blood pressure–lowering medication).

People with CKD and diabetes need to get their *hemoglobin A1C* level—the average blood glucose level over three months—below 7% (usually through careful attention to diet and the use of diabetes medications). If CKD progresses to end-stage renal disease, a kidney transplant or dialysis, in which machines do the job of your kidneys, is required.

Important: If you have CKD, review all your medications, vitamins and herbs with your doctor. In people with advanced kidney disease, fat-soluble vitamins (such as vitamin A) can accumulate in the body, causing vitamin toxicity. In addition, certain herbal medications, such as those containing *aristolochic acid,* can be toxic to the kidneys. Certain medications, including the diabetes drug *metformin* (Glucophage), and nonsteroidal anti-inflammatory drugs, such as *naproxen* (Aleve) and *ibuprofen* (Motrin), can worsen CKD.

People with CKD also should take precautions when undergoing certain medical tests. For example, dyes used as contrast agents for *computed tomography* (CT) scans and other procedures can weaken the kidneys. Oral *sodium phosphate* bowel preparations used for colonoscopies, such as Visicol and OsmoPrep, also can be harmful. If you have CKD, tell your doctor about it before undergoing radiological tests that use contrast agents or taking a sodium phosphate product prior to a colonoscopy.

■ ■ ■ ■

One-Minute Test that Could Save Your Life

Emergency room (ER) doctors misdiagnose one-third of strokes when the only symptom is dizziness, and patients may wait hours for diagnostic MRIs, delaying treatment.

Study: With a one-minute visual exam that looks for abnormal eye movements, such as jerking, doctors diagnosed all 69 stroke victims among 101 ER patients, while MRIs gave eight false negatives.

Best: Dizzy patients should ask for an eye-movement test.

David E. Newman-Toker, MD, PhD, assistant professor of neurology, Johns Hopkins University School of Medicine, Baltimore, and leader of a stroke study.

New Software Helps Patients Pick The Best Stent

Harlan M. Krumholz, MD, professor of medicine (cardiology) and investigative medicine and public health (health policy), Yale University School of Medicine, New Haven, Connecticut.

John Spertus, MD, professor, University of Missouri—Kansas City, director of Health Outcomes, Mid America Heart Institute of Saint Luke's Health System, Kansas City.

What's a heart patient to do? There seems to be no easy answer to the question of whether it's better to have your arteries propped open with a bare metal stent or a higher-tech, drug-eluting one…or none at all. The bare metal stent carries a risk that the blockage will recur…the drug-eluting one brings an increased risk of blood clots…and there are some cases in which stent placement actually worsens outcomes, though clearly doing nothing at all can be dangerous as well. The answers to these complex questions are continually revised as medical research keeps evolving. Stents themselves represent a real breakthrough in cardiovascular medicine—they're faster and less invasive than bypass surgery at opening a blocked artery when a person is having or is at severe risk for a heart attack. However, attempts to refine the technology have failed to produce a clear-cut advantage either way.

Harlan M. Krumholz, MD, is professor of medicine (cardiology), investigative medicine and public health at the Yale University School of Medicine and director of the Yale-New Haven Hospital Center for Outcomes Research and Evaluation. According to Dr. Krumholz, both types of stents are viable options, since doctors have learned how to minimize the risks associated with drug-eluting ones—although there is always some risk involved with any intervention. The best answer ultimately depends on the priorities and risk profile for each patient.

IS IT STILL A CONTROVERSY?

Though it stirred up the cardiology world at the time, Dr. Krumholz said that the controversy about the propensity of patients to develop blood clots after insertion of drug-eluting stents has calmed down, since patients who get this higher-tech medical device are now routinely prescribed anticlotting medications. Proper therapy mitigates the risk, Dr. Krumholz said. Discuss the particulars of your situation with your doctor.

When it comes to cost, however, the questions sort out differently. The costs associated with drug-eluting stents are significantly higher than bare metal stents, which means patients (and doctors) are often faced with trying to decide the most cost-effective form of treatment. Those individuals at lower risk for renarrowing of the blood vessels may do better with the bare metal stent, while others who have difficulty taking the medication and/or are unlikely to take it for the necessary 12 months may need to weigh that as a factor. These issues can only be resolved by asking the right questions and getting honest answers.

A SOFTWARE SOLUTION?

One hospital group in the Midwest has found a solution. There is a new and innovative Web-based program now in use at the Saint Luke's Mid America Heart Institute in Kansas City, Missouri. It is software designed to be used as part of the decision-making process. Cardiac patients and medical staff work through the program together—it creates a customized risk assessment for each type of stent with clear explanation of the risks that accompany each. Called PREDICT and initially designed as a way to improve the informed consent process, the program personalizes the risks in a way that makes it very easy to understand. A study of the system, published in *Circulation: Cardiovascular Quality and Outcomes*, a journal of the American Heart Association, focused on how helpful patients found these individualized risk-assessment/consent forms. Researchers reported that patients who used the PREDICT system understood their risks better, had better recall of the details of the procedure and less anxiety about the treatment process.

Such tools may well represent a new direction for helping to make medical decisions that match patients with the procedure most likely to be successful in their particular case.

■ ■ ■ ■

Better Fix for Abdominal Aortic Aneurysms

In the first two years of an ongoing study, patients who had *endovascular repair* (performed through a catheter inserted into an artery) were no more likely to die than those who had the standard abdominal incision procedure—and they had less blood loss, needed no transfusions and spent less time in the hospital. Until the study is completed, patients with an aneurysm of less than 5.5 centimeters should talk with their doctors about watchful waiting—holding off on repair while continuing observation.

Frank A. Lederle, MD, professor of medicine and director of Minneapolis VA Center for Epidemiological and Clinical Research. The two-year results of his ongoing study of 881 veterans were published in *The Journal of the American Medical Association*.

■ ■ ■ ■

Are You at Risk for DVT?

In a study of 46 men and women with *superficial vein thrombosis* (clotting in blood vessels close to the skin), 24% of the patients were found to also have *deep vein thrombosis* (DVT), a condition in which blood clots form—usually in the leg—and can break away and travel to the lungs or brain, causing stroke or death.

If you have been diagnosed with superficial vein thrombosis: Ask your doctor to evaluate you for DVT.

Barbara Binder, MD, associate professor, department of dermatology, Medical University of Graz, Austria.

■ ■ ■ ■

Dangerous Blood Clots Are Likely Up to 12 Weeks After Surgery

Patients who have recently undergone surgery are up to 110 times more likely to be admitted to a hospital because of potentially fatal *thromboses* (blood clots) than people who have not had surgery.

Self-defense: Anticlotting drugs and physical measures, such as compression stockings, can reduce risk.

Jane Green, MD, PhD, is group head and principal investigator, Cancer Epidemiology Unit, University of Oxford, England, and coauthor of a study of thromboses in 947,454 women, published in *BMJ Online First*.

■ ■ ■ ■

Compression Hose No Help After Stroke

To reduce risk for *deep vein thrombosis* (DVT) a potentially fatal blood clot that typically forms in the legs and may travel to the heart or lungs—immobilized stroke patients sometimes wear thigh-high compression stockings.

Study: Ultrasounds done up to a month after immobilizing strokes revealed almost no difference in DVT rates among patients who wore hose and those who did not.

But: 5% of hose wearers had skin problems (blisters, tissue death), compared with only 1% of non-hose wearers.

Martin Dennis, MD, professor of stroke medicine, University of Edinburgh, Scotland, and leader of a study of 2,518 stroke patients.

■ ■ ■ ■

Test Identifies Risk for Deadly Blood Clots

Researchers followed 8,574 adults for eight years. They found that those with *microalbuminuria* (high levels of the protein albumin in the urine) had a 40% risk for blood clots in the legs or lungs—a condition known as *venous thromboembolism* (VTE)—compared with 12% for those with normal albumin levels. VTE can be life-threatening if a detached clot lodges in the heart, lungs or brain. If you are at risk for VTE (due to family history, for example), ask your doctor about testing your albumin levels annually.

Ron T. Gansevoort, MD, PhD, associate professor of nephrology, University Medical Center Groningen, the Netherlands.

Video Gaming That's Good for Your Health

Gustavo Saposnik, MD, MSc, director, Stroke Outcomes Research Unit, Li Ka Shing Knowledge Institute, St. Michael's Hospital of the University of Toronto, Toronto, Canada.
William Meehan, MD, director, Sports Concussion Clinic, Division of Sports Medicine, Children's Hospital Boston.
American Stroke Association Conference, San Antonio, Texas.

Recovering stroke patients whose physical therapy regimen is built around Wii video games appear to improve better than patients treated with standard therapies, a new Canadian study reveals.

The finding suggests that the enormously popular virtual reality programs could move beyond fun and games into the serious business of physical rehabilitation.

"This is new technology that may potentially help patients with a stroke," said study lead author Gustavo Saposnik, MD, director of the Stroke Outcomes Research Unit at St. Michael's Hospital at the University of Toronto, Canada. "We ran a pilot study to see whether this is doable, safe, and more effective than routine therapy," he said. "And we found it was."

The findings were presented at the international conference of the American Stroke Association in San Antonio, Texas.

THE STUDY

The Wii gaming system—produced by Nintendo, which did not fund the study—allows players to physically interact in real-time with images on TV screens through the use of wireless motion-detection remote controls.

To gauge the promise of a Wii-based rehabilitation program, Dr. Saposnik and his colleagues focused on 20 stroke survivors, average age 61, all of whom were recovering from mild to moderate *ischemic* (caused by blood vessel blockage) or *hemorrhagic* (bleeding) strokes.

The stroke survivors were randomly divided into two groups. One group participated in standard recreational therapy for impaired arms, involving the playing of card games or the block-stacking game Jenga The second group was assigned to Wii-based therapy, either playing virtual tennis or cooking virtually (through "Wii Tennis" or "Wii Cooking Mama").

The Wii-based therapy involved movements that mimic the arm strokes required in a tennis match or those needed for cutting potatoes, peeling onions, slicing meat and shredding cheese.

Both the recreational and Wii-based therapies were administered in eight 60-minute sessions spread over two weeks. Both regimens, which were described by the researchers as "intensive," were launched within two months following stroke occurrence.

THE RESULTS

After two weeks, the Wii group showed greater improvements than the recreational group in the patients' affected arms, as measured in terms of the speed and grip strength necessary for normal motor function. No evidence of safety risk was found among the Wii group.

"Basically, we found that Wii therapy produced a 30% better improvement than recreational therapy in the time it took for the Wii patients to execute a task, and in how well they were able to execute a task," said Dr. Saposnik.

IMPLICATIONS

Dr. Saposnik said that if the apparent benefits of Wii therapy hold up to further scrutiny, the high-tech physical therapy approach could help address two paramount challenges patients face when embarking on a recovery program: time and access.

"Rehabilitation is time-consuming, which can translate into poor compliance," he noted. "And it's not always available to all patients, based on cost and insurance constraints. But the high-intensity, repetitive nature of Wii therapy seems to offer quick benefits, and it's widely available. So this could prove to be very helpful."

LARGER STUDY UNDER WAY

"However, this is just an initial step towards expanding our understanding of the potential benefit this kind of innovative, interactive approach in neurorehabilitation might have following a stroke," Dr. Saposnik cautioned.

"A larger study should be completed before making recommendations," he said. "And that is already under way."

EXPERT REACTION

William Meehan, MD, director of the Sports Concussion Clinic at Children's Hospital Boston, said Dr. Saposnik's early observation makes "a lot of sense."

"In general terms, the use of computer programs with some sort of motor movement component has certainly already been shown to be of benefit in terms of helping patients regain balance control when dealing with a sports-related concussion," he said. "So I think this whole rehabilitation approach has great promise.

"And it is much more convenient than normal therapy, in that patients could perhaps do this kind of thing at home," Dr. Meehan added. "But, I would say it will probably end up best being used to augment standard therapies, because you do always want an actual therapist to monitor patient progress."

info For additional information on recovering from a stroke, visit the Web site of the National Stroke Association, *www.stroke. org,* and click on "Recovery."

■ ■ ■ ■

Better Stroke Recovery

When researchers reviewed 14 studies involving 429 stroke patients, they found that a lower-leg splint supporting the foot and ankle—designed to keep joints properly aligned—immediately helped patients walk faster and improved balance, while an upper-limb splint (such as a wrist splint) did not improve function.

If a loved one has suffered a stroke: Ask his/her physical therapist or podiatrist whether a lower-leg splint might improve your loved one's mobility and balance.

Sarah T. Tyson, PhD, physiotherapist, School of Health, Sport and Rehabilitation, University of Salford, Greater Manchester, England.

■ ■ ■ ■

Music Therapy for Stroke Patients

In a small study of men and women who suffered partial vision loss due to stroke, the patients were better able to identify shapes and lights while listening to music they enjoyed.

Theory: Pleasing music activates brain areas linked to positive emotional responses to stimuli, improving awareness of the visual world.

If you have experienced vision loss due to stroke: Ask your doctor whether music therapy might benefit you.

David Soto, PhD, research fellow, division of neuroscience and mental health, Imperial College, London.

■ ■ ■ ■

Antidepressant Improves Stroke Recovery

Stroke victims' learning and memory skills can be improved by the antidepressant Lexapro, according to a recent study.

Recent finding: Stroke patients who were given a 12-week course of *escitalopram* (Lexapro) after a stroke had higher scores on tests of verbal and visual memory. The drug, a *selective serotonin reuptake inhibitor* (SSRI), helped stroke recovery even if given as much as three months after the stroke, although it should be administered as soon as possible.

Ricardo E. Jorge, MD, associate professor of psychiatry, Carver College of Medicine, University of Iowa, Iowa City, and leader of a study of 129 nondepressed stroke patients, published in *Archives of General Psychiatry*.

Women's Health

Study Touts Success with "Female Viagra" Drug

New industry-funded research suggests that the drug *flibanserin*, an antidepressant that has been touted as a female version of Viagra, can enhance libido in women with low sex drives.

The research compiles the results of several trials, the first to test a treatment for low libido in women that works on the brain, said lead investigator John M. Thorp Jr., MD, a professor of obstetrics and gynecology at the University of North Carolina at Chapel Hill School of Medicine.

BACKGROUND

"Flibanserin was a poor antidepressant," Dr. Thorp said. "However, astute observers noted that it increased libido in laboratory animals and human subjects. So, we conducted multiple clinical trials, and the women in our studies who took it for *hypoactive sexual desire disorder*

reported significant improvements in sexual desire and satisfactory sexual experiences."

Research suggests that 9% to 26% of women in the United States suffer from low sex drive, with the numbers varying depending on age and whether they've reached menopause.

The findings were presented at the Congress of the European Society for Sexual Medicine in Lyon, France.

Boehringer Ingelheim, which makes flibanserin, funded the research.

STUDY DETAILS

The researchers combined statistics from three trials of flibanserin, which together included 1,946 premenopausal women who took either the drug or a placebo for about six months.

Daily doses of 100 milligrams significantly improved symptoms of low sex drive, the researchers found.

UPDATE

A federal advisory board to the FDA has voted against approving the drug, but encouraged

University of North Carolina School of Medicine news release.

the drug maker to continue its research. The panel found that while flibanserin did increase the number of sexually satisfying events experienced by women with low libido, the drug did not increase the women's desire.

Boehringer has said that it will work with the FDA to address the issues raised by the panel. The company has also announced plans to seek approval for the drug in other countries as well.

info The Web site of the American Congress of Obstetricians and Gynecologists has more information on women's sexuality at *www.acog. org*. Type "sexuality and problems" into the search box.

■ ■ ■ ■

High Cholesterol Hurts Women's Sex Lives

In a study of 556 women, researchers found that women with *hyperlipidemia* (elevated cholesterol levels in the blood) reported significantly lower sexual satisfaction than those without the condition.

Theory: Accumulation of fats in blood vessel walls (already linked to erectile dysfunction in men) also may reduce blood flow to female genitals.

If you have experienced a loss of sexual function: Ask your doctor to check your total cholesterol levels.

Katherine Esposito, MD, PhD, researcher, department of geriatrics and metabolic disease, Second University of Naples, Italy.

Good News About The Pill

BMJ (British Medical Journal) press release.

There's good news for women who have used birth control pills. A long-term study finds that those who took oral contraceptives at some point in their lives have a lower

risk of death than women who never took the "Pill."

"Many women, especially those who used the first generation of oral contraceptives many years ago, are likely to be reassured by our results. However, our findings might not reflect the experience of women using oral contraceptives today, if currently available preparations have a different risk than earlier products," said study leader Philip Hannaford, MD, of the University of Aberdeen in Scotland.

However, those who took oral contraceptives are at higher risk of violent or accidental death. The authors of the study, which was published in the journal *BMJ (British Medical Journal)*, aren't sure why this might be so.

STUDY DETAILS
Dr. Hannaford and colleagues tracked 46,000 women for up to nearly 40 years.

In the long term, women who took birth-control pills had a significantly lower risk of death from causes such as heart disease and cancers—even cancers of the uterus and ovary —compared with other women.

Women younger than 40 who took birth control pills had a slightly higher risk of death, the researchers report.

BOTTOM LINE
The authors concluded that "oral contraception is not significantly associated with an increased long-term risk of death—indeed a net benefit was apparent."

However, "the balance of risks and benefits may vary, depending upon the patterns of oral contraception usage and background risk of disease."

info For more about birth control pills, visit the Web site of the independent health information source, HealthyWomen, at *www.healthy women.org,* and search "oral contraceptives."

■ ■ ■ ■

What to Do If You're Bleeding After Sex

Bleeding after sex should be looked into unless you are menstruating or just lost your virginity. Postcoital bleeding could be related to abnormal (precancerous or cancerous) cells on the cervix…a cervical polyp…an intrauterine device (IUD)…a sexually transmitted disease, such as *gonorrhea, chlamydia* or *trichomoniasis*…a uterine fibroid…a yeast infection…or some kind of trauma to the vagina, cervix or perineum. If you experience bleeding after intercourse, it may be a warning sign to see your gynecologist.

Lissa Rankin, MD, obstetrician/gynecologist, Mill Valley, California, and author of *What's Up Down There? Questions You'd Only Ask Your Gynecologist If She Was Your Best Friend* (St. Martin's).

Drug May Shrink Fibroids, Preserve Fertility

Alicia Armstrong, MD, chief of gynecologic services, Program for Reproductive and Adult Endocrinology, National Institutes of Health, Bethesda, Maryland.

Lynnette Nieman, MD, senior investigator, National Institute for Child Health and Human Development, Bethesda, Maryland.

Scott Chudnoff, MD, assistant professor, department of obstetrics & gynecology and women's health, Albert Einstein College of Medicine, and director of gynecology, Montefiore Medical Center, New York City.

European Society of Human Reproduction and Embryology news release.

Preliminary research suggests that a new drug treatment shrinks uterine fibroids and helps women with the noncancerous tumors retain their fertility.

ABOUT UTERINE FIBROIDS

Uterine fibroids, which cause abdominal pain and heavy menstrual bleeding, are a leading cause of hysterectomy. They can also contribute to miscarriage.

"Both the fibroids and the surgical interventions commonly used to treat them can cause significant fertility problems," said Alicia Armstrong, MD, chief of gynecologic services at the National Institutes of Health's Program for Reproductive and Adult Endocrinology.

RESEARCH FINDINGS

In two new studies, researchers tested a drug called *ulipristal acetate* (brand name ellaOne), which blocks ovulation and is used as a form of emergency contraception. It works by adjusting the body's reaction to the presence of the hormone *progesterone*.

In the studies, 57 women, ages 25 to50, with uterine fibroids were randomly assigned to receive treatment with the drug or a placebo. They took the pills once a day for three menstrual cycles.

The fibroids shrank in more of the women who took the drug versus the placebo, and those who took higher doses had better results. Women who took the drug also had less bleeding than those who took the placebo.

The studies show that the drug "is an effective noninvasive treatment for fibroids that can help maintain fertility in women whose only option up to now was to have surgery," said Lynnette Nieman, MD, a principal investigator with the studies.

The studies are both in Phase II, the second in three phases of research required before the federal government will approve a drug for a specific use.

The study findings were presented at a meeting of the European Society of Human Reproduction and Embryology in Rome.

EXPERT COMMENTARY

Scott Chudnoff, MD, a gynecologist and uterine fibroid specialist, said the research could lead to significant new treatments for women with fibroids. But some women might not respond the same way to the treatment, and the fibroids may return when women stop taking the drug, said Dr. Chudnoff, who is director of gynecology at Montefiore Medical Center in New York City.

Still, a new treatment would help doctors do a better job of personalizing their approach to individual patients, he said. The research, he added, is "definitely promising."

For more information about uterine fibroids, visit the Web site of the National Library of Medicine, *www.nlm.nih.gov/medlineplus*, and search "uterine fibroids."

Natural Ways to Boost Fertility

Mark A. Stengler, NMD, naturopathic medical doctor in private practice, La Jolla, California…adjunct associate clinical professor at the National College of Natural Medicine, Portland, Oregon…author of many books, including *The Natural Physician's Healing Therapies* and coauthor of *Prescription for Natural Cures* (both from Bottom Line Books)…and author of the *Bottom Line/Natural Healing* newsletter.

Thirty-nine-year-old Danielle and her husband, Scott, had been trying to conceive for three years. Because of Danielle's age, they feared that time was running out.

Infertility specialists advised them that their only options were *intrauterine insemination*, a process of artificial insemination in which sperm is placed in a woman's uterus…or *in vitro fertilization*, a process of fertilization in which eggs and sperm are combined in a lab and the resulting embryos are implanted. Both techniques require a substantial drug regimen. Worried about the potential side effects of these drugs and the cost, the couple decided to explore other options. Danielle had read one of my books and believed that natural medicine might help her.

The tests that I conducted showed that she did not ovulate regularly and that her levels of the hormone *progesterone* were too low to adequately maintain a pregnancy. Progesterone is needed to build and maintain the lining of the uterus, in which the fertilized egg can grow. Scott's tests by a fertility specialist showed that he had lower-than-normal sperm motility, the ability of sperm to move toward an egg. For the best chance of a successful pregnancy, we needed to treat both Danielle and Scott.

I conducted further tests and found that while Danielle's thyroid hormone level was within the normal range, it was slightly low, which can throw off ovulation. I prescribed Nature-Throid, a natural prescription medicine for patients who have an underactive thyroid or other thyroid problems. Because her thyroid level was within the normal range, none of her other doctors had suggested that she take a thyroid supplement. Danielle was already taking the herb

Vitex agnus-castus, known as chasteberry, which she had learned about in my book. Studies have shown that it can stimulate ovulation and normalize progesterone levels. For Scott, I prescribed the supplements *coenzyme Q10* and *L-carnitine*, which can help to increase sperm motility.

I encourage couples struggling with infertility to be mindful of eating a healthful diet. I suggest that their diet consist of organic foods, with an emphasis on fruits, vegetables, nuts, lean protein and gluten-free grains, such as corn, rice, buckwheat and quinoa, because gluten can cause infertility. I also recommend that they consume essential fatty acids—such as cold-water fish and flaxseed—to promote gland health and hormone balance. Danielle and her husband already ate a healthful diet, so they didn't have to make any changes.

Four months after I began treating her, Danielle was delighted to tell me that she was pregnant! As of the writing of this article, Danielle is scheduled to deliver her baby any day.

Freezing Ovaries Preserves Fertility, Scientists Report

Sherman Silber, MD, director, Infertility Center of St. Louis at St. Luke's Hospital.

Richard J. Paulson, MD, professor of obstetrics and gynecology, chief, Division of Reproductive Endocrinology and Infertility, University of Southern California Keck School of Medicine, Los Angeles.

American Society for Reproductive Medicine annual meeting, San Francisco.

Scientists are reporting the ability to freeze and transplant ovaries, a development that could help preserve fertility in women facing cancer therapy.

"We can transplant ovaries without any loss of ovarian tissue or eggs, and it functions perfectly normally whether it's fresh or frozen," said coresearcher Sherman Silber, MD, director of the Infertility Center of St. Louis at St. Luke's Hospital.

Dr. Silber said women who want to delay having children could also use the technique. He reported the findings at the American Society for Reproductive Medicine annual meeting, in San Francisco.

EGG FREEZING VS. OVARY FREEZING

Currently, women can have their eggs frozen and put back after cancer treatment is complete, Dr. Silber noted. "But there are disadvantages," he said. "If you put all those eggs in one basket, and she goes through *in vitro fertilization* (IVF), she can't have any better chance of pregnancy than 50%. If she is not pregnant from that, then she's finished."

With ovary transplantation, however, "She's got a normally functioning ovary just like she would have if she were younger. Freezing the ovary and putting it back is much more sure for the patient than egg freezing," he said.

OVARY TRANSPLANTATION TO TWIN

In one paper, Dr. Silber reported that he and his colleagues had transplanted an ovary from one identical twin to her twin sister, allowing the twin with premature ovarian failure to conceive a child. One year after the transplant, the twin with the transplanted ovary became pregnant.

OVARY FROZEN AND RESTORED

Dr. Silber and his colleagues also reported at the meeting on one woman who had her ovary removed, frozen and then restored. They said they've done the procedure nine times. "It's very repeatable," Dr. Silber said. "It's not just a fluke."

Dr. Silber said the ability to remove an ovary, freeze it and put it back into the same woman represents the real breakthrough. "We can freeze the ovaries of young women who are going to lose their fertility over time and transplant them back later, and they [the ovaries] won't have aged," he explained.

The technique can benefit cancer patients about to undergo radiation, chemotherapy or bone marrow transplant, which would leave them sterile, Dr. Silber said. "But if we take the ovary out, freeze it, save it and transplant it back later, they will be fertile again," he said.

RECOMMENDATION

Dr. Silber said that if a woman receives a cancer diagnosis, "ask about freezing your ovary. In addition, young women who are going to put off childbearing should also think about having one of their ovaries frozen," he added.

EXPERT COMMENTARY

Richard J. Paulson, MD, chief of the Division of Reproductive Endocrinology and Infertility at the University of Southern California Keck School of Medicine, in Los Angeles, thinks the new reports are encouraging but preliminary.

"This is very exciting," Dr. Paulson said. "Fertility preservation is our next major frontier, because what we have found is that women with cancer are increasingly surviving their chemotherapy but are infertile. It would be very helpful if we could have a method to preserve their fertility."

Although women are having their eggs frozen, many women can't go through the procedure to harvest the eggs, Dr. Paulson said. "It would be very appealing to take the ovary out and freeze it for the future," he said.

However, Dr. Paulson noted that, so far, no woman had become pregnant after her ovary had been removed, frozen and put back.

info For more on infertility, visit the US National Women's Health Information Center's Web site, *www.womenshealth.gov* and search "infertility."

Fake Acupuncture Tied to Higher IVF Pregnancies

European Society for Human Reproduction and Embryology news release.

Compared to real acupuncture, placebo acupuncture was associated with significantly higher overall pregnancy rates among women undergoing *in vitro fertilization* (IVF), says a University of Hong Kong study.

REAL VS. PLACEBO ACUPUNCTURE

In real acupuncture, fine needles are inserted into particular points on the body. In placebo acupuncture, blunt needles that look identical to real acupuncture needles retract into the handle of the needle when pressed on the skin, but still give the sensation and appearance of entering the skin.

THE STUDY

The researchers gave real or placebo acupuncture to 370 women on the day of embryo transfer and found that 55.1% of those who received placebo acupuncture became pregnant, compared with 43.8% of those who received real acupuncture. The findings were published in *Human Reproduction*.

"We found a significantly higher overall pregnancy rate following placebo acupuncture when compared with that of real acupuncture," said study author Ernest Hung Yu Ng, MD, an associate professor in the department of obstetrics and gynecology at the University of Hong Kong.

IMPLICATION

The results suggest that placebo acupuncture may not act as an inert control for real acupuncture and may be having a real effect. That theory is supported by the fact that the researchers noted significant changes in measurements for uterus receptivity and patient stress levels after the women received both the real and placebo acupuncture.

POSSIBLE EXPLANATIONS

There are two possible explanations for the study results.

"Placebo acupuncture is similar to acupressure and therefore is good enough to improve the pregnancy rate," said Dr. Ng, who added it's also possible that real acupuncture may, in some way, reduce the pregnancy rate. Acupressure utilizes the same pressure points as acupuncture, but uses gentle to firm finger pressure instead of needles.

"So far, there is no evidence that real acupuncture would adversely affect IVF outcomes because, in a previous meta-analysis of several acupuncture studies, the pregnancy rate was higher in the acupuncture group than in the control group. However, we cannot draw a firm conclusion about this from our current study, as we did not compare the two groups with a third control group of patients who received neither form of acupuncture. Further studies should be conducted to compare placebo or noninvasive acupuncture and controls without acupuncture," Dr. Ng said.

info For more information on acupuncture, visit the Web site of the US National Center for Complementary and Alternative Medicine, *http://nccam.nih.gov/health/acupuncture/*.

Hormone Might Help Restore Female Fertility

Society for Endocrinology news release.

A hormone called *kisspeptin* may offer a new treatment for infertility, according to British researchers who found that the hormone can activate the release of sex hormones that control the menstrual cycle.

According to the researchers, the hormone kisspeptin is an important regulator of reproductive function. Animals that lack kisspeptin function don't go through puberty and remain sexually immature.

THE STUDY

The study included 10 women who were not menstruating and were infertile due to a hormone imbalance. The researchers injected the participants with either kisspeptin or saline and then measured levels of two sex hormones—*luteinizing hormone* (LH) and *follicle stimulating hormone* (FSH)—essential for ovulation and fertility.

THE RESULTS

The women who received kisspeptin had a 48-fold increase in LH and a 16-fold increase in FSH, compared with those who received the saline. The study is the first to show that kisspeptin can stimulate production of sex hormones in infertile women, according to the study's authors.

The findings were presented at a Society for Endocrinology meeting in the United Kingdom.

IMPLICATIONS

"This research shows that kisspeptin offers huge promise as a treatment for infertility," said study author Waljit Dhillo, PhD, of Imperial College London.

"From our previous results, we know that kisspeptin can stimulate release of reproductive hormones in healthy women. We have now extended this research to show that kisspeptin treatment has the same effect in women with infertility. In fact, our current data show that kisspeptin causes a greater increase in luteinizing hormone production in non-menstruating women than in fertile women in the previous study," Dr. Dhillo said.

"This is a very exciting result and suggests that kisspeptin treatment could restore reproductive function in women with low sex hormone levels. Our future research will focus on determining the best protocol for repeated kisspeptin administration with the hope of developing a new therapy for infertility," he added.

Fruits and Veggies May Improve Sperm Quality

Plataforma SINC news release.

Eating a diet rich in fruits and vegetables plays an important role in semen quality, according to new research from Spain.

THE STUDY

The study included 61 men—30 with reproductive problems and 31 who did not have such issues. It appeared online in the journal *Fertility and Sterility*.

The study found that "men with good semen quality ate more vegetables and fruit (more vitamins, folic acid and fiber and less protein and fats) than those men with low seminal quality," said the lead author, Jaime Mendiola, PhD, a researcher at the University of Murcia.

EXPLANATION

Antioxidants, found mainly in fruits and vegetables, lower the level of oxidative stress that

can affect semen quality, the researchers explained, and also improve sperm concentration and mobility.

MEAT AND DAIRY LOWER SEMEN QUALITY

An earlier study by the same team "showed that men who eat large amounts of meat and full-fat dairy products have lower seminal quality than those who eat more fruit, vegetables and reduced-fat dairy products," Dr. Mendiola said.

But the new study "found that people who consume more fruits and vegetables are ingesting more antioxidants, and this is the important point," Dr. Mendiola said. "A healthy diet is not only a good way of avoiding illness but could also have an impact on improving seminal quality."

FOOD VERSUS SUPPLEMENTS

"What we still do not understand is the difference between taking these vitamins naturally and in the form of supplements," the researcher added. "In the studies we are going to carry out in the United States (where the consumption of vitamins in tablet form is very common), we will be looking at the role of supplements."

info The Web site of the US National Institute of Child Health and Human Development has more about reproductive health at *www.nichd.nih.gov/*. Under "A to Z health & human development topics," choose "R" and click on "Reproductive Health."

Fertility Drugs Do Not Increase Ovarian Cancer Risk

BMJ (British Medical Journal) news release.

Women who take fertility drugs do not have an increased risk of developing ovarian cancer, according to a large study by Danish researchers.

BACKGROUND

There's been ongoing debate about whether fertility drugs boost the likelihood of ovarian cancer. Previous studies have yielded conflicting findings, and concerns endure, especially for women who undergo several cycles of fertility drug treatment or those who never become pregnant.

NEW STUDY

In the new study, Danish Cancer Society researchers analyzed data from 54,362 women referred to fertility clinics between 1963 and 1998. Of those women, 156 developed ovarian cancer. The researchers adjusted for several risk factors and then assessed the effect of four groups of fertility drugs over an average period of 16 years.

The study found no overall increased risk for ovarian cancer after the use of any fertility drug. It also found no increased risk among women who had 10 or more cycles of fertility drug treatment or among women who never became pregnant.

The researchers did note a statistically significant increase in the risk of the most serious type of ovarian cancer among women who took the fertility drug *clomiphene* (Clomid), but indicated they believe this was a chance association.

The study was published in *BMJ (British Medical Journal)*.

STUDY FINDINGS REASSURING

Penelope Webb, PhD, a research fellow at the Queensland Institute of Medical Research in Australia, wrote in an accompanying editorial that the findings are reassuring and provide further evidence that the use of fertility drugs does not increase the risk of ovarian cancer.

STUDY ONGOING

Many of the women in the study had not reached the peak age for ovarian cancer, so the researchers plan to continue to monitor their risk.

info The Web site of the National Infertility Association, *www.resolve.org*, has more information about infertility.

Pregnancy Complication Points to Thyroid Problems Later On

BMJ (British Medical Journal) news release.

New research offers bad news for women who develop a condition known as *preeclampsia* during pregnancy. They are at higher risk for reduced thyroid function in later life.

ABOUT PREECLAMPSIA

Preeclampsia develops in the second half of pregnancy and can cause serious problems, such as extremely high blood pressure. The causes aren't clear, but may have something to do with high levels of proteins in the body.

THE STUDY

Researchers in the United States and Norway looked at two groups of pregnant women—those who developed preeclampsia and those who didn't. The study was published in an online edition of *BMJ (British Medical Journal)*.

In the US study, researchers compared 140 healthy pregnant women who developed preeclampsia with 140 women who didn't. Those who had the condition showed double the levels of thyroid-stimulating hormone, an indication that the thyroid is not functioning properly, as those who didn't develop preeclampsia.

The Norwegian study examined 7,121 pregnant women and found that those who developed preeclampsia, especially in two pregnancies, were more likely to have high concentrations of thyroid hormone 20 years later.

ADVICE

The researchers suggest that doctors should closely follow women who develop preeclampsia, keeping an eye out not just for heart and kidney disease, which are known risks, but also thyroid disease.

info To learn more about preeclampsia, visit the Preeclampsia Foundation Web site, *www.preeclampsia.org*.

Acupuncture May Relieve Heartburn in Pregnancy

Joao Bosco Guerreiro daSilva, MD, PhD, Department of Internal Medicine, Rio Preto Medical College, São José do Rio Preto, Brazil.

Richard Frieder, MD, obstetrician-gynecologist, Santa Monica-UCLA Medical Center, and clinical instructor, obstetrics and gynecology, David Geffen School of Medicine, University of California, Los Angeles

Marshall H. Sager, DO, past president, American Society of Medical Acupuncture, acupuncturist, Bala Cynwyd, Pennysylvania.

Acupuncture in Medicine.

Acupuncture relieves the indigestion and heartburn that bother many women as their pregnancy progresses, a new Brazilian study shows.

"Although small, this study suggests that acupuncture can relieve symptoms of indigestion that are pretty common in pregnancy and may provoke loss of quality of life in the final days, disturbing not only eating but also sleeping," said lead researcher Dr. Joao Bosco Guerreiro da Silva, MD, PhD, from the department of internal medicine at Rio Preto Medical College.

BACKGROUND

Indigestion is common during pregnancy, with up to 80% of moms-to-be suffering heartburn, stomach pain or discomfort, reflux, belching and bloating. Symptoms tend to worsen as the pregnancy progresses, and women who avoid taking medicine for fear of harming the developing fetus might welcome an alternative treatment.

THE STUDY

For the study, the researchers randomly assigned 42 pregnant women with indigestion to dietary counseling plus antacids, or to dietary counseling and antacids plus acupuncture, once or twice a week. The researchers assessed the women's symptoms at the beginning of the study and every two weeks after that for eight weeks.

Heartburn, the main symptom, was reduced by half in 75% of the women treated with acupuncture. Women receiving acupuncture also ate and slept better, he said.

The 20 women who underwent acupuncture and completed the study reported having milder symptoms and took less medication than the 16 women getting conventional therapy, the researchers found.

Fewer than half the women receiving traditional treatment said their heartburn was halved.

Among the 14 women who took antacids, seven in each group, those receiving acupuncture took 6.3 fewer doses, while those receiving conventional treatment upped the amount of medication they took by 4.4 doses, the researchers found.

In addition, 15 women in the acupuncture group said that their eating habits improved by 50%, compared with fewer than one in three in the other group. Fourteen women receiving acupuncture said their sleep had improved by 50%, compared with just one in four women treated conventionally.

The report was published in *Acupuncture in Medicine.*

IMPLICATION

"Dyspepsia [indigestion] in pregnancy is a very common problem," Dr. Guerreiro da Silva said. "Medication is always a concern. Acupuncture can be effective. It is safe and simple to apply and every pregnant woman can be treated."

EXPERT COMMENTARY

Richard Frieder, MD, an obstetrician-gynecologist at Santa Monica-UCLA Medical Center and clinical instructor of obstetrics and gynecology at the David Geffen School of Medicine, University of California, Los Angeles, doesn't think that acupuncture works any better than conventional treatment.

"This is an interesting idea but far from proves any benefit, as the control group did not have any type of placebo treatment, such as fake acupuncture to make the control and test group comparable," Dr. Frieder said.

Indigestion and heartburn are common in pregnancy and usually successfully treated with diet, sleep positioning and medication with no known harmful effects, Dr. Frieder noted.

"Acupuncture might be a nice alternative for women who are inclined to this option, but it is doubtfully more effective than standard treatment if the study had been done in an apples-to-apples comparison," he said.

Another expert thinks that acupuncture does relieve indigestion, but he won't perform it on pregnant women because of concerns about litigation.

"It is a well-done study and it is expected that there would be positive results," said Marshall H. Sager, DO, past president of the American Society of Medical Acupuncture and an acupuncturist in Bala Cynwyd, Pennsylvania.

However, he worries that he would be sued if something went wrong with the pregnancy. "I wouldn't touch a pregnant lady with acupuncture because of the malpractice situation. Not that it's not effective, but that's my problem with the medical/legal aspects of it," he said.

Zinc May Counter Effects of Alcohol in Early Pregnancy

Alcoholism: Clinical & Experimental Research news release.

Zinc supplements may help mothers-to-be reduce the risk for birth defects linked to alcohol use early in pregnancy, Australian researchers report.

The animal study was published in the journal *Alcoholism: Clinical & Experimental Research.*

BACKGROUND

"Alcohol's damage to the fetus depends not only on the amount and duration of alcohol exposure, but also on the timing of the exposure relative to the development of the cells and tissues involved," said study coauthor Peter Coyle, PhD, an associate professor at the Hanson Institute in Adelaide.

"Earlier work had shown that prenatal alcohol, as well as other toxins, can result in fetal zinc deficiency and (developmental malformations) by inducing the zinc-binding protein, *metallothionein*, in the mother's liver. Since then, our group has confirmed the importance of metallothionein in alcohol-mediated birth defects," he said.

NEW STUDY

In this study, Dr. Coyle and colleagues injected either saline or a 25% solution of alcohol into pregnant mice on their eighth day of gestation. In mice, the eighth day of gestation is equivalent to weeks three to eight during a human pregnancy. The mice were fed either a regular or zinc-supplemented diet from conception to day 18 of gestation, when some fetuses were assessed for birth defects. The growth of the surviving offspring was monitored for 60 days after birth.

"There were three key findings," Dr. Coyle said.

"One, fetal abnormalities caused by acute alcohol exposure in early pregnancy can be prevented by dietary zinc supplementation. Two, dietary zinc supplementation throughout pregnancy can protect against post-natal death caused by acute alcohol exposure in early pregnancy. Three, dietary zinc supplementation increases the mother's blood zinc to overwhelm the transient drop in zinc caused by alcohol, which we believe prevents the fetal zinc deficiency and subsequent fetal damage."

IMPLICATIONS

These findings don't mean that taking zinc makes it safe for women to drink during pregnancy, however.

"We have not determined whether zinc protects against all of the possible negative outcomes from alcohol exposure in pregnancy," Dr. Coyle said. "Nor would we recommend that makers of alcoholic beverages include zinc in their product so that women can drink while pregnant. Indeed, we take the conservative stand of a 'no alcohol policy' during pregnancy."

What the studies do indicate is that dietary zinc supplementation could be as important as folic acid in helping to prevent damage to the fetus during pregnancy, according to Dr. Coyle.

The US National Institute of Alcohol Abuse and Alcoholism has more information about drinking during pregnancy at *http://pubs.niaaa.nih.gov.* Under "Publications," click on "Pamphlets/Brochures/Fact Sheets/Posters."

Should You Diet When You Are Pregnant?

Yvonne Thornton, MD, MPH, clinical professor, obstetrics and gynecology, New York Medical College, Valhalla, New York.

Robin Kalish, MD, director, clinical maternal fetal medicine, NewYork-Presbyterian Hospital/Weill Cornell Medical Center, New York City.

Journal of the National Medical Association.

In a study that reinforces recent changes in pregnancy weight gain recommendations, obese women who gained little or no weight while pregnant had better outcomes than obese women who gained more.

BACKGROUND

About 35% of US women are obese, according to the US Centers for Disease Control and Prevention.

Though doctors know that obesity during pregnancy raises the risk for hypertension, gestational diabetes and other complications, no one is certain what the optimal weight gain for pregnant women should be.

THE STUDY

In the new study, published in the *Journal of the National Medical Association*, researchers divided 232 obese women, all with a body mass index (BMI) greater than 30 (a BMI of 30 and over is considered obese), into two groups. One group was given the standard advice to "eat to appetite." The other group was given nutritional counseling, told to keep a food diary and placed on a diet that limited calories to between 2,000 and 3,500 a day, depending on their weight before the pregnancy.

By the end of the pregnancy, the average weight gain in the group of women who stuck to their normal diets was 31 pounds. The average weight gain for women in the calorie-restriction group was 11 pounds. Twenty-three extremely obese women actually lost weight during their pregnancy.

CALORIE RESTRICTION BENEFITS SEEN

The results seem to support less, not more, weight gain during pregnancy. Women in the calorie-restricted group had fewer C-sections and lower rates of gestational diabetes and hypertension and had retained less weight six weeks after delivery.

Fewer women in the calorie-restricted group delivered newborns weighing more than 10 pounds, which can make deliveries risky for both mother and child. There were no growth-restricted babies in either group.

HEALTHY EATING DURING PREGNANCY

"Women who are obese when beginning a pregnancy are, by definition, unhealthy," noted Yvonne Thornton, MD, MPH, a clinical professor of obstetrics and gynecology at New York Medical College and the study's lead author. "To say that they should gain even more weight is counterintuitive, and our study bears that out."

Still, Dr. Thornton does not favor establishing a one-size-fits-all weight gain number for obese women.

Instead, "we need to focus on making these women healthier by getting them to eat a well-balanced diet, similar to the types of moderate calorie-restricted diets that women with gestational diabetes are put on with no ill effects," she said.

"Over the past decade, obstetricians have become more aware that the idea of 'eating for two' is really not a good thing, especially for patients who start out obese," said Robin Kalish, MD, director of clinical maternal fetal medicine at New York-Presbyterian Hospital/Weill Cornell Medical Center.

STUDY AUTHOR'S WEIGHT STRUGGLE

The idea for the study came from Dr. Thornton's own lifelong struggle with weight. During her first pregnancy in the late 1970s, she gained 67 pounds and hit a peak weight of 225 pounds.

After the pregnancy, she signed up for Weight Watchers and lost 20 pounds, only to become pregnant again.

But with her second child, she continued the focus on nutrition and gained less than a half-pound.

"I was the first test case," Dr. Thornton said.

NEW WEIGHT-GAIN GUIDELINES

Experts at the US Institute of Medicine and the National Research Council recently updated their gestational weight gain guidelines to urge that obese women gain only 11 to 20 pounds during pregnancy—down from a minimum weight gain of 15 pounds that had been recommended in 1990.

Mom and Baby Alike May Benefit from Exercise

Raul Artal, MD, chairman of obstetrics, gynecology and women's health, Saint Louis University School of Medicine, St. Louis.

Thomas Wang, MD, Kaiser Permanente, San Diego.

American College of Obstetricians and Gynecologists (*www.acog.org*).

American Pregnancy Association (*www.american pregnancy.org*).

It's natural that a woman might be worried about exercising while she's pregnant. So many changes are occurring in her body, it makes sense to have second thoughts about whether exercise might harm her or her unborn child.

But it turns out that a thoughtful exercise program is good for both mother and child, according to medical experts.

"We know that women who exercise during pregnancy have less chance of developing certain conditions like gestational diabetes," said Raul Artal, MD, chairman of obstetrics, gynecology and women's health for the Saint Louis University School of Medicine. "Not only that, exercise maintains musculoskeletal fitness. Women can cope with the anatomical and physiological changes of pregnancy better when they're in good shape. They also tolerate labor better and recover more quickly from delivery."

The baby also benefits. One study found that when an expectant mother works out, her fetus reaps cardiac benefits in the form of a lower fetal heart rate.

CHOOSING APPROPRIATE EXERCISE

When choosing what sort of exercise to pursue, a woman should take into account the shape she was in before becoming pregnant, said Thomas Wang, MD, a family practitioner for Kaiser Permanente in San Diego.

"A lot of things depend on the level of fitness they had before," Dr. Wang said. A mom-to-be should pursue activities that will provide a good level of exertion without testing the limits of her body's current conditioning. If she's just starting a fitness program to improve her health during pregnancy, she should start out slowly and be careful not to overexert herself.

The American College of Obstetricians and Gynecologists recommends that pregnant women do at least 30 minutes of moderate exercise a day most days of the week. First, though, all women should consult a doctor to make sure it's okay.

ACTIVITIES TO AVOID

But there are certain activities that should at least be undertaken with caution, if not avoided altogether. Pregnant women, for instance, should not go scuba diving, as that activity exposes the fetus to a risk of developing decompression sickness, also known as the bends.

Women also should think twice before engaging in activities where the risk of falling is high, such as gymnastics, horseback riding, downhill skiing and high-intensity racquet sports. And they should avoid contact sports, such as ice hockey, soccer and basketball.

"Anything that involves impact or the chance of abdominal trauma, they should try to avoid," Dr. Wang explained.

SAFE EXERCISE

Exercise that's perfectly safe for expectant mothers includes Kegel exercises (which strengthen the pelvic floor muscles), swimming, walking, light dancing and yoga. Riding a stationary bicycle or working out on aerobic gym equipment—elliptical or stair-climbing machines, for instance—is also fairly safe, as long as care is taken to prevent a fall.

Most pregnant women also can take part in jogging, running and aerobics, especially if those were exercises they regularly performed before pregnancy.

WEIGHT TRAINING

Pregnant women who weight train should emphasize improving their muscle tone, particularly in the upper body and abdominal area, according to the American Pregnancy Association. They should avoid lifting weights above their heads and performing exercises that strain the lower back muscles.

"There have been some studies that show heavy lifting causes a temporary drop in the baby's heart rate," Dr. Wang said. "It usually corrects pretty quickly, but they might want to be careful."

EXERCISE PRECAUTIONS

Other things to keep in mind if exercising while pregnant:

•**Avoid exercising to the point of exhaustion or breathlessness,** as that could affect the oxygen supply to the fetus.

•**Avoid overheating,** which can affect the baby's development. Don't exercise in hot weather.

•**During the second and third trimesters,** avoid exercise that involves lying flat on your back as this decreases blood flow to the womb.

Though that might seem like a lot of precautions for something that's supposed to be safe, doctors insist that women can and should engage in a well-thought-out fitness program during their pregnancy.

"By and large, if there are no medical complications of pregnancy, women can continue engaging in the same type of activities," Dr. Artal said. "Women should be encouraged to continue living an active lifestyle."

info The more information on pregnancy and exercise, visit the Web site of The Nemours Foundation, *http://kidshealth.org/parent,* and search "exercise during pregnancy."

Vaginal Delivery Possible After Cesarean Section

Jeffrey Ecker, MD, maternal-fetal medicine specialist, Massachusetts General Hospital, and associate professor, obstetrics and gynecology, Harvard School of Medicine, Boston.

William Grobman, MD, associate professor, obstetrics and gynecology, and maternal-fetal medicine specialist, Northwestern University's Feinberg School of Medicine, Chicago.

Peter Bernstein, MD, MPH, professor, clinical obstetrics, gynecology and women's health, and director, fellowship program in maternal and fetal medicine, Montefiore Medical Center and Albert Einstein College of Medicine, New York City.

Obstetrics & Gynecology.

Many women who've had a Cesarean section may be candidates for vaginal birth in future pregnancies, say new guidelines from the American College of Obstetricians and Gynecologists.

"These guidelines emphasize again that a trial of labor after Cesarean is an important option for most women," said one of the authors of the new guidelines, Jeffrey Ecker, MD, a maternal-fetal medicine specialist at Massachusetts General Hospital in Boston.

BACKGROUND

Years ago, experts believed that once a woman had undergone a Cesarean birth, she would have to deliver any subsequent pregnancies with a C-section as well. But with changes in surgical procedures and growing evidence to support the possibility of a *vaginal birth after a Cesarean* (VBAC), attitudes began to shift.

However, in the 1980s and 1990s, as the VBAC rate increased, so did complications related to the procedure. Because of concern over complications and possible legal consequences, the VBAC rate dropped dramatically, from 28.3% of deliveries in 1996 to 8.5% in 2006. But repeat C-sections also have a risk of complications for mother and baby, the authors of the guidelines noted.

Currently, nearly one in three mothers delivers by Cesarean in the United States, according to the study.

NEW EVIDENCE SUPPORTS VBAC

More recent studies have supported the idea that many women can successfully deliver vaginally after having had a Cesarean, explained William Grobman, MD, another author of the new guidelines and an associate professor of obstetrics and gynecology at Northwestern University's Feinberg School of Medicine in Chicago. A National Institutes of Health panel came to the same conclusion and said that a Cesarean delivery in the past doesn't mean a woman must automatically have a Cesarean in subsequent pregnancies.

The new guidelines recommend counseling women who've had one Cesarean birth using a horizontal incision low in the uterus (low transverse incision) that they are candidates for VBAC, and offering the option of a trial of labor so they can attempt to deliver vaginally.

Between 60% and 80% of women who attempt VBAC have a successful vaginal delivery, according to the guidelines. Dr. Grobman said that for some women, the success rates may be much higher.

The guidelines, published in *Obstetrics & Gynecology*, suggest that the following women may also be candidates for a trial of labor after a Cesarean…

•**Women who've had two previous C-sections using a low transverse incision.**

•**Women who've had a C-section with a low transverse incision who are currently pregnant with twins.**

•**Women who've had a Cesarean delivery but don't know if they had a low transverse incision.**

WOMEN WHO SHOULD NOT HAVE VBAC

Some women definitely aren't candidates for VBAC. These include women who've had a vertical incision on the uterus or serious pregnancy complications, such as placenta previa (a condition in which the placenta grows in the lowest part of the uterus and covers the opening to the cervix), said Dr. Grobman.

EXPERT REACTION

"For some women, a VBAC remains an inappropriate choice. But for many, if not most women, choosing a trial of labor when you've had a C-section is an appropriate choice," said Dr. Ecker.

The guideline authors hope that women and their health care providers will feel a "sense of shared decision-making," Dr. Grobman said. "Rather than provide a directive of 'you can' or 'you can't' do this, doctors need to provide information about the potential risks and successes and let women have autonomy to make their own decision."

Peter Bernstein, MD, MPH, a professor of clinical obstetrics, gynecology and women's health at the Montefiore Medical Center in New York City, said he's very pleased to see the new guidelines. "Over the last 10 years or so, the pendulum has been swinging too far away from VBAC, and I think they're trying to swing the pendulum back the other way to a more reasonable position and making it available to women who are interested in it," he said.

info To learn more about vaginal birth after a Cesarean delivery, visit the Web site of the National Institutes of Health, *http://consensus.nih.gov/2010/vbacstatement.htm*.

Breast-Feeding Nurtures Scholars-to-Be

Joseph Sabia, PhD, assistant professor, public policy, American University, Washington, DC.

Daniel Rees, PhD, professor, economics, University of Colorado Denver.

David L. Katz, MD, director, Prevention Research Center, Yale University School of Medicine, New Haven, Connecticut.

Journal of Human Capital.

Children who were breast-fed do better in high school and are more likely to go to college than their bottle-fed siblings, researchers report.

While the health benefits of breast-feeding to both infants and mothers is well known, this study suggests the practice may have educational benefits as well. This is the first study using data on siblings to examine the effect of breast-feeding on high school completion and college attendance, the researchers noted.

"We compare sibling pairs—one of whom was breast-fed and one of whom was not, or siblings who were breast-fed for different durations—and find consistent evidence that breast-fed children have higher high school grade point averages and a higher probability of attending college," said study coauthor Joseph Sabia, PhD, an assistant professor of public policy at American University in Washington, DC.

The researchers ruled out factors, such as socioeconomic status, in the connection between breast-feeding and educational achievement, Dr. Sabia said.

The report was published in the *Journal of Human Capital.*

STUDY DETAILS

For the report, Dr. Sabia and his colleague Daniel Rees, PhD, a professor of economics at the University of Colorado Denver, used data from the National Longitudinal Study of Adolescent Health. They looked at the breast-feeding histories and high school grades of 126 siblings from 59 families; high school graduation and college attendance data was obtained for 191 siblings from 90 families.

"If you're breast-fed, your high school GPA goes up substantially, and the likelihood that you go on to college goes up," Dr. Rees said.

For every month you are breast-fed, your high school GPA goes up about 1% and your probability of going to college goes up about 2%, Dr. Rees added.

"We found that more than one-half of the estimated effect of being breast-fed on high school grades can be linked to improvements in cognitive ability and health," Dr. Sabia said. "Thus, we conclude that improvements in cognitive ability and adolescent health may be important pathways through which breast-feeding affects long-term academic achievement," he said.

About one-fifth of the increased likelihood of going to college appears to be due to breast-feeding, Dr. Rees added.

"This is another benefit of breast-feeding," Dr. Rees said. "We know that breast-feeding leads to better health, higher IQ, but the next step is what are the implications, and this is an important implication," he said.

EXPERT REACTION

David L. Katz, MD, director of the Prevention Research Center at Yale University School of Medicine, said this study may not prove a connection between school performance and breast-feeding, but it could be another reason to breast-feed your baby.

"An array of health benefits is convincingly associated with breast-feeding, including a reduced risk of both infections and obesity in the breast-fed child," Dr. Katz said. "Less certain, but long suggested, is enhanced cognitive development in breast-fed children as well."

It could be that factors that determine whether or not a baby is breast-fed are an important piece of the puzzle, Dr. Katz noted. "Why a baby is fed one way or another may matter as much as which way a baby is fed," he said. "A study of association such as this cannot fully resolve that issue."

Natural Therapies For Endometriosis... No Surgery Needed

Victoria Maizes, MD, associate professor of medicine, family and community medicine and public health and executive director of the Arizona Center for Integrative Medicine at University of Arizona in Tucson. She is co-editor of *Integrative Women's Health* (Oxford University). *www.integrativemedicine.arizona.edu.*

W ith *endometriosis*, tissue from the *endometrium* (uterine lining) migrates outside the uterus via the fallopian tubes, then grows on the ovaries, fallopian tubes, rectum, bladder and/or pelvic lining.

During menstruation, this displaced tissue behaves as it would if it were in the uterus—it thickens, breaks down and bleeds. Trapped blood inflames surrounding tissues, which can lead to internal scarring. Resulting pain ranges from mild to incapacitating...scarring can impair fertility. Symptoms usually ease after menopause, though hormone therapy may lead to flare-ups.

Conventional treatment typically involves oral contraceptives, which block the effects of natural hormones on the growths outside the uterus…or the drug *leuprolide* (Lupron), which stops menstruation.

Downside: These drugs can cause weight gain and mood swings. When medication does not bring sufficient relief, patients may be advised to have endometriosis tissue surgically removed or to have a hysterectomy. But as with all surgery, these options carry risks for infection and complications.

Natural approaches may help you avoid drugs and surgery. *Try…*

•**Anti-inflammatory diet.** This reduces the inflammation caused by trapped menstrual blood. To increase intake of anti-inflammatory omega-3 fatty acids, eat more fatty fish (herring, mackerel), flaxseeds and walnuts…and take a daily fish oil supplement. Every day, eat several servings of vegetables and fruits, which are rich in antioxidants. Avoid inflammation-promoting refined carbohydrates (white bread, doughnuts)… eat more whole grains (brown rice, bulgur).

•**Pelvic floor physical therapy.** Chronic muscle tension in the abdomen, legs and pelvic floor may result from a conditioned response to pelvic pain, exacerbating discomfort. Pelvic floor physical therapy from a specially trained therapist can reduce muscle tension and improve day-to-day functioning.

Also helpful: Yoga, stretching.

•**Botanical supplements.** Black cohosh, black haw and/or ginger may help by reducing the effects of inflammatory enzymes and proteins, boosting antioxidants or reducing sensitivity to painful stimuli. Supplements can cause side effects or interact with medications, so consult a holistic doctor for dosage and usage guidelines. Do not take black cohosh or black haw if you have a history of breast cancer. Do not take ginger if you have a bleeding disorder or gallstones.

•**Acupuncture.** Various studies suggest that this can ease the pain of endometriosis, though the exact mechanism is not known.

Find a practitioner: Contact the American Association of Acupuncture and Oriental Medicine (866-455-7999, *www.aaaomonline.org*).

Simplest: Use a heating pad…or take a warm bath to ease discomfort.

■ ■ ■ ■

Faster Prolapse Recovery

With *vaginal prolapse*, the uterus, vaginal wall, rectum and/or bladder drop from the normal position and may protrude outside the vaginal opening.

Breakthrough: Compared with patients who had traditional open surgical repair, those who had less invasive robotic-assisted surgery had fewer complications, shorter hospital stays and faster recovery.

To find a surgeon experienced in this specific technique, inquire at a large teaching medical center.

Daniel S. Elliott, MD, assistant professor of urology, Mayo Clinic, Rochester, Minnesota, and leader of a study of 48 prolapse patients.

■ ■ ■ ■

Help for Hot Flashes

When 454 postmenopausal women who suffered from moderate to severe hot flashes used *estradiol* (Evamist)—a spray-on product containing estrogen—or a placebo spray for 12 weeks, the estradiol group had an average of eight fewer hot flashes per day, compared with an average of four fewer hot flashes daily for the placebo group.

Unlike oral estrogen therapy, the spray form does not appear to increase risk for side effects, such as blood clots.

John E. Buster, MD, professor, obstetrics and gynecology, Warren Alpert Medical School, Brown University, Providence.

■ ■ ■ ■

Menopause Raises Cholesterol, Increasing Heart Disease Risk

The average LDL (bad) cholesterol count jumps by about 9% in the two-year window surrounding the final menstrual period. Total cholesterol levels also increase by about 6.5%.

Important: Women undergoing menopause should take steps to keep their cholesterol under control.

Among the strategies: Regular exercise… maintaining a healthy weight…not smoking… and taking cholesterol-lowering medications.

Karen A. Matthews, PhD, is distinguished professor of psychiatry and professor of epidemiology and psychology, University of Pittsburgh School of Medicine. She is lead author of a study of menopausal transition in 1,054 women, published in *Journal of the American College of Cardiology.*

■ ■ ■ ■

Could Iron Skillets Harm Your Health?

There's no reason to get rid of your skillets. Iron overload—an excessive buildup of iron that can lead to organ damage—is primarily a genetic problem. Though a woman's need for iron is reduced once this mineral is no longer lost during menstruation, you are unlikely to get iron overload from cookware.

However, to be safe, consider using another type of pan when cooking acidic foods, such as applesauce and tomato-based items. Highly acidic foods heated in iron skillets do absorb significant amounts of the mineral—especially when foods are heated for a long time and stirred frequently, as many sauces are.

Harold H. Sandstead, MD, professor emeritus of human nutrition, department of preventive medicine and community health, University of Texas Medical Branch, Galveston.

Deadly Skin Cancer Alert For Women Only

Andrew Bronin, MD, associate clinical professor of dermatology at Yale School of Medicine in New Haven, Connecticut. A dermatologist in private practice in Rye Brook, New York, he also is editor in chief of *DermClips*, an American Academy of Dermatology (AAD) continuing medical education publication, and a recipient of the AAD's Presidential Citation award, given to major contributors in the field of dermatology.

Remember back in the 1960s, at the height of the feminist movement, when women were encouraged to look at their *vulvas* (external genitalia) in a hand mirror in order to learn about their bodies? Turns out there's a medical rationale for this, too—because such self-exams help detect genital skin cancer.

It can be surprising to learn that women can get skin cancer "down there." Though men also get genital skin cancer, a recent study found that women are almost three times more likely to die of the most common type of this disease. It's not clear why women's mortality rates are higher—it might be that women are more susceptible or that this cancer is more aggressive in women…or just that growths are easier to find on male genitalia, so men get treated earlier in the progression of the disease.

The vulva includes the *clitoris, labia* (vaginal lips) and opening to the vagina. There are several types of vulvar cancer. Andrew Bronin, MD, is associate clinical professor of dermatology at Yale School of Medicine in New Haven, Connecticut, and a dermatologist in private practice in Rye Brook, New York. *Here are his prevention and early detection strategies for protecting yourself from…*

•**Squamous cell vulvar cancer.** This skin cancer arises in the squamous cells (the layer of cells on the surface of the skin) and accounts for nearly 90% of vulvar cancers. Risk factors include age (85% of women who contract the disease are over age 50)…chronic vulvar or vaginal inflammation…infection with HIV (the AIDS virus)…or a history of cervical cancer or *lichen sclerosus* (a disorder characterized by thin, itchy vulvar tissues).

•**Squamous cell cancer can be linked to certain strains of human papillomavirus (HPV).** The HPVs are a group of more than 100 related viruses, some of which are also associated with genital warts and cervical cancer. The sexually transmitted strains of HPV usually spread during vaginal, anal or oral sex via skin-to-skin contact (rather than via bodily fluids). Though the virus sometimes clears up on its own, there is no surefire way to eradicate HPV—so prevention is important. *To reduce your risk...*

•**Get tested for HPV.** Like a Pap smear, the HPV test analyzes cervical cells. If you are not infected, ask your doctor whether you should get the Gardasil vaccine, which protects against four of the most troublesome strains of HPV. "Although the vaccine is currently FDA-approved for women age 26 and under, it also may benefit older women," Dr. Bronin said. "Even if you are infected with one strain of HPV, consider vaccination—because it may protect you against three other strains."

•**Even if a man has no visible genital warts, he could have a "preclinical" HPV infection**—meaning that the virus is present and contagious but hasn't yet produced visible symptoms. So if you enter a new relationship, have your partner use condoms. But understand that this is not foolproof since it protects you from infections only in areas covered by the condom.

Also: Be aware that the more sexual partners you've had—and the more partners your partner has had—the higher your likelihood of having been exposed to HPV.

•**Don't smoke!** Smoking increases vulvar cancer risk, especially if you have HPV.

•**Vulvar malignant melanoma.** This type accounts for only about 4% of vulvar skin cancers, but it is the most deadly because it spreads rapidly. Melanoma develops in the melanocytes, the skin's pigment-producing cells. You probably know that sun exposure increases the risk for malignant melanoma—but sun is not a requirement for the development of this disease. In fact, melanoma has the potential to occur anywhere that you have pigment cells...and that's every square inch of your skin, including your vulva. You can get malignant melanoma even where the sun never shines.

"Having moles that are atypical—in other words, funny-looking to the eye and under the microscope—anywhere on your body increases your risk for vulvar malignant melanoma. So does a personal or family history of any malignant melanoma," Dr. Bronin said. Unfortunately, vulvar melanomas have some of the worst prognoses of all malignant melanomas, with a five-year survival rate of only 50%...precisely because they often are not caught until it is too late.

•**Vulvar adenocarcinoma.** This type begins in the gland cells just inside the vaginal opening or in the top layer of vulvar skin. It accounts for about 8% of vulvar cancers. Though less deadly than melanoma, it has a relatively high recurrence rate.

Concern: Diagnosis often is delayed because a cancerous growth may be easily mistaken for a cyst.

KEY: EARLY DETECTION

Catching vulvar cancer early offers the best chance for a good outcome. *Potentially lifesaving strategies...*

•**Give yourself periodic vulvar self-exams.** The frequency depends on your personal risk factors, so ask your gynecologist to recommend a schedule. What to do: "Use a mirror to check the inner and outer labia, vaginal opening, clitoris and perineal area between the vagina and anus. Look for abnormal lumps or growths... red, white or grayish lesions...changes in pigmentation...swelling...or sores that don't heal," Dr. Bronin suggested. If you spot any such signs, see your gynecologist or dermatologist as soon as possible.

•**Also be on the lookout for unexplained itching, tenderness, pain or nonmenstrual bleeding**—and again, alert your doctor without delay.

•**Get an annual gynecologic checkup.** Your doctor will be watching for the disease (among other things)—but it doesn't hurt to ask, "Do you see any signs of vulvar cancer?"

Diagnosis and treatment: When suspicious growths are found, the tissue is biopsied. If the precancerous condition *vulvar intraepithelial neoplasia* is diagnosed, laser therapy or surgery can keep it from turning into a squamous cell cancer. If the biopsy does reveal squamous cell cancer, treatment options include laser therapy, surgery, radiation and/or chemotherapy.

If a pigmented skin lesion is suspected of being malignant melanoma, it should be surgically removed by a dermatologist or gynecologist and examined at a pathology lab. Early recognition and removal of a malignant melanoma can be lifesaving.

For vulvar adenocarcinoma, treatment also is surgical, with the extent of the surgery depending on the extent of the disease. Again, Dr. Bronin emphasized, early detection offers the best chance for limiting the necessary surgery and enhancing the prognosis.

▪ ▪ ▪ ▪

Safer Estrogen Therapy

Estrogen replacement relieves menopausal hot flashes but can raise the risk for potentially deadly blood clots.

Recent study: Women who were at elevated risk for clots used estrogen either orally or transdermally (as a gel, spray or skin patch). After eight weeks, blood tests showed increased clotting in oral estrogen users—but not in transdermal users.

Lila Nachtigall, MD, professor of obstetrics and gynecology, New York University School of Medicine, and director, Women's Wellness Program, NYU Langone Medical Center, New York City. She is coauthor of a recent study of clotting in 84 postmenopausal women.

▪ ▪ ▪ ▪

Oral Estrogen Problem "Leaks" Out

Women who took oral *conjugated equine estrogen* (such as Premarin) to relieve menopausal symptoms were more likely than those taking a placebo to develop or experience a worsening of urinary incontinence.

But: In women using topical estrogen (such as a vaginal cream or ring), incontinence symptoms improved. Estrogen increases breast cancer and stroke risk—so discuss pros and cons of various types with your doctor.

June Cody, methodologist, academic urology unit, University of Aberdeen, Scotland, and lead reviewer of 33 studies involving 19,313 women.

The Baffling Bladder Condition Antibiotics Can't Cure

Kristene E. Whitmore, MD, professor and chair of urology and female pelvic medicine and reconstructive surgery at Drexel University College of Medicine, and medical director of the Pelvic and Sexual Health Institute, both in Philadelphia. She is coauthor of *Overcoming Bladder Disorders* (Harper Perennial). *www.pelvicand sexualhealthinstitute.org.*

Perplexing, painful and inconvenient, the chronic condition known as *interstitial cystitis/painful bladder syndrome* (IC/PBS) affects women more than nine times as often as men. Its symptoms, including bladder pain and frequent urination, often are mistaken for those of a bladder infection—yet tests reveal no bacteria, and antibiotics bring no relief.

Though IC/PBS affects up to 6% of American women, its cause is a mystery.

What is known: The bladder wall becomes inflamed and super-sensitive...pinpoints of bleeding and ulcers often appear...stiffness and scarring may develop.

Many women suffer for years without a proper diagnosis, taking antibiotics for infections that they do not actually have. This delay causes needless pain...raises the odds that resistance to antibiotics will develop...and increases the risk that an IC/PBS–triggered inflammatory reaction will spread to other organs. In severe cases, surgery may be needed to remove part or all of the bladder. IC/PBS cannot be cured—but treatment can relieve symptoms and reduce complications.

GETTING DIAGNOSED

If you have symptoms that suggest IC/PBS, visit your doctor. If no infection is found or symptoms persist despite treatment, consult a urologist or *urogynecologist.*

IC/PBS symptoms…

•**Bladder pain or pressure**

•**Frequent urination** (more than eight times in 24 hours)

•**Urgent need to urinate**

•**Discomfort, pain or pressure in the lower pelvis or vulva**

•**Pain during or after sex**

•**Flare-ups during menstruation.**

There is no definitive test for IC/PBS. Diagnosis involves excluding other conditions, such as a bladder infection, overactive bladder or bladder cancer. Testing may include blood and urine tests, bladder biopsy and cystoscopy (exam of the bladder using a viewing instrument).

Good news: For about 70% of patients, natural remedies ease symptoms with few or no side effects.

SOOTHING DIETARY STRATEGIES

Your diet affects how your bladder feels. *Helpful…*

•**Identify foods that spark symptoms.** A chief culprit is cranberry juice. Yes, this juice combats bladder infections—but with IC/PBS, you aren't fighting an infection. And cranberry juice is acidic, so it irritates a sensitive bladder.

Other top troublemakers: Alcohol…artificial sweeteners…caffeine (coffee, soda, tea)…carbonated drinks…citrus fruits, citrus juices…spicy foods…and tomato products.

For a comprehensive list of problematic foods, visit the Web site of the Interstitial Cystitis Association (*www.ichelp.org,* click on "Patient Resources"). To identify your personal triggers, for one month do not eat anything on the ICA list. Then, reintroduce one food from the list every three to five days. If symptoms flare up, swear off that food.

•**Drink more, not less.** You may think that limiting fluids reduces your need to urinate—but skimping on water makes urine more concentrated and thus more irritating. Drink six to eight cups of water daily—and sip, don't gulp.

•**Take supplements.** With your doctor's approval, try the following…

•Prelief (sold at drugstores) contains *calcium glycerophosphate,* which makes food less acidic.

•CystoProtek (sold at *www.cysto-protek. com*) has antioxidants and anti-inflammatories (*glucosamine, quercetin, rutin*) that help repair the bladder lining.

Note: If you take a multivitamin or other supplement that contains vitamin C, choose one with ascorbate, not ascorbic acid.

MIND OVER BLADDER

Try any or all of the following mind–body therapies…

•**Bladder retraining.** Urinating temporarily relieves pain, so patients use the toilet often—in some cases, up to 60 times a day—but this habit further reduces the bladder's capacity to comfortably hold urine.

Best: Try to increase your typical time between bathroom trips by 15 minutes. After two weeks, increase by another 15 minutes. Continue until you can wait at least two hours.

•**Stress reduction.** Practice relaxation techniques daily, such as deep breathing, meditation and yoga. Also consider *craniosacral therapy* (gentle head and spine massage).

Practitioner referrals: The Upledger Institute, 800-233-5880, *www.upledger.com.*

•**Acupuncture.** This reduces IC/PBS pain for some patients.

Referrals: American Association of Acupuncture and Oriental Medicine, 866-455-7999, *www.aaaomonline.org.*

MEDICAL TREATMENT OPTIONS

Persistent bladder pain eventually can cause pelvic muscles to spasm, worsening IC/PBS. *Helpful…*

•**Intravaginal Thiele massage.** To relieve spasms, a physical therapist massages muscles inside the vagina and/or rectum…and patients learn to do the procedure themselves at home. In one study, this reduced symptoms for 90% of patients.

•**Electrical nerve stimulation.** Stimulating the sacral nerves in the back with a mild current helps pelvic floor muscles function normally. If symptoms are severe, a urologist or urogynecologist can implant a nerve stimulator under the skin near the tailbone for continuous stimulation.

•**Medication.** About 5% to 10% of IC/PBS patients must resort to narcotic prescription painkillers—but these can have adverse effects, including a risk for dependence.

Better: First consider one or more of the following non-narcotic prescription drugs, discussing the pros and cons with your doctor…

•*Dimethyl sulfoxide* (DMSO). A pain-relieving anti-inflammatory and antispasmodic, this drug is infused into the bladder through a catheter and kept in place for about 20 minutes. The procedure typically is done once a week for six weeks. Relief lasts three to 12 months…treatment is repeated as needed. Side effects may include garlic taste in the mouth, headache and dry nasal passages. DMSO is the only drug approved for this treatment, but for some patients, other anesthetics (such as *lidocaine*) work as well with fewer side effects.

•*Pentosan* (Elmiron). This oral drug helps heal the bladder lining. It can thin the blood, however, so it may be inappropriate if you use a blood thinner, such as *warfarin* (Coumadin).

•*Potassium citrate* (Urocit-K). Taken orally, this makes urine more alkaline. Possible side effects include nausea, muscle weakness and irregular heartbeat.

•Urelle. This brand-name oral medication is a five-drug formulation that reduces pain and spasms. Side effects may include nausea, dizziness and blurred vision.

LIFESTYLE CHANGES

To make day-to-day life with IC/PBS more comfortable, try…

•**Modified exercise routines.** When symptoms flare up, reduce the intensity and duration of workouts—for instance, by walking instead of running. Rinse off after swimming to remove irritating chlorine.

•**Bathing.** Soak in bathwater mixed with colloidal oatmeal (sold at drugstores). Avoid bubble baths and bath oils—these can be irritating.

•**A personal lubricant for sex.** This makes intercourse more comfortable.

Try: The organic Good Clean Love line (541-344-4483, *www.goodcleanlove.com*).

Chances Are It's *Not* a Yeast Infection

Cherie A. LeFevre, MD, assistant professor of gynecology and director of the Vulvar and Vaginal Disorder Clinic at Saint Louis University School of Medicine. She is author of numerous scientific articles published in *Obstetrics & Gynecology, Journal of Reproductive Medicine* and other medical journals.

When itching, burning and vaginal discharge make their unwelcome appearance, many women assume that they have a yeast infection—an overgrowth of the *candida* fungus that often is a normal part of the vaginal environment. To end the outbreak, they use a nonprescription anti-yeast medication, such as *miconazole* (Monistat).

Problem: More often than not, yeast is not to blame. In a recent study, 153 women thought they had yeast infections—but in 74% of cases, tests revealed that symptoms actually had a different cause.

This is just one of many common misunderstandings about vaginal infections, a group of conditions collectively called *vaginitis*. Each misunderstanding can lead to misdiagnosis, ineffective treatment and unnecessary suffering. *Here's what you need to know to protect yourself…*

THE LEADING CULPRIT

•**Bacterial vaginosis (BV).** The most common kind of vaginitis, this accounts for 40% to 45% of cases. It is an overgrowth of anaerobic bacteria, a type that doesn't need oxygen. BV develops when (for reasons that are unclear) the vagina's pH changes from a healthy acidic level of 3.8 to 4.2 to a less acidic, more alkaline level of above 4.5. This allows anaerobic bacteria to thrive.

Signs/symptoms: A thin gray discharge…fishy odor…itching…burning during urination.

Diagnosis: If you suspect BV, see your doctor if you've never had the symptoms before (to ensure an accurate diagnosis) or if recurrent BV occurs more than twice a year (to confirm the diagnosis and discuss prevention strategies). To diagnose BV, the doctor performs a physical exam…does a pH test…prepares a wet mount (a sample of vaginal discharge to examine under a microscope)…and conducts a whiff test by adding a chemical solution to the wet mount that, in the case of BV, releases fishy-smelling proteins.

Treatment: Typically a prescription antibiotic, such as *metronidazole* (Flagyl), is used orally for seven days or in topical gel form for five days—or longer for recurrent BV.

Soothing: Twice daily, soak for 10 minutes in a sitz bath of lukewarm water mixed with four tablespoons of baking soda.

Prevention strategies…

•**Launder panties, towels and other articles that come in contact with your genital area using dye-free and fragrance-free detergent,** such as All Free Clear. If you use a stain remover on these articles, soak and rinse them afterward in clear water, then machine-wash. Skip fabric softener and dryer sheets.

•**Wear white 100%-cotton panties and thigh-high nylons,** not panty hose.

•**Use nonperfumed soaps, body washes and lotions.**

Good brands: Basis, Dove Hypoallergenic, Neutrogena, Pears. Never use bubble bath, bath salts or scented bath oils.

•**Use white, unscented toilet paper.** Avoid adult or baby wipes.

•**Do not douche or use feminine hygiene spray.**

•**Avoid deodorized sanitary products.** Use a tampon only when your flow is heavy enough to soak it within four hours—otherwise, use a pad.

•**To keep the groin area dry, apply moisture-absorbing Gold Bond Powder or Zeasorb powder** (not talcum powder) daily…and change your panties if they become damp. Panty liners can keep moisture trapped in—so wear them only on days when menstrual flow is light, not daily.

THE FUNGI

•**Yeast infections.** These account for 20% to 25% of vaginitis cases. Up to 95% of yeast infections are candida *albicans*…the rest are candida *glabrata*, candida *parapsilosis* or another strain. Factors that increase susceptibility to yeast…

•**Weakened immune system** (for instance, from stress, high-dose steroids or chemotherapy drugs).

•**Antibiotics,** which disturb the normal balance of vaginal flora.

•**Elevated blood sugar** due to diabetes or a diet high in potatoes, sugar and/or refined carbohydrates.

Signs/symptoms: A thick, white, cottage-cheeselike vaginal discharge…itching…burning…redness.

Diagnosis: Unlike bacterial infections, yeast infections do not raise vaginal pH—but a normal pH result on an over-the-counter test (such as Vagisil Screening Kit) does not confirm that you have yeast rather than something else. So if you suspect a first yeast infection or if bouts recur more than twice yearly, see your doctor for a yeast culture, physical exam, pH test and wet mount.

Treatment: A doctor-diagnosed first yeast infection or flare-ups that occur twice per year or less can be treated with nonprescription antifungal medication. But for frequently recurring infections, it is better to take a stronger prescription antifungal, such as *fluconazole* (Diflucan), for one to three days. If symptoms persist, ask your doctor about doing a yeast culture to identify and tailor treatment to the species. Do not try to treat yeast with "natural" douches, such as tea tree oil—vaginal tissues are easily irritated.

Prevention: Follow the BV treatment guidelines above—they also guard against yeast—and reduce dietary sugar.

THE STD

•**Trichomoniasis ("trich").** Responsible for 15% to 20% of vaginitis cases, trichomoniasis is the only sexually transmitted form of vaginitis—you can't "catch" BV or yeast from a sexual partner. Trich is caused by a parasitic *protozoan* (single-celled organism) that burrows under the vagina's mucous lining.

Signs/symptoms: Heavy, yellow-green, frothy, foul-smelling discharge and intense itching.

Diagnosis: Again, you should have a physical exam, pH test and wet mount. Trich is the diagnosis with a pH greater than 4.5, the presence of large numbers of inflammatory white blood cells and microscopic detection of the pear-shaped protozoa. If you have trich, your risk for other sexually transmitted diseases rises —so get screened for *chlamydia* and *gonorrhea*, too.

Treatment: A one-day course of metronidazole eradicates trich. Your sex partner also needs antibiotics so you aren't reinfected.

THE MENOPAUSAL MISERY

•**Atrophic vaginitis.** Vaginal tissues are very sensitive to declining estrogen—so this type of vaginitis is common, affecting an estimated 10% to 40% of postmenopausal women to some degree.

Signs/symptoms: Vaginal dryness, itching and burning…smelly yellow discharge…painful intercourse.

Diagnosis: A physical exam reveals dry, thin vaginal and vulvar tissues. When diagnosing atrophic vaginitis, your doctor should rule out other problems that cause similar symptoms, such as *lichen planus* (a skin disorder that involves vulvar tissue degeneration).

Treatment: Vaginal estrogen rings or tablets. However, they are not appropriate for women with migraines or a history of, or increased risk for, breast cancer or cardiovascular disease.

Natural alternative: Twice daily and also before intercourse, gently rub a dab of vegetable oil or solid vegetable shortening onto the vulvar tissues and inside the vagina.

Within six weeks, women who have suffered for years with atrophic vaginitis and painful intercourse often get complete relief.

■ ■ ■ ■

Amino Acid Reduces Compulsive Hair-Pulling

Compulsive hair-pulling—known as *trichotillomania*—primarily affects women. There is no approved medication to treat it.

New study: Trichotillomania patients took 1,200 milligrams (mg) to 2,400 mg of the amino acid *N-acetylcysteine* (NAC) or a placebo. After 12 weeks, 56% of NAC users and 16% of placebo users rated their symptoms as "much or very much improved."

Theory: NAC acts on the *glutamate* system of the brain, which controls compulsive behaviors. NAC is sold in health food stores.

Jon E. Grant, JD, MD, MPH, associate professor of psychiatry, University of Minnesota School of Medicine, Minneapolis, and leader of a study of 50 people.

Natural Ways to Calm Restless Legs

Chris D. Meletis, ND, executive director, Institute for Healthy Aging, Carson City, Nevada, a private practitioner in Beaverton, Oregon, and coauthor of *Great Health* (INA).

In bed, you feel an aching, tingling or "creepy-crawly" sensation in your legs. Moving brings relief, so you can't resist—but then it's hard to fall asleep.

Culprit: *Restless legs syndrome* (RLS), a neurological disorder that's twice as common in women as men. Sedative medications don't fully alleviate symptoms and can cause daytime drowsiness. *Better…*

•**Get screened for underlying conditions.** Diagnosis and treatment of diabetes, Parkinson's, sleep apnea or nerve damage may also relieve RLS.

•**Review medications.** Certain antihistamines, antidepressants, antinausea drugs and blood pressure drugs aggravate RLS. Ask your doctor about alternatives.

•**Take supplements.** Try this daily regimen for a month. If it helps, continue indefinitely—200 milligrams (mg) of alpha-lipoic acid…300 mg of magnesium…1,000 micrograms (mcg) of *methylcobalamin*, a form of vitamin B-12…800 mcg of *5-methyltetrahydrofolate* (5-MTHF), a form of folic acid…and 300 mg of *resveratrol*. As with any supplement regimen, talk to your doctor before beginning.

•**Have your iron tested.** Iron deficiency increases RLS risk.

But: Excess iron can harm the brain and organs. Take iron only if a blood test reveals a deficiency and your doctor recommends it.

•**Use homeopathy.** Try *Arsenicum album* if RLS is accompanied by exhaustion and heaviness or trembling in the legs…*Causticum* if symptoms include burning or cramping in calves and feet…*Ignatia* if you have muscle spasms when dropping off to sleep. Consult a homeopathic practitioner for dosages.

•**Try acupuncture.** Some patients report improvement in RLS symptoms.

Symptom soother: Firmly massage your calves and thighs.

Boost Your Energy Instantly

Evangeline Lausier, MD, director of clinical services at Duke Integrative Medicine and assistant clinical professor of medicine at Duke University School of Medicine, both in Durham, North Carolina. She is an internist specializing in women's health and complex multisystem illnesses, with an emphasis on preventive lifestyle.

When you feel drowsy or droop with fatigue, every task seems monumental and even fun activities feel like work. Fight that fatigue with a double-pronged approach to invigoration—including on-the-spot techniques for an immediate energy burst… plus simple strategies that take just minutes to do. They'll give you long-lasting stamina day after day.

FOR AN INSTANT ENERGY SURGE…

•**Wake up your nose—and the rest of you will follow.** Aromatherapy stimulates the brain's olfactory center and heightens awareness of your surroundings. Dab a drop of therapeutic-grade rosemary essential oil (sold at health food stores) on the pulse points behind both ears, as you would perfume…or dampen a cloth with cool water, sprinkle it with four drops of therapeutic-grade lemon essential oil, then place it on your forehead or the back of your neck for five minutes. Do not dab full-strength essential oil directly under your nose—it could be too strong.

•**Belt out a few bars.** As you sing, you inhale deeply, bringing more energizing oxygen into your lungs and increasing circulation throughout your body…and exhale through your mouth, efficiently expelling the waste product carbon dioxide.

Bonus: Choosing a favorite cheerful song lifts your mood.

•**Give yourself a good stretch.** Stretching opens the chest, straightens the spine, expands the lungs and relieves energy-sapping tension in neck and shoulder muscles. *Try…*

•**Seated stretch.** Sit in a sturdy chair, feet flat on the floor, hands clasped in front of you. As you inhale, straighten arms and slowly raise them over your head, turning your wrists so palms face the ceiling. Gently press arms as far back as possible, holding for a count of five. Slowly exhale, lowering arms to the starting position. Repeat three times.

•**Doorway stretch.** Stand in a doorway, a few inches behind the threshold, with feet about six  inches apart. Raise your arms out to your sides and bend elbows to a 90-degree angle, placing hands and forearms on either side of the doorjamb. Keeping your back straight, lean forward slightly to feel a stretch across your chest. Hold for 15 seconds. Repeat three times.

•**Take 800 steps.** A moderately brisk walk—at a pace of about 100 steps per minute—is an excellent way to get blood flowing

Illustrations by Shawn Banner.

to your heart and brain. Exercise also triggers the release of endorphins, brain chemicals that make you feel alert and energetic. If possible, walk outdoors—the sun's rays activate the synthesis of mood-enhancing vitamin D.

•**Just breathe.** The beauty of this is that you can do it anytime, anywhere, and instantly feel more alert.

Good deep-breathing technique: Inhale deeply through your nose, filling your lungs for a count of four…hold your breath for a count of seven…slowly and deliberately exhale through pursed lips (to regulate the release of air) to a count of eight. Take three normal breaths, then repeat the deep-breathing exercise twice more.

TO REFUEL ENERGY RESERVES…

•**Eat a stamina-boosting breakfast**—one cup of fortified, whole-grain cereal. Whole grains are complex carbohydrates that enter the bloodstream slowly, providing sustained energy by keeping blood sugar levels stable. Avoid starting your day with simple carbohydrates, such as white toast or a doughnut, which cause blood sugar and energy levels to spike and then plummet by mid-morning.

Also: With your cereal, have one-half cup of low-fat milk or fortified soy milk. Its calcium and vitamin D nourish your bones…its protein is used to build and repair muscle and other tissues.

•**For snacks, go nuts.** A handful of almonds, cashews, walnuts or other type of nut provides a sustained energy boost, thanks to blood sugar–stabilizing complex carbohydrates and tissue-building protein.

More benefits: Though relatively high in calories at about 160 per ounce, nuts tend not to cause energy-depleting weight gain because they promote long-lasting satiety and stave off hunger. Nuts also are rich in unsaturated fats that promote cardiovascular health.

•**Take a green tea break three or four times a day.** Green tea contains *catechins,* antioxidant plant chemicals that support the immune system by neutralizing cell-damaging free radicals, fighting bacteria and easing inflammation. When your immune system is operating at its peak, you have more pep. Green tea also boosts metabolism, stabilizing blood sugar and helping to ward off weight gain…and protects against many debilitating chronic conditions, including heart disease and diabetes.

Convenient: If you are going to be out and about during the day, before you leave the house, brew up enough tea to fill a thermos and take it with you.

While green tea does contain some caffeine—enough to provide a slight energy lift—its caffeine content generally is low enough not to interfere with sleep, provided that you avoid drinking it within four hours of bedtime. If you want to minimize caffeine, let the green tea bag steep for just 30 seconds, then discard that water and replace it with fresh hot water, allowing it to steep for several minutes.

If you prefer coffee: Be aware that, with its higher caffeine content, coffee may leave you feeling even more sluggish once the caffeine buzz wears off. Limit caffeinated coffee to no more than 16 ounces per day, and consume it prior to midafternoon so it doesn't interfere with your sleep.

•**Try energizing supplements.** Various supplements help support immune function and/or reduce energy-sapping stress. Each has its own benefits as well as risks (such as possible side effects or interactions with medications or other supplements), so it is important to discuss their appropriateness and dosage guidelines with your doctor before taking them.

Options to consider: Astragalus…calcium plus magnesium…coenzyme Q10…ginseng… *rhodiola*…vitamin B complex.

•**Express yourself to lower stress.** Play the piano, pen a poem, paint a picture or just doodle.

The purpose: Creative self-expression is stimulating—it alleviates energy-draining stress by helping you reconnect with your deep inner well of emotional well-being.

■ ■ ■ ■

Strengthen Thighs to Kick Arthritis

When researchers evaluated the strength of 3,026 adults' *quadriceps* (front thigh muscles), women with the strongest thighs had the lowest incidence of painful knee osteoarthritis. The benefit was less apparent in men, for unknown reasons.

To strengthen your thighs and knees (whether or not you have osteoarthritis): Include quadriceps-building exercises, such as climbing stairs slowly and walking at a moderate pace, in your regular exercise routine.

Neil Segal, MD, director, Clinical Osteoarthritis Research Program, University of Iowa, Iowa City.

■ ■ ■ ■

Yoga Helps Women Stand Taller

Elderly women who spent nine weeks doing yoga gained an average of one centimeter in height because they stood more upright and crouched less. They also walked faster, used longer strides and could balance longer on one leg by the end of the program.

Jinsup Song, DPM, PhD, assistant professor, Temple University, Philadelphia.

The Four Secrets of Radiant Skin

Karen Burke, MD, PhD, assistant clinical professor of dermatology at Mount Sinai Medical Center, and a dermatologist and research scientist in private practice, both in New York City. She is author of *Great Skin for Life* (Hamlyn).

Often women compliment dermatologist Karen Burke, MD, PhD, on her smooth, spotless, glowing skin—and assume that she's had "work done" on her face. But that's not the case. "Instead of resorting to lasers, Botox or surgery, it's often possible to

achieve wonderful results with just the following four products," said Dr. Burke.

•**Mild, moisturizing cleanser.** The goal is to remove oil, dirt and bacteria—without leaving skin overly dry.

New technology: Dove Sensitive Skin Nourishing Body Wash with Nutrium Moisture contains a blend of soybean oil, fatty acids and glycerin to penetrate deep into skin. Use it all over.

To minimize facial sagging: Wash twice a day, gently moving fingertips back and forth across vertical lines by your mouth…and up and out over horizontal forehead, cheek and eye wrinkles.

•**Sunscreen.** To guard against wrinkles, spots and skin cancer, use a sunscreen every day with an SPF of at least 30 (better yet, 40 or more) that protects against both UVA and UVB rays.

Transparent: Sunscreens with the new micronized zinc oxide provide excellent UVA/UVB protection with no telltale white film.

Long-lasting: Anthelios face and body sunscreens contain Mexoryl, which degrades much more slowly than other UVA filters do *(www. Anthelios.com)*.

•**Antioxidant serum.** This helps reverse sun damage by stimulating production of collagen (the protein that gives skin its structure) and neutralizing harmful free radicals.

Transforming: Apply six to eight drops of SkinCeuticals C E Ferulic to your face daily *(www.SkinCeuticals.com)*.

•**Topical retinoic acid** *(tretinoin)*. Ask your dermatologist to prescribe this vitamin-A derivative to rejuvenate skin and help prevent skin cancer.

Thrifty: Generic tretinoin 0.01% gel costs less than brand-name (about $90 for 1.6 ounces, approximately a four-month supply). Apply at bedtime to the face and back of your hands. To minimize flaking, use it every other day to start, working up to daily use.

Note: Nonprescription products are far less effective because they break down quickly.

Women Who Marry Younger Men May Die Earlier

Demography news release.

Women who marry men seven to nine years their junior could be upping their odds of dying sooner, German researchers report.

STUDY FINDINGS

Tying the knot with a significantly younger guy raises a woman's risk of death by 20%, according to a study published in *Demography*.

Not that marrying much older men is much safer. The study, based on data from nearly two million Danish couples, indicates that marrying an older man might also shorten a woman's life, and that the healthiest choice for a husband might be a man around a woman's own age.

POSSIBLE EXPLANATION

"One of the few possible explanations is that couples with younger husbands violate social norms and thus suffer from social sanctions," said Sven Drefahl, from the Max Planck Institute for Demographic Research (MPIDR) in Rostock, Germany.

Such couples could therefore be stigmatized as outsiders—receiving less social support, enduring a more stressful life and perhaps developing poorer health as a result, Drefahl speculated.

MARRIAGE IN GENERAL BOOSTS LONGEVITY

On the positive side, the study authors stressed that, as a whole, marriage is not bad for life expectancy. In fact, both men and women experience a bump in longevity when they get married, relative to unmarried people, the study found.

In addition, few women may be distressed by the new finding on marrying younger men, since many prior studies have shown that women typically prefer men of similar age. In the United States, for example, the average groom is typically 2.3 years older than his bride, the research team noted.

MEN BENEFIT FROM MARRYING YOUNGER WOMEN

In contrast, the study found that men got a health benefit from choosing a younger wife. While men who married older women increased their risk for death, men who exchanged rings with a woman seven to nine years younger cut their risk of dying by 11%, the researchers found.

OLD THEORIES QUESTIONED

The reasons for the apparent gender difference remain unclear, the authors said. The finding does cast doubt on a long-held theory of "health selection" when it comes to May-September relationships. That notion suggests that older men and women who found younger partners were able to do so because they were healthier than average and therefore already faced a longer life expectancy. The theory relies on the notion that a younger spouse would boost the older partner's social and psychological frame of mind on the one hand, while being there to care for him (or her) in old age—all contributing to increased longevity for the older mate. "These theories now have to be reconsidered", Drefahl said.

info For more on marriage and health, visit the Web site of the RAND Corporation, *www.rand.org/pubs/research_briefs/RB5018/index1.html*.

■ ■ ■ ■

Wedding Ring Rash

Wedding-ring dermatitis can cause red, scaly welts on the ring finger, underneath a person's wedding band. It can be caused by moisture and soap trapped under the ring—or by an allergy to nickel, which is usually present in small amounts even in costly rings made of gold, silver or platinum. You can develop a rash even after wearing a ring for years because its protective coating wore away and the nickel has come to the surface.

Self-defense: Stop wearing the wedding ring until the rash heals—one to two weeks. A hydrocortisone cream, such as Cortaid, may help. If you start wearing the ring again and the rash reappears, see a dermatologist to get an allergy test to determine if the rash is caused by a reaction to nickel. You may need to have the ring recoated or buy a new one.

Jeffrey Benabio, MD, dermatologist, Kaiser Permanente, San Diego.

Proven Ways to Help You Forgive Yourself... And Move On

Frederic Luskin, PhD, director of the Stanford University Forgiveness Projects and professor of clinical psychology at the Institute of Transpersonal Psychology, both in Palo Alto, California. He is author of *Forgive for Love* (HarperCollins). *www.LearningToForgive.com.*

Women tend to be hard on themselves, turning isolated errors into cause for sweeping self-condemnation. I failed at that task becomes I am a failure...I gained a few pounds becomes I'm fat and ugly...I hurt someone I love becomes I'm a terrible wife. This often makes it difficult for women to forgive themselves for their mistakes and shortcomings. Fortunately, research has revealed proven techniques that help people pardon themselves.

Why make the effort: Self-forgiveness can lead to improved health, reduced stress, better relationships, personal growth and inner peace. *Steps to take...*

•**Identify your "grievance story."** This is the story that replays in your mind, focusing on your flaws. Write it down...then consider how you vilify yourself.

Example: "My best friend dumped me because I'm clingy and controlling. I deserve to be lonely." Now rewrite this as a "forgiveness story" by emphasizing good intentions and lessons learned—"What I did was done out of love...but now I see that people need space and I'm working to improve my relationships."

•**Challenge unenforceable rules.** Make a list of the rules or beliefs you judge yourself by—that loving mothers don't lose their tempers, that you must always make wise financial decisions.

Ask: "Is it possible for me—or anyone—to adhere to such rules?" If not, change your rules to conform to the reality that people do frequently fail. Doing your best doesn't require perfection.

•**Label your dreams.** A big dream is to find a fulfilling career or a loving lifelong companion...a small dream is that a particular job or a particular romantic relationship is "the one." Failing at a small dream does not doom the big dream. Make a course correction if necessary (for instance, by acknowledging that a career in sales or a long-distance relationship is not right for you), then keep moving toward the real goal—your big dream.

•**Make amends.** We've all been hurtful at one time or another...but making amends allows you to make peace with the past.

What to do: Sincerely apologize to, and practice kindness toward, the people you wronged. If they are not available, use symbolic acts of kindness.

Examples: Volunteer in a nursing home if you blame yourself for not having helped your elderly parents enough...give money to charity if you fudged on your taxes. Even if someone you harmed won't forgive you, trying to make amends helps you forgive yourself.

Index